People and Computers XV – Interaction without Frontiers

10/9/01

Ann Blandford, Jean Vanderdonckt
and Phil Gray (Eds)

People and Computers XV – Interaction without Frontiers

Joint Proceedings of HCI 2001 and IHM 2001

 Springer

Ann Blandford, PhD, BA
School of Computing Science, Middlesex University,
Bounds Green Road, London N11 2NQ, UK

Jean Vanderdonckt, PhD, MSc (CompSci), MSc (Maths)
Institut d' Administration et de Gestion, Université Catholique de Louvain,
Place des Doyens, 1, B-1328 Louvain-la-Neuve, Belgium

Phil Gray, BA, DipCompSci, MSc
Department of Computing Science, 17 Lilybank Gardens,
University of Glasgow, Glasgow G12 8RZ, UK

British Library Cataloguing in Publication Data
A catalogue record for this book is available from the British Library

ISBN 1-85233-515-7 Springer-Verlag London Berlin Heidelberg
A member of BertelsmannSpringer Science+Business Media GmbH
http://www.springer.co.uk

Typeset: by *Winder.*
Printed and bound at the Athenæum Press Ltd., Gateshead, Tyne and Wear
34/3830-543210 Printed on acid-free paper SPIN 10839100

Contents

Preface: Interaction Without Frontiers   xi

Keynote Papers   **1**

As Easy to Use as a Banking Machine   3
Ken Dye

Instrument Mediated Activity in Situations   17
Pierre Rabardel

From 2D Photos of Yourself to Virtual Try-on Dress on the Web   31
Frédéric Cordier, WonSook Lee, HyeWon Seo &
Nadia Magnenat-Thalmann

Computer-mediated Communication   **47**

Privacy in Multimedia Communications: Protecting Users, Not   49
Just Data
Anne Adams & Martina Angela Sasse

Managing Visibility in Ubiquitous Multimedia Communication   65
Environments
Leon Watts & Emmanuel Dubois

Collaborating with Virtual Humans   83
Pascal Le Mer, Laurence Perron, Christophe Chaillou,
Samuel Degrande & Grégory Saugis

Requirements Engineering   **105**

An Interactive Guide Through a Defined Modelling Process   107
Hermann Kaindl, Stefan Kramer & Mario Hailing

Multidisciplinary Practice in Requirements Engineering: Problems   125
and Criteria for Support
Ian Denley & John Long

Improving and Mediating Software-to-Usability Engineering   139
Communication
H Antunes, A Seffah, T Radhakrishnan & S Pestina

Usability Engineering   151

KALDI: A CAUsE Tool for Supporting Testing and Analysis of   153
User Interaction
Ghassan Al-Qaimari & Darren McRostie

Understanding Inspection Methods: Lessons from an Assessment   171
of Heuristic Evaluation
Gilbert Cockton & Alan Woolrych

Developing A Usability Capability Assessment Approach through   193
Experiments in Industrial Settings
Timo Jokela, Marko Nieminen, Netta Iivari, Katriina Nevakivi &
Mikko Rajanen

Revisiting Concepts   211

IDA-S: A Conceptual Framework for Partial Automation   213
Andrew Dearden

Beyond Mode Error: Supporting Strategic Knowledge Structures   229
to Enhance Cockpit Safety
Rachid Hourizi & Peter Johnson

DPI: A Conceptual Model Based on Documents and Interaction   247
Instruments
Olivier Beaudoux & Michel Beaudouin-Lafon

User-centred Design   265

Getting the Story Straight   267
Phil Turner, Susan Turner & Rod McCall

Augmenting the Affordance of Online Help Content 279
Milene Selbach Silveira, Simone D J Barbosa & Clarisse
Sieckenius de Souza

Beyond the Interface: Co-evolution Inside Interactive Systems — 297
A Proposal Founded on Activity Theory
Grégory Bourguin, Alain Derycke & Jean-Claude Tarby

User Interface Modelling 311

A Flexible Methodology and Support Environment for Building 313
Task Models
Cécile Paris, Jean-Claude Tarby & Keith Vander Linden

From the Formal Specifications of Users Tasks to the Automatic 331
Generation of the HCI Specifications
Adel Mahfoudhi, Mourad Abed & Dimitri Tabary

Supporting Context Changes for Plastic User Interfaces: A Process 349
and a Mechanism
Gaëlle Calvary, Joëlle Coutaz & David Thevenin

Computer-supported Collaborative Working 365

Eye-Tracking Explorations in Multimedia Communications 367
J Mullin, A H Anderson, L Smallwood, M Jackson & E Katsavras

Rich Interaction in the Context of Networked Virtual Environments 383
— Experiences Gained from the Multi-player Games Domain
Tony Manninen

Using Workflow for Coordination in Groupware Applications 399
Karim Saïkali & Bertrand David

Mobile Computing 413

ToyMobile: Image-based Telecommunication and Small Children 415
Pekka Ketola & Hannu Korhonen

The Reality Gap: Pragmatic Boundaries of Context Awareness 427
Yun-Maw Cheng & Chris Johnson

Data Capture for Clinical Anaesthesia on a Pen-based PDA: Is It a 439
Viable Alternative to Paper?
Martin Gardner, Meurig Sage, Phil Gray & Chris Johnson

Web Design 457

Interactivity and User Commitment — Relationship Building 459
through Interaction on Websites
Ann Light

Evaluating Multi-modal Input Modes in a Wizard-of-Oz Study for 475
the Domain of Web Search
Alexandra Klein, Ingrid Schwank, Michel Généreux &
Harald Trost

Dynamic Information Presentation through Web-based 485
Personalisation and Adaptation — An Initial Review
Diana Bental, Lachlan MacKinnon, Howard Williams,
David Marwick, Daniel Pacey, Euan Dempster & Alison Cawsey

Speech and Audio 501

Speech Output for Older Visually Impaired Adults 503
M Zajicek & W Morrissey

Using Non-speech Sounds to Improve Access to 2D Tabular 515
Numerical Information for Visually Impaired Users
Rameshsharma Ramloll, Stephen Brewster, Wai Yu & Beate Riedel

Diary in the Sky: A Spatial Audio Display for a Mobile Calendar 531
Ashley Walker, Stephen Brewster, David McGookin & Adrian Ng

Novel Input Devices 541

Input Device Selection and Interaction Configuration with ICON 543
Pierre Dragicevic & Jean-Daniel Fekete

Measuring the Usability of Text Input Methods for Children 559
Janet Read, Stuart MacFarlane & Chris Casey

Beyond the 10-bit Barrier: Fitts' Law in Multi-Scale Electronic   573
Worldsⁿ
Yves Guiard, Frédéric Bourgeois, Denis Mottet &
Michel Beaudouin-Lafon

Author Index   589

Keyword Index   591

Preface: Interaction Without Frontiers

This year's BCS-HCI conference marks another first for the conference series; similarly, this year's AFIHM-IHM conference marks a first for that conference series. For 2001 is the first occasion on which the two conferences have combined to transform the idea of 'interaction without frontiers' into reality. So although the proceedings you are reading looks and feels like a standard proceedings in the BCS-HCI series, it is also the proceedings of the annual IHM conference. This volume, Volume I, contains the long papers of this year's proceedings, all in English, while Volume II, which is published by Cépaduès, contains all other contributions (e.g. short papers, posters, videos, workshops, tutorials) and is bilingual. One of the challenges for readers of Volume I is to spot which papers were originally submitted and reviewed in French, before being expertly translated (by their authors) into English. Just looking at the affiliations of authors will not provide sufficient guide. One of the delights for us, as editors, has been being (so unavoidably) introduced to the work of the other language community. Through the two volumes of proceedings from this year's conference, readers can also become familiar with work that they may not have encountered previously because it has traditionally been presented within the 'other' language community.

As in previous years, the standard of accepted papers has been high: fewer than one in three of submitted papers was accepted for publication and presentation at the conference. We are also very pleased to have received written papers from all three of our keynote speakers this year, to provide a permanent reference to the material of their presentations. These represent diverse approaches to HCI research and practice: from the theoretical psychology-based work of Pierre Rabardel to the innovative technology-oriented work of Nadia Magnenat-Thalmann and the practitioner-focused work of Ken Dye.

The theme of this year's conference is 'interaction without frontiers' — a theme that reflects both the physical realities of the conference (bringing together different communities and languages) and current trends in computing development. As this conference illustrates, old boundaries between interaction devices and modalities are breaking down rapidly, as are the traditional borders between countries, communities and academic disciplines.

The theme of the conference is reflected in many of the papers being presented: on novel styles of interaction — with virtual humans, in virtual environments and in mobile computing — and on non-standard input and output technologies. It is also reflected in the range of work being presented: HCI is no longer viewed as just a branch of applied psychology, or a synonym for implementing and demonstrating novel devices. Rather, HCI is recognised as being a multidisciplinary field of research and practice. So as well as reports of work on novel styles of interaction, we find work that derives from a social sciences tradition (e.g. Adams & Sasse), from engineering (e.g. Al Qaimari & McRostie), from psychology (e.g. Mullin et al.) and from design (e.g. Dragicevic & Fekete). The multidisciplinary nature of the field is considered directly by Denley and Long. To achieve universal usability, we must take every opportunity to cross cultural and linguistic boundaries: this volume represents, in several ways, interaction without frontiers.

Ann Blandford, Jean Vanderdonckt & Phil Gray
June 2001

The Organising Committee

Conference co-chairs:	Phil Gray, *University of Glasgow*
	Alain Derycke, *Université des Sciences et Technologies de Lille*
Treasurers:	Ian Benest, *University of York*
	Christelle Farenc, *Université Toulouse 1*
Publicity:	Tom McEwan, *Napier University*
	Lachlan MacKinnon, *Heriot-Watt University*
	Patrick Girard, *ENSMA*
Website:	Andy Dearden, *Sheffield Hallam University*
	Jean-Claude Tarby, *Université des Sciences et Technologies de Lille*
Group liaison:	Chris Roast (British HCI Group), *Sheffield Hallam University*
	Bertrand David (AFIHM), *ICTT Ecole Centrale de Lyon*
Sponsorship:	Alistair Kilgour, *Real Axis Consulting*
	Jean-Daniel Fekete, *École des Mines de Nantes*
Language issues:	Chris Johnson, *University of Glasgow*
	Jean-Marc Robert, *École Polytechnique de Montréal*
Full papers:	Ann Blandford, *Middlesex University*
	Jean Vanderdonckt, *Université Catholique de Louvain*
Posters and short papers:	David Benyon, *Napier University*
	Philippe Palanque, *Université Toulouse 1*
Doctoral consortium:	John Long, *University College London*
	Laurence Nigay, *Université de Grenoble*
Workshops:	Fabio Paternò, *CNUCE-CNR*
	Bertrand David, *École Centrale de Lyon*
Tutorials:	Fintan Culwin, *South Bank University*
	Patrick Girard, *ENSMA*
Panels and round tables:	Steve Brewster, *University of Glasgow*
	Christian Bastien, *Université René Descartes – Paris V*
Interactive experience:	Xristine Faulkner, *South Bank University*
	Michel Beaudouin-Lafon, *Université Paris Sud*
Videos:	Leon Watts, *UMIST*
	Christophe Kolski, *Université de Valenciennes*
Laboratory and organisational overviews:	Eamonn O'Neill, *University of Bath*
	Franck Tarpin-Bernard, *INSA de Lyon*
Industry day:	Nigel Bevan, *Serco Usability Services*
	Alain Derycke, *Université des Sciences et Technologies de Lille*
Student volunteers:	Anna MacLeod, *South Bank University*
	José Rouillard, *Université des Sciences et Technologies de Lille*

The Reviewers

Mourad Abed	*Université de Valenciennes*
Emmanuel Adam	*Université de Valenciennes*
Yamine Ait Ameur	*ENSAE-SUPAERO /ONERA-CERT*
Francoise Anceaux	*Université de Valenciennes*
C. Baber	*University of Birmingham*
Remi Bastide	*LIHS — Université Toulouse 1*
Christian Bastien	*Université René Descartes*
Gordon Baxter	*University of York*
Mathilde Bekker	*IPO, Center for User System Interaction*
Yacine Bellik	*LIMSI-CNRS*
David Benyon	*Napier University*
Bertrand David	*École Centrale de Lyon*
Staffan Bjork	*Gotenburg University*
Marie-José Blin	*Lamsade/Université Paris-Dauphine*
Richard Boardman	*Imperial College of Science, Technology and Medicine*
Birgit Bomsdorf	*FernUniversitat Hagen*
Marie-Luce Bourguet	*Queen Mary, University of London*
Chris Bowerman	*University of Sunderland*
Stephen Brewster	*University of Glasgow*
Nick Byran-Kinns	*Icon Media Lab*
Jean Caelen	*CLIPS-IMAG*
Sandra Cairncross	*Napier University*
Samantha Campion	*User Centric*
Noëlle Carbonell	*LORIA*
Chaomei Chen	*Brunel University*
Dave Clarke	*Visualize Software*
Gilbert Cockton	*University of Sunderland*
Martin Colbert	*Kingston University*
Karin Coninx	*Limburgs Universitair Centrum*
Jonathan Crellin	*Porstmouth University*
Alison Crerar	*Napier University*
Mary Czerwinski	*Microsoft Research*
Oscar de Brujin	*Imperial College*
Geert deHaan	*Maastricht McLuhan Institute*
Corné (C.P.J.) de Koning	*Test Consultant, Source Software Testing BV*
Brigitte De La Passardiere	*Université Pierre et Marie Curie – Paris VI*
Alain Derycke	*TRIGONE Université de Lille I*
Emmanuel Dubois	*Domaine Université, Grenoble*
Jean-Marc Dubois	*Université Bordeaux 2*
Lynne Dunckley	*Open University*
Mark Dunlop	*University of Strathclyde*
Erik Duval	*Katholieke Universiteit, Leuven*
Thierry Duval	*IRISA (INRIA Rennes)*
Daphne Economou	*Manchester Metropolitan University*
Alistair Edwards	*University of York*

Alain Ejzyn	*ICHEC*
Kees Engelmoer	*KPN Research*
David England	*Liverpool John Moores University*
Christelle Farenc	*Université Toulouse I*
Jean-Daniel Fekete	*École des Mines de Nantes*
Alan Ferris	*AIT plc*
Jonathan Gass	*IBM Silicon Valley Labs*
Claude Ghaoui	*Liverpool John Moores University*
Alain Giboin	*INRIA*
Patrick Girard	*Université Poitiers*
Simon Grant	*Information Strategists*
Phil Gray	*University of Glasgow*
Tom Gross	*FIT Institute for Applied IT.*
Mountaz Hascoet	*LRI, Université Paris-Sud*
Hans-Juergen Hoffman	*Darmstadt University of Technology*
Lars Erik Holmquist	*Interactive Institute*
Kate Hone	*Brunel University*
Steve Howard	*University of Melbourne*
Ismail Ismail	*Totalise*
Francis Jambon	*LISI/ENSMA*
Phillip Jeffrey	*Bell Mobility*
Hilary Johnson	*University of Bath*
Luc Julia	*BravoBrava!*
Alistair Kilgour	*Heriot-Watt University*
Mark Kirby	*University of Huddersfield*
Arthur Kirkpatrick	*University of Oregon*
Christophe Kolski	*University of South Africa*
Eric Lecolinet	*ENST Paris / Dept. INFRES*
Jianfu Liu	*Université Libre de Bruxelles*
John Long	*University College London*
Aran Lunzer	*Hokkaido University*
Wendy Mackay	*INRIA*
Robert Macredie	*Brunel University*
Panos Markopoulos	*Eindhoven University of Technology*
Jean-Claude Martin	*LIMSI-CNRS / Université Paris 8*
Masood Masoodian	*University Waikato*
Jon May	*Sheffield University*
Patrick McAndrew	*Open University*
Sharon McDonald	*University of Sunderland*
Guy Melançon	*Lirmm*
Christophe Mertz	*CENA: Centre d'Etudes de la Navigation Aérienne*
Michelle Mongomery Masters	*Pyrusmalus*
Andrew Monk	*University of York*
David Moore	*Leeds Metropolitan University*
Thierry Morineau	*Université de Valenciennes*
Jocelyne Nanard	*LIRMM-Université Montpellie*
Alok Nandi	*Alterface*
N. Hari Narayanan	*Auburn University, USA*

Ian Newman   *Loughborough University*
Eva Olsson   *Uppsala University, Sweden*
Eamonn O'Neill   *University of Bath*
Sami Paihonen   *Nokia Mobile Phones*
Philippe Palanque   *LIHS Université Toulouse 1*
Fabio Paternò   *CNUCE-CNR*
André Peninou   *Université de Valenciennes*
Simon Polovina   *Hertfordshire University*
Helen Purchase   *The University of Queensland*
Roope Raisamo   *University of Tampere, Finland*
Rakhi Rajani   *Brunel University, Middlesex*
Nina Reeves   *Cheltenham & Gloucester College of HE*
Dimitrios Rigas   *University of Bradford*
Chris Roast   *Sheffield Hallam University*
Laurence Rognin   *Pacte Novation, France*
Tony Rose   *Canon Research Centre Europe Ltd*
Nicolas Roussel   *Université de Fribourg*
Daniel Salber   *IBM T.J. Watson Research Center*
Angela Sasse   *University College London*
Dominique Scapin   *INRIA*
Brian Shackel   *Loughborough University*
Andy Sloane   *University of Wolverhampton*
Mark-Alexander Sujan   *Universität Karlsruhe*
Jean-Claude Tarby   *Institut CUEEP – Université Lille 1*
Franck Tarpin-Bernard   *ICTT-INSA de Lyon*
Mark Treglown   *University of Nottingham*
Jacqueline Vacherand-Revel   *École Centrale*
Peter Van Roy   *University College London*
Carol Vella
Alfred Vella
Paul Vickers   *Liverpool John Moores University*
Nadine Vigouroux   *IRIT, UMR CNRS 5505*
Fred Voorhorst   *The Fantastic Corporation R&D*
Denise Whitelock   *Open University*
William Wong   *Swinburne University of Technology*

Keynote Papers

As Easy to Use as a Banking Machine

Ken Dye

Microsoft Corporation, Redmond, WA 98052, USA

Tel: *+1 425 936 7011*

Email: *kend@microsoft.com*

Over 100 million people use productivity suites such as Microsoft Office to accomplish a huge variety of tasks. Most of those tasks are 'problem solving' tasks that require users to generate novel solutions in novel situations. It is the problem solving nature of work that makes designing productivity software difficult. It is difficult for the designer to anticipate and understand the user's task. As a consequence, productivity suites present difficulties for users and those difficulties are often discussed in the HCI community. Despite the difficulties involved in designing productivity software, suites are 'pretty well' designed and users are successful using them. Productivity software is only 'pretty well' designed because current user research practice is good at locally optimising individual features in products. When users are not successful it is because current user research practices are not very good at understanding the kinds of problem solving tasks that constitute work. Practitioners do not currently have good methods for taking field observations and turning those observations into design. It is only by developing these methods that we can improve the design of productivity software. Understanding how to turn observations into designs is very important to improving the design of productivity software and it is very difficult. Solving this problem will require cooperation between HCI researchers and HCI practitioners.

Keywords: usability, product design, software design, scenarios, foeld research.

1 Introduction

Over the past ten years, Microsoft has done over 8000 user studies involving more than 60,000 participants. That total includes over 500 observational studies involving more than 5000 users. We have, in our archives, over 90,000 hours of videotape of users using software. 8000 user studies is a large amount of effort to design software and solve HCI problems. At CHI'99, I was on a panel[1] with Jakob Nielsen who said , "Microsoft does a lot of usability, why aren't their products well designed." I have two answers to that question. First, there is a fundamental problem of software design that we have not solved. And, second that problem cannot be solved by either researchers or practitioners alone, and researchers and practitioners have not found a way to work together effectively to solve it.

When I say software I really mean what has come to be called 'productivity' software. I will talk about productivity software, and in particular about Microsoft Office, because that is what I have worked on for the last ten years and it is what I know. I believe that Microsoft Office is a good example to use because it is typical of productivity software and is used by millions of people. And, I believe that what I will say about Microsoft Office applies to many kinds of software and many design problems.

In talking about productivity software I would like to make the point that Microsoft Office, and productivity software in general, is not really productivity software in the scientific management sense of productivity. That is, its real value is not in allowing you to do more work or to work faster but rather to help solve an infinite variety of novel problems. It is problem solving software.

The fundamental problem in designing productivity software is that we do not know how to describe the problem solving tasks that users perform. And, even if we can describe the problem solving tasks, we do not know how to take descriptions of what many individual people do, in the form of observational data, and create software that enables them to do these tasks. To design better software we need to understand how to take the complex and messy world that users work in and turn it in to software. According to Bruce Blum in 'Beyond Programming':

> "Consider the perspectives of in-the-computer (i.e. that of programming) and in-the-world (i.e. that which is beyond programming). What is in-the-computer is of interest only to the extent that it is difficult to construct. What is in-the-computer is also in the world, and its utilitarian evaluation depends on its behaviour in-the world. But there are profound differences in form between what is in-the-computer and in-the-world. The former is stable and formally represented, whereas the latter is dynamic and not fully understood." (Blum, 1996)

Because the world is "dynamic and not fully understood" it is difficult to design software that adapts to the world. This is a particularly difficult problem because of the number of people who use productivity software. Gerhard Fischer points out that:

> "One of the fundamental problems of system design is how to write software for millions of users (at design time), while making it work as if it were designed for each individual user (who is known only at use time)." (Fischer, to appear)

---

[1] Panel entitled "What Makes Strategic Usability Fail: Lessons from the Field". Stephanie Rosenbaum, Moderator.

Fischer's solution is to design "context aware applications", which, as he points out, "requires a broader understanding of context".

'Appliances' may be another possible solution. Don Norman has pointed out one of the really difficult issues of designing software for personal computers:

> "Make a single device do everything, and each task will be done in a manner that is adequate, but not superior. As I have explained before, a multipurpose device cannot be optimised for any single task; it has to be a compromise." (Norman, 1998)

Norman's solution is information appliances based on activity based computing:

> "The basic idea is simple: Make it possible to have all the material needed for an activity ready at hand with little or no mental overhead." (Norman, 1998)

The idea of activity based computing seems quite sensible to me and may be the way that products should be designed. Even activity based computing and designing information appliances, however, rely on our ability to understand work through observation and turn those observations into design. The problem does not go away just because we move towards activity based computing. To design better software we must understand the world better and know how to turn that understanding into design. To design better productivity software we must understand work better and know how to turn that understanding into design.

It is my claim that we do not have very good tools for understanding problem solving work or for turning an understanding of problem solving work into design. Developing these tools is a very difficult problem that cannot be solved by researchers alone or practitioners alone. Solving this problem will require cooperation.

2 The State of Productivity Software

It is easy to overstate the case that productivity software is poorly designed. It is in fact 'pretty well designed' given the state of the art of designing software. That does not mean that Microsoft Office is always perfectly adapted to the user. Some users experience frustrations and difficulties with Microsoft Office. And, I think we can extend that statement to cover all productivity software. There are a number of reasons why users sometimes have difficulties but the primary reason is that designers, and HCI professionals in general, do not know how to understand adequately the problem solving work that people do and how to create products that adapt to that work.

If I am to make the claim that Microsoft Office is pretty well designed I should support that claim with data. In November 2000 we did a survey of knowledge workers called the Microsoft Product Satisfaction Study 2000. We asked knowledge workers: "How would you rate the quality of your current Microsoft Office Suite?" 60% rated the quality of Microsoft Office at 8 or 9 (a top box score) on a nine-point scale. 0% rated Microsoft Office quality at 1–4 (bottom box score) on a nine-point scale. Many users seem to believe that Microsoft Office is well designed and built.

A high customer satisfaction score does not mean that Microsoft Office is perfectly designed. It may be that user expectations are very low because of their experiences with software. It may be that for many users Microsoft Office is the only product they use and they have no comparison. But, it does indicate that many users find Microsoft to be useful. And to achieve that level of customer satisfaction Microsoft Office must at least be 'pretty well designed' for users.

At the end of the product cycle for each version of Office we do a 'baseline' study to see how well we did designing Microsoft Office. The results from the baseline study for Office 2000 indicate that users are very successful at a wide range of tasks (see Table 1).

For most 'unitary' tasks users perform quite well. Most of the tasks on which users do not perform very well involve new technology, specifically HTML and The Web.

The goal of the baseline studies is to tell us something about our design process, not make broad claims about the design of Microsoft Office. If I were to use this data to decide whether Office was well designed, my major criticism would be that it doesn't capture the real measure of good design — the ratio between the time the user spends attending to the task and the time the user spends attending to the software. Nor does it specify the task in a way that is meaningful to all users. The first problem is the result of our understanding, at the time, of how to design baseline studies. The second problem is more complicated. We really cannot think of how to represent the task in a way that is meaningful to all or even many users. We just don't understand the tasks well enough. Even so, this data does indicate that, at some level, Microsoft Office is 'pretty well' designed for the tasks it is designed to support.

As HCI professionals we can see many problems with the design of Microsoft Office. Often we can actually provide empirical evidence for those problems. And, when we talk with users we hear about their particular frustrations and difficulties. How can users be satisfied with and perform well with software that is 'pretty well' designed? And, why is Microsoft Office not perfectly adapted to the user's work? The answer to the first question is that users are very smart and find very clever ways to apply the tools we give them. The second question has to do with the current state of software design.

3   Designing Software — Current Practice

At its best, current software design practice begins by specifying some user task in the form of a scenario (Carroll, 1995). The scenario is, or should be, the result of careful field observation of users. Once the task is specified, designers generate a number of possible designs in the form of low-fidelity prototypes. These designs are presented to users to determine which general approach is likely to work best. After selecting an approach, the designer creates more realistic prototypes that are refined through a process of rapid iterative testing.

This practice has evolved over the last ten years. Initially designers relied mostly on rapid-iterative testing. Then they began to do low fidelity prototyping. Recently, designers have begun working with ethnographers to do field observations. This evolution has led to a big improvement over the way software was designed

	Time on Task (secs)	Success Rate
Web Related		
18 Save PPT doc as an HTML doc to Web Folder subfolder	165	77%
22 Find and choose a Theme	166	100%
24 Link to a specified document	191	100%
25 Publish Interactive Spreadsheet to Web Folder	208	21%
26 Make an intra-doc link	197	30%
28a Edit an web page from seeing it in IE	60	90%
28b Save to the HTML file from which web page was opened	24	88%
29 Create an email link	106	100%
File management		
1 Open file from My Docs	16	100%
2 Open file from Desktop	34	93%
3 Save file to Desktop	26	93%
5 Use Office dialog's View Button	83	100%
6 Open a file read-only	93	71%
9 Save doc to My Docs	27	100%
11 Choose and open a file based on appearance	158	69%
Formatting		
22 Find and choose a Theme	166	100%
8 Bullet a list	59	100%
23 Choose custom bullets	123	69%
19 Add a horizontal line	125	77%
21 Add a heading for a list	110	93%
15 Print Preview	29	100%
16 Save to Word 95 format	77	86%
Assistance		
10 Hide the Office Assistant	16	93%
13 Bring the Assistant back from Hiding and ask a question	56	100%
20 Turn Office Assistant off	53	93%
30 Turn Office Assistant back on from Off	42	92%
Minor Command Changes		
5 Use Office dialog's View Button choices	83	100%
6 Open a file read-only	93	71%
7 Office Find by Author	278	54%
11 Choose and open a file based on appearance	158	69%
28b Save to the HTML file from which the web page was opened.	44	73%
No changes		
8 Bullet a list	59	100%
21 Add a heading for a list	111	93%
15 Print Preview	29	100%
16 Save to Word 95 format	77	86%
New To Office 2000		
30 Turn Office Assistant back on from Off	42	92%
20 Turn Office Assistant off	53	93%
22 Find and choose a Theme	166	100%
17 Make a new directory on an established Web site	195	67%
25 Publish Interactive Spreadsheet to Web Folder subfolder	208	21%

Table 1: Results of the Microsoft Office 2000 baseline study (Allen, 1999).

10 years ago and there are many examples of that improvement in Microsoft Office and other software. But, the key to making this process work is specifying the task in a sufficiently rich scenario that is useful to inform the design. Currently, we do not understand how to take field observations and turn them into scenarios that are useful for design. We end up locally optimising individual features as the results from the Microsoft Office 2000 baseline demonstrate. Rapid-iterative testing is still the basic activity of design and rapid-iterative testing is a hill climbing method that leads to local optima. Without the right scenario we do not know if we are climbing the right hill. Creating scenarios is the weakest part of the design process and understanding how to create scenarios is the central problem that HCI researchers and HCI practitioners should work together to solve.

There are other reasons that design is difficult. Some are avoidable and others are not. Legacy issues create difficult trade-offs for designers. Software engineering is largely a craft industry. The work of coding products must be divided up into 'features' for individual developers to code. That leads to optimising those features. An additional problem is that we often design software with technology in mind rather than user tasks. Technology based design was a common theme at the ACM Conference on Computing Technology in March 2000 (Konrad, n.d.). In an effort to apply the latest technology we create scenarios that are not meaningful to users.

Some claims about why software is only 'pretty well' designed are misconceptions. It is sometimes suggested that the problem of poor design is an economic question — that software companies do not care about designing products for their users but instead care only about profits. Two things strike me as wrong about this claim. First, it suggests the problems associated with software design are not difficult and that if companies just adopted the right stance towards the user software would be well designed — just as I once believed that if software companies cared enough about the user to do usability testing they would produce well designed software. Second, it has been my experience that companies do understand the importance of good design for successful products and that good design is one of the many things companies must and do consider when creating products.

4   As Easy to Use as a Banking Machine

One way we have tried to bridge the gulf between HCI practitioners and researchers is to invite researchers to Microsoft to see what we do. It is our hope that they can tell us things that will help us do our job better. It is also our hope that they will come to understand the practical issues involved in designing and shipping software. Several years ago we invited Ben Shneiderman to visit Microsoft while attending a conference in Seattle. It is difficult for me to think of anyone who as made a greater contribution to HCI and my own understanding of HCI than Ben Shneiderman. While in Seattle, Ben gave an interview with a local newspaper in which he said: "Computers should be as easy to use as a banking machine."

Intuitively banking machines are easy to use, although they are not perfect. I recently gave my ATM card and password to a friend from southern Africa and asked her to get some money from an ATM. She had to call me several times before she was successful. And, I have stood in front of a banking machine in London for several minutes waiting for my money when I was supposed to take my card. Banking machines in the US generally give you the money first and then return your card. Never-the-less, as easy to use as a banking machine is a useful goal.

Why is a banking machine easy to use? When you step up to an ATM the software knows a lot about your task. It knows that you want to do one of a few things that it does — withdraw money, deposit money, or check your balance. These are all relatively well-structured tasks. By well structured I mean that the starting point is clear, the goal is clear and the steps for getting from the starting point to the goal are clear. And, we know a lot about that task domain when we insert our bank card. We share an understanding of the task with the machine.

Current observational methods seem to work quite well for designing software for well-structured tasks. But, how much of a user's work involves well structured tasks? Most of the work that people do is not like interacting with a banking machine. Most work involves problem solving, and solving a problem means creating something novel. It is impossible for the machine to understand much about the user's task because the user doesn't know the solution to the problem until she has solved it. A student writing to her parents for money doesn't know what she is going to say until she has written the letter. And, to understand why she eventually says what she says requires understanding the student's financial situation, her relationship with her parents, what she needs the money for and a host of other variables. According to Lucy Suchman:

> "Even in the case of more deliberative, less highly skilled activities, we generally do not anticipate alternative courses of action, or their consequences, until some course of action is already under way. It is frequently only on acting in a present situation that its possibilities become clear, and we often do not know ahead of time, or at least not with any specificity what future state we desire to bring about." (Suchman, 1987)

If the user cannot specify the task in advance, how can the software?

5   Real Work

Shari Schneider, an ethnographer in the Microsoft Mobile Group, recently did a field study of the way people work focusing on work involving mobile devices. She found that users frequently referred to the work they do at their PC as 'real work'. Among other things, real work involved 'gathering thoughts' and 'thinking about complex issues':

> "In comparison to what they can do with mobile devices, participants defined their work pc, home pc and their laptop while mobile as places where they do 'real work'. Participants have identified the following aspects of 'real work':
>
> **Working with Documents**

- Creating, navigating, composing (in terms of both physical data input and 'gathering thoughts'), editing, and reading documents were expressed as types of 'real work'.

- Thinking about complicated issues when composing an email or creating a document. As mentioned above, this concept was expressed consistently by participants, and was defined in terms of the desktop pc as a place where they can get organised in their thoughts as well as in their materials . . .

- Accessing other resources in the office, such as people, files, books and other shared office information." (Schneider, 2000)

Is it possible to specify the tasks that constitute real work in such a way that the designer can adapt software to the task, or does real work involve a number of tools applied in many different situations? A letter to your parents is a relatively simple problem solving task. The typical work product — a report, a plan, an analysis — is much more complex and responds to a much more complex audience and situation. And, the artefact itself may be much more complex. It may contain pictures, symbols, charts, and so on. And the user may need a large set of tools simply to construct that artefact. What can the designer, or the software, know about the user's task? It is enough to know that the user is writing? Is it enough to know that the user is writing a report? It helps. Templates are an attempt to take advantage of our limited knowledge of the user's task. But, each individual problem is new, and exists in situation that is too complex for even the user to fully represent in advance. If it were not, users would create perfect solutions every time.

6   Tools for Novel Tasks

Home repairs is a good analogy to the type of work Knowledge Workers do. In the US we have a chain of stores called Eagle Hardware. Eagle Hardware stores are the largest, most complete, and most confusing hardware stores you can imagine. You can get anything at an Eagle Hardware. Eagle Hardware stores can be fun if you don't actually have to find anything. But, finding things is very difficult.

Most people have a small set of tools at home for doing home repairs — a few screwdrivers, two pairs of pliers, a hammer, a level, and perhaps a few more. For the vast majority of tasks the home-owner performs, these tools are adequate. The hammer might not be the perfect hammer for a particular job, but it works. The home-owner may be using a screwdriver when an awl is the right tool, but the screwdriver works. This is very much the situation with productivity suites. The 80/20 rule, that 80% of users use only 20% of the functionality in Microsoft Office — but not the same 20%, applies to home repair tools, although there are very few home-owners who use 20% of Eagle Hardware's tools.

Occasionally, home-owners come across tasks for which their small, familiar set of tools is not adequate. For example, a home-owner may want to remove some wallpaper, a task few people have ever done or may ever do again. It is very unlikely that the typical home-owner will have the right tools for the task or even understand how to use those tools. So, the home-owner goes to Eagle Hardware.

In many cases the home-owner is not sure what the right tool is or exactly how to use it. In such a case, both the home-owner and Eagle Hardware have a problem. The home-owner wants to get the right tools to get the job done. Eagle hardware wants the home-owner to know what the right tools are so that she will buy them. Occasionally the home-owner can solve the problem by browsing. The home-owner goes to the home decorator sections, finds the various tools for removing wallpaper, reads the packaging, and purchases the right tool. Unfortunately home-owners sometimes buy the wrong tool or don't use it properly with disastrous results.

Because Eagle Hardware has a stake in solving the problem, Eagle Hardware provides various experts to assist the home-owner. The home-owner goes to the home decorator expert and begins a dialogue. The purpose of this dialogue is for Eagle Hardware to understand the users task. Fischer & Reeves show that this dialogue is cooperative problem solving in which both the home-owner and the customer and the sales agent are trying to arrive at a representation of the problem that is satisfactory (Fischer & Reeves, 1995). What kind of wallpaper is it? How was it attached to the wall? What kind of wall is it? If the home-owner can give Eagle Hardware enough information, the expert can select the right tool and, with a little instruction and trial and error, the home-owner can remove the wallpaper.

Thinking, composing, calculating, and communicating is a much larger problem set than home repairs. But, the problem is similar. Every tool at Eagle Hardware has been optimised for some home-owner task. But the difficulty of doing home repairs has not gone away. Every feature in Microsoft Office is locally optimised to some task because that is what we have accomplished with user testing. But the difficulty of doing problem-solving work with computers has not gone away.

Is it possible to understand the novel, ill-structured, problem solving tasks people think of as 'real work'? And, is it possible to instantiate that understanding in software that makes the task simple? These questions are very difficult to answer without good methods for collecting observations and turning them into designs. I am not suggesting that designing can be mechanical, only that good heuristics for understanding how to understand real work and how to adapt software to real work are a critical part of designing software. And, that it is a part of designing software that we don't know enough about.

7 Solving the Design Problem

Part of the reason these problem have not been solved is that they cannot be solved by either researchers alone or practitioners alone. Many researchers have addressed part of the problem of understanding and representing field observations. Lucy Suchman (1987) and Ed Hutchins (1995) are two examples that have influenced our work at Microsoft. John Carroll's (1995) work on scenario based design has also influence our work. Work by William Newman (1997) on defining critical parameters for system design is another example. For most practitioners the primary tool is Contextual Inquiry based on methods developed by Whiteside et al. (1988) and refined by Hugh Beyer & Karen Holtzblatt (1998). At Microsoft we have hired a number of ethnographers over the past five years and used CI and other observational methods extensively. Our experience has been that the strength of CI is that it teaches

designers how to observe users. Its weakness is that it has not helped designers
to generalise those observations and turn them into design. The practical question
is whether it is possible, given the kind of work people do, to successfully turn
observational data into design. Is it ever possible to turn a real world need into a
formal computer program?

Solving this fundamental design problem will involve two kinds of activities.
The first activity is defining the problem and generating the right research issues by
observing many types of users in many different contexts. In other words, we first
have to generate the right set of questions to answer about real work. The second
activity is carefully researching the answers to those questions and testing them in
real software. Practitioners are particularly positioned and skilled at generating the
right set of questions. Researchers are skilled at researching and arriving at answers
to those questions. By combining those two skills HCI can make real progress
towards improving design methods.

Unfortunately, researchers and practitioners do not have a good history of
cooperating to solve HCI problems. In 1993 I was involved in the development of
the Usability Professionals Association along with Janice James, the first president
of UPA, Jack Young, and Dave Rhinehart because most practitioners felt that ACM
SigCHI, the major conference in the HCI field, and other conferences did not address
their needs. Too often, they felt, CHI was focused on the cool new device or the cool
new technology rather than the real problems of designing software.

I do not mean here to discount the contribution of applied research to the
practice of designing software. One of the first articles that influenced user research
at Microsoft was by Wright & Monk (1991). That was followed by Virzi's (1992)
paper on number of subjects and a CHI paper by Nielsen & Landauer (1993).
Finally, discount usability testing became the standard method as formulated in
Jakob Nielsen's (1993b), 'Usability Engineering'. Much of the research that has
influenced practice has been in developing new methods for using empirical methods
to design software and it has improved design practice. But still, the history of
researchers and practitioners working together to generate and solve HCI problems
could have been better.

There are obstacles to researchers and practitioners working together. Most
practitioners work in environments where competitive advantage is, or at least seems
to be important. So, most practitioners are unable to publish their work routinely.
And, intellectual property is often an issue both for researchers and practitioners.
Practitioners and researchers are engaged in very different activities. Practitioners
are engaged in building and shipping software. Researchers are engaged in adding
to what we know about users and software. But practitioners and researchers share
a common goal, designing software that makes peoples lives better even if we go
about it in a different ways and our day-to-day activities are very different.

John Seely Brown and Paul Duguid describe a famous example of the failure of
practitioners and researchers to work effectively together — the failure of Xerox to
turn the work on the Xerox Star into a successful product. This example illuminates
some of the cultural differences between researchers and practitioners:

"In the case of the GUI, however, when the researchers, with their new criteria met the engineers, each side accused the other of arrogance or stupidity (or both). It's easy to blame the corporate side for such exchanges, particularly when the invention goes on the be a success. But where the GUI researchers had had the opportunity to develop their understanding incrementally in practice, the engineers had to make a large conceptual leap in one go." (Brown & Duguid, 2000)

Solving the problem of turning observations into designs will require access to many types of users in many domains. Practitioners routinely have access to large numbers of users as the output from the Microsoft Usability Labs shows. And, practitioners are skilled at implementing and testing solutions for a wide range of users and environments. It is from the practical design of productivity software that some of the problems that researchers can address, at least in this area, should come. Discussing the application of cognitive psychology to system design, Thomas Landauer says:

"It seems to me that mutually beneficial relations between cognitive psychology and system design can never the less occur. The essence of the investigative procedure I advocate is as follows. The investigator, applied psychologist or system designer, should set up a situation in which people doing a task that is, one hopes, to be aided by a computer system can be observed an recorded in some detail. From this the range of problems that are encountered and the things that people, novice or expert, can do well are noted." (Landauer, 1988)

Landauer goes on to advocate a form of rapid iterative usability testing. But, he continues:

"This is fine for system development, but what does it have to do with the science of human cognition? I maintain that the same process is well suited for generating the problems and serving as a testing ground for investigations of true scientific value in cognitive psychology. When particular problems are encountered repeatedly and found to be severe, in the context of a fully working (or partly working system), but the fix or cure for the problems is not obvious to the designer, on has identified a prime candidate for deeper research." (Landauer, 1988)

Landauer is talking about the application of cognitive psychology to system design but his statement holds true for any form of HCI research. Practitioners work with large numbers of users in realistic contexts every day to solve design problems. We have been pretty successful at solving local design problems and locally optimising features. We have been less successful at understanding complex problem solving environments, the type of environment people face at work, and turning that understanding into design. However, practitioners do not have the goal, nor the skills to do the deeper research need to solve the problem. But, the practice of building and shipping software generates a large number of questions that can lead to "investigations of true scientific nature" and for creating software that improves people's lives.

I am aware that I have raised an issue without proposing a practical concrete solution. However, the first step is to understand the nature of the gulf between HCI research and HCI practice so that gulf can be bridged. If we cannot represent the problem correctly, neither community will make much progress towards improving the design of software. I do have some suggestions from my point of view as a practitioner:

- Researchers and practitioners should take each other seriously. Often when I talk to a software designer about some article or line of research that is relevant to the design problem they are working on, I get a responses like "Oh, what products have they shipped" or "They think my job is so easy". When I talk to researchers they sometimes attribute all the problems with software to inept (or worse, unprincipled) practitioners. Researchers should keep in mind that shipping a successful software product is a major intellectual and engineering achievement. Practitioners should remember that many of the designs we take for granted are the result of careful and painstaking research.

- We should provide data for our claims. Some claims about the design of software are little more than conjecture or opinion. For example, the Start button in Windows has become an easy target for criticism recently. Why, critics say, is 'Shut Down' under the start button. It is under the Start button because we did a number of user studies and found that users were very successful shutting down their computer. And, based on those studies, we believe it is because users think of the Start button much like they think of the 'Power' button on their receiver, or an unlabelled light switch. We would love to see other ideas or additional data, but given what we learned in the lab we feel we could support the design decision.

- We should stop focusing on widgets. Andrew Kwatinetz, a program manager at Microsoft, is fond of saying, "Let's save our users hours, not seconds". Interface elements are an important part of product design. But, the issues in product design that will save users hours are in matching the software to the task.

- Let's think carefully about how new technologies affect the user's experience with the computer. Speech recognition, virtual reality, intelligent agents are important lines of research. They are important to researchers because they may lead to new insights about computing. They are important to software companies because software companies cannot allow competitors to develop new technologies that will give them a competitive edge. But HCI researchers and practitioners have the burden of demonstrating that new technologies can be really beneficial to users.

  For example, some people, mostly in industry have believed that solving the speech recognition problem will make computers easy to use. We did a number of 'Wizard of Oz' experiments using a perfect speech recognition system, another human being fully knowledgeable about the system. My conclusion from those studies is that language understanding and speech recognition are not sufficient. For speech to be a useful way of interacting with computers we must overcome a whole host of communication issues.

It is important to include new technologies in software products. But, it is also important to understand that they may cause some difficulties for users. It is important to do research on new technologies, but it is also important, at least for HCI researchers and practitioners, to demonstrate how they might be helpful to users.

- Finally, we need to really understand how to use ethnographic methods and field observations to design software. Ethnographic methods currently have cache. And, using ethnographic methods seems essential to designing good scenarios and good software. But, there is still a lot we do not know about what kind of observations to make, what kind of data to collect, and how to use that data once it is collected.

HCI has borrowed many methods from many disciplines, and ethnographic methods promise to be a useful addition to the HCI toolkit. If ethnographic methods are to fulfil that promise they have to be applied by practitioners who are HCI researchers first and not anthropologists first. And, HCI researchers have to carefully investigate and explore how ethnographic research can lead to better software design.

If our common goal and responsibility as HCI practitioners and HCI researchers is to create software that works for users, we have to find a way to cooperate on that goal. The practitioner's role is to generate the problems that lead to fruitful research, and to find ways to implement the results of research into useful products. The researcher's role is to carefully understand and investigate those problems to come up with novel and interesting solutions. Without this cooperation many of the problems users face will be very difficult to solve.

References

Allen, L. A. (1999), Baseline Usability Study of Office 2000, Unpublished Technical Report. Microsoft Corporation.

Beyer, H. & Holtzblatt, K. (1998), *Contextual Design: Defining Customer-centered Systems*, Morgan-Kaufmann.

Blum, B. I. (1996), *Beyond Programming: To a New Era of Design*, Oxford University Press.

Brown, J. S. & Duguid, P. (2000), *The Social Life of Information*, The Harvard Business School Press.

Carroll, J. M. (ed.) (1995), *Scenario-Based Design: Envisioning Work and Technology in System Development*, John Wiley & Sons.

Fischer, G. (to appear), "Articulating the Task at Hand and Making Information Relevant to It", *Human–Computer Interaction* . Special Issue on Context-Aware Computing. http://www.cs.colorado.edu/ gerhard/papers/hci2001.pdf.

Fischer, G. & Reeves, B. (1995), Beyond Intelligent Interfaces: Exploring, Analyzing and Creating Success Models of Cooperative Problem Solving, *in* W. A. S. B. R M Bæcker, J Grudin & S. Greenberg (eds.), *Human–Computer Interaction: Toward the Year 2000*, Morgan-Kaufmann, pp.823–31.

Hutchins, E. (1995), *Cognition in the Wild*, MIT Press.

Konrad, R. (n.d.), "Scientists, Engineers Rail at PC Industry", ZD Net News, 14 March 2001, http://www.zdnet.com/zdnn/stories/news/0,4586,2696127,00.html.

Landauer, T. K. (1988), Research Methods in Human–Computer Interaction, *in* M. Helander (ed.), *Handbook of Human–Computer Interaction*, North-Holland, pp.905–928.

Newman, W. M. (1997), Better or Just Different? On the Benefits of Designing Interactive Systems in Terms of Critical Parameters, *in* G. C. van der Veer, A. Henderson & S. Coles (eds.), *Proceedings of the Symposium on Designing Interactive Systems: Processes, Practices, Methods and Techniques (DIS'97)*, ACM Press, pp.239–45.

Nielsen, J. (1993), *Usability Engineering*, Academic Press.

Nielsen, J. & Landauer, T. K. (1993), A Mathematical Model of the Finding of Usability Problems, *in* S. Ashlund, K. Mullet, A. Henderson, E. Hollnagel & T. White (eds.), *Proceedings of INTERCHI'93*, ACM Press/IOS Press, pp.206–13.

Norman, D. A. (1998), *The Invisable Computer*, MIT Press.

Schneider, S. (2000), Mobile Tool Taxonomy: An Ethnographic Study, Unpublished Technical Report. Microsoft Corporation.

Suchman, L. A. (1987), *Plans and Situated Actions — The Problem of Human–Machine Communication*, Cambridge University Press.

Virzi, R. A. (1992), "Refining the Test Phase of Usability Evaluation: How Many Subjects is Enough", *Human Factors* **34**(4), 457–68.

Whiteside, J., Bennett, J. & Holtzblatt, K. (1988), Usability Engineering: Our Experience and Evolution, *in* M. Helander (ed.), *Handbook of Human–Computer Interaction*, North-Holland, pp.791–817.

Wright, P. C. & Monk, A. F. (1991), "A Cost-effective Evaluation Method for Use by Designers", *International Journal of Man–Machine Studies* **35**(6), 891–912.

Instrument Mediated Activity in Situations

Pierre Rabardel

Université Paris 8 – CNRS, ESA 7021, 2 rue de la Liberté,
F-93526 Saint Denis Cedex 2, France

Tel: *+33 1 49 40 64 95*

Email: *pierre.rabardel@univ-paris8.fr*

This chapter contributes to the development of the ecological view of human activity with artefacts. It identifies crucial principals for human-centred design and presents a theoretical framework for an understanding of what an instrument is in the eyes of the person using it. The design of instruments is considered as an activity distributed between designers and users. Prospects for human-centred design are put forward.

Keywords: artefact, human-centred design, instrument, affordance, utilisation scheme, tailoring activities, personal view, mediation, formative model.

1 Introduction

This chapter aims to contribute to the development of an ecological view of human use of artefacts as a means for activity[1]. Rasmussen (1997) recently outlined the evolution of models attempting to describe human behaviour:

> "...in several human sciences a common trend is found in modelling behaviour. Efforts are moving from normative models of rational behaviour, through efforts to model the observed less rational behaviour by means of models of the deviation from rational, toward focus on representing directly the actually observed behaviour, and ultimately to efforts to model behaviour-generating mechanisms."

Based on these analyses, Vicente (1999) points out that these evolutions are from normative models to descriptive models and more recently, to formative

---

[1] In this text, we will not treat relations with artefacts and technical systems when they are the objects of the activity, as is the case, for example, in the control process.

models. He describes formative models as approaches where "the workers finish the design".

The approach put forward in this paper springs from this latest generation of models as well as methods of analyzing work and more generally, activity. It offers a theoretical framework to allow an understanding of what an instrument is for the person using it and how users continue design in usage. It also allows the design of artefacts that reflect this point of view and foster the continuation of design in usage: anthropocentred artefacts.

In the first part, I will define, based on the literature, the principles that I feel are essential to theoretical frameworks that foster human-centred design. In the second part, I will use a study of driving vehicles to develop a theoretical framework of the mediated instrument in terms of situations and their different organisational levels. In the third part, I will come back to the meaning of activities by which subjects continue design in usage by suggesting that we consider the design of instruments as an activity distributed between designers and users. I will put forward prospects for design.

2   Principles that Foster Human-centred Design

In this first part, in referring to the literature, I will identify six constituting principles[2] of human design and man/artefact relations suitable for human-centred design.

1. Norman (1991) suggests that we distinguish between two possible points of view on artefacts: the 'personal view' and the 'system view'. He defines these as follows:

   > "Under the system view, the system is composed of the person, the task and the artefact. The artefact enhances the performances of the system. The system view is taken by the designer and or the researcher. Under the personal view, the artefact changes the nature of the task the person is facing. The personal view is taken by the user, the person, the subject."

   Each of these two possible points of view are, of course, legitimate. Engeström (1990) summed up the issues at stake in interaction between design and utilisation processes: it is vital for the user to take the system view whereas the designer must work from the personal view. I share this conclusion wholeheartedly and formulate it as the following principle: *human-centred design must be predominantly organised around the personal view*[3].

2. The system view approach implies, more often than not, that agents have a symmetrical position within the system. Whether they are humans or artefacts, they are considered equally as actors of the system. This position offers the

---

[2]The six principles we identify are definitely not exhaustive. However, we consider them sufficiently crucial to be at the heart of any approach concerning human-centred design.

[3]Of course, the personal view alone is not enough to design efficient and reliable artefacts but it is essential to making them effectively antropocentred.

advantage of considering the different components of the system in a unitary conceptual framework. However, it also throws up major problems for an objective understanding of human activity with artefacts. In particular, it only rarely corresponds to the personal view and as such, does not easily allow the design of anthropocentred artefacts.

The personal view is fundamentally asymmetrical. For this reason, I have formulated a second principle: *the conceptual frameworks most conducive to the design of anthropocentred artefacts are those which are organised around the asymmetry of the relationship between subjects and artefacts, asymmetry being constitutive of the personal view.*

3. Activity theory:

> "...assumes an asymmetric relation between people and things, in contrast to the proposal of a symmetric relationship offered by cognitive science or various brands of computer science, where computer programs and human behaviours are modelled using the same language and methods. Activity theory places computer applications, along with other artefacts as mediators of human activity." (Bødker & Graves Petersen, 2000).

As of 1931, Vygotsky (1978) considered mediation as the main fact of psychological activity. Today, the mediating nature of artefacts is identified by several authors in different scientific fields (Léontiev, 1981; Kaptelinin, 1996; Engeström, 1990). This leads us to the third principle: *artefacts are mediators of their users' action and finalised activity.*

4. Artifacts have a constituting social and cultural element: they are shared within communities and contribute to the accumulation and transmission of culture (Cole, 1996; Wertsch, 1998). The forth principle can be formulated as follows: *mediating artefacts are socially situated and culturally distinctive.*

5. The fifth principle, highlighted by the same authors, is correlative to that above: *mediating artefacts undergo a process of appropriation-development by users.*

6. Finally, the development of research in situated activity Suchman (1987) allows us to put forward a sixth principle: *activity mediated by instruments is always situated and situations have a determining influence on activity.*

I am convinced that the respect of these principles is a necessary prerequisite to the development of human-centred design. However, it is not enough in itself. Designing anthropocentred artefacts also means working based on a theory of the status, the nature and the usage of the instrument by the subject. I will now explore this by organising our presentation around the situated nature of the instrument-mediated activity.

3   Instrument Mediated Activity and Situations

Our study concerns driving a vehicle with a drivers' aid device[4].

The device in question is a semi-automatic gearbox for a truck designed to meet two main objectives:

- The reduction of fuel consumption (a vital consideration for transport companies).

- A reduction in driving effort to improve driver comfort and health.

This gearbox has a computer linked to traditional gearbox mechanisms, a display screen and a gear selector in the cabin. The computer processes information from different sensors. It displays recommended gear ratios based on driving conditions and the state of the vehicle's drive chain. It is designed to give drivers optimum performance at the most fuel-efficient gear ratios. It also aims to reduce wear and tear by avoiding over-revving and handling errors. Its designers consider that the computer is the equivalent of a 'good driver': fast and economical, optimising driving efficiency.

The selector allows the driver to choose between a 'high-performance' mode and an 'economical' mode. It also allows the manual selection of a different gear from the one being used (+1 or -1).

The screen displays the gear being used on the left and the gear recommended by the computer on the right. The computer's recommendation is accepted by depressing the clutch pedal. A beep sounds when the vehicle has moved into the new gear, at which time the pedal can be released.

The designers set themselves certain design principles, which aim to take users' needs into consideration:

- The computer recommends gear ratios but the user makes the decision.

- Depending on his needs, the driver can manually pre-select a gear, or choose between a high-performance mode and an economical mode.

- So as not to disturb drivers, designers attempted to modify the driving cabin as little as possible. For example, they retained the clutch pedal and the gearshift, but changed their functions.

We will see that despite these very positive intentions, the computer developed generates major problems for drivers of the trucks equipped with them. These problems will be analyzed in light of the types of situations in which they appear[5].

---

[4]The research we use here was carried out by Valérie Galinier (1996) as part of her PhD.

[5]Data was collected over five days from four drivers who were novices in using automatic gearboxes. The activity and the environment were filmed, the computer's recommendations, actions on the controls and their effects, as well as information gathering were recorded. The information was completed by interviews.

	Manual gearbox	Semi-automatic gearbox
Aim of action	Changing gear in line with driving conditions	
Object of action	Change gear	Inform computer that recommended gear is accepted
Utilisation scheme	<ul><li>Depress clutch pedal to uncouple</li><li>Selection of chosen gear</li><li>Clutch pedal to recouple</li></ul>	<ul><li>Depress pedal to inform</li><li>Wait for beep</li><li>Release pedal so as not to send other information</li></ul>

Table 1: Comparison of two gear changing situations.

3.1   A Situation of Artifact Usage: Changing Gears

A specific difficulty that drivers encounter is the appearance of 'system breakdowns': they tell the computer to accept the computer's recommendation by depressing the clutch. However, if they do not leave their foot on the clutch long enough, the old gear is deselected, but the new gear does not have time to engage. The vehicle is then in motion but not in gear. Attempts to recover from these incidents often lead to a series of successive system breakdowns.

These incidents are unpleasant as the following example indicates: a driver was going up a steep hill and wanted to change down to increase engine speed. A system breakdown occurred, leading to a drop in engine speed, which obliged him to stop the vehicle and start it up again. It is clear that these incidents can become problematic in other situations. If the driver had been coming down the hill, he would have needed engine braking and the failure would have created a potentially dangerous situation.

System breakdowns are common occurrences: from 10 to 20% of attempted gear changes according to drivers during the first days of using the new gearbox. This rate is still slightly over 2% on the 5th day. Thus, it is not a passing phenomenon that disappears after a brief apprenticeship.

We will now look at why these system breakdowns appear by taking on the user's point of view, i.e. in terms of a personal view. The drivers in question are experienced and developed their skills by driving vehicles with manual gearshifts. They developed 'utilisation schemes' specific to this type of gearbox. It is even more natural that they continue applying these utilisation schemes given that the designers kept the same control devices (clutch pedal and gearshift) in the new semi-automatic gearbox.

Table 1 allows us to compare the two situations during a change of gears. The aim of the gear change is identical: adapting the gear ratio to driving conditions, but for the rest, everything changes, as the following table indicates.

In the manual gearbox, the driver himself performs the gear change. The nature of the action's object changes with the semi-automatic gearbox: the driver only needs to inform the computer that he accepts the recommended gear ratio. We move from 'doing' to 'having done'. The signification of each of the operations and the utilisation scheme changes profoundly, even if, in the first and last operations, the movements required (depressing and releasing the pedal) remain the same.

Thus the driver must carry out actions where the object and signification of the operations making up the action are now completely different. The designers aimed to change the cabin as little as possible so as not to disturb the drivers and so the controls (clutch pedal and gearshift) and realisation modes (depressing and releasing the pedal) of operations remained the same. In short, retaining the surface characteristics of the interface did not at all help drivers. Rather, it camouflaged the nature and extent of the changes they were confronted with. However, this explanation remains specific to the situation we are looking at. I will now give a more general explanation, which will allow us to re-examine the design problem on different grounds.

In reality, drivers trained on a manual gearbox have developed an instrument, in the psychological sense. This instrument, like all instruments, results from the association of an artefact component (in this case, a pedal and a gearshift) and a utilisation scheme component made up of both pre-structured sequences of operations, and representations of the object and conditions of the action [6].

As far as the subject is concerned, the functional instrument is not only the machine or parts of the machine. It is made up of a mix of an artefact and the schemes that together form the functional instrumental whole. It is the association or coupling of artefactual components and schematic components which constitutes the instrument as a mixed functional entity and allows the subject to act on objects of the activity to attain the goals he sets for himself. When the driver wants to change gears to suit driving conditions, it is this instrument, this mix of subject and artefact, that he mobilises and uses. The two components of the instrument are inherently linked. We can consider that they are in a relation of reciprocal affordance [7]: the artefact affords the utilisation scheme and the scheme affords the artefact so as to constitute the functional instrument in situation when the subject needs it.

We can now put forward a more general explanation: the designers' choice led to retaining the artefact component of the 'gear changing' instrument and obliged drivers to restructure the utilisation scheme component. It could even be said, given the extent of the transformation, that they needed to constitute a new scheme. The drivers' task was in fact to destructure a solidly constituted instrument so as to form a new instrument. Paradoxically, the design choice of not changing the commands so as not to disturb users actually increased their difficulties. The controls retained constitute the artefact part of the old instrument and afford schemes pertinent to driving with a manual gearbox.

An analysis of the design project in terms of the instrument, as carried out above, could have been done beforehand and would have predicted the appearance of system breakdowns during use. This analysis would have also led to rethinking the design problem on different grounds, thus avoiding the difficulties encountered, i.e.

---

[6]The notion of the psychological instrument is developed by Rabardel (1995) and Béguin & Rabardel (2000).

[7]The concept of affordance was initially developed by Gibson (1966) to describe the reciprocal relation between perception of the environment and action. It was transposed into ergonomics by Norman (1988).

Acceptance terms	Changing up in lower range	Changing up in higher range
> 5 seconds	4%	18%
From 1 to 5 seconds	52%	53%
< 1 second	44%	29%

Table 2: Acceptance time for changing up.

searching for and putting to use, within the design process, an instrument that already exists in society and which has, for subjects, an equivalent or nearly equivalent functional value to that sought in the specific situation. Do such instruments (in the psychological sense I have defined), which correspond to situations of accepting or validating choices exist in society? Clearly, the answer is yes. An example is the validation button used in automatic teller machines for which most of us have already constituted corresponding utilisation schemes. It would have been possible to transpose this type of instrument (artefact and utilisation schemes) into the context of the driving cabin. This would have allowed the effective respect of one of the designers' criteria: disturbing the user as little as possible.

3.2   Deciding to Change Gears: A Situated Driving Activity

The analysis above looks at an instrument in a usage situation, in this case changing gears. But the decision to change gears occurs before the change is carried out. We will see that at this level also, designers' choices are problematic for drivers given that changing gears is situated in the environment of the driving activity.

Drivers refuse approximately 40% to 45% of changes recommended by the computer. This means that in these cases, the computer's recommendation does not correspond with their wishes or needs at that time. The gap between driver and calculator appraisals is due to deep-seated differences between man and machine in evaluating situations. This is manifested in acceptance times.

Table 2 highlights the great differences in acceptance times when increasing gears (changing up) The differences occur within and between ranges.

The inter-range differences correspond to differences between classes of situations. Changing up in low range (CULR) corresponds to situations of starting the vehicle up again after a stop or a great reduction in speed. Changing up in high range (CUHR) corresponds to situations in which the vehicle has reached cruising speed. It is characterised by a lengthening of acceptance times compared with the low range.

Intra-range differences correspond to differences within the same class of situations. These differences indicate the drivers' treatment of a variety of driving situations in this class. Accepting the recommendation in less than a second indicates that the driver anticipated this recommendation and validated it without even consulting the display. This means that his knowledge of the system (his apprehension of the 'system view') is sufficient to predict the recommendation that will be made in the given situation. A response time of between one and five seconds corresponds to consulting the display, then making a decision quickly based on the immediate context. This is the standard situation targeted by the system's designers: proposing the right gear change at the right time. A response time of over five seconds indicates a pertinent proposal but with a delay due to an evolution in the context.

In total, the extent of refusals (40% to 45%) as well as deferred acceptances, i.e. over five seconds (from 4% to 18% in our examples), indicates that we are a long way off the target objective: proposing a pertinent gear change when the driver would be liable to change gears.

The reasons for this gap are easily identified: the computer's appraisal criteria are different from the driver's. The computer recommends gear changes based on an instant treatment of motor parameters and the state of the drive chain. Drivers, on the other hand, make decisions that incorporate the dynamic and changing character of the immediate driving environment. They anticipate the evolution of the situation based on their knowledge of the particularities of the route and on the activity of other drivers.

In some circumstances, the difference in appraisals can lead to a sort of competition between the driver and the computer. The computer repeatedly recommends a particular gear ratio when the driver wants another[8]. This is the case, for example, when going downhill. The computer recommends a higher gear while the driver wants a lower one to increase the effect of engine braking. Drivers progressively develop ways of forcing the computer to recommend the right gear at the right time. For example, they temporarily go from economical mode to high-performance mode so the computer recommends the desired gear. This action is not destined to increase power and save time, as designers intended. Rather, it allows drivers to take control, using indirect means, of the computer's recommendations.

3.3   The Instrumented Activity in Classes of Situations

Above, we have seen that variable driving conditions lead the driver to demand gear changes that are often different to those recommended by the computer. They even develop strategies to take control of the computer and make it produce the recommendations they want. The computer then becomes, for them, an instrument producing recommendations in line with their own criteria, rather than those implemented in its design.

Yet, as we will now see, the situated nature of driving is not only due to the dynamic variability of circumstances. It also comes from the fact that the situations are organised by drivers into classes of situations, with which they associate instrumented activity schemes and specific instruments. Each of us has a personal experience of driving. Going up or down a hill, turning a corner, driving on a straight and wide or narrow and winding road can all be considered as classes of situations. The situations of each of these classes have characteristics that are sufficiently similar to generate driving modalities. These modalities are both relatively stable and yet different from one class to another.

---

[8]These competitive phenomena were also identified by Evrard & Awada (1994) who point out that in some situations, 'both the pilot and the co-pilot want to drive the vehicle at the same time'.

I will use examples of stop–start situations to illustrate the development of instruments specific to classes of situations.

Drivers will progressively develop their utilisation schemes so they have an instrument adapted to the peculiarities of stop-start situations. This development is the result of a process of instrumental genesis[9], which I will now examine.

1. Initially, the instrumented activity scheme is directly transposed from the situation of driving with a manual gearbox. The driver depresses the clutch pedal (D), allows the automatic computer to select a gear by default (A_s) or attempts to select the gear manually (M_s), then releases the clutch pedal (R).

   This scheme, which I call the 'old scheme', symbolised $(D > A_s/M_s > R)$, leads to many system breakdowns, particularly when the driver attempts to select gears manually. He is then in conflict with the computer. Having depressed the clutch pedal, he has sent the message to move into the gear by default. The outcome of this conflict depends on several factors (the initial state of the computer, the gear the driver is attempting to move into, the length of time he depresses the pedal, etc.).

2. In a second phase, the 'old scheme' is retained, but a second scheme appears and coordinates itself with the first. The resulting instrumented activity scheme is made up of two linked schemes:

   - The first manages the stopping phase: depress pedal, move into neutral (N), release pedal: $(P > N > R)$. I call this the 'stopping scheme'
   - The second manages the starting up phase: $(D > A_s/M_s > R)$. This is the 'old scheme'.

   The new instrumented activity scheme, symbolised $(D > N > R) + (D > A_s/M_s > R)$ allows a definite reduction in system breakdowns because the 'stop scheme' stabilises the initial state of the computer. This indicates that the driver has begun to take the functioning of the computer into consideration.

3. Finally, in the third phase, the 'old scheme' component disappears and two new schemes appear. The resulting instrumented activity scheme is made up of three linked schemes:

   - The first is the preceding 'stop scheme': $(D > N > R)$.
   - The second programs the starting up of the vehicle by pre-selecting a speed (M_s): 'selection scheme'.
   - The third manages the start phase: depressing pedal, releasing pedal $(D > R)$: 'validation scheme'.

---

[9]Processes of instrumental genesis implicate both the subject and the artefact. They concern the development of utilisation schemes and instrumented activity schemes as well as the transformation of functions, functioning or the structure of the artefact. See Rabardel (1995) for a detailed development.

The instrumented activity scheme, symbolised $(D > N > R) + (M_s) + (D > R)$ allows avoidance of all system breakdowns.

The instrumented activity schemes thus appear in the following order:

'old scheme'

⇓

'stop scheme'   +   'old scheme'

⇓

'stop scheme'   +   'selection scheme'   +   'validation scheme'

The above list lays out the stages of the instrumental genesis process by which subjects develop, based on a usage scheme for manual gearboxes and an automatic gearbox artefact (with the original manual controls), a new instrument for managing the stop–start class of situations. The instrument is multi-functional. Each of its functions is clearly differentiated and supported by an associated sub-scheme of corresponding artefacts[10]. This instrument efficiently mediates the subject's activity in stop–start situations because the scheme components organise and coordinate the subject's and the computer's actions. It integrates and subjugates the computer's actions to the structure of all the subject's own actions organised by the instrumented activity scheme. Thus, the instrumented activity scheme not only organises the subject's action but also cooperation between the subject and the computer. It performs an operational and concrete appropriation of the system view so as to serve the personal view.

Once the instrument is constituted, it can be mobilised in all the situations within the class because it corresponds to the situational invariants of this class. Its usage is flexibly adapted to the variability of the situations and contexts. It incorporates the driving activity in line with the constraints of the task and the driver's objectives.

It is possible to benefit from these characteristics when designing. One way is to emulate instruments effectively developed by users and transpose them onto the artefacts of the following generation. Another way, which is more traditional in a sense, would mean in the example of the gearbox, allowing the user to configure it so that it recommends gear changes effectively corresponding to his activity in different classes of situations.

3.4   Classes of Situations Organise Themselves into Domains of Activities

Classes of situations are an organisational level whose pertinence for understanding instrumented activity has been demonstrated above. Classes of situations are themselves organised in groupings at a higher level: domains of activities. Here too, each of us has his/her own experience: driving in the city or driving in the mountains are domains of activity that bring together groups of classes of specific situations.

Domains of activity can be organised around characteristics of the environment, as in the examples above. They can also be organised around other types of

---

[10]To simplify reading, in this presentation of the instrumental genesis, we have only mentioned control artefacts. It goes without saying that schemes also organise information gathering, particularly on the reading and the revolution counter.

driving determinants. Thus, driving vehicles in a professional context is unlike driving for oneself: the constraints and demands of work throw up specific domain characteristics such as delivery deadlines or traffic restrictions.

These demands are liable to have a great impact on the instrument. Thus, the automatic gearbox described above has proven to be totally unusable for driving public transport vehicles. Drivers rejected it because it did not allow them to respect criteria specific to the domain of transporting people.

Another example will indicate that instrumental genesis processes can develop, within a domain of activities, in a totally unexpected manner. We will now look at a navigation aid system for driving in urban areas. Users were familiar with the use of the system. Analyses compared driving with guidance by the system and by a map on paper (Forzy, 1999). Contrary to designers' expectations, use of the system did not significantly improve navigation performance (except for subjects who had particular difficulties with the map). However, the quality of driving improved significantly. Risk taking, errors or breaking rules occurred much less often[11]. Questioning users after the experiment revealed that they considered the system more compatible with driving. The negative consequences of navigation errors are reduced with the system: if directions cannot be followed, an alternative route will always be suggested. As a result, users develop usage modalities that favor security, rather than possible navigation errors that are easily made up for. The instrument developed by users is multi-functional, as in the previous example. Yet its main function for the activity, constituted during a process of instrumental genesis, does not focus on the artefact's main constituting function, but rather, on driving safety.

4   Discussion: Designing Instruments, an Activity Distributed Between Designers and Users

Based on these two examples, we have seen the close ties between users' development of instruments and the situated nature of their activity mediated by these instruments: usage situations, instrumented activity situations, classes of situations, and domains of activity. I will now situate the approach put forward in terms of the diversity of models on which the design process is based. Each of these model types has specific advantages.

Models focussed on technologies and tasks allow the elaboration of reliable technical systems and functions adapted to the domain and the objectives. Yet they do not really allow designers to anticipate the user's activity in as far as this activity is only partly shaped by systems and tasks. Models based on human factors were developed to define the properties of the human component of man-machine systems. This definition looks at the properties of humans independently of their mobilisation in the activity: morphology, properties of perceptive systems, cognitive mechanisms, etc. They are useful to define some of the characteristics that technical systems and artefacts need to have to facilitate man-machine interaction. Yet these models, like technology-based models, only allow designers to partly anticipate users' activity, insofar as human properties only condition the production conditions of activity.

---

[11]Non respect of traffic lights or overtaking restrictions, refusal to cede priority, changing lanes or late braking, inappropriate speeds, deviations in trajectories.

This is why new generations of models focussed on the activity itself have developed over the last few years. These models aim to anticipate and define users' productive activity: the activity of carrying out tasks mediated by instruments. They also aim to anticipate and define the constructive activity by which users develop their instruments and transform their activity situations.

In light of this, let us come back to Vicente's analysis:

"It is well known that workers frequently informally tailor the design of their device and work practices to better meet domain demands. In some cases, workers make *permanent* changes that could have been, but were not, originally introduced by designers ... in contrast the *temporary* changes ... would have been far more difficult, if not impossible, for designers to anticipate completely and reliably. These tailoring activities are responding to local circumstances ... and can be interpreted as attempts at 'finishing the design' of the sociocultural system ... The phrase 'finishing the design' does not refer to relatively permanent modifications made by workers to tailor the interface to their own personal preferences. Instead, it refers to continual adaptations of the structure and state of the sociotechnical system to particular local contingencies." (Vicente, 1999, pp.125–6)

Here, Vicente identifies an essential activity: the tailoring device users employ. However, I feel his ensuing analysis is too restrictive. While it is undeniable that some of the operator's informal activities of adapting artefacts reflect the local variability of circumstances and tasks, another, more significant part corresponds to the development of instruments through a process of instrumental genesis.

This development in usage, this continuation of design within the activity, must, in our opinion, be considered as an intrinsic characteristic of human activity. The existence of instrumental geneses is not primarily the result of insufficiently elaborated design[12], but the expression of the part of design that is in any case carried out by the user.

The design of instruments is an activity distributed between designers and users. Designers' task is to elaborate an instrumental proposal in the form of artefacts and anticipated operational modes. Users will (partly, totally or not at all) take on this proposal to develop their own instruments, in line with their own characteristics and needs. These will be pertinent for the domains of activities and situations in which they constitute resources.

For this reason, I consider that the development of human-centred design requires grounding in conceptualisations and theoretical frameworks that render the reality of instruments within the productive and constructive activities of human subjects:

- Instruments are intrinsically mixed in nature: they are made up of artefact components and utilisation scheme components.

---

[12] Even if instrumental geneses also have to compensate for inadequate design at times.

- Instruments are strongly linked to situations both in terms of the variability of circumstances and the invariants of situations and their different organisational levels: usage situation, activity situation, classes of situations, domains of activities, etc.

- Instruments result from a development process (and not only a learning process), which occurs through instrumental geneses. Instruments born of instrumental geneses organise the coordination of the artefact's and the subject's actions, allowing them to be pertinent and efficient mediators for the subject's activity.

- Instruments are both private, meaning specific to each individual, and social. The social nature of instruments is due to the social nature of artefacts, usage schemes and instrumented activity schemes. These schemes are social in that they have characteristics that are both shared and widespread in communities and collectivities.

The 'instrument-mediated activity' theoretical framework opens up prospects for human-centred design. I have outlined some of these in this text and have developed them elsewhere. I will content myself with running through the principles here:

- Organising the design process around social utilisation schemes available in the society, culture or collectivity to receive the artefact.

- Designing artefacts so they facilitate the continuation of the design process in usage and the development of instrumental geneses.

- Emulating instruments born of instrumental geneses developed by users; developing participatory design processes around instrumental geneses.

The design of anthropocentred artefacts does not mean following to the letter what the user is or wants at a given time. While remaining human-centred, it can also introduce breakdowns in schemes and instruments that the users have already developed and mastered. However, I feel that breaking with and following on from past schemes must be deliberate and made explicit. The design process must aim to give users the means to manage breakdowns and continuations within their activity.

References

Bødker, S. & Graves Petersen, M. (2000), "Design for Learning in Use", *Scandinavian Journal of Information Systems* **12**(1-2), 61–80. Special Issue: Information Technology in Human Activity.

Béguin, P. & Rabardel, P. (2000), "Designing for Instrument Mediated Activity", *Scandinavian Journal of Information Systems* **12**(1-2), 173–90. Special Issue: Information Technology in Human Activity.

Cole, M. (1996), *Cultural Psychology: Once and Future Discipline?*, Harvard University Press.

Engeström, Y. (1990), *Working and Imagining: Twelve Studies in Activity Theory*, Orienta-Konsultit Oy.

Evrard, F. & Awada, A. (1994), Copilote Électronique pour la Conduite Automobile, *in* B.Pavard (ed.), *Systèmes Coopératifs : De la Modélisation à la Conception*, Octares, pp.309–49.

Forzy, J. (1999), "Assessment of a Driver Guidance System: A Multi-level Evaluation", *Transportation Human Factors* 1(3), 273–87.

Galinier, V. (1996), Apports de l'Ergonomie à la Conception d'Instruments : Concevoir Autour des Schèmes d'Utilisation, un Exemple dans le Domaine du Transport Routier, Thèse de Doctorat en Ergonomie, CNAM, Paris.

Gibson, J. J. (1966), *The Senses Considered as Perceptual Systems*, Houghton-Mifflin.

Kaptelinin, V. (1996), Computer-mediated Activity: Functionnal Organs in Social and Developmental Contexts, *in* B. A. Nardi (ed.), *Context and Consciousness: Activity Theory and Human–Computer Interaction*, MIT Press, pp.45–68.

Léontiev, A. N. (1981), *Problems of the Development of Mind*, Progress.

Norman, D. A. (1988), *The Psychology of Everyday Things*, Basic Books.

Norman, D. A. (1991), Cognitive Artefacts, *in* J. M. Carroll (ed.), *Designing Interaction: Psychology at the Human–Computer Interface*, Cambridge University Press, pp.17–38.

Rabardel, P. (1995), *Les Hommes et les Technologies : Approche Cognitive des Instruments Contemporains*, Colin.   Available in English, September 2001 at http://ergoserv.psy.univ-paris8.fr.

Rasmussen, J. (1997), Merging Paradigms: Decision Making, Management and Cognitive Control, *in* R. Flin, E. Salas, M. Strub & L. Martin (eds.), *Decision Making under Stress: Emerging Themes and Applications*, Ashgate, pp.67–81.

Suchman, L. A. (1987), *Plans and Situated Actions — The Problem of Human–Machine Communication*, Cambridge University Press.

Vicente, K. J. (1999), *Cognitive Work Analysis: Towards Safe, Productive and Healthy Computer-based Work*, Lawrence Erlbaum Associates.

Vygotsky, L. S. (1978), *Mind In Society: The Development of Higher Psychological Processes*, Harvard University Press. Edited by Michael Cole, Vera John-Steiner, Sylvia Scribner, Ellen Souberman.

Wertsch, J. V. (1998), *Minds as Action*, Oxford University Press.

From 2D Photos of Yourself to Virtual Try-on Dress on the Web

Frédéric Cordier, WonSook Lee, HyeWon Seo & Nadia Magnenat-Thalmann

MIRALab, University of Geneva, 24 rue du General Dufour, 1211 Geneva, Switzerland
Email: *{cordier,wslee,seo,thalmann}@cui.unige.ch*
URL: *http://www.miralab.unige.ch*

This paper describes a complete methodology for cloning and dressing people by using a website. The input is simple photographs or body measurements that anybody can produce in any environment. Then the Web-based virtual-try-on allows users to see them dressed. The basic methodology uses a pre-calculated generic database to produce personally sized bodies and animate garments on a Web application.

Keywords: made to measure, generic database, body cloning, generic garment, Internet, Web, virtual try-on, 3D clothing.

1 Introduction

The Internet along with the rapidly growing power of computing has emerged as a compelling channel for sale of garment products. A number of initiatives have arisen recently across the world, evolving around the concepts of Made-to-Measure manufacturing and shopping via the Internet. The combination of these new services is now possible by the emergence of technologies, systems and practices, such as 3D whole body scanners, automatic body measurement, the customisation of existing styles and Virtual-Try-On visualisation techniques.

However, high product return rates persist, and most consumers are still either hesitant to purchase garments online or are unsatisfied with their online shopping experience (Beck, 2000). A number of recent studies identified the causes for consumer hesitancy, and of particular notes are the consumer's overwhelming concern with fit and correct sizing, and the inability to try on items. Following a survey by the French company Lectra (see http://www.lectra.com), an estimated 30% of online garment purchases are sent back by consumers.

Consumers that purchase garments online today base their purchase and size-selection decisions mostly on 2D photos of garments and sizing charts. This method is not precise enough and not interactive enough to provide right sizing as well as right choice to the consumer.

In this paper, we present the first link between human cloning and clothing on the Web. We enable people to visualise themselves wearing a variety of garments at home via the Internet. Thanks to this technology, we can virtually try on several styles of garment depending on our preference and dimensions, and produce from our 3D garment the corresponding 2D patterns to send to the manufacturer. The main idea is to use both a generic body and generic garment database. An automatic fitting process of the 3D garment to the cloned 3D body and back to the 2D patterns is discussed. The methodology is based on four parts:

Photo-cloned body with acceptable level of accuracy: The clothing simulation is based on existing software used to dress and animate virtual mannequins. The important issue for the photo-cloned body is the ability for the consumer to try on the garments and to check the fit.

Even though the photographs are easy to input, it is faster or often preferable to directly give body dimensions. We propose another personalised body creation with the measurements input on the Web interface.

Online cloth fitting and simulation: We give a methodology to fit the garments and dress the customer's 3D model with them. Physical simulation for cloth is not appropriate as calculation time is critical for the Web application. Our approach is to use a database of pre-computed garment animations, which are then automatically fitted to the personally sized body.

Output of 2D patterns for manufacturing: By extracting the measurement data from the fitted garments, the corresponding 2D patterns are created and can be sent to manufacturers.

Online Web interface module: A virtual showroom is provided for the user to try on the garments. A window displays the animation of her/his body walking with the garments.

Figure 1 shows the overall flow about our integrated methodology for the individualised garment try-on on the Web. In Section 2, we describe our pre-processing of the generic database, which is the basic idea for the Web-based approach. The photo cloning of bodies is described in Section 3. Section 4 is devoted to the creation of personally sized bodies based on user-input measurements. Then Section 5 explains how a made-to-measure garment can be constructed. The animation of the personalised garments is also explained. Section 6 describes the Web interface with examples to show how the consumer can use the application. The possible manufacturing idea for the made-to-measure garment is described in Section 7. The main point for the manufacturing is how to create 2D patterns back from the 3D personalised garment. Finally, conclusion and future research is discussed.

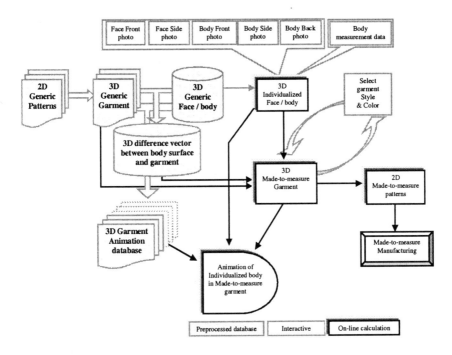

Figure 1: Virtual-try-on overview with cloned body and made-to-measure garment.

2 Generic Database: Bodies and Garments

The most important idea for our approach is to use a pre-calculated generic database for bodies and garments and adapt them to the personal data (photos or measurement data). For the Web application, fast calculation is a critical issue. Our method requires as much pre-calculation as possible for the generic database and then minimise the calculation to make the given generic data to be personalised. We discuss how to prepare the generic body and garment database for several styles.

2.1 Generic Body and Animation

There are numerous possible methods to make a personalised virtual human for the face (Akimoto et al., 1993; Blanz & Vetter, 1999; DeCarlo & Metaxas, 1996; DeCarlo et al., 1998; Escher & Magnenat-Thalmann, 1997; Fua & Leclerc, 1996; Guenter et al., 1998; Ip & Yin, 1996; Kurihara & Arai, 1991; Lee & Magnenat-Thalmann, 2000; Lee et al., 1995; Nagel et al., 1998; Pighin et al., 1998; Proesmans & Van Gool, 1997; Saji et al., 1992) and the body (Addleman, 1997; Gu et al., 1998; Hilton et al., 1999; Kakadiaris & Metaxas, 1995; Kakadiaris & Metaxas, 1996; Plänkers et al., 1999; Zheng, 1994). Here we discuss the creation of the face, body skeleton and body surface. The most popular methods used for both body constructions and animations are to use generic models. The generic model can be one, several or numerous (Blanz & Vetter, 1999) to be adapted to the personal shape and texture. The main advantage of using generic models is that we can give necessary information as a pre-processing and the online calculation can be done quickly and it gives the animation information automatically. The basic idea is to consider an avatar as a combined set of data, including the 3D shape and the structure to animate it. The human modelling approach starts from default virtual human templates, including shape and animation structures, and modifies the shape to create a new virtual actor described in Section 3. More detail about the seamless generic body can be found in other texts — see http://www.H-Anim.org and (Lee et al., 2000).

For the generic body animation, we apply a walking motion obtained from the VICON motion capture system. Six cameras with the sample rate of 120Hz are used along with 25mm markers.

- Several steps are involved in obtaining the animation for the body.

- Obtain a skeleton and its animation data from marker positions.

- Modify the posture of the skeleton together with the skin to locate them properly.

- Convert the original motion data to the new skeleton.

- Attach the skin to the skeleton.

- Perform animation with skin deformation.

After performing all steps necessary, we have a generic body with seamless surface and real-time skin deformation capacity whenever skeleton joints are animated with given animation parameters.

2.2   Generic 3D Garment Using 2D Patterns and Simulation

As described in Volino & Magnenat-Thalmann (2000), we use a similar approach for garment reconstruction and animation on a moving body surface. The garment is made from 2D patterns of garment surfaces. The approach for garment simulation that is going to be used takes its inspiration from the traditional garment industry, where garments are created from two-dimensional patterns and then seamed together. A 3D garment simulator includes the mechanical model, collision engine, rendering and animation. The patterns need then to be discretised into a triangular mesh. Once the patterns have been placed around the body, a mechanical simulation is invoked to make the patterns come together along the seaming lines. Consequently, the patterns are attached and seamed, obtaining the shape influenced by the body shape. The mechanical simulation gives the animation of the garment on the body, accounting for the collision response and friction with the body surface. The final visual look of the garment is displayed through its material properties i.e. colours, shininess, and texture which are some of the rendering parameters. Geometrical complexity is another very important consideration, as the rendering time as well as the computation time for the animations is directly proportional to the number of polygons to be displayed.

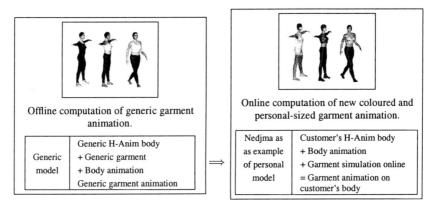

Offline computation of generic garment animation.	Online computation of new coloured and personal-sized garment animation.

Generic model	Generic H-Anim body
	+ Generic garment
	+ Body animation
	Generic garment animation

$\implies$

Nedjma as as example of personal model	Customer's H-Anim body
	+ Body animation
	+ Garment simulation online
	= Garment animation on customer's body

Figure 2: Individual chooses the garment style and colour and then the personalised avatar model wears the garment and animation follows.

Here we discuss the generic 3D garment using generic 2D patterns that define the style (Figure 2). We perform calculation of the generic garment fitting to our generic body and build a database according to the style such as trousers, skirts, pullovers, one-piece dresses, etc.

The garment animation is calculated on a moving generic body with given skeleton animation sequences. For each time frame, we save the garment surface information, which is used later in Section 4 to get Made-to-Measure garment simulation for the online calculation.

3 Cloning Yourself

It is our goal to develop a technique that enables an easy acquisition of the personalised avatar model with acceptable accuracy to be produced at a low cost and properly animated. Many possible methods can acquire input data for modelling from a high-end laser scanner to low-end still photographs. Each of them has its advantages and disadvantages. In our method, we use photographs as input: front and side views for the face and front, side and back views for the body.

Our method is a feature-based modelling of animatable human body. With the generic model described in Section 2.1, we modify the shape and skin colour to be adapted to given photographs. Shape modifications are transmitted to the attached animation structures in order to keep the set of data consistent. We obtain a 'ready to animate' virtual human as the output of the modelling process. Our approach optimises the modelling of virtual humans in order to animate him/her. Feature based approach is useful to provide easy input in robust way and to take the animation structure while the shape resembles the input shape.

The methodology is composed of two major components: face-cloning and body-cloning. The outline of the human cloning is shown in Figure 3. Detailed information for the face cloning can be found in other papers (Akimoto et al., 1993; Ip & Yin, 1996; Kurihara & Arai, 1991; Pighin et al., 1998). The

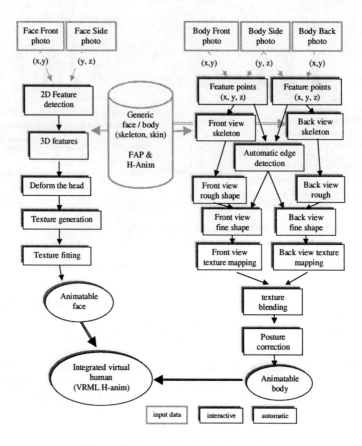

Figure 3: Face and body cloning outline.

body-cloning component uses feature point specification, which enables automatic silhouette detection of the body with an arbitrary background, and then a body modification by using feature points and body silhouette respectively. The final integrated human model with cloned face and body together has photograph-realistic H-Anim humanoid.

Even though the input data is limited to only three photographs for the body, the error is acceptable. This will be discussed in the following section.

We validate the result of the body cloning in two ways. First, we compare laser-scanned data and photo-cloned data in 3D. The laser-scanned data provide three input photographs (front, side, and back views) for the photo-cloning and the output 3D data from photo-cloning and the laser-scanned 3D data are compared using 3D error measurement. Second, we use tailor's measurements with a real-person. We measure several body parts of the person and the photo-cloned body is measured for the same body parts for the comparison. Figure 4 shows two examples of people used for the photo-cloning. Nedjma is much taller than Sabrina and Sabrina is thinner.

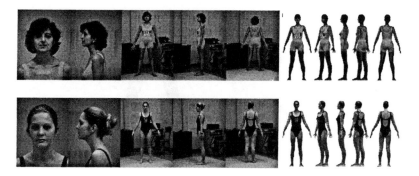

Figure 4: Cloning examples with five photographs. Upper sequence is for Nedjma the lower sequence is for Sabrina.

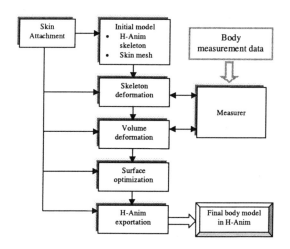

Figure 5: Overview of the body creation process.

4   Body Creation Based on Measurements

Sometimes people are not able to or not willing to provide their photos for the body cloning. In this case, we allow the user to input their key measurement data and create a virtual human of these measurements. Based on modification of the generic body model by deforming several parts of the body, the system is composed of several modules working in a pipeline. Figure 5 gives an overview of the pipeline.

4.1   Body Model

Our generic body model is composed of a skin mesh and a skeleton. The skeleton hierarchy we have chosen to use is the H-Anim Level of Articulation (LoA) 2 one (see http://www.H-Anim.org) as is the case with the photo-cloning (Section 3).

Figure 6: Skin attachment. The 'l_hip' bone (left) and the skin part that are attached to it or affected by the bone (right).

4.2 Adjusting the Limbs

The idea of adjusting the limb lengths and volumes is to firstly define the dependency of the skin part to the skeleton or attach the skin part to the skeleton and then apply the necessary transformation on the bone to derive the natural deformation on the corresponding skin part. The height, the length of the legs and arms fall into this category.

The attachment is considered as assigning for each vertex of the mesh its affecting bones and corresponding weights (Figure 6). To say that a vertex is 'weighted' with respect to a bone means that the vertex will move as the bone is rotated in order to stay aligned with it. At 100% weighting, for instance, the vertex follows the bone rigidly. This method combines for each vertex the transformation matrix of the bones in accordance to their weight.

Figure 7d shows the modification of the limb volume and length we obtained by skeletal deformation. Given the desired measurement value $T_{desired}$ and the current measurement value $T_{current}$, a scale transformation $s = \frac{T_{desired}}{T_{current}}$ will be applied to the corresponding bone to get the desired measurement on the body.

4.3 Adjusting the Volumes of Body Parts

For some parts of the body that concern the volume measurements, deformation means more than the simple transformation of associated bones. Breast or chest, abdomen and hips are such examples.

As the generic model is based on characteristic lines or contours and thus naturally forms a regular grid, we use parametric curves to smoothly deform these parts locally. The deformation in this case takes place in two directions: one along the vertical direction and the other along the horizontal one. Figure 8 shows an example of the deformation of breast region of the mesh.

Along the vertical lines, 6 points are sensibly selected as the B-spline control points. The first and last points are fixed in order not to create discontinuities on the surface. The second and the fifth points as well are just present to give a regular aspect to the surface, i.e. a curve that grows gradually. The third and the fourth points

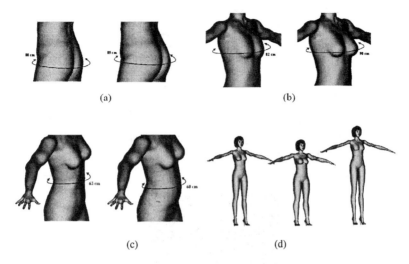

(a)   (b)

(c)   (d)

Figure 7: (a) Deformation of the bottom to obtain different sizes. (b) Deformation of the breast to obtain different sizes. (c) Deformation of the abdomen to obtain different sizes. (d) Variously sized female bodies.

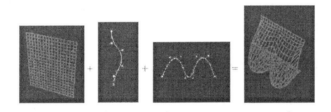

Figure 8: The deformation on the breast.

undergo a translation of factor F, as shown in Figure 9. All the other points in the line are sampled using the Boor–Cox algorithm (Foley et al., 1995).

Along the horizontal direction, the points should be located in such a way that it preserves the shape of the breast. The translations of the control points form a function f, whose evolution takes the shape of the breast as shown in Figure 9b. In other words, the value of the factor F is dependent on the column to which the deformation is applied, multiplied by the degree of displacement desired by the user. Whenever the user increases or decreases the size via the user interface, the resulting measurement values are shown. Figure 7a illustrates some of the results we obtained.

The abdomen region is deformed similarly except that we use Bézier curve in this case. The displacement factor along the horizontal direction in this case takes the form of the abdomen. The resulting modified shapes are shown in Figure 7b. This approach is similar to the one described in (Seo et al., 2000).

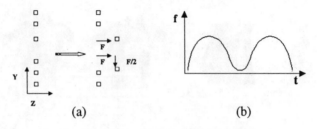

(a)   (b)

Figure 9: (a) Translation of control points along the vertical direction. (b) Function of displacement factor along the horizontal direction.

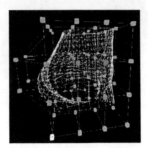

Figure 10: Automatic displacement with 4 control points.

For the bottom part, a simple method of deformation based on the FFD (Free Form Deformation) is used. The bounding box of the bottom is regularly sampled to obtain $4 \times 4 \times 4 = 64$ control points of the Bézier volume. As we move any of the control points, the enclosed surface will be deformed accordingly. We discovered that only certain points of the volume are necessary in most cases. We thus obtain the differently sized bottoms by simultaneously moving these points, which are the four central points of the back face of the Bézier volume as shown in Figure 10. Some of the various female bodies that are produced are illustrated in Figure 7.

5   Fitting Generic Garment Animation to Personally Sized Bodies

Given a body created from a generic model, our method modifies the animation of the generic garment. As described in the previous sections, the program generates bodies from a generic model using the measurement data or photos. The same fitting process applied to the body (from generic to personally sized body) will be also applied on garments. Each generic body goes with a set of generic garments. The generic garment animation is modified to the personally sized body.

On each frame of the garment animation, the vertex position of the garment is adapted to the skin surface of the personally sized body. The method consists on applying a local scale factor on garment vertices. This local scale factor is computed from the transformation matrix of the bones and the influence regions. This is done in two steps:

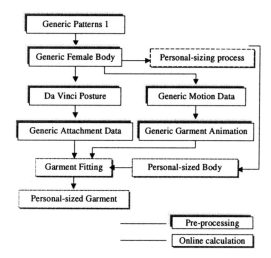

Figure 11: Dataflow diagram for one generic female body and one specific generic pattern.

- The first step consists of defining the influence regions. This has been pre-calculated during the pre-processing phase. This is needed to compute the local scale factor from the transformation matrix of the bones. Around the bones, we define influence regions based on the distance between the garment surface and the bones. The computation of these influential areas is made with the 'Da Vinci posture'.

- The second step is the fitting of the garment surface to the body generated from the measurements or by the cloning program. It is part of the online calculation. Given a personally sized body, and by using the influence region of the bones, the local scale factor is defined for each garment vertex. This scale factor is then used to modify the animation of the generic garment.

Figure 11 gives an overview of the dataflow model and shows the modules for pre-processing (construction of the generic garment database) and online calculation that will be executed for the personally sized bodies.

5.1 Influence Regions on Garments

The influence region is generated in the 'Da Vinci' posture. These regions are defined on the garment; each vertex has a list of weights defined for each bone (Figure 12). This weight defines how much the position of a vertex depends on the bone. This weight has to be defined for each bone, and is inversely proportional to the distance between the vertex and the bone. This data is defined at once in the pre-processing calculation and is used as is during the online calculation. The influence regions on garment are used as generic data. The local scale factor for garment vertex is computed by combining the different local coordinate systems of the bones weighted by the influence value.

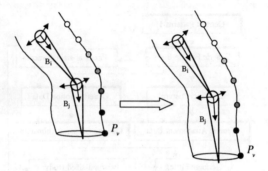

Figure 12: Influence regions on garments.

In Figure 12, P_v is a vertex on the garment. The colour of the vertices along the edge shows the influence areas of the two bones B_i and B_j. In order to avoid discontinuity when fitting the generic garment to the personally sized body, the region boundaries are smooth.

5.2 Calculation of the Garment Using Influence Regions

This method is used for the online calculation. This calculation has to be fast and robust. We have chosen a geometric method that fulfils these two requirements. For a given frame, the position of a vertex is calculated by applying a local scale factor. This local scale factor is defined by combining the weighted transformation matrix of the bones. The resulting position of a vertex P_v is given by the following equation where $M_{v,i}$ is the transformation matrix of the bone, $K_{v,i}$ is the weight of the bone, and $O_{v,i}$ is the position of the garment vertex in the local coordinate system of the bone.

$$P_v = \sum_i M_{v,i} K_{v,i} O_{v,i}$$

In Figure 12, B_i and B_v are the two main bones of the legs. By modifying the length of bone B_j, we move the vertex P_v. As P_v is close to the bone B_i, this vertex position will be mainly affected by this bone.

5.3 Web Interface

The Web interface provides the user with all the functionalities to define his/her body (by measurements or with photos), to choose his/her garment and to visualise himself/herself walking in this garment.

The user interface (see Figure 13) is divided into 3 modules. First, the user is required to complete a page to define his/her measurements or give his/her photos to the photo-cloned program. A second page follows where the user chooses one of the garments available in the library. Some properties of the garment can be customised such as the texture. In the last stage, after the online processing, the users can see themselves walking with the garment in the Virtual Fitting Room.

This Virtual Fitting Room is a 3D viewer. Using the menu, the user can move the point of view. For the 3D viewer, there are a considerable number

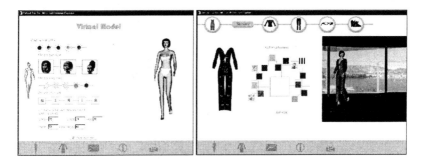

Figure 13: User interface of the Virtual-Try-On Web site.

of 3D technologies (see http://web3d.about.com). We use a Shout3D (see http://www.shout3D.com) loader for our virtual-try-on on the Web. Our Web application fulfils the major considerations that determines the quality of the virtual fitting room application:

Quality of the animation: This depends largely on the number of frames that can be redrawn on the display during a unit of time.

Interactive possibilities: Our graphical interface allows the user to move around the scene and visualise the objects through modification of viewing parameters.

Response time: This should be minimal. The user is not willing to spend more than a few minutes in the Virtual Fitting Room. Our 3D models are optimised to make the whole process of dressing the customer and displaying the animations as fast as possible. By using pre-computed generic bodies and garments, we have dramatically reduced the time for online calculation. The animation of garment provides good realism, including wrinkles, while the computation time takes no more than thirty seconds.

6   From 3D garment to 2D patterns

By the online calculation, the user is able to create the 2D patterns from the personally sized garment. As described in a previous section, the user gives his/her measurements or uses photos to generate the personally sized body. Using this generated model, the generic garment is then modified. And in the final step, the user retrieves the size of personally sized 2D pattern that can be directly used to create the real garment. In this section, we describe how we generate the size of the patterns.

In our model, we keep the information on the 2D patterns that has been used to generate the garment. Both 2D patterns and the garment have some feature points on the seaming. Figure 14 shows two examples.

These feature points are located on the seams mainly on the corners. By measuring the distance of the edges joining two feature points, we extract the length of the corresponding seaming. These lengths are then applied to the 2D patterns. In some cases the extracted lengths of two symmetric seams are not equal, we use the average length.

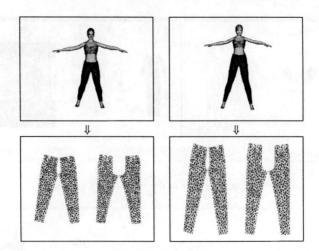

Figure 14: Feature points.

7   Conclusion and Future Research

In this paper, we have developed a methodology to see ourselves at any angle in privacy and try several different styles of garments. We have introduced this idea for Made-to-measure garment simulation on an individualised body using an online Web application. The key points we have shown here are the acquisition of personal virtual body from easy input such as photographs or measurement, the 3D-garment made to exact measurements calculated from 3D virtual cloned body or measurement-oriented body, and then the optimised Made-to-measure garment simulation on the Web. Finally, the 2D patterns are generated from the personally sized garments. These 2D measurements could be directly sent to the cloth manufactures. The speed optimisation for online calculation comes from wide use of generic database of bodies and garments. This research works as a prototype. To have it working on daily basis, it needs to optimise every step.

Acknowledgements

This work is supported by the European Project E-Taylor IST-1999-10549. We are grateful to Chris Joslin for reading the paper and having made useful suggestions as well as Pascal Volino and Marlene Arevalo for their precious help.

References

Addleman, S. (1997), Whole-body 3D Scanner and Scan Data Report, *in* R. N. Ellson & J. H. Nurre (eds.), *Three Dimensional Image Capture and Applications*, SPIE — The International Society for Optical Engineering, pp.2–5.

Akimoto, T., Suenaga, Y. & Richard, S. W. (1993), "Automatic Creation of 3D Facial Models", *IEEE Computer Graphics and Applications* **13**(3), 16–22.

Beck, B. (2000), Key Strategic Issues in Online Apparel Retailing — The Need For An Online Fitting Solution, http://www.techexchange.com/thelibrary/online_fit.html.

Blanz, V. & Vetter, T. (1999), A Morphable Model for the Synthesis of 3D Faces, *in* M. Schweppe (ed.), *Proceedings of SIGGRAPH'99, Computer Graphics (Annual Conference Series)* **33**, ACM Press, pp.187–94.

DeCarlo, D. & Metaxas, D. (1996), The Integration of Optical Flow and Deformable Models with Applications to Human Face Shape and Motion Estimation, *in* B. Bhanu (ed.), *Proceedings of CVPR'96*, IEEE Computer Society Press, pp.231–8.

DeCarlo, D., Metaxas, D. & Stone, M. (1998), An Anthropometric Face Model using Variational Techniques, *in* M. Cohen (ed.), *Proceedings of SIGGRAPH'98, Computer Graphics (Annual Conference Series)* **32**, ACM Press, pp.67–74.

Escher, M. & Magnenat-Thalmann, N. (1997), Automatic 3D Cloning and Real-Time Animation of a Human Face, *in* N. Magnenat-Thalmann & D. Thalmann (eds.), *Proceedings of Computer Animation '97*, IEEE Computer Society Press, pp.58–66.

Foley, J. D., van Dam, A., Feiner, S. K. & Hughes, J. F. (1995), *Computer Graphics Principles and Practice*, reissued second edition, Addison–Wesley.

Fua, P. & Leclerc, Y. (1996), "Taking Advantage of Image-based and Geometry-based Constraints to Recover 3-D Surfaces", *Computer Vision and Image Understanding* **64**(1), 111–27.

Gu, J., Chang, T., Mak, I., Gopalsamy, S., Shen, H. C. & Yuen, M. (1998), A 3D Reconstruction System for Human Body Modeling, *in* N. Magnenat-Thalmann & D. Thalmann (eds.), *Modelling and Motion Capture Techniques for Virtual Environments (Proceedings of the International Workshop CAPTECH'98)*, Vol. 1537 of *Lecture Notes in Computer Science*, Springer-Verlag.

Guenter, B., Grimm, C., Wood, D., Malvar, H. & Pighin, F. (1998), Making Faces, *in* M. Cohen (ed.), *Proceedings of SIGGRAPH'98, Computer Graphics (Annual Conference Series)* **32**, ACM Press, pp.55–66.

Hilton, A., Beresford, D., Gentils, T., Smith, R. & Sun, W. (1999), Virtual People: Capturing Human Models to Populate Virtual Worlds, *in* N. Magnenat-Thalmann & D. Thalmann (eds.), *Proceedings of Computer Animation '99*, IEEE Computer Society Press, pp.174–185.

Ip, H. & Yin, L. (1996), "Constructing a 3D Individual Head Model from Two Orthogonal Views", *The Visual Computer* **12**(5), 254–266.

Kakadiaris, I. A. & Metaxas, D. (1995), 3D Human Body Acquisition from Multiple Views, *in* S. Shafer, A. Blake & K. Sugihara (eds.), *Proceedings of the Fifth ICCV Conference*, IEEE Computer Society Press, pp.618–23.

Kakadiaris, I. A. & Metaxas, D. (1996), Model-based Estimation of 3D Human Motion with Occlusion Based on Active Multi-viewpoint Selection, *in* C. Dyer & K. Ikeuchi (eds.), *Proceedings of the IEEE Conference on Computer Vision and Pattern Recognition*, IEEE Computer Society Press, pp.81–7.

Kurihara, T. & Arai, K. (1991), A Transformation Method for Modeling and Animation of the Human Face from Photographs, *in* N. Magnenat-Thalmann & D. Thalmann (eds.), *Proceedings of Computer Animation '91*, Springer-Verlag, pp.45–58.

Lee, W. & Magnenat-Thalmann, N. (2000), "Fast Head Modeling for Animation", *Image and Vision Computing* **18**(4), 355–64.

Lee, W., Gu, J. & Magnenat-Thalmann, N. (2000), "Generating Animatable 3D Virtual Humans from Photographs", *Computer Graphics Forum* **19**(3), 11–21. Proceedings of Eurographics 2000.

Lee, Y., Terzopoulos, D. & Waters, K. (1995), Realistic Modeling for Facial Animation, *in* R. Cook (ed.), *Proceedings of SIGGRAPH'95 22nd Annual Conference on Computer Graphics and Interactive Techniques, Computer Graphics (Annual Conference Series)* **29**, ACM Press, pp.55–62.

Nagel, B., Wingbermühle, J., Weik, S. & Liedtke, C.-E. (1998), Automated Modelling of Real Human Faces for 3D Animation, *in* A. K. Jain, S. Venkatesh & B. C. Lovell (eds.), *Proceedings ICPR'98*, IEEE Computer Society Press, pp.95–9.

Pighin, F., Hecker, J., Lischinski, D., Szeliski, R. & Salesin, D. H. (1998), Synthesizing Realistic Facial Expressions from Photographs, *in* M. Cohen (ed.), *Proceedings of SIGGRAPH'98, Computer Graphics (Annual Conference Series)* **32**, ACM Press, pp.75–84.

Plänkers, R., Fua, P. & D'Apuzzo, N. (1999), Automated Body Modeling from Video Sequences, *in* A. Hilton & P. Fua (eds.), *Proceedings of the IEEE International Workshop on Modelling People (mPeople)*, IEEE Computer Society Press, pp.51–63.

Proesmans, M. & Van Gool, L. (1997), Reading between the Lines — A Method for Extracting Dynamic 3D with Texture, *in* D. Thalmann (ed.), *Proceedings of VRST'97*, ACM Press, pp.95–102.

Saji, H., Hioki, H., Shinagawa, Y., Yoshida, K. & Kunii, T. (1992), Extraction of 3D Shapes from the Moving Human Face using Lighting Switch Photometry, *in* N. Magnenat-Thalmann & D. Thalmann (eds.), *Creating and Animating the Virtual World,*, Computer Animation Series, Springer-Verlag, pp.69–85.

Seo, H., Cordier, F., Philippon, L. & Magnenat-Thalmann, N. (2000), Interactive Modeling of MPEG-4 Deformable Human Bodies, *in* N. Magnenat-Thalmann & D. Thalmann (eds.), *Proceedings of Deform 2000*, Kluwer, pp.120–31.

Volino, P. & Magnenat-Thalmann, N. (2000), *Virtual Clothing — Theory and Practive*, Springer-Verlag.

Zheng, J. (1994), "Acquiring 3D Models from Sequences of Contours", *IEEE Transactions on Pattern Analysis and Machine Intelligence* **16**(2), 163–78.

Computer-mediated Communication

Privacy in Multimedia Communications: Protecting Users, Not Just Data

Anne Adams[†] & Martina Angela Sasse[‡]

[†] *Department of Computer Science, Middlesex University, Bounds Green Road, London N11 2NQ, UK*
Tel: *+44 20 8411 6946*
Email: *a.adams@mdx.ac.uk*
URL: *http://www.cs.mdx.ac.uk/staffpages/aadams/*

[‡] *Department of Computer Science, University College London, Gower Street, London WC1E 6BT, UK*
Tel: *+44 20 7679 7212*
Fax: *a.sasse@cs.ucl.ac.uk*
Email: *http://www.cs.ucl.ac.uk/staff/a.sasse/*

As the use of ubiquitous multimedia communication increases so do the privacy risks associated with widespread accessibility and utilisation of data generated by such applications. Most invasions of privacy are not intentional but due to designers inability to anticipate how this data could be used, by whom, and how this might affect users. This paper addresses the problem by providing a model of user perceptions of privacy in multimedia environments. The model has been derived from an analysis of empirical studies conducted by the authors and other researchers and aids designers to determine which information users regard as private, and in which context. It also identifies trade-offs that users are willing to make rendering some privacy risks acceptable. To demonstrate how this model can be used to assess the privacy implications of multimedia communications in a specific context, an example of the models application for a specific usage scenario is provided.

Keywords: privacy, multimedia communications, grounded theory, trust, user-centred design.

1 Introduction

The increasing uptake of multimedia communications technology brings risks as well as benefits. The relationship between technology and privacy is particularly complex, and often discussed in emotional, rather than rational, terms (Adams & Sasse, 1999a; 1999b). The discussion of privacy within the HCI community looks likely to continue throughout the new millennium. The CHI99 panel, *"Trust me, I'm accountable: trust and accountability online"* (Friedman & Thomas, 1999) provided a showcase of the difficulties faced by application designers and organisational users. Two positions emerged from the debate:

1. "As the new technology environments develop, users will adapt their privacy expectations and behaviours".

2. "Privacy is a complex problem, but it will not go away. To design successful applications, we have to acknowledge the problem and start tackling it, proactively".

The first type of response may remind veterans of the early days of HCI, when some in the computing industry argued that *"inaccessible user interfaces are not really a problem — people will get used to them, eventually"*. The continued growth of HCI as a discipline shows how misguided that belief was. In our view, designers and organisations who subscribe to the view that *"users will eventually get used to"* having no privacy in computer environments, are similarly misguided.

1.1 Background

The problem with much of the published literature on privacy is that it concentrates on protecting certain types of *data* without establishing what *people* regard as private information (Davies, 1997). Expert opinion on what might be invasive is not a sufficient basis for designing acceptable multimedia communication technology, or effective policies for their usage. Professionals' perceptions of the data captured are not sufficient grounds for determining what will be acceptable to users. In our view, it is vital to identify user's perceptions to predict acts that will be regarded by them as invasive, and why (Adams & Sasse, 1999a; 1999b).

Although previous research (Bellotti, 1996; Bellotti & Sellen, 1993; Lee et al., 1997; Smith & Hudson, 1995) has identified the need for user feedback on, and control of, potentially invasive information, we need to understand when and why users want to exercise this feedback and control. Most privacy research to date has focussed on policies and mechanisms around the concept of *personal information* — data that can be used to identify an individual (Davies, 1997). We argue that such a *data-centric* approach cannot work well in the domain of multimedia communications. The majority of data in this field allows identification of a person (e.g. video image, voice patterns). Labelling all audio and video data as *personal information* — and thus declaring it to be *off limits* — is hardly practical. To define privacy it is important to review an *individual* within society; for being private requires a public context (Wacks, 1989; Goffman, 1969; Agre, 1997). Thus, organisational *culture* (Smith, 1993; Dourish, 1993) and perceptions of the *situation*

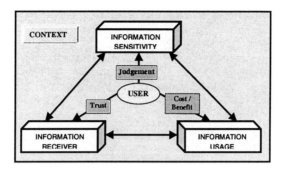

Figure 1: Privacy model factors and issues.

(Harrison & Dourish, 1996; Adams & Sasse, 1999a) will influence what users are prepared to reveal about themselves.

Ultimately, it is important to understand that most multimedia invasions of privacy are not intentional or malicious (Adams, 1999; 2001; Adams & Sasse, 1999a; 1999b). Seeking to address this problem a model of the user perspective on privacy in multimedia environments has been identified. The model helps to determine which information users regard as private, from whom, and in which context. The model also highlights privacy risks users' trade-off against the potential benefits to be gained from using multimedia applications.

2   Research Approach

To generate the model of users' perceptions of privacy (see Figure 1), we drew on an established approach from social psychology. *Grounded Theory* is a structured approach to both qualitative and quantitative data which can be used to model highly complex and sensitive phenomena in a structured empirical yet ethical manner, making it ideal for identifying privacy perceptions (Strauss & Corbin, 1990; Stevenson & Cooper, 1997). This *Grounded Theory* model was developed inductively from an integrated analysis of previous privacy literature and further studies of the phenomenon within multimedia communications (Adams, 2001). Rather than formulate a model and then attempt to prove it, the model was allowed to emerge through the analysis of qualitative and quantitative data collected by the authors and other privacy researchers. The *Grounded Theory* analysis has produced:

- A privacy model of the factors involved in privacy invasions.

- The privacy invasion cycle, which details how these factors lead to privacy invasions.

Designers and organisations wishing to implement multimedia communications should identify user assumptions (see Figure 2) for each privacy model factor and match them to what is actually occurring to identify areas where users' may perceive threats to their privacy. This process should take place prior to, or during, technology

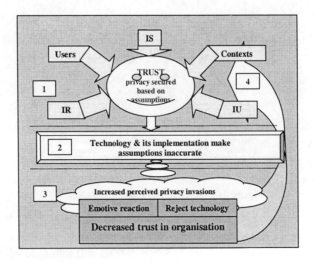

Figure 2: The privacy invasion cycle.

installation. The model can be used as a guide to identifying where potential privacy problems could occur for specific scenarios and where further investigation and consultation may be required. It should be noted that some model aspects require further research to detail pre-emptive solutions to the privacy invasion cycle.

2.1   Privacy Invasion Cycle

The central concept for the *privacy model* is privacy invasion and its story-line (the conceptualisation of a descriptive narrative for privacy invasion) is the *privacy invasion cycle*. The changing process detailed in the privacy *invasion cycle* (PIC) details users' strategies for managing and responding to privacy invasions. PIC (see Figure 2) reveals that most invasions of privacy occur when users realise that a mismatch has occurred between their perceptions and reality.

Trust: Users do not go into every situation ready to assess the privacy benefits and risks of that information exchange (Adams, 1999; Adams & Sasse, 1999a; 1999b). The degree of trust[1] felt by the user in the *Information Receiver*, technology and technology instigators determines the degree of privacy evaluation required.

Assumptions: The trust felt by the user in that information exchange relies, however, on many implicit assumptions surrounding that interaction (Adams, 1999; 2001; Adams & Sasse, 1999a; 1999b).

    1. Users previous knowledge and experiences and their role in the interaction.

---

[1]Users' privacy perceptions often reflect their trust in the organisation, technology and thus expectations for privacy protection, rather than perceived potential privacy risks and responses to those risks.

2. Perceived *Information Sensitivity* (IS).

3. Perceived *Information Receiver* (IR).

4. Perceived *Information Usage* (IU).

5. Perceived Context of interaction.

The technology mediating the multimedia interactions can make those assumptions inaccurate.

Realisation and Response: When users realise that their assumptions were inaccurate, they experience an invasion of privacy. Their responses are likely to be emotive, resulting in a rejection of the specific system, decreased trust in the Information Receiver and the organisation who implemented the technology (Adams & Sasse, 1999a; 1999b).

Decreasing Cycle: The next time the user encounters what they perceive to be a similar scenario (i.e. similar Information Receiver, technology or organisation implementing the technology) their initial trust levels will be lowered, and distorted negative assumptions may prevail which, if confirmed, will decrease users' trust still further (Adams & Sasse, 1999a; 1999b).

The PIC thus details high-level perceptions of privacy invasion and how these perceptions change over time. For designers and those deploying multimedia, however, a detailed account of the factors involved is required to identify potential solutions. The privacy model, therefore, reviews in more detail the factors relevant to PIC.

2.2   Multimedia Privacy Model

Like all mental models, users' privacy perceptions are not necessarily correct — they may be inaccurate, incomplete and biased — but they nevertheless determine user responses (Norman, 1986). It is therefore vital to establish the perceptions and assumptions with which users approach a specific technology in a particular context. This model (see Figure 1) has identified 3 major privacy factors (*Information Sensitivity, Receiver & Usage*) that interact to form the users' overall perception of privacy. There are also two further issues which are important but not specific to privacy (*User, Context*). The context of interaction also produces context issues which interact with and vary the importance of the privacy factors (e.g. Scenario 1: IU > IS or IR, Scenario 2: IR > IU or IS). Within specific scenarios trade-offs occur between the factors making some privacy risks acceptable to users based on their assumptions. This paper presents a summarised version of the model and relevant issues (Adams, 2001). Our aim is to provide designers and organisations with a better understanding of how users will perceive data generated or transmitted by multimedia communications technology, and the way it is used.

2.3   Privacy Factor: Information Sensitivity

The primary factor in this privacy model is *Information Sensitivity* (IS) (Goffman, 1969; Adams, 1999; Adams & Sasse, 1999a, 1999b; 1999c). *Information*

Sensitivity relates to the users' perception of the data being transmitted and the information interpreted by the receiver. This model highlights that contrary to the *personal information* approach to privacy users make adjustable judgements about *Information Sensitivity* (Bennett, 1992; Agre, 1997). Users judgements assess *Information Sensitivity* via a flexible scale rather than making a simple binary private vs. not private distinction. Users' perception of the data transmitted, and how public or private the broadcast situation is, can also affect perceived sensitivity levels.

2.3.1   Primary and Secondary Level Information

A key factor in a user's perception of multimedia data is the degree to which it provides information that defines them personally. Most data can be used to infer at least two levels of information:

1. *Primary level*[2]: The core data being broadcast / the topic of discussion e.g. the medical facts discussed in a video-mediated doctor-patient consultation, or technical opinions of a speaker giving a remote lecture.

2. *Secondary level*: other interpretative social / psychological characteristics of the user broadcasting the data e.g. the body language a doctor adopts when giving a pessimistic diagnosis to a patient, or the speech characteristics of the speaker giving a lecture.

We have found that many privacy invasions can be explained in terms of primary/secondary levels of information: most users fail to appreciate that the data in question can reveal more than primary level information. When they discover the data has a secondary level, which has been used in a way they did not anticipate, they feel that their privacy has been invaded. Consider the case of sales staff that discover the security cameras in their store were also used to evaluate their performance. The secondary level can also emerge over time: students participating in video-mediated tutorials (Adams, 1999) initially rated discussions of their coursework as 'impersonal' and regarded anyone using the data as a 'non-invasive' act. Towards the end of the course, however, the same students regarded the same data as potentially invasive, since someone reviewing several sessions could notice that a particular student was a *social loafer*, i.e. always badly prepared and contributing little to the discussion. Information can thus become invasive depending on what context the information was viewed in, how it was used and who viewed it.

Primary-level information may affect perceived sensitivity of secondary level information, and vice versa. Lacking knowledge of your field of expertise would be more personally detrimental than having an inadequate understanding of a general topic — e.g. the weather (unless you are a meteorologist). Similarly, being emotional (2nd level) in a family argument (1st level) will appear more appropriate than becoming emotive about the weather. Interactions can also occur between the *context* of data, the *Information Receiver*, and its *usage*. It is the increased potential for

---

[2]Highly sensitive primary information, which is personally defining, tends to relate to the traditional paradigm of personal information. Here the sensitive nature of the information is immediately apparent e.g. medical information, personal finance information etc.

ubiquitous technology to vary these factors without the user's full awareness of the repercussions, which increases the likelihood of unacceptable privacy risks.

It is particularly important to review *Information Sensitivity* issues within multimedia communications technology. Firstly, multimedia generates a richer set of data, and this increases the amount of secondary information relayed. Examples include:

- Text with textual cues: information presentation, inappropriate use of language, etc.

- Audio with verbal cues: tone of voice, accent or dialect, gaps in conversation etc.

- Video with visual cues: dress and look of user, mannerisms, body language etc.

Secondly, the speed with which multimedia data can be distributed to a potentially vast audience further increases the risk associated with un-anticipated interpretations of such data.

2.3.2 Situation

How others view us depends on the situation in which we are observed. Harrison & Dourish (1996) point out the importance of our perception of 'place' in social interactions. Certain behaviours may be socially acceptable in a *private* situation, but not in a *public one* — and vice versa. If a user misinterprets how public a situation is, the result may be inappropriate behaviour, thus producing inappropriate expressions of themselves. Adams & Sasse (1999a) report an example where those installing a multimedia application judged the situation (staff common room) as public, and thus saw no problem with broadcasting images over the Internet. The users, however, regarded the situation as private or semi-private, and felt their privacy was being invaded through the installation of a camera. The result was an emotive rejection of the technology, and decreased trust in those who had introduced it. However, it is not just the distinction of *public* vs. *private* that is important, but the users' notion of *place* that is vital in perceptions of how private the information may be (Harrison & Dourish, 1996). Some data may be considered unacceptable for transmission beyond a specific public setting. Adams & Sasse (1999b) reviewed perceptions of audio and video data being broadcast from a public conference. Even though transmitting images of speakers and those asking questions was deemed acceptable, broadcasting video of the audience was not. This issue was emphasised when embarrassing images of a member of the audience sleeping during a session were broadcast; his boss happened to watch the session and reprimanded him on his return. This highlights an interaction between *task* and *situation* factors. The situation for the conference attendee was only acceptably public to those visible to him, whilst the images were used for purposes other than those assumed of information exchange (similar to staff performance monitoring).

Mackay (1995) and Bellotti & Sellen (1993) suggest that people should be made aware that their images are being transmitted. Ultimately this model proposes that allowing users to weigh-up the information value (e.g. audience to obtain overall session perspective) against potential privacy risks involved (e.g. those not consciously on show being viewed) prior to transmission reduces the likelihood of these invasions occurring. It must be remembered that although technology deployers perceptions are important that they are likely to have different situation perceptions from those of users (Adams & Sasse, 1999a).

2.4   Privacy Factor: Information Receiver[3]

The *Information Receiver* (IR) is the user's perception of the person (not necessarily actual person) who receives and or manipulates their data. A range of issues will influence users' assessment of the *Information Receiver* and potential trade-offs made, with trust (often based on relationships, information roles and group membership) playing the most important part (Adams, 2001).

2.5   Privacy Factor: Information Usage

The model identifies that the final privacy factor *Information Usage* relates to users' perception of how their information is currently being used or at a later date. Important usage issues (some of which this paper expands upon) relate to the users' perception of task, recording awareness, repeated viewing, context, editing and risk/benefit trade-offs.

2.5.1   Current Information Usage: Task

This model highlights the importance of *task* factors on users' perceptions of information and related privacy issues, as most multimedia privacy research has not reviewed these aspects. Davies (1997) asserts that the acceptability of CCTV for surveillance (security) in the UK is a manipulation of the concept of public interest. Adams & Sasse (1999a) report a case where the line between awareness and a surveillance technology were crossed according to users' perceptions. Crossing that line violated users' implicit assumptions underlying multimedia environments as a tool for increased cooperation, communication and thus freedom of information. This resulted in an emotive rejection of the technology, and a decrease in users' trust in the organisation.

2.5.2   Later Information Usage: Recording, Repeated Viewing and Editing

Users' anxieties about the use of technology are often said to come down to a fear of the potential *Information Usage*. Recording of multimedia data increases the likelihood of information losing important contextual factors, which can increase the potential for it to become invasive (Dix, 1990). Adams & Sasse (1999b) identified that data recorded without time and date stamps could be potentially invasive when viewed out of context. A professor, for example, presenting her findings via videoconferencing which is recorded and viewed 10 years later could be viewed as an out of date researcher if the information has not even been date stamped. Further contextual information could decrease potential misunderstandings for future *Information Receivers*.

Using recorded multimedia data with secondary level information (see Section 2.3.1) also increases its sensitivity, as the potential to view the data

---

[3]For a detailed full analysis of this complex factor see (Adams, 2001).

repeatedly increases (Mackay, 1995; Bellotti & Sellen, 1993; Adams & Sasse, 1999b). An embarrassing instance (emotional response in a debate, an indelicate physical action) within an interaction could be 'written off' as one of those humiliating moments best forgotten. However, a record of that event can be watched an infinite number of times by numerous people. It must be remembered that if the most guarded of politicians can make embarrassing mistakes on film what is the probability that the rest of us will.

Organisations often assume that a user providing personal data for accepted organisational practices (e.g. providing a service) accepts that this can be used in any way that fits within these parameters. This again makes the mistake of assuming that information remains at the same degree of sensitivity regardless of slight changes in its usage. Using recorded videoconferencing data to evaluate the technology may be acceptable; using the same data to evaluate the technology's effect on people of different ethnic backgrounds may not. Not only should casual access to multimedia data be restricted (Mackay, 1995), but an understanding obtained of how changes in usage can affect sensitivity levels.

As the potential to manipulate and edit data increases, so do associated privacy risks. This becomes doubly important within multimedia communications, as the perception that, *"a picture doesn't lie"*, although inaccurate, still prevails (Mackay, 1995). Although taking a section (in its entirety) out of the whole may appear to be keeping it within its context, evidence shows that users perceive this as a major threat to privacy (Adams & Sasse, 1999b). However, it must be understood that the majority of findings of privacy invasion within multimedia communications result from unintentional acts rather than malicious intent.

2.6 User Issues

Within multimedia communications the term user traditionally refers to people both broadcasting and receiving information. However, it is as the former that we take privacy risks and as the latter that we encounter communication benefits that can be traded off against those risks. This model, therefore, highlights the importance of presenting the user as the person who has data transmitted either directly (primary information — their work achievements, consumption habits, medical records etc.) or indirectly (secondary information — personality, attentiveness, intelligence) about themselves. The model also identifies that for privacy purposes designers and technology deployers must understand that the user may well not be actively using the system and may actually be unaware that their data (their image, voice etc.) is being transmitted (Bellotti & Sellen, 1993; Adams & Sasse, 1999a; 1999b). Ultimately, users' perceptions of the sensitivity of multimedia data will initially be biased by their knowledge of, and previous experience with, the technology and the data it generates. In particular, previous experiences — positive in terms of benefits, negative in terms of privacy invasions — will affect their judgements.

2.7 Context Issues

The context of interaction relates to user perceptions of the technology, social and organisational norms as well as national and international boundaries.

2.7.1   Technology

In the real world, people rely on social and physical cues to appropriately frame interactive behaviour (Goffman, 1969). Within virtual interactions, contextual cues are often lacking or distorted, resulting in user isolation from reality. Most privacy research in HCI has concentrated on distorted perception of information caused by problems at the user interface level. Disembodiment from the context of the interaction and dissociation from one's actions are suggested to be key factors in user isolation. Bellotti & Sellen (1993) argue that users require feedback on, and control of, how they are presenting themselves in multimedia interactions. With regard to perceptions of the information transmitted — and thus its sensitivity — accurate and appropriate feedback is of utmost importance. However, it is not just feedback and control on *when* information is being transmitted that is required, but *what* is being transmitted. Users often make assumptions about the *Information Receiver* (IR) — e.g. that they know how other participants in a videoconference see them — but such assumptions are often incorrect (Thomas, 1996). Interpersonal distance has, in the past, been found to dictate the intensity of a response: faces in a close-up, for instance, are scrutinised more often than those in the background (Thomas, 1996). Reeves & Nass (1996) argue that, because the size of a face is more than just a representation of an individual, it can influence psychological judgements of a person and become an invasive piece of information. Image quality and camera angles may result in a perception of the user, which they regard as inaccurate. It is important that users have feedback on how they are being presented to the IR. Lee et al. (1997) also highlight the importance of the users ability to control and manipulate the image transmitted.

Finally, what data is captured can affect how invasive the information is perceived to be. Audio in isolation is perceived as significantly more invasive than video only (Adams & Sasse, 1999a). A lack of feedback of who may be listening to the information can result in a rejection of the technology. Smith & Hudson (1995) highlighted how, in an awareness application reviewed, users' lack of IR feedback resulted in the audio channel being rejected for even low sensitivity information.

2.7.2   Social, Organisational and National Contexts

There is limited relevant research, but organisational culture has been identified as an important factor (Dourish, 1993; Smith, 1993) whilst some social groups are noted as more at risk of privacy invasion that others (Raab & Bennet, 1998).

3   Multimedia Communication Scenario

To demonstrate how this model can be used to assess the privacy implications of multimedia communications technology in a specific context, a specific usage scenario is evaluated using the model. Although the model can be used as a design tool it is presented here as an evaluation tool for a current multimedia communication application scenario, which actually occurred.

A videoconference seminar was given from a speaker alone in a small London-based office to two audiences: one local (London) and one remote (Glasgow). Both audiences watched the seminar in seminar rooms projected onto a large screen. During the seminar the two audiences either heard audio from the presenter or from

Information Sensitivity (IS)	PIC user assumptions	PIC technology breaches
IS judgements: System interaction levels distort perception of what is transmitted and its sensitivity.	Users could assume the IR is local (IR location is not clearly stated) perceiving the situation as semi-private with local norms (e.g. language, behaviour).	The IR is actually located across the country and may have different perceived norms.
Public/private situation: Although the seminar local images and audio transmitted remotely. Presenter's isolation further distorts situation.		
Primary and secondary levels: Presenter had poor feedback of what the IR received. The degree of media transmitted increased the amount of 2nd information received.	The presenter may assume habits and mannerisms may not be noticeable from the small image feedback they saw.	The IR receives large images where actions are more dramatic and potentially embarrassing.

Table 1: Multimedia scenario evaluated for the *Information Sensititvity*.

the video recording whilst the presenter had all the audio channels open. At the end of the seminar a question and answer session occurred during which all of the audio channels were open.

The audiences had varying degrees of experience with multimedia communication technology, ranging from novice to expert, whilst the presenter was experienced in multimedia communications. Although the participants within each audience knew each other, they did not know the remote audience or the seminar presenter. Consequently, the seminar presenter knew none of the people watching.

All the screens (both audiences and the presenter) displayed 4 tiled windows of the London audience, Glasgow audience, presenter and Seminar slides/video. PowerPoint slides and a video recording of a previous seminar were used as part of the seminar. The slides were transmitted as a vic stream and the recording was also played out from a VCR through this stream (i.e. the image was switched from the slides to the clip, and then back again). The size of the windows displayed to the audiences (at Glasgow and London) were:

> Presenter   *Common Intermediate Format* (CIF)
> Other audiences image   CIF
> Viewing their own image   *Thumbnail*
> Slides / video recording   Super CIF

The presenter saw their images on a desktop screen at window size Quarter CIF whilst the two audiences and the slides/video recording were thumbnail images.

3.1   Scenario Privacy Evaluation

This scenario is evaluated for each of the model factors and Issues (see Tables 1–3 to assess whether the privacy invasion cycle (PIC) could be evoked for some of the participants.

Information Receiver (IR)	PIC user assumptions	PIC technology breaches
Trust levels: Established local audience trust levels for each other may have been at odds with trust in remote viewers.	Users may assume the only IRs are those visible on the screen with associated trust levels.	IRs not on the screen were able to view the session e.g. seminar technicians.
Information Usage (IU)		
Current IU: Participants often attend seminars, not mediated by technology, which are not recorded or re-used.	Users could assume images and audio are only viewed during the seminar.	Images and audio were in reality being recorded and could also be edited and re-used for different purposes at a later date.
Later IU: Participants were not advised or given feedback about seminar recordings later IRs or editing.		

Table 2: Multimedia scenario evaluated for the *Information Receiver and Usage.*

User Issues	PIC user assumptions	PIC technology breaches
Mental models: Poor feedback on technical processes and data transmitted.	Low system interaction levels could produce user assumptions that they are only IRs with a mental model of the scenario as similar to television or cinema.	Video and audio data was captured with two way communication elements which should stimulate a mental model similar to that of the telephone.
System interaction: System interaction levels (direct / indirect), varied throughout.		
Context Issues		
Technology: Poor interface feedback on what information was transmitted and in what context it was received.	Audience users could assume as they can only hear the presenter (not the other users) that all the users can only hear the presenter.	The technology transmits more than is relayed to the user. The presenter, can hear audio from both of the audiences.
Social grouping/Organisational culture: seminar interaction occurred within a specific context (with associated norms) both in time and location.	Users may assume the context of interaction is understood by the IR (e.g. time of day, environmental conditions — cold, poor lighting etc.).	Information broadcaster actions could be mis-interpreted (e.g. shivering, poor concentration) especially when recorded.

Table 3: Multimedia scenario evaluated for the User and Context issues.

3.2 Scenario Privacy Recommendations

The evaluated scenario detailed in Section 3.1 (see Tables 1–3 has been used as a basis for recommendations to decrease the potential for privacy invasions occurring. It is important to identify exactly what degree of *control* and *feedback* (Bellotti & Sellen, 1993) is required, by whom (*Information Broadcaster/Receiver*) and why.

3.2.1 Briefing Session

- System details: A briefing session should be provided detailing how the system works for novices to establish accurate mental models. They must not be allowed to establish the inaccurate 'television/cinema viewing only' mental model of the system.

- Interaction details: The briefing session should establish clearly how public or private the situation is. What may be clearly public to the designer or technology instigator can be just as clearly private to the user (Adams & Sasse, 1999a). The audience must clearly understand that although they are attending a seminar (with low system interaction levels) they can still be viewed and heard remotely. They must also understand:

  1. when they can be viewed and heard; and

  2. who the Information Receiver is.

- Recording details: Clear notification must be given if the seminar is to be recorded stating who will be able to view or edit it at a later date. Participants should be informed that they can leave if they now wish to not take part.

3.2.2 Interface Changes: Information Broadcaster

- Data transmission: Present noticeable feedback on what data (i.e. video, audio) a seminar attendee, or presenter, is broadcasting and receiving. Feedback should also be provided to the presenter of how they are being viewed by the audiences, including the image size.

- Interaction Feedback: Display obvious feedback of who is receiving the data and when. If the receivers are not part of the interaction they should also be detailed. Also show clearly and in an understandable way ('technically related distances' are not acceptable for novices) the *Information Receiver's* current location.

- Recording Feedback: Detail noticeable feedback to the information broadcaster of when transmitted data is also being recorded (e.g. a red light going on with the letters REC underneath)

3.2.3 Interface Changes: Information Receiver

- Contextual feedback: It is important for information to be kept within its original context (Dix, 1990; Adams & Sasse, 1999b). People viewing the session remotely or at a later date must be provided with contextual information (e.g. where transmitted from, why, when — time/date stamp)

- Edited data: Edited versions should be clearly marked and links to original versions detailed (Adams & Sasse, 1999b).

- Information handling: Identify if the *Information Receiver* is using the information for the same task as that perceived by the *Information Broadcaster*. Highlight to both acceptable *Information Usage*, e.g. 'for seminar purposes only'

3.2.4 Policy Procedures

- Recording permission: Users' permission to record sessions should be obtained where possible. If impractical then feedback to users who are recorded must be provided (see interface issues).

- Changed usage: If the information is to be used for another purpose other than those previously detailed to the user a further permission should be obtained.

- Editing: Any editing — even minor — to recorded multimedia information should have permission obtained from the user and be carefully reviewed for potential *Information Receiver*, *Sensitivity* and *Usage* privacy risks.

- Continued privacy evaluation: Assess the usefulness of the information capture against potential risk of privacy invasion to the user. These assessments can save later costly user trade-offs and rejections of the technology e.g. 'I'm not taking part in or presenting a remote seminar'.

4   Discussion and Conclusions

This paper highlights limitations of the current personal information privacy paradigm for multimedia communications. The concept of *personal information* is often employed as an assessment of users' potential privacy worries. However, the majority of multimedia communication is personally identifiable (e.g. user's visual image, email address, name etc.) and it would be impractical to treat it all as sensitive information. In contrast, some multimedia environments allow for complete anonymity, which produces the misguided impression that no sensitive information is released and therefore users' privacy is secured. Ultimately, users' privacy perceptions relate strongly to users' misconceptions due to inaccurate social and physical cues and not to a simplistic categorising of the data transmitted. The *privacy invasion cycle* highlights how these inaccurate assumptions can lead to privacy invasions.

This model has mapped all of the relevant elements of users' privacy perceptions so that further research may detail context specific variations. These variations relate, for example, to different domains, tasks, social norms, organisational culture and national and international norms. Indeed, the importance of culture within multimedia communications is an important factor that is woefully under-researched.

In conclusion, not only must we accept the importance of privacy within multimedia communications, but also the significance of users' privacy perceptions. Application designers and organisations considering using multimedia communications must realise that, even though privacy may initially not be an important concern for some users, they will react strongly when they see that it has been invaded (Adams, 2001; Adams & Sasse, 1999a; 1999b). This model details what guides users' perceptions and a theory of the processes behind privacy invasions in order to aid in the development of multimedia applications acceptable to users. There is a need to counteract privacy problems before they arise thus solving them before people lose their trust and emotively reject the technology.

Acknowledgements

We gratefully acknowledge the help of staff in the Department of Computer Science at UCL. This research was originally funded by BT/ESRC CASE studentship S00429637018

References

Adams, A. (1999), Users' Perception of Privacy in Multimedia Communication, *in* M. W. Altom & M. G. Williams (eds.), *Companion Proceedings of CHI'99: Human Factors in Computing Systems (CHI'99 Conference Companion)*, ACM Press, pp.53–4.

Adams, A. (2001), Users' Perception of Privacy in Multimedia Communication, PhD thesis, School of Psychology, University College London.

Adams, A. & Sasse, M. (1999a), Privacy Issues in Ubiquitous Multimedia Environments: Wake Sleeping Dogs or Let Them Lie?, *in* A. Sasse & C. Johnson (eds.), *Human–Computer Interaction — INTERACT '99: Proceedings of the Seventh IFIP Conference on Human–Computer Interaction*, Vol. 1, IOS Press, pp.214–21.

Adams, A. & Sasse, M. (1999b), Taming the Wolf in Sheep's Clothing: Privacy in Multimedia Communications, *in Proceedings of Multimedia'99*, ACM Press, pp.101–7.

Adams, A. & Sasse, M. (1999c), "The User is Not the Enemy", *Communications of the ACM* **42**(12), 40–6.

Agre, P. (1997), Beyond the Mirror World: Privacy and the Representational Practices of Computing, *in* P. Agre & M. Rotenberg (eds.), *Technology and Privacy: The New Landscape*, MIT Press, pp.29–62.

Bellotti, V. (1996), What You Don't Know Can Hurt You: Privacy in Collaborative Computing, *in* A. Sasse, R. J. Cunningham & R. Winder (eds.), *People and Computers XI (Proceedings of HCI'96)*, Springer-Verlag, pp.241–61.

Bellotti, V. & Sellen, A. (1993), Designing for Privacy in Ubiquitous Computing Environments, *in* G. de Michelis, C. Simone & K. Schmidt (eds.), *Proceedings of ECSCW'93, the 3rd European Conference on Computer-Supported Cooperative Work*, Kluwer, pp.77–92.

Bennett, C. (1992), *Regulating Privacy*, Cornell University Press.

Davies, S. (1997), Re-Engineering the Right to Privacy, *in* P. Agre & M. Rotenberg (eds.), *Technology and Privacy: The New Landscape*, MIT Press, pp.143–65.

Dix, A. (1990), Information Processing, Context and Privacy, *in* D. Diaper, D. Gilmore, G. Cockton & B. Shackel (eds.), *Proceedings of INTERACT '90 — Third IFIP Conference on Human–Computer Interaction*, Elsevier Science, pp.15–20.

Dourish, P. (1993), Culture and Control in a MediaSpace, *in* G. de Michelis, C. Simone & K. Schmidt (eds.), *Proceedings of ECSCW'93, the 3rd European Conference on Computer-Supported Cooperative Work*, Kluwer, pp.125–137.

Friedman, B. & Thomas, J. C. (1999), Trust me, I'm Accountable: Trust and Accountability Online, *in* M. W. Altom & M. G. Williams (eds.), *Companion Proceedings of CHI'99: Human Factors in Computing Systems (CHI'99 Conference Companion)*, ACM Press, pp.79–80.

Goffman, E. (1969), *The Presentation of Self in Everyday Life*, second edition, Penguin.

Harrison, R. & Dourish, P. (1996), Re-Place-ing Space: The Roles of Place and Space in Collaborative Systems, *in* M. S. Ackerman (ed.), *Proceedings of CSCW'96: ACM Conference on Computer Supported Cooperative Work*, ACM Press, pp.67–76.

Lee, A., Girgensohn, A. & Schlueter, K. (1997), NYNEX Portholes: Initial User Reactions and Redesign Implications, *in* S. C. Hayne & W. Prinz (eds.), *Proceedings of International ACM SIGGROUP Conference on Supporting Group Work, Group'97*, ACM Press, pp.385–94.

Mackay, W. (1995), Ethics, Lies and Videotape..., *in* I. Katz, R. Mack, L. Marks, M. B. Rosson & J. Nielsen (eds.), *Proceedings of CHI'95: Human Factors in Computing Systems*, ACM Press, pp.138–45.

Norman, D. A. (1986), Cognitive Engineering, *in* D. A. Norman & S. W. Draper (eds.), *User Centered System Design: New Perspectives on Human–Computer Interaction*, Lawrence Erlbaum Associates, pp.31–62.

Raab, C. D. & Bennet, C. J. (1998), "The Distribution of Privacy Risks: Who Needs Protection?", *Information Society* **14**(4), 253–62.

Reeves, B. & Nass, C. (1996), *The Media Equation: How People Treat Computers, Television and New Media Like Real People and Places*, Cambridge University Press.

Smith, I. & Hudson, S. (1995), Low Disturbance Audio for Awareness and Privacy in Media Space Applications, *in* R. Heller (ed.), *Proceedings of Multimedia'95*, ACM Press, pp.91–7.

Smith, J. (1993), "Privacy Policies and Practices: Inside the Organizational Maze", *Communications of the ACM* **36**(12), 105–22.

Stevenson, C. & Cooper, N. (1997), "Qualitative and Quantitative Research", *The Psychologist: Bulletin of the British Psychological Society* **10**(4), 159–60.

Strauss, A. & Corbin, J. (1990), *Basics of Qualitative Research: Grounded Theory Procedures and Techniques*, Sage Publications.

Thomas, J. C. (1996), The long term social implications of new information technology, *in* R. Dholakia, N. Mundorf & N. Dholakia (eds.), *New Infotainments Technologies in the Home: Demand Side Perspectives*, Lawrence Erlbaum Associates.

Wacks, R. (1989), *Personal Information: Privacy and the Law*, Clarendon Press.

Managing Visibility in Ubiquitous Multimedia Communication Environments

Leon Watts & Emmanuel Dubois[†]

Centre for HCI Design, Department of Computation, UMIST, PO Box 88, Manchester M60 1QD, UK

Tel: *+44 161 200 3383*

Fax: *+44 161 200 3324*

Email: *leon.watts@co.umist.ac.uk*

[†] *Equipe IIHM, CLIPS-IMAG, BP 53, 38041 Grenoble Cedex 9, France*

Users of Ubiquitous Multimedia Communications Environments (UMCE), such as media spaces, have to manage a trade-off between gaining some awareness of colleagues' ongoing activities and the risk posed to their own personal privacy by being 'on permanent display'. UMCEs involve pervasive, continuous and heterogeneous connections between people and spaces. In order to learn more about the mechanisms underlying this trade-off, we studied a UMCE in the form of a minimal media space over a period of three months. We interpreted our results with reference to social identity theory, which casts self-identity as a set of affiliations and externally visible association with them. UMCE users themselves would define, configure and occupy places, or locales, within their spaces as a way of achieving a reliable and low-cognitive-effort management of their self-presentation. It may be that effective interpersonal and inter-group connections of this kind require attention to intra-space heterogeneity as well as heterogeneity in inter-space and technological terms. In this way, it would be possible to avoid the attentional demands of adjusting visibility through manipulations of sensor position or continually fiddling with filters. Instead, one may capitalise on a familiar regime of managing self-presentation by creating and then moving into and out of intra-space locales, each associated with a particular set of identities and audiences.

Keywords: media space, ubiquitous computing, multimedia communication environments, social identity theory, place, privacy.

1   Introduction

For nearly a decade, extensive research and development of media spaces has been underway at a number of academic and industrial laboratories (Fish et al., 1990; Heath & Luff, 1992; Lee et al., 1997; Mantei et al., 1991; Tang & Rua, 1994). Media spaces are typically intended to support low-level and low-effort interpersonal awareness among workgroup members. They exist as a surrogate for a physical milieu where building architecture or physical distribution hinder spontaneous and informal interaction. Indeed, this was a major design goal for Fish and Kraut's pioneering work (Fish et al., 1990). The design intention has been to add to the infrastructure of a work place, conveying on an ongoing basis information about who is where and doing what. The distinctive and necessary feature of the media space, in this role, is its continuous operation.

Most media spaces have been video-based although the concept does not in principle require a literal visibility. Interval Research Corporation has been working on an audio-only media space for some years (Singer et al., 1999). A number of media spaces have also honoured the principle of facilitating interaction by including or integrating companion conferencing facilities. Early media spaces, such as Bellcore's VideoWindow and CRUISER, were based on an analogue of person-to-person face-to-face communication, using point-to-point audio and video connections over a network of media space nodes. To reflect the 'everywhere and always on' nature of the media space, and a continuity with wearable and ubiquitous technologies (Falk & Björk, 2000), they are better understood as a class of technologies called Ubiquitous Multimedia Communication Environments (UMCE) (Adams & Sasse, 1999a; Bellotti, 1997).

Dourish et al., reporting several years of personal experience with an 'office share' media space, suggest that the true potential of a media space is given by the generation of a hybrid space out of the local, physical space and image of the distant space (Dourish et al., 1996). They contrast this with multimedia support for isolated interactions. There is some evidence to suggest that seeing the physical aspects of joint activity (manipulating, pointing etc.) or person-in-place, simply offers a different kind of value than that obtained from seeing a person's face (Watts & Monk, 1996). In other words, the value of transmitted images has more to do with their objective information content than in the subtleties of non-verbal communication cues. At the same time, the propensity for the physical locations themselves to affect mediated interactions has become ever more apparent (Dourish et al., 1996; Watts & Monk, 1998). This trend is evident in UMCE development. Emphasis has shifted away from having several targeted views within a persons work space (Gaver et al., 1993) towards a general awareness of one's group via images of activity at various locations (Daly-Jones et al., 1998; Lee et al., 1997; Rønby-Pederson & Sokoler, 1997).

Despite the fact that much of UMCE research and development has been carried out in commercial laboratories, few of these systems have appeared in the every-day office. The tension between privacy and accessibility seems to be the critical factor. Image filters have been used to safeguard privacy (Hudson & Smith, 1996; Zhao & Stasko, 1998) but seem to be skirting the issue, simply reducing awareness to improve privacy and thereby risking removal of the benefit. The evolution of NYNEX Portholes is a notable exception, in trying to couple filtering regimes with classes of onlooker (Girgensohn et al., 1999). Indeed 'audience awareness', or knowing who are in receipt of personal information, has been argued as one of the cornerstones of privacy maintenance (Adams & Sasse, 1999b). This paper draws upon empirical data to explore the changing ideas behind the UMCE concept, with special reference to the architectural notion of 'place', an account of privacy risk developed by Adams and Sasse, and social identity theory.

The architect Christian Norberg-Schulz defines place as a design concept for architecture, composite of a locality within a physical area and the activities that customarily characterise it. Place defines an 'atmosphere' within which human actions are appropriate or inappropriate, so that the architect's task is to create a culturally and functionally effective facility for people to live in and to use (Norberg-Schulz, 1980). Harrison & Dourish (1996) have argued that the design of collaborative systems needs to take account of this space–place distinction by including the role, function, nature and convention of a space when introducing technologies. Adams & Sasse (1999a; 1999b) have developed a multidimensional framework for privacy with reference to UMCE adoption. They note that privacy is an inextricably subjective construct which, nevertheless, shows common structural characteristics between individuals. For example, the sensitivity of a given piece of information is conditioned by its expected recipient, and the acceptability of transmitting information is governed by obtaining prior permission for its transmission. There is hence no absolute privacy status for any particular piece of information: it is always about permission and control over any information on the part of the person to whom it pertains. Social identity theory concerns how people understand themselves in relation to their peers and also how they affiliate and then demonstrate their affiliations to their peers. Lea & Spears have applied social identity theory to studies of computer-mediated communication and found some marked effects for such media on intra- and inter-group processes. This paper will argue for a connection between place, social identity and UMCE design.

At this laboratory a video-based UMCE, CoMedi, has been under development for some time (Coutaz et al., 1999; Coutaz et al., 1998). In March 1999, a light-weight version of CoMedi was installed in a total of fifteen locations in three physically separated buildings (and across three floors in one of these buildings). Our intention was to examine and extend understanding of the UMCE concept by recording both preconceived ideas of its merits and demerits and then seeing how these attitudes were confronted by real and extended experience. A particular emphasis in our study was placed on the relationship between information in public and private space, and between spaces for work and social space, a distinction that is not always clearly understood (Falk & Björk, 2000). We thus report first a set of assumptions within the community about the vital aspects of media spaces, positive and negative, that were expressed just prior to the CoMedi installation. We report an analysis of the use of CoMedi based on day-to-day observations and examination of diary records, informal discussions with community members and a questionnaire that was intended to bring out some of the themes we felt we had identified during the observational period.

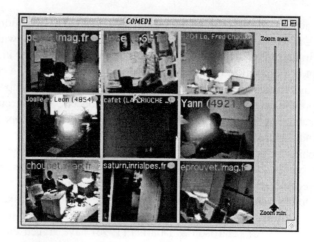

Figure 1: A typical CoMedi window in use, showing images from nine active nodes.

2 The CoMedi Media Space

CoMedi exists in two forms. One is a fully-functioning concept demonstrator, including computer vision as a tool for image filtering and other technically advanced functions. In its other form, CoMedi is a light-weight Java implementation, allowing robust and fully compatible installations on Silicon Graphics, PC and Macintosh computers. Indeed, all three platforms supported CoMedi nodes during the period of our study.

In the following account, a CoMedi node means a workstation running CoMedi software associated with a single camera, not a particular office. Some offices had two CoMedi nodes. The interface and interaction model is deliberately simple and common to all platforms. Starting a CoMedi node causes the local image to be displayed on the local monitor first and in the same form as it is multicast to other nodes. Following automatic network checking for other nodes, images are added to the CoMedi GUI window, automatically resizing each image pane as a function of the total number of current images. Figure 1 shows a typical CoMedi window, comprising nine panes, each containing an image sent approximately every 5 seconds by a distant CoMedi node. Users may select a particular image and enlarge it with the zoom slider, shown on the right-hand edge of Figure 1, in which case other images are contracted to compensate.

CoMedi thus provides each connected user with a view of all other locations containing functioning and accessible CoMedi nodes. CoMedi supports a weak visibility-reciprocity principle. Those who can see others via the media space are normally also visible, since connection is automatic on launching the media space unless permission is explicitly refused. All active nodes, whether or not contributing an image to the local node, are included in an 'audience' list that may be displayed from a CoMedi menu. Besides restricting other nodes from displaying their image (filtering who can see by changing access permission), local users can also select

Figure 2: Image filters on CoMedi image panes showing (clockwise from top left), local filter, no filter, motion filter and venetian blind filter.

one of two software filters to degrade the view of his/her office (filtering what can be seen). Filters once applied affect images for all audiences by:

- Providing a 'venetian blind' style of mask (see Figure 2, bottom left-hand image pane).

- Transmitting only a representation of office activity (see Figure 2, bottom right-hand image pane).

Additionally, CoMedi includes an explicit 'accessibility' signal in the form of a coloured circle. These are visible in Figure 2 in the top right-hand corner of each pane. Users can choose 'available' (green), 'busy' (yellow) or 'do not disturb' (red).

3 Community and Experience

We carried out a number of complementary data collection exercises over a three-month period, each building on data gathered to date. In this paper, we focus on observations made by ourselves and diary comments left by the community of users.

3.1 The User Community

CoMedi was established within a large French research institute: of the order of 100 people would have experienced it on a fairly regular basis during the study period. It was installed on 15 workstations in research laboratories located in three different buildings. Of these, 14 were situated in offices to be hosted on volunteers' workstations and one in a communal rest and coffee area simply known as the 'Cafette'. Members of five separate research groups within the institute responded in the written data resources (initial survey, diaries and final questionnaire) although it is likely that some of the comments made in a communal diary were left by people outside the Institute. Relations between members of the community are characterised by cordiality and informality, with much shared social time. In contrast, working practices did not extend to very much shared formal activity between the groups. The group that developed CoMedi formed the largest single response group (contributing about half of all data gathered) and this was split over two floors in one of the buildings. Within this group, working practices involve extensive and continuous interaction on a range of projects.

3.2   Observations of CoMedi in Use

The physical deployment of media space technologies is known to be important, whether as a matter of competition for limited amount of 'desktop real-estate', or as a difficulty in arranging camera and position to give an honest view of occupancy/audience (Dourish et al., 1996). We found our users very willing to exploit the physical configuration of camera and monitor to adjust the visibility of themselves and, more critically for the thrust of this paper, their space. In the first place, camera angles were adjusted frequently and seemingly without hesitation. The cameras at all CoMedi nodes were light-weight, compact and had fixed and generous depths and fields of view (with the exception of the Cafette camera, discussed below). This meant that users had a lot of freedom to choose how much of their space (i.e. which of their places) they displayed, at the cost of however much self-visibility they were prepared to tolerate. It is clear that this flexibility meant every user could put a cast-iron guarantee on privacy, simply by keeping their camera pointed away from themselves or other colleagues. In office settings, this was an extremely rare occurrence. Members of the community seemed to settle on a degree of visibility that varied from full-image head-and-shoulders to just profile or 3/4 view occupying a fraction of their CoMedi image (contrast the lower right pane with the upper centre pane in Figure 1).

Secondly, some parts of users' spaces were more sensitive places than others. In Figure 1, three users (top and centre left, centre right) have used strips of clear sticky tape to obscure only part of their spaces, leaving the remainder free for others to see. This became so conventional that we considered it to be part of the official repertoire of image filters (see Figure 2, top left pane). It selectively restricted available information by partitioning the space strictly in terms of the camera's image. Hereafter, this practice shall be referred to as **locale filtering**.

People who adopted locale filters applied them both to their own habitual seating positions, so that they themselves were obscured (although still visible in a degraded form) or to their working areas (notably, obscuring the content of computer screens). People who adopted locale filters tended not to move their cameras: to do so would have changed the filtered place within their space. It seemed that people in offices resolved the privacy-availability trade-off by choosing between the visibility of a restricted subset of their space in a generalised or selective way, where the direction of the camera achieved the former and the locale filters were the mechanism for the latter. Depending on the configuration they arrived at, users could maintain enough presence within CoMedi for other users to determine that they were individually located within the Institute and to some extent how appropriate some contact would be, given current evidence of activity. This evidence of activity could be any or all of interacting with objects, such as components or papers, computers or people.

The central pane in Figure 1 shows an image from the Cafette. The camera was fitted with a lens given a particularly narrow field of view, only showing a small part of the room at a time. This limited the likelihood of any given Cafette user appearing on camera at any moment since more of the Cafette space was 'out of shot' than 'in shot'. Frequently they were people who did not encounter CoMedi in office contexts and also were less familiar with the content and function of the CoMedi display. Furthermore, the 'Russian roulette' of the five-second image update meant that the current image of the Cafette was of limited use for determining what would be shown next. Worse still, if they were captured for the next frame, their image would persist for the next five seconds or so. Several users complained that they lacked confidence in being out of frame, as they desired, and so directed the camera out of the window. The benefit of so doing was seeing an image that was unequivocally not of the Cafette interior (the limbs and leaves of a tree) and so reduced concern about wandering into the camera's field of view without realising it. Users enforced a field of view that did not include any path between, for example, the coffee machine and easy chairs. From the point of view of any other connected office, this had an immediate and catastrophic effect on audience awareness: one could never be sure who was present in the Cafette and consequently who might be 'looking in'. And yet there was no evidence of retaliatory behaviour by office-based users on these occasions.

On several occasions, the directibility of the camera was also capitalised upon to set a welcoming tone for the Cafette. The camera was occasionally pointed at brioche or pizza for all in the building to enjoy, as a general announcement to come and be sociable. The link here between the Cafette as a space and the Cafette as a cultural central point for the user community is clear. The community exploited the connection between image from a known space and an atmosphere consistent with the social meaning of that place. There was never an instance of an office user pointing their camera at a pizza, for example, although on one occasion an office user pointed their camera at their white board with an announcement of a particular success.

Every CoMedi pane carried an identification label integrated with the image. By default, this was set to the workstation's network name. However, the label could be reset very simply via a CoMedi menu to a text string. To accommodate longer strings, the display font contracted according to the number of characters used (note differences between top left and top right panes in Figure 1). Users variously displayed their own names, office locations, phone extensions, email addresses or short messages. This underlines the role of CoMedi as a UMCE despite being designed as a minimal awareness tool. It was explicitly used to send interpersonal and intergroup messages, both through the text label and symbolic acts or in combination. The centre pane of Figure 1 was altered to LA BRIOCHE following the use of the Cafette camera to advertise the presence of this French delicacy on a coffee table there. It is interesting to note that whereas office nodes frequently took individuals' names, this was never true of the Cafette. In so far as personal labelling signifies personal ownership, it highlights an individual-collective dimension to the differences between office and Cafette nodes in parallel with the private-public distinction.

Occasionally, cameras were re-directed to local whiteboards (including in the Cafette) to show messages. These were commonly humorous but included occasionally vitriolic complaints from Cafette users about the CoMedi installation there. Group-level effects were thus in clear evidence in both positive, cohesive and negative, devisive guises. Interestingly, these were relatively rarely matched by comments in the Cafette log. The communal display of upset in this way, within the very medium itself, suggests that the disembodied CoMedi manifestation was identified as an agency in its own right, as opposed to the CoMedi evaluators who would read the book.

3.3 Data from CoMedi Users

Log books were kept with each CoMedi installation, including the Cafette, and comments solicited. Notes were also made from informal conversations about CoMedi experiences. Three months following the installation, a formal evaluation was undertaken, including circulation of questionnaires and interpretation of the responses with reference to the other materials.

3.3.1 Informants

Informants were recruited anonymously by email. In addition, copies of the questionnaires were left in the Cafette itself and a URL with a version of the questionnaire was publicised. 26 completed questionnaires were returned, 4 of which were discarded because they were spoiled or the respondents used the Cafette for less than 5 visits per week. The remainder were from people who rated their usage of the Cafette as greater than 20 visits per week, including 14 office + Cafette users and 8 Cafette-only users.

3.3.2 Diaries and Discussions

Seeing an unoccupied space strongly implies that it is empty, but the validity of this inference strictly depends on the camera's field of view. The consequence is that empty images are always untrustworthy. During the observation phase, it seemed that this was more disturbing for the Office than the Cafette-only group.

Diaries and informal discussions showed that Office users were initially worried by "le sentiment d'etre épié" (the feeling of being spied upon) but learnt that the image definition was so low that relatively little could be learnt by remote viewers, at least compared to their original concerns. Visibility and legibility of computer screen content was mentioned several times, for example.

For Adams & Sasse, Information Usage is a strong determinant of the perception of privacy risk. We explicitly stated that we would not be filming from the video feeds to the media space. Even so, residual worries were there for some members of the community. One wrote:

> "at the start, my impression was negative ... in fact, taking stock, we weren't really being filmed live as the images that everyone else could see were updated after a certain delay."

So in two accidental ways, the technical limitations of CoMedi worked to the advantage of Office users by placing a bottleneck on the quality and frequency of information transmission.

French: « Je n'étais pas en mésure de savoir si quelqu'un se trouvait dans les parages en consultant seulement le media space »

English: "I couldn't tell if someone was around just by looking at the media space display"

Désaccord (Disagree)   Accord(Agree)

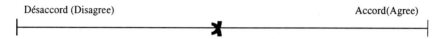

Figure 3: The inverse presence item as an example of the analogue-scale format questionnaire, with English translation, showing a response half way between Disagree and Agree (=0.5 as proportion).

Location was a strong and recurrent theme in the diaries and in conversation: knowing just where someone else was so that they could be sought out without wasting a journey. As a consequence of the degree of mobility within the community, it was often hard to find someone and so CoMedi really did seem to fill a niche — at least for the Office subgroup with members of their own research group also connected. For other Office users, this value was not relevant and several commented on the fact.

The working practices of the community involve a great deal of face-to-face contact inspite of telephones in every room, and a culture where everyone is constantly within email reach. Despite these other communications technologies, several people regretted the lack of a text ping to precede a visit. The implication is the CoMedi fell short of its aim to support accessibility awareness. This is surprising, given the existence of an explicit circular indicator within the CoMedi image panes. However, this indicator was almost never used. It seemed that people just liked CoMedi to be there, available at a glance and that using menus to change status settings a greater cost than the gain of maintaining a proper reflection of their accessibility through this mechanism. The contrast with the menu usage for changing text strings is striking. Accessibility is something that changes as a function of activities orthogonal to a UMCE: an additional effort would be required to harmonise a UMCE indicator in this way that inevitably interferes with the accessibility-moderating activity. Where the UMCE is operating as a low-level awareness device, it cannot require more than low-level or incidental activity to change its state.

3.3.3 Questionnaire

The questionnaire for the second study comprised 33 items on analogue differential scales, made up of issues that had been identified by the community in an intial round of opinion-gathering supplemented by Adams & Sasse's privacy model. These scales offer more subtlety of response than a conventional 7 point Likert scale without adding an appreciable analytic burden and have proven sensitive devices in other studies of mediating technologies (Daly-Jones et al., 1998; Watts et al., 1996). An example of such a scale is given in Figure 3.

Data presented in this section compare responses in terms of experience group: whether just in the Cafette (Cafette) or in both offices and in the Cafette (Office).

Group	Atmosphere	Location *	Presence	Rapprochement	Accessibility *
Cafette	0.47	0.27	0.20	0.27	0.28
	(0.41)	(0.31)	(0.31)	(0.19)	(0.23)
Office	0.48	0.67	0.36	0.45	0.57
	(0.33)	(0.29)	(0.32)	(0.28)	(0.27)

Table 1: Ratings of potential advantages (mean ratings as a proportion of the analogue scale, standard deviations of the mean). Asterisks indicate significant difference between the groups at the 0.05 level.

In each case a rating figure is given as the mean rating point on the analogue scale, ranging from 0 (very negative rating) to 1 (very positive rating). Thus, mid-scale ratings indicate uncertainty about the issue for the respondents.

Table 1 summarises questionnaire data for the mooted benefits of CoMedi. Cafette and Office users were non-committal about the value of CoMedi for the atmosphere at a connected node. Neither group were convinced that CoMedi was much use for telling in a general sense whether a particular person was in the building. Rapprochement, the extent to which intra and intergroup cohesion might improve, seems to contrast the two groups but the difference did not reach significance ($t(17) = 1.31$; $p = 0.207$)[1]. The groups contrast strongly on the ability to tell exactly where a person was (location: $t(20) = 3.08$; $p = 0.006$) and how appropriate it would be to initiate contact with a person (accessibility: $t(20) = 2.84$; $p = 0.013$) with office users expressing more confidence on both counts.

Table 2 summarises responses to questions about potentially problematic aspects of living with CoMedi. The similarity of privacy rating between groups was somewhat surprising, just failing to reach significance ($t(20) = 2.01$; $p = 0.073$). Two items on the questionnaire were intended to expose this factor. We noticed that one asked about the acceptability of sending information on the respondents activities and the other directly about privacy violation. There was good agreement on these two items for the Cafette group (Pearson's $r = 0.90$) but not for the Office group (Pearson's $r = 0.20$). This difference may reflect the personal nature of judgements about privacy violation, as discussed by Adams and Sasse. For this reason, only the explicit privacy invasion item contributed to Table 2. Individual differences in the Office group seem to underline the control issues for self-presentation discussed above. Interference, how much CoMedi changed patterns of behaviour, differentiated the groups strongly, with the Cafette group equivocating about changes to their patterns of activity whereas Office users responded clearly that their behaviour had been affected ($t(20) = 2.60$; $p = 0.017$).

Uncertainty about 'audience awareness' covers two issues. We wanted to know how clearly users felt they knew who could see them and whether, if they did not know, this was worrying. As Table 2 indicates, neither group felt that they really knew who was watching but, at the same time, they did not find this uncertainty

---

[1] Not all respondents chose to rate this item.

Group	Privacy	Misleading Reciprocity *	Interference *	Self-presentation Control	Audience Identity	
					Worry	Aware
Cafette	0.56	0.37	0.58	0.24	0.50	0.18
	(0.38)	(0.27)	(0.34)	(0.35)	(0.43)	(0.28)
Office	0.27	0.73	0.24	0.23	0.33	0.24
	(0.22)	(0.27)	(0.26)	(0.31)	(0.30)	(0.28)

Table 2: Ratings of potential disadvantages (means, standard deviations of the mean). Asterisks denote statistical signficance.

particularly worrying. The difference between Cafette and Office user ratings did not reach significance. Both of these findings should be interpreted in the context of the observations reported in the previous section. Users routinely positioned cameras so that they were barely visible, or with highly restricted fields of view. This both meant that the images were relatively unrevealing to an observer and uncompromising for the observed. Finally, following up on this point, respondents were asked about their perception of control over self-visibility. Both groups rated themselves as having very limited self-presentation control. Since their level of mechanical control extended to absolute invisibility, this is rather surprising. An interpretation is that the sophistication of control they wanted was far from the level of control they had. Misleading reciprocity describes the confusion between being present to a CoMedi display but invisible for its camera, or person-node discontinuity. The Cafette group, as occasional users, were considerably less concerned about this than the Office group $(t(20) = 2.72; p = 0.028)$.

4 Discussion

Several issues for UMCE design persisted throughout our period of study, whilst others dropped away with familiarity or the evolution of work-arounds. The flexibility of the physical equipment making up our media space mitigated against great interference in day-to-day activity, although it clearly did happen, whilst early-expressed concerns about being distracted by the presence of a CoMedi seemed to evaporate. The cost of physical manoeuvring may be measured in time and effort: both are mainly in terms of an additional attentional demand. Furthermore, in the Cafette, the transience of occupation and frequency of 'sensor reconfiguration' (i.e. camera movement) meant that the position of the media space camera had to be checked on every visit. For Office users, it was less likely to shift from where it was last placed. Privacy concerns are always complex: they were resolved at least to a level of tolerance for some whilst for others they were never adequately addressed.

4.1 The Hybridity of Places

Reporting on their own experiences, Dourish et al. (1996) wrote:

> "the spaces we have been dealing with are hybrids of the physical and the electronic ... (creating) new spaces, which become distinctive places as sets of appropriate orientations arise within our communities.

Our ability to appropriate, transform and reuse space is rooted in the
flexible switching which media spaces afford."

Our study found that flexible switching lead to an unpredictability that is at odds
with this account. It is worth re-emphasising the complexity of the Cafette in this
respect. We found that the ability to 'appropriate and reuse' was a function of group
membership within the community as whole. The ability to appropriate is strictly
conditioned by ownership and kind of place; its very sociality. The placeness of the
Cafette was heavily ingrained and resistant to change, by virtue of its identity resting
on an idea of sociable comportment among a large number of individuals.

Perception of place is in terms of appropriateness of behaviours and readiness
for their expression: a clear link exists between what a place stands for and the
normed comportment of social groups. It follows that the appropriateness of an
individual's self-presentation in the context of a given place is a matter of their
evolving perceptions of the norms of place. This is important as placeness owes not
only to a physical location but also to its contents, including people and artefacts, and
these contents (especially people!) changed in the Cafette on a fairly unpredictable
basis and often invisibly to CoMedi users. The mobility of our users within
physical space, a motivating factor for the installation of our UMCE, suggests that the
placeness of a location is subject to continual adjustment with its occupancy. Indeed,
the volatility of certain locations in this regard might itself be thought of as one of the
defining characteristics of our CoMedi study. So the rigidity of place is indivisible
from the 'inertia' of expectation on the part of its users. We see this inertia as a
function of the number of people who share an understanding of place and also the
extent to which expectations are entrenched on the part of particular individuals or
groups. Activities across a UMCE begin from pre-existing ideas about its placeness
but are then blended with the personalities and 'atmosphere's of switched-in places,
as a composite of the behavioural propensities of persons, groups and affordances of
the contributing locales.

Self-presentation is a key concept in social identity theory (Tajfel & Turner,
1986). People belong to many groupings, each of which is associated with norms
of conduct. In order to maintain in-group identity, one must act within the limits of
conduct recognised as appropriate for the group. Importantly, social identity theory
posits the existence of, and need to actively maintain, multiple identities. For a
number of years, Lea & Spears have leveraged social identity theory to study the
influence of anonymity on group normative behaviour, so-called 'deindividuation
effects', in text-based communication media (Postmes et al., 1998; Spears et al.,
2001). They have demonstrated that filtering out interpersonal cues can give rise to
more opportunity for the influence of group-level cues for identity and consequently
affect group-level processes. In particular, they argue that mediating technologies
can exert a very strong influence on the extent to which an individual feels able to
express behaviour in line with a particular identity.

It should be understood that expression of identity-relevant behaviour is as
much about volunteering information as it is about its withholding. As a minimal
UMCE, there are some challenging contradictions between the coupling of CoMedi's
linguistic poverty with its intermittent, obscured and low-resolution visual cues

and the visually impoverished nature of text-based communication. Although the non-verbal role of appearance is usually associated with posture, gesture and dress (Argyle, 1988), personal effects (family photos, ornaments, sports gear etc.) were included in CoMedi images. These effects were located within distinct zones of physical space, locales understood as appropriate for social self-presentation. An approach to designing self-presentation fluent UMCEs based on social identity theory is perfectly congruent with the Adams and Sasse framework. Whereas Adams and Sasse posit structural similarities between individuals' agreement to participation in a UMCE, social identity theory would predict that the structures are in terms of the compatibility of self-presentation norms among concurrently connected social groups. In effect, this means that Adams and Sasse's framework is a very useful but incomplete design tool.

There are some serious problems for the prospect of multiple concurrent connections for this reason. One might imagine a number of views on a space, each optimised to an audience group in terms of self-presentation, based on configuration of technological filters and user-defined locales. Inevitably, there is a practical limit on the number of variables and, still more importantly from a social identity perspective, the transparency of such configurations. Moving aspects of configuration into real space eases matters but does not then give carte blanche for an infinite set of UMCE connections.

In non-technological contexts, the processes for recognising place are invariably over-learnt and very low effort. For the UMCE designer, the challenge is to create a facility that would allow individuals to build hybrid places at which they are multiply present, based on the physical and cultural reality of the places they objectively inhabit. Only then can individuals properly manage each of their places in terms of their own self-presentation.

4.2 Coping with Sensitivity of Hybrid Places

CoMedi's filters are general, in that once selected they apply to the images displayed on all CoMedi workstations. Self-presentation, including both showing and hiding aspects of self, may be governed with acceptable limits for some colleagues but be entirely inappropriate for others. Furthermore, the highly transient nature of Cafette occupancy made it difficult for individuals to decide on the criteria for self-presentation. The perception of office space was not subject to the same level of ambiguity. It is here that we return to the idea of place. Place can stand for group-level affiliation and so support the identities associated with them. Although occupancy of the offices in our study was uncertain, the fact that they were offices set usable limits on expectations of the expression of behaviours. Our users seemed to manage their self-presentation by deciding on areas of risk in terms of their behaviour and translating these into constrained locales within their spaces. The locales were then filtered to a level of clarity consummate with the risk of transgressing group norms. Furthermore, the office space was more stable and so more easily controllable for the office users. The space was understood to represent different degrees of risk and this risk could be seen, on a social identity interpretation, to be in terms of potential norm violation or exposure to unwelcome attention from out-group members.

5 Conclusion

UMCE connections explicitly link spaces and implicitly link people. They do this by generating a set of hybrid interaction zones, made up of constellations of people and places. As a design problem, the disambiguation of connections between people and spaces is very significant. Not only are they fluid but, in order to fulfil their infrastructural or background design brief, they must maintain a low attentional demand. Critical points for CoMedi seemed to be that there were limited opportunities to tailor self-presentation for different audiences, that partitioning of a physical space into locales of differential sensitivity helped with this process, and that ownership and control could not be satisfactorily resolved in the communal place.

Girgensohn et al. (1999), describing the issue as 'awareness of audience', consider it to be mainly a matter of poor interface supporting for reciprocity, and have proposed some inventive strategies for teasing apart levels of audience in relation to self-presentation. There is a clear need for mechanisms to support multiple self-presentations via communications technologies. It was clear at the outset of our study that the Cafette was quite explicitly a 'place' rather than a space. It was perhaps less clear that the same could be said of offices, and that placeness could be refined to govern the status of locales within offices. We have argued that placeness is intimately related to personal presence and self-presentation, linking the filtering of activity through ad-hoc manipulation of self-image to social identity theory. It may be that effective interpersonal and inter-group connection by UMCE requires attention to intra-space as well as inter-space and technological heterogeneity, grounded in terms of self-presentation. The architectural notion of 'place' suggests that one might design media spaces in terms of the interpersonal and cultural significance of areas within physical spaces. Places must be defined by UMCE users themselves according to the static (appearance) and dynamic (activity-based) forms of self-presentation they wish to project to members of the on-looking community. In this way, individual visibility to a UMCE network would be managed by physical positioning in a local area, rather than through the onerous and cumbersome business of constantly adjusting visibility through manipulations of a camera's global field of view.

Acknowledgements

This work was supported by the European Union 'TACIT' TMR network (contract ERB FMRX CT97 0133) and France Télécom. We would like to thank Joëlle Coutaz, Yann Laurillau for technical support and the PRIMA-INRIA group, Montbonnot, France, Lorna Goulden for discussion of 'place', and all the members of CLIPS-IMAG, Grenoble who participated in this study.

References

Adams, A. & Sasse, M. (1999a), Privacy Issues in Ubiquitous Multimedia Environments: Wake Sleeping Dogs or Let Them Lie?, in A. Sasse & C. Johnson (eds.), *Human–Computer Interaction — INTERACT '99: Proceedings of the Seventh IFIP Conference on Human–Computer Interaction*, Vol. 1, IOS Press, pp.214–21.

Adams, A. & Sasse, M. (1999b), Taming the Wolf in Sheep's Clothing: Privacy in Multimedia Communications, *in Proceedings of Multimedia'99*, ACM Press, pp.101–7.

Argyle, M. (1988), *Bodily Communication*, second edition, Methuen.

Bellotti, V. (1997), Design for Privacy in Multimedia Computing and Communications Environments, *in* P. Agre & M. Rotenberg (eds.), *Technology and Privacy: The New Landscape*, MIT Press, pp.63–98.

Coutaz, J., Berard, F., Carraux, E., Astier, W. & Crowley, J. L. (1999), CoMedi: Using Computer Vision to Support Awareness and Privacy in Mediaspaces, *in* M. W. Altom & M. G. Williams (eds.), *Companion Proceedings of CHI'99: Human Factors in Computing Systems (CHI'99 Conference Companion)*, ACM Press, pp.13–16.

Coutaz, J., Berrard, F., Carraux, E. & Crowley, J. (1998), Early Experience with the Mediaspace CoMedi, *in* S. Chatty & P. Dewan (eds.), *Proceedings of EHCI'98, the IFIP Working Conference on Engineering for Human–Computer Interaction*, North-Holland, pp.57–72. See also http://iihm.imag.fr/publs/1998/EHCI98_CoMedi.ps.gz.

Daly-Jones, O., Monk, A. & Watts, L. (1998), "Some Advantages of Video Conferencing Over High-quality Audio Conferencing: Fluency and Awareness of Attentional Focus", *International Journal of Human–Computer Studies* **49**(1), 21–58.

Dourish, P., Adler, A., Bellotti, V. & Henderson, A. (1996), "Your Place or Mine? Learning from Long-term Use of Audio–Video Communication", *Computer Supported Cooperative Work* **5**(1), 33–62.

Falk, J. & Björk, S. (2000), Privacy and Information Integrity in Wearable Computing and Ubiquitous Computing, *in* G. Szwillus, T. Turner, M. Atwood, B. Bederson, B. Bomsdorf, E. Churchill, G. Cockton, D. Crow, F. Détienne, D. Gilmore, H.-J. Hofman, C. van der Mast, I. McClelland, D. Murray, P. Palanque, M. A. Sasse, J. Scholtz, A. Sutcliffe & W. Visser (eds.), *Companion Proceedings of CHI2000: Human Factors in Computing Systems (CHI2000 Conference Companion)*, ACM Press, pp.177–8. Also available at http://www.viktoria.informatik.gu.se/groups/play/publications/2000/wear-ubi.pdf.

Fish, R. S., Kraut, R. E. & Chalfonte, B. L. (1990), The VideoWindow System in Informal Communications, *in* D. G. Tatar (ed.), *Proceedings of CSCW'90: Third Conference on Computer Supported Cooperative Work*, ACM Press, pp.1–11.

Gaver, W., Sellen, A., Heath, C. & Luff, P. (1993), One is Not Enough: Multiple Views in a Media Space, *in* S. Ashlund, K. Mullet, A. Henderson, E. Hollnagel & T. White (eds.), *Proceedings of INTERCHI'93*, ACM Press/IOS Press, pp.335–41.

Girgensohn, A., Lee, A. & Turner, T. (1999), Being in Public and Reciprocity: Design for Portholes and User Preference, *in* A. Sasse & C. Johnson (eds.), *Human–Computer Interaction — INTERACT '99: Proceedings of the Seventh IFIP Conference on Human–Computer Interaction*, Vol. 1, IOS Press, pp.458–65.

Harrison, R. & Dourish, P. (1996), Re-Place-ing Space: The Roles of Place and Space in Collaborative Systems, *in* M. S. Ackerman (ed.), *Proceedings of CSCW'96: ACM Conference on Computer Supported Cooperative Work*, ACM Press, pp.67–76.

Heath, C. & Luff, P. (1992), "Collaboration and Control: Crisis Management and Multimedia Technology in London Underground Control Rooms", *Computer Supported Cooperative Work* **1**(1–2), 69–94.

Hudson, S. E. & Smith, I. (1996), Techniques for Addressing Fundamental Privacy and Disruption Tradeoffs in Awareness Support Systems, *in* M. S. Ackerman (ed.), *Proceedings of CSCW'96: ACM Conference on Computer Supported Cooperative Work*, ACM Press, pp.248–57.

Lee, A., Girgensohn, A. & Schlueter, K. (1997), NYNEX Portholes: Initial User Reactions and Redesign Implications, *in* S. C. Hayne & W. Prinz (eds.), *Proceedings of International ACM SIGGROUP Conference on Supporting Group Work, Group'97*, ACM Press, pp.385–94.

Mantei, M. M., Bæcker, R. M., Sellen, A. J., Buxton, W. A., Milligan, T. & Wellman, B. (1991), Experiences in the use of a Media Space, *in* S. P. Robertson, G. M. Olson & J. S. Olson (eds.), *Proceedings of CHI'91: Human Factors in Computing Systems (Reaching through Technology)*, ACM Press, pp.203–8.

Norberg-Schulz, C. (1980), *Genius Loci: Towards a Phenomenology of Architecture*, Rizzoli.

Postmes, T., Spears, R. & Lea, M. (1998), "Breaching or Building Social Boundaries? SIDE-effects of Computer-mediated Communication", *Communication Research* **25**(6), 689–715.

Rønby-Pederson, E. & Sokoler, T. (1997), AROMA: Abstract Representation of Presence Supporting Mutual Awareness, *in* S. Pemberton (ed.), *Proceedings of CHI'97: Human Factors in Computing Systems*, ACM Press, pp.51–8.

Singer, A., Hindus, D., Stifelman, L. & White, S. (1999), Tangible Progress: Less is More in Somewire Audio Spaces, *in* M. G. Williams, M. W. Altom, K. Ehrlich & W. Newman (eds.), *Proceedings of the CHI99 Conference on Human Factors in Computing Systems: The CHI is the Limit*, ACM Press, pp.104–11.

Spears, R., Lea, M. & Postmes, T. (2001), Social Psychological Theories of Computer-mediated Communication: Social Pain or Social Gain?, *in* H. Giles & W. P. Robinson (eds.), *The Handbook of Language and Social Psychology*, second edition, John Wiley & Sons.

Tajfel, H. & Turner, J. C. (1986), The Social Identity Theory of Intergroup Behaviour, *in* S. Worchel & W. G. Austin (eds.), *Psychology of Intergroup Relations*, Nelson-Hall, pp.220–37.

Tang, J. C. & Rua, M. (1994), Montage: Providing Teleproximity for Distributed Groups, *in* B. Adelson, S. Dumais & J. Olson (eds.), *Proceedings of CHI'94: Human Factors in Computing Systems*, ACM Press, pp.37–43.

Watts, L. A. & Monk, A. F. (1996), Remote Assistance: A View of the Work AND a View of the Face?, *in* M. Tauber, V. Bellotti, R. Jeffries, J. D. Mackinlay & J. Nielsen (eds.), *Companion Proceedings of CHI'96: Human Factors in Computing Systems (CHI'96 Conference Companion)*, ACM Press, pp.101–2.

Watts, L. A. & Monk, A. F. (1998), "Reasoning About Tasks, Activity and Technology to Support Collaboration", *Ergonomics* **41**(11), 1583–606.

Watts, L. A., Monk, A. F. & Daly-Jones, O. (1996), "Inter-personal Awareness and Synchronization: Assessing the Value of Communication Technologies", *International Journal of Human–Computer Interaction* **44**(6), 849–75.

Zhao, Q. A. & Stasko, J. T. (1998), Evaluating Image Filtering Based Techniques in Media Space Applications, *in Proceedings of CSCW'98: ACM Conference on Computer Supported Cooperative Work*, ACM Press, pp.11–8.

Collaborating with Virtual Humans

Pascal Le Mer, Laurence Perron, Christophe Chaillou, Samuel Degrande & Grégory Saugis

France Télécom R&D–2, Avenue Pierre Marzin, 22307 Lannion Cedex, France

Tel: *+33 2 96 05 20 59, +33 2 96 05 16 03, +33 2 96 05 07 41*

Fax: *+33 2 96 05 11 29*

Email:
{pascal.lemer,laurence.perron,gregory.saugis}@francetelecom.com

Laboratoire d'Informatique Fondamentale de Lille, USTL Cité Scientifique – Bât M3, 59655 Villeneuve d'Ascq Cedex, France

Tel: *+33 320 434 720*

Fax: *+33 320 434 043*

Email: *{lemer,chaillou,degrande}@lifl.fr*

In real work group situations we naturally and unconsciously use the non-verbal channel to communicate. In Collaborative Virtual Environments (CVE) anthropomorphic avatars can be used to provide this channel.

Indeed, anthropomorphic avatars are relevant to several aspects relating to reproducible behaviour. However, there is no single and ideal concept that specifies the data entering into the system, the technical devices to be implemented and the way in which the anthropomorphic avatars must be animated so that they communicate.

In this article we emphasise the problems linked to the difficulties in acting and communicating simultaneously in non-immersive CVE. We propose a computer architecture model centred on interpersonal communication within CVE. This proposal has been formed on the basis of studies relating to the various functions of human gestures. We also discuss our approach

to assessing the model. It is an iterative and multidisciplinary approach based on the comparison of real and mediated group activities.

Keywords: non-verbal communication, gesture, collaborative virtual environments, human/avatars/human interaction.

1   Introduction

In real group work situations, we naturally and unconsciously use the non-verbal channel to communicate and manage communication. By non-verbal channel, we mean the elementary information on each person's intentions, expressions and actions, that are instantaneously visible to all through the movements of the body. The quantitative and qualitative importance of the information exchanged through this channel can be shown in face to face situations (Corraze, 1980). But when communication is remote, i.e. beyond the range of our senses, it then becomes dependent on the extension which is afforded to it by the tools of telecommunication. Communication is therefore constrained by the more or less developed technical nature of the systems: visioconferencing, Collaborative Virtual Environments, etc.

Non-verbal information almost exclusively refers to the image of each interlocutor. In practice, visioconferencing has shown its limits, particularly with regard to group activities (Perin & Gensollen, 1992). The severing of collaborative space unity is one of the limits. Indeed, in visioconferencing, the location referential is not the same for everybody, and questions such as 'Who is doing what?' or 'Who is talking to whom?' become difficult. This problem remains awkward even if people can compensate verbally (as in the case of conference calls), but we nevertheless believe that certain activities such as 'teletraining' or 'teledesigning' are far more affected by the problem (introducing a parasite task that is added to the main task).

One solution that would avoid severing collaborative space unity would be to project and represent the users into a virtually unique environment. This is why we are working on a Collaborative Virtual Environment project into which we have introduced anthropomorphic avatars to provide a representation of each user. To meet the needs of industrialists (Car design processes, telemedicine, etc.) equipped with desktop terminals, we are focusing our study on non-immersive CVEs. However, the use of avatars to mediate communication in this type of environment involves studying concepts such as: 'the identification' of the user with his avatar, the interaction system, and the users' perception with regard to these forms of representation.

We will deal with the problems linked with the difficulty of acting and communicating simultaneously within non-immersive CVEs (i.e. desktop terminals) and we will propose a computer architecture model centred on interpersonal communication. Our proposals will be founded on the various functions of human gestures. We will also discuss our assessment approach based on the comparison of real and mediated group activities.

2 Levels of User Representation by an Avatar

Group communication within the CVE requires that parameters be met that are necessary in terms of the representation of the user. We can quote a few of them from Benford et al.'s (1997) work:

- Presence — The perception of users in the environment.

- The location of the person.

- Identification — Recognition of an actor.

- The view point — Focus.

- The action point — Pointing, selection, action, designation.

- The level of presence — Status.

- Expressions and gestures.

It is clear that, depending on the context of use, certain parameters may vary in significance or be simply achieved technically. If representing the user with an avatar is significantly beneficial in terms of the behaviours that are to be synthesised, there are no corresponding generic models of user representation to date.

Indeed, there is no exhaustive model for the specification of input data, technical devices and ways in which the data must be processed, so that the avatars allow the users to collaborate with one another as if in natural situations or at least to an acceptable degree.

We have determined five types of user representations, with which the users do not identify themselves in the same way with their avatar:

The 'mimetic' avatar: this is an isomorphic representation of the user's behaviour in a voluntary and conscious way. An analysis technique makes it possible to restore the user's behaviour to his avatar in front of his screen in an identical manner (e.g. facial expressions, gestures, etc.). This technique currently makes it possible to detect gestures (Marcel et al., 2000a) and facial expressions and to re-synthesise them with 'real time' inverse kinematics (Tolani & Badler, 1996; Chin, 1996) or mesh distortion (Breton, 2001) algorithms. Figure 1 depicts the capture of facial expressions and their reproduction. Figure 2 depicts the capture of gestures by magnetic means as well as their reproduction through an avatar (Viaud & Saulnier, 1995).

The 'puppet' avatar: this consists of 'controlling' an avatar like puppeteers. The user must use a specialised input device (for example: a Dataglove) or a graphical interface to animate his avatar. The use of an input device is often 'intrusive' and limits interactions. Figure 3 shows an example of implementation. There are many such examples in the world of television: Cléo from Canal+, Bill from 'Bigdil', etc.

Figure 1: Expression detection and facial animation.

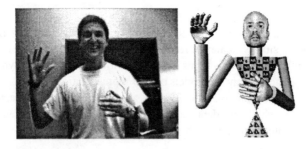

Figure 2: Movement capture and animation by inverse kinematics.

Figure 3: Puppeteer.

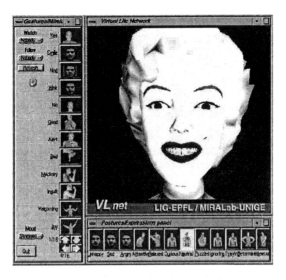

Figure 4: Animation based on a library of behaviours.

The 'symbolic-emotion' avatar: this consists of animating an avatar by means of a library of symbolic behaviours. Very much used in 'body chat', these systems prompt the user to express emotional or affective states, moods or levels of presence by choosing a finite series of behaviours by means of an interface. Figure 4 shows an HCI example from the VLNET project (Guye-Vuillème et al., 1999).

The 'symbolic-action' avatar: the analysis of the user's actions in the CVE produces the animation of the avatar with a library of symbolic behaviours. The idea is to endow the avatar with a behaviour so as to relate each person's actions within the environment. It is then the system that manages the behaviours. Figure 5 and Figure 6 illustrate this type of implementation in the field of games (Quake 3 Arena). Figure 5 shows the interface that allows the user to interact with the world, Figure 6 depicts the avatar's behaviour symbolising his actions (see Figure 5). Figure 7 shows a user interacting with a CVE and Figure 8 shows his representation from the view point of another user[1].

The comparison of these four figures emphasises the effect of the representation of the environment on the user identification mechanisms with regard to his avatar. Indeed, in certain 'collaborative' games, one has a partial view, an integral view or no view of the avatar. For this reason, the avatar is perceived rather as an autonomous agent to whom one issues certain commands.

---

[1] For more information see http://www.crg.cs.nott.ac.uk/research/projects/Coven

Figure 5: View point of user A in action.

Figure 6: Visual rendering of the actions of user A.

Figure 7: Manipulation and action in COVEN — 'actor' view point.

Figure 8: Manipulation and action in COVEN — 'observer' viewpoint.

Figure 9: Autonomous avatar behaviour.

The 'agent' avatar: the analysis by the system of the CVE's activity makes it possible to implement symbolic animation of the avatar based on a library of behaviours. The difference with the previous concept is that the avatar can have a behaviour that is totally independent of the user's actions depending on what is happening in the CVE. This type of concept is used in certain 'chat rooms' that use autonomous agents (cf. Figure 9) (Cassell & Vilhjálmsson, 1999).

For example, in Figure 9 when an avatar comes near the user's avatar, the user's avatar greets it. This is an example of autonomous behaviour which does not require any action from the user.

3   Limits of the Representations and New Problems

3.1   *Limits of the Representations*

The drawback of implementing 'mimetic' avatars is that it monopolises the user's hands which makes direct actions with objects in the interface difficult. Another disadvantage with the 'mimetic' is that it makes the avatar's and the user's spatial behaviours incoherent since they are not in the same space. The 'symbolic-emotion', 'symbolic-action' and 'agent' avatars only offer a limited register of semantic information that cannot be easily combined.

Co-verbal gestures are not very compliant with rules of construction and use. Indeed, they are subject to a great degree of intra and inter-individual variability. This is why they are fairly complex to process by artificial systems without losing any of their richness (Lebourque, 1998). This is even more significant if one attempts to mediate signed gestures (i.e. gestures that replace speech or disambiguate it).

Consequently, one can see that depending on the concept that is used and the associated technical means, it is difficult to mediate the user's gestures of expression (e.g. pointing to somebody with the arm and nodding one's head) and gestures of action and apprehending the world (e.g. handling an object in the virtual world, changing one's view point to see a masked object) simultaneously. This leads us to examine the question of non-verbal communication and particularly the implemented repertoire of actions and expressions depending on the fields of application.

3.2   *Action and Communication: the Gesture Problem*

Claude Cadoz (1994) explains that the gesture is both a means of action in the world and a bi-directional informational means of communication:

> "... on peut considérer trois fonctions différentes mais complémentaires et imbriquées: une fonction d'action matérielle, modification, transformation de l'environnement, que nous appellerons ici ergotique, une fonction épistémique, c'est-à-dire de connaissance de l'environnement et enfin une fonction sémiotique, c'est-à-dire d'émission d'informations à destination de l'environnement. Chacune de ces trois fonctions prises séparément fait intervenir à des degrés variables chacune des deux autres."

which can be translated:

> "... one can consider three different functions that are linked and that complement one another: a material action function, modification, transformation of the environment, that we will call ergotic[2], an epistemic[3] function, meaning a function relating to the knowledge of the environment and finally a semiotic function, meaning a function relating to the broadcasting of information aimed at the environment. Each of these three functions taken separately involves each of the other two to varying degrees."

---

[2]The root 'erg' relates to the fact that the gesture in question would mean an exchange involving energy between the operator and the physical object to which the gesture applies.

[3]The root 'epistem' supposes that the gesture relates to knowledge.

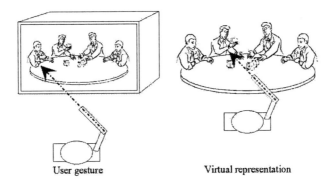

User gesture   Virtual representation

Figure 10: Scale ratio problem for mimetism.

Cadoz concentrated on the hand, but his observations can be extended to other organs. Furthermore, the gesture is defined as "all of the body's movements, mainly the hand's, the arm's and the head's, whether carrying any significance or not". Thus the eyes have a semiotic and an epistemic function. The face has a mainly semiotic function that is very important in interpersonal communication. The relation between the eyes and the face is, let it be noted, particularly close.

The semiotic function is as important as it is complex. Solely in terms of co-verbal behaviours, which are most common in situations of collaborative activity, several classifications are found. For example, that proposed by Ekman & Friesen (1972) distinguishes the following: sticks, ideograms, deictic movements, spatial movements, rhythmic movements, kinetographs, pictographs and emblematic movements. The relevance of such a typology does not reside in seeking to understand the functioning of human non-verbal communication, but rather to have functional criteria of communication assessment with a view to mediating.

For example, in a non-immersive situation, deictic and spatial movements must be taken into account to facilitate collaboration. Indeed, Figure 10 underlines the problems posed by non-immersive CVEs for these gestures (i.e. perceived gestures ≠ gestures made by the user).

Below, we will work on four gestural functions: addressed and non-addressed semiotics, ergotics and epistemics.

3.3 Analysing the Systems

It would seem sensible to cross the five levels of avatar representation in relation to the expected system functions, which will make it possible to enrich communication within the CVEs (cf. Table 1).

Considering the results that appear in this table, one may assume that information technology, such as it is today, does not make it possible to mediate all human gestural functions simultaneously and in a sufficiently rich manner.

On the one hand, the 'video' analysis of the user's behaviour is interesting because it is non intrusive and is the only analysis that can fully transcribe the

| Gesture functions/ | Semiotic Function | | Ergotic | Epistemic |
Avatar concept	Non addressed	Addressed	Function	Function
Mimetic	++	0	0	0
Puppet	++	++	+	++
Symbolic-emotion	+	+	+	+
Symbolic-action	0	+	++	++
Agent	0	+	++	++

Table 1: Analysis of the concepts of avatar use in relation to gesture functions. The gesture function possibilities are classed according to 3 levels: 0 means that the function is not supported or only supported in a very minimal way, + means that the function is not supported completely and ++ means that conceptually the function is implemented in an equivalent way to reality and that the limitations are essentially technical.

user's expressions (cf. 'mimetic'). However, because of spatial shifting, it does not make the transcription of deictics possible and remains limited in terms of action gestures. Furthermore, action peripherals are generally optimised to ensure a particular function. The tool therefore dissociates functions that are not so in reality. Here are two examples: the mouse allows pointing and selection in the WIMP[4] environments and the screen makes it possible to display it. If you wish to give the action peripheral a 'proprioceptive' function, a force feedback peripheral is selected; and if you wish to give the screen an action function, you get a touch screen.

However, if you wish to use peripherals supporting such functions as: expression, action and perception in a sufficiently rich manner for a collaborative activity, when they exist, they remain too intrusive for desktop terminals. Peripherals are predominantly used in immersive environments to allow the user to act and communicate simultaneously.

3.4 Issues

We believe that collaborative activities require the virtualisation of the three gesture functions (ergotic, epistemic and semiotic) for reasons of communication quality. However, none of the concepts presented previously is appropriate. Our study therefore centres on seeking a non-intrusive device in a non-immersive environment that integrates these three functions. The system will have to offer solutions for critical cases such as behaviours relating to space, facial expressions or the possibility of combining gesture functions (e.g. acting on something whilst designating somebody).

This type of study is only meaningful if the notion of device acceptability for the user is integrated. In so doing, we are restricted both humanly and technically.

Another objective is to ensure collaboration through making communication primitives available. This implies studying the mechanisms linked to the Human/avatar/Human model (visual rendering of the avatars and perception of the users during activity).

[4]WIMP: Window Icon Mouse Pointer.

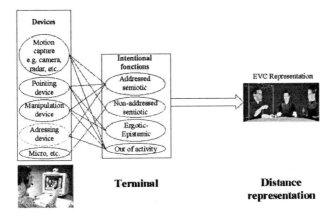

Figure 11: Basis of the interaction model.

4 Computer Architecture Model

Our proposal is based on the architecture of a system of analysis.

4.1 The Basis of the Analysis Model

The various gesture functions can be supported in an independent manner from one another by known devices. Table 1 is an aid in mapping levels of avatar representation to the system's expected functions.

The 'Mimetic' function which consists of the isomorphic representation of the user's behaviour (which seems to be the best concept to ensure the gesture's non-spatial semiotic function) can be supported by a system of user movement capture. The analysis of the user's actions, mapping to a library of behaviours, with a view to animating his avatar, seems to be a good way to synthesise the gesture's ergotic and epistemic functions. However, in the field of non-immersive environments, we have not found an ideal concept to ensure the semiotic function relating to virtual space.

Figure 11 represents a summary of a system that makes it possible to provide the gesture's various functions independently. We will use it as a basis for our future thoughts.

The diagram features the following: on the left, the system interaction peripherals (input data); in the middle, the intentional functions managed by the system and on the right, the visual rendering on the CVE screens. The visual rendering of the avatars is the remote representation of the gestural functions that the user must be able to carry out using the system. Each function of the central module represents a system state, and the links indicate the possible use of the input peripherals.

4.1.1 Addressed Semiotic Function

This function refers to expressive gestures relating to an avatar or an object in virtual space.

We have seen that these gestures are problematic in non-immersive environments. We are therefore considering two solutions to provide this function:

- Using the user's gestures of expression to allow him to define this gestural function himself; the difficulty then resides in differentiating between addressed semiotics and non-addressed semiotics.

- Using logical or physical instruments to provide the means to develop a repertoire of gestures.

4.1.2   Non-addressed Semiotic Function

In contrast to its previous function, the non-addressed semiotic function does not refer to an object in virtual space. The user's mimetism is therefore ensured.

4.1.3   Ergotic-epistemic Function

Our system must be able to adapt itself to various remote collaborative activities (games, teledesigning, teleeducation, telemedicine, etc.). These activities generally require specialised access peripherals such as a 'doll's head' (Hinckley et al., 1994) in medicine.

4.1.4   Out of Activity Function

The aim of this function is to provide information on the user's level of presence. Indeed, the relevance of a non-immersive terminal is to avoid restricting the user by taking into account notions such as multitasking, pauses and activity changes.

4.2   Various Modes of Interaction

From an IT point of view, ensuring the various functions of the gesture by combining non-intrusive devices would imply management of the different modes by the system. Switching from one mode to the other can be done on the initiative of the user or the system.

In the first case, it is the user who activates the mode change whereas in the second case, the system would detect it. The first case can be rejected because it equates to adding an additional task for the user — his objective is to collaborate with other users in order to carry out a task and not to enter commands to animate an avatar in order to communicate at distance.

We have therefore chosen to focus on detection by the system. However, since technology in this field is not very mature, only a 'hybrid' system would seem satisfactory in terms of our restrictions. The 'hybrid' character of our system is based on the user adaptation. On the one hand, the mechanism consists of endowing the system with a gesture recognition module and on the other hand of requiring the user to learn to perform gestures that can be differentiated by the system. We are therefore working on a command interface system with intention detection.

In the first instance, we will study the techniques that are required for gesture recognition and more specifically the intention detection module. We will then discuss the representation that the user can achieve according to the various levels of 'virtualisation' of his avatar. We will finally explain how to animate an avatar on the basis of our architectural model.

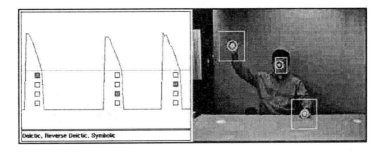

Figure 12: Intention detection.

4.3 Intention Detection

In order to be able to support the various gesture functions (outside immersion), we have introduced an intention detection module into our architecture. Its role is to distinguish action movements from gestural communication movements.

Figure 12 shows video analysis of the user's gestures. Without accessing the gesture's semantic level, it uses known influence zones and gestural trajectory signatures to determine — for example — whether a gesture belongs to one of the following types: deictic, symbolic or neutral (Marcel et al., 2000b). To analyse trajectories, one can use 'neural network' techniques that are developed to learn to distinguish the various types of gesture.

Other types of information coming from the action peripherals or from the virtual environment itself provide other indications on the user's gesture.

We are therefore going to develop a new interaction mode that admittedly compels the user to express himself through a repertory of learned gestures, but which, following acquisition, allows him to combine ergotic, semiotic and epistemic gestures.

Figure 13 depicts how the detection module is inserted into the general synoptic. At input, the module controls the information of all the peripherals and at output, it operates a mode selector.

The mode selector is not a binary system. It must differentiate the head's and the hands' gestures. Thus, the systems will be able to have different statuses at the same time and, for example, manage a situation in which the user uses one hand to act and the other hand and/or head to express himself.

Let it be noted at this point that such a system is restricted by the use of action peripherals that do not prevent the user from performing gestures with his hand.

4.4 Various Degrees of Gesture 'Virtualisation'

Assuming the system is sufficiently reliable to categorise gestural modalities, we must still verify the system's usability. If the system can have various operating statuses, will the user understand the various underlying logics and the mode changes?

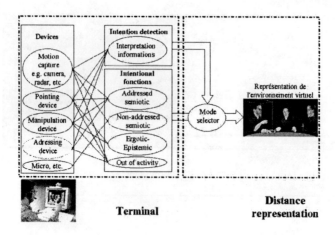

Figure 13: Intention detection within the model.

We talk about various degrees of gesture virtualisation. Indeed, gestures can be used to operate a tool, to handle an object in three dimensions and possibly to express one's self. If we are currently far from having solved the technical problems, the user's place must not be underestimated. Will the user be willing to act and communicate with an avatar, considering all the problems that can be sensed and are underlying with these different levels of virtualisation.

4.4.1 What Cognitive Representation?

Can the user naturally imagine the various levels of virtualisation of his gestures? In order to envisage an interaction 'virtualisation', Verna & Grumbach (1998) propose a model that represents man's cognitive interaction in his environment. They put forward the following fact:

> "Un monde virtuel ne doit pas seulement être un environnement que l'on peut percevoir, mais il doit également répondre aux commandes de l'utilisateur."

which can be translated:

> "A virtual world must not only be an environment that one can perceive, but is must also respond to the user's commands."

The therefore propose the MRIC model, which clearly decouples the mental representation of the action over the world, from that of the control of the body; and he then lists the various possible levels of 'virtualisation'.

This model provides few answers to our question; however, our problem is identical to that described by Verna & Grumbach. In our model, the extension of the action is carried out through a tool, whereas expression can be carried out through a virtual body. If this model is likely to work, it must necessitate the handling and compensation of feedback such as proprioceptive feedback that allow us to act in the real world and to apprehend our environment.

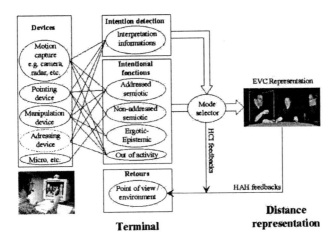

Figure 14: Visual feedback in the model.

4.4.2 Feedback

If the system automatically detects certain referenced gestures, it means that the user must be aware of this mechanism and must be able to imagine the various levels of 'virtualisation' of his gestures. We believe that feedback is required for each level of virtualisation. Thus, we will be able to use the visual feedback as a potential indicator that can be used in the regulating loop.

Learning and communication are based on the feedback notion and consequently the Human/Machine dialog. This is also the case with interpersonal communication that is mediated by avatars where feedback on linguistic acts plays an essential part. This therefore means studying a new interaction mode on the "Human/avatars/Human" model.

Figure 14 depicts this module that is part of the system's general model.

To give an example of visual feedback, one can try to define the way in which the designation gesture will be 'virtualised'. In reality, we at least have proprioceptive feedback on this gesture. In order to virtualise it, one can propose the use of the concept depicted in Figure 15. Addressing is carried out via ray tracing and the metaphor of the hand makes it possible to identify the system's mode.

Until now we have only studied visual feedback, but we are considering the use of other types of feedback (e.g. proprioceptive, olfactory, aural, etc.) depending on the task, the users' profiles, the context of use.

4.5 Avatar Synthesis

The next challenge is to determine what rendering will make it possible to establish the communication and the management of the various 'action and expression' gestural repertories. The use of an avatar to represent the user makes it possible to achieve interpolations between the various postures. The system is therefore able to carry out a fluid switch from one mode to another in terms of visual rendering. However, it is not enough to achieve fluid rendering.

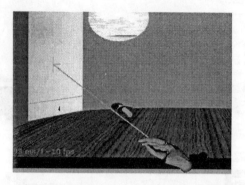

Figure 15: Visual feedback of an addressed gesture.

Figure 16: A terminal development mode.

If the user must have good visual feedback from the 'virtualisation' of his various gestures, from the point of view of interpersonal communication, he must also have good visual feedback on what the other avatars are doing and expressing. Consequently, validating our model requires an excellent 'intermediation' of Human/Avatar/Human communication!

The choice of implemented technologies to ensure this must be taken into account in the assessment of interactions. This is why, before we touch on our assessment approach, it seems important to first describe the way in which we have implemented our concepts within a CVE.

5   Implementation of the Model Within a CVE

5.1   The Terminal and the CVE

The collaborative virtual environment that allows us to carry out our experimentation is SPIN-3D (Saugis, 1998). Figure 16 shows the means of interaction with the environment and the graphical interface.

In order to carry out experimentation, various technical and software means have been implemented.

Figure 17: Video replacement sensor.

5.2 Implemented Technologies

Since video capture systems are not yet sufficiently efficient or integrable; we have chosen to use magnetic motion capture peripherals temporarily (see Figure 17).

In order to restore an elementary behaviour in a quasi- mimetic way, we have integrated an inverse kinematics algorithm (Tolani & Badler, 1996) that makes it possible to animate the avatar in 'real time' based on a flow of positions and orientation of the user's hands and head. To increase realism, we have also integrated a few heuristics to generate arm abductions in particular.

For reasons of technological integration, mimetism does not include the reproduction of the fine movements of the fingers and does not take into account facial expressions. Nevertheless, we have decided to synthesise the movement of the lips associated with voice because it seemed to us to be a good indicator of the speaker's location. The association of the labialisation and the lateralisation of sound makes it possible to be congruent in terms of location indicators.

One could also imagine the integration of facial expressions linked to prosody when it is technically detectable. We also use random facial micro-movements and micro-expressions to give the avatar a more lifelike aspect.

So far as symbolic behaviours are concerned, a library has been developed via a posture editor (see Figure 18).

The avatar's behaviour can be compared to that of an autonomous agent. Indeed, it must partly perceive the environment and act upon it according to messages it receives from the network and according to rules. For example, the designation of an object in a scene depends on the spatial relation existing between the designator and the object. These positions in space are perceived according to the relative position of each user (cf. view point notion). If one uses the analogy to define an agent (Ferber, 1998), the avatar is THE communication support with the other agents. In our model however, the avatar can neither supply nor receive information from the other avatars; neither can it react to the environment's actions in an autonomous way. This limits the aforementioned analogy.

5.3 Intention Detection

We describe below how we supply the user with intentions and reproduce them via avatars according to our typology.

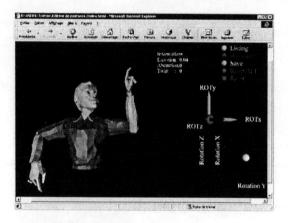

Figure 18: Posture editor.

5.3.1   Ergotic Gestures

The detection takes place as soon as an acquisition is carried out through a peripheral.

5.3.2   Epistemic Gestures

The detection takes place as soon as an action is carried out via a manipulation peripheral (for our application, a SpaceMouse). For example, changing the viewpoint on the scene via a rotation of the banner causes a movement of the head and arms of the avatar that represents the acting user.

5.3.3   Non-addressed Semiotic

The movement of the arms carried out in certain areas around the space of the body is captured in order to reproduce gestures of expression.

5.3.4   Addressed Semiotic

Depending on the contexts of use (free hand or not), detection takes place via a peripheral (pointing with a mouse) or movement capture (Marcel et al., 2000b). These two modalities must make it possible to detect the deictics in any case.

5.4   First Results

A development mode of each of these functions has been integrated into the system and a minimal detection system has been implemented.

An initial test has made it possible to validate certain system functions for limited registers of behaviour: hand and head deictics, non-addressed gestures of an arm, and a behaviour symbolising certain basic actions. It is nevertheless apparent that the lack of feedback on the gesture can be a hindrance especially when the gestures must be precise (e.g. in the event of contacts with the body).

The minimal functions implemented in the system will allow us to test the model in a mediated group activity context.

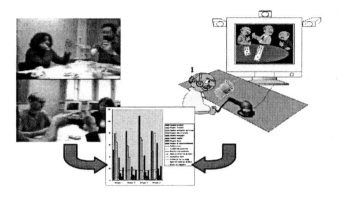

Figure 19: Behavioural study methodology.

6 Collaborative Activities in SPIN-3D

At the same time as technical studies, ergonomic studies have been carried out to analyse collaboration activities in natural situations in order to categorise the observed non-verbal behaviours (Nunez, 2000). The approach consists of observing a real activity with the aim of 'virtualising'.

Today, we are seeking to asses the way in which the means of communication are apprehended by users.

6.1 Assessment Approach

We are considering several stages and techniques to assess our theoretical model (with a focus on the interference of action gestures with communication):

- 'Action' centring with injection of gestures of expression.

- 'Communication' centring with injection of behaviours symbolising ergotic gestures.

- 'Collaboration' centring with the mixing of addressed and non-addressed semiotic gestures.

We believe we have made sufficient progress at the technological level to implement a collaborative activity and to carry out acceptability and usability tests. Indeed, we believe that the double technical and human constraint requires an iterative approach. By implementing a card deck activity into the system and by carrying out ergonomic studies, our purpose is to advance the architecture model, the interaction concepts, the state of the art in the field, and the technical devices (cf. Figure 19).

On the basis of the initial real activity observations, we are able to mediate elementary communication functions.

7 Conclusion

We have developed an architecture model that makes it possible to combine the various concepts of avatar animation for the CVE. From a functional point of view, this combination may be categorised as being 'symbolic-mimetic'. From a technical point of view, this model seems effective. Our next objective is therefore to instantiate our model through a new application so as to carry out an ergonomic assessment

8 Discussion

Implementing a gesture recognition module in the system compels the user to learn and also to adapt himself to the system; this choice is questionable because it contradicts a basic ergonomic principle which is that the user must only make a minimum effort to use the software.

On the one hand, it is also difficult to apprehend the accommodation capacity of the potential users and, on the other hand, the gesture distinguishing capacities of the intention detection module in view of the variability of users and of the contexts of use.

The initial thoughts on the feedback notion require a more in-depth study. Indeed, it is a major determinant of the model's acceptability. In particular, aspects relating to the user's representation via an avatar and possibly to one's self image: should you see yourself? To what extent? In what form? If the five categories of previously defined avatars seem to offer adapted functional solutions, what about 'symbolic-mimetic' avatars? Only an iterative approach such as we have taken can answer the questions we are asking.

References

Benford, S., Bowers, J., Fahlen, L., Greenhalgh, C. & Snowdon, D. (1997), "Embodiments, Avatars, Clones and Agents for Multi-user, Multi-sensory Virtual Worlds", *Multimedia Systems* 5(2), 93–104.

Breton, G. (2001), FaceEngine, A 3D Facial Animation Engine Designed for Realtime Applications, *in Proceedings of Web3D 2001 Conference*, ACM Press, pp.15–22.

Cadoz, C. (1994), "Le Geste Canal de Communication Homme–Machine — La Communication Instrumentale", *Techniques et Sciences Informatique* 13(1), 31–61.

Cassell, J. & Vilhjálmsson, H. (1999), "Fully Embodied Conversational Avatars: Making Communicative Behaviours Autonomous", *Autonomous Agents and Multi-Agent Systems* 2(1), 45–64.

Chin, W. K. (1996), Closed-form and Generalised Inverse Kinematic Solutions for Animating the Human Articulated Structure, BSc project report (stident number 938345B), Department of Computer Science, Curtin University of Technology, Perth, Western Australia. Supervisors Brian von Konsky & Andrew Marriott.

Corraze, J. (1980), *Les Communications Non-verbales, Le Psychologue*, Editions Presses Universitaire de France.

Ekman, P. & Friesen, W. (1972), "Hand Movements", *Journal of Communication* **22**, 353–74.

Ferber, J. (1998), *Les Systèmes Multi-agents, Vers une Intelligence Collective*, InterEditions.

Guye-Vuillème, A., Capin, T., Pandzic, I., Magnenat Thalmann, N. & Thalmann, D. (1999), "Nonverbal Communication Interface for Collaborative Virtual Environments", *Virtual Reality* **4**, 49–59.

Hinckley, K., Pausch, R., Goble, J. C. & F., K. N. (1994), Passive Real-world Interface Props for Neurosurgical Visualisation, *in* B. Adelson, S. Dumais & J. Olson (eds.), *Proceedings of CHI'94: Human Factors in Computing Systems*, ACM Press, pp.232–242.

Lebourque, T. (1998), Spécification et Génération de Gestes Naturels — Application à la Langue des Signes Française, PhD thesis, LIMSI-CNRS, France.

Marcel, S., Bernier, O. & Collobert, D. (2000a), Approche EM pour la Construction de Régions de Teinte Homogènes : Application au Suivi du Visage et des Mains d'une Personne, *in Proceedings of 6èmes Journées d'Études et d'Échanges "COmpression et REprésentation des Signaux Audiovisuels" (Coresa 2000)*.

Marcel, S. G., Bernier, O., Viallet, J. & Collobert, D. (2000b), Hand Gesture Recognition using Input–Output Hidden Markov Models, *in Proceedings of International Conference on Automatic Face and Gesture Recognition*, IEEE Computer Society Press, pp.456–61.

Nunez, L. (2000), La Communication Interpersonnelle à Travers des Clones Anthropomorphiques, Technical Report, Provence University, France.

Perin, P. & Gensollen, M. (1992), "La Communication Plurielle : l'Interaction dans les Téléconférences", Documentation Française, Coll. Technique et Scientifique des Télécommunications.

Saugis, G. (1998), Interface 3D pour le Travail Coopératif Synchrone, une Proposition, PhD thesis, Université Lille I France.

Tolani, D. & Badler, N. I. (1996), "Real-time Inverse Kinematics of the Human Arm", *Presence* **5**(4), 393–401.

Verna, D. & Grumbach, A. (1998), Can We Define Virtual Reality? The MRIC Model, *in* J. Heudin (ed.), *Proceedings of Virtual Worlds '98*, Vol. 1434 of *Lecture Notes in Artifical Intelligence*, Springer-Verlag, pp.29–41.

Viaud, M. & Saulnier, A. (1995), Real Time Analysis and Synthesis Chain, *in Proceedings of International Workshop on Automatic Face and Gesture Recognition*, IEEE Computer Society Press.

Requirements Engineering

Requirements Engineering

An Interactive Guide Through a Defined Modelling Process

Hermann Kaindl[†], Stefan Kramer[‡] & Mario Hailing[†]

[†] *Siemens AG Österreich, PSE, Geusaugasse 17, A-1030 Wien, Austria*

Tel: *+43 51707 43288*

Fax: *+43 51707 53270*

Email: *{hermann.kaindl,mario.hailing}@siemens.at*

[‡] *Albert-Ludwigs University Freiburg, Department of Computer Science, Georges-Köhler Allee Geb. 79, D-79110 Freiburg i.Br., Germany*

Email: *skramer@informatik.uni-freiburg.de*

We address the problem of getting started in using a yet unfamiliar CASE (computer-aided software engineering) tool in a purposeful way. We propose a solution based upon a defined modelling process of a method that is to be supported by the tool in question. This process defines in a systematic way how to model functional requirements, scenarios and goals as well as their relations. An explicit representation of this process enables an interactive *process guide* integrated in the tool to instruct and support the user while already working on real problems. This automated guide proposes primary tasks (according to the method) to be performed by the user. In addition, it supports the user performing them as well as all the secondary tasks involved. For example, if any instruction cannot be understood and executed, the users can let the guide execute this instruction on their behalf. We describe this interactive guide for getting started in using a CASE tool for requirements engineering according to a defined modelling process, and evaluate its implementation.

Keywords: development tools, CASE tools, process guide, scenarios.

1   Introduction

New users of a tool immediately want to start using it for real work (or fun), not to learn to use it. However, extensive training in courses or tutorials (paper-based as well as online) takes the approach that the user learns the use of the tool, before its actual use. If users try to use a tool without going through such a learning phase, errors are likely to occur, which often results in frustration on the side of the novice user. This may even lead to not using the tool at all.

This issue arises prominently with CASE (computer-aided software engineering) tools, since their use often not only involves mastering a new user interface but also new and difficult modelling tasks to be performed with the tool. For example, a CASE tool for object-oriented analysis (OOA) should be used for modelling according to an OOA method that the tool is intended to support. If the new user of such a tool, however, is also unfamiliar with a method to be supported by the tool, purposeful use of it is unlikely. Note the difference to first using, e.g. a word processor for simply writing letters, when prior knowledge of writing them with a typewriter can be transferred.

If someone neither knows the tool nor a related method, the question may arise why to use them at all. The deeper problem, however, is that people are facing difficult tasks like developing useful software. Methods for OOA and requirements engineering are intended to help them accomplish such a task, and appropriate tools should support the methods.

We think that it is a real challenge for designers of CASE tools to improve the human–computer interaction of first-time usage. This issue is vital to the successful support of methods for software development through these tools, since novice users may simply not know how to use a CASE tool according to the method. Instead of focusing on support for learning to use the tool before its actual use for real work, we suggest guiding the novice user interactively through its first use.

Assuming the availability of a method to be supported by a given CASE tool, purposeful use of the tool should follow the process defined in this method. According to (Preece et al., 1994), a *primary task* is a task that someone wants to (or is supposed to) carry out in the first place, and a *secondary task* is a task of mastering enough of a tool to accomplish a primary task. Since the process only prescribes the primary tasks, a user knowing them still has to figure out how to perform all the required secondary tasks. Even worse, a novice user may not even be familiar with the process and therefore the primary tasks. This is the most important case of those addressed by our approach.

The thesis of this paper is that a CASE tool may itself provide automated process guidance for novice users getting started. In support of this thesis, we devised and implemented an interactive *process guide* for the scenario-based modelling process proposed by Kaindl (2000) on top of our modelling tool RETH (Requirements Engineering Through Hypertext). In a nutshell, RETH combines requirements definition in natural language with OOA, providing a uniform hypertext interface in the tool. Requirements, goals and domain entities are all modelled as objects in RETH. Classes and instances are distinguished, and each of them is described in one hypertext node in the tool. In this way, descriptions in natural language of, e.g. requirements statements or glossary entries are integrated in the object-oriented structure. For an overview of this tool and the method supported by it, we refer the interested reader to, e.g. (Kaindl, 1996; Kaindl, 1997).

We gathered empirical evidence about the usage of this process guide by novice users. The results of a usability test and a more formal experiment as well as the feedback from real users in practice suggest that our process guide provides effective guidance according to the given method. Subjectively, users that have the guide available tend to feel better and more secure about what they do and their achievements than users without the guide at their disposal.

This paper is organised in the following manner. First, we present our process guide through an example session. Then we summarise and discuss our approach more generally. After reporting some empirical evidence, we relate our approach to previous work.

2 The Process Guide

Rather than starting the presentation of our approach with a dry theoretical explanation, we first illustrate a sketch of a typical session of a novice user guided by the process guide. We assume a novice user who is unfamiliar with the method and the tool, and we focus on supporting the very first phase of getting started. After this example session, we summarise the major features of our approach and discuss it more generally.

2.1 Sketch of a Typical Session

Immediately after a user starts the modelling tool RETH for the first time, it explains briefly some essential features of its own user interface. Figure 1 illustrates a typical window of this user interface. Figure 2 shows the explanatory text, which is also available at any time through the help system. This user interface looks much like that of Microsoft Office products, and the hypertext user-interface approach is like that of Netscape Navigator and Microsoft Internet Explorer. We assume that the explanation of the main part of the user interface for the user of the tool as shown in Figure 2 is also sufficient for the reader of this paper.

The major design rationale for building this kind of user interface was that many people have experience with these tools. The users of our tool are assumed to have such experience, and in our environment this assumption is true. So, most users do not have problems with secondary tasks like opening files or following hypertext links. However, as long as they are not yet familiar with the method to be supported by this tool, they have problems with what to do with it, i.e. modelling appropriately by applying the process of this method. They have problems with the primary tasks in the first place and do not know which secondary tasks are required for their achievement.

Immediately after this introduction of the basic user interface of the tool, it asks whether help from the process guide is wanted or not. If the user gives an affirmative answer, the process guide introduces itself briefly.

Then the process guide immediately addresses the major issue that the user might not know which primary tasks to perform with the tool as defined in the

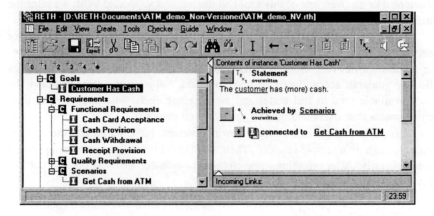

Figure 1: A typical window of the tool's user interface as explained in Figure 2.

> The left part of the window shows the hierarchy of hypertext nodes. Each node represents either a class, labelled with the symbol ("C"), or an instance ("I"). These can be classes or instances of domain objects as well as, e.g. requirements objects.
>
> The right part of the window shows the content of the node that is selected in the left part. Every node consists of one or more so-called partitions. Their content can be expanded or shrunk in the user interface, and they represent attributes and relations of objects.
>
> *Menus:*
> Through the menu bar at the top of the window, every function of the tool is accessible.
>
> *Hypertext links:*
> The source of hypertext links is shown through blue and underlined text. Such links can be followed through selecting this text. Note, that also in the help text you will find such links, that will lead you to glossary entries explaining the corresponding notions.

Figure 2: Explanatory text.

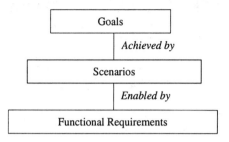

Figure 3: Part of the entities to be represented.

process. It presents a list of conceptual entities to choose from. So, users can choose, under guidance, which conceptual entity they want to represent in the model, e.g. a goal or a scenario. We focus here on a small but essential part of the method as described in more detail by Kaindl (2000), that contains (among other entities) goals, scenarios and functional requirements as well as their relationships (see Figure 3). According to this part of the method, goals are *achieved by* executing scenarios (see also Figure 1), and the execution of (actions in) scenarios is *enabled by* functions. Taken together, these relations help to show how the functions of a system to be built will serve goals of its users through their use in scenarios.

According to the minimalist instruction approach of Carroll (1998), the user has preferably a real task to perform, which involves modelling such entities, anyway. In such a situation, the motivation is usually much higher than in a tutoring environment where a hypothetical problem is dealt with that the user is not very interested in.

For the presentation here, let us assume that the user picks a reasonable task to model using the system, e.g. to model a scenario that is envisaged for using the system modelled now. As an example of such a scenario, consider the typical way of getting cash from an ATM (automated teller machine), which is also the example that the process guide provides to the user in order to illustrate what is meant here. Modelling such a scenario is a primary task in the course of the modelling process supported by our approach.

In order to perform such a primary task with the given tool, however, certain secondary tasks must be performed that may require some understanding of this modelling approach. So, the process guide now offers active help for performing them. Figure 4 shows a screen dump of the window presented to the user, which provides a sequence of instructions for performing those secondary tasks. The guide presents the whole sequence corresponding to a primary task at once, so that the user can see the context and gain an overview. The next instruction to be followed in the current situation is highlighted. For example, the last instruction in Figure 4 is to enter a textual description for a newly defined scenario.

If the user is able to follow this instruction successfully, the process guide recognises the corresponding state change and provides positive feedback to the user. Now the subsequent instruction is highlighted as the one to be followed, etc.

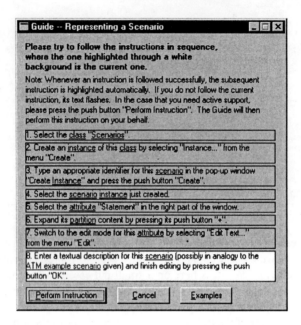

Figure 4: Instructions for representing a scenario.

A novice user, however, may not be able to follow one or the other of these instructions for various reasons. For example at step 1 of Figure 4, he or she may simply not yet know what a class of scenarios is or how to find it in the user interface. So, at any time during this guidance through the process the users may have the process guide perform the current instruction on their behalf (by pressing the push button "Perform Instruction" in the window shown in Figure 4, which has the same effect as if the user would have performed this instruction through the regular user interface).

Still, let us assume that the novice user ends up in a situation where he or she tries to follow an instruction but fails for whatever reason. The process guide recognises that an instruction has not been followed and provides feedback about this fact by flashing the instruction for each new action by the user that does not follow the instruction successfully. Concurrently, the button for having the process guide perform the instruction on the user's behalf is flashing in order to emphasise this option.

A special instruction in the course of representing a scenario is, of course, the one to enter a textual description for it (the last one in Figure 4). While the secondary task of typing in the text need not be supported specifically for the kind of user we focus on, writing a good scenario description is certainly a difficult primary task. So, the process guide tries to provide at least some rudimentary and traditional support by offering access to an example scenario (through pressing the push button "Examples" or through a hyperlink from the underlined string "ATM example scenario" in the instruction text).

Connect with Goals

Each <u>scenario</u> should be connected with at least one <u>goal</u> that can be achieved through its execution.

The underlying idea is to model scenarios that are both necessary and useful. In addition, a scenario may be better understood when some corresponding goal is known.

In the case that a scenario cannot be connected appropriately with any goal that is already represented, either some goals may yet be missing in the representation or this scenario may not serve any goal of the user.

Figure 5: Methodological advice for linking a scenario with goals.

Let us assume now that the instructions for modelling such a scenario as illustrated in Figure 4 have been followed successfully and completely by some interaction of the novice user with the process guide. That is, the first primary task suggested by the guide and chosen by the user has been completed successfully. However, the novice user might again not know what to do next.

Therefore, the process guide provides in this situation methodological support by suggesting to link the scenario representation with a goal that is to be satisfied by an execution of the scenario (see Figure 3 again). An example of such a goal is the one of having (more) cash money after having used an ATM machine. More precisely, a window pops up, giving the related methodological advice and some rationale for it online (Figure 5 shows the text). From the hyperlinks (shown underlined), glossary text including examples can be looked up. Next, the window shown in Figure 6 pops up, which provides instructions and support for the secondary tasks required for connecting a scenario with already existing goals.

If no goals are represented yet, or none would be satisfied through the scenario execution, the modelling process prescribes that such a goal should be inferred and specified. In order to perform this primary task under guidance, the user just needs to press the button for representing a new goal. The guide provides the corresponding instructions analogously to those for scenarios shown in Figure 4.

The process guide leads the user through these and analogous instructions as long as the user desires. Whenever the user wants to stop or to continue without guidance, he or she may simply terminate the process guidance at any time.

2.2 Summary of the Essential Features

After this example session, let us summarise and highlight the essential features of our process guide and provide some rationale for their design. The support for the primary tasks is both its most important and unique feature. However, for really supporting a novice user, support for the required secondary tasks is also essential. In particular, the process guide can perform an instruction on the user's behalf. In

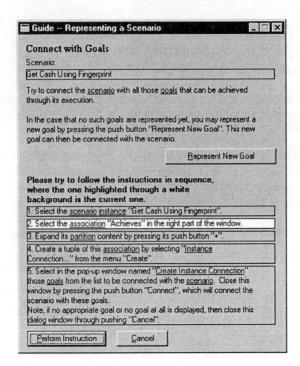

Figure 6: Instructions for connecting a scenario with already existing goals.

addition, it is necessary to provide a novice user with conceptual information while being guided.

The process guide supports the *primary tasks* of modelling (according to (Kaindl, 2000)) in the following manner.

- *Presenting a choice of conceptual entities to be modelled*

    Up-front, the process guide offers a choice of the conceptual entities to be modelled (e.g. scenarios and goals). In this way, it suggests to its user reasonable tasks to be performed with the tool. Since the process supported is flexible with respect to the order in which such entities are modelled, the process guide provides this flexibility as well. So, users are guided to model entities that are important according to the method, but they have a certain freedom in choosing the order in which they want to model them.

- *Providing example descriptions of conceptual entities*

    Using a rather conventional approach, the process guide also provides example descriptions of conceptual entities. Providing such descriptions is certainly not novel, but it helps people to provide descriptions by analogy. A disadvantage of this approach is, however, that the given examples tend to have a strong impact on what the users write, which may sometimes lead to suboptimal descriptions. Still, it is a feasible approach to provide some help, and the process guide provides easy access to the examples at the time they are most needed. A more elaborate approach is to provide style and content guidelines for authoring scenarios (Ben Achour et al., 1999), which could be integrated in our process guide as well.

- *Guidance in linking entities according to the method*

  A strong impact of the process guide on the models produced by its users is that it leads to links between entities according to the method (e.g. links between concrete scenarios and concrete goals). Unless someone has a good understanding of the method, he or she may otherwise not be in a position to install such semantically relevant links. In order to motivate these links, the process guide does not just explain that such a link should be installed, but also why. Providing this rationale seems to be important both for the acceptance of this instruction and for having the users link entities in a meaningful way.

The process guide supports the *secondary tasks* by guiding the user through actually creating representations of instances of the conceptual entities and through linking these representations. This approach is implemented in the process guide in the following manner.

- *Active guidance through step-by-step instructions and monitoring*

  A general characteristic of our approach is that the instructions provided are not just "plain text", but actively supported by the process guide. The guide monitors the user's interactions with the tool and keeps track of the current state of the model representation. Thus it is able to highlight the instruction to be followed next.

- *Immediate feedback at each point*

  Since our guide monitors the user's interactions with the tool, it is able to provide immediate feedback at each point. Technically, it provides positive feedback by highlighting the subsequent instruction and negative feedback by briefly flashing the instruction.

  The guide gives feedback without blocking the rest of the tool. So, a situation may arise where the user interrupts following the instructions of the process guide momentarily to perform some other task, but plans to resume later. While our guide recognises that an instruction has not been followed, it cannot distinguish this situation from an unsuccessful attempt to follow the instruction. Consequently, the negative feedback provided does not necessarily indicate an error, but just serves as a reminder of the fact that the step has not been performed successfully.

- *Possibility of letting the system perform the current step on one's behalf*

  Alternatively, the users can let the tool execute any instruction on their behalf. (Of course, certain information like the name of a scenario or its description need to be entered by the users even in this case.)

When dealing with both primary and secondary tasks, novice users in particular may sometimes not know the meaning of a technical term used in the given instructions. So, conceptual information about the modelling method is obviously very important for the users to perform their tasks. Thus, all textual descriptions provided by the process guide are interlinked with a hypertext that contains definitions of important terms as well as examples. This relates to a certain kind of support information, namely conceptual information, according to the minimalist instruction approach of Carroll (1998). Using the process guide, conceptual information in a hypertextual form is available at any point in time: when choosing a conceptual entity to be represented, while following the instructions, etc. Whereas conceptual information is provided in the form of a hypertext, "procedural knowledge" about the process is provided by "active" step-by-step instructions.

2.3 *Discussion*

Our concrete implementation of the process guide certainly depends on the method supported and the tool it is integrated with. However, the approach of our process guide is presumably more generally applicable. We can imagine that such a process guide would be useful in many CASE tools for modelling which support a defined method. In a general word processor without any defined method for purposeful use, our approach for guiding primary tasks is certainly not applicable, but also not necessary.

One obvious prerequisite of this approach is that primary tasks are defined in a process, another that all the instructions on secondary tasks for achieving those primary tasks are known beforehand.

In this sense, the process guide "knows" what to do and what to suggest to the user. Still, the user needs to provide the information and knowledge of the concrete application. After all, the guide cannot model the domain on its own.

If the process guide were the only interface to the modelling tool, it would certainly over-constrain its use. There may well be other ways of using a CASE tool in addition to a predefined process. Such a process defines certain ways of purposeful use, but advanced users and experienced modellers can still be more creative in their approaches and use a tool with some purpose not covered by the underlying process of the guide. An advanced user, therefore, need not necessarily use the guide and follow its instructions.

Therefore, the basic user interface, which is like that of today's Microsoft Office products, is still necessary and useful, because it leaves the user some freedom of performing operations and actions without being guided. We would even argue that the user interfaces of the basic tool and the process guide should be kept more or less separate, much as they are in the current implementation. Otherwise the users may mix up the levels of abstraction on which they wish to perform their actions (e.g. renaming some node vs. adding and linking a new scenario).

Surprisingly, even an advanced user might take advantage of such a process guide in a way it was not originally designed for. As long as users work along the lines of a defined process as supported by the guide, they may simply and quickly let it perform the instructions on their behalf. According to preliminary experience, this can free users from the cognitive overhead involved with selecting entities and applying operations to them in the original user interface. In this sense, such a process guide can be viewed as a high-level interface for faster and easier use of the tool in a prescribed and purposeful way.

So, while originally devised for support of the initial stages of using a tool, the guide may even be useful for advanced users. This is one of the reasons why our concern is not so much that users learn quickly, but rather that they are guided and supported. The fact that the process guide supports real work immediately distinguishes it from a tutoring system.

3   Empirical Evidence

Still, the question remains in which sense or how much the tool integrated with the process guide is really better than the basic tool without. So, we try to provide empirical evidence in order to answer this question at least partly.

3.1   Use in Practice

From the use of the basic tool RETH in practice (as well as observations with other modelling tools), it was clear that without any extra instructions or consultation, users lacking information about a method do not really know what to do with the tool. That is why the process guide was developed in the first place.

Until the time of this writing, we have delivered the RETH tool to its users together with the integrated process guide for almost two years. From these users we already received feedback that the process guide indeed helps to answer the question of what to do at least in most cases. Whenever we had the opportunity (in the course of consulting) to watch users when they used RETH with the process guide for the first time, we have been able to see their positive reactions directly.

3.2   Design of Usability Test and Experiment

We also designed and conducted an informal usability test as well as a formal experiment to evaluate our approach and its implementation in a more rigorous way. Unfortunately, it seems very hard to make an experimental comparison for validating this experience from practice. Unless some instructions on what to do are given to users of the basic tool, they would be unable to perform a task where the performance or the results could finally be compared with those of having the process guide available.

So, we first designed a rather informal usability test where the process guide was available all the time. Primarily we were interested in the effects of the process guide on the users' behaviour, and whether it was really able to guide the users through the process of modelling with the tool. The given overall task during this usability test was to model some aspect of any real problem that the participants were facing in a project, in order to keep their motivation as high as possible. For dealing with their task, the participants used our modelling tool RETH with the process guide in charge at the start, but they were allowed to switch it off at any time. The duration was on average about one hour.

In the subsequent experiment, however, we wanted to see a comparison of having the process guide available or not. So, this experiment design included precise (but high-level) descriptions of tasks to be performed. We defined a task T

as a sequence of three subtasks. For subtask T_1 the given instruction was to represent a scenario "Get Cash from ATM". Subtask T_2 was to represent a goal "Customer Has Cash" and T_3 to link them. The text for the scenario and goal was given in a file to simply copy it in. In fact, a similar text was also available in the examples section of the help text (as mentioned above). Since only the text was available there, however, the experiment was not biased.

We designed this experiment to test the hypothesis *Direct Utility*:
If the process guide is available and used, a task supported through it can be performed faster than without. (Of course, other criteria can be defined for the utility of the process guide like the quality of the results, but for an objective comparison the time used seems to be appropriate, if the quality is comparable. In our experiment, quality was not an issue since all the subjects succeeded to perform the given task T successfully.)

For performing the usability test, 3 subjects without any prior knowledge about our method and tool were selected by the management. For the experiment, 14 subjects interested in our tool volunteered. The profile of the subjects matched that of real users of our tool closely, but none had used it before. So, they are mostly experienced designers and software developers. All subjects were familiar with Microsoft Office products and one of the major Web browsers. Finally, they had some average familiarity with requirements engineering, object-oriented approaches and hypertext.

The set of subjects for the experiment was divided into two disjoint experimental groups. Subjects were balanced across groups according to whether they had already attended a presentation of our tool, to their gender and to their educational level. Apart from that they were assigned randomly.

We asked subjects in one experimental group to perform task T by using the process guide, and subjects in the other without. Through comparing the times needed for task T, we tested our hypothesis *Direct Utility*.

Since we wanted every volunteer to have the opportunity to use the process guide, we asked the subjects of the second group to perform an additional task using the guide, that was not related to our hypothesis. The times needed for this were not taken into account. However, we gathered the subjective opinion about the guide also from these subjects.

We gave every subject up to 30 minutes to perform task T and we informed them beforehand of the time limit on the task.

While the subjects worked with the tool, we made notes and recorded the reactions of the subjects for both the usability test and the experiment. We were able to enhance these notes with more detailed observations when analysing video tapes capturing the whole usability test and experiment. In particular, the tapes allowed us to measure the times used precisely.

3.3   Experimental Results

It was observable in both the usability test and the experiment (also in detail on video) that all of the subjects were able to represent, e.g. scenarios and goals as well as their connection according to the method when supported by the process guide.

The major observation in the usability test was that the subjects indeed found something useful to do with the tool, although no specific tasks were given to them. So, there is some empirical evidence that our process guide can help a novice user unfamiliar with the method to identify and perform reasonable primary tasks with the tool.

Now let us summarise the other major observations:

- Sometimes subjects got stuck, since they could not figure out how to perform a given instruction. Through letting the guide perform it on their behalf, they were able to continue successfully.

- In addition to the active process guide itself, its embedding with more conventional help features turned out to be important. We observed that having the hypertextual access to glossary information about the underlying concepts and to examples was important for understanding and executing the instructions of the process guide.

From the experiment, we have measurable results in terms of how long subjects needed to perform the given task, which all of them succeeded to do. On average, subjects in the group supported by the process guide (mean = 728.86s, median = 441s) were faster on task T than subjects in the other group (mean = 797.71s, median = 636s). In fact, one subject in the first group needed much more time, otherwise this result would be more pronounced. So, there is some indication in favour of the validity of hypothesis *Direct Utility*.

3.4   Subjective Results

For collecting the subjective opinions, we asked every subject immediately after the experiment to fill in a subjective questionnaire. We designed this questionnaire according to (Dumas & Redish, 1993, p.208–12). Primarily, it consists of closed questions, where the respondent is asked to select an answer from a choice of alternative replies, with an additional line for optional comments in free text. We use a multi-point rating scale, more precisely a *Likert scale*. As an example, one of the key questions is to rate whether interacting with the process guide was (*very easy, easy, neither easy nor difficult, difficult, very difficult*). Such closed questions are organised in several sections: background information, the modelling tool itself, the central section on the process guide, and a general section.

Now let us summarise the answers in the questionnaire:

- All of the subjects found the process guide *useful* or *very useful*.

- Nearly all subjects found interacting with the process guide *easy* or *very easy*.

- All of the subjects believe that they have learned how to work with the modelling tool through being guided.

- All but one subjects believe that they would have faced problems without the availability of the process guide. This corresponds well with our previous experience that led us to develop this process guide.

- All but one subjects stated that they would use the process guide again.

In addition to the information from the questionnaire, subjective opinions of the subjects were available through their utterances in the course of performing the tasks. A major finding here was that some subjects felt better and more secure about their results achieved without the guide, once they worked with the guide on the additional task.

4 Related Work

Online tutorials can have certain advantages over paper manuals for the computer user (Al-Awar et al., 1981). Our approach also has these advantages, but tries to let users immediately address their real primary task.

As compared to tutors in the sense of intelligent tutoring systems, we do not attempt to model the users and the current state of their knowledge about the task in question. It would be unrealistic to assume that within the first ten or so minutes of getting started, it would be feasible to infer a user model. In addition, our focus is on guiding a novice user through work on a real problem of this user rather than tutoring.

Since we also strive for letting users act immediately, our approach is more a development in the spirit of providing *minimalist manuals* (Carroll, 1998). As in the minimalist instruction approach, we do not support learning in constructed learning situations, but focus on performing real tasks. However, our approach is different from minimalist instruction in providing guidance for users and in having much less emphasis on learning through instructions. In addition, we do not focus on supporting or easing search in manuals for information to solve problems. Instead of providing a manual (printed or online), our tool checks the fulfilment of instructions and provides immediate feedback both for cases in which they are fulfilled and cases in which they are not. Additionally, the process guide can be asked to perform the instruction on the user's behalf.

An important point is that the instruction sequences provided by our process guide can also be viewed as scenarios. That is, scenarios are in this view also involved on a meta-level. In fact, we develop the modelling tool by using scenarios according to our own approach, and some of these scenarios of interacting with our tool are "implemented" in the instruction sequences of the process guide.

The *Scenario Machine* of Carroll & Kay (1988) is also based on this view of scenarios. It has been designed to overcome problems with the *Training Wheels* word processor, by providing more guidance to a user in the initial stages of learning. It provides additional information explaining why advanced user-interface functions are not available and what options the user could try instead. This is clearly focusing on the secondary task of mastering the tool, while we focus on the primary task of modelling. In contrast to the Scenario Machine, our approach works without blocking tool functionality. The major purpose of the Scenario Machine was on the support of learning to use a tool, while our approach focuses on guiding a user.

Our primary task of modelling is strongly related to *task analysis* — for an overview see, e.g. (Preece et al., 1994, Chapter 20). A task can be viewed as a piece of work that a person or other agent has to perform (or wishes to). Note particularly, that we support tasks of a user who tries to model tasks. Concrete ways of performing tasks can be described in scenarios such as those in our approach. Similar constructs to scenarios have occasionally been called *methods* or *plans* in the context of task analysis.

According to our view of a scenario as a cooperative plan (Kaindl, 2000), developing a scenario can be viewed as a plan construction process, and this view helps us and people using our approach to focus the interactions towards goals. Suchman (1987) has analysed problems with the plan execution approach of an expert help system for using a photocopier. In contrast to the situations investigated there, our tool has full information about all the events on the user interface. In general, this analysis does not invalidate every planning approach, and in particular, not every planning *view*. Scenarios viewed as cooperative plans are still scenarios much like those described, e.g. in the collection (Carroll, 1995). In addition, we do not even assume that any reasonable set of scenarios can be complete for a real-world problem. However, our view of scenarios as cooperative plans allows us to make use of cognitive theories of planning and understanding like the one described by Schank & Abelson (1977) and it is useful for relating scenarios with goals.

A more elaborate approach to process space analysis was proposed for analysing the complex science inquiry process (Quintana et al., 1999). Its motivation was to support high-school science students, who are novices in this domain. Of course, the process that our guide supports is much simpler. But since it is also well-defined and procedural, we were able to focus in more detail on concrete guidance of novice users of the related CASE tool. In some sense, this approach and ours seem to be complementary.

Our process guide provides *performance support*, much as *wizards* and *guides* as distinguished by Dryer (1997). Its implementation combines features of such wizards and guides, but it is more similar to a guide according to (Dryer, 1997). We are not aware, however, of any such guide that would provide methodological support or such comprehensive guidance through sequences of instructions for related secondary tasks like our process guide.

In the world of commercial off-the-shelf software, we found different sorts of assistants and wizards in Microsoft Office products. Some of them are trying to hint at features that might be relevant for the user's task, which is clearly different from our approach. Others (e.g. for MS Excel) are trying to "replace" the original GUI. While our process guide may also be useful in this way, its primary purpose is to guide the user in using the tool for modelling according to a method by use of the *GUI as is*. In addition, the actions in the original interface are still transparent in the sense that their effects can be seen even though the guide performs them. In the help system of MS Word, we found a few "Show me" buttons, which users can press in order to let the tool perform selected instructions on their behalf. In contrast to this feature, our guide allows this for any of its instructions and provides a more comprehensive approach of *guiding* through them: It also highlights the next instruction to be performed and provides immediate feedback at each point.

Whether or not there are similarities of our process guide with existing assistants or wizards with regard to the interactions for supporting secondary tasks, we are not aware of any assistant or wizard that supports *primary tasks* according to a method. Such higher-level methods do not even seem to be defined in the domains where assistants or wizards are currently available. A major contribution of our guide is that it suggests primary tasks according to a defined method to the user.

Many CASE tools support modelling according to defined methods, especially CASE tools for object-oriented development. However, we are not aware of any support comparable to our process guide in these tools at the time of this writing.

5   Conclusion

Making use of a defined process of a method as described by Kaindl (2000), we proposed a new approach to automated and interactive process guidance for using a CASE tool in a purposeful way. The major innovations in our process guide are:

- its support for the primary tasks of modelling; and

- its comprehensive approach to guiding through sequences of instructions for related secondary tasks, which involves

  - monitoring the user's interactions with the tool and keeping track of the current state of the model representation,

  - providing immediate feedback at each point,

  - highlighting the instruction to be followed next, and

  - letting the tool perform any of these instructions on the user's behalf.

Having such a process guide available in our CASE tool RETH for requirements engineering, even novice users of this tool can immediately start using it for modelling according to the defined process (that they usually do not know a priori). This seems to avoid many of the frustrations of having to find out otherwise how to make use of the tool functionality for creating a model representation without guidance. In this way, our approach seems to ease the use of such a tool and of the underlying process in practice.

Acknowledgements

We would like to thank John Karat and Alistair Sutcliffe for very fruitful and useful discussions on the topic of this paper. Vahan Harput and anonymous reviewers provided useful comments on previous versions of this paper. This work was supported in part by the Forschungsförderungsfonds für die gewerbliche Wirtschaft (FFF) under contract 800489.

References

Al-Awar, J., Chapanis, A. & Ford, W. R. (1981), "Tutorials for the First-time Computer User", *IEEE Transactions on Professional Communication* **24**(4), 30–7.

Ben Achour, C., Rolland, C., Maiden, N. & Souveyet, C. (1999), Guiding Use Case Authoring: Results of an Empirical Study, *in Proceedings of the 5th International Symposium on Requirements Engineering (RE'99)*, IEEE Computer Society Press, pp.36–43.

Carroll, J. M. & Kay, D. S. (1988), "Prompting, Feedback and Error Correction in the Design of a Scenario Machine", *International Journal of Man–Machine Studies* **28**(1), 11–27.

Carroll, J. M. (ed.) (1995), *Scenario-Based Design: Envisioning Work and Technology in System Development*, John Wiley & Sons.

Carroll, J. M. (ed.) (1998), *Minimalism Beyond the Nurnberg Funnel*, MIT Press.

Dryer, D. C. (1997), Wizards, Guides, and Beyond: Rational and Empirical Methods for Selecting Optimal Intelligent User Interface Agents, *in Proceedings of the 1997 International Conference on Intelligent User Interfaces (IUI '97)*, ACM Press, pp.265–8.

Dumas, J. S. & Redish, J. C. (1993), *A Practical Guide to Usability Testing*, Ablex.

Kaindl, H. (1996), How to Identify Binary Relations for Domain Models, *in Proceedings of the 18th International Conference on Software Engineering (ICSE'96)*, IEEE Computer Society Press, pp.28–36.

Kaindl, H. (1997), "A Practical Approach to Combining Requirements Definition and Object-oriented Analysis", *Annals of Software Engineering* **3**, 319–43.

Kaindl, H. (2000), "A Design Process Based on a Model Combining Scenarios with Goals and Functions", *IEEE Transactions on Systems, Man and Cybernetics* **30**(5), 537–51.

Preece, J., Rogers, Y., Sharpe, H., Benyon, D., Holland, S. & Carey, T. (1994), *Human–Computer Interaction*, Addison–Wesley.

Quintana, C., Eng, J., Carra, A., Wu, H.-K. & Soloway, E. (1999), Symphony: A Case Study in Extending Learner-centered Design Through Process Space Analysis, *in* M. G. Williams, M. W. Altom, K. Ehrlich & W. Newman (eds.), *Proceedings of the CHI99 Conference on Human Factors in Computing Systems: The CHI is the Limit*, ACM Press, pp.473–80.

Schank, R. & Abelson, R. (1977), *Scripts, Plans, Goals and Understanding*, Lawrence Erlbaum Associates.

Suchman, L. A. (1987), *Plans and Situated Actions — The Problem of Human–Machine Communication*, Cambridge University Press.

Multidisciplinary Practice in Requirements Engineering: Problems and Criteria for Support

Ian Denley[1] & John Long

Ergonomics & HCI Unit, University College London, 26 Bedford Way, London WC1H 0AP, UK

Tel: *+44 20 7679 7557*

Fax: *+44 20 7580 1100*

Email: *ian.denley@systemc.com, j.long@ucl.ac.uk*

This paper is concerned with multidisciplinary practice (MDP) in the emerging field of requirements engineering (RE). It is argued that multidisciplinary requirements engineering practice is ineffective. MDP in RE is introduced, exemplified, and problems identified. The incommensurability of conflicting paradigms may be a possible underlying cause of such problems. Accommodation of alternative paradigms is discussed, and criteria for support to overcome the problems of MDP are proposed.

Keywords: requirements engineering, paradigms, multidisciplinary practice.

1 Introduction

This paper is concerned with multidisciplinary practice (MDP) in the requirements engineering (RE). It argues that multidisciplinary requirements engineering practice is ineffective. MDP in RE is introduced, exemplified, and its problems identified. The incommensurability of conflicting paradigms may be a possible underlying cause of these problems. The accommodation of alternative paradigms is discussed, and criteria for support to overcome the problems are proposed.

---

[1] Now at System C Healthcare Ltd.

Figure 1: Independent MDP in RE

2   Multidisciplinary RE

RE is an emerging field. There is little consensus as to its nature and scope. Its emergence is characterised by a proliferation of perspectives, and a profusion of concepts. Concomitantly, there is increasing interest in the notion that RE may be multidisciplinary in nature (Scaife et al., 1994).

> "Requirements engineering is the elicitation, definition, modelling, analysis, specification and validation of the needs of a computer system. It is multi-disciplinary and draws on techniques from software engineering, knowledge acquisition, cognitive science and the social sciences to improve software engineering practice".
> British Computer Society: Requirements Engineering Specialist Group 1994.

Surprisingly little attention has been paid to the nature of MDP *per se*. The next section has the following aims: to distinguish between possible types of MDP in RE; to illustrate and exemplify them; and to review some examples.

2.1   Types of Practice Involving Multiple Disciplines

We distinguish between two general types of practice:

- Independent MDP — each contributing discipline addresses its own RE problems without influence on or by, other disciplines.

- Dependent MDP — contributing disciplines exert a mutual influence upon one another.

2.2   Independent MDP

In independent MDP, the contribution provided by one discipline and its practitioners does not affect the contribution of other discipline and their practitioners. Each discipline addresses its own RE (see Figure 1).

Supposing the directors of a hospital are re-designing their Accident and Emergency (A&E) department to cope with increasing demands and diminishing resources. This redesign might consist of:

- Redesign of the department's organisation and management structures.

- Procurement of a new information system.

Figure 2: Dependent MDP in RE

If the re-design is carried out by independent MDP, the organisational structures could be re-designed without consideration of the new information system, and vice versa. Practitioners of the discipline of organisational/management psychology (management consultants) might identify a requirement to change the hierarchical structure of A&E staff to multi-professional team-working. However, practitioners of the discipline of software engineering (SE — specialist software developers) might identify a requirement to design the A&E information system around an official NHS minimum data set for A&E (including generic tasks such as registering patients; triaging patients etc.) without consideration of a new team-working structure.

Knowledge and practices from the discipline of organisational/management psychology would be applied independently of knowledge and practices from of SE.

2.3 Dependent MDP

In dependent MDP, the contribution to the RE process provided by one discipline and its practitioners occurs in the context of the other disciplines and their practitioners also offering contributions. Disciplines exert a **mutual influence** upon one another (see Figure 2).

In system development, the disciplines of human factors (HF) and SE exert a mutual influence on the design of behaviours at the user interface. Similarly, the disciplines of HF and sociology exert a mutual influence on the design of behaviours for multi-user systems.

Extending the A&E example, imagine the hospital directors have identified a business requirement to introduce electronic communication between the A&E department and the pathology laboratory, because paper-based investigation requests often go 'missing'. Using knowledge and practices (task analysis), the system developer identifies that doctors currently fill-out and sign the paper-based investigation request forms, including all data. The developer suggests this task should continue to be allocated to the doctor, and suggests that doctors also complete the electronic investigation request forms, including all data. However, an ethnographic study by the system developer discovers that A&E doctors perceive data input tasks to be administrative (and to detract from caring for patients), and only use the computer for information retrieval. The doctors consider data input should be performed by nurses. The system developer cannot simply utilise the two discipline contributions independently of one-another. Instead, the developer must understand how the contributions are related, and how they should influence each other in a requirement for the design of the investigation ordering system.

2.4   Types of Dependent MDP

How might dependent MDP be carried out?

We identify four types of dependent MDP: by concept; by product; by process; by practitioner.

MDP by *concept* occurs if the very foundations of Disciplines 1 and 2 were integrated within a common framework or theory (a hybrid discipline). No such theories or frameworks exist within RE at present.

MDP by *product* occurs when a practitioner of Discipline 1 commissions a requirements study from a practitioner of Discipline 2, and receives a product (the results of an analysis) to be considered with products of their own discipline. MDP is organised around the use of substantive discipline knowledge. Sommerville et al. (1998) use a *viewpoints* framework to make explicit the relationships between multiple discipline perspectives in the requirements for an on-board train protection system.

MDP by *process* occurs if a practitioner of Discipline 1 learns a technique from Discipline 2 and incorporates it into his/her repertoire. MDP is organised primarily around the use of methodological knowledge. This type of MDP is often advocated. Macaulay (1996) suggests requirements engineers should acquire a range of RE techniques; and Sutcliffe (1997) also proposes a technique combination approach.

MDP by *practitioner* occurs if a practitioner of Discipline 1 collaborates with a practitioner of Discipline 2. Both practitioners use their training and judgement to respond to specific concerns. The practitioners themselves act as channels for their respective discipline knowledge. This paper is primarily concerned with dependent MDP by practitioner.

2.5   Examples of Dependent MDP by Practitioner

Three case-studies of MDP in RE were examined, involving collaboration between the disciplines of: psychology and SE; sociology and SE (Denley, 1999). Each case is an example of dependent MDP by practitioner.

2.6   Psychology and SE

1. Gasson (1995) studied MDP between psychologists and software engineers to develop computerised support for interactive student learning. The study analysed design documents from the development team (psychologists and software engineers), and interviews with team members. The project plan required the team to follow an integrated development process model. This model aimed to support collaboration. This RE model failed almost immediately. Gasson speculates there was a dichotomy between the two disciplines, and team members from both failed to understand the requirements of the other or to learn from each other.

2. Scaife et al. (1994) report a multidisciplinary project aimed to develop a software tool for fashion designers. The development team comprised software engineers and psychologists/cognitive scientists. The study focuses

- Dichotomy of approach between the two disciplines.
- Problems of viewpoint, and the different interests of the disciplines.
- Lack of shared assumptions (about the system development process).
- Irreconcilable differences between alternative methodologies.
- Failure of team members to understand each other's disciplines or learn from each other.
- Problems in understanding what the other discipline practitioners do.
- The need for each discipline to make undesirable compromises.
- Problems with understanding terminologies across disciplines.
- Entrenched philosophical positions.

Table 1: Problems in Dependent MDP by Practitioner

on some of the difficulties of software development arising from their interaction. Such difficulties were marked in the early stages of the project, during the translation of empirical data requirements into specifications. The case study identified a number of specific problems, including: a lack of shared assumptions about the development process; problems understanding terminologies across disciplines; and methodological differences about the 'correct' way of working.

2.7   Sociology and SE

This case-study concerns the requirements for a user interface to a flight database providing real-time information to air traffic controllers. The study was constructed from four reports of the project; two from the software engineers (Sommerville et al., 1993); and two from the sociologists' perspective (Hughes et al., 1993). This case-study also represents an example of MDP by practitioner. Multidisciplinary interactions were organised around monthly debriefing meetings.

Both the sociologists and the software engineers retain positive views on their collaboration. However, both groups report problems. There is a wide gulf between their disciplines due to entrenched philosophical positions. The case study identified a number of specific problems, including: communication problems due to different terminologies; methodological differences; and problems understanding 'what the other discipline practitioners actually do'. Future successful collaboration would require both disciplines to question further their own assumptions and working methods.

2.8   Problems in Dependent MDP by Practitioner

These case studies identify similar problems: see the list of Table 1.

In sum, even though we have only examined a small sample of case-studies, there appear to be serious obstacles to effective MDP by practitioner. Next we explore their possible causes.

3 Dependent MDP: Problem with Paradigms

To understand such problems, we need first to understand disciplines. The notion of a *paradigm* (Kuhn, 1962; 1970; Burrel & Morgan, 1979; Guba & Lincoln, 1989; 1994) is used to guide reasoning about the nature of disciplines in terms of the types of problem they address, the practices they employ and the knowledge that supports those practices (Long & Dowell, 1989). Paradigms can be understood as fundamentally different sets of assumptions about the nature of the world and how to obtain knowledge about it. Paradigms are the bedrock on which disciplines are built.

Furthermore, a possible underlying cause of problems in dependent MDP is that paradigms are philosophically **incommensurable**. Paradigms have no common measure, and cannot be mixed together (Jackson & Carter, 1991). However, dependent MDP by practitioner may only be possible if we concede the possibility of the practical **accommodation** of alternative paradigms. Finally, some criteria are proposed which, if met, would support such practical accommodation.

3.1 Disciplines and Paradigms

Long & Dowell (1989) suggest that most definitions of disciplines assume three primary characteristics: *knowledge*; *practice*; and a *general problem* with a particular scope. The scope of general (discipline) problems can also be decomposed resulting in sub-disciplines.

The division of a discipline into sub-disciplines is useful. It allows us to classify disciplines and examine their commonalities and differences. The discipline of science is a sub-discipline of a super-ordinate discipline whose scope might include metaphysical beliefs about the nature of the world, the human individual's place in it, and possible relationships between human beings and the world. Such a discipline addressing sets of basic assumptions and beliefs is known as a *paradigm* (Burrel & Morgan, 1979; Guba & Lincoln, 1989; Guba & Lincoln, 1994)[2]. In their perspective, a paradigm may be viewed as a set of **basic beliefs** that represent a world-view defining for its holder the nature of the 'world', the individual's place, and relationships to that world. The beliefs are basic, in that they can only be accepted on faith (however well the beliefs are argued). There is no way to establish their ultimate truthfulness. They define a paradigm as:

> "the basic belief system or world-view that guides the investigator, not only in choices of method but in ontologically and epistemologically fundamental ways."

These basic beliefs are summarised by how their proponents respond to three fundamental questions. The answer to any one question, taken in any order, constrains answers to the others.

Ontological question: what is the form and nature of reality, and therefore, what can knowledge be about?

---

[2]Note that both these perspectives on the notion of 'paradigm' are somewhat broader in scope than that of Kuhn (1962; 1970).

Epistemological question: what is the relationship between the knower and what can be known?

Methodological question: how can the knower find out about whatever he or she believes can be known?

Guba & Lincoln (1994) believe the order of these questions reflects a logical, if not necessary, primacy. They also argue that they can be answered in different ways, and each formulation constitutes a different paradigm. Answers to these questions, cannot be proven. They further argue that answers given are human constructions; all inventions and hence subject to error. Advocates of any particular construction must rely on its **persuasiveness** and **utility** rather than proof.

3.2 Discussion on the Accommodation of Paradigms

Despite their differences, all three earlier perspectives share a common feature: they all believe paradigms are philosophically **incommensurable**, that is, having no common measure, and cannot be mixed together (Jackson & Carter, 1991; Sankey, 1994). Conversely, a re-occurring theme is the possibility of achieving some other kind of **accommodation** between them at a *practical* level.

3.3 Incommensurability of Paradigms

That paradigms are distinct and cannot be mixed is based on the notion of irreconcilable conflicts between their philosophical positions on certain key features including: criteria; facts; meaning; and values — after Kitchener (1986). Each feature is considered.

Criteria: Competing paradigms select different problems, as the most important to solve, and employ different standards, against which to judge the success of the solution. Incommensurability is typically taken to imply no common measure among paradigms of inquiry; rival paradigms cannot be comparatively evaluated by a neutral set of rules or criteria (Lincoln, 1990).

Facts: Rival paradigms do not share a common body of data providing a neutral standard for their comparison; their fundamentally different theoretical viewpoints lead to different perceptions and interpretation of the facts. There are no neutral facts, free of all theory and empirically given. All facts are relative with respect to a particular paradigm. Similarly, the *content* of paradigms cannot be compared, since they are logically and epistemologically incompatible.

Meaning: Paradigms cannot be compared because there is no language independent of theory. Languages categorise the world in different ways, and in the transition between paradigms words change their meanings or conditions of applicability (Kuhn, 1970).

Values: Guba & Lincoln (1994) adopt an unashamedly relativistic position, when they say that all paradigms are human constructions, products of the human mind and subject to error. For them:

"the basic beliefs of paradigms are essentially contradictory ...
value freedom and value boundedness, cannot coexist in any
internally consistent metaphysical system."

In summary, then, paradigms are incommensurable since the rules for action,
for process, for discourse, for what is considered knowledge and truth, are different
and lead to diverse, disparate, distinctive and typically antithetical ends (Lincoln,
1990).

Given the incommensurability of paradigms, some authors suggest that it may
be possible to **accommodate** different paradigms within multi-disciplinary **practice**
within a given field — see, for example, (Weaver & Gioia, 1995) for organisational
studies and (Chua, 1986) for accountancy. Such practical accommodation might
take place either through the collaborative work of groups of practitioners, (**social-
community** accommodation), holding different paradigms, or via the practice of
individuals[3] (**individual** accommodation) — after Skrtic (1990).

3.4   Social-community Accommodation of Paradigms

The implication outlined earlier is that a scientific community is premised on meta-
theoretical assumptions, defined by a paradigm. Without a paradigm, there can be
no scientific community (Skrtic, 1990). We still might ask whether advocates of
alternative paradigms can live with (and learn from) each other? — after Austin
(1990).

The emphasis, then, of the social-community accommodation is on
communication between different schools of thought. Accommodation involves
understanding the key issues of each paradigm, appreciating the different views
of others, allowing multiple contributions to the same inquiry (constructing
requirements for the redesign of an information system, for example).

However, this type of accommodation has its dangers, both for practitioners
and paradigms. First, social-community accommodation may be *more apparent
than real*. Multi-disciplinary teams are ways to provide different perspectives.
Their differences produce a wide range and diversity of points of view. However,
apparently different theorists may be located within the same paradigm even if
they do not share identical perspectives (Burrel & Morgan, 1979). Socio-technical
theory still operates within a traditional functionalist paradigm, despite its social
perspective. Multi-disciplinary teams, therefore, often fail to give an all-round view.
The second danger is *incorporation*. Alternative paradigms may be regarded as
simply points of view to be considered, and if possible, rebuffed or incorporated
within the dominant orthodoxy. Such a view favours incorporation as the line of
intellectual development.

The third danger is that non-dominant paradigms are forced to take up the role
of *handmaiden* to the dominant paradigm (Guba & Lincoln, 1989). This situation
occurs when an alternative paradigm is used to make good the deficiencies of the
dominant one without calling that one into question. An ethnomethodological
approach to inquiry may be tacked onto a conventional software development

---

[3]Note that both of these types of accommodation would be required to support dependent
multidisciplinary practice by practitioner.

process to unearth social issues of interest that can be passed onto the software engineer to inform the 'real design work'.

Despite these dangers, the social-community accommodation of paradigms has been pursued in RE. Macaulay (1996) proposes to improve the communication process between different disciplines in the early phases of information systems design. A number of requirements methods attempt to integrate methods from different paradigms, e.g. MEASUR (Stamper, 1994). All these methods attempt to integrate a social/organisational perspective (such as Checkland's (1981) soft systems methodology) with a software engineering perspective (such as JSD or Object Oriented Analysis).

Finally, although for social-community accommodation it is not necessary for each researcher to be able to operate within different paradigms, each researcher should appreciate other views from alternative paradigms. However, the individuals involved may not even be able to reach this level of appreciation.

The depth of the paradigm socialisation processes leads to a fourth danger. Each paradigm may be sufficiently divergent, and the emotional and political commitments so high, that accommodation within either research or practice, may produce only *dissonance* and *incoherence* (Lincoln, 1990).

In sum, then, we conclude that the social-community accommodation of paradigms has a number of dangers that need to be appreciated, and avoided, for communication between paradigms to be successful.

3.5   Individual Accommodation of Paradigms

A further implication from earlier arguments is that the socialisation of individuals into accepting the assumptions of a paradigm might lead to a fundamental separation of people in one paradigm from another. Paradigms and their communities may constrain the behaviour and beliefs of their individual members. Such constraints may lead individuals, having only limited exposure to alternative perspectives, to conclude that theirs is the only way to think and operate. Representatives of different paradigms, then, may live in different worlds, hold mutually exclusive beliefs, use different vocabularies and have different ways of seeing. Despite such differences, however, we might still ask whether, "an individual researcher or practitioner can accommodate various paradigms?" — after (Austin, 1990).

Firestone (1990) believes that paradigm accommodation depends on one's stance on the nature of paradigms, the philosophical principles and research practice. Those who argue that paradigms are incompatible view them as systems of rules that are largely deductive; where assumptions about the nature of the world (ontology), and how one knows it (epistemology), govern the conduct of the research. Firestone suggests an alternative conception that views the paradigm-practice relationship as bi-directional, rather than uni-directional. In practice, researchers use a variety of imperfect approaches to enhance the credibility of their arguments.

In short, Firestone believes that an accommodation of paradigms is possible at the level of the individual, and argues that individuals should let the various paradigms inform practice to the extent that they are useful. The methods that characterise paradigms can be combined by the individual to solve particular problems and answer particular questions. With respect to RE, Macaulay (1996) suggests that a requirements engineer might develop a portfolio of techniques which can be drawn upon, depending on the given situation, and be used in combination as required.

Although Firestone's bi-directional understanding opens up the possibility of personal accommodation, few practitioners consciously articulate the paradigms from which they borrow techniques. They are unlikely to understand the implications of using such techniques. Such practitioners are content to live with internal inconsistencies that they neither recognise nor even particularly value (Crandall, 1990).

Individual accommodation of paradigms, then, requires that the role of the paradigm be brought into the realm of conscious thought. Schon (1983) suggests that such a conscious use of paradigms may be a difficult, but not an impossible task. Given a sufficient understanding of alternative paradigms, then, an individual may behave congruently with selected paradigms.

Lincoln (1990) believes that learning to use and possibly adopting a new paradigm is an intensely personal process, evolving not only from intellectual, but also personal, social and possibly political transformations. Reinharz (1981) has developed a model of the process by which individuals develop a commitment and ability to operate within a different paradigm.

We conclude that individuals may be able to operate in more than one paradigm; but that such practical accommodation can only take place over time, either by conversion or critical reflection.

4   Criteria for Support for Dependent MDP in RE

Earlier, we explored the general notion of dependent MDP in RE, and have highlighted a number of problems with dependent MDP by practitioner (Table 1). We have argued that the root cause of such problems lies in the philosophical incommensurability of paradigms.

We propose that dependent MDP by practitioner relies upon the practical accommodation of alternative paradigms. Overcoming the problems of dependent MDP by practitioner relies upon: communication between different 'schools of thought' (i.e. social community accommodation); and the need for individual practitioners consciously to articulate, reflect upon, and perhaps even operate within, alternative paradigms (i.e. individual accommodation).

In Table 2, we have condensed the discussions of this paper into a set of non-exhaustive *criteria* which, if met, would support the practical accommodation of paradigms and hence support dependent multidisciplinary requirements engineering practice.

This paper suggests that overcoming the problems associated with dependent MDP by practitioner depends upon the practical accommodation of alternative paradigms. We have proposed a number of criteria that any type of support (such as methodological support) should aim to meet in order to facilitate the practical accommodation of paradigms, and hence overcome some of the paradigmatic constraints acting upon dependent MDP.

A. Criteria for the social-community accommodation of paradigms

Any approach that aims to support the practical accommodation of paradigms should:

1. Support multi-paradigmatic contributions to the same inquiry (Austin, 1990).

2. Help practitioners understand the key issues of each paradigm (Crandall, 1990).

3. Help practitioners appreciate the views of those operating in a different paradigm (Austin, 1990).

4. Allow each paradigm to express itself independently of the other (Burrel & Morgan, 1979).

5. Help improve communication between practitioners of different paradigms (Guba & Lincoln, 1989)

6. Help practitioners understand the practical implications of alternative paradigm positions (Skrtic, 1990).

7. Help practitioners understand alternative beliefs (Burrel & Morgan, 1979).

8. Help practitioners understand the values and norms of alternative paradigms (Schon, 1983).

B. Criteria for the individual accommodation of paradigms

Any approach that aims to support the practical accommodation of paradigms should:

9. Bring the role of the paradigm into the realm of conscious thought (Schon, 1983).

10. Support practitioners in the conscious articulation of alternative paradigm positions (Crandall, 1990).

11. Help practitioners change their own behaviour and beliefs (LeCompte, 1990).

12. Help practitioners use different vocabularies (Jackson & Carter, 1991).

13. Support practitioners in the enumeration of specific paradigm positions and criticisms (Reinharz, 1981).

14. Support practitioners in the management of commitment and critical reflection (Reinharz, 1981).

Table 2: Criteria for Support for the Practical Accommodation of Paradigms.

References

Austin, A. E. (1990), Discussion on Accommodation, *in* E. G. Guba (ed.), *The Paradigm Dialog*, Sage Publications.

Burrel, G. & Morgan, G. (1979), *Sociological Paradigms and Organisational Analysis*, Heinemann.

Checkland, P. B. (1981), *Systems Thinking, Systems Practice*, John Wiley & Sons.

Chua, W. (1986), "Radical Developments in Accounting Thought", *Accounting Review* **61**(4), 601–632.

Crandall, D. (1990), Peering at Paradigms through the Prism of Practice Improvement, *in* E. G. Guba (ed.), *The Paradigm Dialog*, Sage Publications.

Denley, I. (1999), Dialectic Approach to Multidisciplinary Practice in Requirements Engineering, PhD thesis, University College London, London, UK.

Firestone, W. (1990), Accommodation: Towards a Paradigm-Praxis Dialectic, *in* E. G. Guba (ed.), *The Paradigm Dialog*, Sage Publications, pp.105–24.

Gasson, S. (1995), User Involvement in Decision Making in Information Systems Development, *in* B. Dahlbom, F. Kämmerer, F. Ljundberg, J. Stage & C. Sørensen (eds.), *Proceedings of IRIS 18*, Gothenberg Studies in Informatics, Report 7. http://iris.informatik.gu.se/conference/iris18/iris1826.html.

Guba, E. G. & Lincoln, Y. S. (1989), *Fourth Generation Evaluation*, Sage Publications.

Guba, E. G. & Lincoln, Y. S. (1994), Competing Paradigms in Qualitative Research, *in* N. K. Denzin & Y. S. Lincoln (eds.), *The Handbook of Qualitative Research*, Sage Publications, chapter 6, pp.105–17.

Hughes, J., Randall, D. & Shapiro, D. (1993), "From Ethnographic Records to System Design: Some Experiences from the Field", *Computer Supported Cooperative Work* **1**(3), 123–41.

Jackson, N. & Carter, P. (1991), "In Defence of Paradigm Incommensurability", *Organization Studies* **12**, 109–27.

Kitchener, R. (1986), *Piaget's Theory of Knowledge*, Yale University Press.

Kuhn, T. S. (1962), *The Structure of Scientific Revolution*, University of Chicago Press.

Kuhn, T. S. (1970), *The Structure of Scientific Revolution*, second edition, University of Chicago Press.

LeCompte, M. D. (1990), Emergent Paradigms: How New? How Necessary, *in* E. G. Guba (ed.), *The Paradigm Dialog*, Sage Publications, pp.167–87.

Lincoln, Y. (1990), The Making of a Constructivist, *in* E. G. Guba (ed.), *The Paradigm Dialog*, Sage Publications, pp.67–87.

Long, J. & Dowell, J. (1989), Conceptions of the Discipline of HCI: Craft, Applied Science and Engineering, *in* A. Sutcliffe & L. Macaulay (eds.), *People and Computers V (Proceedings of HCI'89)*, Cambridge University Press, pp.9–34.

Macaulay, L. A. (1996), *Requirements Engineering*, Springer-Verlag.

Reinharz, S. (1981), Implementing New Paradigm Research: A Model for Training and Practice, *in* P. Reason & J. Rowan (eds.), *Human Inquiry: A Sourcebook of New Paradigm Research*, John Wiley & Sons, pp.415–36.

Sankey, H. (1994), *The Incommensurability Thesis*, Avebury.

Scaife, M., Curtis, E. & Hill, C. (1994), "Interdisciplinary Collaboration: A Case Study of Software Development for Fashion Designers", *Interacting with Computers* **6**(4), 395–410.

Schon, D. A. (1983), *The Reflective Practitioner: How Professionals think in Action*, Basic Books.

Skrtic, T. M. (1990), Social Accommodation: Towards a Dialogical Discourse in Educational Inquiry, *in* E. G. Guba (ed.), *The Paradigm Dialog*, Sage Publications, pp.125–35.

Sommerville, I., Rodden, T., Sawyer, P., Bentley, R. & Twidale, M. (1993), Integrating Ethonography into the Requirements Engineering Process, *in Proceedings of the International Symposium on Requirements Engineering (RE'93)*, IEEE Computer Society Press, pp.165–173.

Sommerville, I., Sawyer, P. & Viller, S. (1998), Viewpoints for Requirements Elicitation: A Practical Approach, *in Proceedings of the 4th International Symposium on Requirements Engineering (RE'98)*, IEEE Computer Society Press, pp.74–81.

Stamper, R. (1994), Social Norms in Requirements Analysis — An Outline of MEASUR, *in* M. Jirotka & J. Goguen (eds.), *Requirements Engineering: Social and Technical Issues*, Academic Press.

Sutcliffe, A. G. (1997), A Technique Combination Approach to Requirements Engineering, *in* J. Mylopoulos (ed.), *Proceedings of the 3rd International Symposium on Requirements Engineering (RE'97)*, IEEE Computer Society Press, pp.65–74.

Weaver, G. & Gioia, D. (1995), "Paradigms Lost: Incommensurability vs. Structurationist Inquiry", *Organization Studies* **15**(4), 565–589.

Improving and Mediating Software-to-Usability Engineering Communication

H Antunes, A Seffah, T Radhakrishnan & S Pestina

Department of Computer Science, Concordia University, 1455 de Maisonneuve W, Montreal PQ H3G 1M8, Canada

Tel: *+1 514 848 3024*

Fax: *+1 514 848 2830*

Email: *{antunes,seffah,krishnan,pestina}@cs.concordia.ca*

URL: *http://www.cs.concordia.ca/*

In the last five years, many software development teams have tried to integrate the user-centred design techniques into their software engineering lifecycles, in particular in the use case driven software engineering lifecycle. However, because of lack of understanding and communication between two diverse teams and cultures, they often run into problems. One problem arises from the fact that the software engineering community has their own techniques and tools for managing the whole development lifecycle including usability issues, and it is not clear where exactly in this usability engineering techniques should be placed and integrated with existing software engineering methods to maximise benefits gained from both. This paper identifies the principles of a cost-effective communication line between human factors/usability specialists and software development teams. It also describes a tool that can help to understand, define and improve this communication line while facilitating the integration of usability in the software development lifecycle. As a case study, we will consider two popular requirements engineering processes: user-centred requirements process as defined in ISO 13407 and implemented in RESPECT and the use case driven requirements process as defined and implemented in the Rational Unified Process.

Keywords: usability engineering, software development lifecycle, use cases user-centred design, human-to-human communication.

1   Introduction

For small-size projects, software development teams can mostly avoid the direct involvement of usability experts, due in particular to the availability of design guidelines and usability patterns, heuristics for evaluation or tasks flowcharts to supplement the functional requirements analysis. However, for large-scale projects it is necessary, almost impossible, not to involve explicitly usability specialists, at least during the requirements analysis and usability testing steps. Culled from our day-to-day experience, four different ways, for involving usability expertise in the software development teams, are possible:

1. resort to third part companies specialised in usability engineering;

2. involve a consultant expert in usability;

3. form/create a usability team; and finally

4. provide training to some members of the development team that can act as the champions of the usability.

However, whatever the approach chosen for involving usability engineers in the software development lifecycle, the difficulties of communication between the software development team and the usability specialists could seriously compromise the integration of the usability expertise in software development lifecycle. Among the difficulties of communication, one can mention the educational gap, the use of different notations, languages and tools, as well as the perception of the role and importance of the design artefacts. For example, in spite of the similarities existing between use cases and task analysis (Artim et al., 1998; Forbrig, 1999; Seffah & Hayne, 1999) and the advantages by their complementarity uses, the software and usability engineers often try to substitute one by other.

The ultimate objective of our research is to build a framework, while contrasting and comparing the software and usability engineering lifecycles, for improving and mediating the communication between the software development teams and usability engineers. This framework is governed by the questions below we are addressing:

- How can the software engineering lifecycle be re-designed so that end users and usability engineers can act as active participant throughout the whole lifecycle?

- Which artefacts collected and generated in the usability engineering lifecycle are relevant and what are their added values and relationships with software engineering artefacts?

- What are the usability techniques and activities for gathering and specifying these relevant artefacts?

- How can these artefacts, techniques and activities be presented to software engineers (notations), as well as integrated (tool support) in the software development lifecycle in general?

2   Background and Related Work

The following are only some of the many investigations that, over the last few years, have tried to answer such questions.

Artim et al. (1998) emphasises the role of task analysis by providing a user-centric view of a suite of applications, and then emphasises use cases by providing each application with a method of exploring user-system interaction and describing system behaviour.   Jarke (1999) points out that scenarios are used in software engineering as intermediate design artefacts in an expanded goal-driven change process.   They provide a task-oriented design decomposition that can be used from many perspectives, including usability trade-off, iterative development and manageable software design object models.   Ralyte (1999) in the CREWS project develops a framework for integrating different kinds of scenarios into requirement engineering methods.   Constantine & Lockwood (1999) suggests that use case specifiers first prepare lightweight use case model descriptions (*essential use cases*) that do not contain any implicit user interface decisions. Later on, the user interface designer can use these essential use cases as input to create the user interface without being bound by any implicit decisions. Nunes (1999) proposes to annotate use cases using non-functional requirements at the level of abstraction at which they should to be considered. Rosson (1999) proposes combining the development of tasks and object-oriented models, which are viewed as a refinement of rapid prototyping and an extension of scenario-based analysis. Krutchen (1999) introduces the concept of *use case storyboard* as a logical and conceptual description of how a use case is provided by the user interface, including the interaction required between the actor(s) and the system.

3   A brief Description of the Processes Investigated in Our Case Study

As starting point of our investigations and a research case study, we are considering the following two requirements processes (Figure 1):

- The use case driven requirements workflow as defined in the Unified software engineering Process (UP) proposed by Rational Software Inc. (Booch et al., 1999).

- The RESPECT framework (**RE**quirements **SPEC**ification in **T**ematics), which is concerned with the capture and specification of end-user requirements (Maguire, 1998).

3.1   Capturing User Requirements as Use Cases in the Unified Process

The goal of the requirements process, as defined in the unified process (UP), is to describe what the system should in terms of functionalities do in terms of functionalities, and allow the developers and the customer to agree on this description. Use cases are the most important requirements artefact. It is used by:

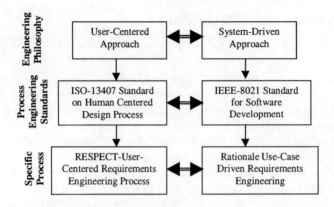

Figure 1: A view of our research case study and framework.

1. the customer to validate that the system will be what is expected in terns of functionalities, and

2. by the developers to achieve a better understanding of the requirements and a starting point for technical design.

A Use case storyboarding, which is a logical and conceptual description of how use cases are provided by the user interface, includes the required interaction between the user(s) and the system. Storyboards represent a high-level understanding of the user interface, and are much faster to develop than the user interface itself. The use case storyboards can thus be used to create and evaluate several versions of the user interface before it is prototyped designed and implemented (Krutchen, 1999).

One of the weaknesses of use case driven requirements workflow is that the use cases attempt to describe representative ways in which the user will interact with the software but is not comprehensive. Another weakness of this process is that the main people involved in this process are stakeholders and technical persons including the use case specifier and the user interface developer. The end-user is not directly involved. The use case specifier details the specification for a part of the system's functionalities by describing the requirements aspect of one or several use cases.

3.2 User Requirements Engineering in RESPECT Framework

RESPECT is a user-centred requirements engineering framework developed by European Usability Support Centres. The RESPECT process is a concrete implementation of the iterative user-centred design process for interactive software suggested by the ISO 13407 Standard (ISO, 1999). The RESPECT process starts from the point where project is summarised from the end user point of view. By the end of the process, it produced different text-based forms that detail the user interface, user support and help, the physical and organisational context, equipment and hardware constraints, usability goals that must be achieved, as well as the system installation procedure.

Although RESPECT is a highly detailed process for capturing and validating context of use and usability requirements with the active involvement of end-users and stakeholders, the text-based forms produced are not easily understandable by software development teams. They are also a source of ambiguity and inconsistency, especially when they are compared to the use cases.

4   Principles for Improving Human-to-Human Communication

Our first step for improving and mediating software-to-usability communication involved identifying complementarities between the use-case requirements and RESPECT processes.   The four principles outlined below summarise these complementarities.

Firstly, RESPECT captures a complete description of the context of use including user characteristics, task analysis, as well as the physical, technical and organisational environments in which the system will be used. Although in theory use cases have the potential to gather the non-functional requirements that are a simplified description of the context of use, in practice, use cases have been used for gathering the system functionalities and features including technical capabilities and constraints. Therefore:

Principle 1: *Context of use and functional requirements should be considered as two views of the requirements picture. The software view on this picture is a set of artefacts describing the functionalities and the technical requirements of the system. The usability view is a set of artefacts describing the context of use and the usability goals/factors in which the functionalities will be used.*

To a certain extent, this principle means that both the software and the usability views are important. Table 1 indicates the software and usability views for each of the processes that we considered in our case study. Such classification of the artefact can facilitate the identification of potential relationships between artefacts.

Secondly, in RESPECT, the context of use is described using a non-formal notation which is easy to understand by end-users and stakeholders. However, these forms are a cause for inconsistency and ambiguity when used by software developers. The artefacts that are produced and the semi-formal notation used in use case approach are more understandable by software developers. Use cases as a notation can also support, in a certain extent, automatic generation of code (Krutchen, 1999; Booch et al., 1999).

Principle 2: *As Artim et al.'s (1998) discussed about "one model, but many views and notations". We strongly share his belief that different notations for the same concept may foster communication between persons. This means that we can use different notations to describe the artefacts related to the functional and context of use including text-based forms and use cases. However, this requires maintaining the correspondence between multiple views at an abstract level using a high level notation. As we will discuss it the next section, we selected XML as an abstract description of requirements.*

	RESPECT	UP Requirements Workflow
Software View	General system characteristics System functions and features User interface	Use case diagram Requirements attributes Boundary class Use case storyboard User interface prototype
Usability View	Organisational structure Task scenario and interaction steps Technical environment User support Physical environment Social and Organisational environment	Stakeholder and users needs Additional requirements
Other artefacts that cannot be classified.	Standards and style guides to apply Test plan Implementation plan	Vision document Glossary

Table 1: Relationship between RESPECT and UP requirements artefacts.

Thirdly, in RESPECT as in other similar approaches, usability specialists use the *context of use* as an important input for usability testing. Software developers use the functional requirement artefacts as a starting point for technical design and implementation.

Principle 3: *A common step to the two processes should include activities for reviewing and validating the integrity and consistency of all requirements artefacts from both the usability and software views. After validation, we should generate a usability testing and implementation portfolios.*

For example, the usability-testing portfolio should include the entire usability requirement artefacts that will be used during usability testing. The implementation plan should include the artefacts that required for implementing the system.

Fourthly, it is important for usability-to-software engineering collaboration and for consistency and coherence of requirement artefacts to gain a high-level understanding of the system and this from the beginning. Therefore:

Principle 4: *The requirements should start when a representative set of users and/or stakeholders are invited to summarise the system from the future user's perspective. They are mainly asked to answer different questions that we organised in a system summary form. Users and stakeholders, the main contributors during this step, are invited to give brief answers to these questions. All completed forms are then analyzed and compiled in a unique system summary form by usability engineers. This compiled form is approved by software developers, stakeholders and users. It is used as a roadmap during the requirement process and represents a general consensus on the system.*

Questions	Assumptions
What is the purpose of the system?	ISO 9000-based quality system over an Intranet.
Why is this system necessary?	Supporting the development of the company outside the country (new clients, remote offices.)
Who will use the system?	Employees and some of the company's clients.
What will the users accomplish with the system?	Access to quality procedures and associated forms. Learn the quality system and the ISO 9000 standard
Where will the system be used?	Standalone workstations and personal digital assistants.
How will users learn to use the system?	Introductory course and online assistant.
How will the system be installed?	By a Webmaster for the server version, and by employees on their PDA (download from the server).
How will the system be maintained?	By a Webmaster and a quality control manager.

Table 2: An Example of the System Summary Form.

Table 2 is an example of the system summary form that we developed. User-centred requirements frameworks such RESPECT and use case-driven approach supporters (Constantine & Lockwood, 1999) suggested similar questions.

5 A Framework for User-centred and Use-case Driven Requirements Engineering

Based on these principles, we iteratively defined, used and validated a framework for improving software-to-usability engineering communication (Figure 2). This framework clarifies how usability expert activities can be incorporated in the software development lifecycles. It also clarifies the relationships between activities done by software engineers and usability experts.

Mainly the framework has been used in 10 projects we conducted at CRIM (Computer Research Institute of Montreal) between 1997 and 2000. All the projects are related to Web-based interactive systems including, for example, an environment for managing ISO 9001 documentation, a tool for sharing resources as well as a Web-based training system. RESPECT and use case-driven approaches were used simultaneously by software and usability experts. At the end of each project, we conduct a series of ethnographic interviews where all participants were interviewed. We asked them to describe their activities during the projects and to highlight the difficulties in term of communication. We also reviewed the framework with all participants and asked them about potential improvements.

6 Toward An XML-Based Tool for Identifying, Studying and Mediating Human-to-Human Communication

As part of the SUCRE project (Software and Usability Concurrent Requirement Engineering), we developed a tool (called SUCRE Mediator) for studying and

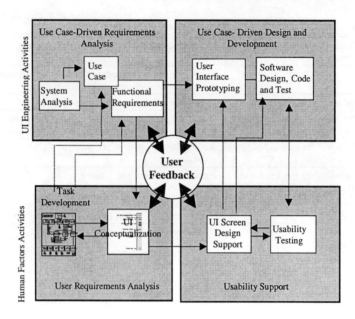

Figure 2: A framework for user-driven and use case-based user interfaces engineering.

comparing processes, as well as for mediating the communication between usability and software engineers. The tool can be used by researchers and software process engineering groups (SPEG) that are generally responsible for defining, implementing and improving software development processes.

In SUCRE Mediator, a process describes *who* is doing *what, how,* and *when.* It is represented by the four process modelling elements: actor, the 'who', activities, the 'how', artefacts, the 'what', and tool, the 'when'. Each activity is characterised by a description, a status, actors involved, artefacts used or produced by the activity, etc. Activities can have different kinds of relationships between them. The membership relationship defines the relation between an activity and a step. In the same way, the dependence relationship between activities is useful to infer the status of an activity from its predecessor activities.

Within SUCRE Mediator, processes are described and stored in an XML database. We choose XML as a process markup language because of its high compatibility with the Internet, which is a convenient medium for mediating human-to-human communication.

The SUCRE Mediator helps to visualise processes in a cognitively acceptable way. This tool supports three different basic representations:

- DYNAMIC TREE displays activities as leaves in a tree of processes and steps.

- GRAPH displays the interdependence of activities inside one process, illustrating the dependence relationship.

- MATRIX displays any membership relationships between elements in different level of representation, e.g. a step has activities, the user wants to see the activities of the current step, or in an higher level all the activities for all the steps of the current process. The set of views is not closed yet; we may add other views if they are considered useful.

The user can open simultaneously different processes that he or she wants to compare. By default, the processes will be displayed using a DYNAMIC TREE representation. When the user selects a specific node, SUCRE Mediator displays the related views. When the user selects a specific activity or artefact presented in a view, a popup menu triggered by a right mouse button click, allows the user to change the activity status, to add or remove activity's artefacts, resources and actors. The activity status can be changed with the only following constraints:

- If the new status is APPROVED, then the predecessors could block the change in case these predecessor activities are not approved yet

- If it's about a return to non-approved, then the successors could block the change in case when all the successor activities are approved.

By changing the status of activities, new precedence relationships are created between this activity and other activities. This new 'generated' process can be saved in a new XML file on the disk. The colours assigned to each status value can be visualised and changed. This new configuration could be saved for later utilisation into a XML configuration file. The user can switch between any of the previously described views offered for the same process in order to identify for example the critical activities may have different name in different processes, or the possible relationships between the 2 processes, for instance between the artefacts produced at different steps in the 2 development processes.

7   Conclusion and Further Investigations

In this paper, we presented our investigations on how to improve and mediate the communication between usability expert and software development teams. With respect to experimentation, two specific processes constitute the focus of our interests: use case-driven and the user-centred requirements engineering processes. Further to the framework for improving software-to-usability engineering communication we defined, we identified the following principles that we consider as critical issues.

First, the requirements of an interactive system must be defined on two levels, but not independent of one another as it is today. The first level is concerned with the specification of the context of use, and the second focuses on functional requirements. Different specification notations may be used for the two levels, but they should exploit an integrated representation of all the requirements artefacts. In our case, we adopted the text-based forms as used in RESPECT and the graphical representation of use cases as defined in Unified Modelling Language.

Secondly, the list of artefacts describing the context of use ensures a good usability specification. Better still, this list can assist with generating functional requirements, at least to a limited extent. This result is fundamental because it can minimise requirements artefacts inconsistency and improve communication between software and usability engineers.

These results encourage us to pursue our investigations by developing more the XML-based tool described in this paper. Within this tool, software engineers can understand the issues of:

1. how to redesign the software engineering lifecycle so that end users and usability engineers can be active participants, and

2. how the artefacts collected and generated in the user-centred design could be integrated in software development lifecycle.

References

Artim, J., van Harmelen, M., Butler, K., Gulliksen, J., Henderson, A., Kovacevic, S., Lu, S., Overmyer, S., Reaux, R., Roberts, D., Tarby, J. & Linden, K. (1998), "Incorporating Work, Process and Task Analysis into Commercial and Industrial Object-oriented Systems Development", *ACM SIGCHI Bulletin* **30**(4), 198.

Booch, G., Rumbaugh, J. & Jacobson, I. (1999), *The Unified Modelling Language User Guide*, Addison–Wesley.

Constantine, L. & Lockwood, L. (1999), *Software for Use: A Practical Guide to the Models and Methods of Usage-centered Design*, Addison–Wesley.

Forbrig, P. (1999), Task and Object-Oriented Development of Interactive Systems — How Many Models are Necessary?, *in* D. J. Duke & A. Puerta (eds.), *Design, Specification and Verification of Interactive Systems(DSVIS) '99*, Springer-Verlag, pp.124–36.

ISO (1999), "ISO 13407 International Standard. Human-centred Design Processes for Interactive Systems". International Organization for Standardization, Genève, Switzerland.

Jarke, M. (1999), "Scenarios for Modeling", *Communications of the ACM* **42**(1), 47–8.

Krutchen, P. (1999), Use Case Storyboards in the Rational Unified Process, *in* A. M. D. Moreira & S. Demeyer (eds.), *Object-oriented Technology, ECOOP'99 Workshop Reader*, Vol. 1743 of *Lecture Notes in Computer Science*, Springer-Verlag, pp.244–56. Workshop on Integrating Human Factors in Use Case and OO Methods.

Maguire, M. (1998), RESPECT User Centered Requirements Handbook, WP5 Deliverable D5.3, EC Telematics Applications Program, Project TE 2010 RESPECT.

Nunes, N. (1999), A Bridge Too Far: Can UML Finally Help Bridge the Gap?, *in* A. Sasse & C. Johnson (eds.), *Human–Computer Interaction — INTERACT '99: Proceedings of the Seventh IFIP Conference on Human–Computer Interaction*, Vol. 1, IOS Press. A paper at the Doctoral Consortium.

Ralyte, J. (1999), Reusing Scenario Based Approaches in Requirement Engineering Methods: CREWS Method Base, *in Proceedings of the First International Workshop on the Requirements Engineering Process — Innovative Techniques, Models, Tools to Support the RE Process*, IEEE Computer Society Press.

Rosson, M. (1999), "Integrating Development of Tasks and Object Models", *Communications of the ACM* **42**(1), 49–56.

Seffah, A. & Hayne, C. (1999), Enhancing Use-cases Driven Process with Elements of a User-centered Requirements Framework, *in* A. M. D. Moreira & S. Demeyer (eds.), *Object-oriented Technology, ECOOP'99 Workshop Reader*, Vol. 1743 of *Lecture Notes in Computer Science*, Springer-Verlag, pp.244–56. Workshop on Integrating Human Factors in Use Case and OO Methods.

Usability Engineering

KALDI: A CAUsE Tool for Supporting Testing and Analysis of User Interaction

Ghassan Al-Qaimari & Darren McRostie

Department of Computer Science, RMIT University, Melbourne, Victoria, 3001 Australia

Tel: *+61 3 9225 3213*

Fax: *+61 3 9662 1617*

Email: *{ghassan, mcrostie}@cs.rmit.edu.au*

URL: *http://www.cs.rmit.edu.au/~ghassan*

In this paper we describe the design and implementation of KALDI, a Computer Aided Usability Engineering (CAUsE) tool, built to automate many of the tedious and time consuming aspects of empirical usability testing. KALDI, uses only software techniques to record precise user actions as well as to capture a video-like recording of the user interface being tested. It also allows for the detailed analysis of the recorded user actions through the use of a sophisticated visualisation of data.

The KALDI tool has many advantages over other techniques, including the ability to conduct tests without using specialised equipment, visually represent user actions at different levels of detail, record user performances from remote locations, perform automatic classification of abstract event data into user actions and the synchronised display of video-like playback with an indication of the corresponding recorded action/event.

Furthermore, we discuss in this paper the benefits of integrating this class of CAUsE tool in future User Interface Management Systems (UIMS). These benefits include helping to encourage usability testing throughout the development lifecycle, as well as providing a basis for interactive system designers and usability specialists to make sound design decisions more efficiently.

Keywords: , CAUsE tools, evaluation, GOMS, cognitive walkthrough

1 Introduction

The benefits of conducting usability evaluations throughout the development lifecycle of a software product have been well demonstrated through many case studies (Karat, 1997). These benefits include increasing productivity of the users, increasing the likelihood of a product being used to it's full potential, reducing training costs and increasing the marketability of a product (Bevan & Macleod, 1994).

Usability testing can be achieved by carefully examining and video taping a number of test users attempting to accomplish a pre-determined series of tasks using the interactive software (or a mock-up of the software) to be tested. The video recording is then analyzed by logging the actions the users perform as well as the time each action takes. From this detailed study, the analyst can choose the best approach to take in an interface design, and can identify key problem areas in the usability of the system (Nielsen, 1993a; Rubin, 1994).

This technique provides good results if undertaken correctly, but requires a number of sample users, specialised video equipment for both recording and playing back (with accurate time information), and takes a significant amount of time for a skilled usability specialist to analyze (Nielsen, 1993a; Crellin et al., 1990). Because of the expense in both time and equipment required to undertake this form of empirical user testing, other techniques have been devised for faster, cheaper evaluations. These techniques fall into two categories: analytical and inspection.

Analytical techniques rely on a skilled usability expert to understand and simulate the way a user would attempt to accomplish tasks using the interface under test. Two such techniques are Cognitive Walkthrough (Lewis, 1997; Wharton et al., 1992) and GOMS (Card et al., 1993; Kieras, 1997). The Cognitive Walkthrough evaluates systems by analyzing the mental processes required of users. This technique helps determine how easy it is to explore and learn a system, identifies potential problems and reasons for these problems. The technique is useful for evaluating the usability of systems which users have not yet seen. It reveals how successfully does a particular design guide the unfamiliar user through to the completion of their task. GOMS attempts to evaluate how efficient an interface will be by looking at the actions required to achieve goals and summing the estimated duration for each action. This technique helps decide between different interface options and can detect potential problems, however it does not identify the reasons behind these problems. GOMS methods are applicable in cases where users have already become familiar with the system, and they have the required cognitive skill (Card et al., 1993).

Inspection techniques (Nielsen, 1992), on the other hand, use a set of guidelines or rules with which an interface design is compared, and are usually performed by one or more usability experts. One such technique is a Heuristic (or Expert) evaluation, in which a number of evaluators compare the interface to a set of nine heuristics or design principles. This technique can uncover potential usability problems and the reasons for these problems, but it does not effectively reveal user confusion, nor does it measure user speed of performance.

Although faster and cheaper, analytical and inspection techniques have two main problems: Firstly, neither of the techniques utilises test users, instead relying on a simulation of the user. This may lead to problems if the usability expert did not fully understand the users of the system, which may lead to major problems being undetected. Secondly, they both require the use of skilled usability specialist whose time and availability is usually limited (Newman & Lamming, 1995).

Due to the expense and difficulty involved in conducting usability activities, usability evaluation of any kind is often left out of the software development lifecycle or performed only towards the end of the cycle where it's usefulness is limited. For usability evaluations to have a significant affect on the quality of an interactive system, they must be conducted throughout the entire software development lifecycle, whenever crucial design decisions must be made.

Currently, there is a recent trend towards developing automated tools for making usability analysis methods and empirical testing more effective. These tools are termed Computer Aided Usability Engineering (or CAUsE) tools. In this research work, we introduce KALDI[1] (**K**eyboard/mouse **A**ction **L**ogger and **D**isplayInstrument), developed to combine an event logging and screen recording tool which forms part of the Java Abstract Windowing Toolkit (AWT) (Geary, 1999) with a Java based analysis and playback tool. The analysis tool displays the logged events in a graphical notation showing the description and duration of the recorded user action, which is combined with a linked video playback of the program output and mouse movements. KALDI demonstrates that usability testing can easily and cheaply be conducted at any stage of the development lifecycle, giving the developers the ability to measure the performance and detect the problems of an interactive system.

Further more, we will also propose in this paper that CAUsE tools such as the one we developed should be integrated in future graphical toolkits and UIMSs in order to reduce the gap between design/implementation and usability evaluation. This integration would promote active and ongoing usability assessment during the entire development lifecycle.

The paper is organised as follows: Section 2 contains background information; Section 3 reviews existing CAUsE tools; Section 4 provides a detailed description of the KALDI tool, and summarises its advantages and limitations; Section 5 presents our conclusions.

2   Usability and User Centred Design

According to the International Standards Organisation, ISO 9241-11 (ISO, 1998), usability is defined as "the extent to which a product can be used by specified users to achieve specified goals with effectiveness, efficiency and satisfaction in a specified context of use." Effectiveness refers to the accuracy and completeness with which users achieve specified goals. Efficiency refers to the resources (time, money, mental

---

[1] According to legend, Kaldi was an Abyssinian goat herder who learned of the effects of the coffee bean when he noticed that his normally docile heard had become lively for no apparent reason. On further inspection he noticed that the goats had been nibbling on some bright red berries of a nearby plant, and so coffee was discovered (Baxter, 1995).

effort etc.) expended in relation to the accuracy and completeness with which users achieve goals. Satisfaction refers to freedom from discomfort, and positive attitudes to the use of the product. Context of use refers to the users, goals, tasks, equipment (hardware, software and materials), and the physical and social environments in which a product is used.

Producing highly usable interfaces on the first attempt (even when the most skilled usability specialists are involved) is rare. An iterative and user-centred approach is usually required, with the results of usability evaluations being fed back into the development process, steering the development effort towards an acceptable level of usability (Nielsen, 1993b; Hix & Hartson, 1993).

Traditional software development methods, such as the waterfall and spiral lifecycles, do not allow for this type of user-centred and iterative process (Hix & Hartson, 1993; Boehm, 1988; Norman & Draper, 1986; Ryan & Al-Qaimari, 2000). Users are typically involved in contributing to the early stages and late delivery/acceptance stages of the cycle, while the steps from specification to delivery are treated as a linear progression of development, with only limited iterations between adjacent stages. With such a methodology, an incomplete assessment of the users needs during the specification or design stages will not be detected until the product is delivered and the users find it does not fit their tasks.

In HCI literature, user-centred design and development methodologies, such as the Star lifecycle (Hix & Hartson, 1993), have been proposed for interactive systems. The Star lifecycle is highly iterative and self-correcting through placing usability evaluation in the centre of the lifecycle, and emphasising the importance of prototyping. Therefore, usability activities become an integral part of the development process. The Star lifecycle is also multi-disciplinary, as it recognises the need to involve different skills, such as human factors and instruction theory, in the design and development process.

The task of design involves a complex set of processes. Design is a goal directed process in which the goal is to conceive and realise some new thing. But, with some training and a lot of practical experience, the accuracy of performance increases and people become or are labelled as 'experts' (Jeffries et al., 1981). Central to this notion is that there is a positive correction of accuracy and performance. There is a vast range of definitions of expert used in the literature and the definition of novice also varies widely. Most studies use experience as an operationalisation of expertise rather than actual performance. One approach to defining expert and novice is to take less experienced performers and more experienced performers and call the former novices and the latter experts. In many skill domains the distinction between experts and novices is clear: experts perform far better than novices do. First there are significant differences in domain knowledge, second there are differences in problem representation, third there are differences in problem perception, and fourth are differences in problem solving. As training and experience increase, people become significantly more accurate and so are labelled expert (Chi et al., 1988). Research shows that these differences in expertise are accompanied by changes in cognitive processes: experts know more than, represent and perceive problems differently from, and have different ways of solving problems from novices (Soloway et al., 1988).

A major problem in research in investigating the transition from novice to expert status, is research design and measurement. In laboratory-based studies, much behavioural data used to investigate cognitive processes have little ecological validity, and may not capture the expertise in the performance of expert subjects. How faithful is the laboratory task to the real thing? Self report data however may not reliably reflect the cognitive processes of subjects especially expert subjects. First their validity depends on high self-insight and second, the ability of the method to be uninvasive. These are just some of the issues in research methodology and measurement which are posed in studies of novice/expert designs in HCI. The present investigation attempts to address these issues by automating the process of user testing to produce more reliable data.

3   CAUsE Tools

There is currently a trend towards improving the effectiveness of the different usability evaluation techniques, discussed earlier, by using computer-based tools to automate repetitive aspects and provide means of viewing the detailed and complex usability data in a simple and meaningful way (Macleod & Rengger, 1993; Nielsen, 1993b). There are few of these Computer Aided Usability Engineering (CAUsE) tools in existence. In this subsection we review three of the more notable ones.

3.1   DRUM

DRUM (Diagnostic Recorder for Usability Measurement) is a video logging and video player control tool (Macleod et al., 1997). It is a commercially available product that runs on an Apple Macintosh computer and is capable of driving several high-end video tape players (with computer interface cards). DRUM assists in the mark-up and logging of video taped sessions. The usability tester plays the videotape (which is controlled and monitored by the computer) and logs the start and end of tasks or critical actions. These log entries are stored along with a videotape index number that allows the computer to cue or rewind the tape to the exact log position.

Once a session has been manually logged by the usability tester, analysis and metric calculation routines can be activated which provide useful statistical information regarding the logged tests. The logs can be viewed and analyzed, but the system does not provide for a graphical view of the information (text based time log only). It is suggested that DRUM is much more efficient than manual video logging. This is because the statistical calculations and overhead of marking up video tape and measuring elapsed times are automated — two to three hours per hour of tape, as opposed to manual logging which often takes ten hours per hour of video (Macleod & Rengger, 1993). However, the actual mark up is manual, needing an experienced usability specialist to mark start and end of user actions, with little scope for automation. Determining the start and end times of actions is also error prone and reliant on the accuracy of the video recorder, amount of tape stretch and the diligence of the human operator.

DRUM uses specialised equipment that requires careful set up and calibration for both the recording and analysis of the usability testing session. This increases the cost and means that the equipment must be available and configured before a usability evaluation can be undertaken, which in turn reduces the likelihood of regular testing.

3.2   UsAGE

UsAGE (User Action Graphing Effort) is an operating system event-logging tool that graphically displays and compares the logs (Uehling & Wolf, 1995). It is a prototype tool which aims to automate the analysis of an empirical usability test and presents the results in a graphical representation. The tool takes a different approach to DRUM. Instead of using a video recording and manual logging, it directly logs the UIMS events as they are generated, and stores them with a time stamp.

UsAGE attempts to automate analysis by graphically comparing the recorded event logs of expert and novice users. The expert actions are displayed as a graph of nodes that extend horizontally across the display. Novice events are displayed as a sequence of nodes that are matched to expert events, with arcs displaying the sequence of the events. Matched events are placed vertically below the expert event, with unmatched events being placed below previously matched events. In UsAGE, nodes are labelled with the UIMS event name, and the events displayed are at a very low conceptual level, making it hard for the analyst to understand how the events relate to the actual operation of the application. To overcome this, UsAGE allows the recorded events to be fed back into the application user interface, which replicates and displays the recorded user's actions.

The UsAGE tool overcomes some of the limitations of pure video tape analysis tools (DRUM for example), and provides a means of graphically viewing and comparing logged actions, and ensures very accurate time information. However the tool has some limitations. As UsAGE displays all logged events, understanding what the user was attempting to accomplish can be missed due to being overwhelmed by large volumes of data.

Although this tool requires no specialised equipment to record and playback the test session, it does require that a copy of tested software is available, with any other supporting data. This may be a problem where the data used by the system is changing in nature (like Internet applications and database systems) or with interfaces that might show unpredictable behaviour as a result to a given action, as is the case with intelligent interfaces.

3.3   Integrated Data Capture and Analysis Tool

The Integrated Data Capture and Analysis tool described by (Hammontree et al., 1992) is a combination of an operating system event logger and video player control tool. It combines the advantages of video based logging tools, as in the case of DRUM, with the benefits of UIMS event loggers, as in UsAGE. The tool uses filters to aggregate the user-generated events into meaningful classifications of the user's actions. This converts verbose system based event records into more useful and simple descriptions of the user's actions. The tool also can be used to control a video tape player, using the time stamped system events as index points on the videotape. This allows the usability tester to easily see how the filtered events relate to the actual application.

This tool removes the need for manual videotape logging while retaining ability to play back, search and quickly retrieve logged events. It also keeps accurate system level logs of the user interaction and presents the data at a higher conceptual level which is more useful to the usability analyst.

Although this tool makes a good attempt at combining the advantages of event logging and video techniques, it still has some limitations. Firstly, it relies on specialised video equipment with a computer-controlled interface. Secondly, it does not present the log data in a graphical way, and it does not allow the usability tester to change the level of detail of the log view to suit the current analysis task. Finally, the tool does not support the concept of hierarchical classifications of user actions, which may lead to the automatic classification presenting the high level user action without the low level actions that contributed to it.

3.4 Summary

The development of CAUsE tools is a new trend, and we can expect to see many more tools in the coming years. The three tools described above are representative of existing CAUsE tools that aim to assist empirical usability testing. They are also representative of the limitations of current tools.

Limitations of video logging tools include:

- Do not possess accurate and precise measurement of time.

- It is possible to miss actions performed by the user that are not highly visible.

- Automation of the classification of actions is very difficult.

- The tools require expensive specialised videotape equipment.

Event logging and automatic filtering tools, on the other hand, possess the following limitations:

- Difficult to conceptually understand how the raw events relate to the interface.

- Difficult to communicate and demonstrate usability problems once they are detected.

- Events capture without automatic filtering generally produces a volume of data, which is difficult to analyze.

- Events capture with automatic filtering can possibly obscure finer interaction details, which may be of importance.

4 KALDI

In this section we present our CAUsE Tool, known as KALDI (Al-Qaimari & McRostie, 1999), which has been developed to address many of the limitations mentioned above. KALDI is a hybrid tool that both logs system events and records the interface display. The tool is designed to graphically display the logged events and allow them to be displayed at different levels of conceptual abstraction. The tool docs not use videotape, but stores screen images directly to the hard drive, and therefore does not limit the frequency of usability tests due to specialised equipment. The tight mapping between the event visualisation and the video-like playback of captured events gives context to otherwise abstract events.

KALDI is implemented using SUN SWING SET (Geary, 1999), and is applicable for currently emerging interface technologies, such as collaborative network based applications. The tight integration with the graphical toolkit provides KALDI with the means of recording internal program state information, as well as the visible program output, which would assist in evaluating and improving adaptive and intelligent interfaces.

The KALDI is a suite of three individual tools: *the live capture tool*; *the live monitoring tool*; and *analysis tool*. The design of each tool within the suite is described in the following subsections.

4.1   The Live Capture Tool

It forms part of the Java Abstract Windowing Toolkit (AWT), and involves monitoring events, taking screen shots, if necessary, and transmitting the data along the network connection. Events in Java are objects that contain information regarding the event, including a reference to the widget that the event is targeting. The live capture tool reads this event information as it is generated and transmits it over the network along with a date-time stamp.

A screen shot is taken whenever an event occurs that might have caused the screen to update. To take a snapshot, a blank in-memory image is created and the widget targeted by the event is 'printed' into the image. The image is then converted to a byte array and transmitted over the network.

The live monitor tool has no user interface of it's own as it forms part of the Java core library, and is invoked remotely from the monitor tool.

4.2   The Monitor Tool

The monitor tool (Figure 1) is a small interactive program that is used by the usability specialist while a test session is being recorded. This tool invokes the capture tool and receives the event and screen capture information, which it displays to the usability specialist and saves to permanent storage.

As the screen capture playback is being displayed, the usability specialist can insert comments and categorise the user's interaction with the software under test by grouping the events into tasks and actions.

The monitoring tool is not fully implemented yet. The current prototype version is capable only of receiving the network connection, saving the data and playing back the live video capture.

After a few test recordings, it became obvious that the saved events and screen captures would consume considerable disk space during lengthy recordings. Compression is applied to the data as it is being saved (using the GZIP algorithm) which reduces the size of the save file by approximately 95%. For example, a one-minute recording of a small sample application produces a save file consuming 2.43megabytes, which is reduced to 24.6kilobytes after compression is applied.

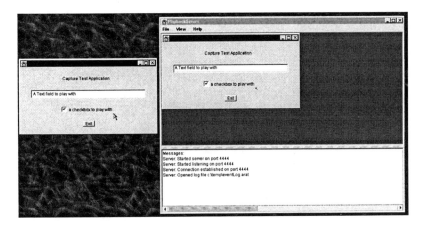

Figure 1: The monitor tool interface recording a sample application beside it.

4.3 The Analysis Tool

The analysis tool is used by the usability specialist after the recording of a test session. It gives the usability specialists the ability to classify the user's interaction with the system, compare user performance and analyze results. This component allows for the playback of recorded screen capture data, the reclassification of raw event data into hierarchical actions and tasks, and provides the usability specialist with an easy way to see how a user performed.

The analysis tool interface is divided into three functional areas (see Figure 2): *the event viewing area* (top right-hand side sub-window), where the raw events, action groups, and tasks are displayed graphically; the playback area (bottom right-hand side sub-window) in which the recorded sessions are played back; and the index area (left-hand side sub-window) in which tasks can be easily selected for display or playback in the opposite two areas. The following sub-sections describe the three areas.

Event Viewing Area It is in this part of the interface that the usability tester classifies the raw events into user actions and tasks. Classification of events is achieved by creating an action group and encapsulating the events (or other action groups) within the new action group. The usability specialist assigns a description to each action group and the encapsulated events are removed from the display and replaced with the action group. Action groups can be expanded by the usability specialist to examine and modify the contents if necessary.

Action groups give meaning to a series of seemingly unrelated raw events. For example, a series of events consisting of: mouse pressed, mouse moved to (x_0, y_0), mouse moved to (x_1, y_1), mouse moved to (x_2, y_2), mouse released, may be encapsulated in an action group with the description 'Drag and Drop'. Action groups may also contain other action groups. This allows the usability specialist to

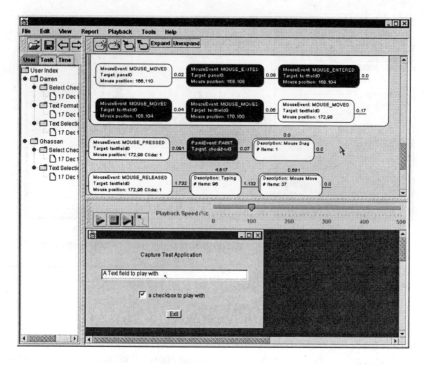

Figure 2: The analysis tool.

create higher-level action groups such as 'Delete file' (which may consist of 'open browser window', 'select file icon', 'drag and drop' action groups).

Events and action groups are encapsulated into a high-level group called a Task. Tasks behave in a similar way to action groups in that they contain other items and may be expanded to show that containment. Tasks are identified with a name, specified by the usability tester, and are also associated with the test user who performed the task.

Both tasks and action groups may be expanded to display their contents. This is achieved by double clicking the task/action group representation or by using the toolbar or menu. When a task/action group is expanded, its box grows and the encapsulated action groups and raw events are displayed inside the expanded task/action group. Once expanded, the encapsulated items can be selected and manipulated (see Figure 3).

Toolbar buttons associated with the event viewing area exist for the following operations:

- Creating a new action group and placing all selected items within the new group.

- Creating a new task and placing all selected items within the new group.

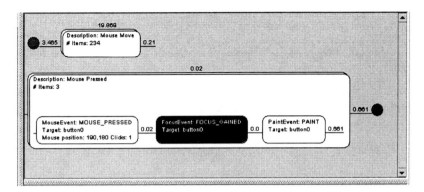

Figure 3: The event display area showing an unexpanded and expanded action group. The blue highlight indicates the currently selected event.

- Expanding (showing the contents) or contracting (hiding the contents) a selected action group or task.

- Moving adjacent or contained items into, or out of, an action group or task.

- Editing the properties of an action group or task (such as the action name).

- Playing the video-like screen captures for the selected items.

Playback Area   The playback area displays the captured screen images and displays the recorded location of the mouse, providing a smooth full motion playback of the recorded session. As each frame is displayed, the corresponding event in the event viewing area is highlighted. In the event display area, the blue highlights signify selected events, while the green highlight shows the event being played back in the playback display area. This synchronised event view/playback display gives the usability tester immediate understanding of the event display, and provides important context information about the interface as a whole.

The playback area displays each recorded frame in sequence, beginning with the first event selected in the event viewing area, ending with the last event selected (or the last displayed event if only one event was selected). The display pauses for an amount of time equal to the difference between the time stamps of the currently displayed event and the next event, multiplied by the user specified playback speed factor, for each playback frame. A 'ghost' mouse pointer is displayed in the playback area to show the recorded location of the mouse pointer during playback, and by changing colours, the recorded state of the mouse buttons.

The usability tester can display the historic location of the mouse pointer by toggling a mouse tail option. The mouse tail shows where the mouse has been by displaying a series of dots on the playback area. The size of the tail is limited by elapsed time, which gives the effect of a tail that follows the mouse around, growing longer as the pointer moves faster, and growing shorter as the pointer slows. This playback enhancement gives a simple and effective historic record of the mouse movements.

Toolbar buttons associated with the playback area exist for the following operations:

- Starting the playback from the item (event, task or action group) selected in the event view area. The playback will stop at the last item selected (if more than one item is selected) or the last item in the event view area.

- Stopping the playback. If the playback is started again, it will commence from the first selected item.

- Pausing the playback. If the playback is started again, it will continue from the last displayed event.

- Changing the playback speed.

- Changing the length of the mouse tail.

Index Area   The index area (Figure 2, right-hand side sub-window) gives the usability specialist the ability to quickly find and display recorded tasks. It does this by presenting the task names, grouped by associated user names and recording times in a tree structure. Once the desired task is located, it can be selected and displayed in the task view area as well as replayed in the playback area.

The index allows the usability specialist to find all tasks performed by a given user, all users who performed a given task or a list of all tasks in chronological order. The index is automatically generated from the manipulated recording, and is updated as new tasks are added or removed.

The index area shows a tree with all the tasks displayed on first level branches. Once a branch is expanded, the names of all users who attempted the task are displayed on the second level branches. Expanding a user name branch displays a date and time for each occurrence of the expanded task commenced by the expanded user. Alternatively, another index can also be displayed which places the user name on the first level branches and the task names on the second level branches. This allows for finding all tasks performed by a specified use.

A third index is available which is displayed in a table form, showing all tasks, user names and date/time of the task's commencement, sorted by date/time. This index view is useful for locating tasks by the date/time they were started and for scheduling future experiments.

4.4   Action Display Notation

Display of event information as a textual event log can be tedious to read, and it is difficult to communicate the hierarchical nature of the action groups and tasks. A graphical notation is more compact, allows for direct manipulation, is easier to read and captures the hierarchical nature of action groups and tasks by having one representation graphically contain another.

The items in the notation represent the start and end of a recording session, raw events, action groups and tasks, and consist of a series of boxes connected with arcs. Each box contains textual information identifying and qualifying the item it represents, and if the item has duration, it is displayed above the box (in seconds). Each arc is labelled with the time difference between the end of the first item and the start of the second item, which are connected by the arc.

Raw events are represented in the notation as rounded boxes (see Figure 3). Text within the box identifies the class and type of event (e.g. MouseEvent: MOUSE_PRESSED), the target for the event (e.g. button0), and (if available) the coordinate of the event.

Action groups are represented in the notation as two stacked events. Text within the box shows the action group description and the number of items contained within the action group. A label above the box shows the number of seconds between the start of the first and the end of the last contained item. Action groups may be expanded to show the contained items. When expanded, the box is enlarged and all contained items are displayed below the text within the box.

A task is represented in the notation as a beveled box. Text within the box shows the task name, the name of the user who attempted the task, and the date/time that the task commenced. Tasks also show the duration and may be expanded.

Filled circles mark the start and end of a single contiguous session. An arc (and the time difference label) does not connect start and end markers.

4.5 Automatic Classification Filters

For the event log, video playback and timing information to be accurate, all events need to be captured. These results in a large volume of information being displayed in the event display area, making it difficult for the usability tester to determine what the user was attempting. Mouse movements in particular generate a large number of events, which can be represented more usefully as a single action group.

Two prototype filters were designed for this work. The first filter groups mouse movement events as well events that occur as a consequence of the mouse moving around the interface. These events included MouseMove events (which are generated very rapidly as the mouse moves over the interface), MouseEntered and MouseExited events (which are generated as the mouse enters or leaves a control on the interface).

The second filter groups events related to typing, which are generated as keys are pressed and released, as well as when the contents of a control (edit field for example) changes due to keyboard input.

The two example filters were designed to demonstrate the utility of automating event grouping, and is invoked by selecting an automatic filtering option from the main application menu bar.

4.6 Summary of Advantages and Limitations

The advantages of our approach over current video taping and event logging techniques including:

- Flexibility in use, allowing for testing on multiple platforms using multiple styles of empirical testing.

- Practicality in use, by reducing the need for specialised and expensive equipment or complex, time consuming set up.

- Precision in its ability to measure events and the time they occurred.

- Transparency to the test user, with little impact on the software being tested, and no intimidating video cameras or usability testers.

- Ability to archive and compare results of multiple test performances, as well as the ability to easily copy and share results (via e-mail for example).

- Remote usability testing, allowing a greater base of test users, with only a small additional cost.

- Tightly integrated quantitative data (through event logging) and qualitative data (through the video-like screen capture playback).

The visualisation of events described within this work provides the usability specialist with a means of managing the data presented. The main advantages to the visualisation approach used in this work include:

- Viewing the data at various levels of complexity, with the ability to reveal details of interesting sections of data.

- The tight mapping between the event visualisation and the video-like playback of captured events, giving context to otherwise abstract events.

- The ability to nest event classifications and record the hierarchical nature of user actions and tasks.

We have also demonstrated in this work the importance of integrating a CAUsE tool with the graphical toolkit, which we believe, is a trend that will continue in the future. The close association between the CAUsE tool and graphical toolkit makes the tool more accessible throughout the development of interactive software, giving the interface designers a ready means of evaluating and improving interface design decisions. Tight integration with the graphical toolkit provides KALDI with the means of recording internal program state information, as well as the visible program output, which would assist in evaluating and improving adaptive and intelligent interfaces.

KALDI is still an evolving tool, and as such, is limited in its current functionality. We intend to implement the following components and enhancements in order for the tool to be fully utilised:

- Provide the ability to monitor multiple windows and multiple applications.

- Provide facilities in the live monitor tool to categorise events and insert comments as the data is being received.

- Provide the ability to display multiple tasks at the same time and compare them.

- Modify the graphical display of events to communicate not only the user actions and the interface feedback, but also the state of both the interface and the underlying model after every action.

- Add the ability for the tool to measure machine performance, so that test results will not be biased by machine lag.

- Provide statistical reporting on the event data.

- Evaluate the applicability of the tool to test multiple users in collaborative environments.

Informal software and usability evaluations were conducted throughout the development of KALDI. Further studies are to be undertaken in the future to formally evaluate the usability and utility of KALDI and the visual representations it supports.

We also intend to evaluate the dynamics of KALDI: skill acquisition, metacognitive strategies and knowledge elicitation during software navigation. The study aims at implementing an interactive theoretical and empirical orientation whereby benefits accrued from the KALDI tool may aid psychological and human factors theorising. Alternatively such psychological theorising may guide the ongoing development of KALDI.

5 Conclusions

Usability analysis methods and empirical user evaluations are the standard accepted techniques for developing usable systems. It is widely agreed that these techniques, which are inherited from Human Factors, do indeed work when carefully applied (Crellin et al., 1990). However, many HCI researchers have agreed, for example see Nielsen (1992; Butler et al., 1989), that empirical user testing is too slow and expensive for modern software development practice, especially when hard-to-get domain experts are the target user group. In this research work we discussed usability analysis and testing activities, and described the design and implementation of KALDI, a prototype CAUsE tool developed to automate these activities.

KALDI is still an evolving prototype. It was developed to demonstrate the advantages of automating usability activities using purely software techniques. The tool helps integrating usability testing into the development lifecycle. It enhance the collaboration between interactive systems developers and usability specialists, and consequently improves their ability to make sound design decisions.

The recent trend towards implementing CAUsE tools to support usability evaluation represents a significant development in this area. In this paper we demonstrated the benefits of integrating such tools in future graphical toolkits and UIMSs to reduce the gap between design/implementation and usability evaluation. This integration would promote interactive and ongoing usability assessment during the entire development lifecycle.

Acknowledgement

The authors wish to thank Dr Janice Langan-Fox for her invaluable comments and continuous support.

References

Al-Qaimari, G. & McRostie, D. (1999), KALDI: A CAUsE Tool for Supporting Testing and Usability Analysis of Human–Computer Interaction, *in* J. Vanderdonckt & A. Puerta (eds.), *Computer-Aided Design of User Interfaces II*, Kluwer, chapter 30, pp.337–355.

Baxter, J. (1995), *The Book of Coffee — The Connoisseurs Handbook*, Quintet Publishing.

Bevan, N. & Macleod, M. (1994), "Usability Measurement in Context", *Behaviour & Information Technology* **13**(1-2), 132–45.

Boehm, B. W. (1988), "The Spiral Model of Software Development and Enhancement", *IEEE Computer* **21**(5), 61–72.

Butler, K., Bennett, J., Polson, P. & Karat, J. (1989), "Report on the Workshop on Analytical Methods: Predicting the Complexity of Human–Computer Interaction", *ACM SIGCHI Bulletin* **20**(4), 63–79.

Card, S., Moran, T. & Newell, A. (1993), *The Psychology of Human-Computer Interaction*, Lawrence Erlbaum Associates.

Chi, M., Glaser, H. R. & Farr, M. J. (1988), *The Nature of Expertise*, Lawrence Erlbaum Associates.

Crellin, J., Horn, T. & Preece, J. (1990), Evaluating Evaluation: A Case Study of the Use of Novel and Conventional Evaluation Techniques in a Small Company, *in* D. Diaper, D. Gilmore, G. Cockton & B. Shackel (eds.), *Proceedings of INTERACT '90 — Third IFIP Conference on Human–Computer Interaction*, Elsevier Science, pp.329–35.

Geary, D. M. (1999), *Graphic Java 2: Mastering the JFC – Volume 2, Swing Components*, The Sun Microsystems Press Java Series,, third edition, Prentice–Hall.

Hammontree, M., Hendrickson, J. & Hensley, B. (1992), Integrated Data Capture and Analysis Tools for Research and Testing on Graphical User Interfaces, *in* P. Bauersfeld, J. Bennett & G. Lynch (eds.), *Proceedings of CHI'92: Human Factors in Computing Systems*, ACM Press, pp.431–2.

Hix, D. & Hartson, H. R. (1993), *Developing User Interfaces: Ensuring Usability through Product and Process*, John Wiley & Sons.

ISO (1998), "ISO 9241-11 International Standard. Ergonomic Requirements for Office Work with Visual Display Terminals (VDTs). Part 11: Guidance for Specifying and Measuring Usability". International Organization for Standardization, Genève, Switzerland.

Jeffries, R., Turner, A., Poison, P. & Atwood, M. (1981), The Processes Involved in Designing Software, *in* J. Anderson (ed.), *Cognitive Skills and Their Acquisition*, Lawrence Erlbaum Associates, pp.255–83.

Karat, J. (1997), "Evolving the Scope of User-centred Design", *Communications of the ACM* **40**(7), 33–8.

Kieras, D. E. (1997), A Guide to GOMS Model Usability Evaluation using NGOMSL, *in* M. Helander, T. K. Landauer & P. V. Prabhu (eds.), *Handbook of Human–Computer Interaction*, second edition, North-Holland, pp.733–66.

Lewis, C. (1997), Cognitive Walkthroughs, *in* M. Helander, T. K. Landauer & P. V. Prabhu (eds.), *Handbook of Human–Computer Interaction*, second edition, North-Holland, pp.717–32.

Macleod, M. & Rengger, R. (1993), The Development of DRUM: A Software Tool for Video-assisted Usability Evaluation, *in* J. Alty, D. Diaper & S. Guest (eds.), *People and Computers VIII (Proceedings of HCI'93)*, Cambridge University Press, pp.293–309.

Macleod, M., Bowren, R., Bevan, N. & Curson, I. (1997), "The MUSiC Performance Measurement Method", *Behaviour & Information Technology* **16**(4–5), 279–93.

Newman, W. & Lamming, M. (1995), *Interactive System Design*, Addison–Wesley.

Nielsen, J. (1992), Finding Usability Problems Through Heuristic Evaluation, *in* P. Bauersfeld, J. Bennett & G. Lynch (eds.), *Proceedings of CHI'92: Human Factors in Computing Systems*, ACM Press, pp.373–80.

Nielsen, J. (1993a), "Iterative User-Interface Design", *IEEE Computer* **26**(11), 32–41.

Nielsen, J. (1993b), *Usability Engineering*, Academic Press.

Norman, D. A. & Draper, S. W. (eds.) (1986), *User Centered System Design: New Perspectives on Human–Computer Interaction*, Lawrence Erlbaum Associates.

Rubin, J. (1994), *Handbook of Usability Testing*, John Wiley & Sons.

Ryan, C. & Al-Qaimari, G. (2000), The Orbital Model: A Methodology for the Development of Evolving Interactive Software Systems Based on Complex Domains, *in* M. Torres (ed.), *Proceedings of the IIIS International Conference on Information Systems Analysis and Synthesis (SCI/ISAS'00)*, pp.99–105.

Soloway, E., Adelson, B. & Ehrlich, K. (1988), Knowledge and Processes in the Comprehension of Computer Programs, *in* M. Chi, R. Glaser & M. Farr (eds.), *The Nature of Expertise*, Lawrence Erlbaum Associates, pp.127–52.

Uehling, D. & Wolf, K. (1995), User Action Graphing Effort (UsAGE), *in* I. Katz, R. Mack, L. Marks, M. B. Rosson & J. Nielsen (eds.), *Proceedings of CHI'95: Human Factors in Computing Systems*, ACM Press, pp.290–1.

Wharton, C., Bradford, J., Jeffries, R. & Franzke, M. (1992), Applying Cognitive Walkthroughs to More Complex User Interfaces: Experiences, Issues and Recommendations, *in* P. Bauersfeld, J. Bennett & G. Lynch (eds.), *Proceedings of CHI'92: Human Factors in Computing Systems*, ACM Press, pp.381–8.

Understanding Inspection Methods: Lessons from an Assessment of Heuristic Evaluation

Gilbert Cockton & Alan Woolrych

School of Computing, Engineering and Technology University of Sunderland, PO Box 299, Sunderland SR6 0YN, UK
Tel: *+44 191 515 3394, +44 191 515 3447*
Fax: *+44 191 515 2781, +44 191 515 3752*
Email: *{Gilbert.Cockton,Alan.Woolrych}@sunderland.ac.uk*

The Heuristic Evaluation method was applied by 99 analysts working in groups to an office application's drawing editor. The use of structured problem report formats eased merging of analysts' predictions and the subsequent association of a set of actual problems, which was extracted from user test data. The user tests were based on tasks designed to ensure that all predicted problems would be thoroughly addressed. Analysis of accurate and inaccurate predictions has supported the derivation of the DR-AR model for usability inspection method effectiveness. The model distinguishes between the discovery of candidate (possible) problems and their subsequent confirmation (or elimination) as probable problems. We confirm previous findings that heuristics do not support the discovery of possible usability problems. Our results also show that heuristics were most used appropriately to confirm possible problems that turned out to have low impact or frequency. Otherwise, heuristics are used inappropriately in a way that could lead to poor design changes. Heuristics are also very poor at eliminating improbable problems (65% of all predictions were false), and thus mostly incorrectly confirm false predictions. Overall, heuristics provide a poor analyst *resource* for the successful elimination/confirmation of im/probable problem predictions. Analysis of false predictions reveals that more effective analyst resources are knowledge of users, tasks, interaction, application domains, the application itself and design knowledge from HCI. Using the DR-AR model, we derive a strategy for UIM improvement.

Keywords: evaluation, usability inspection methods, heuristic evaluation, usability engineering, DR-AR model.

1 Usability Inspection Methods and their Assessment

A key goal of Human–Computer Interaction (HCI) research is to support predictive analysis of software designs. Two complementary approaches have been developed from the outset of HCI research. *Model-based* approaches draw on the formality of computer science and/or theoretical models from cognitive psychology, for example Cognitive Complexity Theory, (Kieras & Polson, 1985). Such approaches could be sound application vehicles for the results of scientific research in computer science and psychology. Clearly, as HCI is an extremely complex phenomenon, such scientific approaches could require decades of research before coming to fruition. As a result, Usability Inspection Methods (UIMs) have also been developed as an alternative approach. These vary in their independence of scientific knowledge. At one extreme, *discount methods* make little attempt to ground themselves in any disciplined corpus of interaction data. They are distillations of the informed opinions of HCI experts. Heuristic Evaluation (Molich & Nielsen, 1990) is the best known example. More sophisticated approaches do draw on a corpus of interaction data. *Cognitive Dimensions* (Green, 1991) was developed within the Psychology of Programming community by Green and collaborators. Each proposed dimension can be related to experimental results from this community. Lastly, *Cognitive Walkthrough* (Lewis & Wharton, 1997) was initially based on a theory of novice learning.

The difference between model-based and inspection-based approaches is thus not the presence or absence of theoretical underpinnings, but their methods and goals. Model-based approaches use explicit representations of systems (devices) and/or users that are suited to the application of approximate theories. Their goal for the foreseeable future will be to develop and assess the quality of the underlying theories. Inspection-based approaches are presented as loose procedures. Their goal is to have the best possible immediate impact on interactive systems design at the lowest possible cost. They do not require specific 'theory-friendly' representations, although, for example, Cognitive Walkthrough can be applied to UAN specifications (Lavery & Cockton, 1997a), and Cognitive Dimensions have been used in conjunction with Entity-Relationship diagrams (Green, 1991).

The test of a UIM is not its performance relative to model-based approaches, since the latter are insufficiently developed. The true benchmark is *expert evaluation*, which we restrict to the application of tacit expert knowledge in an unsystematic manner. While UIMs do have the advantage of being communicable and repeatable, they must still improve analyst prediction, which has not yet been convincingly established because UIMs have been so poorly assessed. They thus come with little guarantee of quality. Still, Heuristic Evaluation (HE) was the most used usability method in a recent major survey (Rosenbaum et al., 2000). Usability professionals take risks with UIMs for two reasons:

- Model-based approaches remain limited or immature. They are expensive to apply and their use is largely restricted to research teams, e.g. Gray et al. (1992). UIMs are cheap to apply, have been applied to many commercial designs by practitioners, and are seen as a low-cost and low-skill. Where resources rule out user testing, UIMs are the best available practical approach — some usability is better then no usability.

- UIMs complement user testing. They can be used before a testable prototype has been implemented and can be iterated without exhausting or biasing a group of test participants. They can be used to identify probable problems as a focus for user testing.

Given that practitioners will use UIMs and that high quality model-based approaches will most probably not be available within this decade, we need to keep improving UIM quality. The starting point is an accurate assessment of what each UIM can and cannot do. With this, usability experts could combine properly scoped methods effectively. No such scoping yet exists, which is not surprising given fundamental methodological problems with many evaluations of UIMs (Gray & Salzman, 1998).

Assessments of reliability have tended to concentrate on simple 'percentages' of usability problems that a UIM accurately predicts. There are four basic problems with this approach, all far less subtle than the methodological issues addressed in Gray & Salzman (1998). Firstly, to calculate a percentage, 100% must be known with some confidence. It is not clear how one could ever know all of the usability problems associated with a computer application. Secondly, it relies on problem counts and classifications that are rarely checked for inter-rater reliability, but such counts are typical unstable and wholly dependent on evolving research protocols. Thirdly, even if 90% of problems were predicted, the 10% missed could be the most serious. Fourthly, it must be established that predictions are due to the UIM and not to expert judgement or an analyst's intuitions.

2 Improving the Assessment of Usability Inspection Methods

UIM evaluation must be improved. The urgent need is to abandon simple (and highly flawed) percentage yields of predicted problems in favour of *scoping* what UIMs do and do not predict. With that in place, practitioners can combine UIMs to cover all product-critical problem types. Also, researchers can then suggest why prediction failures occur, which supports UIM improvement.

Scoping UIMs may appear to be a simple extension to calculating percentage yields, since it requires identification of predicted problems and unpredicted problems. However, it also requires identification of unrealised predictions, that is *false positives*. A UIM that generates a high proportion of false positives will undermine its main advantage of efficiency at low-cost. Dealing with large numbers of false positives will both waste development effort and undermine the credibility of usability practitioners. Further, scoping requires analysis of the actual role of a UIM in making predictions, whether or not they turn out to be true or false. A UIM can only be said to have really predicted a problem if there is evidence that it was actually applied during problem identification.

Our approach to improving UIM assessment is more straightforward than that advocated by Gray & Salzman. We have not tried to address general problems of validity, but instead have addressed five concrete confounding procedural variables:

- *Quality of analyst understanding of the UIM:* misunderstandings can result equally in false positives, missed problems, or predicted problems with inappropriate analysis.

- *Reliability of prediction merging:* errors in forming a single set of predictions for each analyst (group) and then all analysts will corrupt the problem count, as well as distorting the counts of (in)appropriate UIM applications.

- *Ability of user testing to expose actual problems,* which would result in miscoding (as false positives) problems that a UIM can in fact predict.

- *Reliability of known problem extraction:* errors in forming the set of actual problems from user testing again risks miscoding predicted problems as false positives.

- *Reliability of matching predicted to actual problems,* which risks miscoding predicted problems as false positives or vice versa.

By addressing the above, we have increased confidence in our results. While we do not claim to have satisfied the ideals of Gray & Salzman, we would argue that our assessment of HE is the most searching to date, even though there is still significant room for improvement. By applying and improving our research methods, the quality and/or use of UIMs could be greatly improved. Our specific tactics for addressing the five procedural variables above are now each described.

2.1 Quality of Analysts' Understanding of the UIM

Analysts who do not understand a UIM can readily both predict many false positives and fail to predict problems. Both would misrepresent a UIM's quality. We addressed this in two ways:

- *Expert tuition* of the individual analyst (second author) and a pair of analysts (two visiting masters students) — the individual analyst prepared three sets of Heuristic Evaluation (HE) predictions. Coaching focused on specific reporting of separate problems and appropriate use of heuristics. The coach (first author) never inspected the application version under analysis. The visiting students prepared two Cognitive Walkthroughs and an expert evaluation (as a check on user test task selection, Section 2.3). All three analysts were supplied with training manuals on the UIMs (Lavery et al., 1996; Lavery & Cockton, 1997a) and a structured report format (Lavery & Cockton, 1997b).

- *A lecture and tutorial* from the second author on HE for 96 student analysts in the group study — as part of their final year undergraduate HCI class, students were supplied with the HE training manual and had to use a standard report format. The second author provided no support or guidance during the (unassessed) exercise.

The above approaches increase confidence in the analysts' understanding of HE. The training manuals included self-assessment materials that check understanding of a heuristic and its appropriate application. In our studies, it would thus be

---

Problem No. 1/ Usability group 1

Brief Description

After drawing a shape, the 'selection tool' is automatically selected.

Likely Difficulties

Users cannot draw multiple lines or shapes without re-selecting the appropriate drawing tool.

Specific Context (if applicable)

When drawing multiple shapes of the same type.

Assumed Causes

Application does not appear to support drawing multiple shapes of the same type.

Relevant Heuristic

Breaches H3 (user control and freedom), breaches H5 (error prevention), and breaches H7 (flexibility and efficiency of use).

Figure 1: Example completed student problem report.

---

unreasonable to wholly attribute inappropriate use of heuristics and unpredicted problems to analysts' *misunderstanding* of HE.

2.2 Reliability of Prediction Merging

By constraining analysts to use a common report format, we made it easier to merge their predictions. Figure 1 shows an example completed report from one student group. The report format requires analysts to briefly describe the problem, hypothesise likely difficulties (with specific contexts where applicable), and to state their assumed causes and breached heuristics. This format improved the quality of predictions by forcing analysts to hypothesise likely difficulties in context, rather than to just focus on problem features. It made analysts more reflective and less likely to propose problems with little justification. Where predictions still turned out to be false, we could understand analysts' reasoning. Note however that the example prediction is *bogus*, in that drawing tools can be locked by double-clicking, but not surprisingly few analysts found this. The informed prediction here would be that tool locking is difficult to find, with likely difficulties as in Figure 1. As it was, such difficulties never transpired, since users employed copy and paste for multiple object creation, and without apparent annoyance, frustration or inefficiency. We return to *bogus* problems in Sections 3.3 and 4.3.

2.3 Ability of User Testing to Expose Actual Problems

UIMs are assessed by comparing predictions with actual problems. Initially, actual problem sets were simply 'known' to the researchers, with later studies actually collecting them via user testing! However, testing alone cannot rule out the possibility of miscoding predictions as false positives. We must be certain that user testing would indeed expose all predicted problems that really exist. We addressed this by systematically deriving task sets for user testing from the initial set of analyst's predictions (second author's). Tests using this task set provided an initial set of actual problems. However, once the results of the subsequent analyses by the visiting masters students and undergraduate groups were available, we could identify predictions that had not been adequately covered by initial user testing. We ran extra participants with an extended task set in order to address such new predictions. Two video cameras, a highly sensitive boundary microphone and direct screen recording in our usability laboratory recorded 15 users overall.

This approach should ensure that false positives are correctly coded. It does not of course ensure that *all* usability problems have been elicited. That is simply not possible. All actual problem sets are a lower bound. There will always be some unknown problems, albeit eventually of low severity or (by implication) low frequency. Problems that cannot be detected by changing the test user population within fixed task user testing can be addressed in other ways such as field studies, instrumented applications and free test usage. However, for our study, extending the actual problem set would only reduce HE's percentage yield (which we don't trust anyway!) and thus enlarge the set of unpredicted problems (thus potentially further restricting the UIM's scope). Such additions should *not* reduce the number of false positives if the task set has been properly derived from earlier predictions.

2.4   Reliability of Actual Problem Extraction

Covering a wide range of usability problems in user testing does not ensure that such problems will make it to the final documented problem set. In one study (Jacobsen et al., 1998), four usability experts extracted significantly different problem sets from the same video tapes using the same problem identification criteria. The SUPEX method (Cockton & Lavery, 1999) has been developed to increase reliability in problem set extraction. This method was still under development during the study reported here, and thus SUPEX could not be applied. However, general principles from SUPEX such as transcription, segmentation, difficulty isolation and generalisation were all applied in the hope that problem extraction would be improved.

We stopped difficulty generalisation just above the level of simple instances, resulting in a relatively high problem count (further generalisation would by definition reduce the number of problem types). As an aside, note that, as difficulties can be organised into hierarchies, one can select a problem count at any level in the hierarchy, i.e. a few or hundreds, which is another reason for mistrusting percentage yields and naïve success/failure analyses of UIMs (Dutt et al., 1994)! Informed interpretation of problem counts requires explicit levels of problem generalisation. Similarly, confidence in coding predictions as (un)successful also requires knowledge of the abstraction level for the actual problem set.

2.5   Reliability of Matching Predicted to Actual Problems

Our problem format allows matching on one or more components of a problem prediction. This overcomes a major problem in UIM assessment. UIMs tend to focus on the *causes* of likely difficulties, without necessarily being specific about

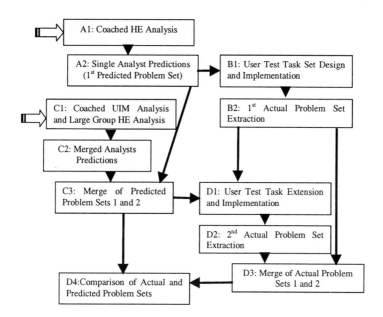

Figure 2: Overview of the research process.

what these observable difficulties could be. Conversely (and thus *unmatchably*), user testing highlights actual difficulties (*effects*) without necessarily being able to identify their causes. We did not use our standard report format for user test problems. Instead we directly associated instances of actual problems with predicted problems. The report format eased such associations, and let us avoid the 'liberal' feature-based matching of those studies where any problems matched if they concerned the same design feature (Lavery et al., 1997)! Where no matches were made on the first pass, we could double-check that all false positives had been properly coded by scanning all transcribed video data from user tests for possible unmatched problems.

3   An Assessment of Heuristic Evaluation

This paper reports the first detailed analyses of the results of HE predictions from a single analyst, a pair of analysts and 96 undergraduate analysts in 23 groups. The extended version of HE in our training manual was used (Molich & Nielsen's ten heuristics and three extra from Lavery et al. (1996)). The design for analysis and test was the drawing editor of Microsoft PowerPoint (Version 4.0). Figure 2 presents the research procedure. The study spanned four phases, indicated by the letters A, B, C and D.

3.1   Phase A: Single Analyst's Predicted Problem Set

Phase A began with an application of HE by the second author. Three refinements of a set of problems were prepared, guided by coaching from the first author (Woolrych,

2001). This addressed the first potential confounding variable when assessing UIMs: Quality of Analysts' Understanding of the UIM (2.1 above). The analyst's predictions from the third refinement were formed into a problem set (A2).

3.2   Phase B: First Actual Problem Set

A task set (B1) was derived from the analyst's problem set (A2). Twelve volunteers of varying computing experience attempted these tasks (B1). This addressed the third potential confounding variable when assessing UIMs: Ability of User Testing to Expose Actual Problems (2.3 above). An actual problem set was derived from the results of this user testing (B2). Appropriate use of concepts from the SUPEX method addressed the fourth potential confounding variable when assessing UIMs: Reliability of Known Problem Extraction (2.4 above).

3.3   Phase C: Multiple Analysts' Predicted Problem Sets

Phase C repeated Phase A, but with two visiting masters students (not using HE) and a final year undergraduate class as the analysts (C1). Their predictions had to be merged into a single set (C2) and then further merged (C3) with the first analyst's predictions (A2). The 96 undergraduate analysts received a lecture and tutorial on HE. The first author coached the masters students on Cognitive Walkthrough and Expert Inspection. These two interventions addressed the first potential confounding variable when assessing UIMs: Quality of Analysts' Understanding of the UIM (2.1 above). Merging of all analysts' problems (A2 and C2 into C3) benefited from the standardised problem report format, thus addressing the second potential confounding variable: Reliability of Prediction Merging (2.2 above). C3 contained 40 predicted problems (including 14, some repeated, from A2). Five group's predictions were of such poor quality (very incomplete problem reports) that they were discarded. This could be attributed to the fact that the exercise was not assessed, but had it been, then other problems, notably excessive or careless predictions, could have resulted.

Predictions in C3 were coded in two ways by the second author. Firstly, some predictions were clearly *bogus* and would be impossible to match to an actual problem for one of two reasons. Either they were *factually bogus*, that is due to an error of fact, usually about allegedly missing features or feedback. Alternatively, they were *logically bogus* — based on major errors of HCI judgement, usually a flawed argument that an alternative design would be superior, when in fact a reverse-engineered rationale for the feature would indicate otherwise. Note that this coding does not require us to ignore an analyst's predictions, but it does require us to exclude them from the count of predicted problems since they simply cannot happen (bogus problems did not arise with coached analysts). This is not to say that a factually bogus problem is not evidence of a potential problem. For example, some analysts missed prompting in the message bar to 'double click' to end a freeform object, but even though this is easy to miss, this feature caused no problems. As with the Figure 1 bogus prediction, translation to a similar non-bogus prediction is possible, but no such translation could be matched to an actual problem. For non-bogus ('true') false positives, even though some analysts judged that a heuristic was breached, no actual problem emerged, despite the falsification design used for user test tasks (D1, Section 3.4).

Heuristic applications for non-bogus problems in C3 were further coded as being (in) appropriate. We used explicit criteria from our HE training manual (Lavery et al., 1996), which provides conformance questions that state "What the system should do, or users should be able to do, to satisfy the heuristic." Such questions are answered with conformance evidence, i.e. the "design features or lack of design features that indicate partial satisfaction or breaches of the heuristic." For many heuristic applications, these criteria were clearly ignored.

For heuristics to be shown to have a role in problem discovery or analysis, *appropriate* heuristics must be associated with problems. Reference to inappropriate heuristics is evidence that an expert rather than a heuristic evaluation is being applied. Such evidence was abundant in our study. For example, Problem 11 (graphical representation of tools) was predicted by 12 of the 18 analyst groups. The reported problem was that the graphics on the various tool icons did not accurately convey their function to the user. The following heuristics were considered to have been breached by analyst groups (where more than one group applied the heuristic, this is indicated in brackets):

Aesthetic and minimalist design	User control and freedom (3)
Error prevention (2)	Help and documentation
Flexibility and efficiency of use	Recognition rather than recall (3)
Consistency and standards	Visibility of system status

No analyst(s) chose the most appropriate heuristic for Problem 11, *match between system and real world*! Many toolbar icons in the version under test do not intuitively communicate their function by failing to follow appropriate real world conventions. There is a plausible argument for *aesthetic and minimalist design*, especially 'minimalist'. There is too much information on a small icon, making it indistinguishable from similar ones. Less convincingly, although *error prevention* is generally applicable (for any problem elements that causes errors, better design fixes them!), this heuristic should not be applied without identifying actual likely errors (via the difficulties section of our problem reports). Associations between problems and heuristics become even weaker as superficial linguistic cues cut in, e.g. *flexibility and efficiency of use*. Hard to guess icons do reduce efficiency, but this heuristic actually covers elements such as shortcuts and accelerators. Similar arguments apply to *consistency and standards*, as perhaps standard icons exist that are not used. However, beyond this, heuristics have clearly been 'attached' to the problem after identification, for example, neither *user control and freedom* nor *help and documentation* are remotely applicable. Lastly, it can be argued that two of the heuristics have not been breached at all: icons are meant to support *recognition not recall* and in various states they can support *visibility of system status*. Despite this apparent conformance to heuristics, problems still arose with toolbar icons, suggesting that heuristics could lead analysts to eliminate probable problems from their predictions.

3.4 Phase D: Second Actual Problem Set

Phase D repeated Phase B, but with a supplementary task set (D1) derived from problems in the second predicted problem set (C3) that were not in the first set of actual problems (B2) but could not have been exposed by the first task set (B1). Three additional volunteers used the extended task set (D1), resulting in some new actual problems (D2). These were merged with the initial set (B2) to form a composite set of actual problems (D3).

There were 19 actual problems in D3. Note that in the analysis below, some figures vary from a short report of this work (Woolrych & Cockton, 2000). In particular, the seven missed problems in (Woolrych & Cockton, 2000) have been reduced to five (one was reassociated with an existing predicted problem, the other was thresholded out as not really being a usability problem). This bears out the importance of rigorous problem extraction. A full version of the SUPEX extraction method (Cockton & Lavery, 1999) was not ready for this study. So, as would be expected by advocates of structured problem extraction, we created an unstable problem set! This reinforces the hazards of solely basing assessments on percentages of problems found and missed, since all problem counts are somewhat fluid and open to re-interpretation. This apart, the approach that we did take reduced risks associated with the fourth potential confounding variable when assessing UIMs: Reliability of Known Problem Extraction of the UIM (2.4 above).

Scoping a UIM's effectiveness requires more than simple problem counts. For actual problems, we explored two aspects of problems that were (not) predicted: their frequency and impact. Frequency was coded as *high* (over 20% of users), *medium* or *low* (one user). However, as one predicted problem was so severe that user testing could not proceed without bypassing it, only 18/19 predicted problems were analysed. Problem impact was classified as *severe* (task failure, over 2 minutes wasted or major impact on task quality), *nuisance* (under 2 minutes wasted or minor quality impact), and minor (immediate recovery or no task impact).

We also explored effort required to discover problems in D3, coding them as follows. The easiest problems to discover are *perceivable*, and can usually be discovered by simply looking at the display. The next easiest problems to find are *actionable*, where one to a few interaction steps (e.g. clicks) will reveal the problem. The hardest problems to find are *constructable*, as only several interaction steps involving multiple application objects may reveal a problem.

Phase D ended with associating actual problems in D3 with predicted problems in C3. The process here addressed the fifth potential confounding variable when assessing UIMs: Reliability of Matching Predicted to Actual Problems. The resulting problem set D4 allowed us to assess the actual impact of HE when evaluating a small user interface. The results of this analysis are now presented.

4 Analysis of Results

We applied the following measures to the final problem set D4:

- Superficial effectiveness: a simple percentage measure of actual problems predicted by HE.

- Actual effectiveness: three separate measures of HE's ability to predict the most frequent, most severe and most complex actual problems, plus a measure of the actual role played by HE in forming predictions.

	Missed Problems		Analysable Predicted		All Actual Problems	
High	40%	2	69%	9	61%	11
Medium	0%	0	8%	1	6%	1
Low	60%	3	23%	3	33%	6

Table 1: Comparative problem frequency distribution.

	Missed Problems		Analysable Predicted		All Actual Problems	
Severe	60%	3	31%	4	39%	7
Nuisance	40%	2	54%	7	50%	9
Minor	0%	0	15%	2	11%	2

Table 2: Comparative problem impact.

- Inefficiency: the simple measure of false positives as a percentage of all predictions.

- Failure distribution: frequency of factually and logically bogus false positives.

For superficial effectiveness, one or more analyst groups predicted 74% (14/19) of actual problems. HE apparently thus predicts most usability problems, replicating existing assessments of the UIM.

4.1 Actual Effectiveness

Table 1 shows the distributions of problems by frequency. Table 2 shows distributions by impact (the bypassed problem can be regarded as severe). Fisher's exact test indicates no significant difference between distributions of predicted and missed problems (2x2 test for either High+Medium vs. Low, High vs. Medium+Low, Severe+Nuisance vs. Minor and Severe vs. Medium+Minor).

HE predicted most actual problems, mostly of high to medium frequency and severe to nuisance impact. However, UIM assessment should not simply focus on success rates. Where and how UIMs fail are of vital relevance to their selection, application and combination. Also, even if missed problems are not an issue, it is wrong to uncritically attribute successful predictions to the UIM. For HE, it needs to be established that heuristics do indeed aid prediction.

The severity and frequency of the five missed problems is indeed a cause for concern. Even though on balance, HE does not miss proportionally more severe impact and high frequency problems than were found, it does still miss them. Table 3 shows the impact by frequency of the unpredicted problems. There were no medium frequency or minor impact unpredicted problems. Although no statistical significance (Fisher's Exact Test) attaches to the relative distributions of problem impact for predicted and unpredicted problems, nevertheless 43% of severe impact problems were missed (as opposed to 18% of high frequency), and severe problems formed 39% of the total actual problems (whereas 61% of all problems were high

	High Frequency	Low Frequency
Severe Impact	2	1
Nuisance Impact	0	2

Table 3: Impact of Unpredicted Problems by Frequency.

	Missed Problems		Analysable Predicted		All Actual Problems	
Perceivable	0%	0	38%	5	28%	5
Actionable	20%	1	54%	7	44%	8
Constructable	80%	4	8%	1	28%	5

Table 4: Comparative discoverability.

frequency). This failure of HE to predict 43% of severe problems introduces major risks when relying on it as a replacement for user testing. To explore why such problems go unpredicted, we applied a further analysis to the final merged problem set (D4) to see if HE tended to only find the more discoverable problems.

Table 4 shows the distributions of perceivable, actionable and constructable problems (3.3 above) for missed, predicted and all actual problems. Fisher's exact test indicates a highly significant difference between the distributions for predicted and missed problems ($p = 0.008$ for Perceivable+Actionable vs. Constructable). There is thus strong evidence that HE rarely predicts constructable problems, which for our data mostly have severe impact (the rest are nuisance). Were HE systematically guiding analysts, then we would not expect this distribution of problem 'discoverability'. We will return to this trend after presenting the remainder of the analysis.

HE thus does little to guide analysts towards hard to find problems. UIM usage is essentially a search problem — usability problems have to be found and confirmed in a manner similar to 'generate and test' strategies used in early AI. However, rather than generate possible moves or solutions, UIM analysts must discover *possible problems*. From Table 4, we conclude that HE does not guide analysts well, who may only find problems that can be readily seen or appear after a few clicks at most.

Note that the masters students' predictions are not separated out in any analysis here. However they predicted the only constructable problem and via expert evaluation (after coaching in Cognitive Walkthrough) and not via HE. Their search strategy of copying diagrams from computing books forced them to address constructable problems. This suggests that problem discovery can be improved within UIMs by explicitly exploiting domain knowledge.

The last measure of actual effectiveness shows whether heuristics supported predictions. For the 13 accurately predicted problems, 71 heuristics were applied (an average of 5.5 per problem). The bypassed problem from user testing had to be bypassed again, since the prediction of this problem came from a class debriefing of the 96 analysts (one group had failed to report it, although aware of it, which

Severe		Nuisance		Minor		All	
Correct	Incorrect	Correct	Incorrect	Correct	Incorrect	Correct	Incorrect
3	11 (79%)	15	24 (62%)	10	8 (44%)	28	43 (61%)
High		Medium		Low		All	
Correct	Incorrect	Correct	Incorrect	Correct	Incorrect	Correct	Incorrect
19	29 (60%)	1	5 (83%)	8	9 (53%)	28	43 (61%)

Table 5: Inappropriate heuristic applications by problem impact and frequency.

opens up further issues about UIMs!). Of the 71 applications 28 (39%) were appropriate, and 43 (61%) inappropriate, according to the procedure described above (Section 3.3). This hardly suggests that HE guided analysts in problem confirmation. So what did? The distribution of appropriate and inappropriate heuristics (Table 5) by both problem frequency and severity offers some clues.

There is a clear (but not statistically significant, Fischer's exact test, 3×2) tendency for heuristic application to become more appropriate as problems become less frequent. For impact, the trend is less clear, but heuristics were still best applied to minor problems. One explanation is that the predicted problems that turned out to be severe and very frequent were 'more obvious' than low frequency/impact ones. Analysts could thus rely on their HCI common sense to confirm such problems and paid little attention to heuristics. Conversely, where a problem was not overwhelmingly obvious, analysts spent more time on heuristic selection to confirm a possible prediction as probable, our first example of the well known cognitive phenomenon of *confirmation bias* (see Section 4.3). HE actually looks more like user testing with a sample of one, but this changes when the frequency of false positives is considered (4.2 below)!

4.1.1 Implications for Software Development

UIMs need to be improved or combined to avoid missing problems of such severity or frequency. Missed high frequency severe impact problems will cause high product support costs (as well as problems for users, organisations, and product image). HE predictions miss too many severe and/or highly frequent problems. Note however that the 19 problems revealed by testing are a lower bound. Test design mainly sought to flush out all genuine predicted problems. The five missed problems are thus a minimal set, and the real picture for unpredicted problems is likely to be (much) worse.

Also, the use of inappropriate heuristics for higher frequency and severity problems will generate poor solution recommendations. Misapplied heuristics, if actually considered during solution generation, will result in the wrong fix to the right problem, wasting development effort by failing to remedy a successfully predicted problem. This should discredit UIMs, leave some usability problems unresolved and result in new usability problems.

	True False Positives		Logically Bogus	
Perceivable	23%	3	43%	3
Actionable	69%	9	14%	1
Constructable	8%	1	43%	3

Table 6: Comparative discoverability for false positives.

4.1.2 Implications for Improving UIMs

The implications of missed problems and misdiagnosis of successfully predicted ones is sufficiently severe to require urgent attention to improving HE and related UIMs. Missed problems indicate that HE provides at best limited support for candidate problem discovery. This is particularly poor given the severity and frequency of the missed problems.

Overall, HE clearly adds little to analysts' common sense, and we have firm evidence that little distinguishes HE from expert evaluation. The tendency to most use appropriate heuristics for possible problems that turn out to have minor impact and/or low frequency indicates that HE provides little support for confirming possible problems as probable ones. Analysts appear to reach for heuristics 'as a last resort', with their problem reports clearly indicating that they draw on other resources to confirm possible problems. UIMs should be extended to better exploit such resources.

4.2 Inefficiency

HE's inadequacies extend beyond poor support for discovering and confirming probable usability problems. Of the problem predictions, 65% (26/40) turned out to be false. With most predictions 'false' in some sense, we coded false predictions using the classes described in Section 3.3.

4.3 Distribution of False Positives

There were 6 factually bogus, 7 logically bogus and 13 'true' false positives. Table 6 shows the distribution by discoverability of factually bogus, logically bogus and *true false positives*. Using Fisher's exact test, no statistically significant results arise from this table, but it is nevertheless interesting that constructable predictions are common for logically bogus problems. As these involve the construction of mistaken design rationales, it is not surprising that more complex interactions are considered. However, the motivation here is less due (if at all) to HE and more to the stubbornness and tenacity of the analyst! As with the appropriate application of heuristics to carefully rationalise minor problems, a similar misplaced determination may lead analysts to abductively rationalise an implausible pet prediction. In both cases, analysts are falling prey to confirmation bias (Griffin & Tversky, 1992), retaining their belief that a problem exists and looking for confirmatory evidence. In the former case, confirmation bias appears to drive analysts to carefully examine possibly relevant heuristics. In the latter case, analysts contrive design rationales as evidence.

Where analysts misunderstood neither design nor the application under test, the resulting false positives were often due to underestimating users' intelligence and adaptability. For example, one prediction claimed that users would be confused by different behaviours for resizing text and other objects, despite their identical handles. No users were affected by this apparent inconsistency.

4.3.1 Implications for Software Development

The most important adverse consequence of a torrent of false positives for the usability community is the risk of embarrassment and a loss of credibility. Experienced usability professionals with a human sciences training and substantial product design experience would most probably avoid many of the false positives in our student analysts' predictions. However, the route for HE into most development settings will be some user advocate, who could be a developer, a technical writer or customer relationship specialist. Such 'barefoot' usability novices will lack the resources that keep seasoned usability professionals out of trouble. Any substantial take-up of UIMs depends on the wider army of keen usability amateurs. HE quite simply fails them, leaving them exposed to the errors of fact, reason and judgement that generate far more false positives than accurate predictions.

The best outcome is for the developers' better judgement to prevail and reject all false positives, but this will progressively eliminate the credibility of usability advocates. Where usability advocates' views prevail, the result will be unnecessary reworking of adequate features, with the strong risk of introducing usability problems that would not otherwise exist. In practice, developers could quickly eliminate bogus, but not other false positives. However, without user test data to separate the wheat from the chaff, 'true' false positives and good predictions can look equally convincing.

4.3.2 Implications for Improving UIMs

Elimination of false positives is a major objective for UIM improvement. *Heuristic Walkthrough* (Sears, 1997) attempts this by preceding HE with a simplified Cognitive Walkthrough (which could result in more constructable problems from its task base). HE alone eliminates very few false positives from a set of candidate problems. However, beginning with such an inherently constructive method as Cognitive Walkthrough could reduce the yield of actionable and perceivable problems that can be rapidly discovered without a task focus. Thus Heuristic Walkthrough runs the risk of reducing false positives at the expense of obstructing the discovery of the most obvious possible problems.

Our study indicates that, while analysts' common sense is mostly adequate for confirming possible problems as probable ones, it is wholly inadequate for eliminating possible problems as improbable (or even impossible) ones. HE apparently does nothing to counterbalance the lack of faith in user ability reflected in many predictions. Factually bogus problems also indicate that HE's lack of support for problem discovery extends to *feature* discovery. This challenges the received wisdom in UIM development that analysts should have empathy with users, and be denied full knowledge of the product. The aim of UIMs is to find and confirm probable usability problems and not to mimic potential users. Indeed, logically bogus predictions indicate that empathy with the *designer* could be more useful. The ability to reverse-engineer sound design rationales could reduce such predictions.

In summary, analysis of false positives indicates the need for better support for eliminating improbable and impossible predictions. Better product knowledge will channel analyst efforts into problems that really could exist. Better design and task knowledge will divert analyst efforts away from rationalising logically bogus predictions. Better knowledge of users and interaction will also support elimination of improbable predictions. HE's only current support here is the association of loose design rationales with some heuristics. Analysts only appear to consider these when their common sense fails them. When analysts mistakenly trust their common sense and misconfirm an improbable problem, they fail to exploit heuristics as a last resource.

5 The DR-AR Model for UIM Effectiveness

We now present a model that explains three key findings of this study:

1. Severe high frequency problems tend to get missed.

2. Successfully predicted high frequency and/or severe impact problems tend to be associated with inappropriate heuristics.

3. Far too many false positives are not successfully eliminated.

We attribute the first finding to HE's poor support for problem discovery in general, but in particular for the discovery of constructable problems that require consideration of several interaction steps and application objects. We explain the second finding by referring to our analysts' problem reports, which do at times successfully draw on knowledge of users, interaction, design principles and rationales, product details and domain knowledge. With these familiar resources at their disposal, analysts appear to have little motivation for correctly selecting a heuristic (if indeed there is a correct heuristic for the problem, but that requires a separate analysis). Resources at an analyst's disposal are such that, for high frequency and/or severe impact problems, confirmation need not consider heuristics. Only for low frequency and/or minor impact problems are analysts forced onto heuristics to rationalise a problem that may otherwise be rejected.

We attribute the third finding to analysts' failure to apply sound HCI knowledge to eliminate improbable predictions. True (non-bogus) false predictions generally seriously underestimate users' capabilities, indicating that relevant critical resources were not applied to eliminating improbable problems (e.g. understanding the beneficial effects of selective attention — users were never misled by incorrect message bar prompts that they never read!) Presumably, elimination is more challenging than confirmation (or simply too unpleasant for certain egos), which may explain the high proportion of false positives from many UIMs.

The above tentative explanations can be integrated into a model of UIM effectiveness that explains successful prediction in terms of discovery and confirmation. Figure 3 shows this DR-AR model of UIM effectiveness. Discovery is related to the difficulty of finding a possible problem, and thus we model the

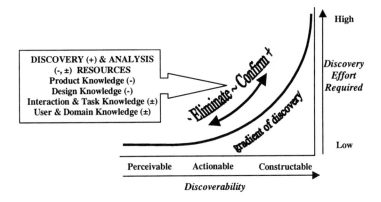

Figure 3: The DR-AR Model for UIM Effectiveness.

Perceivable-Actionable-Constructable continuum as an ever-steepening gradient that the analyst can only ascend via discovery resources (DR) that take analysts deep and wide into the product usage search space. By considering more constructable problems, fewer (severe) problems should be missed. Discovery resources promote such consideration and are indicated with a + (actually, these resources are also analysis resources and are thus marked ± in Figure 3). Existing discovery resources are product knowledge gained from an informal first-pass exploration (HE, as recommended by Nielsen) or the use of task scenarios (Cognitive Walkthrough). We need more expert and informed approaches to search space construction and investigation, driven by extensive knowledge of the product, domain *and* interactive systems design. For example, the masters students used domain artefacts (diagrams in computing texts) to force them to examine complex constructable problems. The undergraduate students do not appear to have used either product or domain resources, and this skimmed over surface features of the test application.

Having discovered *possible* problems, reducing these to a set of *probable* problems requires a wide range of analysis resources (AR). Given a possible problem, knowledge resources are required to confirm or eliminate it as a probable problem. These are marked – for elimination resources and ± for both/either in Figure 3. The process of confirmation and elimination requires more in-depth research. From our problem reports, confirmation clearly happens and does draw on a range of resources, but we have no evidence as yet of how analysts actually confirm problems. However, we do have evidence of elimination from the coaching of the second author and the masters students, with product and HCI knowledge both being common reasons for eliminating possible problems from a set of predictions.

Thus user empathy could be irrelevant to problem discovery, leaving consideration of likely user interaction to elimination of improbable problems. 'User empathy' can all too quickly degenerate into the misrepresentation of users as helpless imbeciles with no problem solving resources. Our prediction reports contain many examples of failure to apply user, design or product knowledge to eliminate improbable or bogus problems. In particular, analysts fail to grasp the dynamics of learning within interactive environments, and especially the role of distributed cognition in problem solving. A better understanding of interaction would lead analysts to eliminate possible problems that are unlikely to arise because users will be able to use the display and the dynamics of interaction as a knowledge resource. Such understandings depend on taking analysis beyond what can be perceived or 'actioned' to constructions of realistic interaction sequences. Interaction and task knowledge can thus be both a discovery resource and an analysis resource for elimination.

6 Conclusions and Future Work

UIMs have been an important development in HCI research and practice. They are 'quick to market' vehicles for both craft knowledge and theory. They have done much to popularise HCI and usability engineering in particular. They provide a more easily won legitimacy for 'barefoot' usability advocates than 'unbranded' expert evaluation. This is all fine for initial take-up of usability engineering in the difficult and challenging circumstances of competitive commercial software development, but not for the long term credibility of usability engineering. It is not enough for HE to be fast and cheap, as even the lowest expenditure must be worthwhile. Given the missed problems, highly frequent false positives and misapplied heuristics, HE's cost-benefit ratio could be very low. The value of predicted problems is significantly undermined by their flawed analysis and missed problems. False positives can significantly increase HE's whole lifecycle costs.

UIM assessment must be improved to improve UIMs. The urgent need is to abandon simple (and highly flawed) percentage yields of predicted problems for a UIM in favour of scoping of what UIMs do and do not predict. We have demonstrated how frequency, severity, discoverability and error analysis of false positives can be applied to scoping HE. Our verdict is that HE can function largely as 'placebo' expert evaluation method with a high yield on finding actual problems, but also with an unacceptably rich harvest of misleading and inaccurate predictions. It is best suited for finding problems that are easy to discover. It is not suited to finding complex multi-object multi-step problems that are typically of nuisance to high severity and mostly of high frequency. HE does not successfully suppress analyst errors of both type 1 (missed problems) and type 2 (false positive).

With HE thus scoped, practitioners could select complementary UIMs to cover all product-critical problem types. Unfortunately, this does not seem possible given the performance of other UIMs relative to our DR-AR model. All existing UIMs appear to be weak on *discovery resources*. None leverage domain knowledge beyond selection and specification of task scenarios, which really must be combined with other domain and product knowledge to ensure full coverage. For example, task-centred domain knowledge can fail to exploit knowledge of typical and critical domain artefacts that would more rapidly and reliably expose usability problem. Only ERMIA based approaches to Cognitive Dimensions (Green, 1991) exploit product knowledge (as high level ERMIA specifications). In addition, many Cognitive Dimensions such as *viscosity* describe inherently constructable problems. In this sense, Cognitive Dimensions may even outperform user testing, which will not reveal constructable problems if (as often happens) the test designer focuses on perceivable and actionable problems (Lee, 1998).

Similarly, UIMs are restricted in their provision of *analysis resources*. HE inconsistently associates loose design rationales with some heuristics. Cognitive Walkthrough only provides a theory of novice learning and (initially at least) an approach to assessing a system's fit to goal structures in the application domain. Cognitive Dimensions provide a distillation of experience from the Psychology of Programming community. UIMs thus need collectively to become more comprehensive in their use of analysis resources, and they could draw opportunistically here on model-based approaches that draw on richer theories from cognitive science.

The advantage of our research approach is that new complementary UIMs could be developed to concentrate on problem types that are outside any existing UIM's scope. We should know what these are to advise usability specialists about problems that currently can only be exposed by user testing. Indeed, user testing could profitably be designed to concentrate on such problems.

We intend to apply the DR-AR model to improving UIMs. Our analysis suggests that, to improve UIMs, (i) analysts must maximise their search space; (ii) analysts must draw on a range of knowledge and (pseudo) -theory to successfully confirm or eliminate candidate problems. Heuristics in their current form are no substitute for such resources. Thus although UIMs could be significantly improved by improving analyst search, analysts must be fixed by better HCI education. Our future work will address both problems via both extensions to UIMs and by complementary resources that could support several UIMs.

In summary, we have developed and refined a research approach that can show what HE and other UIMs can and cannot do, propose reasons for successes and failures, guide UIM improvement and assess the effectiveness of these improvements. As a result, UIMs could move beyond being legitimation devices for usability specialists' common sense and become true complements and extenders of analysts' knowledge and judgement. As a result, usability specialists could be transformed from a role demanded by the prevalence of usability problems into a role that actually earns its keep by systematically eliminating them.

Acknowledgements

Darryn Lavery developed most of the critical research resources used in our study. Sam Marin and Christophe Grosjean, 2000 Matrisse candidates at Facultés Universitaires de Notre-Dame de la Paix (Namur, Belgium) carried out a Cognitive Walkthrough and Expert Evaluation during their 1999 Matrisse research placement at SCET, University of Sunderland. Alan Woolrych's MPhil research studentship was part-funded by a European Social Fund grant to the University of Sunderland.

References

Cockton, G. & Lavery, D. (1999), A Framework for Usability Problem Extraction, *in* A. Sasse & C. Johnson (eds.), *Human–Computer Interaction — INTERACT '99: Proceedings of the Seventh IFIP Conference on Human–Computer Interaction*, Vol. 1, IOS Press, pp.347–55.

Dutt, A., Johnson, H. & Johnson, P. (1994), Evaluating Evaluation Methods, *in* G. Cockton, S. Draper & G. Wier (eds.), *People and Computers IX (Proceedings of HCI'94)*, Cambridge University Press, pp.109–21.

Gray, W. D. & Salzman, M. (1998), "Damaged Merchandise? A Review of Experiments that Compare Usabilty Evaluation Methods", *Human–Computer Interaction* **13**(3), 203–61.

Gray, W., John, B. & Atwood, M. (1992), The Precis of Project Ernestine, or, An Overview of a Validation of GOMS, *in* P. Bauersfeld, J. Bennett & G. Lynch (eds.), *Proceedings of CHI'92: Human Factors in Computing Systems*, ACM Press, pp.307–12.

Green, T. R. G. (1991), Describing Information Artifacts with Cognitive Dimensions and Structure Maps, *in* D. Diaper & N. Hammond (eds.), *People and Computers VI: Usability Now! (Proceedings of HCI'91)*, Cambridge University Press, pp.297–316.

Griffin, D. & Tversky, A. (1992), "The Weighing of Evidence and the Determinants of Confidence", *Cognitive Psychology* **24**(3), 411–35.

Jacobsen, N. E., Hertzum, M. & John, B. E. (1998), The Evaluator Effect in Usability Tests, *in* C.-M. Karat, A. Lund, B. Bederson, E. Bergman, M. Beaudouin-Lafon, N. Bevan, D. Boehm-Davis, A. Boltman, G. Cockton, A. Druin, S. Dumais, N. Frischberg, J. Jacko, J. Koenemann, C. Lewis, S. Pemberton, A. Sears, K. T. Simsarian, C. Wolf & J. Ziegler (eds.), *Companion Proceedings of CHI'98: Human Factors in Computing Systems (CHI'98 Conference Companion)*, ACM Press, pp.255–6.

Kieras, D. E. & Polson, P. G. (1985), "An Approach to the Formal Analysis of User Complexity", *International Journal of Man–Machine Studies* **22**(4), 365–94.

Lavery, D. & Cockton, G. (1997a), Cognitive Walkthrough: Usability Evaluation Materials, Technical Report TR-1997-20, Department of Computing Science, University of Glasgow, UK.

Lavery, D. & Cockton, G. (1997b), Representing Predicted and Actual Usability Problems, *in* H. Johnson, P. Johnson & E. O'Neill (eds.), *Proceedings of the International Workshop on Representations in Interactive Software Development*, Queen Mary and Westifeld Colelge, University of London, pp.97–108.

Lavery, D., Cockton, G. & Atkinson, M. (1996), Heuristic Evaluation for Software Visualisation: Usability Evaluation Material, Technical Report TR-1995-16, Department of Computing Science, University of Glasgow.

Lavery, D., Cockton, G. & Atkinson, M. P. (1997), "Comparison of Evaluation Methods using Structured Usability Problem Reports", *Behaviour & Information Technology* **16**(4-5), 246–66.

Lee, W. (1998), Analysis of Problems Found in User Testing Using an Approximate Model of User Action, *in* H. Johnson, L. Nigay & C. Roast (eds.), *People and Computers XIII (Proceedings of HCI'98)*, Springer-Verlag, pp.23–35.

Lewis, C. & Wharton, C. (1997), Cognitive Walkthroughs, *in* M. Helander, T. K. Landauer & P. V. Prabhu (eds.), *Handbook of Human–Computer Interaction*, second edition, North-Holland, chapter 30, pp.717–32.

Molich, R. & Nielsen, J. (1990), "Improving a Human–Computer Dialog", *Communications of the ACM* **33**(3), 338–48.

Rosenbaum, S., Rohn, J. & Humburg, J. (2000), A Toolkit for Strategic Usability: Results from Workshops, Panels, and Surveys, *in* T. Turner, G. Szwillus, M. Czerwinski & F. Paternò (eds.), *Proceedings of the CHI2000 Conference on Human Factors in Computing Systems*, *CHI Letters* **2**(1), ACM Press, pp.337–344.

Sears, A. (1997), "Heuristic Walkthroughs: Finding the Problems without the Noise.", *International Journal of Human–Computer Interaction* **9**(3), 213–34.

Woolrych, A. (2001), Assessing the Scope and Accuracy of the Usability Inspection Method Heuristic Evaluation, MPhil Thesis, School of Computing, Engineering and Technology, University of Sunderland, UK.

Woolrych, A. & Cockton, G. (2000), Assessing Heuristic Evaluation: Mind the Quality, Not Just Percentages, *in* S. Turner & P. Turner (eds.), *Proceedings of HCI'2000: Volume 2*, BCS, pp.35–6.

Developing A Usability Capability Assessment Approach through Experiments in Industrial Settings

Timo Jokela*, Marko Nieminen†, Netta Iivari*, Katriina Nevakivi‡ & Mikko Rajanen*

* PO Box 3000, 90014 University of Oulu, Finland
Email: {timo.jokela,netta.iivari,mikko.rajanen}@oulu.fi

† Helsinki University of Technology, Otakaari 4, 02150 Espoo, Finland
Email: marko.nieminen@hut.fi

‡ Buscom, Elektroniikkatie 4, 90570 Oulu, Finland
Email: katriina.nevakivi@buscom.fi

Usability capability assessments are carried out to analyse the capability of a development organisation in performing user-centred design (UCD). We carried out four experimental usability capability assessments to learn how to perform assessments effectively in industrial settings. Our starting point was traditional software process assessment based on ISO 15504 ('SPICE'). The recent ISO/TR 18529 was used as the process reference model of UCD. Our experiments showed that the focus of ISO 15504 process assessments — management of activities — did not exactly meet the needs of assessments in our context. These experiences led us to a modified assessment approach where the focus is in performance of UCD. Its main characteristics are:

1. a refined UCD process model;
2. a three-dimensional capability scale; and
3. implementation of an assessment as a workshop rather than a series of interviews.

Keywords: UCD, usability capability, usability capability assessment, usability maturity models.

1   Introduction

The challenge to improve the position of UCD (UCD) in development organisations has been recognised in many presentations and panels in conferences and seminars. For example, there have been papers (Rosenbaum et al., 2000), tutorials (Bloomer & Wolf, 1999), panels (Rosenbaum, 1999) and interviews (Anderson, 2000) at CHI conferences. A European TRUMP project has also addressed this topic.

A typical approach to start organisational improvement efforts in any domain is to carry out *current state analysis*. Through current state analysis, one can identify the strengths and weaknesses of an organisation, and thus get a good basis for planning and implementing improvement actions. For example, in software engineering, current state analysis is a widely used practice in the form of *process assessment*. Recognised process assessment approaches are *CMM* (Paulk et al., 1995), *Bootstrap* (Kuvaja et al., 1994), and *ISO 15504* (ISO, 1998a). When we examine the recognised *process improvement models* of software engineering, for example IDEAL of Software Engineering Institute (McFeeley, 1996) and ISO/TR 15504-7 (ISO, 1998b), they essentially include process assessment as a step in an improvement process.

In UCD, similar activity called *usability capability assessment* (UCA) seems to gain popularity. According to a study of Rosenbaum et al. (2000), 16 organisations out of 134 (12%) reported using 'organisational audits' as a means for enhancing 'strategic usability'. *Our research problem is to learn how to perform usability capability assessments effectively in industrial settings.*

In this research, our hypothesis was the traditional software process assessment, as defined in ISO 15504[1], using the recent *ISO/TR 18529* (ISO, 2000) as the process reference model of UCD. A pre-version of the model is the *UMM Processes* (Earthy, 1999). It was originally developed in the European *INUSE* research project and further elaborated during another European research project, *TRUMP*. In the beginning of our research, ISO/TR 18529 was not yet approved, and our reference was the UMM Processes model. — In this paper, however, we use consistently the term ISO/TR 18529.

ISO/TR 18529 is a process model developed specifically for process assessment. The format of its process definitions complies with the requirements of ISO 15504. Altogether, ISO/TR 18529 identifies seven UCD processes. Five of them are derived from the standard ISO 13407 (ISO, 1999). The processes are further divided into base practices. In an assessment, the capability of a process is typically determined through performance of *base practices*. The result of an assessment is a *capability profile*: each UCD process is given a capability rating. There are six levels of *capability*, from 0 (lowest) to 5 (highest). — The processes of ISO 13407 are illustrated in Figure 1. ISO/TR 18529 is discussed more detailed in Bevan & Earthy (2001).

---

[1] Also known as 'SPICE'

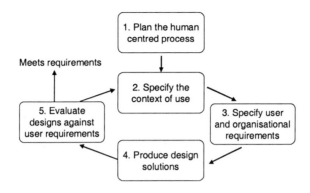

Figure 1: Activities of UCD as defined in ISO 13407.

2 Overview of the Assessments

We carried out four experimental usability capability assessments in three industrial companies in Finland. We started at *Buscom* with a traditional process assessment by using the ISO/TR 18529 process model as a reference in May 2000. Thereafter we performed an assessment at *Teamware* in June 2000. The third assessment (NET 1) was carried out at *Nokia Networks (NET) IMN* user interface team in October-November 2000. The biggest methodological step took place during this assessment. We developed revised process and capability models based on the experiences from the two previous assessments. The fourth assessment (NET 2) was at Nokia Networks in a customer documentation team in December 2000. This time we implemented the assessment as a workshop rather than as a series of interviews. The flow of the assessments is illustrated in Figure 2.

We describe each of the four assessments one by one, pointing out the main characteristics of the assessments and lessons learned. We describe the basics of the evolved models as part of the discussion of the NET 1 case.

3 Assessment at Buscom in May 2000

Buscom develops fare collection systems for transportation systems — especially for bus companies. The company has two features that make an assessment a special case. First, the company is small — about 60 employees. Another specific feature is that at the time of assessment, the company had only limited background in UCD. Still the company found it sensible to start development of UCD processes with an assessment.

3.1 Implementation of the Assessment

There were altogether six members in our assessment team. Two members of the team were trained process assessors. One of the team was the usability person of the company.

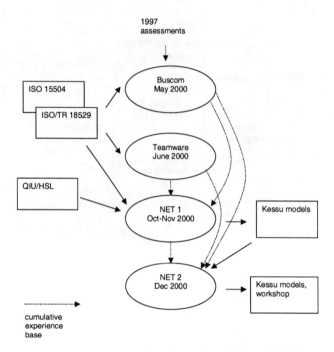

Figure 2: Summary of the assessments.

Based on our previous experience from assessments in 1997, reported in (Kuutti et al., 1998), we decided to assess to the level 1 only. In other words, we focused on assessing the substance of UCD — not on how the activities are managed. We interviewed the representatives from a number of development projects during two weeks' time, having altogether 10 interview sessions. There were one, two or three interviewees in each interview session. The total amount of interviewed persons was 20. On many days, we had two interviews per day.

We used base practices of the ISO/TR 18529 model as our reference in the interviews. We put effort in understanding what is meant with each base practice and in understanding to which extent the base practice was performed in the development process of the organisation. To do this, we assigned a responsible person for each process in our assessment team.

Rating the capability of processes, however, was not as successful as we had planned. During the assessment, we decided to give up giving ratings on the basis of base practices. The reasons for this were partly the tight schedule, partly the difficulties in the interpretation of base practices. The assessment team felt that it was difficult to give valid capability ratings. Our decision was the rate the processes informally, based on professional judgement rather than on the based practice driven capability-rating algorithm. We reported the results emphasising the qualitative findings.

3.2 Feedback from the Assessment

We gathered feedback from the assessment by using questionnaires delivered to the audience in the results presentation session. The staff reported that they generally found results of the assessments useful. A clear result was that those who were interviewed learned more about UCD than those that attended the result presentation session only. The core processes of ISO 13407 were perceived understandable. The results reporting session that lasted one hour, however, was perceived somewhat 'boring'.

In addition to gathering feedback with questionnaires, we later conducted some in-depth interviews of some key persons. The interviews revealed some interesting points that were not covered by the questionnaires. For example, we had presented a definition of processes and the related base practices in the form of ISO/TR 18529 model. The usability person reported afterwards that the interviewees had found the definitions of the processes and base practices difficult to understand. Some of the staff had a perception that the assessment was "academic stuff driven by the interests of the university".

The usability person of the company said that the assessment was personally a very positive learning experience. She learnt a lot not only about assessments but also got a more thorough understanding of the practices and principles of UCD and of the current ways of working in different units of the organisation. The assessment team found generally the UCD processes of the model sensible. The main problem was, as said, in the interpretation of the base practices.

3.3 Lessons Learnt

Based on these experiences it seems that assessment is not only about identifying strengths and weakness but also about communicating about usability and UCD to the organisation. We did not find as a very good result that many members of the staff had perceived 'not understandable' the things that we had presented. We conclude that improvement in the assessment process should be done in the following areas:

- From the assessors point of view, the main lesson learnt was that more precise and unambiguous interpretations of the base practices of the processes are required.

- The assessment should be carried out in slower pace. Too frequent interviews did not allow time to 'stop and think'. Two interviews a day may be appropriate for routine assessment, but not for research.

- The assessment process should be planned better and scope of the assessment should be only a very limited number of projects.

- Communicating the basics of UCD and the results of an assessment is a challenge. Results should be presented both qualitatively and quantitatively in a concise form.

The positive lessons learnt were:

- Limiting the assessment to level 1 of capability was the right choice: it made sense to examine only the essential performance of UCD. Assessment of management issues (levels 2 of capability and above) had not been meaningful in this case.

- The basic concepts of ISO 13407 (processes, definitions of usability etc.) are useful. They give a good basis for assessments.

- Interviews were experienced to be effective learning processes by the interviewees and the usability person.

4   Assessment at Teamware in June 2000

Teamware Group is an international software development company with several years' experience in UCD. Its main business is Internet based solutions for communities. A UI design team within the company, Ergo Team, has operated for years, and has influenced remarkably in the improvement of the user-centred development practices in the company.

This assessment followed an assessment that was conducted at Teamware in November 1997, reported in Kuutti et al. (1998). Even if we found some problems with the ISO/TR 18529 model in the assessment at Buscom, the approach was not changed for this assessment. One reason for this was that Teamware wanted to have comparative results with the assessment that was carried out earlier. Another reason was that the lead assessor was from a different organisation.

4.1   Implementation of the Assessment

The assessment team consisted of seven persons. Additionally, one representative of the assessed organisation was present in all assessment sessions. Most members of the assessment team had participated software process assessment training according to Bootstrap method (Kuvaja et al., 1994) after the assessment at Buscom.

All the processes of ISO/TR 18529 (HCD.1-7) were on the focus of assessment. The assessment method was traditional: the capability of the processes was determined using the base practices. The goal was to assess the processes up to level 3 of process capability if applicable — as was done in 1997. The focus of the assessment was in the early phases of development although all processes were assessed. The customer defined the focus.

The assessment lasted one week. Eight interview sessions (nine persons) took place during the week. The results were reported to the representatives of the organisation on the last day.

4.2   Feedback from the Assessment

We delivered questionnaires to the audience in the results presentation session. The questionnaires revealed that most interviewees felt that the interviews handled meaningful issues. Some pointed out that due to the insufficient information provided by the opening briefing they could not prepare themselves well enough. Most of the interviewees reported on gaining new ideas concerning their work. However, managers felt that the interviews did not handle very meaningful issues.

In results reporting session, the respondents considered all the UCD processes to be very important — if not for them, then for the company. Otherwise, they criticised the assessment results. They felt that many important areas related to the UCD were not discussed at all in the interviews. They felt that model had limited discussions sometimes to even irrelevant topics. Consequently, some felt that the results did not describe reality very well. The respondents also criticised that we did not explain well enough the terminology used or the maturity scales presented. We presented the results qualitatively, but the audience wished for the qualitative results, too.

The assessment team experienced the assessment week rather frustrating. The biggest problem was — as was at Buscom — in the interpretation of base practices. The interpretations caused even more disputes within the assessment team than at Buscom — now there were members from two organisations in the assessment team. Especially, there were disagreements whether a process truly reaches level 1, and wheter it makes sense to examine upper levels of capability. Some members of the assessment team experienced a problem in the validity of the interview style: interviewing the processes through base practices one by one. Many members of the assessment team felt that they did not get a good picture of essential practices of the company. These problems also led to difficulties in rating the capability of the processes. The capability scores were given but the interpretation of the findings remained contradictory.

We show some examples of base practices in Table 1. We had trouble in agreeing on interpretation with practices such as "Analyse the tasks and worksystem" and "Analyse the implications of the context of use". One the other hand, there were no problems to interpret a base practice such as "Describe the characteristics of the users".

4.3 Lessons Learnt

We got confirmation to our understanding that an assessment is not only about identifying strengths and weaknesses but also about increasing the awareness and commitment of the personnel towards UCD. Interviews were found to be an effective learning process to the interviewees, at least to the designers. Also the experience of the company from the previous assessment confirms those who were interviewed got committed to UCD.

Most of the lessons learnt are in line with the lessons learnt from the assessment at Buscom. Our main conclusion, again, was that we need a *clear, unambiguous interpretation of the process model*. We can also repeat most of the lessons learnt from the Buscom assessment: the assessment should be carried out in slower pace; one should learn new ways for discussing with management; the assessment process should be planned better; results should be presented both qualitatively and quantitatively, etc.

5 Assessment at Nokia Networks IMN User Interface Team in October 2000

Nokia Networks (NET) IMN organisation develops base stations for the mobile networks. The software developed by the IMN user interfaces team is used for configuring, installing, and maintaining of the base stations.

Context of use process	
Outcomes as defined in KESSU process model	Base practices as defined in HSL model
• Identification of user groups • Description of the characteristics of users • Description of the environment of use • Identification of user accomplishments • Description of user tasks • Identification of user task attributes	• Define the scope of the context of use for the product system • Analyse the tasks and worksystem • Describe the characteristics of the users • Describe the cultural environment/organisational / management regime • Describe the characteristics of any equipment external to the product system and the working environment • Describe the location, workplace equipment and ambient conditions • Analyse the implications of the context of use • Present these issues to project stakeholders for use in the development or operation of the product system

Table 1: Illustration of differences between outcomes and base practices. Example: Context of use process.

5.1   Implementation of the Assessment

Based on the experiences in the previous assessments, the main research driver in this assessment was to develop more unambiguous interpretations of the base practices. We used the *QIU* model (Earthy, 2000), which is the earlier version *HSL* model (Earthy, 2001) — together with the ISO/TR 18529 and ISO 13407 — as references in our interpretation work. The QIU model was recently distributed to a large audience of reviewers, and feedback was desired about it. In addition, we knew that the QIU model was an improved — although more complicated — version of the ISO/TR 18529 model.

This time we had a clear focus in the assessment: one development project. We interviewed the personnel of the company during two weeks' time, having altogether five interviews. In each interview session, there were one or two interviewees. In each interview session, we examined one or two UCD processes.

5.2   Development of New Process and Capability Models

The interpretation of the base practices realised to be quite a challenge. The work led to developing something different than interpretation of base practices. Jointly with the usability experts of NET, we decided to carry out the assessment up to

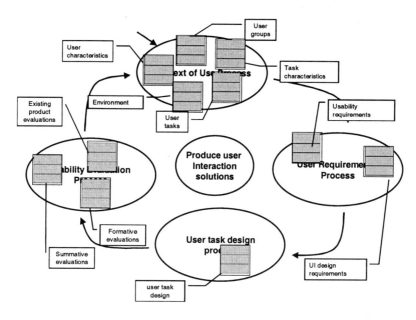

Figure 3: The KESSU Process model.

level 1 based on concrete *outcomes* of processes. In contrast with the outcomes of processes in ISO/TR 18529 (the model defines also outcomes, in addition to base practices), we limited the outcomes to include only concrete deliverables. The outcomes of our *KESSU*[2] Process model and base practices of the HSL model is illustrated in Table 1. As one can see, we have transformed some of the base practices into concrete outcomes. The substance of those base practices that do not produce concrete deliverables are covered by new capability dimensions (see discussion to follow).

Another distinctive feature is that we have split the 'Produce Design Solutions' process of ISO/TR 18529 (and ISO 13407) into two parts. Visually, in its former position there is a 'User Task Design' process. In the centre, there is a new process, 'Produce User Interaction Solutions'. The process model — including the outcomes — is illustrated in Figure 3. We identify five main processes: Context of use process, User requirements process, User tasks design process, Produce user interaction solutions process, and Usability evaluation process.

The reasoning behind splitting the Produce Design Solutions process is that the process is always existent and produces 'full outcome' (the system and user interface) — even in cases where the development process in not user-centred. All the other processes are characteristic to UCD: they provide user-driven information for the design process.

---

[2]KESSU is the name of our national research project that aims to develop methods for improving user centred-design in development organisations.

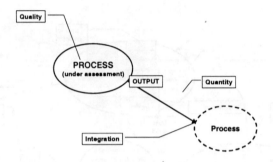

Figure 4: KESSU dimensions of process capability.

The outcome driven assessment led also to new kind of capability dimensions. The capability scale evolved to have three different dimensions as illustrated in Figure 4:

- The *quantity* of outcomes of the process. The more extensively an outcome exists, the higher performance score it gets.

- The *quality* of the outcomes. With this dimension, we examine the quality and validity of the outcomes. For example, we want to make a difference whether an outcome is based on someone's opinions or derived by using recognised user-centred methods and techniques.

- The *integration* of outcomes with other processes. The more extensively the outcomes are communicated and incorporated in other relevant processes, the higher rating is given to integration.

The integration aspect has also been addressed in the HSL model. Its solution is, however, different: a process has a specific base practice that addresses integration. An example is shown in Table 1 ("Present these issues to project stakeholders for use in the development or operation of the product system").

The different process and capability models led also to a different way of presenting the results. We present the capability profile in one visual picture, using different symbols to denote the different dimensions, as illustrated in Figure 5.

Altogether, we consider that we have developed new process and capability models. We call the models as *KESSU Process Model* and *KESSU Process Capability Dimensions Model* respectively. They are documented in project reports Jokela (2001b) and Jokela (2001a).

5.3 Feedback from the Assessment

We gathered feedback from the assessment again with questionnaires delivered in the opening briefing, after each interview and finally in the results presentation session. The interviewees found that the assessment approach made a lot of sense. They reported that the interview sessions had pointed out targets for improvement, and

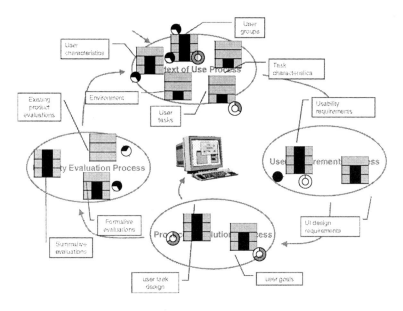

Figure 5: Example of capability profile presentation.

some of the interviewees had received confirmation to their own thoughts on how UCD should be developed.

The feedback from results presentation session was generally good. Especially, the audience reported high motivation for getting training in UCD and for trying UCD approaches in their work. They regarded UCD activities very important in the development.

All those members of the assessment team who had attended the previous assessments found this assessment more successful and sensible than the earlier ones. One illustrative comment from an assistant assessor was: "Interview by interview, the models became clearer. This is the way we should have done from the beginning: to make a clear interpretation of our own about the reference models". The definition of outcomes and assessing through the outcomes was found easier and to give a better picture about the UCD in the organisation than assessment through base practices. Assessors felt that this time they got a good picture about the UCD activities in the organisation.

5.4 Lessons Learnt

A clear feeling after the assessment was that "we want to try this approach again". However, there were also places to improve. The overall role and position of an assessment in the organisational context should be rethought. One organisational problem was, for example, that very few developers attended the opening session of the assessment. In addition, definitions for the levels of rating the capability dimensions should be created, and some terms should be made easier to understand, for example 'summative' and 'formative'. The assessment report should be quicker to produce.

6   Assessment at Nokia Networks IMN Customer Documentation Team

This assessment had a different object domain than the earlier ones: the object of the assessment was the development process of customer documentation. Three key persons from the customer documentation and a two-person assessment team participated the assessment.

The customer documentation group has experience about UCD for some years. For example, they have organised user evaluations of user manuals in laboratories and in the field. There is clear enthusiasm towards UCD in the group. The group is further developing their documentation processes, and was motivated to get feedback from an external evaluator.

The assessment had one significant difference compared with the earlier ones. It was decided to carry it out in half a day workshop. The reason for this was practical: there was no time for an assessment with multiple interviews.

6.1   Implementation of the Assessment

We used the process and capability models developed in the previous assessment. Our plan for the assessment was to follow a cycle that is used in typical assessments: interview, wrap-up of the findings by the assessment team, and agree on the results with the interviewees. At this time, we just hoped to cover all the relevant processes in a time that normally is reserved for one long interview.

In the interview part, we asked the project team to describe the activities of the development process of the user manual and quick reference guide. We did not describe our reference model beforehand but used it as our reference in the interview.

In the results session, the findings were contrasted against the process model. The lead assessor explained the model step by step, and interpreted the information received in the interview session against the model. We agreed on the areas where the organisation had strengths and weaknesses. The session was finished in about 1.5 hours. Some refinements and clarifications were made on the process model during the discussion.

6.2   Feedback from the Assessment

One immediate feedback came actually when we finished the workshop. One of the participants said that she already had started to challenge herself on how to implement improvements in one specific area. We asked feedback from the project team through email. Comments were received from the team on the same afternoon. They reported for example:

- "The assessment pointed out many issues to consider in the following documentation projects."

- "Now we know that task analysis is important. We also need to work on usability requirements."

- "We found that your model worked well also in our domain."

The assessment team found the assessment as a positive experience. We succeeded in getting a credible picture of the development process in a short time. We had felt that there was a positive atmosphere in the workshop.

6.3 Lessons Learnt

This assessment confirmed that we would experiment the revised process and capability models in the forthcoming assessments. The definitions of processes seem to make UCD concrete to the organisation. The capability dimensions point out the areas of improvement, and give a means to discuss the project at an appropriate level of abstraction.

The specific implication of this assessment is to try the workshop approach again. It is efficient — one workshop instead of a series of interviews. Moreover, a workshop may be a solution to one problem that we have faced: people being in different positions in assessments (those who are interviewed, and those who are not).

7 Discussion

Our target was to learn how to perform effective usability capability assessments through experiments in industrial settings. For that, we carried out four experimental usability capability assessments.

In the beginning of the research, we used an ISO 15504 style process assessment approach with one capability dimension, rating capability through base practices, and an assessment method with a number of interviews. During the assessments, we found that in our context it sensible to focus on the performance — not management — of UCD activities. As a result, we developed an assessment approach with an outcome-driven process model, three-dimensional capability model, and an implementation the assessment as a workshop.

Our process and capability models seem to make the assessment and UCD more understandable to the audience and easier for the assessors in our context. The workshop type of assessment makes an assessment efficient and spreads UCD knowledge to larger part of the staff than interviews of a limited number of people.

We, however, want to emphasise that our assessment approach is a complementary one to the traditional process assessment. Compared with ISO 15504 assessment, we can say that we examine the UCD activities thoroughly 'below the level 1 of capability'. Traditional process assessment should be used in contexts where it is applicable to examine the management of UCD activities at higher levels of capability.

7.1 Contrasting the Results with Experiences of the TRUMP Project

Bevan & Earthy (2001) report about recent assessment case studies carried out in the European TRUMP project. They carried out assessments in two organisations: at Inland Revenue (IR) at UK and at Israel Aircraft Industries (IAI). In both assessments, they used the ISO/TR 18529 as a reference. The IR assessment was a 'full' process assessment with twelve interviews while the assessment at IAI was a light assessment, a one-day workshop. Bevan & Earthy report that both assessments were successful.

One can regard the assessment at IR and our assessment at Teamware methodologically similar: traditional process assessment based on the same process model. The assessment at IR, however, was seemingly a more successful than the one at Teamware. One potential explanation may be the fact that the lead assessor in the IR assessment was the main author of the ISO/TR 18529 model. The assessment team at IR was also probably more experienced in process assessment than we are. In addition, we find that there are many other factors that potentially affect the success of an assessment. These factors include: the business and products of the company; general situation in the organisation (e.g. whether there has been recent big changes); the culture of the organisation; the tradition of carrying out development projects and improvement programs; the position of the sponsor of the assessment; how the assessment is planned, organised and conducted; how the project(s) to be assessed are selected; how successful are the presentations; the way the processes and base practices are communicated in the interviews; the characters and attitudes of individuals; the position of usability persons in the organisation etc. Not only the assessment approach but these kinds of non-technical factors may have a great impact to the success of the assessment.

The assessment at IAI resembles our last workshop at NET. They both were successful, too. The reference models were a bit different — IAI was assessed by using base practices while we used KESSU process model as reference. One may ask whether we would have succeeded with base practices, too. It may be possible. We find 'outcome based assessment' working probably because it makes things concrete — the outcomes are deliverables. Using 'concrete' base practices might work as well.

Bevan & Earthy's report that the success of the improvement efforts in the TRUMP trials has been very good. We have not yet carried out subsequent assessments to monitor our success. We assume that our success has not generally been at the same level. On the other hand, we find that the success of improvement actions does not depend on the success of an assessment only. Success in improvements depends on many factors — as do the assessments.

7.2   Limitations

There are some limitations to be considered when making decisive conclusions about our assessments experiences. First, the organisational situations may be very different, and one assessment approach that is suitable for one organisation may not be the best choice for another one. Therefore, comparing the success of assessments based on the feedback from the organisations assessed is problematic. On the other hand, we find as an advantage in our research that the assessment team was almost the same in all assessments. The assessment team was able to compare the different assessments.

Second, our goal for the assessments was to give a good basis for improvement actions in UCD. From this viewpoint, issues such as spreading knowledge about UCD to the staff and getting them committed to UCD improvement actions are important.

A different target for assessment could be for example to get exact ratings of usability capability for selection of contractors. This was not our goal. Another viewpoint that we excluded is standardisation that has been one driver of the ISO/TR 18529 and HSL models.

Third, each assessment is a different instance, even if the same approach is used. Assessment is a very human process, and its success may depend on many human issues — both the organisation assessed and the composition of the assessment team have influence on it. Specifically, an assessment necessarily has 'a look' of the lead assessor.

Fourth, one limitation is related to the assessment with the ISO/TR 18529 and HSL models. The assessments were very much based on the interpretations, experience and style of the lead assessors. The interpretation of the ISO/TR 18529 model is based on documentation. Some other person may have conducted the assessments in a different way.

Fifth, a specific feature in our assessments is that all organisations represented geographically limited industrial settings.

7.3 Implications for Next Assessments

We started with assessments with a number of interviews using a traditional process assessment approach, and finished with an assessment that was half a day workshop. What are our choices for the next assessment? In our environment, we most probably go for a workshop. We were able to get a clear picture of the position of UCD in the organisation, and to analyse and communicate the results in a very short time in the last assessment at NET. Next time, however, we will assign more time — probably one day — for the workshop.

We will continue with the KESSU process model and capability scale (probably with refinements). We find that the outcome-driven process model makes discussions concrete, and the three-dimensional capability scale makes possible to have an appropriate level of abstraction in the assessment.

For those who have not carried out assessments before, our main advice is that one should understand that an assessment is a research effort, no matter which model the assessment is based on. There exist very few reported experiences on assessments. No assessment approach — inclusive the one that we use — is so matured that one can totally rely on its validity.

7.4 New Research Topics

As said, each new assessment should be considered a research activity. A researcher should try to get access for following assessments and for gathering feedback from them. There is definitely space for improvements both at the model and in the assessment method (steps of assessment) levels. We will carry out further assessments, and regard each of them also as a research effort. — Actually, we just finished another assessment that was implemented as a workshop. The most important findings of this assessment are that one should understand the organisational improvement context before planning an assessment and take carefully into accout the human aspects. We will report the findings of this assessment in a forthcoming paper.

The next step in our research is of very constructive nature: to document the assessment approach as a handbook. We assume that the creation of such a document is not a one-time effort but it will be revised after trials. Another artefact we plan to develop is a template to make the assessment efficient. We hope to have an online documentation in the workshops, and deliver the results immediately.

One interesting challenge is how to reliability verify the success of an assessment. We have gathered a lot of feedback in our assessments. However, it still is difficult to make definite conclusions. For example, we find that the assessments should be also training occasions where the understandability of models and results is important. Some others may disagree with the importance of this criterion.

Acknowledgement

There are a number of people who have contributed this work. We wish thank the personnel of the partner companies, especially Erkki Jylhä-Ollila, Risto Rauhala and Timo Salmu from Buscom; Pirkko Jokela and Eija Suikola from Teamware; Pekka Suhonen, Marjo Favorin, Tuula Strömberg, Jouko Salo, Johanna Tapio and Tanja Petrell from Nokia Networks; and Petri Hyyppä from Nokia Mobile Phones. We also wish to express thanks to the other project members of the KESSU project: Pekka Abrahamsson, Mikko Jämsä, Tero Posio, Tonja Molin-Juustila, Mikael Johnson, Samuli Saukkonen, and Kari Kuutti; and to the national funding organisation TEKES.

References

Anderson, R. (2000), "Organisational Limits to HCI. Conversations with Don Norman and Janice Rohn", *Interactions* 7(3), 36–60.

Bevan, N. & Earthy, J. (2001), Usability Process Improvement and Maturity Assessment, *in* J. Vanderdonckt, A. Blandford & A. Derycke (eds.), *Proceedings of IHM-HCI'2001, Joined Conference on Human–Computer Interaction: Volume 2*, Cépaduès-Editions.

Bloomer, S. & Wolf, S. (1999), Successful Strategies for Selling Usability into Organizations, *in* M. W. Altom & M. G. Williams (eds.), *Companion Proceedings of CHI'99: Human Factors in Computing Systems (CHI'99 Conference Companion)*, ACM Press, pp.114–5.

Earthy, J. (1999), Usability Maturity Model: Processes, Project Report, Lloyd's Register of Shipping, London, UK.

Earthy, J. (2000), Quality In Use: Processes and Their Integration — Part 2, Assessment Model, Project Report, Lloyd's Register of Shipping, London, UK.

Earthy, J. (2001), Ergonomics — Human System Interface — Human-system Life Cycle Processes Proposal, Project Report, Lloyd's Register of Shipping, London, UK.

ISO (1998a), "Software Process Assessment — Part 2: A Reference Model for Processes and Process Capability", Project Report. International Organisation for Standardization, Genève, Switzerland.

ISO (1998b), "Software Process Assessment — Part 7: Guide for Use in Process Improvement", Project Report. International Organisation for Standardization, Genève, Switzerland.

ISO (1999), "ISO 13407 International Standard. Human-centred Design Processes for Interactive Systems". International Organization for Standardization, Genève, Switzerland.

ISO (2000), "Human-centred Lifecycle Process Descriptions", Project Report. International Organisation for Standardization, Genève, Switzerland.

Jokela, T. (2001a), KESSU Process Capability Dimensions, v0.1, Project Report, Oulu University, Oulu, Finland.

Jokela, T. (2001b), KESSU Process Model, v0.2, Project Report, Oulu University, Oulu, Finland.

Kuutti, K., Jokela, T., Nieminen, M. & Jokela, P. (1998), Assessing Human-centred Design Processes in Product Development by Using the INUSE Maturity Model, *in* S. Nishida & K. Inoue (eds.), *Proceedings of the 7th IFAC/IFIP/IFORS/IEA Symposium on Analysis, Design and Evaluation of Man–Machine Systems (MMS'98)*, IFAC, pp.89–94.

Kuvaja, P., Similä, J., Kranik, L., Bicego, A., Saukkonen, S. & Koch, G. (1994), *Software Process Assessment and Improvement — The BOOTSTRAP Approach*, Blackwell.

McFeeley, B. (1996), IDEAL SM: A User's Guide for Software Process Improvement, Project Report CMU/SEI-96-HB-001, Software Engineering Institute, Pittsburgh, USA.

Paulk, M. C., Weber, C. V., Curtis, B. & Chrissis, M. B. (eds.) (1995), *The Capability Maturity Model: Guidelines for Improving the Software Process*, Addison–Wesley.

Rosenbaum, S. (1999), What Makes Strategic Usability Fail? Lessons Learned from the Field, *in* M. W. Altom & M. G. Williams (eds.), *Companion Proceedings of CHI'99: Human Factors in Computing Systems (CHI'99 Conference Companion)*, ACM Press, pp.93–4.

Rosenbaum, S., Rohn, J. & Humburg, J. (2000), A Toolkit for Strategic Usability: Results from Workshops, Panels, and Surveys, *in* T. Turner, G. Szwillus, M. Czerwinski & F. Paternò (eds.), *Proceedings of the CHI2000 Conference on Human Factors in Computing Systems*, *CHI Letters* **2**(1), ACM Press, pp.337–344.

Revisiting Concepts

IDA-S: A Conceptual Framework for Partial Automation

Andrew Dearden

School of Computing and Management Sciences, Sheffield Hallam University, Howard Street, Sheffield S1 1WB, UK

Tel: *+44 114 225 2916*

Fax: *+44 114 225 3161*

Email: *a.m.dearden@shu.ac.uk*

IDA-S (Information, Decision, Action and Supervision) is a conceptual framework for thinking about partial automation, i.e. systems in which the delivery of a system function is performed by a combination of human and automated activities. The framework offers a generic decomposition of any function into a number of elements that can be considered as primarily performed by the machine, or primarily performed by the human user or operator.

The framework can be used in automation design to support the generation of design alternatives, the expression of distinctions between alternative designs, and to create operational specifications of chosen designs.

IDA-S was developed to support automation design for advanced aircraft systems, and has been extended to deal with systems engineering for naval systems. This paper explores how the IDA-S framework could be applied in the design of innovative consumer products, and explores possible differences between such an application and applications in large-scale systems engineering.

Keywords: function allocation, partial automation, design models, systems engineering, IDA-S, design space analysis.

1 Introduction

This paper presents a conceptual framework for thinking about partial automation. The framework can be used to support analysis and design of future systems, and takes the perspective of 'allocation of function' (McCarthy et al., 2000), i.e. it considers how different aspects of a task or function might be distributed between humans and machines. By systematically considering a series of distinct aspects, the framework can be used to describe or to explore different ways in which humans and automated systems can interact. At the same time, the framework can provide a common language that allows human factors experts, users and systems engineers to discuss design possibilities. In particular, the framework is sufficiently detailed to support the early specification of requirements for partially automated systems.

The framework was developed to support allocation of function discussions in the design of advanced aircraft flight-decks (Dearden et al., 1998), has been applied to automated support for supermarket pricing policy (Armature Ltd., 2000), and is being evaluated for use in Naval systems design (Johnson et al., 2000). This paper considers how the framework could be used to support reasoning about the use of automation in innovative consumer products such as personal digital assistants.

1.1   *Structure of the Paper*

The next section examines the background and motivation for the development of the IDA-S framework. Section 3 discusses minimal requirements for a framework to support design and specification of partial automation, focusing on the goals of generating design concepts, expressing distinctions between concepts during design discussions, and developing operational specifications of selected design concepts. Section 4 examines existing conceptual frameworks for partial automation, and Section 5 presents an overview of the IDA-S framework. Section 6 examines how the IDA-S framework can be used in the activities of generating design concepts, supporting discussion of those concepts and creating operational specifications of a chosen concept. Section 7 discusses evaluation and further work.

2   Background and Motivation

The increasing power, improved connectivity and diminishing cost of computational systems opens many opportunities for innovation in the design of consumer products and services. Many such innovations are based around automating activities that were previously performed manually. For example, modern mobile phones allow a user to establish a call by speaking the receiver's name, rather than dialling the receiver's telephone number. Refrigerators that can automatically order goods when supplies are running low, have been suggested (Financial Times, 2000). Businesses are increasingly using Internet and intranet technologies to automate transactions. Aircraft have long been controlled via automated systems, as have the physical devices used to deliver major services, e.g. communication networks, power generation and distribution.

Turning innovative ideas for automation into usable products challenges designers to consider how human users will interact with such systems. Where the use of automation is well established, it is now widely understood that inappropriate automation may result in systems that: fail to deliver hoped for benefits, are not used, or increase the risk of accidents (Woods et al., 1994; Billings, 1997; Palmer et al., 1993). In the design of consumer products, the primary hazard may be a failure to create an attractive commercial proposition.

In systems engineering the possible benefits and pitfalls of using automation are discussed during the early stages of design within a process called 'allocation of function' (MOD, 1989). Although there is considerable confusion about the use of the term function within the literature (Cook & Corbridge, 1997), this paper adopts the following as a working definition:

> A *function* is a service or benefit required of the completed human-machine system, described in a way that is independent of any particular division of work between humans and machines.

Using this definition, a function for an aircraft system might be 'fly following a previously specified route', a function for a personal digital assistant could be 'book theatre tickets'. Allocation of function involves human-factors experts, systems engineers, project managers, user representatives and other stakeholders examining and discussing alternative ways of applying automation to realise the functions suggested. Such discussions help to uncover possible implications of alternative designs for the users and for the development project. The discussion does not lead to a 'correct' design prescription. Rather, it helps the design team to agree an initial specification that reduces the risk that the system will fail to deliver intended benefits, be unsafe or will be delivered late and over budget.

In the context of the design of innovative consumer products, these initial stages of conceptual design are typically conducted using brainstorming techniques to generate initial ideas, and applying storyboards and scenarios to explore these ideas in increasing detail (Schuler & Namioka, 1993; Carroll, 1995). This paper examines how IDA-S might be used to complement such practices.

3   Requirements for a Framework

Any abstract framework to support the design and specification of interactive systems should exhibit (minimally) three key properties. Dearden & Harrison (1997) name these properties as: generativity, expressivity and operationality. The meaning of these terms can best be understood by examining roles that an abstract framework might play in design and development process.

Firstly, a framework can be used to help the design team to explore a wide range of different design alternatives. The degree to which a framework supports the generation of alternative proposals can be termed the *generativity* of the framework.

Secondly, a framework may be used, to reason about the relative advantages and disadvantages of alternative proposals. To support such assessments the framework must support shared understanding of design proposals between participants drawn from different domains of expertise (Ehn & Kyng, 1991; O'Neill, 1998), and that understanding must be sufficiently detailed to allow comparison of alternative designs with respect to relevant criteria. The degree to which a framework supports a design team in evaluating different proposals can be termed the *expressivity* of the framework.

These first two activities of generating alternatives and expressing distinctions can be related to the idea of design options and applying assessment criteria in discussions of design rationale and design space analysis (MacLean et al., 1991).

Thirdly, a framework may be used to communicate design ideas to the developers who are charged with delivering those concepts. To support this role, a framework should support the designers in producing a representation of the selected design that provides clear guidance to engineers during the later stages of development. The degree of support that a framework provides for this role can be termed the *operationality* of the framework. Notice that the concept of operationality is a refinement of the concept of the readability of a representation. Operationality focuses on the 'reading' of the representation for a specific purpose, namely imagining and constructing an artefact that matches the specification.

4   Existing Frameworks

The problems arising from the use of automation in domains such as aviation, manufacturing and undersea exploration have given rise to a number of frameworks that seek to distinguish different types or 'levels' of automation.

The simplest such distinction assumes that a function can be realised in one of three ways, either by human action, by machine action, or by a combination of the two (Older et al., 1997; Goom, 1996). More sophisticated systems generate a wider range of options for how a function might be shared. Table 1 presents a framework developed by Sheridan & Verplanck (1978), see also Sheridan (1992), which suggests eight intermediary levels between manual control of an operation and fully automatic operation. Shoval & Borenstein (1993) suggest a space of 6 levels, depending on the allocation of sub-tasks of 'perception' 'cognition' and 'action' to humans or machines. Semple (1998) suggests a similar three-stage model of 'information', 'decision' and 'action'. Kaber & Endsley (1997) provide a different 10-point scale of 'levels' of automation. In this framework they consider four elements of a function: 'generating options', 'selecting an option', 'implementing the option' and 'monitoring'. Each of these four components might be allocated to the human, shared between human and machine, or allocated to the machine. Billings (1997) suggests 5 different types of sharing between 'direct manual control' and 'autonomous operation' of functions in aircraft. For example, Billings distinguishes between 'management by delegation' in which a human operator (pilot) commands a particular function that the automation carries out consistently, from 'management by consent' in which the automation must seek confirmation from a human operator before executing significant changes of state.

Each of these different schemes generates a different perspective on the space of possible designs that might be available to realise a function. The different schemes are also capable of expressing different types of distinction between alternative designs. For example, Billings distinguishes four very different supervisory relationships when a human operator turns over control to an automated system, whereas Kaber & Endsley only consider whether the human and or the machine are involved in 'monitoring' the ongoing process. On the other hand, Kaber & Endsley (and Sheridan & Verplanck) make a distinction between generating decision options and selecting a particular option, whereas Billings simply suggests the possibility of applying decision support. Each of these distinctions may have important consequences for the feasibility and desirability of systems. No single

Level	Description
1	The human does all the planning, scheduling, optimising etc. and turns task over to computer for merely deterministic execution.
2	Computer provides options, but human chooses between them, plans the operations, and then turn task over to computer for execution.
3	Computer helps to determine options, and suggests one for use, which the human may or may not accept before turning task over to computer for execution.
4	Computer selects options and plans action, which human may or may not approve, computer can reuse options suggested by human.
5	Computer selects action and carries it out if human approves.
6	Computer selects options, plans and actions and displays them in time for the human to intervene, and then carries them out in default if there is no human input.
7	Computer does entire task and informs human of what it has done.
8	Computer does entire task and informs human only if requested.
9	Computer does entire task and informs human if it believes the latter needs to know.
10	Computer performs entire task autonomously, ignoring the human supervisor who must completely trust the computer in all aspects of decision making.

Table 1: Sheridan & Verplanck's 10 level framework, see Levis et al. (1994).

scheme drawn from this set, can express every distinction that can be made by at least one other scheme, i.e. no scheme dominates all the others in terms of expressivity (Dearden et al., 1998).

In terms of their operationality, these schemes vary in their ability to generate specifications that can be easily interpreted by developers. Schemes similar to Billings' have been found in practice to be difficult for systems engineers to understand without having extensive prior training in HCI (Warren, 1997). Frameworks such as those suggested by Kaber & Endsley, Shoval et al. and by Sheridan & Verplanck, benefit from a fixed decomposition of elements for each function that can be allocated to the human or the machine. For example, if 'navigate to a specified destination' is a function required in a future vehicle, and a design team selects the 'Decision Support' level of Kaber & Endsley's framework, it is then possible to specify the following use-case:

- The user specifies a destination.

- The system generates a number of possible routes to reach the destination.

- The user suggests an alternative route.

- The user selects one of the routes.

- The user and system monitor progress towards the destination.

- The user drives to the destination following the selected route.

Such requirements may require further refinement, but a use-case described at this level is accessible and understandable by systems engineers (who may not have an extensive training in human-factors or HCI). Hence, the schemes provided by Kaber & Endsley and by Sheridan & Verplanck appear to be more operational than Billings's framework.

A further limitation of these previous frameworks is their failure to address issues of information automation. Research in distributed cognition has shown how representational support can change the nature of the cognitive work required of a human operator (Hutchins, 1995; Zhang & Norman, 1994). Vicente et al. (1995) have demonstrated how automated processing of information prior to display can support improved human-machine interaction. None of the above frameworks generates a space of alternatives for information automation, nor expresses distinctions between different information automation solutions.

In summary, it is clear that all of these previous frameworks are lacking in either generativity, expressivity, or operationality. IDA-S was developed to subsume these previous frameworks and address these deficiencies.

5   The IDA-S Framework

IDA-S stands for 'Information, Decision, Action and Supervision'. These four components correspond to Semple's (1998) three steps with an additional component 'Supervision'. Supervision is added because of the wide recognition in automation literature that the ongoing supervision of automation is a major contributor to the complexity of working with such systems (Woods et al., 1994; Billings, 1997; Moray, 1986). Each 'component' is further decomposed into a set of 'elements'. To use the framework designers consider alternative ways in which the elements might be distributed between humans and machines. Hence each element gives rise to a question that might be asked of a possible design. A brief outline of the elements within each component is given below. For a more detailed treatment, the reader is referred to (Dearden et al., 1998).

5.1   Information

The information component is decomposed into the following elements.

Collect: How is information required to perform a function to be collected? Will it be collected electronically via sensors or by a human operator, or by some combination of the two?

Integrate: How is the collected information to be integrated? Will the human be responsible for integration? Could automation support integration via techniques such as ecological interface design (Vicente et al., 1995)? Will the automation be entirely responsible of integration using data fusion techniques?

Configure for problem solving: When the collected information indicates a need for some function to be performed, it is often necessary to configure resources to support the problem solving action, for example by switching to a particular page of a display, or by taking control of some resource. Such reconfiguration might be the responsibility of a human user, or might occur automatically as is the case with 'electronic centralised aircraft monitoring' systems on aircraft which respond to subsystems failures by presenting details of the particular subsystem affected.

Initiate response: When information indicates a need for a function to be performed, the initiation of a response may rely on the human operator deciding to that action is required, or automation might present an alarm to initiate action from the human operator.

Note: The ordering of the elements should not be understood as representing a fixed temporal sequence, although this particular order may be relevant for many functions. Alternative orderings may be possible, for example, when a human initiates a response to some information they have collected and integrated, the response might begin by configuring a (sub-)system to support further collection and integration of information.

5.2 Decision

The structure of the decision element is based, in part, on the elements identified by Sheridan & Verplanck (1978) of generating proposals, selecting proposals and approving actions. However, these are supplemented by two additional elements, evaluation and modification.

Propose: Given a recognition that a function should be performed, proposals for how that function could be delivered may be made by either a human operator, automation, or both might be permitted to make suggestions.

Evaluate: Having derived one or more proposals for action, an assessment of the different proposals may be possible. A human operator might want to evaluate proposals taking into account specific contingencies in the current work situation. An automated system might perform some algorithmic evaluation of proposals against pre-defined criteria.

Modify: The initially generated proposals might be modified by either the human or the automation. For example, a human operator might modify a route proposed by an automated navigator, or the automated navigator might modify the operator's suggestion to avoid travelling the wrong way along a one-way street.

Select: If more than one proposal is under consideration, the operator might be permitted to select a particular one, alternatively, an automated system might make the selection according to some scoring algorithm.

Approve: Finally, when only one candidate proposal is under consideration, there may be a step in which approval is required for that action. Such approval might be required from the human operator, or, in some systems, the automation might have a final approval step. For example a command to raise the landing gear on some aircraft will not be approved by the automation if the aircraft is flying below 1500 feet.

Again, the order of elements in the framework does not imply a particular temporal sequence. In fact, it may not be possible to distinguish separate activities of selection and approval, the act of a human selecting a particular option might constitute approval for the application of that option. Similarly, proposal, evaluation, selection and modification may be interleaved in many different ways.

5.3 *Action*

The action component is not decomposed into elements. If an action cannot be understood as being assigned completely to either the human or the automation, the IDA-S framework can be re-applied to the action to explore how the work is distributed between the two agents.

5.4 *Supervision*

The supervision component is perhaps the most complex to understand. The rationale for this particular decomposition chosen is based on Billings's (1997) concepts of management by delegation, consent and exception, and on Sheridan & Verplanck's (1978) treatment of undersea tele-operators. The elements are described below:

Monitor ongoing operation: Will the operator be required to monitor the ongoing progress of the function, or will the monitoring be conducted by automation with limited feedback unless exceptional conditions arise.

Identify exceptions: Will the operator be responsible for deciding whether some exceptional condition has arisen requiring a change of behaviour, or will the automation be required to determine this by computing some threshold. Alternatively, there may be no concept of an exceptional condition, as in Billings' concept of management by delegation.

Refresh Authority[1]: When exceptional conditions are identified, does the automation require further authority to be granted by the human operator (as in Billings' concept of Management by Consent), or can it renew its own authority unless the human operator explicitly intervenes (Billings' concept of management by exception).

Determine output content: During automated operation the information fed back to a human operator is often selective. The attributes included or excluded within the feedback might be fixed, might be varied by the operator requesting particular information, or might be varied dynamically by the automation. This element captures these distinctions that are identified in Sheridan & Verplanck's (1978) work.

Detect completion: Some functions can be defined in terms of achieving a particular goal. For example, attaining a particular temperature or altitude. Will the human operator be required to recognise whether this has occurred, or will this be a required feature of the automation?

Terminate process: If a function has a clear end or goal point, then if an operation is required to terminate the process that has been used to achieve that goal, will that operation be the responsibility of the human or the machine. For example, if the goal is to grind a piece of metal until it has no surface blemishes greater than one micron, will the automation terminate the grinding process when that goal is reached?

Again, no temporal ordering is implied.

6 Applying the IDA-S Framework in Automation Design

Section 3 identified roles that a design framework could play within a design process: helping to explore the possible design space; expressing distinctions during discussions of alternative designs; and the creating operational specifications to communicate to other participants in later development processes. This section discusses how IDA-S can support these roles.

6.1 Generating Design Concepts

To use IDA-S as a generative tool, each function required or suggested for a system is selected and the 'elements' used as keywords to structure a brainstorming session. This usage is similar to the usage of keywords to drive the HazOps (Hazard and Operability Studies) safety technique (Villemeur, 1992). For each function the team considers each element in turn, generating as many ideas as possible related to the individual keyword. The keywords give rise to particular questions. So, for example, the keyword 'Collect' suggests questions about, what information might be relevant to the function and how might the human-machine system obtain such information. The keyword 'Evaluate' suggests questions about how might alternatives be compared, what different criteria might be relevant to the beneficiary of the function (in this case the user). What types of algorithmic evaluation might be possible? Thus, the keywords enable a systematic exploration of a space of alternative design possibilities. For example, in developing a design for a personal digital assistant, a possible function suggested could be 'book cinema tickets'. Using the keywords a range of design proposals can be generated. Table 2 shows one collection of concepts generated (by the author) in this way.

At this stage, the no system designs have been created, rather a space of possibilities has been constructed. Each keyword can be understood as representing a dimension that can be used to distinguish between different design alternatives. The set of keywords then defines a multi-dimensional coordinate space, with each point in the space representing a particular way of distributing work between the human and the machine to realise the function.

The process of exploring the design space may also lead to new understandings of the function, its possible inputs and outputs. For example, does the function 'book cinema tickets' lead to entries in the user's diary, does it include authorising the financial transaction, and does it include activities related to getting to the cinema. In the context of large-scale systems engineering, the functions required of a system may have been defined in more detail in advance of applying the IDA-S framework for concept generation. However, early observations of systems engineers applying

Keyword	Concepts
Collect	Films showing, times, prices, reviews, recommendations from friends, public transport timetables, seat availability, current engagements, friends timetables.
Integrate	Generate a film preference rating, identify possible slots, identify times in friends diaries when they might be available.
Configure	Log into a chat room, connect to a relevant network, present 'entertainment' display, set up a call to a friend.
Initiate	Trigger an alarm, phone the user, begin collecting reviews .
Propose	A film to see, a time, a place, transport arrangements.
Evaluate	Rate alternative plans, present reviews of films, compare with TV listings, relate to current bank balance, compare timings with respect to existing commitments.
Modify	Different time, place, film, seat, friends, different activity (e.g. theatre, club, pub).
Select	Specify a particular booking and a diary entry.
Approve	Confirm the ticket purchase / payment.
Monitor	Monitor whether the plan is being executed: is the user running to time, is the friend running to time.
Identify Exceptions	Fire at the cinema, user makes different booking in diary, arrival likely to be late, friend likely to be late, public transport problems, traffic congestion.
Refresh authority	Can the machine automatically contact friend to apologise for lateness?
Determine output content	What information will be available in the display following the booking transaction, does the user need to query to find out details such as the amount transferred or the seat number allocated?
Identify completion	Not applicable
Terminate process	Not applicable
Action	Place booking, transfer funds, record appointment in diary, confirm with friends diary.

Table 2: Concepts for a function 'book cinema tickets'.

---

the technique also indicate that an initial functional decomposition may be (locally) renegotiated as different automation options are explored.

Table 2 can be understood as a range of alternative ordinates that can be identified along each dimension. To create individual design proposals, designers can select points within the coordinate space by selecting one value along each dimension. Table 3 shows how one such point could be represented using IDA-S. By choosing different mixes of elements performed by the human and the machine, a variety of different design concepts can be generated and documented.

In comparison to the previous frameworks, if used in this way, IDA-S should generate a wider range of design alternatives. Distinctive features IDA-S are: the inclusion of elements dealing with information automation taking into account work by authors such as Vicente et al. (1995) and Zhang & Norman (1994); the

Information	
Collect	System collects information about films at nearby cinemas, times and reviews.
Integrate	User integrates information.
Configure	System configures by presenting a menu of relevant tasks (e.g. read reviews, check times, select cinema, phone a friend).
Initiate	User initiates by selecting a function 'book film' and indicating a date and approximate time.
Decision	
Propose	System proposes films that the user might like to see.
Evaluate	User evaluates reviews, prices, times; system supports evaluation by presenting information about times, prices, availability and film reviews.
Modify	User modifies number of seats, type of seat.
Select	User selects one film and showing time.
Approve	User approves booking.
Supervision	
Monitor	System monitors progress of the transaction.
Identify exceptions	System alerts the user if no seats are available / insufficient funds.
Refresh authority	User must refresh authority if different seats offered.
Determine output content	Not applicable, output content is deterministic.
Identify completion	System reports that transaction has been completed.
Terminate process	System terminates connections when transaction completed.
Action	System implements plan by placing booking with cinema booking system, authorising transfer of funds and entering film into users diary.

Table 3: A possible allocation for the function 'book cinema tickets'.

incorporation of the different aspects of supervision covered by Billings and by Sheridan & Verplanck, and the inclusion of the idea of evaluation and modification of proposals.

6.2 Expressing Distinctions Between Design Alternatives

Given a collection of alternative design proposals, a design team will want to consider the advantages and disadvantages of each proposal. In the QOC design rational approach (MacLean et al., 1991) this stage would correspond to the investigation of options with respect to selected criteria.

The function allocation method described by Dearden et al. (2000) involves comparing the effect of different design options within a series of rich scenarios. Design options, defined using the IDA-S framework, are discussed with operators (pilots), human-factors experts and systems engineers to investigate their beliefs about expected benefits or disadvantages of each design option within the chosen scenario.   In early trials using IDA-S, domain experts, systems engineers and human-factors professionals have been willing to rank the relative advantages and disadvantages of competing proposals in terms of their likely impact on criteria such as performance, technical feasibility, development cost, operator situation awareness or operator workload.   On the basis of these early results, IDA-S appears to be an expressive representational framework to support design discussions in these specialised settings.

There are, however, limits to the expressiveness of a framework such as IDA-S, which may be more apparent when consumer products are being considered. In large-scale systems design, functions and scenarios such as 'replanning a route' (Dearden et al., 2000) or combating a ship-board fire (Johnson et al., 2000) may be well defined with readily agreed design criteria (e.g. technical feasibility, speed, accuracy, operator workload).   In consumer product design, some criteria may be more difficult to establish, and many criteria may be beyond the expressive scope of an abstract framework such as IDA-S. For example, subjective emotional responses to a particular proposal, or the ability of a customer to relate a design to her own wants and needs may be as important as issues of functional complexity. Whilst an IDA-S model might help in the assessment of criteria such as technical feasibility, development cost and perhaps support initial estimates of the time that might be required to complete a function, it cannot support assessment of these more subjective criteria. To incorporate such criteria into design discussions alternative approaches would be needed to complement IDA-S modelling. Standard collaborative design techniques such as storyboards, scenarios, paper-prototypes or Wizard of Oz experiments (Carroll & Aaronson, 1988) would also be needed. In this setting the IDA-S descriptions could be used as a reference point when setting up scenarios to ensure that scenarios presented were consistent with the range of designs that were currently under consideration.

In comparison with previous frameworks, it can be shown that any two designs distinguished by any of the frameworks, can also be distinguished within IDA-S. Also, by combining insights from the different frameworks, new distinctions may be expressed. For example, a distinction can be drawn between different forms of Billings's 'Assisted Manual Control'.   Automation might assist by generating proposals, e.g. a traffic collision advisory system (TCAS) proposing avoidance manoeuvres, or by supporting a pilot in evaluating actions, e.g. a flight director indicating how the aircraft's flight compares to an 'ideal' approach path.   See Dearden et al. (1998) for a detailed examination of the theoretical expressiveness of IDA-S. Hence, IDA-S can be regarded, in this specific sense, as being at least as expressive as the combination of these predecessors.

6.3   Communicating Operational Specifications

The third role that IDA-S can play is to provide a framework for specification of a selected design, which can then be communicated to other participants in development. In this role, IDA-S is similar to previous frameworks such as Kaber & Endsley's (1997) or Sheridan & Verplanck's (1978). Using the generic elements, the design concept can be transformed to generate a series of explicit requirements that define a boundary between the system that is to be constructed, and the user or operator of that system. Examples of such statements are:

> 'the system shall support the user in evaluating films by presenting information about reviews, times and prices of films, and ticket availability.'

> 'the system shall alert the user if the booking transaction encounters exceptional conditions, such as lack of funds or seats not available'

Such statements can be presented at a level that abstracts away from the low-level details of interaction design, and may be combined within use-cases. For example, the above statement about evaluation does not commit the designers of the system to any particular modality (visual vs. audio presentation), any particular presentational format (star ratings for films, or full textual reviews). Using the IDA-S framework delays the need to make such commitments to later stages of the development process. Johnson et al. (2000) discuss how IDA-S can be integrated with UML to support use-case authoring.

7 Evaluation and Further Work

The discussion in this paper presents some theoretical evaluation, relative to the criteria of generativity, expressivity and operationality (Dearden & Harrison, 1997). In addition, the framework has been applied to a number of case studies relating to large scale systems design problems, see Dearden et al. (1998) and Johnson et al. (2000). It is being used and evaluated by BAE SYSTEMS within a major development project. It has been used by Armature Ltd. in the design of an automated aid to support supermarket pricing (Armature Ltd., 2000). It has also been applied in a naval domain in an evaluation workshop attended by systems engineers, human-factors experts and domain experts. Preliminary feedback from these exercises has been favourable.

Some concerns have been raised in respect to the presentation of the framework, particularly with regard to the definition of the different elements. Examples are: the separation between selecting an option and approving that decision option — these might occur in an atomic interaction; and possible confusion about the distinction between the information component, intended to connote the handling of information about the broader environment, and the 'monitoring' element of supervision, connoting the management of information about the behaviour of the automation. In response, some changes in the names of elements have been made between the initial presentation of the framework in Dearden et al. (1998) and in this presentation. A carefully designed handbook with examples might also improve the usability of the framework. Finally, it should be recognised that IDA-S does not, in its current form deal directly with the issue of adaptive automation. Further development is required to consider how this can best be achieved.

The framework has not previously been applied to the design of innovative consumer products. This paper has focused on the possibility of applying the framework in this area. Further evaluation is planned examining the performance of students in applying the framework in design exercises.

Acknowledgements

IDA-S was developed in collaboration with Dr Peter Wright and Professor Michael Harrison at the University of York. The initial development was funded by BAE SYSTEMS. The author would particularly like to thank Peter Gosling, Peter Wilkinson, Nigel Cox and Martin Curry of BAE SYSTEMS for their helpful contributions during the development of the framework.

References

Armature Ltd. (2000), Retail Price Desk Data Sheet, Available at http://www.armature.com.

Billings, C. E. (1997), *Aviation Automation. The Search for a Human-centered Approach*, Lawrence Erlbaum Associates.

Carroll, J. & Aaronson, A. (1988), Learning by Doing with Simulated Intelligent Help, Technical Report RC 13453, IBM Research Division, TJ Watson Research Centre, Yorktown Heights, NY, USA.

Carroll, J. M. (ed.) (1995), *Scenario-Based Design: Envisioning Work and Technology in System Development*, John Wiley & Sons.

Cook, C. & Corbridge, C. (1997), Tasks or Functions: What are we allocating?, *in* E. Fallon, L. Bannon & J. McCarthy (eds.), *ALLFN'97 Revisiting the Allocation of Functions Issue: New Perspectives*, IEA Press, pp.115–24.

Dearden, A. M. & Harrison, M. D. (1997), "Abstract Models for HCI", *International Journal of Human–Computer Studies* **46**(1), 151–77.

Dearden, A. M., Harrison, M. D. & Wright, P. C. (1998), IDA-S: A New Framework for Understanding Function Allocations, Technical Report COE/TR/98/03, University of York Centre of Excellence in Cockpit Automation, Department of Computer Science, University of York, UK.

Dearden, A. M., Harrison, M. D. & Wright, P. C. (2000), "Allocation of Function: Scenarios, Context and the Economics of Effort", *International Journal of Human–Computer Studies* **52**(2), 289–318.

Ehn, P. & Kyng, M. (1991), Cardboard Computers: Mocking-it-up or Hands-on the Future, *in* J. Greenbaum & M. Kyng (eds.), *Design at Work: Cooperative Design of Computer Systems*, Lawrence Erlbaum Associates, pp.169–96.

Financial Times (2000), "Bluetooth: Wireless Wonders All Set to Change the Way We Live", *Financial Times: Information Technology* . 5th April.

Goom, M. (1996), Function Allocation and MANPRINT, *in* D. Beevis, P. Essens & H. Schuffel (eds.), *Improving Function Allocation for Integrated Systems Design*, Crew Systems Ergonomics Information Analysis Center, Wright-Patterson Airforce Base, Ohio, USA, pp.45–61. Technical Report SOAR 96-01.

Hutchins, E. (1995), *Cognition in the Wild*, MIT Press.

Johnson, P., Harrison, M. & Wright, P. (2000), The Integration of the Enhanced Function Allocation Representation with Systems Engineering Methods and Tools, Technical Report DERA Project, Deliverable 2.5, HCI Group, Department of Computer Science, University of York, York YO10 5DD, UK.

Kaber, D. & Endsley, M. (1997), The combined effect of level of automation and adaptive automation on human performance with complex, dynamic control systems, *in Proceedings of the Human Factors and Ergonomics Society 41st Annual Meeting*, Human Factors and Ergonomics Society, pp.205–9.

Levis, A. H., Moray, N. & Hu, B. (1994), "Task Decomposition and Allocation Problems in Discrete Event Systems", *Automatica* **30**(2), 203–16.

MacLean, A., Young, R. M., Bellotti, V. M. E. & Moran, T. P. (1991), "Questions, Options and Criteria: Elements of Design Space Analysis", *Human–Computer Interaction* **6**(3-4), 201–50.

McCarthy, J., Fallon, E. & Bannon, L. (2000), "Editor's Preface — Special Issue: Dialogues on Function Allocation", *International Journal of Human–Computer Studies* **52**(2).

MOD (1989), *Defence Standard 00-25. Human Factors for Designers of Equipment. Part 12: Systems.* Available at http://www.dstan.mod.uk.

Moray, N. (1986), Monitoring Behaviour and Supervisory Control, *in* K. R. Boff, L. Kaufman & J. P. Thomas (eds.), *Handbook of Perception and Human Performance*, John Wiley & Sons, chapter Chapter 40, pp.40.1–40.51.

Older, M., Waterson, P. & Clegg, C. (1997), "A Critical Assessment of Task Allocation Methods and Their Applicability", *Ergonomics* **40**(2), 151–71.

O'Neill, E. J. (1998), User-developer Cooperation in Software Development. Building Common Ground and Usable Systems, PhD thesis, Queen Mary and Westfield College, University of London. Available at http://www.maths.bath.ac.uk/ maseon/thesisPDF.html.

Palmer, E., Hutchins, E., Ritter, R. & Vancleemput, I. (1993), Altitude Deviations: Breakdowns of an Error Tolerant System, Technical Memorandum DOT/FAA/RD-92/7, NASA.

Schuler, D. & Namioka, A. (eds.) (1993), *Participatory Design: Principles and Practices*, Lawrence Erlbaum Associates.

Semple, W. G. (1998), Information, Decision or Action? — The Rôle of IT in Fast Jet Mission Systems, *in Proceedings of the 1998 AGARD Conference MP3*, NATO Advisory Group on Aerospace Research and Development. Reference taken from preprint supplied by the author.

Sheridan, T. & Verplanck, W. (1978), Human and Computer Control of Undersea Teleoperators, Technical Report, Man–Machine Systems Laboratory, Department of Mechanical Engineering, MIT, Cambridge, MA, USA. See (Sheridan, 1992) for a discussion of the concepts in this report.

Sheridan, T. B. (1992), *Telerobotics, Automation and Supervisory Control*, MIT Press.

Shoval, S.and Koren, Y. & Borenstein, J. (1993), Optimal Task Allocation in Task Agent Control State Space, *in Proceedings of the IEEE Conference on Systems, Man and Cybernetics*, IEEE Computer Society Press, pp.27–32.

Vicente, K., Christoffersen, K. & Pereklita, A. (1995), "Supporting Operator Problem-solving Through Ecological Interface Design", *IEEE Transactions on Systems, Man and Cybernetics* **25**(4), 529–45.

Villemeur, A. (1992), *Reliability, Availability, Maintainability and Safety Assessment*, Vol. 1, John Wiley & Sons.

Warren, C. (1997), Allocation of Function: A Brief Review, Technical Report JS13076, BAE Systems, Sowerby Research Centre, Bristol, UK.

Woods, D. D., Johannesen, L. J., Cook, R. I. & Sarter, N. B. (1994), Behind Human Error: Cognitive Systems, Computers and Hindsight, Technical Report SOAR 94-101, Crew Systems Ergonomics Information Analysis Center, Wright Patterson Air-force Base, Ohio, USA.

Zhang, J. & Norman, D. A. (1994), "Representations in Distribution Cognitive Tasks", *Cognitive Science* **18**(1), 87–122.

Beyond Mode Error: Supporting Strategic Knowledge Structures to Enhance Cockpit Safety

Rachid Hourizi & Peter Johnson

University of Bath, Bath BA2 7AY, UK
Tel: *+44 1225 826006*
Fax: *+44 1225 826492*
Email: *{R.Hourizi,P.Johnson}@bath.ac.uk*
URL: *http://www.bath.ac.uk/~maprh,*
http://www.bath.ac.uk/~maspj

In the contextual complexity of modern, computerised systems, the current system state can come as an unpleasant shock to even an experienced user. In this paper, we show that errors, which occur within such complexity, cannot easily be described in terms of individual tasks and their component actions. We use this starting point to examine the dominant thinking in this field (Palmer, 1995; Palmer et al., 1993; Degani et al., 1996; Rushby, 1999). We show this dominant position, which suggests that much of this 'automation surprise' (Palmer, 1995) results from mode error, is a fundamental misclassification of the human factors involved. We then show the existence of a deeper problem, which we identify as a knowledge gap (Johnson, 1992) between operator and system. We next assert the existence of a second, higher level of activity, which encompasses the strategies used by operators to manage tasks within a complex, changing environment. We show that the knowledge gap identified arises as the result of a failure in such a strategy and develop a new design solution, based on this re-classification. We then evaluate this new approach through the redesign of interfaces in a simulation of a well-documented air-incident. The results of our evaluation show the redesign to be significantly less prone to the depicted error. We conclude by considering the implications of these results in terms of our knowledge-based approach.

Keywords: aviation, safety, automation surprise, mode error, user interface redesign, knowledge structures, task and strategy.

1 Automation Surprise

Despite the existence of uniquely comprehensive incident reporting systems (e.g. ASRS, CHIPS) and a great deal of research time and effort, little progress has been made in reducing the impact of human factors on aircraft safety. Accident rates per take off have remained almost unchanged over the last twenty years (De Keyser & Javaux, 1996) and human error is listed as a key causal element in an increasing number of crashes (Harrison, 2000).

Inadequate integration of safety promoting principles and procedures (e.g. CRM) has been identified as a contributory factor to this lack of improvement. Equally the failure of the principles and procedures themselves to address fundamental flightdeck issues such as high workload and tight schedules have been important negative elements (Johnson & Love, 2000).

In fact, the combination of this high workload and the changes in flight control activity, caused by the introduction of computerised, 'glass' cockpits has thrown up a new type of 'human error' — automation surprise — a phenomena which involves operator confusion about the status of the auto flight control system, particularly its modes, and the subsequent behaviour of the aircraft (Degani et al., 1996). This new class of error provides a focus for our paper.

2 Air Inter Flight F-GGED

In order to better understand both this new error class and its potential solutions, we will use a well-reported instance to underpin our study:

At 18:20 hours, on the 20th January 1992, an Airbus A320 passenger jet, flying a short journey from Lyon to Strasbourg (Air Inter flight F-GGED), crashed into the foothills of Mont St-Odile in eastern France, killing all but six of the passengers and the entire crew. When the surviving cockpit voice recorders were retrieved from the wreckage, it was found that the crew had shown no sense of panic during the final moments of the flight, had attempted no evasive action and had, apparently, been entirely unaware that a crash was imminent, until an altitude alarm had sounded 200 feet above ground level — too late to avoid impact. No mechanical failure could be identified as leading directly to the crash, nor was any significant human malpractice to blame. (Bureau Enquetes Accidents, 1992)

Though the causes of such a crash are inevitably complex, there is agreement (Bureau Enquetes Accidents, 1992; De Keyser & Javaux, 1996) that inappropriate entry to the autopilot was central to the events leading to the disaster:

The pilot and co-pilot had been refused permission to land on their first request and, were about to make a second attempt using navigation assistance from the local air traffic control. At the time of the error, both pilot and co-pilot were extremely busy, needing to correct their lateral course, get the landing gear down, run through the pre-descent checklists and enter an appropriate rate of descent.

The overloaded pilot entered a speed of descent of 3300feet per minute in the place of an angle of 3.3degrees (Both are entered through the bimodal VS/FPA dial — see below). The desired entry would have given a relatively gentle descent, whilst the error lead to a steeper drop, culminating in the plane crashing into a mountainside short of the airfield.

Figure 1: Airbus A320 FCU (original) (Meriweather, 2000).

In order to better understand this erroneous entry, a basic description of the plane's Flight Control Unit (FCU) is needed, see Figure 1.

Essentially the FCU is made up of switches, which affect the entry format of related bi-modal dials. An example is the Speed/Mach dial, which allows plane speed to be entered as either a number of multiples of the speed of sound (Mach) or as a number of feet per minute (Speed), depending on the setting of the Speed/Mach switch.

Parameters can then be entered either individually or in combination (e.g. go to an altitude of 15,000feet at a vertical speed of 400feet per second).

Finally, an autopilot setting is then chosen, using one of six buttons towards the bottom of the FCU. These buttons dictate which autopilot is used to execute the instructions entered and the manner of execution. An example would be the AP 1 button, which engages Autopilot 1, after an automatic delay of four seconds.

If we combine this understanding of the FCU with the events of flight F-GGED, we can identify two pivotal human 'failures' in the causal chain leading to the accident. Firstly, the pilot entered a seemingly correct parameter value on the correct entry dial, whilst the panel was in an unappreciated mode. Subsequently, both the pilot and co-pilot failed to notice the (unintended) rapid descent of the aircraft until shortly before impact. In other words, they were surprised by the performance of the system (plane) — an example of the phenomenon described in Section 1. These errors are summarised in the schematic outline of events in Figure 2.

3   Task Analysis

Having identified the key events leading to the crash of flight F-GGED, we must next understand how the human 'error' occurred and how it can be avoided or its results mitigated.

In theory, a traditional task based approach, such as GOMS (Card et al., 1983) or HTA (Annett et al., 1971) could be used to address this problem. In either variant, individual tasks would be identified and deconstructed within a temporal structure (i.e. first A would occur, then B, then C etc.). The top level of this deconstruction would be a series of goals and sub-goals beneath which would be a series of actions, required in their achievement. The action step(s) at which human error occurred could then be identified and a solution proposed, based on simplification or support at a key moment. Alternatively, the entire action sequence could be altered to prevent the error conditions from arising.

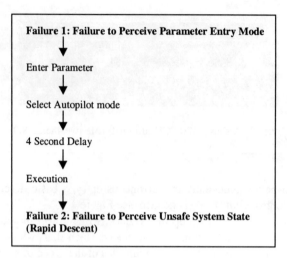

Figure 2: Erroneous instruction entry, Air Inter flight F-GGED.

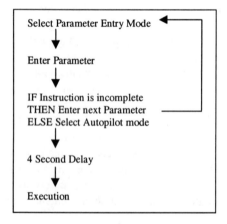

Figure 3: Instruction entry task (original interface).

This basic form can be extended to include simple conditional structures. Both GOMS (Card et al., 1983) and HTA (Annett et al., 1971) use this extension to create a simple conditional tree, describing a task in terms of component actions and decision points. This allows a procedural description of simple cockpit tasks, such as the completion of checklists or a basic altitude change.

In terms of traditional task analysis, the 'enter instruction to autopilot' task, derived from the accident report Bureau Enquetes Accidents (1992) and Meriweather's (2000) instructions for use, could, therefore be summarised as per Figure 3.

Though this approach provides a clear description of the actions required for accurate instruction entry, it does little to explain the crash on flight F-GGED.

Issues such as high workload, require a deeper understanding of the problem domain. One task in isolation may be easily achievable by an experienced pilot with nothing else to do. This level of performance may be reduced, however, if the pilot is also responsible for other activities (Kirsh, 2001), some of which may be triggered by contextual factors like weather, the actions of a colleague or terrain over-flown. For example, it is extremely unlikely that a pilot, concentrating only on a simple altitude change would be surprised by the state of the autopilot or its current mode. The same pilot attempting to correct a lateral course setting, whilst executing pre-descent checklists in tandem with a co-pilot and listening for instructions from local ATC may, however lose track of one system setting whilst concentrating on another.

Description based solely on the actions required for routine execution of a task provide little insight into these contextual factors.

Furthermore, the combination of contextual input and time constraints may require the operator to coordinate multiple goals, some of which may induce the suspension or cancellation of existing activities e.g. the execution of an altitude change may be interrupted by an incoming message from ATC. The interruptions and resumptions of activity, which result from this multitasking play a significant causal role in the production of human error (Dismukes, 2001; Kirsh, 2001) and must, therefore be incorporated both in any system description or model and in an eventual interface design.

Equally, temporal relationships between multiple activities may be more complex than the simple serial approach described above. Related activities can be performed by multiple agents in parallel or can be interleaved by one or more participant. Some activities may require an absolute block of time ('enough' time) for completion. In either case, the execution of an otherwise simple task may be negatively affected (Johnson & Gray, 1996).

The problem with an approach based on actions grouped into individual tasks is that it does not support a link between the contextual factors (described above), which affect automation surprise, and the effects, which they produce. In other words, these approaches describe 'what' occurs but not 'how' or 'why'.

4   Mode Error

One approach, which attempts to deal with the complex social environment in which automation surprise occurs is that based upon 'mode error'. Under this approach, analysts look beyond the theoretical actions required for isolated task completion and base their investigation upon a common error, which can occur in a busy multi-agent system, such as the modern flightdeck:

Many of the examples of cockpit automation surprise involve such an error (e.g. Failure 1 in Figure 2), i.e. they involve a failure to perceive the current system mode. For this reason, the dominant description of the surprise lists mode error, as a key causal factor in the accident model (Palmer, 1995; Palmer et al., 1993; Degani et al., 1996; Rushby, 1999). These modal errors, as described, fall under the category of perceptual slips i.e. the pilot (or operator) fails to notice the current mode of the system and, therefore, ends up with a system which reacts to his/her input in an unexpected way.

This type of error and indeed perceptual slips in general describe a failure to correctly identify an important detail within the execution of an otherwise well understood activity (In our example, the 'select parameter entry mode' action). In light of this, the temptation is to provide a solution at the action level i.e. to reduce the likelihood that the activity will be poorly executed. Having identified a slip as the pivotal issue in the causal structure of an accident, many authors (sensibly) go on to describe solutions, which involve the prevention of that slip. For example, Rushby (1999) builds models, which identify systems and interfaces that are 'prone' to such errors, suggesting individual features, which need reworking. Palmer (1995) suggests lock-ins, to prevent the passage from mode-confusion to hazardous state.

This approach, then, moves on from an understanding of activity based on expert execution in sterile surroundings. It allows for the existence of a contextually influenced error type and attempts to lessen or mitigate it. What it does not do, however, is provide an explanatory account for the class. We understand that errors, such as those observed on flight F-GGED can occur and what they might entail, but are still unable to explain why.

We can demonstrate the insufficiency of this approach by returning to flight F-GGED:

Though Failure 1 (from Figure 2) is covered by a mode error based description, Failure 2 is not. The second 'mistake' — the misperception of the unsafe system state (following the erroneous entry) — is not directly caused by the mode error. Why, then, does it occur? In the case of flight F-GGED, the pilots had information which could have led them to understand that a sustained, rapid drop was taking place both from the instrument panel, had they chosen to consult it and from the raw physical sensation of quick descent. They took neither into account. De Keyser & Javaux (1996) describes this as 'fixation error', an error during which the pilots are presented with considerable evidence that the system is not performing the intended action but continue to believe that they have correctly grasped the system state.

Given that perceptual slips are not generally followed by 'fixation' in other circumstances (Reason, 1990), their regular occurrence in cases of automation surprise suggests that a more fundamental explanation exists which links the two 'failures' described above. This explanation would, if extracted, provide a better explanation of the surprise than mode error alone.

5   A Knowledge Based Approach

In order to find the common element which links the two failures, described in the previous section, we re-examined the failures themselves. We found that the combination of 'confirmation bias' i.e. a tendency to confirm an existing world view in the face of contradictory evidence (e.g. the 'fixation' error, also described above) and 'selectivity' i.e. a focus on only those factors which support the current world view (e.g. the Air-Inter pilots' concentration on the VS/FPA entry dial to the exclusion of the underlying entry mode) were common occurrences in failures caused by a lack of operator knowledge (Reason, 1990). Neither was common in examples of skill-level failure i.e. the failure to execute a well-rehearsed procedure (as would be implied by an explanatory account based on mode error alone). In this context, mode errors become a symptom of the underlying problem (the operators lack of knowledge of the current system state), rather than the cause.

Further examples of both selectivity and confirmation bias can be found in the 1988 Air France crash at Mulhouse-Habsheim (Degani et al., 1996), where the pilots continued to believe that they could avert disaster by fighting with the plane's joystick, despite the fact that their actions were not affecting the flight path as expected and in the China Airlines crash during a descent into Nagoya, where the pilots continued to believe that they could safely land the plane using the joystick, whilst a mistaken engagement of full forward thrust made it practically impossible to do so. Both incidents support the view that knowledge gaps lie behind many examples of automation surprise.

6 Task Knowledge Structures

Having identified knowledge gaps as a major factor in an explanatory account of automation surprise, our next step is to identify improvements in flightdeck interaction, which will eliminate them (or at least mitigate their effects) and, by doing so, improve cockpit safety.

In order to achieve this we need to understand the relationship between human-system interaction and the operator's knowledge (both actual and required). A starting point in this area is provided by the concept of Task Knowledge Structures (TKS) (Johnson et al., 2000):

The TKS approach asserts that operators store the knowledge required for an activity domain (e.g. the flightdeck) in identifiable and predictable structures. Specifically, it contains a notion of procedural dependency, which states that individual actions within a common goal structure will be similarly grouped within the operator's knowledge structures. It also asserts that interaction designed in conformance with these structures will reduce the cognitive load on the user and, therefore, be less prone to error. (Johnson et al., 2000). In other words, interaction organised in a way that matches the operator's knowledge will lead to more accurate execution.

This will be particularly important in our example of automation surprise, since, as we have shown above, high workload contributed significantly to the accident on flight F-GGED. Interaction design, which lessens the cognitive load on the pilots is, therefore of immediate benefit.

7 Tasks, Activities and Strategies

Before we attempt to improve the interaction described in Figures 2 & 3, however, one further element is needed. We have demonstrated above that the pilots' errors on flight F-GGED stem from a lack of knowledge of system state. We have equally shown that interaction based upon existing knowledge structures will lead to lower error rates. We have not, however, identified either the activities or the underlying knowledge structures, which allow the pilot to maintain their understanding of system state and autopilot actions.

This is particularly important in light of our assertion that routine, proceduralised activities do not provide sufficient insight into complex, contextually influenced interaction, such as that observed in the cockpit. Re-examination of such standardised 'Tasks', even with the assistance of TKS seems unlikely to provide the explanatory account for automation surprise we have sought throughout this paper.

With this in mind, we propose to draw a distinction between the broad set of 'Activities', which covers all interaction in a complex environment and its subset of 'Tasks', which describes only those well-defined, proceduralised, activities which can, therefore, be defined independently of context and modelled using the simple conditional structures, described in Section 3.

At this point, both our examination of flightdeck activity and the logic of describing tasks as only one subset of all possible activity points to the existence of a second, higher level group of activities. These are certainly not tasks in the narrow sense defined above but involve the organisation of lower level activity in response to context. Activity on this higher level includes organisation, interruption and problem solving. An understanding of this cognitive level will be key during the post hoc improvement we intend to describe for the Airbus A320 flight control unit.

If we are to model this second set of activities, we must develop a notion of strategy. This notion would encompass the knowledge structures, which would allow a system operator (in our example, a pilot) to coordinate, monitor and (potentially) alter a lower level activity or 'Task', according to the particular context in which they found themselves. In other words, it would describe the management activity needed to perform a group of lower level tasks in a complex, changing, interactive environment (an approach, which fits well with Huettner's (1998) assertion that the pilots role is changing from one of hands on operator to that of process manager).

Such strategies may involve the simplification of contextual inputs (i.e. allow safe execution through focus on a few key points) or insulate the task execution from the effects of its environment (i.e. provide sufficient checks, that poor execution can be identified and dealt with). We need to find an appropriate strategy to minimise or eliminate the types of knowledge gap, which occurred on flight F-GGED.

8   Modelling Cockpit Interaction

From our discussion of the flight F-GGED crash, above, we know that our safety enhancing strategy must lessen the occurrence of pilot-system knowledge gaps i.e. in this case, it must coordinate the desired instruction (to the autopilot) with the instruction actually registered.

In the highly formalised environment of flight control, there are many examples of such coordination, including that between ATC and the cockpit, pilot and co-pilot and even cabin crew and flying staff. Unlike the relatively newer problem of the human–computer interface, these interactions have existed for many decades and have the benefit of research, implementation, re-examination and correction over that time.

The benefit to the designer is the fact that a coordinated approach has been developed to the transfer and checking of information, formalizing the passage of instructions between human agents involved in the task of flight control. The aim of this approach (detailed in the following sections) is both to update the knowledge base of the actors in each role (flying pilot, non-flying pilot and ATC) and to check that this knowledge base has been synchronised after each instruction. This is achieved through the use of acceptance, repetition and confirmation procedures.

At this point, we need to make a key assumption — that all activity related knowledge (both 'strategic' and 'task') is stored, retrieved and processed in a similar way. Since far less research attention has been paid to strategies than to tasks, this is largely untested, but, if true, it allows us to extend the TKS principle of procedural dependency (Johnson et al., 2000) to improve the failed cockpit interaction on flight F-GGED. We will discuss the results of this assumption below and will further develop the idea in future research.

If our working assumption is correct, we should be able to apply the formal coordination approach (described earlier in this section) to the interaction between pilot and autopilot and thereby significantly lessen the occurrence of automation surprise.

The next step is to develop and test this assertion — a step we achieved by returning flight F-GGED.

9 Sources

In order to redesign the interface, we need an activity model for the transfer of coordinated instructions within the cockpit. As per Johnson (1992), a starting point in this analysis is the identification of appropriate sources for the study of goals, tasks, subtasks and procedures. Unfortunately, a number of approaches (interviews, questionnaires, direct observation) were not available, since we had no direct access to pilots or ground crew.

On the other hand, the accident report of flight F-GGED does include a transcript of the conversations between flying pilot (PF), non-flying pilot (NFP) and Air Traffic Control (ATC) during the final 30minutes of the journey (Bureau Enquetes Accidents, 1992). Though a somewhat narrow basis for study, we can be re-assured that the commission of enquiry (including experienced aviators) made only minor criticisms of the interaction amongst the crew/ATC. We can therefore conclude that we have a relatively reliable source of indirect observation of a flight deck, which can be considered for our analysis.

In order to avoid the omission of key details, which could, by chance, not to show up on these (fairly short) transcripts, we have also cross-checked our results with other sources (the accident report Bureau Enquetes Accidents (1992) and the Palmer et al. (1993) study on altitude change procedures). These other sources also provide valuable input to our model.

Analysis of the interaction between ATC and cockpit and between pilot and co-pilot yielded the strategic activity structure described in Figure 4.

10 Analysis

A comparison of the task model described in Figure 2 (Original FCU) and the strategic activity model described in Figure 4 (Coordinated Cockpit Instruction

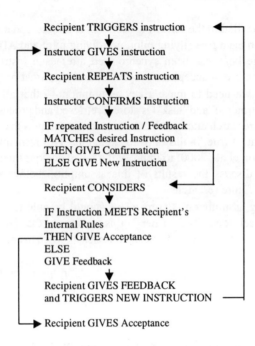

Figure 4: Strategic activity model: Coordinated cockpit.

Transfer) shows that the task of using the original interface is significantly different from the equivalent intra-cockpit task:

1. No full repetition of the desired instruction is provided.

2. No confirmation is required from the pilot — the instruction is automatically executed after a four second delay.

3. No internal rule check is performed by the recipient (autopilot). Simple errors, such as 'fly to a dangerously low altitude' (e.g. into the ground!) are therefore not subject to any lockout.

4. The feedback given to the instructor (pilot) is both distributed i.e. given parameter by parameter and passive i.e. the instructor has to make an effort to look for it.

These omitted elements constitute the core of the coordination strategy outlined in Section 7, above. The principle of procedural dependency (the reliance on familiar task knowledge structures during interface usage) (Johnson et al., 2000) would suggest that their inclusion in a redesigned interface would reduce the underlying knowledge gap and, therefore, the system error rate.

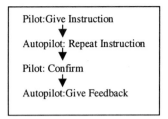

Figure 5: Redesigned task model.

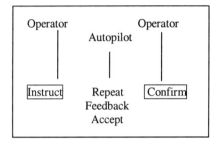

Figure 6: Abstract user interface design.

11   Redesign

Our next objective was, therefore, to match the workflow required by the interface to the underlying activity structure.

Since this structure was essentially linear (i.e. it contained relatively few conditional branches), we opted for a linear design, where the user started at one side of the interface (we chose the left) and worked across to the other (the right). This gave the blueprint described in Figure 5.

We then modified this model to give the autopilot a single 'voice' i.e. we collected all autopilot output into a single area. The strict linear interpretation of Figure 5 would have called for at least two areas of output, the first for repetition and the second for feedback. However, prototype designs showed this to be confusing for users and we simplified the design. This, in turn, left us with the schema described in Figure 6.

The final step was to flesh out the design. Many details were refined according to the usability principles of user control, consistency, forgiveness, perceived stability, feedback, modelessness and progressive disclosure. The most noteworthy design decision, however, was to make the entry options surrounding each parameter more explicit by grouping mutually exclusive choices in columns. The users activity was now represented as a journey from left to right, with a selection to be made from each column passed.

Our final design is shown in Figure 7.

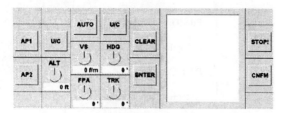

Figure 7: Airbus A320 FCU (Redesign — final result).

12   Usability Testing

In order to analyse the improvements (if any) offered by our redesign, we ran usability tests on the two interfaces (original and redesigned). Conscious of the potential risk of unrepresentative results obtained by an artificially created scenario, we returned again to the transcripts of flight F-GGED.

Though we were unable to test the interfaces on commercial pilots within the time frame of the project, a group of ten regular but non-professional computer users were found who would give sufficiently reliable results for an initial evaluation.

First, we created a condensed version of the transcripts by eliminating long periods of silence and all casual conversation, which had no bearing on the navigation of the plane.

Next we recorded the abbreviated version onto tape in order to ensure that each subject would receive identical instructions with consistent timing across the tests.

We divided the ten subjects into two equal groups. The first were trained on the original interface, before attempting to enter the taped instructions in real time, whilst the second underwent the same process, but using the redesigned interface.

The subjects were observed during the simulation and their entries for each individual instruction were recorded. In this way, we could measure and analyse not only the raw success/failure of each instruction, but, in the case of an error, the false entry sequence. Finally, we recorded the time taken for each instruction entry.

A narrow measure of success was to be the elimination of the entry sequence, which played such a prominent part in the crash of flight F-GGED, but we also considered a wider set of results, including the number of errors made on each instruction, each dial and within each of a set of pre-determined categories.

13   Data

Within the narrow measure of success (the elimination of the specific error which caused the crash on flight F-GGED), we had remarkable success. 40% of the test group, asked to use the original interface to enter instructions, made the same inappropriate error as the actual pilot, leading to a theoretical crash (see Figure 8).

The second test group (those using the re-design), however returned zero occurrences of this mode confusion, supporting the idea that the re-design had achieved its most obvious purpose.

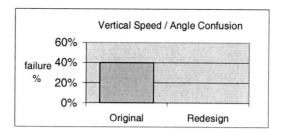

Figure 8: Vertical speed / flight path angle confusion errors by interface.

Figure 9: Summary of total error rates by interface.

Behind this rather crude measure, however, a more detailed examination of the results also gave cause for optimism, though, rather inevitably, further work will be needed before a definitive conclusion can be reached.

Overall, error rates were reduced by over 40% (see Figure 9) and entry times also fell by 10%. This combination of more accurate entries, with no corresponding drop in input speed suggests that our interface redesign had helped to diminish the task knowledge gap identified above.

Equally encouraging is the spread of error rate reduction. Drops were seen across the different entry parameters (see Figure 10 below), supporting the view that we had not simply solved a problem within the use of a particular dial or button but had rather improved the usability of the entire interface.

Having examined recorded errors by entry parameter, we next grouped the errors into the following categories:

- No Entry: The subject attempted no entry for the given instruction.

- Magnitude Error: An error was made in the order of magnitude of a given parameter e.g. an altitude of 100feet in the place of 10,000feet.

- FPA/VS Confusion: A vertical speed was entered in the place of an angle of descent (flight path angle) — see flight F-GGED accident description above.

- Other: Errors not falling into any of the previous three categories.

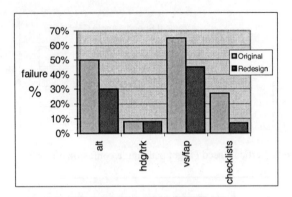

Figure 10: Error rates by entry parameter.

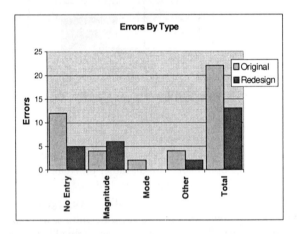

Figure 11: Number of errors by type.

In three of the four categories, we found marked improvement with our redesign (see Figure 11 above). A potential design solution for the fourth category will be discussed below.

14 Discussion

14.1 Test Results

The residual error rate, even on our re-designed interface remained at just over 20%.

Though the types of error observed could, to some extent, be explained by the operator's unfamiliarity with the domain, we were unhappy with the idea of dismissing them, on this basis alone. For this reason, we developed three further elements for future inclusion in our interface environment, which, we believe, would remove the larger error groups. A short summary of these elements is as follows:

1. For the 'No Entry' errors observed, subjects gave an inability to remember the complete instruction in a 'rushed' environment as a major causal factor. Though the use of a tape to provide instructions has many advantages, it does have the drawback of limited interactivity, removing the state-check-confirm procedure seen between instructor and recipient in the real cockpit. For this reason, we intend to adjust our test environment to include repetition of instructions before parameter entry, believing that by focusing attention in this way we will aid subjects ability to remember their goals.

2. Next, whilst looking at the group of magnitude errors, we found that our subjects encountered great difficulty with the language of the cockpit. Notably, they confused target 'levels' (given in hundreds of feet) with absolute altitudes (given in feet). Though it could be argued that this would not be a factor amongst commercial pilots, who would be familiar with such language, we felt that further amendments to the interface could make the issue clearer, even for experienced pilots, thus reducing the likelihood of such errors occurring. We will therefore change the input displays to emphasise the link between the two formats. e.g. 12,000feet (a level of 120) could be portrayed as '120 00'.

We also feel that the set procedures surrounding the coordination task could be extended to encourage the pilot(s) to revisit feedback information before confirmation. Examples of such an extension could be the reading aloud of an entered instruction for acceptance by a colleague or the autopilot.

14.2   Strategies and Activities

Our approach in this paper has been underpinned by the belief that the activities observed in complex interactive environments cannot be sufficiently described using traditional task-based approaches. A description of the higher level, strategic activity, used to manage the interaction between the individual tasks and their context, is also required.

Though we have asserted the existence of such strategic level activity on the flight deck and proposed that failure on this level (rather than task execution failure) underpins automation surprise, a great deal of work is needed to make this classification robust. We suggest three phases of further research into this area, which would, in combination support the production of safer flightdeck interaction.

1. Clearer definition of strategic activity.

2. Development of a modelling framework for strategies.

3. Development of design principles, which translate understanding of strategies into tangible HCI design benefits.

14.2.1   Clearer Definition of Strategic Activity

In this paper, we have defined strategies as those activities which involve the management of groups of lower level tasks, within a complex contextual setting. Further research could provide insight into the following questions:

- How do we identify strategies currently employed in complex interactive settings?

- How are these strategies used?

- To what extent do strategies change according to domain, user, context etc.

- Which data collection methods are suitable for the task of gathering information in this area?

14.2.2   Development of a Modelling Framework for Strategies

Though an informal description of strategies can be useful in early stages of research, a deeper understanding requires formal identification of properties and structures present in their make-up. Interesting research questions in this area include:

- What similarities exist between different strategies (are there any universal commonalities)?

- Which potential differences must be allowed within a common modelling framework?

- How can we formally define the boundary between task and strategic activity (or do we need to?) i.e. how are the cognitive processes which underlie strategies different from those which underpin low level activities (or are they actually very similar)?

- What level of abstraction should be attempted?

- Do strategies, at some level, exist independently of domain e.g. could we use the coordination strategy identified in this paper in the design of an interface at a nuclear power plant?

14.2.3   Development of Design Principles, which Translate Understanding of Strategies into Tangible HCI Design.

In many ways, this is the most important step of all. An abstract understanding of strategic cognition will not, in itself, produce any tangible safety benefits. The understanding gained must be extended to produce design approaches and principles which allow interface designers 'in the field' to produce safer interfaces.

Important questions in this area include:

- To which types of errors is strategic cognitive activity particularly prone?

- How can these errors best be prevented?

- How should this prevention be systematically included in interface design?

15 Conclusions

In conclusion, we have described a level of activity on the flightdeck, which cannot be adequately described by approaches based on traditional task analysis. We described this level of activity as strategic-management. We then went on to focus on the 'automation surprise' class of human error and found it to involve such strategic level activity.

We then examined the dominant 'Mode Error' approach to this area and found it to be rooted in a traditional task based, rather than strategic activity and show this to be founded on a misclassification of the human factors involved.

We went on to assert that an extension of existing knowledge-based analysis can be used to provide causal accounts of strategic as well as task level failure. We then use such a knowledge-based approach to demonstrate that a more insightful description of these situations would show that coordination problems give rise to a knowledge gap on the part of the user

By looking at other, relevant Air Traffic Management procedures, we have identified a generic coordination activity, designed to avoid the occurrence of such a knowledge gap.

Applying the knowledge principle of procedural dependency (Johnson et al., 2000), we then produced a new design solution, which by facilitating and enforcing a process of checks and confirmations supported this coordination strategy. In this way, we addressed the cause of the surprise (knowledge deficiency), rather than its symptoms (amongst others, mode error).

We then tested the new interface empirically, using a simulation of a well-documented air incident. We found that the new interface supported more accurate and faster instruction entry and would, therefore, have lessened the likelihood of the accident, had it been both available and in use.

This enhancement to cockpit safety provides support for our assertion that knowledge surrounding strategic activity is stored, retrieved and processed in similar ways to that which underpins individual tasks. It also promotes the idea that existing approaches to interface design, based upon an understanding of the underlying activity knowledge structures, can be extended into the strategic area and provide a basis for safer interaction design within complex interactive environments.

Acknowledgements

Professor Johnson's research on this project is supported by EPSRC grant PRIDE: Task Related Principles for Interface Design and Evaluation.

References

Annett, J., Duncan, K., Stammers, R. & Gray, M. (1971), *Task Analysis*, number 6 *in* "Training Information", HMSO.

Bureau Enquetes Accidents (1992), Rapport de la Commission d'Enquête sur l'Accident Survenu le 20 Janvier 1992 près du Mont Sainte-Odile (Bas Rhin) à l'Airbus A 320 Immatriculé F-GGED Exploité par la Compagnie Air Inter, Technical Report, Bureau Enquetes Accidents.

Card, S. K., Moran, T. P. & Newell, A. (1983), *The Psychology of Human–Computer Interaction*, Lawrence Erlbaum Associates.

De Keyser, V. & Javaux, D. (1996), Human Factors in Aeronautics, *in* F. Bodart & J. Vanderdonckt (eds.), *Design, Specification and Verification of Interactive Systems '96*, Springer-Verlag, pp.105–22.

Degani, A., Shafto, M. & Kirlik, A. (1996), Modes in Automated Cockpits: Problems, Data Analysis and a Modeling Framework, *in Proceedings of the 36th Israeli Annual Conference on Aerospace Sciences.*   Also available at http://human-factors.arc.nasa.gov/IHpublications/degani/modeusage/modes2.html.

Dismukes, K. (2001), Remembering Intentions in Dynamic Environments, http://human-factors.arc.nasa.gov/projects/ihi/remembering.html.

Harrison, M. (2000), Interaction Analysis and Human Error Tolerance, http://www.cs.york.ac.uk/hci/tolerance/.

Huettner, C. (1998), Chapter 1: The History of Aviation Safety, http://www.aero-space.nasa.gov/library/ch1.htm.

Johnson, C. & Gray, P. (1996), "Temporal Aspects of Usability", *ACM SIGCHI Bulletin* **28**(2), 32–33.

Johnson, C. & Love, L. (2000), Using Diagrams to Support the analysis of System 'Failure' and Operator 'Error', http://www.dcs.gla.ac.uk/~johnson/papers.

Johnson, P. (1992), *Human–Computer Interaction: Psychology, Task Analysis and Software Engineering*, McGraw-Hill.

Johnson, P., Johnson, H. & Hamilton, F. (2000), Getting the Knowledge into HCI — Theoretical + Practical aspects of Task Knowledge Structures, *in* J. M. Schraagen, S. F. Chirman & V. L. Shaun (eds.), *Cognitive Task Analysis*, Lawrence Erlbaum Associates, pp.201–14.

Kirsh, D. (2001), "Réflexions sur la Surcharge Cognitive (A Few Thoughts on Cognitive Overload)", *Intellectica* **2000/1**(30), 18–52.   http://icl-server.ucsd.edu/~kirsh/Articles/Overload/published.html.

Meriweather, J. (2000), Airbus A320 Flight Deck, http://www.Meriweather.com/a320.

Palmer, E. (1995), "Oops, It Didn't Arm". A Case Study of Two Automation Surprises, *in* R. S. Jensen & L. A. Rakovan (eds.), *Proceedings of the Eighth International Symposium on Aviation Psychology*, OSU, pp.24–7.   http://human-factors.arc.nasa.gov/ihi/papers/publications/palmer/_Oops/PalmerOops.html.

Palmer, E., Hutchins, E., Ritter, R. & Vancleemput, I. (1993), Altitude Deviations: Breakdowns of an Error Tolerant System, Technical Memorandum DOT/FAA/RD-92/7, NASA.

Reason, J. (1990), *Human Error*, Cambridge University Press.

Rushby, J. (1999), Using Model Checking to Help Discover Mode Confusions and Other Automation Surprises, *in* D. Javaux (ed.), *Proceedings of the 3rd Workshop on Human Error, Safety, and System Development.* http://www.csl.sri.com/papers/hessd99/.

DPI: A Conceptual Model Based on Documents and Interaction Instruments

Olivier Beaudoux[†‡] & Michel Beaudouin-Lafon[‡]

[†] *Département Génie Informatique, Réseaux et Télécoms, Ecole Supérieure d'Electronique de l'Ouest, 4 rue Merlet de la Boulaye, 49009 Angers, France*
Tel: *+33 2 41 86 67 67*
Email: *olivier.beaudoux@eseo.fr*
URL: *http://www-ihm.lri.fr/~beaudoux*

[‡] *Laboratoire de Recherche en Informatique, Université Paris-Sud, Bâtiment 490, 91405 Orsay, France*
Tel: *+33 1 69 15 69 10*
Email: *mbl@lri.fr*
URL: *http://www-ihm.lri.fr/~mbl*

The DPI model (Documents, Presentations, Instruments) offers an alternative to current application-centred environments by introducing a conceptual model based on documents and interaction instruments. DPI makes it possible to edit a document through multiple simultaneous presentations. The same instrument can edit different types of content, facilitating interaction and reducing the user's cognitive load. DPI includes a functional model, aimed at the user interface designer, that describes implementation principles in terms of properties, services and representations. The DPI model offers a first but essential stage in designing and implementing a new generation of document-centred environments based on a new interaction paradigm.

Keywords: conceptual model, document-centred interaction, instrumental interaction, compound document, interactive work-space, desktop environment, metaphor, action, perception.

1   Introduction

Most current desktop environments are based on applications, each dedicated to handling a particular type of data, such as text, image or vector-based drawing. Windows were introduced to facilitate switching among applications and techniques such as copy-paste were created to enable the transfer of contents from one application to another. Unfortunately, many tasks require multiple applications. A user may be forced to juggle four or five applications in order to create a single web page or technical document. Software vendors use three strategies to reduce the resulting complexity and higher cognitive load.

The first creates "mini-applications" within a larger application. For example, Microsoft Office has three applications (Word, PowerPoint and Excel) that each include functions for vector-based drawing. Not only do these offer significantly fewer functions than a full-scale vector-drawing application, which is still needed for complex drawings, but the user interfaces are somewhat different and the data formats are incompatible. This approaches duplicates functionality without solving the problem.

Open architectures offer another approach, allowing third parties to develop and market extensions called *plug-ins*. For example, Adobe Photoshop (Gray, 1997) offers a wide variety of plug-ins to edit images, including creation of vector-based drawings and simple 3D models. Other image-editing applications are compatible with Adobe Photoshop's plug-ins so software vendors who develop Photoshop plug-ins have a larger market. The market of plug-ins for QuarkXPress (page layout) and Macromedia Director (multimedia authoring) is also very active, and some plug-ins are more expensive than the parent application. Users install plug-ins to extend and specialise applications according to their needs, and can use the same plug-in in different applications. However, the user interfaces of plug-ins are often poorly integrated into the parent application and are accessible only through bulky dialogue boxes.

The third approach explicitly produces multiple applications with compatible user interfaces. The best example is the Adobe suite: Photoshop (image edition), Illustrator (drawing), GoLive (Web site design) and InDesign (page layout) have the same visual presentation of the interface and similar tool palettes. All support layered documents, and layers created in one application can be imported into another application. Sometimes the link can be "live": the imported layer is automatically updated when it is edited in its original application. However, this approach does not relieve users from dealing with multiple documents for a single task: For a live link to work, the document holding the imported layer must be kept on disk. In addition, applications that do not belong to the suite cannot take advantage of the integration of functions within the suite.

The goal of all these approaches is to put the document, rather than the application, at the centre of the interaction. Unfortunately they all fail because users must still juggle multiple applications and/or multiple documents for a single task. They try to make applications less visible by blurring the boundaries between applications, but the underlying logic is still application-centric. Historically, the Xerox Star (Johnson et al., 1989) was the first major system to adopt a document-

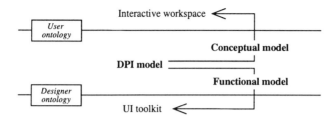

Figure 1: The two levels of the DPI model.

centred approach. More recently, frameworks such as OpenDoc (Apple, 1994) and OLE (Brockschmidt, 1995) have made applications less visible by supporting *compound documents*: a document is not managed by an application dedicated to its type, but each of its parts is handled by a specialised application or *part editor*. These approaches do not discard applications but make them less visible. For example, when a part of a document is clicked, menu bars and tool palettes are reconfigured to allow editing its content. This is similar to switching between applications. The main advantage is the *in-place* editing that saves copy-pasting between applications. But the transition from one document part to the next creates a break in the interaction since each part manages its own interface: there is no sharing of tools among part editors.

In summary, even though systems are becoming more document-centric, the user interfaces are still application-centric. The goal of this paper is to explore the problem of document-centred interaction. We propose the Documents–Presentations–Interactions (DPI) model, a conceptual model that separates document *contents* from document *interaction*.

The DPI model combines a document model compatible with XML (W3C, 2000a) and an interaction model based on instrumental interaction (Beaudouin-Lafon, 1997). We present two levels of the DPI model: the conceptual model that matches a *user ontology*, and the functional model that matches a *designer ontology* (Figure 1). A concrete implementation of the DPI model must define an interface model that matches the conceptual model and a software architecture that supports the functional model. Our longer term goal is to create a toolkit for building a new generation of document-centred environments.

The next two sections describe the conceptual and functional models, respectively. We then compare DPI with related work and conclude with a discussion of future work.

2 Conceptual Model

In a user ontology[1] the concepts of document and instrument are natural: the document is a data repository and the instrument is a means for creating and

---

[1]The term *ontology* here means a description of the concepts and relationships that are meaningful to a subject (in our case, the users and designers of interactive systems).

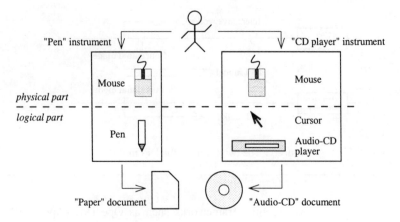

Figure 2: Instrument description

modifying documents. Therefore the DPI model is based on the document metaphor and the instrument metaphor.

2.1   The Instrument Metaphor

In daily life, we often use tools or instruments to operate on physical objects. For example, we use a pen to write on a sheet of paper. This observation forms the basis of the instrumental interaction model (Beaudouin-Lafon, 1997; Beaudouin-Lafon, 2000). According to this model, an instrument mediates between a user and *target object* (or object of interest).

An instrument has two facets: physical and logical. The physical facet exists outside the system. It includes input-output transducers used by the instrument. Input transducers capture the physical actions of the user and output transducers provide feedback information. The logical facet exists inside the system and its state is made perceivable outside the system. It includes methods for transforming user actions onto the logical instrument (input), and the representation of the instrument itself (output).

Instruments can be more or less direct. For example, using a pen to write on paper is more direct than using a CD player to play a CD. A similar indirection occurs when the pen or the CD player is simulated by an interactive system and is operated with a mouse (Figure 2).

Most instruments modify existing objects. However instruments can also be used to change the *perception* of an object, as with magnifying glasses (Perlin & Fox, 1993) and Magic Lenses (Bier et al., 1993). Such instruments create *alternate presentations* of documents (see next section). In general, these instruments are direct but the manipulation affects the way the instrument operates rather than the target object.

Interaction instruments can be organised into three categories:

- *Direct instruments*: The users acts *directly* on the document. For example, clicking the mouse on an object and moving the hand moves the object. The action of the hand on the instrument and its effect on the target object are perceived as similar.

- *Indirect instruments*: The user acts *directly* on the instrument but *indirectly* on the document. For example, entering a number in a dialog box changes the font size of the selected text. The action of the hand on the instrument and its effect on the target object are perceived as related but different.

- *Perception instruments*: The user acts *directly* on the instrument but *not* on the document. For example, moving the thumb of a scrollbar changes the part of the document that is being viewed. The action of the hand on the instrument affects the presentation of the target object, not its contents.

2.2   The Document Metaphor

In the physical world, documents such as books have two facets:

- *Persistence*: the document provides on-going support for its contents, e.g. the paper absorbs the ink. When writing on a document, the user perceives the persistent result of his actions. When reading a document, the user perceives what has been made persistent and then interprets it.

- *Presentation*: the document has a concrete appearance. The appearance is intrinsic to the document: a document has a single presentation which is a direct result of the persistent information it contains.

Persistence and presentation are naturally coupled in physical documents. However they are decoupled in electronic documents. The file system manages persistence, and output devices, such as screens, manage presentation. This decoupling is evident when a document that appears on the screen must be explicitly saved onto a persistent storage medium.

An advantage of this decoupling is the ability to view several presentations of a document at the same time, e.g. an outline or page layout presentation of a text document, or a visual or audio presentation of a musical partition. While this is useful from the user's perspective, it breaks the physical document metaphor. In the user ontology, we want to hide the decoupling between document and presentation as much as possible.

2.3   Multiple Presentations Abstraction

If each document had only one presentation, the notion of presentation would be unnecessary in a user ontology. However, the advantages of multiple presentations are well-known (see the Zelig system, Celentano et al. (1992), for an example). So our goal is to follow the physical document metaphor while supporting multiple presentations: from the users' point of view, any presentation of the document should be the document itself.

We could introduce multiple presentations by using the cameras and monitors metaphor from X_{TV} (Beaudouin Lafon et al., 1990): a document is filmed by one or more cameras and can be visualised by the equivalent of video monitors. This metaphor is easy to understand. Users may edit a document with its *natural* presentation, and visualise it through *alternate* presentations provided by the monitors. This approach preserves the initial document metaphor, but goes against the principle of direct manipulation (Shneiderman, 1983) since the alternate presentations are passive.

The DPI model extends this metaphor by making alternate presentations active, i.e. the document can be edited through *any* presentation. This introduces a fundamental requirement: editing results must be *synchronous* across presentations. This ensures that the abstract idea of multiple presentations becomes concrete to users. They observe that multiple presentations are updated synchronously and are therefore the *same* document.

Multiple editable presentations also open the way to *shared editing*, i.e. supporting simultaneous editing of the same document by multiple users from their respective workstations. This groupware extension to DPI is beyond the scope of this article.

2.4   Compatibility between Model Components

The DPI conceptual model describes how users manage documents by using instruments on their presentations and how they perceive the results of their actions. Based on Norman's action theory (Norman & Draper, 1986), the diagram in Figure 3 presents the model as an action and perception flow diagram with three levels: user, instrument and document.

- The *user level* states that users specify their intentions through actions and interpret the results using their senses.

- The *instrument level* describes how instruments transform user actions. Instruments support three main functions: navigation, perception and editing. Navigation can be carried out by an indirect instrument such as a search instrument, by a direct instrument such as a scrollbar or by a perception instrument such as a radar view. Editing can be carried out by an indirect instrument such as a spell checker or by a direct instrument such as a pen. Perception is carried out either directly by the natural document presentation, or indirectly by perception instruments that provide alternate presentations, such as a magnifying glass.

- The *document level* reveals the double role of documents: persistence of user actions and presentation of contents.

According to the ecological theory of perception (Gibson, 1979), action and perception are strongly coupled: the user must perceive before acting, e.g. by locating an object before selecting it, and must act in order to perceive, e.g. by navigating through a document in order to locate an object. This is supported in DPI by the three functions of instruments, editing, navigation and perception. However an effective coupling between action and perception requires additional *compatibility rules* among the three levels of the model:

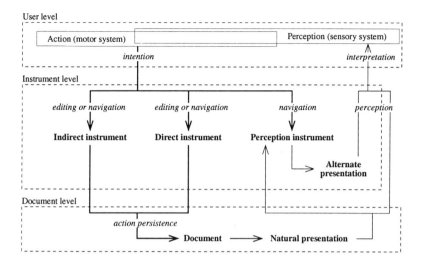

Figure 3: DPI conceptual model as an action-perception diagram. Thick lines represent the action flow and thin lines represent the perception flow. For clarity, the perception of instruments is omitted.

1. *User ↔ instrument* compatibility: interaction with an instrument should match its function. For example, a brush-like instrument should be used to change an object's colour. This relates to the concept of *affordance* (Gibson, 1977): instruments must express their functions in a directly-perceivable way.

2. *Instrument ↔ document* compatibility: an instrument works with specific types of documents. For example, a pen is adapted to a sheet of paper because paper can receive ink. This compatibility defines the possible interactions between instruments and documents.

3. *Document ↔ user* compatibility: the natural presentation of a document should be suited to our senses. For example, a sheet of paper is compatible with visual perception, while a Braille display is compatible with tactile (and possibly visual) perception.

We take compatibility in physical documents for granted; we are not aware of compatibility *per se* but rather the lack of it. The goal of the DPI conceptual model is to generate a comparable set of possible combinations among electronic documents, instruments and presentations. By separating instruments from documents, the DPI model supports instruments that can act on documents of different types, increasing the number of possible combinations. These combinations should simplify interaction and reduce the users' cognitive load while offering a rich set of functions. For example, the same instrument could be used to change the colour of a title in a text document and the colour of an arrow in a drawing. Current desktop environments do not support these kinds of facilities.

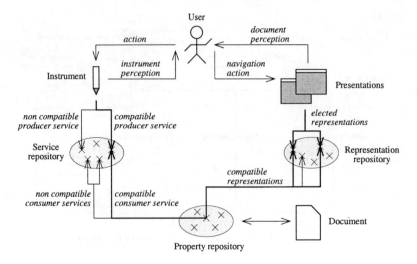

Figure 4: DPI functional model. Thick lines represent a sample instrument to presentation interaction path. Thin lines represent other possible interaction paths.

---

3 Functional Model

The functional model transcribes the conceptual model for the interface designer. We express it in a designer ontology by reifying the conceptual model's relationships into primitives (Figure 4), described in sections Sections 3.1–3.3. We then combine these into documents and presentations (Section 3.4) as well as devices and instruments (Section 3.5).

3.1 Persistence Primitive: The Property

A document and its presentations are defined by their *properties*. A property *definition* is a pair *(name, type)* and a property *value* is a pair *(name, value)*. A property can be *atomic* (it defines a single value), *composite* (it defines a value composed of a predefined set of properties), or a *set* (it defines a value composed of an arbitrary set of properties).

Name-value associations are defined in documents and form their states. *Name-type* associations define the properties' *schema*. Document properties are visualised through presentations and edited using instruments. Some properties cannot be edited, such as a document's creation date. This information, i.e. that it cannot be edited, is stored in the schema.

The properties in the DPI document model provide fine-grained access to the contents of a document. Interaction instruments can act on specific properties, independently of document types. Moreover, the document format is open and extensible because the properties' schemas are available and extensible. For example, the document format could be based on XML (W3C, 2000a) and the property schemas on DTDs or XML schemas. In contrast, OpenDoc or OLE provide coarse-grained access at the level of *parts*[2], and parts are stored in a proprietary format.

3.2   Action Primitive: The Service

All objects involved in the interaction process are connected through *services*. A service is the means by which user actions are transmitted along the action-perception chain. *Producer services* can activate *consumer services* in a chain from input devices to document properties via instruments. The *activation* of a service is based on the instrument $\rightarrow$ document compatibility described in the conceptual model. Activation of consumer service S_{in} in consumer C by producer service S_{out} in producer P is defined as follows:

1. P and C are *likely to interact* if P is a direct instrument geometrically pointing at C, or if P is an indirect instrument targeting C.

2. If P and C are likely to interact, a *compatibility* test is carried out between each consumer service $(S_{out,i})_{i=1..n}$ of P and each producer service $(S_{in,j})_{j=1..p}$ of C. A *connection* $S_{out,i} \rightarrow S_{in,j}$ is made for each compatible pair $(S_{out,i}, S_{in,j})$.

3. A connection $S_{out,i} \rightarrow S_{in,j}$ is *activated* when the service $S_{out,i}$ is invoked. The producer must choose the invoked service if there is an ambiguity. For example, an instrument that can move and resize an object provides two services. Once the two services are connected, this instrument provides the user with a means of choosing which one to activate, for example by offering two activation buttons.

4. Services remain connected as long as P and C are likely to interact.

The simplest compatibility test between services is the equality of their names. However, it is useful to define more generic compatibility rules. For example, services can be organised in a tree so that two services S_1 and S_2 are compatible if and only if S_1 is an ancestor of S_2. An instrument that provides the generic move service would then be compatible with properties that provide specialised services such as move_icon or move_note if move_note and move_icon were descendants of move in the service tree.

Services reify the traditional notion of a command: a service is a command that an instrument can apply to a target document property. Generic (or polymorphic) instruments directly result from the compatibility rule: the same instrument can edit different kinds of properties as long as it is compatible with them. Thus, the concept of service embodies the reification and polymorphism principles of Beaudouin-Lafon & Mackay (2000). From an interaction point of view, instrument services define a fine-grained interaction, at the instrument and property levels, while OpenDoc part editors (Apple, 1994), for example, define a coarse-grained interaction at the editor and part levels.

---

[2]A document is composed of parts, each with a specified data type such as formatted text or vector-based drawing.

3.3   Perception Primitive: The Representation

Properties are perceived by users through *representations*, *elected* among those
compatible with the property. Some standard (or canonical) representations are
provided for simple types (e.g. integer, character string), composite types (e.g. date,
time) and set types (e.g. trees, lists, icons). Perception instruments can transform
properties of a document-specific schema into properties of a well-known schema
with standard representations.

Electing representations works like activating services: a representation
provided by a document is selected if it is compatible with the presentation medium.
In order to create a presentation, a representation is elected either automatically or
with user assistance. This election mechanism corresponds to the document → user
compatibility of the conceptual model.

As for services, the use of representations allows a fine-grained control of the
document presentation, at the property level, whereas in OpenDoc, part editors are
coarse-grained, at the part level.

3.4   Documents and Presentations

The DPI model does not make any assumption about the organisation of documents.
The model of Dourish et al. (1999) is a better candidate than a traditional hierarchical
file system because it uses collections and dynamic queries and it is based, like
DPI, on document properties (see Beaudoux (2000) for more details). Documents
can also be used to represent workspaces, collections, and even instruments. This
homogeneity should help users organise their environment. For example, documents
could be queried by specialised languages such as XPath (W3C, 1999) and XML
Query (W3C, 2000c).

A document is a tree of property values and a presentation is a tree of
representation property values. For graphical interaction, these representations
include geometric properties such as location and size. A direct instrument targets a
document property through its presentation, therefore representations must maintain
a link back to the properties they represent. Moreover, presentations may contain
properties that do not correspond to any document property. For example, in
a representation using icons, the positions of icons are unlikely to correspond
to properties of the underlying document. Thus, presentations must store their
own properties with their associated documents. This means that a style sheet
approach such as XSL (W3C, 2000b) cannot be used to transform a document into a
presentation: a more powerful mechanism is necessary.

Multiple presentations make it possible to edit a document according to several
perspectives. Consider a scenario involving the creation of material for a course,
composed of handouts for the students, slides for the presentation and notes for
the teacher. The natural presentation of the document is an outline that facilitates
navigation through the course hierarchy and editing at the semantic level. At the
layout level, each facet of the course (handouts, slides and notes) has a dedicated
alternate presentation with appropriate formatting of figures and text. These four
presentations make it easy to edit various aspects of the course in parallel.

Representations are defined in a *repository* that changes dynamically. When a document is (down)loaded into the system, associated presentations may have elected representations that are not defined in this repository. In this case, the necessary representation definitions can be (down)loaded as well. This is similar to loading plug-ins into a Web browser.

3.5   Devices and Instruments

3.5.1   Physical, Logical and Simulated Devices

Input devices provide producer services and are defined as a tree of sensors — see Beaudoux (2000) for more details. For example, a one-button mouse has three sensors: two potentiometers and one button, and produces three services: single-click, double-click and drag-and-drop. In order to support a wide variety of platforms and input devices, the DPI model defines physical, logical and simulated devices.

A *physical device* corresponds to a hardware peripheral such as the above one-button mouse.

A *logical device* is built from one or more devices. For example, a logical three-button mouse can be built by combining the physical one-button mouse with two keyboard keys used as additional button sensors. This follows Myers (1989) *Interactors* model.

A *simulated device* emulates a physical device. For example, the Xerox Star (Johnson et al., 1989) displays soft keyboards on the screen to input special characters such as mathematical formulas with the mouse. X_{TV} (Beaudouin-Lafon et al., 1990) supports the creation of arbitrary simulated devices. *Metamouse* (Maulsby et al., 1989) uses a simulated mouse to demonstrate procedural actions.

3.5.2   Functional Model of Instruments

An instrument receives the user actions from an input device and transforms them into commands sent to the target property of a document (Figure 5). The *physical part* of the instrument defines its consumer services, i.e. what input it accepts. For example, a move instrument may accept two services: drag-and-drop and constrained drag-and-drop. The instrument may use an existing device or create a dedicated logical device as described in the previous section. For example, the instrument may create a logical device that combines the one-button mouse with the keyboard's shift key in order to provide both drag-and-drop and constrained drag-and-drop services. When multiple devices are available, the instrument may ask the user or use a document that specifies priorities and preferences. Once the device is selected, the producer services of the elected input device are connected to the consumer services of the instrument (1).

The *logical part* of the instrument defines its producer services. For example, the move instrument provides the change-position service. When an instrument's consumer service is activated by a user action on a device, it is transformed into a producer service (2), which in turn activates a consumer service of the document (3). For example, a drag-and-drop action on the mouse is transformed into a change-position command applied to the target property of the document.

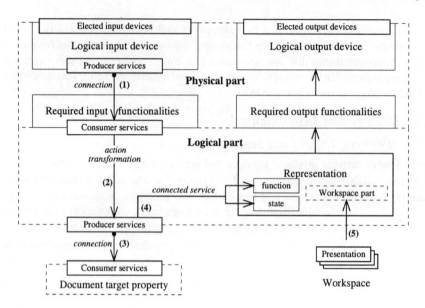

Figure 5: Functional model of an instrument

Instruments must themselves be represented on output devices. This representation should include the function and state of the instrument (4). Perception instruments must also manage the alternate representation of their target documents (5), e.g. magnifying glasses must generate magnified presentations of the documents underneath them.

The persistence of instrument properties is managed transparently by an associated document. This document contains the instrument state, configuration (logical device, behaviour, representation), and online help. Sleeter (1996) discusses the importance of online help in document-centred systems. Online help tends to be centralised in traditional environments while document-centred systems must provide help at different levels: workspace, documents and instruments.

The generic aspect of instruments with respect to documents results from the generic aspect of services with respect to properties (Section 3.2). The same instrument can be used in several contexts. For example, a pen can be used to enter text in any writable document, to write annotations in any document, and to edit the label of a workspace element, e.g. the name of a document. The service compatibility between instruments and document properties results in the ability to dynamically create contextual palettes of instruments. Traditional contextual menus are predefined by the application and depend only on their target object. The DPI model makes it possible to dynamically compute the palette of activatible instruments for a given set of properties.

Finally, instruments can be *chained* together. For example, combining a pen (direct instrument) with a magnifying glass (perception instrument) permits precision drawing as the pen operates *through* the magnifying glass, as with Magic Lenses (Bier et al., 1993). To our knowledge, no other general system supports such facilities.

Instruments, like representations, are declared in a *repository* that changes dynamically. When a document is (down)loaded into the workspace, related instruments can also be (down)loaded. This offers greater flexibility than plug-ins.

4 Related Work

4.1 Document Models

OpenDoc (Apple, 1994) was the most advanced attempt at creating a document-centred system, although it was developed in the context of an existing application-centred environment (MacOS). Dykstra-Erickson & Curbow (1997) explain that users do not have to interact with applications in order to edit documents: they interact with the documents themselves. The document model is based on the metaphors of paper and *parts*. A document is a set of parts, and each part can be handled by a specialised *editor*. In our approach, documents are *not* the single most important entity in the system: instruments are the main interaction component, while documents handle persistence and are the targets of instruments. The main differences between OpenDoc and DPI can be summarised as follows:

- OpenDoc editors have a finer grain than traditional applications, but a coarser grain than DPI instruments. Similarly, OpenDoc parts have a coarser grain than DPI document properties.

- OpenDoc editors do not separate interaction from display whereas DPI instruments are decoupled from presentations.

- OpenDoc editors are specialised for a given part type while DPI instruments can be generic and DPI presentations can be canonical.

DPI supports a more seamless style of interaction than OpenDoc: in OpenDoc, the interactive environment, e.g. menu bars and palettes, changes when navigating from part to part, whereas a single DPI instrument can be used across all documents in the workspace.

The OLE framework (Brockschmidt, 1995) uses inter-application communication to allow multiple applications to operate on the same document. OLE is not a document-oriented system, but does make it possible to edit compound documents. Within the Microsoft Office suite, applications have homogeneous interfaces and the interaction through OLE is relatively seamless. However this continuity breaks down when using other applications.

OOE (Backlund, 1997) is a NextStep system extension that manages composite documents in a simple way: clicking a part invokes its creator application. The display of compound documents takes advantage of *display PostScript*. Since in-place part editing is not available, OOE is in fact application-centred.

HotDoc (Buchner, 2000) is a Smalltalk extension to the well-known MVC design pattern. It supports compound documents by defining the PartApp,

`PartView` and `PartController` classes. Unlike OLE and OOE, HotDoc does support multiple views (or presentations) of the same model (or document). HotDoc is based on a part-based model similar to OpenDoc, with similar drawbacks.

4.2   Interaction Models

Myers (1989) *Interactors* encapsulate interaction in a small number (seven) of object types. An interactor is not based on an input device type but on the *nature* of the interaction, e.g. defining a point or selecting an item in a list. This approach emphasises the separation between interaction and visualisation and the ability to use various devices for the same task.

Our contribution consists of separating devices from instruments and supporting physical, logical and simulated devices. Logical and simulated devices are transparent to the user and appear only in the designer ontology. Also, DPI is not limited to seven basic devices or instruments. In fact, instruments can be strongly typed or highly generic, according to their function.

The instrumental interaction model is the foundation of the DPI model, but does not constitute a conceptual model. By combining the concepts of interaction instruments and compound documents, we have created general and homogeneous conceptual and functional models. In particular, DPI services ensure independence between documents and instruments.

4.3   Software Architecture Models

The model, view and controller components of the MVC design pattern (Krasner & Pope, 1988) are similar to DPI's document, presentation and instrument components. However, MVC, like other architecture models, describe the synchronisation between its components and not a conceptual model of interaction. In contrast, the design of DPI is explicitly driven by the user ontology. The conceptual model is based on the observation that physical instruments mediate interaction between users and documents. The functional model obtains from this instrument metaphor.

5   Conclusion and Future Work

The Documents–Presentation–Instruments (DPI) conceptual model attempts to break the complexity barrier of desktop environments. DPI is based on document-centred interaction, using both a user ontology *and* a designer ontology. The user ontology employs document and instrument metaphors and introduces the *multiple presentations* abstraction. The designer ontology employs properties for persistence, services for user actions and representations for perception, and the concept of compatibility.

This article uses examples to illustrate the expressiveness of the DPI model, and compares it with other systems. However, the DPI model is abstract and must be validated through a concrete implementation. A partial validation has been carried out with the design and implementation of CPN2000 (Beaudouin-Lafon & Mackay, 2000; Beaudouin-Lafon & Lassen, 2000). This application's conceptual model is a simplified version of DPI that addresses a single document type. CPN2000 has implemented and validated independence between documents and instruments, generic instruments and instrument representations.

The next stage is to define a concrete interface model and test it with realistic use cases. After this validation, we plan to implement the full DPI model and test it by building documents and instruments in a real-world setting. We also plan to extend the model to support *groupware* (shared document editing) and investigate other environments such as mobile systems and augmented reality. In summary, the DPI model offers a first but essential stage in designing and implementing a new generation of document-centred environments based on a new interaction paradigm.

Acknowledgement

We thank Wendy Mackay and the anonymous reviewers for comments on earlier drafts of this paper.

References

Apple (1994), OpenDoc Technical Summary, Technical documentation, Apple Computers.

Backlund, B. E. (1997), "OOE: A Compound Document Framework", *ACM SIGCHI Bulletin* **29**(1), 68–75.

Beaudouin-Lafon, M. (1997), Interaction Instrumentale : de la Manipulation Directe à la Réalité Augmentée, *in Actes des 9èmes Journées IHM, Poitiers*, Cépaduès-Editions.

Beaudouin-Lafon, M. (2000), Instrumental Interaction: An Interaction Model for Designing Post-WIMP Interfaces, *in* T. Turner, G. Szwillus, M. Czerwinski & F. Paternò (eds.), *Proceedings of the CHI2000 Conference on Human Factors in Computing Systems, CHI Letters* **2**(1), ACM Press, pp.446–53.

Beaudouin-Lafon, M. & Lassen, H. M. (2000), The Architecture and Implementation of CPN2000, A Post-WIMP Graphical Application, *in Proceedings of the 13th Annual ACM Symposium on User Interface Software and Technology, UIST2000, CHI Letters* **2**(2), ACM Press, pp.181–90.

Beaudouin-Lafon, M. & Mackay, W. (2000), Reification, Polymorphism and Reuse: Three Principles for Designing Visual Interfaces, *in* V. Di Gesù, S. Levialdi & L. Tarantino (eds.), *Proceedings of the Conference on Advanced Visual Interface (AVI2000)*, ACM Press, pp.102–9.

Beaudouin-Lafon, M., Berteaud, Y. & Chatty, S. (1990), Creating Direct Manipulation Applications with XTV, *in Proceedings of the European X Window System Conference (EX'90)*.

Beaudoux, O. (2000), Paradigmes et Éléments Architecturaux d'une Boîte à Outils Post-WIMP, Rapport Technique, Computer Science Research Laboratory, École Supérieure d'Électronique de l'Ouest and LRI, Université Paris-Sud (Orsay).

Bier, E. A., Stone, M. C., Pier, K., Buxton, W. & DeRose, T. D. (1993), Toolglass and Magic Lenses: The See-through Interface, *in Proceedings of SIGGRAPH'93 20th Annual Conference on Computer Graphics and Interactive Techniques, Computer Graphics (Annual Conference Series)* **27**, ACM Press, pp.73–80.

Brockschmidt, K. (1995), *Inside OLE*, second edition, Microsoft Press.

Buchner, J. (2000), "HotDoc: A Framework for Compound Documents", *ACM Computing Surveys* **32**(1), 33–8.

Celentano, A., Pozzi, S. & Toppeta, D. (1992), A Multiple Presentation Document Management System, *in Proceedings of the 10th Annual International Conference on Systems Documentation (SIGDOC'92)*, ACM Press, pp.63–71.

Dourish, P., Edwards, W. K., LaMarca, A. & Salisbury, M. (1999), Using Properties for Uniform Interaction in the Presto Document System, *in Proceedings of the 12th Annual ACM Symposium on User Interface Software and Technology, UIST'99, CHI Letters* **1**(1), ACM Press, pp.55–64.

Dykstra-Erickson, E. & Curbow, D. (1997), The Role of User Studies in the Design of OpenDoc, *in* G. C. van der Veer, A. Henderson & S. Coles (eds.), *Proceedings of the Symposium on Designing Interactive Systems: Processes, Practices, Methods and Techniques (DIS'97)*, ACM Press, pp.111–20.

Gibson, J. J. (1977), The Theory of Affordances, *in* R. Shaw & J. Bransford (eds.), *Perceiving, Acting and Knowing*, Lawrence Erlbaum Associates.

Gibson, J. J. (1979), *The Ecological Approach to Visual Perception*, Houghton Mifflin.

Gray, D. (1997), *The PhotoShop Plug-ins Book: Category Listings, Instructions and Examples*, Ventana Communications Group, Incorporated.

Johnson, J., Roberts, T. L., Verplank, W., Smith, D. C., Irby, C., Beard, M. & Mackey, K. (1989), "The Xerox "Star": A Retrospective", *IEEE Computer* **22**(9), 11–29.

Krasner, G. E. & Pope, S. T. (1988), "A Cookbook for Using the Model-View-Controller User Interface Paradigm in Smalltalk-80", *Journal of Object Oriented Programming* **1**(3), 26–49.

Maulsby, D. L., Witten, I. H. & Kittlitz, K. A. (1989), Metamouse: Specifying Graphical Procedures by Example, *in Proceedings of SIGGRAPH'89, Computer Graphics* **23**(3), ACM Press, pp.127–36.

Myers, B. A. (1989), Encapsulating Interactive Behaviors, *in* K. Bice & C. H. Lewis (eds.), *Proceedings of CHI'89: Human Factors in Computing Systems*, ACM Press, pp.319–24.

Norman, D. A. & Draper, S. W. (eds.) (1986), *User Centered System Design: New Perspectives on Human–Computer Interaction*, Lawrence Erlbaum Associates.

Perlin, K. & Fox, D. (1993), Pad: An Alternative Approach to the Computer Interface, *in Proceedings of SIGGRAPH'93 20th Annual Conference on Computer Graphics and Interactive Techniques, Computer Graphics (Annual Conference Series)* **27**, ACM Press, pp.57–64.

Shneiderman, B. (1983), "Direct Manipulation: A Step beyond Programming Languages", *IEEE Computer* **16**(8), 57–69.

Sleeter, M. E. (1996), Building Online Help for a Component-Oriented Architecture, *in Proceedings of the 14th Annual International Conference on Marshaling new Technological Forces: Building a Corporate, Academic, and User-oriented Triangle*, ACM Press, pp.87–94.

W3C (1999), XML Path Language (XPath) Version 1.0, W3C Recommendation, W3C.

W3C (2000a), Extensible Markup Language (XML) Version 1.0, W3C Recommendation, W3C.

W3C (2000b), Extensible Stylesheet Language (XSL) Version 1.0, W3C Recommendation, W3C.

W3C (2000c), XML Query Data Model, W3C Working Draft, W3C.

User-centred Design

Getting the Story Straight

Phil Turner, Susan Turner & Rod McCall

HCI Research Group, School of Computing, Napier University,
Edinburgh EH14 1DJ, UK
Email: *{p.turner,s.turner}@dcs.napier.ac.uk*

We argue that the use of a user-centred design approach necessarily involves some form of story telling or narrative. Given that both the potential end-users and the designers themselves often (perhaps usually) have different interests and points-of-view to present, the resultant co-constructed narrative describing the desired interactive system is inevitably the product of compromise. We describe how such an unwanted compromise can arise and how the process by which it arose can be unpicked using Bakhtin's approach to the analysis of narrative.

Keywords: narrative, user-centred design, collaborative virtual environments, requirements.

1 Introduction

Anyone who has used the techniques of user-centred design will agree that the process is far from fool-proof. It is not unusual to be surprised by the fickleness and wilfulness of users. Here we describe not so much a surprise but a *volte face* in an account of the use of a user-centred design approach to the design of a collaborative virtual environment (CVE). In an attempt to understand why this had occurred, we have investigated the usefulness of narrative as an explanatory framework. This paper, then, is a story about stories: a narrative about narrative. The focus of this narrative is the relationship between narrative itself, e.g. (Pentland, 1999), and the use of user-centred design, e.g. (Bødker & Grønbæk, 1998; Holtzblatt & Beyer, 1998). We show how the co-construction of a narrative about the requirements on the CVE created a myth of homogeneity and consistency. In particular, we are interested in how the multiple 'voices' of the end-users were apparently harmonised.

Our starting point is the recognition that user-centred design has some form of story telling at the heart of the process. A typical user-centred design intervention comprises a series of 'design episodes' which may take a variety of forms ranging from workshops to individual and group interviews. These design episodes are frequently characterised by the planned and spontaneous use of scenarios by analysts and end-users respectively, each contributing to the co-constructed overall story of what artefacts will be created and how they will be used. To understand the structure and dynamics of these design episodes we need an appropriate scheme of analysis (or at the very least, a means of expression) which allows important points of detail to be captured while preserving their context and thus their essentially situated nature. We propose an overall narrative structure for the process (cf. Lloyd (2000) who analyses an engineering design case study as a socially constructed narrative). Within this overall structure can be found individual narrative episodes which in turn comprise a series of utterances (the use of this term is described in Section 1.2).

We believe that this framework offers us a means of understanding both the structure and dynamics of this particular user-centred design process, and by extension, other ventures of this nature. Accordingly, this paper begins with a brief review of narrative methods in user-centred design and the contribution of Mikhail Bakhtin, as applied to the current context. We then introduce the DISCOVER project, its aims and participants. We continue with a discussion of the intended and unintended aspects of the design process in DISCOVER, highlighting aspects of story and myth within a multi-voiced narrative framework. The paper concludes with a discussion of the moral of our cautionary tale and some tentative recommendations arising from it. (Note: we use the terms 'user-centred design' and 'the design process' as a general label for the set of activities from requirements to design via iterative early evaluation.)

1.1   A brief Account of Narrative Applied to User-centred Design

Aspects of narrative in user-centred design are primarily evident in the well-known body of work which has developed and promoted the use of scenarios and associated stories as a means of communication between users and designers. These stories typically involve enabling exploration of design options and documenting of intended usage — e.g. (Bødker et al., 1993); the PICTIVE method (Muller, 1993); (Carroll, 1995); prompted reflection (Kensing, 1998); contextual design (Holtzblatt & Beyer, 1998); (Imaz & Benyon, 1999); among very many others. As will be seen, scenarios and stories of varying degrees of structure have been central to the design process in the current study.

Secondly, analysis informed by narrative methods has been brought to bear as a means of understanding everyday activities. Recent instances include Davenport et al. (2000) who employ narrative as a framing device for their enquiry into domestic use of new media devices. More directly relevant for our current case, however, are Lloyd's (2000) ethnographically-based study of engineering designers and the argument presented in Pentland (1999) for the exploitation of the components of narrative as a basis for generalisation beyond individual case studies while preserving "the details and the drama".

Lloyd makes four main points about the role of narrative in the design process: in the explanation of the design process to others; in the construction and telling of stories by individual designers; as competing accounts of the same object, so a specification may be regarded as a flexible resource for efficient selling in the salesman's discourse, but a defined starting point for the designers (cf. Bakhtin's multi-voicedness, next section); and as the socially constructed meta-story of the process itself. All these can be found in the project case study under discussion here.

Pentland's paper advances a more generic argument for narrative as a framework for research in collaborative systems. It is contended that much existing research in this domain measures and compares individual variables at the expense of context, or removes narrative fragments from their original setting, often reorganising such fragments thematically, or produces descriptive accounts of individual cases from which it is almost impossible to generalise. Pentland's argument draws *inter alia* on Bruner (1986), who suggests that narrative is central to an individual's understanding of the world, and Heritage (1984) and Goguen (1997) who emphasise the importance of the way narrative accounts of one's actions embody the values of the relevant social context. It is thus proposed that since narrative is central to social life, narrative analysis should similarly be central to research in collaborative systems, affording a medium between the idiosyncrasies of individual cases and the de-contextualised comparison of variables. As a practical means of incorporating narrative methods into the analysis of a collaborative system, Pentland advocates an adaptation of Burke's (1969) framework for the dramaturgical analysis of narrative. This comprises the actor, the act undertaken, the scene (or context), the agency (or tool) and the purpose. It is suggested that the framework can be used to highlight, for example, between two apparently similar systems for computer-related problem reporting. Differences in usage of the systems could be accounted for in terms of purpose.

Our approach to the collaborative activity of the DISCOVER design process has much in common with Pentland, although, for reasons to be discussed below, we have used Bakhtins's approach to narrative.

1.2 Bakhtin's Approach to Narrative

The Russian academic, Mikhail Bakhtin (1895–1975) has written widely on narrative, though for reasons of space, this brief introduction cannot do him justice. We have restricted our introduction to Bakhtin's work to those areas we believe are relevant to user-centred design, namely, the role of utterance, voice and, indirectly, dialogicality. While the majority of the commentaries and applications of Bakhtin's work have been literary, Moro (1999) and Wertsch (1991, 1998) have un-picked many interesting aspects which have particular relevance to both situated and mediated action and, as we hope to demonstrate, to user-centred design.

Wertsch (1998) introduces Bakhtin's work in the context of his own socio-cultural research. Wertsch argues that "language is a cultural tool" and "speech is a form of mediated action" (ibid., p.73). According to Bakhtin, speech comprises utterances. An utterance is "oriented towards an addressee, towards who that addressee might be: a fellow-member or not, of the same social group, someone connected with the speaker by close social ties or not" — Bakhtin, quoted in Moro (1999, p.168). Thus in the context of user-centred design, language mediates the interplay between designer and user with the utterance being the appropriate unit of analysis.

1.2.1   The Role of Utterance

An utterance is speech terminated by a change of speaker. Utterances exchanged between speaker and listener are the "links in the chain of speech communication".

Bakhtin observed that each speaker [or, author of an utterance as he phrased it] constructs each utterance as a response to "other viewpoints, world views, trends, theories, and so forth" embodied in the utterance to which he or she is replying. This turn taking between speaker and listener is active on both sides: "the person or persons from whom the author [speaker] expects a response — "the addressee" — is an active participant in the chain of speech communication, for whom the entire utterance is constructed in anticipation of the response" (this introduces the concept of *addressivity*). Thus utterances are "determined by whose word (utterance) it is and for whom it is meant" (ibid., p.86)

Utterances also comprise repeatable and unrepeatable components. The repeatable elements of the utterance, are for example, the words while the unrepeatable components include the context in which the utterance was spoken, its stress and intonation and its " honesty, truth, goodness, beauty and history" (Bakhtin, 1986). However most importantly to attend to one at the expense of the other is fundamentally misleading.

1.2.2   Voices

The notion of an utterance is closely linked to that of a voice. A voice is "the speaking personality, the speaking consciousness". An utterance reflects a point-of-view which is Bakhtin's definition of a voice. A voice is similar to the English use of the word 'hat' to indicate a temporarily adopted role or point-of-view — as in "speaking with my research hat on I think x, but with my teaching hat on I believe y". Voices exist in a social milieu and cannot exist outwith a social context.

Meaning can only come into existence when two or more voices interact — the voice of the speaker and the voice of the listener. Thus he insisted that **both voices** should be taken into account (again a reference to the *addressivity* of an utterance).

1.2.3   Bakhtin in Summary

We have established:

- That an utterance requires an active listener. An utterance is unrepeatable and highly contextual and that an utterance depends upon a voice which reflects the point-of-view of a speaker. The chain of speech communication, in the case of user-centred design, is the effectively the current state of the design or statement of requirements.

- Casting ourselves in the role of 'honest broker' or 'facilitator' in a user-centred design intervention is necessarily disingenuous as we are active participants pursuing our own agenda; inevitably participating and directly influencing the design process rather than simply neutral collators and sorts of information as it is so often portrayed.

So, given a user-centred design approach, we may have a potential framework for understanding the structure of design episodes (narrative) and their dynamics (Bakhtinian utterances and voices).

2   The DISCOVER Project — Background and Methods

Our case study draws upon the DISCOVER project. DISCOVER intends developing a collaborative virtual environment to support training in safety critical skills for the offshore and maritime industries. Effective safety-critical training in these domains is crucially important. The undertaking is almost prohibitively expensive, since trainees are co-located at a specialist training site for several days at a time, or in the case of the offshore industry, hugely complex disaster simulations which are created *in situ* involving the coordination of large numbers of personnel and multiple agencies. DISCOVER will provide a series of collaborative simulations which could dramatically reduce the need for senior mariners and oil rig workers to have to attend courses or run quite so many expensive exercises. It is envisaged that while the system will be made available at existing training centres, it will also be used offshore or on board ships more frequently and in, perhaps, an ad hoc manner. The CVE will enable trainees to practice dealing with emergencies within a safe virtual world. For example, practising the management of extinguishing a fire while at sea and evacuating passengers.

The immediate intended end-users of the DISCOVER CVE are four training organisations. One of these organisations is concerned exclusively with the offshore domain (i.e. oil platforms) while the other three DMI, ISSUS and WMC train senior mariners. For the sake of simplicity we confine our discussion to the maritime domain only.

Using a perspective which is itself informed by narrative methods, we now consider the effect of story telling techniques as part of the user-centred design in our case study, and speculate on the reasons for some unintended effects.

2.1   First Phase Requirements Elicitation — A Story is Constructed

This first phase of the requirements elicitation employed a number of uncontroversial approaches primarily drawn from established user-centred methods. A first phase of requirements elicitation was followed by a second iteration using an early prototype of the DISCOVER collaborative virtual environment and techniques drawn from the Contextual Design method. The first iteration of the requirements work comprised:

Six periods of observation of training sessions.	Two periods of observation of training sessions at DMI.
Interviews with officials from training validation bodies.	Interviews and use of what-if scenarios with trainees and trainers at WMC, DMI and ISSUS.

This yielded a set of high level requirements which were subsequently prioritised by stakeholders using the MoSCoW technique from Dynamic Systems Development Method (Stapleton, 1997). A sample of these requirements is as follows (headings are those stipulated by DSDM, numbers were added for convenient identification):

Must have	Should have	Could have	Want to have but won't have ...
1. Robustness and reliability of simulations. 2. Support for role-playing, and switching of roles. 3. ...	67. Validation of trainee identity throughout training. 68. A familiar user-interface. 69. ...	82. Ability to simulate fully detailed instances of individual ships and off-shore installations. 83. ...	102. Measures of training transfer. 103. Integration of pre-training psychological or aptitude testing. 104. ...

The requirements were agreed by all parties to the project, and subsequently embodied, together with sample usage scenarios, in a document supplied to our sponsors, the European Commission. And here was the first instance in which the demands of constructing a common set of requirements and thus a cogent story for an outside audience (an activity which in itself helped the project to cohere) may have obscured rather than resolved underlying multi-perspectives of the users (i.e. their multi-voicedness). As can be seen, the requirements are both high level and uncontroversial, although many of the full set could not have been predicted before the fieldwork had been undertaken. Few would gainsay, for example, that simulations must be reliable, or that it should be possible to confirm the identity of trainees undergoing training. However, it was possible to sign up to this version of events in good faith, and still hold quite radically different assumptions and intentions in mind, as will be evident later.

2.2   Losing the Plot in Exploring the Prototype

Using an early prototype is, of course, a well proven technique for eliciting further requirements on the complete system. A working prototype system was created and demonstrated to trainers and prospective trainees at all three maritime training sites. Our intention was to give the end users a clear impression of what a CVE is, how it could be used and to elicit feedback.

Demonstrations and simple hands-on tasks were followed by interviews and questionnaires. What happened in practice is that, because of the early stage of development of the software, usability issues assumed such a degree of prominence that users could not be induced to speculate in depth about how the system might be used, or how training delivered through such a medium might relate to existing practice. For example, it is difficult to convince the captain of one of the world's largest passenger vessels of the possibilities of the new medium after difficulty with movement control has 'trapped' him for some minutes in a corner of the virtual bridge. However, some indications emerged of divergent usage intentions and underlying purposes, and triggered much debate about the detailed design features which would be necessary to support these.

The developers in the project now urgently required a unified, detailed, concrete design specification which would nonetheless support each intended context of use. This was to be achieved by means of a workshop involving each of the three maritime organisations.

2.3 Mythmaking: The Requirements-to-design Workshop, Day 1

At this two day event, trainers from the three organisations met with the representatives from one of the software developer organisations and two facilitators from the user-centred design team (the first and third authors).

The agenda was very simple: to agree the *detailed* features of the maritime simulator in the light of how it was expected to be used in practice. We adapted elements of Contextual Design (Holtzblatt & Beyer, 1998) to facilitate the process, principally a variant of the affinity diagram technique, which supports the identification of common themes from a mass of contextual data. We began by asking each training organisation to revisit what they wanted of DISCOVER in terms of the 'w' words (familiar to user-centred design practitioners), i.e. why, when, who, where and, of course, how. It should be said that we did not hear anything we had not heard before but we used this restatement as both a starting point and trigger for exploring the design features of the DISCOVER collaborative virtual environment. As the representatives from the training organisation spoke we noted each issue or explicit design feature on a Post-IT™note. These were summarised as a word or two and in some cases a short phrase. At the end of the process we had gathered over 400 Post-ITs of which approximately 10% were subsequently discarded as duplicates or irrelevant.

The trainers (rather than the analysts in the canonical use of Contextual Design) were then invited to create an affinity model which required them to sort the issues into logical groups as illustrated in Figure 1. Emerging groupings included the layout and configuration of the virtual ship, the appearance and functionality of the avatars and the context of use of the completed system. Throughout this process the software designer helped ground the design details, i.e. he commented upon whether or not the desired functionality could be achieved. At the end of the first day we had co-constructed an affinity model and subsequently a communications model and an artefact/physical model (ibid.) and of the environment to be recreated.

Informal discussion with the three trainers afterwards revealed that they thought that the day had gone well. All three agreed that they felt that we (the project) were all closer to agreeing on the final form of the CVE.

2.4 A Myth Unmasked: What Happened Next, Day 2

> *He went like one that hath been stunned,*
> *And is of sense forlorn:*
> *A sadder and a wiser man,*
> *He rose the morrow morn.*
>
> Coleridge (1798)

Day 2 of the workshop found us together again, this time with the object of getting the representatives from the three training organisations to agree the details of

Figure 1: End users creating an affinity diagram.

how the CVE was to be used in training practice. (The high level features of this had been agreed early in the requirements phase.) As a starting point for this, personnel from the WMC training organisation had previously created a detailed training scenario for a typical exercise to be conducted in the DISCOVER collaborative virtual environment. The scenario was a refinement, but not a significant rewrite, of an earlier version used in the project. It now emerged that the training scenario did not reflect some aspects of practice at DMI and ISSUS but after discussion they agreed to adopt it. We then used the training scenario to create a series of extended, annotated storyboards. The annotations held low level design details and sequencing information which the designers and implementers required.

Approximately an hour into this process one of the trainers identified a fundamental problem with the design which was so great that he said that his organisation would not and could not use it. (While this was pivotally important to the DISCOVER project the details are less relevant to this narrative and consequently are consigned to a footnote[1].) So, after spending 12 person months of carefully co-constructing an agreed story among the intended end-users as to the specification and early design of the CVE we found to our horror in the space of two minutes on the final day of the final workshop that no such consensus had ever existed.

---

[1]The difficulty hinged on the nature of the training itself. The DISCOVER collaborative virtual environment was intended to support the command and control training of senior mariners. This does not directly involve fire fighting or throwing a rope to a man overboard. Instead it is about organising and collecting information from the men fighting the fire or pulling a man out of the water and then acting on that information.

As one of the trainers from the dissenting organisations explained, a mariner in a (real) room with 4 telephones receiving information from the outside world would be more effective than the proposed system. All the visual trappings and interaction of a collaborative virtual environment were largely irrelevant.

In contrast the other two training organisations specifically wanted a collaborative virtual environment to enrich the experience of their trainees.

So, how can we account for the events of the second day of the workshop? In the preceding months we had collectively agreed and consolidated the requirements and initial design of the CVE. We recognise, of course, that these processes of compromise and consolidation involve the systematic rejection of some requirements in favour of others and the integration of multiple perspectives. Indeed we had experienced a not untypical range of technical, inter- and intra-organisational compromises. However we remained puzzled. We had elicited requirements from the key stakeholders, namely, trainers, trainees and senior training managers and we also recognised that these individuals hold multiple roles. We had checked, validated and prioritised these requirements regularly. We had used the well proven techniques of observation, interviewing, artefact collection (e.g. sample training scenarios), scenarios and use of a prototype. We had explored both training and usage scenarios with all concerned from an early stage, but apparently to little avail.

3   A Missing Voice?

In eliciting requirements on the DISCOVER CVE we had focused on the stakeholders and their roles we had identified. When interviewing these individuals they spoke with a particular voice. People with the job title of 'trainer' spoke as maritime trainers, prospective end-users and project members. We as analysts listened as analysts. We together co-constructed a narrative which embodied the design, functionality and behaviour of the DISCOVER system. However what we had failed to appreciate fully that we as listeners necessarily shape what is said. This is a multi-layered process: as well as Bahktin's concept of the active listener, narratologists argue that a narrator assumes a narratee or narratees with a particular set of taken-for-granted knowledge and values.

On reflection, it is apparent that the trainers spoke with multiple voices and it is almost certain that we all failed to differentiate among them. The voices of the maritime trainer (expressing concerns about training effectiveness), project team member (displaying willingness to cooperate) and prospective end-user (concerned about the ease of use of the system) had been seamlessly woven together. We suspect that much of the time these narrators were tailoring their text to an audience of 'fellow project members'. As listeners, we had very likely amplified a chorus of consensus. And it was only when the fine details of usage were discussed that the specific voices of the maritime trainer *talking to fellow trainers* were brought to the fore. This revealed a competing narrative thread was revealed embodying the belief that a collaborative virtual environment was not an optimal solution. To go down this route would require a substantial revision of training materials and mode of working which may only have become apparent once the detail was closely considered. So rather than the maritime trainer's voice perhaps we had witnessed a "reluctant or resistant to change maritime trainer's voice" or "concerned about his/her job voice"). This occurred on the second day of the final workshop, when the trainers spoke solely as trainers, with inevitable conflicts between what they were saying and the voices they had used in the past.

4 Revisiting User-centred Design

We conclude by proposing a number of modifications (or, at least, caveats) to the user-centred design approach.

Firstly, there is a strong case for refining the idea of a largely static and clearly defined stakeholder with that of multiple voices each reflecting a point of view or facet of their stake in the design process. This would not be a trivial endeavour as we have described above. Voices may be ephemeral and consequently easily missed. Voices may well overlap and be mistaken for each other. Voices may also come into existence as a consequence of changes of the design process as we witnessed in the case study described above.

Secondly, there is a need for a reference point which can be used to focus or refocus the individual design episodes. This could take the form of a statement of purpose for the system as a whole (as in various structured design methods, e.g. Yourden) or some kind of statement of the relevant system (as in Checkland's Soft Systems Methodology) or objectified motive as in Leontev's theory of activity.

Thirdly, we would caution against inadvertently de-contextualising requirements and design details. Examining a sample of the Post-Its generated at the workshop reveals such items as "E3: standard graphic signs", "A11: ash tray in cabin" and "E22: Panel for electrical power" which are snippets and snapshots of the utterances of the trainers (E refers to environmental requirements; A refers to the design of the accommodation on board). Instead a practical means of capturing the utterances, which necessarily capture mood, context and a whole host of other potentially relevant factors, is needed. As Pentland (1999) advocates, narrative may afford a structure for this.

Finally, story telling is a universal characteristic of humans. Ask a group of intelligent, articulate people to tell a story about a speculative piece of software which might embody something they know well and it is very likely that they will. Support the process with the tricks and trappings of user-centred design and the likelihood rises. And there is all too strong a tendency to co-construct coherent, simple stories with a beginning, a middle and an end. We believe that is what happened in the case study we have presented here. Perhaps user-centred design is a little too good at eliciting stories, at constructing narrative. Perhaps people become too cooperative and compliant when they are encouraged to talk about subjects they know and care about. Perhaps established requirements methods are too effective in harmonising multiple voices. And perhaps the occasional excursion into reality, through the reiteration of underlying purpose, a measure of scepticism towards apparently consolidated requirements and the more explicit documentation of multiple narratives is needed to balance the account.

Acknowledgements

We gratefully acknowledge the contributions of our colleagues on the DISCOVER project in providing the sites and subjects for the fieldwork herein described and in developing the DISCOVER software. The project is financially supported by the EU ESPRIT programme.

References

Bakhtin, M. M. (1986), *Speech Genres and Other Late Essays*, University of Texas Press. Edited by C. Emerson & M. Holquist, translated by V.W. McGee.

Bødker, S. & Grønbæk, K. (1998), Users and Designers in Mutual Activity, *in* Y. Engeström & D. Middleton (eds.), *Cognition and Communication at Work*, Cambridge University Press, pp.130–58.

Bødker, S., Grønbæk, K. & Kyng, M. (1993), Cooperative Design: Techniques and Experiences from the Scandinavian Scene, *in* D. Schuler & A. Namioka (eds.), *Participatory Design: Principles and Practices*, Lawrence Erlbaum Associates, pp.157–75.

Bruner, J. (1986), *Actual Minds, Possible Worlds*, Harvard University Press.

Burke, K. (1969), *A Grammar of Motives*, University of California Press.

Carroll, J. M. (1995), Introduction: The Scenario Perspective on System Development, *in* J. M. Carroll (ed.), *Scenario-Based Design: Envisioning Work and Technology in System Development*, John Wiley & Sons, pp.1–17.

Coleridge, S. T. (1798), "The Rime of the Ancient Mariner". Longmans.

Davenport, E., Higgins, M. & Somerville, I. (2000), "Narrative of New Media in Scottish Households: The Evolution of a Framework of Inquiry", *Journal of the American Society for Information Science* **51**(10), 900–12.

Goguen, J. A. (1997), Toward a Social, Ethical Theory of Information, *in* G. C. Bowker, S. L. Star, W. Turner & L. Gasser (eds.), *Social Science, Technical Systems and Cooperative Work: Beyond the Great Divide*, Lawrence Erlbaum Associates, pp.27–56.

Heritage, J. (1984), *Garfinkel and Ethnomethodology*, Polity Press.

Holtzblatt, K. & Beyer, H. (1998), *Contextual Design: Defining Customer-centred Systems*, Morgan-Kaufmann.

Imaz, M. & Benyon, D. (1999), How Stories Capure Interactions, *in* A. Sasse & C. Johnson (eds.), *Human–Computer Interaction — INTERACT '99: Proceedings of the Seventh IFIP Conference on Human–Computer Interaction*, Vol. 1, IOS Press, pp.321–8.

Kensing, F. (1998), "Prompted Reflection: A Technique for Understanding Complex Work", *Interactions* **1**(1), 7–15.

Lloyd, P. (2000), "Storytelling and the Development of Discourse in the Engineering Design Process", *Design Studies* **21**(4), 357–73.

Moro, Y. (1999), The Expanded Dialogical Sphere: Writing Activity and Authoring of Self in Japanese Classrooms, *in* R. M. Y. Engeström & R.-L. Punämaki (eds.), *Perspectives in Activity Theory*, Cambridge University Press, pp.165–205.

Muller, M. (1993), PICTIVE: Democratizing the Dynamics of the Design Session, *in* D. Schuler & A. Namioka (eds.), *Participatory Design: Principles and Practices*, Lawrence Erlbaum Associates, pp.211–237

Pentland, B. T. (1999), Narrative Methods in Collaborative Systems Research, *in Proceedings of the 32nd Hawaii International Conference on Systems Sciences*, IEEE Computer Society Press, pp.23–32.

Stapleton, J. (1997), *DSDM: Dynamic Systems Development Method*, Addison–Wesley.

Wertsch, J. V. (1991), *Voices of the Mind*, Harvard University Press.

Wertsch, J. V. (1998), *Minds as Action*, Oxford University Press.

Augmenting the Affordance of Online Help Content

Milene Selbach Silveira[†‡*], Simone D J Barbosa[†‡] & Clarisse Sieckenius de Souza[†‡]

[†] *Informatics Department, PUC-Rio, R. Marquês de São Vicente, 225, Gávea, Rio de Janeiro, 22453–900, Brazil*

Tel: *+55 21 512 2299*

Email: *{milene,sim,clarisse}@inf.puc-rio.br*

[*] *Informatics Faculty, PUCRS, Av. Ipiranga, 6681, Porto Alegre, RS, 90619–900, Brazil*

[‡] *TeCGraf/PUC-Rio, R. Marquês de São Vicente, 225, Gávea, Rio de Janeiro, 22453–900, Brazil*

Traditional online help is often function-oriented, unrelated to users' tasks and not situated at users' current context of interaction. This is due mainly to the help development strategy, and to the lack of a help model that takes into account typical users' task flows. In addition to a help model, we also need adequate access structures to the various components of the help system, each providing a different perspective on help content. This paper proposes the integration of a help model with communicability concepts, both built upon the principles of Semiotic Engineering. Our goal is to provide users with better help access and content, which are designed to clarify users' specific doubts, as expressed by users themselves, during interaction.

Keywords: help systems design, communicability utterances, help systems model and architecture, semiotic engineering.

1 Introduction

Help systems are typically used as a last resort. Users may not see an immediate benefit from accessing online help, because of past frustrating experiences. As designers, we must take great care in providing both clear access and relevant information to users via online help systems.

In previous work (Silveira et al., 2000), we have proposed a model and a corresponding architecture for online help systems. In our view, the designer's knowledge about the application must be elicited throughout the application development process. This view is based on a theoretical framework called Semiotic Engineering (de Souza, 1993), which aims at conveying, through the user interface, designers' intentions and design decisions.

But, why should we capture these design decisions and convey them to users? Users frequently work with an application without knowing the underlying objectives and technological concepts. Their only goal is to perform their tasks correctly and efficiently. It is when users can't seem to be able to do it, i.e. when a breakdown occurs, that the design rationale may play a major role in fostering users' understanding of the application. The design rationale may help users to recover from a breakdown and learn more about the application and the reasons things are the way they are. We were first inspired by an idea presented in Winograd & Flores (1986), that the design should "anticipate the forms of breakdowns and provide a space of possibilities for action when they occur". Additional studies about improvisation, carried out by Dourish (1997), have also pointed to the need for providing users with resources and information for supporting local decision-making processes.

According to Semiotic Engineering, the interface is a message from designers to users. It is a special kind of message, because it is a message about how users exchange messages with the application interface, i.e. it is a meta-message. It represents, implicitly or explicitly, how the designers convey the application and how they built it, and why. As part of this meta-message, the online help system is an important component, because there designers are better able to explicitly convey how they conceived the application.

In previous research, we felt the need to further investigate the kinds of information users may require while interacting with an application. A sample request for contextual information may be illustrated by the expression *What's this?*, available in many existing applications.

In this paper, we propose an attempt to solve users' contextual needs for information, by using communicability utterances (Prates et al., 2000b; 2000a) to access help information at various levels of affordance (Norman, 1988; 1999): operational, tactical, and strategic — for a discussion about different levels of affordance, see de Souza et al. (2000).

2 Existing Help Model

Our first approach for designing online help (Silveira et al., 2000) is based on Semiotic Engineering, which considers help systems as a distinguished meta-message from designers to users (de Souza, 1993). In this case, the designer is explicitly saying what he/she believes are the users' problems or tasks, what he/she think is the best solution for them, and how he/she intends to make it available to users' practical use.

We propose that this designer's vision — sent to users through the help system — be captured *during* the design and development processes. This knowledge elicitation (capturing the designers' knowledge about the application designed and developed by themselves) is based upon questions for the designers, classified into three major topics. From the **designers' point-of-view**:

1. What are the users' problems/needs?

2. What is the best solution for these problems? And what are the alternatives?

3. How was this made available for operational use?

These questions summarise our conclusions after relating research about available technical literature (taxonomies for online help systems (Roesler & McLellan, 1995); context-sensitive help (Marx & Schmandt, 1996; Sleeter, 1996); help for the web (Chamberland, 1999; Priestley, 1998; Rintjema & Warburton, 1998) and user-system dialogues (Chu-Carrol & Carberry, 1998; Hansen et al., 1996; Johnson & Erdem, 1997; Kedar et al., 1993; Mittal & Moore, 1995; Raskutti & Zukerman, 1997), among others) and practice in the design and development of online help systems for groupware applications on the web.

Each topic can be extended into subtopics, whose answers constitute the semantic dimension of the message from designers to users about the application. These are:

1. What are the users' problems and needs?

> *What is the application domain?*
> *What is the nature of work in this domain?*
> *Who are the actors?*
> *What role do they carry out?*
> *What tasks do they do?*

2. What are the best solutions for these problems and needs?

> *What is the application?*
> *How will this technology affect the domain?*
> *What is possible to do with it (goals)?*
> *What is the application useful for?*
> *What are the advantages of the application?*

Technology

> *What computational environment is presumed for the full operation of the application?*
> *What does the user need to know in order to use this application?*

Activities
> *What activities (tasks) can be carried out in the application environment?*
> *What are the available options in the current version?*

3. How can all of this be put to operational use?

Computer–Human Interaction Analogy
> *What is the basic computer–human interaction analogy used?*

Tasks
> *What does each task mean?*
> *How can/must users do that? When?*
> *Where in the application can users do this task?*
> *How can users do and undo (parts of) tasks?*
> *Why is it necessary to do this or that task?*
> *Examples of performing the task (scenarios)*
> *Who is or isn't affected by a task or part of a task?*
> *What do we do after finishing a task? Until when can we do that?*
> *How do we know if we have (successfully) finished the task?*

Given an actual context of interaction, the user must be able to answer:
> *What can I do now?*
> *Where am I?*
> *Where can I go?*
> *Where did I come from?*
> *What happened?*

We can analyse these questions from four different perspectives: Domain, Tasks, Agent (inspired by van der Veer & van Welie (n.d.) and Application. These perspectives are used to define a preliminary help model (Figure 1). The expressions in boldface represent the corresponding help information. In parentheses, we present the questions for the designers, whose answers will be used to build the actual content of the help topics.

In this model, we find the answers to almost all of the described questions, except the contextualised ones (*What can I do now? Where am I? Where can I go? Where did I come from? What happened?*). The entities' attributes become the answers to the preceding questions, which are listed under each corresponding entity. The questions of a contextual nature are generated at execution time, according to the task and the actual application state.

3   Communicability Concepts for Help Systems

In the communicability evaluation method (Prates et al., 2000b), utterances are used as an attempt to characterise users' reactions when a communicative breakdown occurs during interaction. It is argued that these breakdowns occur when the user cannot perceive the designers' intended affordances. It is an indication that the designer has failed in conveying his/her message through the interface application.

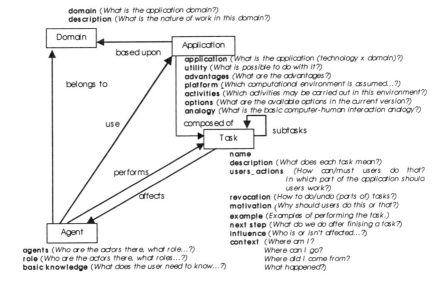

Figure 1: A model for representing information in help systems.

The utterances used for communicability evaluation are: *Where is? What now? What's this? Oops! I can't do it this way. Where am I? What happened? Why doesn't it? Looks fine to me. I can't do it. I can do otherwise. Thanks, but no, thanks. Help!* The symptoms that allow us to identify each utterance in the context they occur is presented in Prates et al. (2000b).

In de Souza et al. (2000), we see that the designer has fostered a successful communication with users when they can perceive the intended application affordances. These affordances may be classified at three levels: operational, tactical, and strategical.

Affordances at the **operational level** are related to users' immediate and individual actions they need to perform. They are closely related to the interactive codes employed in the application. We may consider questions such as **What's this?** as being answered at this level.

Tactic-level affordances are related to a plan, or sequence of actions, for executing a certain task. In general terms, information at this level answers questions such as **How?**

Finally, there are **strategic-level** affordances, which are related to conceptualisations and decisions involved in certain problem-solving processes and in the embedded technology.

Communicability utterances, besides being used in communicability evaluation of human–computer interaction, may allow us to provide a novel technique for accessing online help. Users would be able to express themselves using these utterances whenever they experienced a communicative breakdown during interaction

Question	Communicability Utterance
What is each task?	What's this?
How can it be performed? When?	I can't do it.
	What now?
How do I do and undo (parts of) tasks?	(*)
	Oops!
Why do I have to do this or that task?	(*)
Sample usage (scenarios).	(*)
Whom does this task affect?	(*)
What do I do after the end of this task?	What now?
Until when can this be done?	
Contextual questions	
Where am I?	Where am I?
Where can I go to?	What now?
Where did I come from?	(*)
What happened?	What happened?

Table 1: Users' questions and the corresponding communicability utterances.

It may be argued that many applications already provide access to specific help information by means of the expressions such as *What's this?*. This is typically afforded by specific interface elements, such as popup menus, for instance. The ideas presented here extend this approach to all levels of help content, providing relevant, context-sensitive information at varying granularity.

At first, we have tried to relate users' questions from the model (representing their doubts) to existing communicability utterances. Due to the nature of these utterances, we have considered mostly task-related questions. Strategic questions, related to the domain and to the application as a whole, will not be considered in this analysis. Table 1 summarises the utterances that cover the remaining questions dealt with in our model.

The left column presents the questions whose answers will make up the help **content** that may be **accessed** via the corresponding communicability utterance in the right column. Since not all the questions presented in the model were covered by the existing communicability utterances (as marked with an asterisk [*]), we proceeded the analysis in the opposite direction: from the utterances to the corresponding breakdowns and levels of affordance.

4   Communicability and Help Content

In this section, we analyze the relation between each communicability utterance, the corresponding communicative breakdown, and the affordance level in which it occurs. Our goal is to gain insights for designing coherent help systems that provide content at various levels, and for designing consistent access for each piece of content.

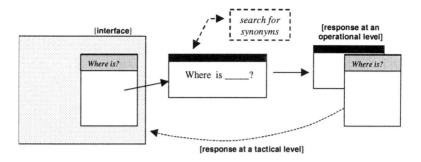

Figure 2: Response for a Where is? question at operational and tactical levels.

4.1 Communicability Utterances

4.1.1 Oops!

Oops! occurs when the user realises he/she has just done something wrong, and wants to reverse the previous action(s). The help response is either **operational** or **tactical**, depending on the complexity of the steps to be performed. For instance, a single *Undo* would be considered an operational response, whereas a sequence of interaction steps that lead to the desired state would be tactical.

4.1.2 Where Is?

The problem here is that the user has an idea of what he/she needs, but cannot find the corresponding interface level. The help response is, at first, **operational**: it tells where the element is. It may be necessary to actually show where the element is, depending on the interaction steps required for reaching it. In this case, the response is considered **tactical**, showing how the user may reach the element (Figure 2).

It is important to note that, in the case of this utterance, the user must specifically describe or identify the element he/she is querying about, since its location is unknown. It is possible that the user does not know the specific name or expression the designer chose to refer to the element, so we should be aware of this problem and provide a variety of synonyms for the terms employed throughout the application.

Where is? utterances can also occur from within help content that was first accessed via other utterances. In this case, the user has been told what to do, but does not know where the necessary interface element is, for carrying out the instructions. For instance, let us consider some help content related to an Oops! utterance, which tells the user what to do to reverse the previous actions. If there is an element the user cannot find in the interface, he/she would further utter Where is? in order to find out the location of (operational) and/or interaction steps required for accessing (tactical) the element (Figure 3).

4.1.3 What Now?

This utterance occurs in two different situations:

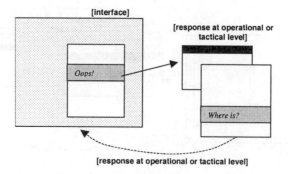

Figure 3: Sequence of Oops! and Where is? utterances.

1. when the user has carried out a few interaction steps but does not know how to proceed with the task at hand; or

2. when the user needs to perform task that he/she cannot even formulate in terms of the available interface elements.

In the first case, the response is **operational**, showing the user what to do (what's the next step). If the user utters *What now?* again, in this context, the response becomes **tactical**, showing the user how to do what is needed.

In the second case, the response would be **strategic**, presenting to the user the tasks the application was designed to support, from a user's perspective, i.e. using the terms he/she should be familiarised with, according to the corresponding domain.

4.1.4 What's This?

The user utters *What's this?* when he/she needs a description of an interface element or its usage. The response is, at first, **operational**, describing the element. If the user wants further information, such as how, where, and when the element is used, we have another *What's this?*, this time at a **tactical** level, describing the element's usage. In many cases, both levels can be presented at once, saving users' an additional interaction step (Figure 4).

Another usage of *What's this?* may occur when the user has heard about some application object or functionality, but could not identify or locate it. In this case, the access to the utterance would be like the one for *Where is?*, in which the user is prompted for additional input.

4.1.5 What Happened?

This utterance occurs when the user does an action expecting a response, and he/she gets another response, or no response at all. The corresponding help content is both **operational** and **tactical**. It reveals what happened, and how it resulted from the previous interaction steps.

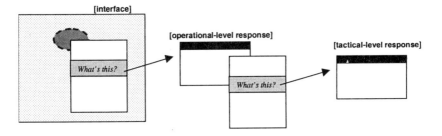

Figure 4: What's this? utterance at various levels of affordance.

4.1.6   Why Doesn't It?

Why doesn't it? occurs when a user retries an operation more than once, because he/she is convinced that he/she is doing the right thing. The response is both **tactical** and **strategic**. It shows the consequences of the interaction steps taken, and why they provide those results.

4.1.7   I Can't Do It

I can't do it. could be accessed from a piece of help content, whenever the user fails in following procedural instructions. The response is presented at a **tactical** level, guiding the user through the preconditions necessary for that task to be performed. It may also present **operational** instructions, at a finer level of interaction detail.

4.1.8   Help!

This utterance gives access to a traditional facet of the help system, when uttered within the application interface. Moreover, it can also be uttered within the help system itself, and in this case, provides information about all kinds of help that are available to users. In this context, it can be used again to ask when and how to access the various portions of the help system.

4.2   *Additional Help Utterances*

Up to this point, the existing communicability utterances have covered only part of the questions presented in the help model, as shown in Table 1. We will now discuss the questions that were not cover by the original utterances, and utterances that did not find a particular place in the model.

The utterances *I can't do it this way.; Where am I?; Looks fine to me.; I can't do it.; I can do otherwise.; Thanks, but no, thanks.* are not used as a direct access to help, but they may be used in the design of help content. In order to access them, a new utterance is proposed: *How do I do this?* In addition, we propose a few other utterances: *Where was I? Why should I do this? Who is affected by this? On whom does this depend?* Following is a description of the breakdowns they intend to solve, and the levels at which they function.

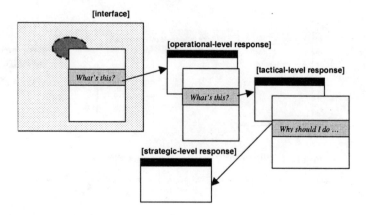

Figure 5: The occurrence of a Why should I do this? within a tactical What's this?

4.2.1　Where was I?

This breakdown occurs when the user needs to retrace his/her previous steps in order to understand the state in which he/she currently is. The response is at both the **operational** level, with an identification and a description of the previous steps, and at the **tactical** level, with an identification of larger tasks that may comprise these steps.

4.2.2　Why should I do this?

Why should I do this? could be accessed from a piece of help content, whenever the user doesn't understand the reasons underlying certain instructions. The response is presented at a **strategic** level, revealing the designer's perspective on that topic.

This utterance is particularly important to Semiotic Engineering, because the designer can use it to explicitly state his/her rationale of the application. The response may also describe the importance he/she assigns to a certain task or operation within a larger context.

For instance, *Why should I do this?* could be used from within a piece of help content previously accessed via a tactical *What's this?*. In this situation, the user would want to know not only what a task is and how to perform it, but also its importance within the application as a whole (Figure 5).

4.2.3　Who is Affected By This? On Whom Does This Depend?

These utterances may occur when work processes and roles are modelled, and roles are responsible for interdependent tasks. The response may be considered **operational**, listing the roles affected by the selected task.

4.2.4　How Do I Do This?

When the user does not know how to perform a certain task in an application, he/she may utter *How do I do this?* and provide additional input in order to obtain the corresponding help information. The response is at a **tactical** level, describing how

Existing Communicability Utterances	Help Utterances
Where is? What now? What's this? Oops! I can't do it! What happened? Why doesn't it? Help!	How do I do this? Why should I do this? Whom does this affect? On whom does this depend? Where was I? Is there another way to do this?

Table 2: Final set of utterances for designing help systems.

he/she should proceed. Typically, it consists of step-by-step instructions.

Within this help context, users may utter *How do I do this?* again, in case an instruction isn't clear. If, on the other hand, he/she tries to perform the operation and doesn't succeed, it is a case of *I can't do it*.

4.2.5   Is There Another Way To Do This?

This utterance comprises both *I can do otherwise* and *Thanks, but no, thanks*. In this case, the response is both **tactical** and **strategical**. For each alternative path of interaction, it should present the steps required to perform the task (tactical), and the motivation for following that path (strategical).

This utterance is also characteristic of our Semiotic Engineering approach, since it allows the designer to explicitly convey his/her design decisions and intentions.

4.3   Summary of Findings

As presented earlier, some utterances can be accessed immediately from the user interface, such as *What's this?* and *What happened?*. Others, however, require additional input, such as *Where is?* and *How do I do this?*. Moreover some utterances may occur from within the help system itself, such as *Why should I do this?*, for example.

Some of the existing communicability utterances are inadequate for accessing help information. For instance, the user would never utter *I can't do it.*, but rather ask *How do I do this?*. The utterances *I can do otherwise* (missing of affordance) and *Thanks, but no, thanks.* (declination of affordance) wouldn't probably be uttered either, because the user would have successfully completed his/her task. However, we present some information in the direction of varying affordances as a response to the *Is there another way to do this?*.

Table 2 illustrates the set of utterances we will use for designing our help system.

5   An Example

In this section, we illustrate two different approaches to accessing help content. We have chosen a small portion of the help system found in MS-Word97. We will show

how we may follow the required steps for accessing a given help topic according to the application's help system, and then compare it to how it would work out when following our approach. Let us consider the following usage scenario:

> *Jack and John are writing together a report due tomorrow. After joining their writings, John was to review the whole report, and discuss his ideas and doubts with Jack. Since they cannot meet in person, John has used a tool within his word processor to highlight the changes he has made. The problem is that Jack is not familiar with this tool. He tries to erase a portion of the revised text, but the only thing that happens is that the text appears in another colour and format. He tries to call John, but he can't reach him. What now? He accesses the help system ...*

> 1. *Upon asking the assistant for the term **Review**, he gets a help topic called **Review a document** (Figure 6 a), which provides a description of the reviewing task, and the following options: Insert a Comment, Modify a Comment, and **Track changes while you edit.***

> 2. *Upon selecting the last option, he gets a help topic explaining how to start making changes (Figure 6 b), but not how to deal with the existing revision marks (in Word's terms, accept or reject). Moreover, there are some elements in the help topic that he doesn't understand. He clicks on each of them, in order to get more information, and a popup window is shown for each: **toolbar** (Figure 6 c) and **revision marks** (Figure 6 d).*

> 3. *Since he still couldn't find what he wanted, he decides to browse and search the help index, looking for terms that would seem related to his doubts. He clicks on the **Tracking changes** item, and selects the **reviewing comments** subitem. He is presented with a small popup window with two options: **Incorporate or reject changes made with revision marks**, and **Review the comments in a document**.*

> 4. *He selects the first option, and finally gets to the help content he needed (Figure 7).*

It is noteworthy that the user's first attempt did not get him to the necessary help content. In our approach, we try to increase the benefits provided by the help system by providing contextualised help. We do that by coupling terms that characterise the application and the supported tasks with the user's perceptions about his/her doubts, as expressed via a communicability utterance. This way, we can provide less information, following a minimalist approach (Carroll, 1998), but more focussed on user's current doubt. He/she can access more detailed levels of information as needed. In our approach, the following steps could have been carried out:

> 1. *User right-clicks on a piece of revised task, and a popup appears, showing the utterances he may use for accessing help about the*

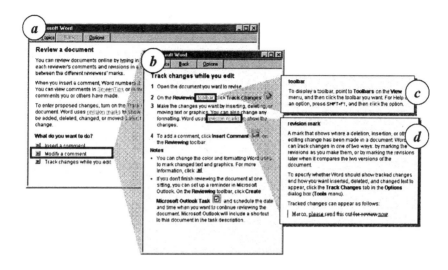

Figure 6: A user's first attempt at accessing help about "Review".

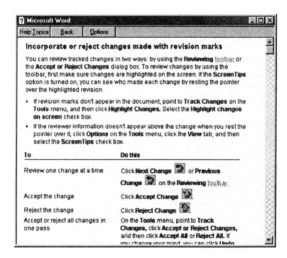

Figure 7: Help content window that contains the required information to our user's task.

*clicked item. He chooses **How do I do this?**, hoping to find information about how to deal with revised text. A help message is shown, such as "The reviewing functions may be accessed through the Track changes option under the Tools menu."* [1]

2. *If the user still doesn't understand how to do it, he may ask again **How do I do this?** about the Track changes expression. The corresponding help message could be like the following: "From the Tools menu, select the Track Changes option. If you want to turn on/off the reviewing mode, select the Highlight changes ... subitem. If you would like to accept or reject each or all of the current revisions, select Accept or Reject Changes .... Finally, if you would like to compare two documents, select Compare Documents ...."*

3. *The user now gets that he can deal with the existing revision marks by selecting Accept or Reject Changes .... However, he would like to know if there is another way to accomplish this task. He then asks **Is there another way to do this?** on the Accept or Reject Changes ... subitem. Another message appears, informing the user that he can also show a Reviewing toolbar and use its buttons.*

6   Proposed Help Model and Architecture

From the aforementioned analysis, we found it necessary to include some kinds of information in our help model. In the following, we will present the enhanced help model and the proposed architecture for designing help systems.

6.1   Enhanced Help Model

The previously proposed help model (Figure 1) did not cover all the information required for supporting the results obtained from our analsys. In particular, we have included a new entity, called **Flow**, from which we derive all the contextual information, and the alternative paths of interaction (along with the underlying rationale). The resulting model is presented in Figure 8.

6.2   Proposed Help Architecture

Taking the enhanced help model as a starting point, we now describe the proposed help architecture that supports users' most frequent doubts, under a Semiotic Engineering perspective. Our architecture provides two means for accessing help: via a Main Help Module, and via Users' Utterances.

The **Main Help Module** is what might be called a traditional help system. It provides answers to all of the questions in the model, and it is typically disconnected from the application (for instance, an independent window). It describes the whole application, from the general domain conceptualisations, the tasks supported by

---

[1] If a message contains an underlined expression, one or more help topics are also available for it, via communicability utterances.

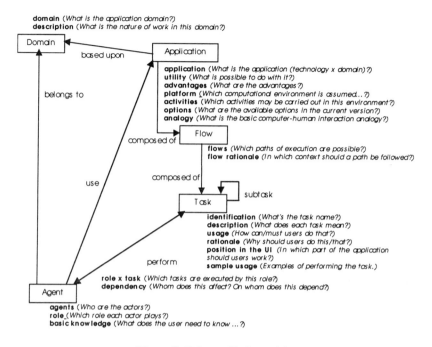

domain *(What is the application domain?)*
description *(What is the nature of work in this domain?)*

Domain

based upon

Application

belongs to

application *(What is the application (technology x domain)?)*
utility *(What is possible to do with it?)*
advantages *(What are the advantages?)*
platform *(Which computational environment is assumed...?)*
activities *(Which activities may be carried out in this environment?)*
options *(What are the available options in the current version?)*
analogy *(What is the basic computer-human interaction analogy?)*

composed of

Flow

flows *(Which paths of execution are possible?)*
flow rationale *(In which context should a path be followed?)*

use

composed of

Task

subtask

identification *(What's the task name?)*
description *(What does each task mean?)*
usage *(How can/must users do that?)*
rationale *(Why should users do this/that?)*
position in the UI *(In which part of the application should users work?)*
sample usage *(Examples of performing the task.)*

perform

role x task *(Which tasks are executed by this role?)*
dependency *(Whom does this affect? On whom does this depend?)*

Agent

agents *(Who are the actors?)*
role *(Which role each actor plays?)*
basic knowledge *(What does the user need to know ...?)*

Figure 8: Enhanced help model.

the application, to the user's manual, with scenarios exemplifying the usage of the application.

Users' Utterances provide a great shift in perspective. Instead of just asking for local information by means of a hint over an interaction element, which only answers *What's this?* questions, in the proposed architecture the user may ask for help by means of a predefined set of utterances (Table 2). In addition to providing varying access to help information in accordance with users' doubts, our approach guides the designer in composing the help content, taking into account the different levels of affordance implied by utterances. This content must be organised in a way that allows layering (Farkas, 1998), i.e. it should provide clearly marked opportunities for accessing alternative or complementary help content, via utterances within the help system. Thus, users will be able to navigate throughout the help content, at different levels of affordance, and according to their immediate need for information, as expressed via the utterances.

In addition to offering help upon users' requests, the application can also volunteer help information, by means of Direct Instructions and Error Messages. **Direct Instructions** are explicit warnings the designers sent to users, to inform them how to proceed at a given moment, or the preferred path of execution for a task. **Error Messages** are generated in case users perform an action incorrectly, or when a system failure occurs. These two components were already present in our first model proposal, and have been implemented in a case study (Silveira et al., 2000).

In addition to these components, additional features were also identified that may be desirable for enhancing help systems:

FAQ generator: the application may monitor users' utterances, and build a list of their most frequent doubts for faster access. It seems to be especially useful within a multiuser environment, where a user may benefit from other users' previous doubts. It can also be a valuable resource for future application redesigns.

Search engine: since the users' terminology may differ from that used in the application, we must provide synonyms for the expressions used for accessing help, both through utterances and the main module.

Annotation module: this module allows users to bookmark or annotate help topics, for future reference (their own, or other users'). This might also be considered a user-defined FAQ list.

7 Discussion

Help systems shouldn't be seen either as useless or as a remedy for all intrinsic design problems (Sellen & Nicol, 1990). In order to try to meet users' needs and promote their understanding of applications, we use this model based on Semiotic Engineering, exploring the direct and indirect messages from designers to users.

Users access help when there is a breakdown in their understanding of an application. Since the designers have only an indirect participation in the interaction scenario, we try to maximise users' comprehension of the application from the designers' point-of-view.

Our approach differs radically from traditional help systems, with explanations that are disconnected from the situation at hand and from users' needs. Instead, we try to bring some of the designers' world, their concepts and perceptions, to users. Typical help systems are very impersonal and sometimes abstract, providing definitions that are separate from the current (intended) context of use. Sometimes a little of the designers' rationale appears in tutorials, but usually not in the help content itself. By following our approach, we bring to help systems more insight about the software, a more accurate perception about the underlying reasons behind every implemented element and operation. We presume that a better informed user will be able to perform better.

The study of communicability utterances has urged us to extend to our original model in order to cope with additional communication breakdowns that occur during interaction, and that can be detected by the communicability evaluation method. These communicative utterances allow users to investigate, from different perspectives, what is going on during interaction. This new help access, taking into account what the designer predicts are possible communicative breakdowns that may occur during interaction, opens up new possibilities for users, in an attempt to minimise their doubts and help deal with their needs using the system.

Apart from impacting the help system itself, our approach can also be beneficial to the design process, because it prompts designers to explicitly give answers to many questions that remain unanswered throughout the development process. This happens typically because too many things are taken for granted, which perhaps shouldn't be, from a user's point-of-view. As a result, many design decisions are not recorded and cannot be retrieved later, if a problem occurs or another, perhaps conflicting, decision must be made.

Acknowledgments

We would like to thank the Semiotic Engineering Research Group at PUC-Rio for invaluable discussions about some of the ideas contained in this paper. The authors would like to thank PUCRS, PUC-Rio, TeCGraf, and CNPq for supporting their research.

References

Carroll, J. M. (ed.) (1998), *Minimalism Beyond the Nurnberg Funnel*, MIT Press.

Chamberland, L. (1999), Componentization of HTML-based Online Help, *in Proceedings of the Seventeenth Annual International Conference on Computer Documentation (SIGDOC'99)*, ACM Press, pp.165–8.

Chu-Carrol, J. & Carberry, S. (1998), "Collaborative Response Generation in Planning Dialogues", *Computational Linguistics* **24**(3), 355–400.

de Souza, C., Prates, R. & Carey, T. (2000), "Missing and Declining Affordances: Are these appropriate concepts?", *Journal of the Brazilian Computer Society* **7**(1), 26–34.

de Souza, C. S. (1993), "The Semiotic Engineering of User Interface Languages", *International Journal of Man–Machine Studies* **39**(5), 753–73.

Dourish, P. (1997), Accounting for System Behavior: Representation, Reflection, and Resourceful Action, *in* M. Kyng & L. Mathiassen (eds.), *Computers and Design in Context*, MIT Press, pp.145–70.

Farkas, D. (1998), Layering as a Safety Net for Minimalist Documentation, *in* Carroll (1998), pp.247–74.

Hansen, B., Novick, D. & Sutton, S. (1996), Systematic Design of Spoken Prompts, *in* G. van der Veer & B. Nardi (eds.), *Proceedings of CHI'96: Human Factors in Computing Systems*, ACM Press, pp.157–64.

Johnson, W. & Erdem, A. (1997), "A Interactive Explanation of Software Systems", *Automated Software Engineering* **4**(1), 53–75.

Kedar, S., Baudin, C., Birnbaum, L., Osgood, R. & Bareiss, R. (1993), Ask How it Works: An Interactive Intelligent Manual for Devices, *in* S. Ashlund, K. Mullet, A. Henderson, E. Hollnagel & T. White (eds.), *Proceedings of INTERCHI'93*, ACM Press/IOS Press, pp.171–2.

Marx, M. & Schmandt, C. (1996), MailCall: Message Presentation and a Navigation in a Nonvisual Environment, *in* G. van der Veer & B. Nardi (eds.), *Proceedings of CHI'96: Human Factors in Computing Systems*, ACM Press, pp.165–72.

Mittal, V. & Moore, J. (1995), Dynamic Generation of Follow on Question Menus: Facilitating Interactive Natural Language Dialogues, *in* I. Katz, R. Mack, L. Marks, M. B. Rosson & J. Nielsen (eds.), *Proceedings of CHI'95: Human Factors in Computing Systems*, ACM Press, pp.90–7.

Norman, D. (1999), "Affordance, Convention and Design", *Interactions* **6**(3), 38–42.

Norman, D. A. (1988), *The Psychology of Everyday Things*, Basic Books.

Prates, R., Barbosa, S. & de Souza, C. (2000a), A Case Study for Evaluating Interface Design through Communicability, *in* D. Boyarski & W. A. Kellogg (eds.), *Proceedings of the Symposium on Designing Interactive Systems: Processes, Practices, Methods and Techniques (DIS2000)*, ACM Press, pp.308–16.

Prates, R., de Souza, C. & Barbosa, S. (2000b), "A Method for Evaluating the Communicability of User Interfaces", *Interactions* **7**(1), 31–8.

Priestley, M. (1998), Task Oriented or Task Disoriented: Designing a Usable Help Web, *in Proceedings of the Sixteenth Annual International Conference on Computer Documentation (SIGDOC'98)*, ACM Press, pp.194–9.

Raskutti, B. & Zukerman, I. (1997), "Generating Queries and Replies during Information-seeking Interactions", *International Journal of Human–Computer Studies* **47**(6), 689–734.

Rintjema, L. & Warburton, K. (1998), Creating an HTML Help System for Web-based Products, *in Proceedings of the Sixteenth Annual International Conference on Computer Documentation (SIGDOC'98)*, ACM Press, pp.227–33.

Roesler, A. & McLellan, S. (1995), What Help Do Users Need? Taxonomies for On-line Information Needs and Access Methods, *in* I. Katz, R. Mack, L. Marks, M. B. Rosson & J. Nielsen (eds.), *Proceedings of CHI'95: Human Factors in Computing Systems*, ACM Press, pp.437–41.

Sellen, A. & Nicol, A. (1990), Building User-centered Online Help, *in* B. Laurel (ed.), *The Art of Human–Computer Interface Design*, Addison–Wesley, pp.143–53.

Silveira, M., Barbosa, S. & de Souza, C. (2000), Modelo e Arquitetura de Help Online, *in* M. Pimenta & R. Vieira (eds.), *Proceedings of III Workshop on Human Factors in Computer Systems, IHC'2000*, Instituto de Informatica, UFRGS, pp.122–31.

Sleeter, M. (1996), OpenDoc — Building Online Help for a Component-oriented Architecture, *in Proceedings of the Sixteenth Annual International Conference on Computer Documentation (SIGDOC'96)*, ACM Press, pp.87–94.

van der Veer, G. & van Welie, M. (n.d.), "Groupware Task Analysis", Notes from a Tutorial at CHI'99. http://www.cs.vu.nl/ martijn/gta/.

Winograd, T. & Flores, F. (1986), *Understanding Computers and Cognition: A New Foundation for Design*, Ablex. From 1988, an Addison–Wesley publication.

Beyond the Interface: Co-evolution Inside Interactive Systems — A Proposal Founded on Activity Theory

Grégory Bourguin, Alain Derycke & Jean-Claude Tarby

Laboratoire TRIGONE, Institut CUEEP, USTL, 59655 Villeneuve d'Ascq, France

Tel: *+33 3 20 43 32 70*

Email: *{gregory.bourguin,alain.derycke,jean-claude.tarby}@univ-lille1.fr*

Task oriented and object oriented traditional interactive system design methods show more and more shortcomings in the light of recent evolutions. These evolutions are both external (organisational) and internal (technological) to the developed systems. The two main problems of traditional methods are their linearity and rigidity. Once a system has been introduced, it can only evolve through maintenance. These methods follow several steps segmenting time, actors, and work to be realised. Taking results from the human sciences, and particularly from Activity Theory, we show how we have defined the co-evolution concept as a solution for the above-mentioned problems. We also present the DARE system that we have developed for supporting this concept.

Keywords: co-evolution, evolving system, reflective system, design method, activity theory, task, exception.

1 Introduction

For many years, we have been involved in the design of interfaces for interactive and complex systems (IS) supporting collaborative and distributed human activities through the Internet. One of our main application domains is the E-Learning, i.e. implementation of interactive systems supporting distant and flexible learning activities. These activities may be individual as well as collaborative (Derycke &

Viéville, 1994; Viéville, 1998). We have particularly focused our research activities on the design of users environments offering real support for cooperative learning (Derycke & Kaye, 1993; Viéville & Derycke, 1998).

Since our first implementations, we have recognised that our technological platforms should offer functional malleability, i.e. create generic platforms supporting adaptation to specific needs, and organisational malleability supporting adaptation to the organisational contexts encountered. Our design approach was to try to provide solutions to deliver this malleability (Derycke, 1998). However, this flexibility was only provided to the designers, and only during the creation phase of a particular instance of our platform corresponding to a well-identified and well-defined need. We have encountered important problems during our experiments. These problems were particularly significant during real use: the users (tutors, administrators and learners) were faced with usability problems, as well as problems closely linked to the rigidity of their systems. They wanted the ability to adapt the existing running systems in order to respond to changes happening in the definition of their activity and/or in its organisational context. This brought us to deeply re-examine the way we design interactive systems by finding new theoretical foundations for creating a new approach. We have found that this work challenges the assumptions underlying traditional HCI design approaches. Our proposition has been implemented in a technological infrastructure called the DARE project that we briefly describe in this paper. We focus here on the fundamental aspects of our work and on the analysis of our approach regarding the general evolution of HCI science.

1.1 Criticisms of Traditional HCI Design Approaches

Recent technological developments such as the Internet in computer and network sciences are posing new problems and issues to the HCI community. However, we can focus on two different types of factors that we consider essential.

1.1.1 Factors External to the HCI Design

The first factors are the rapid evolution of interaction technologies and the new uses they are being put to, integrated as they are into everyday life and not limited to professional activities. The potential of these new technologies seems to be unlimited. However, this potential is still hidden behind the usability and the socio-cognitive appropriation problems that face the users.

We can add under the heading of new generic needs a strong demand coming from human organisations that their information systems require more flexibility and reactivity to remain in equilibrium with a rapidly evolving environment. These transformations of management, which can also be applied to the learning organisation concept (Senge, 1990), can be understood from a system viewpoint as the ability to support changes.

1.1.2 Factors Internal to the HCI Design Process

From our point of view, it seems clear that traditional methods for designing and developing interactive systems are not adequate any more. We would particularly like to show that most of the past approaches are founded on *separation* principles:

- Separation appears in the temporal divisions applied to the interactive system lifecycle; however, they enable iterations and concurrent engineering.

- Separation between the actors' roles: designers, users, maintenance agents.

- Separation between the results coming from human sciences (the role of the human sciences specialists) and the results coming from computer science (the role of the computer scientists), and the difficult problem of creating bridges between these two worlds (Bowkers et al., 1997).

At the HCI level, these separation principles have resulted in separating design objectives. We find:

- *Usability*: linked to ergonomics and interface/interaction design science.

- *Usefulness*: linked to the functionalities of the system, its deep design.

- *Acceptability*: a more social dimension that is linked to the introduction strategy, to the local culture, etc.

1.1.3 Towards a New Interactive Systems Lifecycle

We are convinced that the separation principles presented above are not well adapted to facing the new information systems and their new associated needs, particularly concerning evolution and change management. We believe in a re-foundation of the design process that would make separations disappear. Presenting similar approaches, we note that voices have emerged over recent years, calling for a new vision of HCI (Bannon & Kuutti, 1993).

1.2 Voices for a New HCI Approach

1.2.1 Calls for a More Anthropocentric Approach

Since the middle of the 80's, there have been many sources questioning the traditional HCI approach:

- Sources founded on theories or practices coming from disciplines such as philosophy and linguistic pragmatics (Winograd & Flores, 1986), or coming from social sciences such as ethnography (Suchman, 1987).

- Results coming from the Scandinavian school with its more political approaches such as participative design, involving the end-users more in the design process (Schuler & Namioka, 1993).

- Finally and more recently, e.g. in (TOCHI, 2000), some authors emphasise the problems for future interactive systems designers in the context of an ubiquitous computer science.

Hollan et al. (2000) show that distributed cognition provides a theoretical and experimental framework for building new HCI foundations as well as an integrated framework for this research area. In their conclusions, which converge with ours, these authors emphasise the limits of classical HCI approaches founded on a psychology that considers the human as an information processor. They also argue that there are important opportunities for designing and building interactive systems capturing and exploiting their own past history of use. This proposition is similar to ours but, due to the difference of the theoretical foundations that are used (Activity Theory for us), we believe that the scale of the objects studied and the temporal granularity of the evolutions are different.

1.2.2   The Needs Concerning Tasks Evolution and the Treatment of Exceptions

The treatment of exceptions appears today as one of the most explored approaches trying to satisfy the management of change arising in the user context, at a technical level as well as an organisational level. This approach has recently been followed in the HCI domain by studies of the impact of the changes to the task, which is considered the most important attribute of a usable system (Wild & Macredie, 2000). Classical design methods for usability, founded on task analysis and modelling, do not really address change management and its role in the organisation. Wild & Macredie propose an extension of certain tasks analysis methods to make them more flexible in accommodating changes. They introduce the *exception* concept that represents something unexpected in the normative task model, another information source concerning the evolutions needed and the alteration of the system's needs. This approach is interesting but we have to notice that in the complex socio-technical systems we are interested in, exception is the rule. Moreover, we believe that the users themselves holds an important place in the cooperative treatment of exceptions. The nature of exceptions is indeed unpredictable and change is the norm (Vicente, 2000).

1.2.3   Towards Co-evolution in Evolving Interactive Systems

Our belief is that the Evolving Interactive Systems (EIS) produced have to support the users' emerging needs by adaptation. They also have to take care of the evolution of the context of use and the technologies involved. These EIS can be seen as mediating between their designers and their users in two ways:

- Mediating between the needs, the capabilities, the wishes ... of the users and the constraints, technological or others, the capabilities and the wishes of the designers. The system is an implementation reflecting the local equilibrium, temporary, negotiated, depending on both parties.

- Mediating for supporting maintenance and evolution of the system over time. It is clear that in most of the classical HCI development approaches or methods the user is abandoned after the test and deployment phases (Wild & Macredie, 2000). It is thus necessary that the developed interactive system serves itself as a bridge between the two parties, through the artefact itself. We will argue later that this implies that the EIS have to contain their own representation (a meta-model) and to feature reflective properties (introspection and intercession).

Using the experience developed in the CSCW community, we believe that this continuous transformation possesses a collective and historical dimension. The computerised artefacts have to be adapted inside the community of practice, thus crystallising the capabilities and attitudes of its members. This idea brought us to the study of Activity Theory.

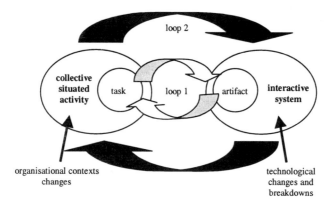

Figure 1: The co-evolution.

Co-evolution means that EIS have to be continually evolving but not in an autonomous way. They do not have to be auto-adaptive but to reflect a conscious evolution of the needs, attitudes and capabilities of the users, evolving individually and/or collectively. However, the system does not to evolve alone. The user also has to transform and adapt his/her practices and working methods to satisfy the evolving needs (Vicente, 2000). This introduces a larger view than the task/artefact cycle proposed by Carroll & Rosson (1986), who tried to expose the dialectical relationship existing between the specification of needs through task expression and the artefact that results from a design process. The co-evolution exposes the continuous, negotiated and socially situated adjustments of the practices as well as the adjustments of the interactive system's behaviour. This is illustrated in Figure 1, reflecting the fact that the global environment determines the task's context (Kirsh, 1999).

2 The Results from the Human Sciences and their Limits

2.1 Social Sciences Results for HCI and their Limits

It is impossible to summarise here all the relevant results from the social sciences and psychology. However, in the framework of the anthropological approaches and the users' needs analysis, we can distinguish those founded on ethnography and on ethnomethodology.

Considering ethnography, Hughes et al. (1995) note that results from needs analysis are too general for technical specialists. Unfortunately, these results propose constraints for system design instead of defining functional specifications (Sommerville et al., 1994).

The case of ethnomethodology is different because it aims at being more than a tool for observing, and has a large audience in the CSCW research domain. Its objective is to provide a conceptual framework for revealing and understanding everyday social actions rather than proposing a new method for ethnology. However and until now, ethnomethodology is mainly used during the preliminary phases of the design (analysis of existing needs) and during the last phases (system evaluations and resulting criticisms about usability and appropriation).

The Technomethodology that has been proposed by Dourish & Button (1998) tries to go past this simple contribution by capitalising on results coming from ethnomethodology and the CSCW research domain at the design process level. Key concepts of ethnomethodology are used as a foundation for the system's conceptual model. This proposition is based on the authors' solid experience in interactive and collaborative system design. This experience brought them to use some computational reflective properties for implementing the desired characteristics.

Due to our previous design work centred on the activity concept, we have chosen Activity Theory (AT) as a theoretical foundation for our design. One can notice that AT today has a growing impact in the new learning technologies research domain, our main application domain (Bourguin & Derycke, 2001). For a more detailed explanation of our choice of AT the reader can refer to (Bourguin, 2000).

2.2   Activity Theory and its Use in Information Systems Design

As presented by Nardi (1996), Activity Theory (AT) is another strong influence from social science that has a wide audience in the fields of HCI and CSCW. AT has its foundation in the Soviet cultural historical school of psychology, founded by L. Vytgosky, A. Leont'ev & A. Luria. AT has been identified as a hot issue for HCI and CSCW over the 10 last years, due to contributions from Engeström (1987), Kutti (1991b; 1991a; 1996) and Bødker (1991). For example, for Kuutti (1991b) the concept of activity is seen as a basic unit of analysis for CSCW research. One can note that in HCI design for usability, it is the task concept that plays this role (Wild & Macredie, 2000). AT has gradually emerged as a body of concepts whose aim is to unify the understanding of human activity, providing a bridge towards other approaches such as those we mentioned in Section 2.2.1.

We are aware that this theoretical framework is itself still evolving and that its complexity does not allow us to take into account all its potential contributions for the EIS design problem. However, we have begun the foundations of a new solution. Our contribution is built on the contribution of Engeström (1987) and Engeström et al. (1997), which gives a simple structural model of the concept of activity, expressing the mediation between the subject (the individual or the subgroup) and the object (raw material or problem space at which the activity is directed) through the instrument (tools and signs). It has been used, with extensions from Kuutti (1993), to replace human activity modelling or analysis in the framework of the organisational context 'in the large' and to introduce the concept of *expansiveness*. This concept is very interesting to us because it corresponds to the dynamic construction of activity by making changes in the nature and composition of the elements constituting the interactive system. These concepts and mechanisms coming from AT constitute the core of the DARE system.

2.3   Towards a Meta-model and a Meta-level Architecture: A New Foundation and a New Framework for EIS Design

Our approach for future EIS design is represented in Figure 2.   In classical approaches, the contributions from human and computer sciences are well-separated

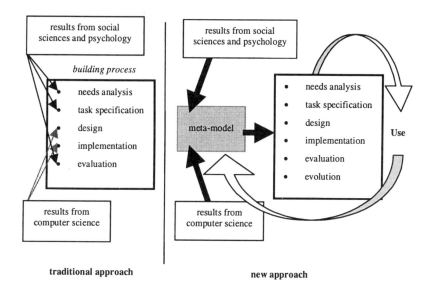

Figure 2: Integrating results from computer and human sciences.

and have only weak interrelationships. In contrast, in our approach, we try to integrate both the human and technological dimensions at the central — conceptual modelling and implementation — level. We want to fuse them into a common theoretical framework. This is realised principally by introducing a meta-model framing the generation of particular EIS and their change management. This meta-model is the key to reflective behaviour and is used for understanding the system's behaviour (introspection) and/or for transforming/adapting the system (intercession) in order to satisfy the task evolutions as well as their execution context transformations. We will show later that in DARE this reflective aspect is directly inspired by our understanding and use of AT. This reflective need is totally in concordance with our previous argument: evolving needs or changes are treated by and through the system. This is where we meet approaches like Technomethodology as presented above and research about information system reflective development practices (Mathiasen, 1998).

Our meta-level architecture developed in the DARE project aims to offer generic software support in a distributed object oriented approach, thus providing a favourable milieu for evolution management of different EIS while adopting a psycho-socio-historical perspective founded on Activity Theory.

3 Our Proposition: The DARE system

3.1 Our Understanding of Activity Theory

We consider the expansiveness property of human activity as one of the main features of Activity Theory. Human activity is expansive in the sense that it can transform

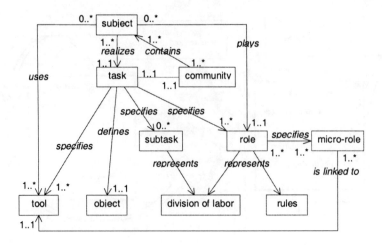

Figure 3: DARE's concepts.

itself in response to the feedback provided by the context in which it executes. This relation is in fact dialectical because the activity in return transforms its context. In particular, the tools that are used in an activity form a part of the activity's context. As such, a tool helps but also influences the realisation of a task. If a computer tool does not fit the user's needs, the user will try to understand its foundations and adapt it to their needs. If they are not able to do this, the tool will certainly be abandoned, maybe for another one. Thus activity is influenced by a context that it, in turn, continually changes. This explains why it seems impossible to predetermine exactly what the users needs from a computer system or tool are, because these needs are emerging during the realisation of the activity where the system is used.

Expansiveness is closely linked to the reflective property of human activity. Any activity involves a meta-activity. The activity level corresponds to the realisation of a task. The task describes the elements creating the context of the activity. We consider activity as an instance of a task. The meta-activity level is a reflection about and a transformation of the activity's context, i.e. a transformation of the task and its elements.

3.2 Our Use of the Concepts and Mechanisms Coming from AT

DARE aims to offer specific contexts for particular activities. Such a context is called an activity-support (AS). Each activity-support corresponds to the specific computer support offered by DARE to the users involved in a specific activity. To support the properties introduced above, DARE allows its user communities to co-evolve their AS during their execution.

An activity-support contains a set of elements corresponding to different concepts directly inspired by AT. These concepts are presented in Figure 3. It is not our aim to present each one of these concepts in detail here. For more information the reader can refer to (Bourguin, 2000).

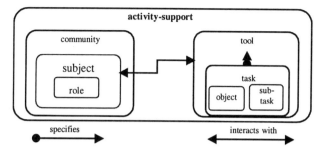

Figure 4: Activity-support — task: a reflective system.

These concepts are used in the definition of the AS conceptual model (cf. Figure 4). This model introduces mechanisms supporting the reflective properties of activity: an AS contains a community of subjects (users) interacting through a set of tools that they use depending on their role. The activity's object (objective), the set of tools, roles and subtasks are defined in the task. To support expansiveness, the task is made accessible inside the AS through particular meta-level tools allowing actions at the meta-activity level. A causal relationship between the AS and its task implies that any modifications of the task have direct repercussions on its instances, i.e. AS. Thus, each AS is an instance of a task it is able to modify. This defines a reflective system. One can note that meta-level tools are managed in the same way as other (cooperative) tools. Thus, the meta-activity is part of the cooperative activity and DARE may be considered as a mediating artefact of the cooperative activity it supports.

Finally, because a task may be used for instantiating many AS and because a task may evolve during activities, it constitutes the element crystallising and enabling reuse of the subjects' experience developed for and through the use of the system.

3.3 Realisation of a Technological Infrastructure for DARE

DARE has to support many different types of activities so that many different types of AS can be created in the system. For this purpose, we have defined the generic AS object model that can be specialised for specific needs. (cf. Figure 5).

Our main objective is to support the co-evolution of the AS at run-time. In traditional design, the generic AS model would only be known by the system's designers. From this viewpoint, the model is a set of abstract classes that can be specialised through implementation in an object oriented programming language. This operation involves mastering the class, attribute, method or even inheritance notions. The question is:

> "How can our generic AS model be made usable from the end-users viewpoint?"

This has been achieved through the DARE meta-model.

A meta-model is a model of a model. For example, the UML meta-model defines the entities and relations that are used to create UML object models. The role of our

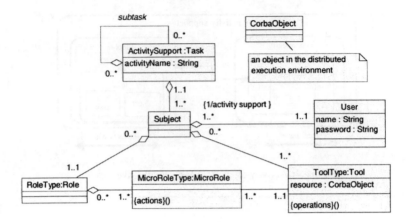

Figure 5: Generic model of an activity-support (UML notation).

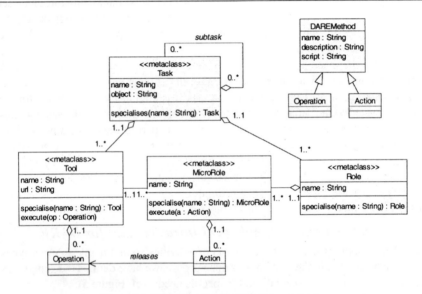

Figure 6: DARE's meta-model (UML notation).

meta-model is similar to the UML one. The main difference is that it defines the basis of a language oriented towards our domain of interest, i.e. AS modelling.

We have show that an AS is an instance of a task. In other words, an AS model is a task. Thus, our meta-model reifies what is a task, i.e. what its structure and components are. As shown in Figure 6, a task specifies a set of role types, micro-roles types, tools types and subtasks.

Thus, modifying an AS can be performed from DARE and by its own users without using object oriented languages entities, but using domain dependent terms like task, tool, role, action, etc. This provides a generic execution environment in

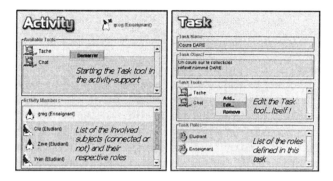

Figure 7: Activity and Task tools.

which users are enabled to co-evolve AS on their own, and are facilitated in doing so in the context of use.

DARE has been implemented using the Smalltalk and Java reflective mechanisms. It provides a CORBA based distributed architecture. It is not our aim to present this implementation here in detail. Further information can be found in (Bourguin, 2000).

However, Figure 7 illustrates the system's user environment in the current implementation. The user accesses the AS through a standard Web browser using a tool (an applet) called *Activity*. This tool offers a representation of the AS that depends on the user's role.

Figure 7 also shows the meta-level tool called *Task* that makes it possible to manipulate the meta-level of the AS (the task), i.e. that can be used for examining and/or modifying the system. This example illustrates DARE's reflective properties because the *Task* tool, managed in the same way as the other tools, can be used to redefine its own use. For more details about the potential of DARE's properties in the E-Learning domain, the reader can refer to (Bourguin & Derycke, 2001).

4 Conclusion

We have proposed a new approach for the lifecycle of interactive systems. This approach takes care of the management of the system changes that are needed, partially performed by users and better supporting the evolution of users' tasks. Keeping in mind the evolution phenomenon and its impact on the underlying HCI, we have adopted a human perspective where transformations are not automatic or unconscious, but result from a cooperative process involving different types of actors: users, designers, computer scientists, etc. Using theoretical propositions, we have tried to create new system foundations including theoretical concepts as first class objects. These concepts may constitute a coherent framework for really taking care of the evolution property of instrumented human activities. Our proposition has resulted in a technological support called DARE that provides a meta-level architecture enabling the design and implementation of Evolving Interactive Systems. Our first uses of this proposition (Bourguin & Derycke, 2000; Bourguin

& Derycke, 2001) demonstrate the great potential of our approach for solving practical problems such as appropriation and acceptance that were emphasised in the introduction of this paper, all the work that still remains and the new problems that have emerged!

It seems necessary to integrate more tools into this platform to make this EIS design and implementation approach more general. We want to create more software components and better formalisms that make DARE easier to use. This work has been started while trying to create bridges between the CSCW and the workflow domains (Le Pallec & Bourguin, 2001). The hardest problem is to find a visual formalism that allows users to understand the system's foundations and to collaboratively transform it according to their emerging needs. Even if our current meta-model is activity domain oriented and thus closer to the user's application domain, the user oriented design language still remains hard to create. By analogy, we are now investigating further the different systems implementing graphical languages for the domain of business process descriptions.

Finally, this work raises problems associated with change management from the temporal viewpoint and the negative impact that too many changes may have in a short space of time when the are not collectively agreed. Continuous transformations in the users' environment may indeed raise a usability problem due to the inability of the users to learn how to work with the system. In other words, some stability is necessary for making efficient use possible. This converges with Carroll's (1991) remark about the usability problems introduced by evolving systems: people invest time in learning and improving the system. Evolutions may produce interferences and cause certain inefficiency when performing the supported tasks. This is a real and important problem. However, we believe that our approach proposes an implicit solution because it addresses other time scales than those addressed in auto-adaptive HCI systems: changes accepted after negotiation should be followed by stable phases that may last a relatively long time, for example, months. Our approach is intended to support the entire EIS lifecycle.

References

Bannon, L. & Kuutti, K. (1993), Searching for Unity Among Diversity: Exploring the "Interface" Concept, *in* S. Ashlund, K. Mullet, A. Henderson, E. Hollnagel & T. White (eds.), *Proceedings of INTERCHI'93*, ACM Press/IOS Press, pp.263–8.

Bødker, S. (1991), *Through the Interface: A Human Activity Approach to User Interface Design*, Lawrence Erlbaum Associates.

Bourguin, G. (2000), Un Support Informatique à l'Activité Coopérative Fondé sur la Théorie de l'Activité : le Projet DARE, PhD thesis, Université des Sciences et Technologies de Lille, France. Informatique, no. 2753.

Bourguin, G. & Derycke, A. (2000), A Reflective CSCL Environment with Foundations Based on the Activity Theory, *in* G. Gauthier, C. Frasson & K. van Lehn (eds.), *Proceedings of ITS'2000, Fifth International Conference on Intelligent Tutoring Systems,*, number 1839 *in* "Lecture Notes in Computer Science", pp.272–81.

Bourguin, G. & Derycke, A. (2001), Integrating the CSCL Activities into Virtual Campuses: Foundations of a new Infrastructure for Distributed Collective Activities, *in*

P. Dillenbourg, A. Eurelings & K. Hakkarainen (eds.), *Proceedings of Euro-CSCL 2001, Fifth European Perspectives on Computer-supported Collaborative Learning*, McLuhan Institute, pp.123–30.

Bowkers, G., Leigh Star, S., Turner, W. & Gasser, L. (1997), *Social Science, Technical Systems and Cooperative Work: Beyond the Great Divide*, Computer, Cognition and Work, Lawrence Erlbaum Associates.

Carroll, J. M. & Rosson, M. B. (1986), Usability Specifications as a Tool in Iterative Development, *in* H. R. Hartson (ed.), *Advances in Human–Computer Interaction*, Ablex, pp.1–28.

Carroll, J. M. (ed.) (1991), *Designing Interaction: Psychology at the Human–Computer Interface*, Cambridge University Press.

Derycke, A. (1998), Integration of the Learning Processes into the Web: Learning Activity Centred Design and Architecture, *in Proceedings of the Webnet'98 Conference*, Association for the Advancement of Computing in Education. CD-ROM publication.

Derycke, A. & Kaye, A. (1993), Participative Modelling and Design of Collaborative Learning Tools in the CO-LEARN Project, *in* G. Davis & B. Samways (eds.), *Proceedings of the IFIP Teleteaching 95 Conference*, North-Holland, pp.191–200.

Derycke, A. & Viéville, C. (1994), Real-time Multimedia Conferencing System and Collaborative Learning: Collaboration Dialogue Technologies in Distance Education, *in* F. Verdejo & S. Cerri (eds.), *Collaborative Dialogue Technologies in Distance Learning*, number 133 *in* "NATO ASI Series", Springer-Verlag, pp.236–56.

Dourish, P. & Button, G. (1998), "On 'Technomethodology': Foundational Relationships between Ethnomethodology and System Design", *Human–Computer Interaction* **13**(4), 395–432.

Engeström, Y. (1987), *Learning by Expanding: An Activity-theoretical Approach to Developmental Research*, Orienta-Konsultit Oy.

Engeström, Y., Brown, K., Christopher, L. & Gregory, J. (1997), Coordination, Cooperation and Communication in the Courts, *in* M. Cole, Y. Engeström & O. Vasquez (eds.), *Mind, Culture and Activity*, Cambridge University Press.

Hollan, J., Hutchins, E. & Kirsh, D. (2000), "Distributed Cognition: Toward a New Foundation for Human–Computer Interaction Research", *ACM Transactions on Computer–Human Interaction* **7**(2), 174–96.

Hughes, J., King, V., Rodden, T. & Anderson, H. (1995), "Ethnography in Interactive Systems Design", *Interactions* **11**(2), 57–65.

Kirsh, D. (1999), Distributed Cognition, Coordination and Environment Design, Proceedings Of the European Cognitives Sciences Society, http://icl-server.ucsd.edu/~kirsh/articles/italy/published.html.

Kuutti, K. (1991a), Activity Theory and its Applications to Information Systems Research and Development, *in* H. Nissen, H. Klein & R. Hirschheim (eds.), *Information systems Research: Contemporary Approaches and Emergent Traditions*, North-Holland, pp.529–49.

Kuutti, K. (1991b), The Concept of Activity as a Basic Unit of Analysis for CSCW Research, *in* M. Robinson, L. Bannon & K. Schmidt (eds.), *Proceedings of ECSCW'91, the 2nd European Conference on Computer-Supported Cooperative Work*, Kluwer, pp.249–64.

Kuutti, K. (1993), Notes on Systems Supporting "Organisational context" — An Activity Theory Viewpoint, Deliverable D1.1, COMIC Project. p.101–117.

Kuutti, K. (1996), Activity Theory as a Potential Framework for Human–Computer Interaction Research, *in* Nardi (1996), pp.17–44.

Le Pallec, X. & Bourguin, G. (2001), "RAM3 : Un Outil Dynamique pour le Meta-Object Facility", *l'Objet* **7**(1), 79–94. Proceedings of LMO'01.

Mathiasen, L. (1998), "Reflective Systems developpment", *Scandinavian Journal of Information Systems* **10**(1 & 2), 67–117.

Nardi, B. A. (ed.) (1996), *Context and Consciousness: Activity Theory and Human–Computer Interaction*, MIT Press.

Schuler, D. & Namioka, A. (eds.) (1993), *Participatory Design: Principles and Practices*, Lawrence Erlbaum Associates.

Senge, P. M. (1990), *The Fifth Discipline: Art and Practices of the Learning Organization*, Currency Doubleday.

Sommerville, I., Bentley, R., Rodden, T. & Sawyer, P. (1994), "Cooperative Systems Design", *The Computer Journal* **37**(5), 357–366.

Suchman, L. A. (1987), *Plans and Situated Actions — The Problem of Human–Machine Communication*, Cambridge University Press.

TOCHI (2000), "Special Issue on Human–Computer Interaction in the New Millenium, Part I & II", *ACM Transactions on Computer–Human Interaction* **7**(1 & 2).

Vicente, K. J. (2000), "HCI in the Global Knowledge-based Economy: Designing to Support Worker Adaptation", *ACM Transactions on Computer–Human Interaction* **7**(2), 263–280.

Viéville, C. (1998), An Asynchronous Collaborative Learning System on the Web, *in* R. Hazami, S. Hailes & S. Wilbur (eds.), *The Digital University — Reinventing the Academy*, CSCW Series, Springer-Verlag, pp.99–113.

Viéville, C. & Derycke, A. (1998), Self Organised Group Activities Supported by Asynchronous Structured Conversations, *in* F. Verdjo & G.Davies (eds.), *Proceedings of the IFIP conference "Virtual Campus: Trends for Higher Education and Training"*, Chapman & Hall, pp.191–204.

Wild, P. J. & Macredie, R. D. (2000), On Change and Tasks, *in* S. McDonald, Y. Waern & G. Cockton (eds.), *People and Computers XIV (Proceedings of HCI'2000)*, Springer-Verlag, pp.45–59.

Winograd, T. & Flores, F. (1986), *Understanding Computers and Cognition: A New Foundation for Design*, Ablex. From 1988, an Addison–Wesley publication.

User Interface Modelling

A Flexible Methodology and Support Environment for Building Task Models

Cécile Paris*, Jean-Claude Tarby[†] & Keith Vander Linden[‡]

* *CSIRO/CMIS, Locked Bag 17, North Ryde, NSW 1670, Australia*

Tel: *+61 2 9325 3160*

Fax: *+61 2 9325 3200*

Email: *Cecile.Paris@cmis.csiro.au*

URL: *http://www.cmis.csiro.au/Cecile.Paris*

[†] *Laboratoire Trigone, Institut CUEEP, Université des Sciences et Technologies de Lille, 59665, Villeneuve d'Ascq Cedex, France*

Tel: *+33 3 2043 3262*

Fax: *+33 3 2043 3279*

Email: *Jean-Claude.Tarby@univ-lille1.fr*

URL: *http://www-trigone.univ-lille1.fr/jean_claude*

[‡] *Department of Computer Science, Calvin College, Grand Rapids, MI 49546, USA*

Tel: *+1 616 957 7111*

Fax: *+1 616 957 6501*

Email: *kvlinden@calvin.edu*

URL: *http://www.calvin.edu/~kvlinden*

Task modelling helps to ensure the usability of interactive systems by producing models that are useful for a variety of reasons, and by forcing designers to view the system from the users' point of view. Unfortunately, it is a difficult process, so most designers either don't do it at all, or they model only certain aspects of the system, potentially using different formalisms that are hard to consolidate. As a result, a complete and coherent model of all the levels of a system is seldom if ever built. To address this problem, this paper proposes a flexible methodology for the construction of task models and an environment that supports this methodology. The methodology, which is based on industrial experience, identifies a sequence of levels for which models should be built, and the environment provides tools for building them, either from scratch or from existing sources.

Keywords: task modelling, requirements analysis, system design.

1 Introduction

The HCI community has advocated task modelling as a way to ensure the usability of interactive systems. To be effective, this modelling should be performed at different levels of abstraction, moving from high-level, user-oriented models to more detailed, system-oriented models. Each level serves a different purpose within the system development life cycle.

The high-level user task analysis comes at the beginning of the development life cycle, allowing the designers think about the system from the users' point of view. It ensures that the designers understand how a prospective system can fit into the users' environment, what functionalities are required, and how they should be organised. The results of this task analysis can be codified in a high-level model and fed into the user requirements analysis, the system's specification and design stages, documentation production, and finally, usability evaluation, e.g. Balbo & Lindley (1997).

Task analysis and modelling can also be done at more detailed levels. Here, the designer might focus on the sequence of interface actions that the user must perform when interacting with the system. Task models at this level are at a low level of abstraction. They can be used to specify the interface to be built, to estimate the time that will be required for each user's goal and actions, or, if the system has already been developed, to perform a comparison of the actual and expected performance, e.g. Balbo (1994).

Ideally, task models at all of these levels of abstraction would be constructed for any system being developed. They are useful as individual models, and become particularly useful when coupled together. For example, the automated production of user documentation requires one to link the expressions of detailed sequences of interface actions with the highest-level goal that they achieve (Paris & Vander Linden, 1996). Similarly, usability evaluations require one to know the goal that a specific sequence of actions is intended to achieve. We thus claim that it is useful to produce a complete set of task models for a system under development, and that this set should be represented in some coherent formalism that allows the models to be properly interconnected. The richer the set of models and interconnections, the more useful they become.

Unfortunately, the process of building task models is tedious and difficult. This is particularly true of the more system-oriented information represented at the lower levels. Consequently, most system designers do not build task models at all. Those who do are likely to focus on a particular aspect of the system such as the highest-level user goals or the user functions supported by the system. Those that model different aspects of the system may potentially use different formalisms to represent each aspect. For example, they may represent high-level user goals using UML use-cases (Booch et al., 1999) or MAD (Scapin & Pierret-Golbreich, 1990; Sebillotte, 1995), and then represent low-level interface events using UAN (Hix & Hartson, 1993) or GOMS (Card et al., 1983). These different formalisms are difficult to consolidate.

The consequence of this is that regardless of how useful a complete and coherent set of task models might be, such a set is not typically built. This denies us the advantages mentioned above, and makes it less likely that we would develop other uses for task models. To address this, we propose a development methodology that employs a sequence of four task models, along with a flexible modelling environment in which to build those models. The methodology, which is based on industrial experiences with subsystems and smaller devices, identifies the important levels at which to build models, and the environment, called ISOLDE, provides tools for building the models from scratch, and for consolidating task information from heterogeneous sources.

This paper begins by describing the work on which the methodology and the environment are based. It then describes the methodology, defining the four modelling levels and giving a list of features required of the modelling environment. Finally, it discusses the ISOLDE environment and the particular set of tools that we have implemented to support the methodology.

2 Related Work

Numerous task model formalisms and methodologies have been developed, including GOMS (Card et al., 1983), UAN (Hix & Hartson, 1993), CTT (Paternò et al., 1997), MAD (Scapin & Pierret-Golbreich, 1990; Sebillotte, 1995), DIANE+ (Tarby & Barthet, 1996), GTE (van der Veer et al., 1996), some aspects of UML (Booch et al., 1999) including use-cases, scenarios and statecharts (Horracks, 1999), and adaptations of statecharts (Harel, 1987) and Petri Nets (Palanque et al., 1993). Taxonomies of task models can be found in Brun & Beaudouin-Lafon (1995) and Balbo et al. (1999), and a recent survey of task modelling notations and tools can be found in Bentley (2000). A study of the role of change in Task Analysis can be found in Wild & Macredie (2000). Though the models may differ in syntax and in particular emphasis, they all attempt to model the users' interaction with a system via hierarchies of related tasks and goals. Because they are usually built manually, occasionally on paper or with general purpose drawing packages, they are also alike in that they tend to be difficult to build and maintain. It is not surprising, therefore, that tools for building them have been developed.

Tools for building and maintaining task models include QGOMS (Beard et al., 1996), CTTE (Paternò et al., 2000; CTTE, 2001), EUTERPE (van Welie et al., 1998), and Rational Corporation's Rose modelling tool for the task modelling elements listed above. These tools are helpful in building electronic versions of their chosen modelling formalism, allowing the resulting models to be maintained more easily and to be used by automated routines of various sorts. These tools don't typically support the automatic (or even partially automatic) acquisition of the models. Thus, the difficulty of actually acquiring the model is not addressed. Furthermore, if the goal is to produce a complete collection of task models that represents all levels of abstractions of the user's interaction with the system, the use of one of these tools would dictate that tool and its chosen modelling formalism be used for all the levels of analysis. One exception to these weaknesses is CTTE, which comes with a companion tool, UL-TM (Paternò, 1999). This tool facilitates the construction of skeleton task models from written task narratives and one can imagine coordinating its use with the facilities described in this paper and vice versa.

Another area of work relevant to this paper is the recording of user interface events (Hilbert & Redmiles, 2000). Event recorders work within the GUI call-back architecture, recording all the GUI events that transpire during a user session. The sequences of recorded events can be seen as a form of task model whose typical use is in post analysis of system use and usability. These models have little if any knowledge of general user goals, but are quite detailed models of low-level interaction between the user and an implemented system.

3 A Flexible Approach to Building Task Models

In this paper we argue that, to be most useful, task models must have two key characteristics:

1. they should be *complete* in the sense that all levels of user interaction should be included, i.e. there should be a collection of task models at the different levels of abstraction; and

2. they should be *coherent* in that a uniform representation language should be used.

With respect to the first, we are obliged to characterise what a complete model is and how it might be built, and with respect to the second, we must propose some flexible environment in which a coherent task model can be built without imposing unrealistic constraints on the design process. This section will discuss each in turn.

3.1 A Coordinated Set of Task Models

To be complete, a collection of task models should have the following 4 levels:

- General User Requirements Specification (GURuS)

- Detailed User Requirements Specification (DURuS)

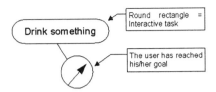

Figure 1: GURuS for the drink machine.

- General Specification of the System (GeSS)

- Detailed Specification of the System (DeSS)

These levels are linked together. The GURuS and DURuS levels are strongly coupled, because the second refines the first. Similarly, the DeSS refines the GeSS. In the first two levels, the task model is focused purely on the user's point of view, while in the last two levels, the focus is on the user's interaction with a specific system and interface.

3.1.1 General User Requirements Specification (GURuS)

The objective of GURuS is to identify the main tasks and the main objects that are relevant for the user. Here, the level of abstraction is very high; the tasks are *black boxes* and the objects are objects that the user employs. The GURuS corresponds to the user's point of view; the system is hidden in this level, and the focus is on the user. This level is independent of the user interface and the platform. It must not integrate constraints from the operating system or the hardware.

Examples of tasks at this level are: duplicate a document (task=*to duplicate*, object=*a document*), or drink something (task=*to drink*, object= *a drink*). A specific example for the design of a drink machine is shown in Figure 1.

To obtain the GURuS, the designer must ask users: *What do you want to do with the system?* From the corpus of information gathered, the designer then keeps all the information that refers to the user's actions and objects, eliminating references to specific interaction events (e.g. *click, cut/copy/paste, open file, select menu*). These are kept, as they may be of use for the specification of the GeSS and DeSS, but they do not belong at this high level of abstraction. Information at this level can also be gathered from:

1. the stake holders (e.g. users and managers);

2. the users' manuals and documentation, if a system already exists; and

3. the prospective system being replaced.

3.1.2 Detailed User Requirements Specification (DURuS)

The DURuS more precisely specify the nature of the user participation and system feedback. As with the GURuS, this level is independent of the platform. It is still at a high level of abstraction, and independent of any specific user interface. The system

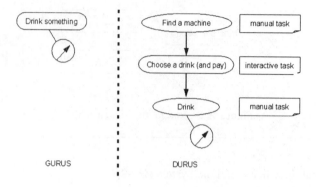

Figure 2: GURuS (on the left) and DURuS (on the right) for the drink machine.

is hidden, but the feedback from the system is more present than in the GURuS. For example, a DURuS may include a general specification for feedback such as *display the availability of the selected drink*. Note that nothing as specific as *display the drink-selection dialog box* will be given.

To obtain the DURuS, the designer refines the GURuS by interviewing users, or writing and exploiting scenarios, e.g. U-Tel (Tam et al., 1998) and EL-TM (Paternò & Mancini, 1999). To build this level of specification, we recommend the use of words that describe actions implying the participation of the user, e.g. *the user chooses a drink*. If necessary, words that describe global actions from the system can also be employed — e.g. *the system displays the price of the drink*. Note that, at this stage, paper or implemented mock-ups can be elaborated to validate the task model.

Continuing our example of the drink machine, the DURuS for this machine would include the following actions (as illustrated in Figure 2):

- *Find a machine*, a manual action.

- *Choose a drink (and pay)*, an interactive action because the users need the system to obtain their drink (*pay* is also required, although is not something the user necessarily wants).

- *Drink*, a manual action.

3.1.3   General Specification of the System (GeSS)

The objective of the GeSS is to identify how the system satisfies the user's goal. At this level, we finally introduce the system. This implies that we now exploit automatic tasks and specify more precise interaction actions, such as *cancel* and *validate*. We now also introduce the constraints due to the platform, for instance user interface guidelines with standard behaviours (e.g. cut/copy/paste, open/save), or hardware with a touch screen, voice recognition, etc.

In the last two steps, we didn't take the system into consideration. We assumed that the system was present, and it did what we wanted. At this level, we are now

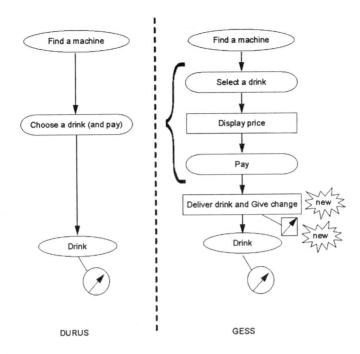

Figure 3: GeSS of the drink machine (on the right).

looking at how the specific system must satisfy the user's goals. To that end, we must specify when the goal is reached from the system's perspective, meaning that the system itself cannot do anymore. Consequently we are introducing: (1) the system's point of view at this level through automatic tasks (tasks which are done only by the system); (2) more low-level interactions; and (3) constraints due to the platform.

Based on our experiences building GeSSs and working with software engineers, we think that it is unrealistic to expect software designers to write GeSSs for large systems by hand. We thus do not assume that our collection of task models will necessarily include this level. This level is, however, useful (and more practical) for sub-systems or for systems with smaller task models (e.g. mobile phones or smart cards).

Note at this point that the goal for the system may not be the same as the user's goal. At this level, we have to specify how the system knows that the user can reach their goal. In the drink machine example, the system assumes that it has finished its work when it has delivered the drink. The terminal event may not be the same for the system as for the user. Consequently, we differentiate them. The system's terminal event is represented as a small square marked with "new" in Figure 3. Also note that some new tasks may be introduced to satisfy the user's goal from the system's point of view. For instance, in Figure 3, the GeSS contains a new automatic task (i.e. "deliver drink and give change"). This task must be completed by the system to allow the user to drink.

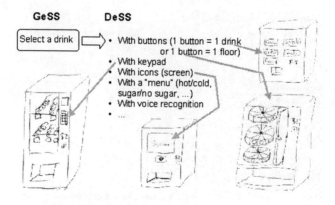

Figure 4: Mock-ups for the drink machine's DeSS.

3.1.4   *Detailed Specification of the System (DeSS)*

The objective of the DeSS is to specify:

- *How the system must be used* — For the drink machine example, the step *the user chooses a drink* must be now changed into *the user chooses between Coca, Pepsi, Vittel and Evian*, and the specific ways the user interacts with the system must be specified (selecting menu items, clicking buttons, etc.).

- *How the system reacts to the user's actions with the system* — This means that all feedback (e.g. icon/cursor modifications and dialog boxes) and all system's decisions (e.g. normal/abnormal task endings and task suspensions) must be indicated.

As with the GeSS, we know it is unrealistic to expect software designers to build these specifications manually. Yet, this detailed level of specifications is very useful for at least three purposes: (1) it can inform the design of the interface proper, (2) it can guide the production of instructions (manually or automatically), (3) it can support usability evaluation, both to check whether the implemented system embodies the early design, and to compare actual and desired user activities. While it is unrealistic to expect the construction of such specifications for large system, as with the GeSS, it is possible to write them for small applications or sub-systems.

For example, the DeSS for the drink machine is probably too complex to write by hand. As a partial solution, a designer can provide alternative interface implementations for the interactions and feedback required. For instance, *Select a drink* can be implemented in an interface in various ways, such as: *select with buttons*, *select with keypad*, *select with icons*, *select with menus*, and so on, as illustrated in Figure 4. Given these specifications, mock-ups or prototypes embodying the different interface solutions can be drafted (again see Figure 4).

In some cases, the designer may choose (or be obliged) to build prototypes (cf. Figure 5) to test the interaction specifications. In such cases, a GUI event recorder can

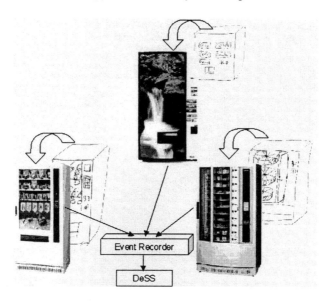

Figure 5: From mock-ups and prototypes to DeSS.

be exploited to fill in the DeSS automatically, as we will see in the next section. We believe that specifying user interface options such as those in Figure 4 and exploiting an event recorder when the prototype is built can drastically cut the work required to build the DeSS, yet providing the benefits of having one.

3.2   Requirements for a Task Modelling Environment

To support the methodology outlined this section, we would like to have an environment that provides an extensible set of tools for building, maintaining, and exploiting the required task models. To enforce coherence in this environment, all of the tools should be built on top of a unified modelling formalism. Clearly, requiring all designers to work with a single formalism, no matter what it is, is unrealistic. Therefore, they should be allowed to use whatever tools and formalisms they'd like at the various levels of the design, and our environment should then be able to port that knowledge into the unified formalism. For example, software engineers may build UML use-case models, designers may write narratives of proposed system use, and programmers may build system prototypes. Our environment could provide tools that extract task knowledge from these disparate sources, representing it in a coherent form. As a fall-back, the environment should also provide a modelling tool that allows the designer to build any aspect of the models from scratch, directly in the unified formalism.

It may be difficult to support a unified formalism, but the advantage is that resulting models can then be exploited for a variety of purposes. For example, tools could be built that take the knowledge in the models and automatically produce user documentation, perform task analyses, or drive training scenarios in simulated

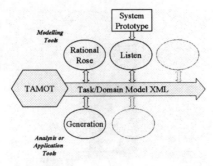

Figure 6: The ISOLDE Environment.

environments. To support these things, the formalism itself must be flexible enough to represent the range of models described in the previous section. It should also allow the elements of one level to refer to the elements of another. In addition, certain applications will require that it represent not only task knowledge but also domain knowledge. Task knowledge includes the basic tasks and their procedural relationships. Domain knowledge includes more detailed knowledge about the actors, actions, and objects involved in each task. This latter type of knowledge can serve to support automated documentation and potentially other features as well.

4   The ISOLDE Environment

This paper now presents ISOLDE as an example of the sort of flexible task modelling environment motivated in the previous section. The ISOLDE environment, shown in Figure 6, provides a task model editor, TAMOT, and an extensible list of modelling, analysis, and application tools all integrated using a common XML task and domain model description. This section will discuss some of the modelling components in the context of a running example. The running example is a recursive example, showing a task model for the use of the TAMOT tool itself. We won't focus on the application tools. For a discussion of the documentation generation tool, see Vander Linden et al. (2000) or Balbo et al. (1998).

4.1   The Task Model Editor

TAMOT is a general purpose task model editor based on the DIANE+ formalism (Tarby & Barthet, 1996). It supports the construction of task models at all levels of abstraction. In addition, it is able to obtain portions of the models automatically from other sources, as will be described in the next subsections.

Figure 7 shows TAMOT being used to edit a task model. As we'll see below, this model was created with other tools, but TAMOT could just as well have been used to build it manually. On the left-hand side, TAMOT displays a hierarchy of user tasks and links between them. On the right, it displays a set of windows showing the graphical representation of the tasks at various points in the hierarchy. In this example, we see the tasks required to achieve the goal of opening a new task model

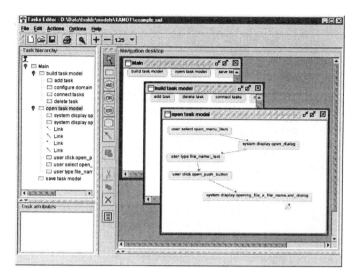

Figure 7: TAMOT, the Task Model Editor.

in TAMOT. The level of specification of the task model shown in this example corresponds to a partial DeSS, the detailed system specifications, as it includes the specific interaction events that users must do to accomplish their goal and the exact system's feedback. To open a new task model, the user must select the open menu item, type a filename, and click the open button. The system responses to these user actions are shown as rectangles in DIANE+. Here, the system displays the *open* dialog box and an *opening file* dialog box at various points in the procedure. Although this example shows only a simple sequence of actions (for reasons we'll see below), DIANE+ allows the designer to model various flows of control at each level, including alternate and conjoined paths, and conditional links and tasks.

4.2   The Task Models

The task models produced by TAMOT can be saved and read back in using an XML format. Because this format is standardised and open, it is possible to build other tools that can read and write these DIANE+ models. These tools may be able to translate task information from other sources into the DIANE+ format, or they may allow the user to create DIANE+ models in other ways. We could also integrate existing tools that can read and/or write XML specifications, e.g. U-Tel (Tam et al., 1998). This is the key to the flexible task modelling environment provided by ISOLDE.

In the next sections, this paper will briefly describe two tools we have developed that illustrate this feature. The first translates task information from another modelling language, and the second constructs new task information. They are only examples of the tools that could be integrated into the ISOLDE environment.

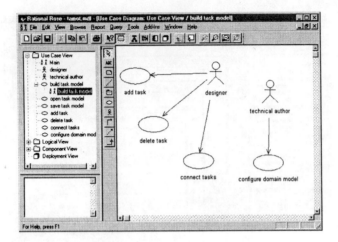

Figure 8: A use-case model in Rational Rose.

4.3   Rational Rose

It is unrealistic to assume that all designers and software engineers could be convinced to adopt the DIANE+ task formalism as part of their design process. Indeed, if a software engineer does any modelling at all, it is more likely to be represented using a software-oriented language like UML. Although UML models are very system-oriented, they can contain some user-oriented information. For example, use-case analyses can identify types of users and their goals with respect to the system. Figure 8 shows part of a use-case diagram for the TAMOT system represented in Rational Rose. There are two different types of users, designers and technical authors, and four different tasks that these users might want to perform with the TAMOT tool.

The ISOLDE environment does not actually include a use-case tool, but it allows designers to use Rational Rose to build use-cases and then export them into the DIANE+ task modelling formalism as basic task models (Lu et al., 1999). This allows the designers to work with the tools they prefer, but then to maintain a single coherent set of task models in the DIANE+ format. Because use-case analysts are not required to follow a careful, user-oriented approach to use-case modelling, the resulting DIANE+ model may have problems that will need to be touched up using the TAMOT tool or some other tool. Yet, this functionality provides support for constructing the GURuS and DURuS from models already constructed in Rose if they exist.

4.4   The GUI Event Listener

If designers use task analysis and modelling at all, they are more likely to do it at the GURuS and DURuS levels. Seldom are they willing to build task models at the GeSS and DeSS levels, as these models are very time-consuming to build even for small projects. Designers are much more likely to build prototypes of the user

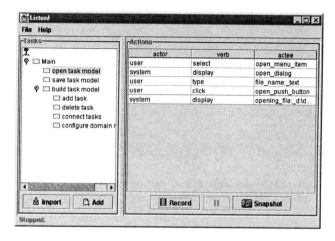

Figure 9: LISTEN, the GUI event recorder.

interface at this level. They can then compare the operation of the prototype with the requirements of the GURuS and DURuS models.

While this approach may be effective, it doesn't produce the explicit system-oriented models that are required by various forms of detailed usability profiling and analysis, or for user-oriented documentation generation. If these models are required, they must be built by hand after the system interface is already implemented. As an alternative, designers are beginning to make use of GUI event recorders in this situation (Hilbert & Redmiles, 2000). These tools record sequences of the lowest level of GUI events as the interface or its prototype is being used. These sequences, if linked to the goals that they are intended to achieve, can be built into task models.

To explore this approach, we have built a GUI event listener and have integrated it into the ISOLDE environment. Figure 9 shows part of the tool in operation. On the left, you see a hierarchy of user tasks, very similar to the one shown in the TAMOT interface itself (see Figure 7). The event recorder cannot easily infer these tasks from the sequence of low-level GUI events it is recording, so it requires the user either to build them by hand (by clicking the Add button) or to import them from another source. Currently, the user is able to import them from either a TAMOT task model or from a UML use-case diagram (the latter was done in this example). The user can then select one of the high-level tasks and start the event recording. In this example, the user has recorded a sequence of events intended to achieve the goal of opening a task model in TAMOT. This sequence is shown on the right as a vertical sequence of actor-action-object triples. Currently the actor can be either the system or the *generic* user. The actions are those common to GUI interfaces (e.g. select, click). The objects being operated on are taken from the set of GUI objects defined in the interface. The recorded sequence shown in Figure 9 results in the task model shown earlier in Figure 7.

Event recorders such as these have been implemented in a number of ways, frequently by modifying the application program to dump the events as the user performs them. The recorder described here is implemented as an extension of two Java Accessibility Utilities. The first, the SwingEventMonitor monitors events in the Java Virtual Machine, and the second, Monkey, produces a tree of all the GUI components used by the system. Because it taps into the Java virtual machine, the designers don't have to modify the original application at all; they simply need to tell Java to activate the recorder when a Java application is started. The recorder then does its job passively, allowing the designers to start, stop and pause recording as appropriate.

This approach to recording low-level tasks for task models is easier than building them by hand, but it does have some limitations. From the implementation point of view, the recorder's use is limited to Java applications built using the Swing widget set, although one could imagine building other tools for other types of interfaces and incorporating them into the ISOLDE environment.

The key limitations of this approach concerns the nature of event sequences. First, they are strict sequences. Where a typical DIANE+ task model may contain alternate paths, conditional arcs, and hierarchical decomposition, the recorded events are always sequences of low-level events. To help address this problem, the recorder allows the user to select a user task from the task hierarchy first, and then record a sequence of events for that task. This allows the user to record event sequences as the leaves of an existing hierarchy of tasks. In addition, the recorder could allow the user to record alternate event sequences for achieving a particular goal (although is currently not implemented). Also, because the recorder is part of the ISOLDE environment, the user can easily port the recorded model to TAMOT and make modifications there as necessary.

A second limitation is that the recorder sorts through all of the GUI events, including countless mouse motion events and other details which are frequently too low level to be of much use, even at the DeSS level. To help address this problem, the recorder masks out GUI events that it is not interested in by exploiting the masking capabilities provided by the Sun recording tool. Currently the recorder listens by default for Action and KeyType events. It also provides the ability to add or restrict other events interactively.

A third limitation is that the recorder receives only low-level GUI events. Because the recorder is independent of the application, it has no knowledge about the domain of the application. For example, it would be difficult for the recorder to infer that the string selected by the user from the text box is a filename, a title, or anything else. We have implemented some heuristics to help with this issue. Repeated events on the same object are collapsed into one event. For example, repeated keystrokes in a text field are reduces to a single *typing string* event. Similarly, repeated AddComponent events for a dialog box are grouped into a single *display dialog* event. We also make simple assumptions about common interface actions. For example, the action performed on buttons is assumed to be a *click* action, the action on menu items *select*, etc. The information still missing can be manually added within the TAMOT tool.

The event recorder, therefore, provides a way of easily recording portions of the lowest-level task models and connecting them to the user goals represented in the higher-level task models. The recorder can also be used to record both *ideal* use scenarios (i.e. the path through the system the designer intended the user to follow) and *actual* use scenarios (what users actually do), thus allowing them to be compared quantitatively.

5 Conclusion

This paper has proposed a flexible methodology for the construction of task models as well as an environment that supports this methodology. The methodology identifies a complete sequence of four levels for which task models should be built during system development, ranging from the highest level user goals down to the lowest level GUI events. Because working with these sets of task models is difficult and time-consuming, the paper also proposed a flexible task modelling environment, which allows designers to build, maintain, and use the task models. The environment, called ISOLDE, supports a coherent formalism for the task models identified in the methodology, and provides an extensible architecture in which to develop them. Although it does not yet fully support the simultaneous representation of all four levels discussed, we are working to extend the facilities to do this. We have presented a number of tools already build within this architecture, and hope that with further development this environment will encourage designers to use the complete methodology for the development of interactive systems.

Acknowledgements

The authors wish to thank the members of our team including Michael Brasser, Nathalie Colineau, Thomas Lo, Shijian Lu, Nadine Ozkan, Maryline Specht, Robert Tot, and Stephan Wan, as well as the anonymous reviewers. Sandrine Balbo also made contributions when she was part of the team. We gratefully acknowledge the support of the Office of Naval Research (ONR grant N00014-96-0465), CSIRO and Calvin College.

References

Balbo, S. (1994), Evaluation Ergonomique des Interfaces Utilisateur : Un Pas Vers L'Automatisation, PhD thesis, Université Grenoble I, France.

Balbo, S. & Lindley, C. (1997), Adaptation of a Task Analysis Methodology to the Design of Decision Support Systems, *in* S. Howard, J. Hammond & G. K. Lindgaard (eds.), *Human–Computer Interaction — INTERACT '97: Proceedings of the Sixth IFIP Conference on Human–Computer Interaction*, Chapman & Hall, pp.355–61.

Balbo, S., Ozkan, N. & Paris, C. (1998), Task Models in Industrial Context: How do They Fit?, http://www-ihm.lri.fr/ihm98/contributions/.

Balbo, S., Paris, C. & Ozkan, N. (1999), Characterising Task Formalisms: Towards a Taxonomy, *in Proceedings of the ECOOP'99 Workshop on Integrating Human Factors into Use Cases and OO Methods*, pp.246–7.

http://www.cs.concordia.ca/~faculty/seffah/ecoop/program.htm. Also available as CSIRO/MIS Technical Report 98/221.

Beard, D., Smith, D. & Danelsbeck, K. (1996), QGOMS: A Direct-manipulation Tool for Simple GOMS Models, *in* G. van der Veer & B. Nardi (eds.), *Proceedings of CHI'96: Human Factors in Computing Systems*, ACM Press, pp.25–6.

Bentley, T. (2000), Task Modelling Review, Technical Report 2000/155, CSIRO/MIS.

Booch, G., Rumbaugh, J. & Jacobson, I. (1999), *The Unified Modelling Language User Guide*, Addison–Wesley.

Brun, P. & Beaudouin-Lafon, M. (1995), A Taxonomy and Evaluation of Formalisms for the Specification of Interactive Systems, *in* M. A. R. Kirby, A. J. Dix & J. E. Finlay (eds.), *People and Computers X (Proceedings of HCI'95)*, Cambridge University Press, pp.197–212.

Card, S. K., Moran, T. P. & Newell, A. (1983), *The Psychology of Human–Computer Interaction*, Lawrence Erlbaum Associates.

CTTE (2001), ConcurTaskTrees Environment, http://giove.cnuce.cnr.it/ctte.html.

Harel, D. (1987), "Statecharts: A Visual Formalism for Complex Systems", *Science of Computer Programming* **8**(3), 231–74.

Hilbert, D. M. & Redmiles, D. F. (2000), "Extracting Usability Information from User Interface Events", *ACM Computing Surveys* **32**(4), 384–421.

Hix, D. & Hartson, H. R. (1993), *Developing User Interfaces: Ensuring Usability through Product and Process*, John Wiley & Sons.

Horracks, I. (1999), *Constructing the User Interface with Statecharts*, Addison–Wesley.

Lu, S., Paris, C. & Vander Linden, K. (1999), Towards the Automatic Generation of Task Models from Object Oriented Diagrams, *in* P. Dewan & S. Chatty (eds.), *Proceedings of the IFIP Working Conference on Engineering for Human–Computer Interaction, Heraklion, Crete, Greece, September 14–18*, Kluwer, pp.169–90.

Palanque, P. A., Bastide, R., Dourte, L. & Sibertin-Blanc, C. (1993), Design of User-driven Interfaces Using Petri Nets and Objects, *in* C. Rolland, F. Bodart & C. Cauvet (eds.), *Proceedings of CAISE'93 (Conference on Advance Information System Engineering)*, Vol. 685 of *Lecture Notes in Computer Science*, Springer-Verlag, pp.569–85.

Paris, C. & Vander Linden, K. (1996), "An Interactive Support Tool for Writing Multilingual Instructions", *IEEE Computer* **29**(7), 49–56. Special Issue on Interactive Natural Language Processing.

Paternò, F. (1999), *Model-Based Design and Evaluation of Interactive Applications*, Springer-Verlag.

Paternò, F. & Mancini, C. (1999), Developing Task Models From Informal Scenarios, *in* M. W. Altom & M. G. Williams (eds.), *Companion Proceedings of CHI'99: Human Factors in Computing Systems (CHI'99 Conference Companion)*, ACM Press. Proceedings of the CHI'99 Workshop "Tool Support for Task-Based User Interface Design". http://www.upb.de/fachbereich/AG/szwillus/chi99/ws/.

Paternò, F., Ballardin, G. & Mancini, C. (2000), Modelling Multi-Users Tasks, Technical Report, The GUITARE Project. http://giove.cnuce.cnr.it/Guitare/document.html.

Paternò, F., Mancini, C. & Meniconi, S. (1997), ConcurTaskTrees: A Diagrammatic Notation for Specifying Task Models, *in* S. Howard, J. Hammond & G. K. Lindgaard (eds.), *Human–Computer Interaction — INTERACT '97: Proceedings of the Sixth IFIP Conference on Human–Computer Interaction*, Chapman & Hall, pp.362–9.

Scapin, D. & Pierret-Golbreich, C. (1990), Towards a Method for Task Description: MAD, *in* L. Berlinguet & D. Berthelette (eds.), *Proceedings of Work with Display Unit '89*, Elsevier Science, pp.371–80.

Sebillotte, S. (1995), Methodology Guide to Task Analysis with the Goal of Extracting Relevant Characteristics for Interfaces, Technical Report Esprit project P6593, INRIA, Rocquencourt, France.

Tam, R. C., Maulsby, D. & Peurta, A. R. (1998), U-TEL: A Tool for Eliciting User Task Models from Domain Experts, *in Proceedings of the International Conference on Intelligent User Interfaces (IUI'98)*, pp.77–80.

Tarby, J.-C. & Barthet, M.-F. (1996), The Diane+ Method, *in* J. Vanderdonckt (ed.), *Proceedings of the 2nd International Workshop on Computer-aided Design of User Interfaces (CADUI'96)*, Presses Universitaires de Namur, pp.95–119.

van der Veer, G. C., Hoeve, M. & Lenting, B. F. (1996), Modelling Complex Work Systems — Method meets Reality, *in* T. R. G. Green, J. J. Cañas & C. P. Warren (eds.), *Cognition and the Worksystem, Proceedings of the 8th European Conference on Cognitive Ergonomics (EACE)*, University of Granada Press, pp.115–20.

van Welie, M., van der Veer, G. C. & Eliens, A. (1998), EUTERPE: Tool Support for Analyzing Co-operative Environments, *in* T. R. G. Green, L. Bannon, C. Warren & J. Buckley (eds.), *Proceedings of the Ninth European Conference on Cognitive Ergonomics*, University of Limerick, pp.109–14.

Vander Linden, K., Paris, C. & Lu, S. (2000), Where Do Instructions Come From: Knowledge Acquisition and Specification for Instructional Text, *in* T. Becker & S. Busemann (eds.), *IMPACTS in Natural Language Generation: NLG Between Technology and Applications*, DFKI document D-00-01, pp.1–10.

Wild, P. J. & Macredie, R. D. (2000), On Change and Tasks, *in* S. McDonald, Y. Waern & G. Cockton (eds.), *People and Computers XIV (Proceedings of HCI'2000)*, Springer-Verlag, pp.45–59.

From the Formal Specifications of Users Tasks to the Automatic Generation of the HCI Specifications

Adel Mahfoudhi[†], Mourad Abed[‡] & Dimitri Tabary[‡]

[†] *Department of Computer Science, Science Faculty of Sfax, Rte Soukra km 3.5, BP: 802–3018 Sfax, Tunisia*

Tel: *+216 4 27 43 90*

Fax: *+216 4 27 44 37*

Email: *adel.mahfoudhi@fss.rnu.tn*

[‡] *LAMIH (UMR CNRS 8530), Université de Valenciennes, BP: 311–59304, Valenciennes Cedex 9, France*

Tel: *+33 3 27 51 14 66*

Fax: *+33 4 27 51 13 16*

Email: *{mourad.abed,dimitri.tabary}@univ-valenciennes.fr*

This paper presents an approach to the construction of a task model of a method, named TOOD (Task Object Oriented Design), used for the development of an interactive system. This approach is based on a formal notation, which gives quantitative results which may be checked by designers and which provide the possibility of performing mathematical verifications on the models. The modelling formalism is based on the joint use of the object approach and high level Petri nets. The concepts borrowed from the object approach make it possible to describe the static aspects of tasks and the Petri nets enable the description of dynamics and behaviour. We also describe a software aid tool for the manipulation of these models, which allows the editing and the simulation of a task model. In order to facilitate the comprehension of the method, an extremely simple example of the air traffic control will be given.

Keywords: task analysis, HCI specification, complexity evaluation, formal method, object approach, Petri nets.

1   Introduction

Several research projects have been dedicated to the modelling of user tasks in the field of interactive system design (see, for example, the work concentrating on the following methods: MAD (Scapin & Pierret-Golbreich, 1990), DIANE (Barthet, 1988), GOMS (Card et al., 1983). However, their actual use is far from being a widespread practice. One of the possible reasons for this is that they do not use truly formal methods, which make it possible to provide the task models with conciseness, coherence and non-ambiguity (Palanque, 1997). What is more, these projects suffer not only from their lack of integration into a global design process covering the entire lifecycle of the Human–Computer Interface (HCI) but also from the lack of modelling support software. In order to overcome these problems, current research projects are oriented towards a methodological framework which covers all stages from the first activity analysis stage up to the stage of the detailed specification of the HCI: The methods MAD* (Gamboa-Rodriguez, 1998), DIANE+ (Tarby & Barthet, 1996), GLADIS++ (Ricard & Buisine, 1996), ADEPT(Johnson et al., 1995) and TRIDENT (Vanderdonckt, 1997) go in this direction. These design methodologies are based on several models (task model, user model, interface model) and are aided by tools for the implementation of these models.

Our research work falls into this category, but we emphasise the formal aspects of model representation and their transformation throughout the stages of the design process. The TOOD method is based on the representation that the user has of the task, apart from the considerations of computer processing. Like the UML/PNO method (Delatour & Paludetto, 1998), HOOD/PNO (Paludetto & Benzina, 1997) and ICO (Palanque et al., 1997), the TOOD method uses the object approach and the object Petri nets to describe, on the one hand, the functional aspects and the dynamics of the user tasks, and on the other hand the behavioural aspects of the HCI and of the user in order to specify how the tasks are performed. Its formalism aims at covering the entire development cycle from the analysis of what exists, up to the detailed design and implementation.

The description of TOOD method is illustrated by an example concerning the air traffic control. Explanations on supporting software for TOOD are also provided. The reader will find a more detailed description of the method in (Mahfoudhi, 1997).

2   TOOD and the Cycle of Development of the HCI

The TOOD design process can be divided into four major stages, (Figure 1):

- The *analysis of the existing system and of the need* is based on its user's activity and it forms the entry point and the basis for any new designs.

- The *Structural Task Model (STM)* is concerned with the description of the user tasks of the system to be designed. It makes it possible to describe the user task in a coherent and complete way. Two models are created at this level: the Static Structural Task Model (SSTM) and the Dynamic Structural Task Model (DSTM), in order to be able to use it for the HCI specification.

- The *Operational Model (OM)* makes it possible to specify the HCI objects in a

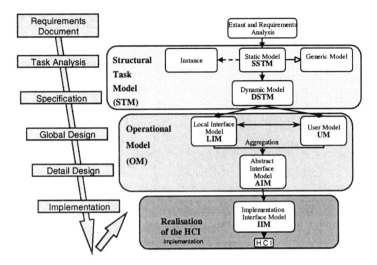

Figure 1: TOOD and the development cycle for the interface.

Local Interface Model (LIM), as well as the user procedures in a User Model (UM) of the system to be designed. It uses the needs and the characteristics of the structural task model in order to result in an Abstract Interface Model (AIM) which is compatible with the user's objectives and procedures.

- The realisation of the HCI is concerned with the computer implementation of the specifications resulting from the previous stage, supported by the multi-agent software architecture defined in the Interface Implementation Model (IIM).

The TOOD method is supported by an editor developed in Visual C++. It makes model capture and syntactic checking easier. Moreover, it supports the test and simulation activities of the dynamic task model. Examples of screen pages are given later by illustrating them with models, which come from a description of tasks related to air traffic control.

3   Analysis of the Existing System

To know what the operator is presumed to do using the new system, we must know what is achieved in real work situations (the activity analysis) using an existing version of the system or a similar system.

In TOOD, this first stage starts with the production of two models: the user model and the system model.

3.1   User Model (UM)

It is based on the analysis of the activity in real work situations. The User Model (UM) models the operator's observable behaviour (actions on tools, reading of

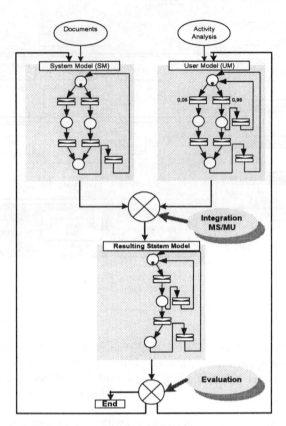

Figure 2: Integration of User Model and System Model.

information, etc.) and his reasoning (mental activities) permitting the production of the observable behaviour.

Observation techniques together with other means of data collection, in particular interviewing, makes it possible to get some objective 'data' on the operators' activity, which are necessary for the construction of the user model.

The user model is described by an Imprecise Petri Net in which places represent states of the system and transitions stand for the necessary actions for the execution of a task. The imprecise marking of the net (Figure 2), represented by the presence of the probability index, models the imprecision of users in their different choices and actions.

3.2   The System Model (SM)

The System Model (SM), represented by an Object Petri Net (OPN) (Sibertin-Blanc, 1985), describes the treatments of the interactive system as it is described by its inventor. In the OPN, the system is modelled by a token provided by a set of attributes. These attributes describe the features and properties of the system.

The set of operations and functions of the interactive system is represented by transitions of its OPN. These operations permit the evolution from one state to another.

3.3 Analysis of the complexity: US/SM integration

This is about a model of the complexity evaluation of the interactive system. It consists of the integration of the user model and the system model through several iterations. (Figure 2).

After every iteration, some modifications in the system model are proposed (addition, suppression or modification of places and transitions). This process continues until the resulting system model is judged satisfactory and compatible with the user model.

The final objective of this stage is to mark all positive and negative aspects of the existing system.

4 Structural Task Model (STM)

After the stage of the existing system analysis and its user's activity, the structural task model (STM) makes it possible to establish a coherent and complete description of tasks to be achieved on the future system, while avoiding the inconveniences of the existing system and adding the new required functions and features. For that, two types of model are elaborated: a static model (SSTM) and a dynamic model (SDTM).

As in MAD* (Gamboa-Rodriguez, 1998) and Diane+ (Tarby & Barthet, 1996), the STM is conceived as a means to take into account the user and his task in the development cycle. The objective is to provide a methodological tool to development teams enabling them to abstract the information about the user task necessary for the formal conception of the HCI and to permit its integration into the computer development cycle. It is a working language facilitating the dialogue and exchanges of information between participants of a development team.

The construction of the structural model is composed of four iterative stages:

- Hierarchical decomposition of tasks.

- Identification of objects and their components.

- Definition of the dynamics of the elementary tasks.

- Integration of the task competition.

4.1 Static Structural Task Model (SSTM)

The structural model enables the breakdown of the user's stipulated work with the interactive system into significant elements, called tasks. Each task is considered as being an *autonomous* entity corresponding to a goal or to a sub-goal, which can be situated at various hierarchical levels. This goal remains unchanged in the various work situations. In order to perfect this definition, TOOD formalises the concept of tasks using an object representation model, in which the task can be seen as an *Object*, an instance of the *Task Class*. This representation, consequently, attempts to model the task class by a generic structure of coherent and robust data, making it

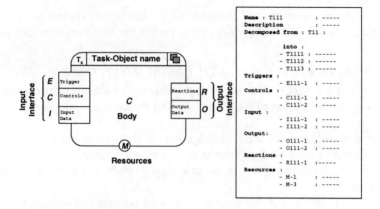

Figure 3: Generic structure of the class-task.

possible to describe and organise the information necessary for the identification and performance of each task.

Two types of graphical and textual document, as shown in Figure 3, define each task class.

The task class is studied as an entity using four *components*: the Input Interface, the Output Interface, the Resources and the Body. We also associate a certain number of *identifiers* to these describers, which makes it possible to distinguish the Task Class amongst the others: *Name, Goal, Index, Type* and *Hierarchy*. This parallel with software engineering guarantees a strong link between a user-centred specification based on ergonomic models and the software design based on the object model. There are defined as follows:

Name: action verb followed by a complement (object treated by the task), reflecting the treatment to be performed by the task. It is preferable for the name to include vocabulary used by the users in order to respect the terminology during the development of the interface.

Goal: explanation in natural language of the goal which the user or application wishes to reach via the task.

Index: formal identifier of the task formed using the number of the master task, to which the sequential number corresponding to the said task is added.

Type: nature of the task; this designates its category: human, automatic or interactive.

Hierarchy: number of task classes composing it; it is represented by a series of small squares.

Body: central unit of the task class. For intermediate or hierarchical tasks, it gives the task procedure diagram, that is to say the logical and temporal relations

Type of task	Human Resource	System Resource
Manual	1..1	0
Automatic	0	1..N
Interactive	1..1	1..N
Cooperative	2..N	0..N

Table 1: Type of task.

of the sub-tasks. These relations reflect, in a certain way, the user's work organisation. On the other hand, for terminal tasks, it defines the action procedures for the HCI/user couple. The specification for these procedures is produced in the task operational model.

Resources: human users and/or interactive system entities involved in the performance of the task. Therefore, four types of task are defined: Manual, Automatic, Interactive or Cooperative (Table 1).

A manual task is accomplished by one and only one user. An automatic task can be done by one or several system resources. An interactive task is accomplished by a user's interaction with a set of system resources. Finally, a cooperative task requires the activity of two or several users that interact between them (human cooperation) or on a collection of system resources (interactive cooperation).

The input interface specifies the initial state of the task. It defines the necessary data to the task execution. These data are considered as the initial conditions to be satisfied at the beginning of the task. It is composed of three categories of information (Table 2).

The output interface specifies the final state of the task. It is composed of two types of data (Table 2).

The resources, and the information of the input and output interfaces are modelled by objects, called 'describer objects', instances of describer classes. These objects, from a computing point of view, represent the components of a task class. Whereas from a user point of view, they constitute the mental image of the entities manipulated in a task. They will, thus, have a final image in the interactive system.

The first stage of the TOOD methodology is the identification of the tasks of the future system. By a hierarchical decomposition, it organises the identified tasks-objects in a hierarchical tree form. It starts from the global task-object (the hierarchical tree's root) passing through the least abstract task-objects (the branches) and finishes with the terminal task-objects (the leaves). If we consider air traffic control, 'to configure the flight entry' can be regarded as a task-object. In order to reduce its abstraction, this task-object can be decomposed into three child task-objects: 'T_{111}:to take knowledge of a new flight' (terminal task-object), 'T_{112}:to take a decision about flight' and 'T_{113}:to verify the position on radar screen' (terminal task-object). It is to be noticed that the events which activate the same task-object

		Description
Input Interface	Triggers	Events which bring about the performance of the task. They are classed into two categories: • Formal or explicit trigger events, which correspond to external triggers. They appear in an observable way in the work environment (information on screen, button press, communication, ...). The tasks triggered by this type of event are considered as being compulsory; that is, their performance is vital. • Informal or implicit trigger events, which correspond to triggers, brought about following a user decision, from information characterising its work situation. Unlike the formal events, they are not visible to an outside observer, but may be expressed verbally
	Contextual conditions	Information which must be checked during the performance of the task. These conditions affect the way in which the task is performed.
	Input data	Information necessary during the performance of the task.
Output Interface	Reactions	Results produced by the performance of the task. Their content indicates the following type of modification: • Physical and, in this case, it indicates the modification of the environment (application call, change of state, ...). • Mental, indicating the modification or a new representation of the situation by the user. The Reactions thus determine whether the aims are attained or not and, in such a case, the task will be repeated after a possible development of the situation.
	Output data	Data transformed or created by the performance of the task.

Table 2: Input and Output Interface components.

---

are shared out among the child task-objects. As shown by the Figure 2, the task-object 'T11:to configure the flight entry' can be activated by two events 'E11–1: Arrival of a new flight' and 'E11–2: Proposition of an entry level (EFL)'. Yet those events activate two different children task-objects, which means that both events ask for two different processings of the task-object 'T11: to configure the flight entry'. Thus the event E11-1 activates the task-object 'T_{111}: to take knowledge of a new flight' to read information about the new flight while the event E11-2 supposes that the flight information has been read and it activates the task-object 'T_{112}: to take a decision about flight'.

Once all future system tasks are identified, the second stage of TOOD concerns the specification which defines all the execution conditions and the effects of each task-object. It consists in listing and identifying all the descriptors or attributes.

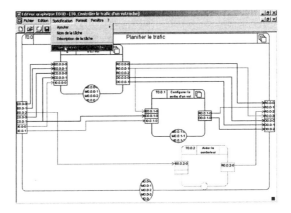

Figure 4: A graphic specification of the task-object 'T11: to configure the flight entry'.

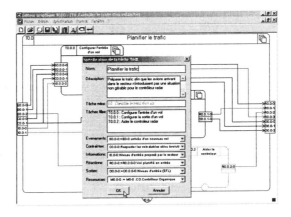

Figure 5: Textual specification of the task-object 'T11: to configure the flight entry'.

The resulting document of this specification includes two kinds of descriptions: a graphic description for a clean, legible and exploitable representation, (Figure 4) and a textual one for a complete description of the descriptors of each task-object (Figure 5).

4.2 Dynamic Structural Task Model (DSTM)

The Dynamic Structural Task Model (DSTM) aims at integrating the temporal dimension (sequencing, synchronisation, concurrency, and interruption) by completing the static model. The dynamic behaviour of tasks is defined by a control structure, called TCS (Task Control Structure), based on an object Petri net (RPO). It is merely the transformation of the static structure. This TCS describes the input interface's describer objects, the task activity, the release of describer objects from the output interface as well as the resource occupation.

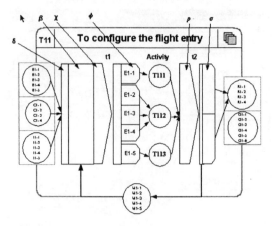

Figure 6: TCS Task Control Structure.

Each TCS has an input transition t1 and an output transition t2 made up of a selection part and an action part. The functions associated with each transition allow the selection of objects and define their distribution in relation to the task activity (Figure 6).

The selection part of transition t1 is made up of three functions: δ, β, χ:

Priority function δ makes it possible to select the highest priority trigger for the task. This function is the basis of the interruption system. It allows the initiation of a task performance, even if another lower priority task is being carried out. However, the performance of the task in relation to this trigger remains subject to the verification of the completeness and coherence functions.

Completeness function β checks the presence of all the describer objects relating to an observed event, that is to say the input data, the control data and the resources used to activate the task class in relation to a given trigger event.

Coherence function χ assesses the admissibility of these describers in relation to the conditions envisaged for the task. This function is a set of verification rules which use simple logical or mathematical type operators and which obey a unique syntax making their formulation possible.

The selection part of transition t2 has a **completeness function** ρ which checks the presence of output data and resources associated with the reactions released by the body of the task.

The hierarchical tasks are considered to be **control tasks** for the tasks of which they are composed. Consequently, the action parts of the input and output transitions of their TCS possess respectively an emission function ϕ and a synchronisation function σ. Function ϕ defines the **emission rules** (constructors of the input

	Constructor	Symbol	Transition	Order of priority	Sharing of resource	Description
Input Transition	Junction and distribution (simultaneity)			Cst	No	n tasks are performed at the same time by m different resources. These tasks may be triggered by the same trigger or else by different triggers.
	Transfer (Or)			Yes	Yes	n tasks are performed in order of trigger priority. The tasks share data and resources. These tasks can be interrupted.
	Transfer with condition			Yes	–	n tasks are performed in order of trigger priority which will satisfy certain conditions. The tasks share data and resources. These tasks can be interrupted.
	Transfer alternative			Yes	–	One single task is triggered. The triggers are similar, but only one is taken according to the context.
Output Transition	Synchronisation			–	–	n sub-tasks must be finished so that the management task may be finished. The management task releases either R_j reactions or new reactions.
	Or			–	–	The management task is finished when at least one of these sub-tasks is finished.
	Alternative			–	–	The management task is finished when only one of its 'daughter' tasks is finished.

Table 3: Constructors of the input transition and Constructors of the output transition.

transition) for transition t1, for the activation of the sub-tasks, as well as the distribution of data used by these sub-tasks. Function σ defines the **synchronisation rules** (constructors of the output transition) for the sub-tasks. These rules are defined in Table 3.

5 Operational Model (OM)

This stage has as an objective the automatic passage of the user tasks description to the specification of the HCI. It completes the external model describing the body of terminal task-objects in order to answer the question how to execute the task? (in terms of objects, actions, states and control structure).

At this level we integrate resources of every terminal task-object in its body. These resources become, in this way, component-objects, belonging to the classes Interface, Machine, Application and Human Operator. The modelling of the class application is not addressed in this paper.

The specification of the HCI passes through two stages. The first corresponds to the specification of component-objects of every terminal task, and by a process of aggregation of these component-objects. The second stage makes it possible to specify the HCI objects.

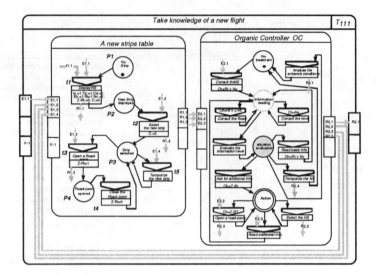

Figure 7: A graphic Specification of the component-objects 'New Strips Table' and 'Organic Controller'.

5.1   Specification of Components-object

All the component-objects cooperate in a precisely defined manner in order to fulfill the aim of the terminal task-object in response to a given functional context. A component-object shall be defined from its class (Interface or Operator) and provided with a set of states and a set of operations (or actions) which allow the change of these states. For example, from the P3 state (strip selected) of the component-object 'new strips table' the operator has the possibility to carry out two actions: t3 (open a road-zoom) or t5 (temporise the new strip), as shown in Figure 7. On the other hand, the set of states and operations of an Operator component-object represents the different possible procedures for the execution of the terminal task. Indeed, the procedure represents the different activity phases of a human operator: situation apprehension, goals identification, preparation of an action plan, application of this action plan, control of the situation, correction (Norman & Draper, 1986).

Graphically, the component-object is presented in an identical structure to the one of a task-object in the structural model. However its internal control structure called Object Control Structure 'ObCS' is modelled by an Object Petri Net 'OPN'. The OPNs are characterised by the fact that the tokens which constitute the place markings are neither atomic nor similar entities, but they can be distinguished from each other and take values, making it possible to describe the characteristics of the system.

In addition to its formal aspect, the ObCS enjoys a simple and easily understood graphical representation, making is possible to represent, with the places of the OPN, all the possible states of the component-object, and with the transitions, to represent all the operations and actions that can be taken from these states.   The graphic representation used for the ObCS is inspired by the cooperative and interactive objects formalism proposed by (Palanque, 1992).

The communication between the component-objects is carried out through their input and output interfaces. So, an action 'A' executed by a component-object 'X' (operator) on the component-object 'Y' (interface) can be read as the component-object 'X' executes its operation reaction corresponding to the query of the action A. This execution is rendered by a reaction R in the output interface of the component-object X. The output interface transmits the reaction R to the input interface of the component-object Y. So the reaction R becomes an event E. And lastly this event activates the service operation of the component-object Y corresponding to the action A asked by the component-object X.

An example from air traffic control, corresponding to the terminal task-object "take knowledge the new flight" taken from (Mahfoudhi, 1997), needs the use of two component-objects: 'a New Strips Table: NST' and ' Organic Controller: OC' (Figure 4). The behaviour of the component-object 'a New Strips Table' is defined by four states P1, P2, P3 and P4. From each state the Organic Controller can carry out a group of actions (transitions). From the P3 state (strip selected), for example, he has the possibility to achieve two actions: t3 (open a road-zoom) or t5 (temporise the new strip).

For the component-object 'Organic Controller', the set of states and operations represents the different possible procedures to execute the terminal task 'Take knowledge of a new flight' in reply to a given functional context. So, the display of a New Strip NS in the component-object 'new strips table' invokes, by the event E2,1, the operation service 'Consult the NS' of the component-object 'Organic Controller OC'. According to his selection 'Ch=', the organic controller carries out a first reading of the NS information ('Consult the road' or 'Consult the level'). After this reading, he changes his state into cognition in order to evaluate his information level. Then he decides to "read again the basic information" or to "ask for additional information". The asking for additional information expresses itself by a change of his state into 'Action' in order to 'select the NS' and to 'open the Road-Zoom'. Both actions transmit R2,2 and R2,3 reactions to the component-object 'new strips table'. It should be noted that the organic controller carries out the action 'open a road-zoom' only after receiving the event E2,2 confirming that the action 'Select the NS' has been carried out. Once the Road-Zoom has been opened, the Organic Controller changes his state into 'information reading' in order to read the additional information and then into the 'situation evaluation' state to decide either to read the information again, or 'to temporise the NS' or to invoke the terminal task-object 'T112: to analyze the entrance conditions'.

5.2 Aggregation Mechanism

In order to realise the HCI in its real structure, the construction of the object classes of the HCI suggests the aggregation of the different component-objects which have the same name, specified during the description of the internal model of each terminal task-object. This aggregation mechanism is comparable to the composition relation of the HOOD method called the parent/child relation.

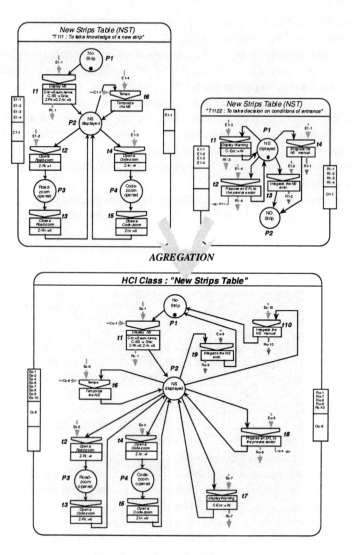

Figure 8: Aggregation mechanism.

Thus, an object class of the HCI is built according to the duplication of all the elements (triggers, contextual conditions, input data, reactions, output data and ObCSs) of the component-objects which have the same name.

The explanatory example in Figure 8 corresponds to the class 'new strips table' constructed by aggregation of the component-objects 'new strips table' of the terminal task-object 'T111:To take knowledge of a new strip', and the one of the terminal task-object 'T1122:To take decision on conditions of entrance'.

6 HCI Implementation

The HCI implementation model in the TOOD methodology is the presentation specification of the final interface as it will be seen by the user. It corresponds to the specification of the Presentation components of the Seeheim model or presentation and action languages.

The construction of this model takes place through the translation of objects, states, actions and ObCS to screens, menus, windows, icons, This translation depends on a collection of criteria and ergonomic rules (Bastien & Scapin, 1995), of guides (Vanderdonckt, 1994) and of heuristics (Nielsen & Molich, 1990).

The following figure (Figure 9) schematises the prototype of simulation of the future objects oriented interface of the PHIDIAS system (HEGIAS) that corresponds to the development of the Implementation Model. This development, made by the CENA, concerns the position of the Organic Controller (OC). It includes four objects:

A radar picture that displays the limits of the controlled sector, the plane tracks, and labels associated with the plane tracks. A clock (HH:MM) is presented in a permanent way.

A new strips table situated in the upper left part of the screen. Strips are presented according to an automatic ordering by geographical flow.

A built-in strips table situated in the left bottom part of the screen.

A work zone situated in the right bottom part of the screen. It is reserved for displaying one of the following entries: the list of flights in account, help in entrance, help in exit or strips withdrawn by anticipation.

There are four input tools: a mouse, two tactile screens, and a mini-keyboard. With these tools, the OC has the possibility to act directly on the interface. He can integrate a new flight, consult a road-zoom, consult help in entrance or in exit for a flight, etc.

7 Conclusion

The use of the object oriented approach and object Petri nets presents several advantages for the modelling of the user task. Indeed, the TOOD task model, through its static and dynamic description, allows the modularity of specifications, the expression of interruptions and concurrency. The addition of describer objects to the task entity enables a connection to a programming language, which simplifies the passage to implementation.

Moreover, the TOOD method can contribute towards helping with communication between the different actors in the design process through its formal description.

The operational model leads to the specification then to the generation of the HCI. This model is developed from the structural model while using the same formalisms which ensures the semantic stability of the TOOD method.

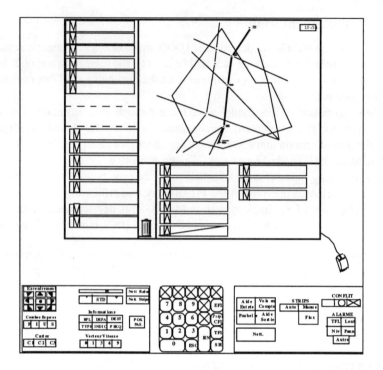

Figure 9: Simulation Prototype of the future air traffic control interface (HEGIAS) specified by TOOD.

References

Barthet, M.-F. (1988), *Logiciels interactifs et ergonomie, modèles et méthodes de conception*, Dunod Informatique Ed., Paris.

Bastien, J. & Scapin, D. (1995), "Evaluating a User Interface With Ergonomic Criteria", *International Journal of Human–Computer Interaction* 7(2), 105–21.

Card, S. K., Moran, T. P. & Newell, A. (1983), *The Psychology of Human–Computer Interaction*, Lawrence Erlbaum Associates.

Delatour, J. & Paludetto, M. (1998), De HOOD/PNO à UML/PNO : Une Méthode pour les Systèmes Temps Réels Basée sur UML et Objets à Réseaux de Petri, Technical Report 98248, LAAS–CNRS.

Gamboa-Rodriguez, F. (1998), Spécification et Implémentation d'ALACIE : Atelier Logiciel d'Aide à la Conception d'Interfaces Ergonomiques, Thèse en Sciences, Université Paris XI, France.

Johnson, P., Johnson, H. & Wilson, S. (1995), Rapid Prototyping of User Interfaces Driven by Task Models, *in* J. M. Carroll (ed.), *Scenario-Based Design: Envisioning Work and Technology in System Development*, John Wiley & Sons, pp.209–46.

Mahfoudhi, A. (1997), TOOD: Une Méthodologie de Description Orientée Objet des Tâches Utilisateur pour la Spécification et la Conception des Interfaces Homme–Machine, PhD thesis, Université de Valenciennes, France.

Nielsen, J. & Molich, R. (1990), Heuristic Evaluation of User Interfaces, *in* J. C. Chew & J. Whiteside (eds.), *Proceedings of CHI'90: Human Factors in Computing Systems*, ACM Press, pp.249–256.

Norman, D. A. & Draper, S. W. (eds.) (1986), *User Centered System Design: New Perspectives on Human–Computer Interaction*, Lawrence Erlbaum Associates.

Palanque, P. (1992), Modélisation Par Objets Coopératifs Interactifs d'Interfaces Homme–Machine Dirigées par l'Utilisateur, PhD thesis, Université Toulouse I.

Palanque, P. (1997), Spécifications Formelles et Systèmes Interactifs, Habilitation à Diriger des Recherches, University of Toulouse I, France.

Palanque, P., Bastide, R. & Paternò, F. (1997), Formal Specification As a Tool for the Objective Assessment of Safety Critical Interactive Systems, *in* S. Howard, J. Hammond & G. K. Lindgaard (eds.), *Human–Computer Interaction — INTERACT '97: Proceedings of the Sixth IFIP Conference on Human–Computer Interaction*, Chapman & Hall, pp.323–30.

Paludetto, M. & Benzina, A. (1997), Une Méthodologie Orientée Objet HOOD et Réseaux de Petri, *in* J.-C. Hennet (ed.), *Concepts et Outils pour les Systèmes de Production*, Cépaduès-Editions, chapter Part5-3, pp.293–325.

Ricard, E. & Buisine, A. (1996), Des Tâches Utilisateur au Dialogue Homme–Machine: GLADIS++, une Démarche Industrielle, *in Proceedings of IHM'96*, AFIHM, pp.71–6.

Scapin, D. & Pierret-Golbreich, C. (1990), Towards a Method for Task Description: MAD, *in* L. Berlinguet & D. Berthelette (eds.), *Proceedings of Work with Display Unit '89*, Elsevier Science, pp.371–80.

Sibertin-Blanc, C. (1985), High-level Petri Nets with Data Structure, *in* K. Jensen (ed.), *Proceedings of the 6th European Workshop on Application and Theory of Petri Nets*, pp.141–70.

Tarby, J.-C. & Barthet, M.-F. (1996), The Diane+ Method, *in* J. Vanderdonckt (ed.), *Proceedings of the 2nd International Workshop on Computer-aided Design of User Interfaces (CADUI'96)*, Presses Universitaires de Namur, pp.95–119.

Vanderdonckt, J. (1994), *Guide Ergonomique des Interfaces Homme–Machine*, Presses Universitaires de Namur.

Vanderdonckt, J. (1997), Conception Assistée de la Présentation d'une Interface homme–Machine Ergonomique pour une Application de Gestion Hautement Interactive, Thèse, Faculté Notre Dame de la Paix, Louvain, Belgique.

Supporting Context Changes for Plastic User Interfaces: A Process and a Mechanism

Gaëlle Calvary, Joëlle Coutaz & David Thevenin

CLIPS-IMAG, BP 53, 38041 Grenoble Cedex 9, France

Tel: *+33 476 514 854*

Fax: *+33 476 446 675*

Email: *{Gaelle.Calvary,Joelle.Coutaz,David.Thevenin}@imag.fr*

URL: *http://iihm.imag.fr/*

Mobility coupled with the development of a wide variety of access devices has engendered new requirements for HCI such as the ability of user interfaces to adapt to different contexts of use. We define a context of use as the set of values of variables that characterise the computational device(s) used for interacting with the system as well as the physical and social environment where the interaction takes place. A user interface is plastic if it is able to adapt to context changes while preserving usability. In this paper, we present a process and a software mechanism that support context changes for plastic user interfaces. We propose to structure adaptation as a three-step process: recognition of the situation, computation of a reaction to cope with the situation, and execution of the reaction. Reactions are specified in an evolution model which, in turn, is executed by a context supervisor. This supervisor is notified of context changes by a software probe that automatically detects deviations from the current situation. When notified, the supervisor executes the evolution model, and, when possible, adapts the user interface to the new context of use.

Keywords: plasticity, adaptation, context of use, platform, environment.

1 Introduction

Recent years have seen the introduction of many types of access devices including Personal Digital Assistants (PDAs) and mobile phones (cf. Figure 1). Systems like CyberGuide (Abowd et al., 1996), the office assistant (Yan & Selker, 2000)

Figure 1: A wide variety of access devices.

and Welbo (Anabuki et al., 2000) all aim at providing the user with context-relevant information as the user moves around. New interaction techniques are being developed to support human tasks while hiding the computer away. These include transforming the PDA into a universal remote controller (Schilit et al., 1994), transferring data between PDAs by picking and dropping (Rekimoto, 2000), and augmenting real world objects with computational facilities (Bérard et al., 2000; Lee et al., 2000). Flexibility becomes more important: when the battery gets low, users may want to switch from their portable PC to the PDA without losing any contextual data. Similarly, they may want to switch from the PDA to a wall-sized electronic white board to share information in a more efficient way with a colleague passing by. These examples demonstrate that adaptation of interactive systems to context changes is becoming a major issue in HCI.

In this article, we address the problem of adaptation to context changes for plastic user interfaces (Thevenin & Coutaz, 1999; Calvary et al., to appear). We recall the definition of our notions of plasticity and context of use, then describe the process and a software mechanism we propose for supporting adaptation to context changes. We illustrate the discussion with the EDF home heating control system, a system we have developed according to our plasticity-related principles.

2   An Example: The EDF Heating Control System

A heating control system allows users to set the level of comfort in the home for different periods of the day. It also provides facilities for programming standard heating behaviour during weekends and vacations. The heating system is controlled with a dedicated wall-mounted device. EDF (the French Electricity Company) is willing to offer new interaction modalities using a variety of access devices suitable for different environments.

The various contexts of use envisioned by EDF include:

- At home, using a PDA connected to a wireless home-net.

- In the office, with a web server running on a standard workstation.

- Anywhere with a WAP-enabled mobile phone.

Clearly, the user interface of the heating control system cannot be the same for every access device: the variation of interactional resources requires specific solutions. Figure 2 shows three versions of the system:

(a) No navigation   (b1) Thumbnail-based navigation

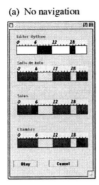
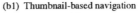

(b2) Menu-based navigation

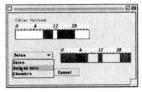

Figure 2: a) Large screen. The temperature of all the rooms of the home are available at a glance; b1 and b2) Small screen. The temperature of a single room is displayed at a time. A thumbnail or a menu allows the user to switch between rooms.

- In Figure 2a, the system displays the current temperature for each of the rooms of the house (the bedroom, the bathroom, and the living room). The screen size is large enough to make observable the entire system state. The user does not need to navigate between the rooms.

- In Figures 2b1 & b2, the screen is too small to display the whole system state. The temperature of a single room is shown at a time. In contrast with Figure 2a, the system state is not observable, but browsable (Gram & Cockton, 1996). As a result, a thumbnail must be introduced to navigate between the rooms (Figure 2b1), whereas in (Figure 2b2) navigation is based on a pull-down menu. The choice between the pull-down menu and a thumbnail depends on the shape of the screen as well as on the number of the rooms.

Figure 3 shows the interaction trajectory for setting the temperature of a room with a WAP-enabled mobile phone: On the left, the user selects the room (e.g. the living room — le salon). In the centre, the system shows the current temperature of the living room (i.e. 18°C). By selecting the editing function ('donner ordre'), the user is able to modify the current settings for that particular room (cf. the right most picture).

When compared to the situation depicted in Figure 2a, two navigation tasks (i.e. selecting the room, then selecting the edit function) must be performed to reach the desired state. In addition, a title must be added to every page to remind the user of the current location within the interaction space.

The user interfaces shown in Figures 2 & 3 have been produced with ARTStudio (Calvary ct al., to appear), a tool for developing plastic user interfaces.

Figure 3: On mobile phones, screen size as well as the absence of direct manipulation require additional articulatory tasks: a navigation task to browse the rooms and a task to enter the edit mode.

3 Plasticity of User Interfaces

The term *plasticity* is inspired from the property of materials that expand and contract under natural constraints without breaking, thus preserving continuous usage. Applied to HCI, plasticity is "the capacity of an interactive system to adapt to changes of the context of use while preserving usability" (Thevenin & Coutaz, 1999).

In this definition:

- A context of use is defined as the couple 'Platform/Environment' where *Platform* denotes the set of variables that characterise the computational device(s) used for interacting with the system. Typically, memory size, network bandwidth, screen size, etc. are determining factors. The *environment* covers the set of entities (e.g. objects, persons and events) that are peripheral to the current task(s) but that may impact the system and/or the user's behaviour, either now or in the future. According to this definition, an environment may encompass the entire world. In practice, the boundary is set up by domain analysts whose role is to elicit the entities that are relevant to the case at hand. These include surrounding noise, lighting conditions, user's and objects location, social ambience, etc.

- Adaptation is a reaction to context changes. Depending on the nature of the change, adaptation may consist of remodelling the user interface (as in Figure 2 when switching to a smaller screen). It may result in a task migration such as turning the heat on when the temperature is too low or hiding confidential information when someone gets too close to the owner's screen. The adaptation is for the well being of the user, but is not targeted at the user's current mental state. The user is supposed to have a predefined profile specified during the early phase of the development process.

- Usability is preserved if the properties elicited at the design stage for the particular system are kept within a predefined range of values. These properties may be selected from general HCI properties such as those identified in (Gram & Cockton, 1996).

In summary, plasticity is a kind of adaptation. It results from a Situation $\Longrightarrow$ Reaction process where:

- Situation denotes a context change (of the platform state and/or of the environment) that requires a reaction.

- Reaction corresponds to the procedure that the system and/or the user executes to preserve usability.

In the next section, we focus the discussion on the adaptation process.

4 The Adaptation Process

Plastic adaptation is structured as a three-step process: recognition of the situation, computation of a reaction, and execution of the reaction.

4.1 Situation Recognition

Recognising the situation includes the following steps:

- Sensing the context of use (e.g. current temperature is 22 °C).

- Detecting context changes (e.g. temperature has raised from 18 °C to 22°C).

- Identifying context changes (e.g. for the heating control system, transition from the *regular* context to the *comfortable* context).

In turn, the identification of context changes may trigger a reaction. There are two general types of trigger: entering a context and leaving a context. Schmidt (2000) suggests a third type of trigger, not considered in our discussion: being in a context. Triggers are combined with the AND/OR logic operators. For example, 'Leaving(C1) AND Entering(C2)' is a trigger that expresses the transition from Context C1 to Context C2. Having recognised the situation, the next step consists of computing the appropriate reaction.

4.2 Computation of a Reaction

The reaction is computed in the following way: Identify candidate reactions, select one of them, and apply the selected reaction.

- Identification of the candidate reactions. So far, we plan the following generic reactions:

  – Switch to another platform and/or to different environmental settings (e.g. switch from a portable PC to a PDA as the battery gets low, or turn the light on because the room grows dark).

  – Use another executable code: the current user interface is unable to cover the new context. It can't mould itself to the new situation and, in the meantime, preserve usability.

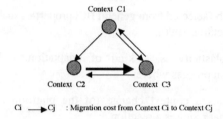

Context C1

Context C2   Context C3

Ci ——▶Cj   : Migration cost from Context Ci to Context Cj

Figure 4: Graphical representation of migration costs between contexts. An arrow denotes the existence of a transition between two contexts. The thicker the arrow, the costlier is the transition.

- Adapt the user interface but keep the same executable code (e.g. switching from Figure 2a to Figure 2b1 when the screen gets too cluttered).

- Execute specific tasks such as turning the heat on. In this case, adaptation does not modify the presentation of the user interface, but it may impact the dialogue sequence.

- Selection of a candidate reaction according to an acceptable migration cost. Every reaction has a migration cost that expresses the effort the system and/or the user must put into this particular reaction. The effort is measured as a combination of criteria selected in the early phase of the development process. Figure 4 shows a graphical representation of migration costs between multiple contexts. An arrow denotes a potential transition. The thickness of an arrow expresses the cost. In the example of Figure 4, it is cheaper to switch from C1 to C2 than to migrate from C2 to C3. There is a potential transition from C1 to C2, but the reverse is impossible.

- The selected reaction is now applied.

4.3   *Execution of the Reaction*

The execution of the reaction consists of a prologue, the execution *per se*, and an epilogue:

- The prologue prepares the reaction. The current task is completed, suspended, or aborted; the execution context is saved (such as the specification of the temperature under modification); if not ready for use, the new version of the user interface is produced on the fly (e.g. a new presentation, a new dialogue sequence, etc.).

- The execution of the reaction corresponds to the commutation to the new version (e.g. the new presentation, the new dialogue sequence, or the execution of a specific task).

- The epilogue closes the reaction. It includes the restoration of the execution context (e.g. temperature settings, resuming of the suspended task).

Each one of the above steps is handled by the system, by the user, or by a cooperation of both. A step occurs on the fly or offline. When a step is performed offline, subsequent steps are also performed offline. Transition between steps means transition between states. Transition between states has been analysed since the early developments of HCI. Norman's evaluation gap, Mackinlay et al.'s (1991) use of graphical animation for transferring cognitive load to the perceptual level, the notion of visual discontinuity (Gram & Cockton, 1996) etc., have all demonstrated the importance of transitions. A transition between two platforms, between executable codes, between user interfaces, etc. is therefore a crucial point that deserves specific research.

The process described so far applies whether the user, the system or a combination of both performs adaptation. In the rest of the paper, we concentrate the discussion on system-handled adaptation. For the reaction to be automatic, we suggest the implementation of the following concepts and mechanisms:

- The concept of a plasticity domain to identify the contexts a particular user interface is able to cover.

- An evolution model that specifies reactions to context changes.

- A context supervisor for handling adaptation.

These issues are discussed next in more detail.

4.4   Plasticity Domain and Plasticity Threshold

As defined above, a plastic user interface is able to adapt to different contexts of use while preserving usability. Figure 5 makes explicit the association of a platform with an environment to define a context of use. Given a particular application, the platforms and environments envisioned for this system are ranked against criteria computed from their attributes. For example, screen size, computational power and communication bandwidth, are typical attributes of the platforms planned for the EDF control system. Using these attributes, a PC would be ranked lower than a PDA since it imposes fewer constraints on the user interface. Similarly an environment with no noise would be ranked lower than an open area such as a street if speech recognition is planned as an interaction technique. Then, as shown in Figure 5:

- the *plasticity domain* of a user interface is the surface formed by all couples 'platform/environment' that this user interface is able to accommodate;

- the boundary of this surface defines the *plasticity threshold* of the user interface; and

- a *plasticity discontinuity* occurs when a change of context lies beyond this boundary

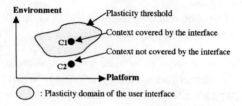

Figure 5: Context coverage and plasticity threshold of a user interface.

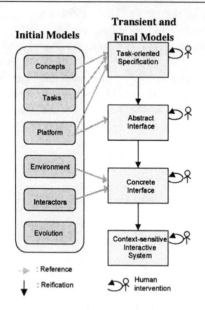

Figure 6: Development process of plastic user interfaces (Calvary et al., to appear).

For example, in Figure 5, Context C1 is covered by the user interface whereas Context C2 is outside its plasticity domain.

The model-based approach we apply for the development process of plastic user interfaces provides a sound framework for identifying the plasticity domain of a particular user interface. As shown in Figure 6, our framework for the development of plastic user interfaces:

- builds upon known models such as the concepts and the task models; and

- introduces new models that have been overlooked or ignored to convey contexts of use: the platform, the interactors, the environment and the evolution models.

These models, which serve as input descriptions to the development process, are called 'initial'. The process uses a combination of reification (vertical transformation shown in the picture) and translation (horizontal transformation not shown in the picture) to transform the initial models into transient models (i.e. the task-oriented description, the abstract and the concrete interfaces) until the final context-sensitive interactive system is produced.

The initial models can be referenced at any stage of the reification (translation) process. Delaying the reference to context models (i.e. the platform, environment, and interactors model) at later stages, results in a larger plasticity domain.

The evolution model, which is an initial model, has a specific role in the adaptation process. We describe it next.

4.5   *The Evolution Model*

The evolution model specifies the reaction to be applied when the context changes. For every triggering condition, the designer may specify a prologue, a reaction, and an epilogue. For example:

- When connecting to an Ethernet Network (triggering condition), set the system in 'Office' mode (reaction).

- When memory is tight, save the state of the running applications as well as the state of the working documents (prologue), reboot the system (reaction) then re-open the working documents (epilogue).

Prologues and epilogues are good locations for specifying transitions that have been tested to alleviate discontinuities between context changes. As mentioned above, the design of *articulatory user interfaces*, that is, portions of user interfaces dedicated to transitions between nominal situations, is an open issue.

The specifications of the prologue, as well as of the reaction and the epilogue, are optional:

- If no prologue is specified, no task is executed before the reaction.

- Similarly, if no epilogue is specified, no task is executed after the reaction *per se.*

- If no reaction is specified, the system computes a reaction depending on the case at hand (cf. Figure 7).

In Figure 7, consider Transition C1→C2 and the four possible situations:

- Case a: C1 and C2 belong to the plasticity domain of the current user interface. As a result, the current user interface is plastic enough to cover the new situation.

- Cases b and c: C1 and C2 belong to different plasticity domains. The current user interface does not apply any more. The set of user interfaces that cover C2 must be identified. In b there is one such candidate whereas in c and c' we observe multiple target user interfaces, including the current user interface (cf. c').

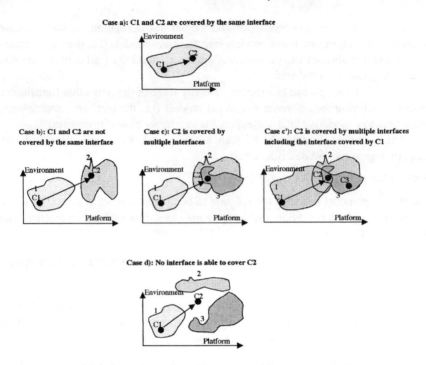

Figure 7: Four situations when migrating between contexts. In a) and c'), the current user interface remains valid; in b) and c) the user interface must be changed; in d) no user interface is able to cover the new context. In c) and c'), criteria must be used to decide between multiple target user interfaces.

- Case d: C2 is not covered by any user interface. The user's task is degraded, nay impossible to perform.

When the new context is supported by multiple user interfaces (cases c and c'), criteria such as migration costs, must be brought to bear to guide the selection process. Case c' deserves additional comments: although the current user interface remains valid for C2, the adaptation process may decide to switch to a different user interface (e.g. that of C3) by anticipating further context transitions. Anticipation can be based on a history mechanism that records context transitions along with their migration costs as the user runs the system across multiple sessions. Considering the transition C1→C2 with Figure 7c', the target user interface may be selected according to the following rule: if the history mechanism indicates that the user is very likely to switch from C2 to C3, and if the migration cost from C2 to C3 is known to be high (as in Figure 4), and if there exists a target user interface U that covers both C2 and C3, then it is sensible to choose U when switching from C1 to C2.

In practice, the evolution model is not necessarily implemented as a centralised process. Instead, it may be distributed among the various user interfaces designed for the interactive system.

Our adaptation process structures the solution space for the problem of adapting user interfaces to context changes. In this space, a number of researchers are concerned with the definition of the notion of context (Dey & Abowd, 2000; Salber & Abowd, 1998). Others are developing new sensing devices such as the Smart Floor (Orr & Abowd, 2000), smart localisers (Harter et al., 1999) and audio sensors (Clarkson et al., 1998) while software architecture models are being devised for capturing context at various levels of abstraction (Dey et al., 1999; Salber et al., 1999; Schmidt et al., 1999). Based on Salber's work (Salber et al., 1999), we are developing a programming model for capturing the context in terms of *contextors* (Rey, 2001). In the following section, we address the detection of context changes using a probe.

5 The Probe: a Software Mechanism for Detecting Context Changes

We have implemented a probe for automatically detecting deviations in user's performance and system properties (Calvary, 1998). This probe is part of CatchIt (Critic-based Automatic and Transparent tool for Computer–Human Interaction Testing) that combines both predictive and experimental approaches to usability testing. We are re-using the principles and mechanism of the CatchIt probe to detect context changes.

5.1 The CatchIt Probe

As a predictive tool, CatchIt verifies that general system properties such as observability, are satisfied by the system. As an experimental tool, CatchIt is able to detect whether the actual user's behaviour conforms to the designers' expectation. For doing so, designers specify *Situation → Reaction* rules that describe users' expected behaviours. For example, *If battery level gets low → switch to another platform*. From the rules specification:

- CatchIt predictively checks the observability of the concepts referred to in the *Situation* description. (In our example, if the battery level is not observable, there is little chance that the user will be aware of the situation).

- When the system is run with subjects, CatchIt experimentally checks whether users perform the expected actions (e.g. switching to another platform as the battery gets low).

In the current implementation of CatchIt, *situations* are expressed as Smalltalk statements. These statements make reference to the software objects that implement the concepts relevant to the situation. For example, *Platform Battery Level IsLow* is a statement that returns a boolean value to denote whether the current power level of the battery is low or sufficient.

Based on the *Situation → Reaction* specification, spy statements are automatically inserted in the source code of the application at the appropriate location. The mechanism is very similar to that of a debugger which modifies the application code without the programmer being aware of it.

Following up our example, suppose that:

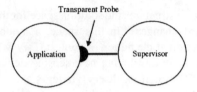

Figure 8: The context probe notifies the context supervisor with context events that may result in context changes.

- Class *Platform* has an attribute *Battery*.

- In turn, Class *Battery* has an attribute *Level*.

- Method *IsLow* of the class *Battery* compares *Level* with a class variable *Threshold*.

From the rule *Platform Battery Level IsLow → switch to another platform*, CatchIt is aware that Object *Level* of the battery must be traced. As a result, every method of the source code that has write access to a *Level* object is modified. Typically, write access methods include initialisation methods (*initialise* and *initialiseWith: aBattery*) and methods that modify an object attribute (for example *setLevel: anInteger* of the class *Battery*).

Spy statements, which are inserted at the very end of every write access method of traced objects, divert code execution and send trace events to a supervisor. A trace event contains the type of the write access method (i.e. creation, modification, or destruction), the method name being diverted and the traced object. In turn, the supervisor takes the appropriate action based on the *reaction* parts of the description rules.

Although CatchIt is intended for usability testing, the probe mechanism applies to the detection of context changes. Figure 8 illustrates the principle of the context probe.

5.2 The Probe for Detecting Context Changes

In the following discussion, we suppose that:

- Designers have modelled the context of use in terms of objects that denote the platform as well as the environment characteristics for the system at hand.

- Context is sensed and modelled as software objects at the appropriate level of abstraction as in (Salber et al., 1999).

As in CatchIt, write access methods to context objects are automatically augmented with spy statements that notify the context supervisor with context events (cf Figure 9). On receiving an event context, the supervisor infers the prologue, the reaction and the epilogue either:

- from the evolution model, when it exists; and/or

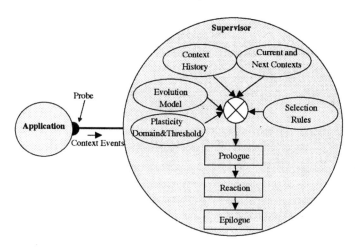

Figure 9: The adaptation process to context changes based on a transparent probe mechanism.

- from the plasticity domain of the current user interface coupled with selection rules and the history of previous contexts.

The supervisor then executes the selected prologue, the reaction and the epilogue. The context probe for plastic user interfaces is under implementation in Java using a *Listener* based approach.

6 Conclusion

This article extends our ongoing work on user interface plasticity. It focuses on the adaptation process and proposes a software mechanism that fits the general framework we are experimenting with for the development of plastic user interfaces. We show how adaptation can be supported at run time by a context supervisor coupled with a transparent context probe that automatically detects context changes. Adaptation is computed by the supervisor based on an evolution model and on the notions of plasticity domain, plasticity threshold and migration costs.

This work leaves opened a large number of issues including recommendations and heuristics for ranking environments and platforms. These are prerequisites for the computation of the plasticity domain and the plasticity threshold of a particular design solution. More importantly, research needs to be deployed in a systematic way to address seamless transitions between contexts.

Acknowledgement

This work has been supported by EDF, France.

References

Abowd, G., Atkeson, C. G., Hong, J., Long, S., Kooper, R. & Pinkerton, M. (1996), Cyberguide: A Mobile Context-aware Tour Guide, Technical Report GIT-GVU-96-27, GVU.

Anabuki, M., Kabuka, H., Yamamoto, H. & Tamura, H. (2000), Welbo: An Embodied Conversational Agent Living in Mixed Reality Space, Videos of the 2000 Conference on Human Factors in Computing Systems (CHI'2000).

Bérard, F., Coutaz, J. & Crowley, J. (2000), Le tableau Magique : Un Outil pour l'Activité de Réflexion, *in* D. L. Scapin & E. Vergisson (eds.), *Actes de la Conférence ErgoIHM'2000*, CRT ILS & ESTIA, pp.33–40.

Calvary, G. (1998), Proactivité et Réactivité: de l'Assignation à la Complémentarité en Conception et Evaluation d'Interfaces Homme–Machine, PhD thesis, Université Joseph-Fourier-Grenoble I, France.

Calvary, G., Coutaz, J. & Thevenin, D. (to appear), A Unifying Reference Framework for the Development of Plastic User Interfaces, *in* R. Little & L. Nigay (eds.), *Proceedings of the 2001 Engineering of Human–Computer Interaction Conference (EHCI'2001)*, Lecture Notes in Computer Science, Springer-Verlag.

Clarkson, B., Sawhney, N. & Pentland, A. (1998), Auditory Context Awareness via Wearable Computing, *in* M. Turk (ed.), *Proceedings of the 1998 Workshop on Perceptual User Interfaces (PUI'98)*, pp.37–42. http://www.cs.ucsb.edu/PUI/PUIWorkshop98/Proceedings/Proc-Papers.html.

Dey, A. & Abowd, G. (2000), Towards a Better Understanding of Context and Context-awareness, *in* G. Szwillus, T. Turner, M. Atwood, B. Bederson, B. Bomsdorf, E. Churchill, G. Cockton, D. Crow, F. Détienne, D. Gilmore, H.-J. Hofman, C. van der Mast, I. McClelland, D. Murray, P. Palanque, M. A. Sasse, J. Scholtz, A. Sutcliffe & W. Visser (eds.), *Proceedings of the CHI 2000 Workshop on The What, Who, Where, When, Why and How of Context-awareness*, ACM Press, p.371.

Dey, A., Salber, D., Futakawa, M. & Abowd, G. (1999), An Architecture To Support Context-Aware Applications, Technical Report GIT-GVU-99-23, GVU.

Gram, C. & Cockton, G. (1996), *Design Principles for Interactive Software*, Chapman & Hall.

Harter, A., Hopper, A., Steggles, P., Ward, A. & Webster, P. (1999), The Anatomy of a Context-aware Application, *in* T. Imielinksi & H. Korth (eds.), *Proceedings of the Fifth Annual ACM/IEEE International Conference on Mobile Computing and Networking (MobiCom'99)*, ACM Press, pp.59–68.

Lee, J., Su, V., Ren, S. & Ishii, H. (2000), HandSCAPE: A Vectorizing Tape Measure for On-site Measuring Applications, Videos of the 2000 Conference on Human Factors in Computing Systems (CHI'2000).

Mackinlay, J. D., Robertson, G. G. & Card, S. K. (1991), The Perspective Wall: Details and Context Smoothly Integrated, *in* S. P. Robertson, G. M. Olson & J. S. Olson (eds.), *Proceedings of CHI'91: Human Factors in Computing Systems (Reaching through Technology)*, ACM Press, pp.173–9.

Orr, R. & Abowd, G. (2000), The Smart Floor: A Mechanism for Natural User Identification and Tracking, Technical Report GIT-GVU-00-02, GVU.

Rekimoto, J. (2000), Multiple Computer User Interfaces: "Beyond the desktop", Direct Manipulation Environments, Videos of the 2000 Conference on Human Factors in Computing Systems (CHI'2000).

Rey, G. (2001), Le Contexte en Interaction Homme–Machine, Diplome d'Etudes Approfondies (DEA), Université Joseph Fourier–Grenoble I, France.

Salber, D. & Abowd, G. (1998), The Design and Use of a Generic Context Server, *in* M. Turk (ed.), *Proceedings of the 1998 Workshop on Perceptual User Interfaces (PUI'98)*, pp.63–66. http://www.cs.ucsb.edu/PUI/PUIWorkshop98/Proceedings/Proc-Papers.html.

Salber, D., Dey, A. & Abowd, G. (1999), The Context Toolkit: Aiding the Development of Context-enabled Applications, *in* M. G. Williams, M. W. Altom, K. Ehrlich & W. Newman (eds.), *Proceedings of the CHI99 Conference on Human Factors in Computing Systems: The CHI is the Limit*, ACM Press, pp.434–41.

Schilit, B., Adams, N. & Want, R. (1994), Context-aware Computing Applications, *in Proceedings of the IEEE Workshop on Mobile Computing Systems and Applications (WMCSA'94)*, IEEE Computer Society Press, pp.85–90.

Schmidt, A. (2000), "Implicit Human–Computer Interaction through Context", *Personal Technologies* 4(2-3), 191–9. Originally a paper in Brewster, S & Dunlop, M (eds), Proceedings of the 2nd Workshop on Human–Computer Interaction with Mobile Devices, p.23-7, 1999.

Schmidt, A., Aidoo, K. A., Takaluoma, A., Tuomela, U., van Laerhoven, K. & van de Velde, W. (1999), Advanced Interaction in Context, *in* H.-W. Gellersen (ed.), *Proceedings of the 1st International Symposium on Handheld and Ubiquitous Computing (HUC'99)*, Vol. 1707 of *Lecture Notes in Computer Science*, Springer-Verlag, pp.89–101.

Thevenin, D. & Coutaz, J. (1999), Plasticity of User Interfaces: Framework and Research Agenda, *in* A. Sasse & C. Johnson (eds.), *Human–Computer Interaction — INTERACT '99: Proceedings of the Seventh IFIP Conference on Human–Computer Interaction*, Vol. 1, IOS Press, pp.110–7.

Yan, H. & Selker, T. (2000), Context-aware Office Assistant, *in* H. Lieberman (ed.), *Proceedings of 2000 International Conference on Intelligent User Interfaces (IUI 2000)*, ACM Press, pp.276–9.

Computer-supported
Collaborative Working

Eye-Tracking Explorations in Multimedia Communications

J Mullin, A H Anderson, L Smallwood, M Jackson & E Katsavras

Multimedia Communications Group, Department of Psychology, University of Glasgow, 58 Hillhead Street, Glasgow G12 8QB, UK

Tel: *+44 141 330 5424*

Fax: *+44 141 337 1922*

Email: *jim@mcg.glasgow.ac.uk*

Two studies are reported exploring the usefulness of eye-tracking techniques in illuminating computer users' behaviour in conducting collaborative tasks while supported by multimedia communications. We describe how the technology was deployed and the data we derived to explore the use of visual cues in computer-supported collaborative problem solving. Participants made modest use of the video-link to their remote collaborator, devoting most of their visual attention to other onscreen resources. Varying the quality of this video-link did not influence its use. Eye-tracking was found to be a viable and useful evaluation technique in CSCW.

Keywords: multimedia, CSCW, eye-tracking, evaluation, videoconferencing.

1 Introduction

In this paper we report two experimental studies that use eye-tracking to explore participants' behaviour whilst engaged in computer-supported collaborative working (CSCW) supported by multimedia communications. We also report methodological guidelines based on our experience of using a remote eye-tracker in this context. We wished to discover whether eye-tracking, which has been used widely in other disciplines, could be a useful addition to the repertoire of investigative techniques in CSCW.

We considered that eye-tracking had potential benefits in this area of HCI because it had produced unique scientific insights in a range of other disciplines most notably psychology. Eye-tracking has been used to explore a range of cognitive processes in psychological research particularly in reading and perception, see for example (Yarbus, 1967; Just & Carpenter, 1976; Rayner, 1995; Traxler & Pickering, 1996). Researchers in these areas have used eye-tracking devices which restricted the movements of the experimental participants, often via head rests or bite bars and so are not suitable for research which wishes to investigate how people deploy their visual attention when interacting with a collaborator. Other less restrictive forms of eye-tracking utilising helmet mounted devices have been used in psychological research on communication (Tannenhaus et al., 1995).

Although such systems allow the participants to communicate freely, the strange appearance of an individual wearing a full-face helmet device makes this approach unsuitable if collaborating participants are visible to one another especially in real world contexts. Newer less invasive forms of eye-tracking technology have been developed and one of our goals was to explore to what extent such systems could be utilised to explore CSCW supported by multimedia communications technologies. We wished to know if this additional information about users' behaviour would provide useful design insights for the development of future CSCW systems.

In addition to these methodological goals, we had related scientific questions that we wished to address. One salient issue for multimedia systems that are intended to support remote communication and collaboration, is the way in which visual signals are utilised. We wished to investigate how visual signals are used in videoconferencing interactions and how this compared to the way such signals are used in face-to-face interactions.

In face-to-face conversations it is known that a rich variety of visual cues are used to facilitate smooth and effective interaction, (Kendon, 1967; Argyll, 1969). In our own earlier research we have been able to chart a whole range of aspects of the communication process which are altered when speakers do not have access to visual signals. These include the way turn-taking is accomplished, the amount of talk required to complete a shared task, the content of the dialogues and even the articulatory quality of the speech sounds produced (Boyle et al., 1994; Anderson et al., 1997a).

Eye-tracking techniques have been used in earlier HCI research, notably as a new form of interface control, either for users for whom conventional input devices are difficult or in application domains where the user is already heavily engaged in other tasks, for example (Jacob, 1991; Gips et al., 1995; Goldberg & Schryver, 1995). Eye-tracking has also been advocated as a more natural, less effortful form of interacting with the interface, for example (Bolt, 1981; Sibert & Jakob, 2000; Tanriverdi & Jacob, 2000).

There have been a few published studies of using eye-tracking techniques to explore usability issues in HCI. Where they exist, these have generally used short artificial tasks involving an individual user, often using helmet or head mounted eye-trackers, for example (Benel et al., 1991; Aaltonen et al., 1998; Ellis et al., 1998; Zellweger et al., 2000). As recently as CHI 2000, Schnipke & Todd (2000) were reporting on the considerable difficulties they have experienced in eye-tracking even single users engaged in on-screen reading using a head mounted sensor and report they are reverting to a more cumbersome helmet-mounted eye-tracking system. The challenges we faced in using such techniques to explore computer-supported collaborative working seemed formidable.

2   Developing the Eye-tracking Methodology

As our studies were designed to explore video-mediated communication, we had to use an eye-tracking system that neither unduly restricted the natural movements of our participants nor altered their appearance. We used a Remote Eye-tracking Device (RED) manufactured by SMI GmbH (http://www.smi.de/).

The two participants in each trial each sat at approximately 70cm from a 19″ computer screen displaying a window containing task relevant information and displaying a video picture of the other person. Participants wore an unobtrusive headphone/microphone set.

For the participants being eye-tracked, the RED was positioned just below the video monitor. Infrared light was directed at the subject's eye and the reflected radiation received by programmable mirrors in front of the RED camera. The picture of the eye is a highly magnified infrared image with an extremely shallow depth of field. A third computer controlled the mirrors to compensate for mild head movements to physically track the head/eye movements and to receive the resulting eye-position data. The point of regard was calculated as a function of the distance between the centre of the pupil and the corneal reflection. Software was written for the operation of the cooperative computer working environments and to enable the calibration of physical points of regard on the eye-tracked participant's screen with readings received from the RED. A calibration criterion was imposed whereby calibrations conducted at the beginning and end of sessions agreed to within 1.5% degrees of visual angle.

It took much longer than we expected to properly set up the eye-tracker and the testing environment, to check our calibration techniques, and to acquire sufficient dexterity in manipulating the tracker whilst live. Tracking is lost at various times, and, when the RED cannot rediscover the eye position, a human operator who is continually monitoring the operation, must manually put it on track again. It takes acquired skill and experience to do this quickly. In all, 163 extensive testing sessions were run for some 400 hours during preparatory work before we felt sufficiently confident in our techniques to begin recording reportable data. The guidelines reported below are derived from this extensive pilot work and from the recorded experimental sessions which followed.

For some months we were rather pessimistic of getting adequate data from the eye-tracker in the situations which we wanted to explore. For example, we found that one serious problem was movement in the radial plane towards and away from the computer screen by participants. This was particularly important, as the RED cannot compensate for movement in this plane. Coupled with the extremely shallow depth of field of the camera, this meant that even rapid manual adjustment by a practised operator resulted in sessions with too much data loss for adequate analysis. Although

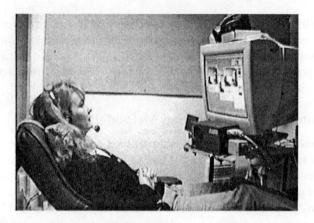

Figure 1: A view of an eye-tracked participant. She is wearing an audio headset. The eye-tracker is the black box below the screen. A video camera sits on top of the screen.

our experimental scenarios required that the subjects be free to move and to express themselves, we eventually found a way of 'naturally' restricting their movement in the radial plane. This involved sitting the subject in a reclining chair with the computer monitor and the eye-tracker cantilevered at a position above their hips. In this position the subject was sitting comfortably but their own weight naturally restricted their movement towards the eye-tracker. Such tactics finally enabled us to acquire reasonable amounts of data from most subjects. A view if the eye-tracked participant is presented in Figure 1.

3 Methodology Guidelines

Based on our experience, we list some indicative guidelines we have derived and which we recommend should be taken into consideration when contemplating eye-tracking in CSCW research:

- Where participants can see one another, eye-tracking devices that cause participants to look strange may influence the communication task and hence such devices should be avoided.

- Using a RED device avoids the problem of causing one participant to look strange to the other participant(s).

- A RED device allows a participant to move relatively naturally whilst still maintaining tracking. However:

- Although an eye-tracked individual can move about to some extent and the device will compensate and follow the head and eye movements, gross movements are difficult to follow and data will be lost.

- If the individual moves significantly to a new position with respect to the viewed scene during the eye-tracked session, then the calibration, and hence the data, may be invalid for some or most of the session. Thus calibration is required at least at the beginning and the end of a session.

- Notwithstanding the foregoing, if the individual moves to a new position for a while, then moves back to the original position, the fact that they moved, and that their data whilst in their new position may be invalid, may not have been noticed. The operator must watch out for this.

- Movement in the radial plane (towards or away from the RED) cannot be automatically dealt with. The depth of focus is only a few centimetres at best. An operator must intervene to re-focus on the fly. This is relatively difficult and, in general, operators must be skilled, as learned pattern recognition and manual dexterity are necessary to restore tracking when the device loses track.

- In order to maintain a natural communication situation or working environment, the eye-tracked participant must be free to move, but contrarily must be restrained in order to get reliable data. Methods must be devised (such as the reclining chair we have described) to 'naturally' restrict movement of the participant. This does not always work to the same extent for all participants.

- We have found that up to 50% of gaze is still lost for many participants in these situations.

- We had to discard between about 20% and 40% of participants' data, as they did not meet the criterion of being successfully tracked for 50% of their gaze.

- Spectacles, contact lenses (especially hard lenses), dark eyebrows, etc. all cause various problems.

- Setting up and calibrating a RED is a time consuming task to begin with. There are many parameters to be manipulated and settings to be chosen. However, researchers can learn to repeat setting-up procedures quickly once these are operational.

- Much raw data is produced which has to be stored and techniques of data interpretation and analysis have to be learned.

4   Study 1

Following our initial 163 equipment testing, calibration and learning sessions, we conducted two experimental studies. In Study 1 we addressed the following questions:

- Can we successfully track the eye movements of users of a video-mediated communication system while they are engaged in problem solving with a remote collaborator?

- Are the recorded eye movements systematic across a sample of users?

- Are the recorded eye movements informative about how users distribute their visual attention during a technologically mediated interaction?

- How often do users look at images of their remote collaborator?

- How does the distribution of eye gaze compare between face-to-face and video-mediated interactions?

4.1   Methodology

Fourteen volunteers were recruited from the student population at the University of Glasgow. They were paid a small fee for participating in the study. They took part in pairs in a collaborative problem-solving task, the Map Task (Brown et al., 1983), which we have used extensively in previous studies of communication. In this task participants both have copies of a schematic map, but they are warned that there may be differences between the two versions of the map, and indeed only some landmarks are shown on both maps. One member of the pair is assigned the role of Instruction Giver, and her copy of the map has a route shown on it. Her task is to instruct her partner (the Instruction Follower) how to draw the route on his copy of the map. Both participants are encouraged to communicate freely to complete the task.

In this study the participants were supported by a high quality videoconference link (image size 145mm× 102mm) which relayed images of their collaborator, these being refreshed over 24 times per second. The copies of the maps were also displayed on screen and the instruction follower used the mouse to draw the route on screen. The participants were placed in rooms on different floors of the laboratory and linked both by video and high quality, full duplex, analogue audio connections.

Each participant took part in two map tasks, swapping between the instruction giving and following roles. The eye gaze of each participant in the instruction giving role was tracked as described above. Three participants' data were discarded due to loss of eye-tracking data. Sessions were discarded unless the participants' gaze was onscreen and tracked for more than 50% of the time. All interactions were tape-recorded and then transcribed, checked and the lengths of interactions in terms of words, turns and words per turn were calculated. Figure 2 illustrates a typical screen display, incorporating the onscreen map and a video window of one participant. The screen display in this case has been overlaid with data captured from the eye-tracker.

4.2   Results

Three areas of the screen were defined for the analysis of eye gaze, the onscreen map, the videoconference window where the collaborator's image as displayed, and a blank area of similar size. The gaze analyses were conducted in several ways. The percentage of time spent looking at the screen was subdivided by screen location and by different lengths of fixations.

There are a priori reasons for electing to analyse the data differentially according to fixation length. A participant may glance at video picture of their remote collaborator to briefly check that the other person is actually present (e.g. the other may have been quiet for some time). They may wish to briefly check what the other person is doing at the time (e.g. tracing the route on the map). Alternatively,

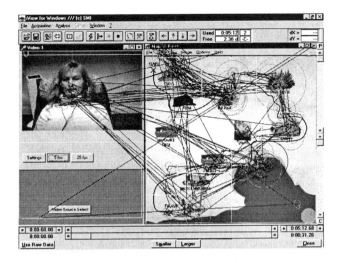

Figure 2: Screen-shot of map task with overlaid data captured from the eye-tracker.

Fixation Length	Map	Video Window	Blank Area
20–80ms	76.3	14.9	4.4
100–380ms	83.3	11.4	0.0
Over 400ms	76.8	19.9	0.0
Overall Average	78.8	15.4	1.4

Table 1: Instruction Givers' gaze by screen location as a percentage of time spent looking at the screen.

they might wish to scrutinise in detail the video image of the other participant at a point of misunderstanding in their dialogue in order to attempt to pick up non-verbal clues that could aid their understanding. These different monitoring behaviours might optimally demand different length gazes. Accordingly the data were split into different fixation lengths in order to explore the possibility that the video picture of the other participant might be used more for one or other type of monitoring behaviour.

These data are shown in Table 1. A small amount of data is lost due to blinks etc. so the figures for each length of gaze do not quite total 100%.

Separate Analyses of Variance were conducted on these data for each fixation length. Each analysis revealed a similar pattern of results, with location always being a significant main effect, and pair wise comparison showing each location differed significantly from the others. (Main effects for short, medium and longest gaze lengths were $F(2,18) = 226.7, 283.5, 272.6$, respectively, $p < 0.01$ for all, with $p < 0.05$ for all pair wise comparisons). There were no other significant main effects or interactions.

These analyses provided clear answers to our initial experimental hypotheses. Firstly patterns of eye gaze can be reliably tracked using non-restrictive techniques for the majority of computer users even whilst they are engaged in computer-supported collaborative working. Secondly the patterns of eye gaze are sufficiently consistent across different users to provide useful information about how computer users distribute their attention during a technologically mediated interaction.

The data loss we suffered in this experiment (21% of participants' sessions discarded) is at least as good as that reported in recent HCI eye-tracking studies which use much less demanding tasks and techniques. Studies which report such data have recorded data losses ranging from 23% (Tanriverdi & Jacob, 2000), 25% (Zellweger et al., 2000), 38% (Sibert & Jacob, 2000) to 62%, (Schnipke & Todd, 2000).

Computer users' visual attention reflects a distribution probably based on task salience and the relative importance of competing information spaces to these tasks. Virtually no time is spent looking at a non-informative blank area, and the majority of time is devoted to the onscreen map, which is the stimulus for the instructions the eye-tracked participant has to produce. A smaller but still noticeable proportion of about 10–20% of the time is spent looking at the image of the collaborator, presumably monitoring their reactions or listening to their spoken contributions to the dialogue. There was no evidence to suggest that participants differentially gazed for longer or shorter times at any particular area of the screen.

4.3   Comparing Eye-Gaze in Video-Mediated and Face-to-Face Interactions

But how does this behaviour compare to what occurs in face-to-face interactions? In particular how frequently do instruction givers look at their partners? To answer that question we turned to our existing HCRC Map Task Corpus. This consists of face-to-face interactions between pairs of participants completing the map task. These have been recorded, transcribed and for a videotaped sub sample, laboriously hand coded for participants' gaze patterns with associated time stampings. A comparable subset of face-to-face dialogues (N = 14) were extracted and compared to our video-mediated interactions.

The two sets of dialogues were compared in terms of task performance (as measured by the accuracy of the completed maps), the lengths of the dialogues in words, turns and words per turn. No significant differences were found. We therefore went on to compare gaze behaviour in the two data sets. This was done in three ways. First we compared the average percentage of time spent by the instruction giver looking at their partner, then the number of times the instruction giver glanced at their partner. Finally we compared the number of glances as a proportion of the length of each dialogue: that is the mean number of glances per turn of speaking were calculated. These data are shown in Table 2.

Separate independent t-tests were conducted for each analysis. These showed that instruction givers spent a significantly greater percentage of their time looking at their partners in face-to-face interactions than in video-mediated interactions ($t(23) = 2.47$, $p < 0.05$), but the frequency and proportion of glances did not differ significantly between the different communicative contexts.

Communication Medium	Face-to-face	Video-Mediated
Mean percentage of time per dialogue Instruction Giver looks at Instruction Follower	22.6	14.7
Mean number of glances per dialogue by Instruction Giver at Instruction Follower	50.3	63.0
Mean number of glances per turn by Instruction Giver at Instruction Follower	0.42	0.6

Table 2: A comparison of gaze behaviour in face-to-face and video-mediated interactions.

4.4 Discussion

In our earlier research on the role of visual signals in face-to-face communication (Boyle et al., 1994; Anderson et al., 1997a) we highlighted the fact that, although visual signals do have a wide range of impacts on the process of communication, the extent to which the visual channel is exploited in face-to-face interactions is relatively modest. In face-to-face interaction particularly in contexts such as a collaborative problem-solving task with other relevant visual material to be monitored, interlocutors do not spend the majority of their time looking at one another. Rather they glance at one another occasionally to monitor their partners' understanding or to signal their own communicative difficulties.

In video-mediated interactions the quality and timeliness of the visual information which is transmitted can vary widely. In the present study, the visual signal is frequently updated, and the audio signal is instantaneous. There should be few of the problems associated with low frame rate video systems where the visual signal is often not synchronised with the audio signal or both are delayed because of bandwidth restrictions. Nevertheless the quality of the visual information which can be picked up from a relatively small on-screen video window is inevitably less than that available in a face-to-face interaction.

Our data on gaze behaviour show no evidence that computer users attempt to compensate for these limitations. Indeed the data suggest that instruction givers spend less time monitoring the visual link to their collaborators than they do in face-to-face interactions. This may be because the quality of the visual information is inferior and so less useful. Alternatively, it may be because the increased cognitive demands or unfamiliarity of communicating via a remote communication system mean that they feel less able to devote time to what seems a less critical component of the task than studying the map in order to formulate their next instruction.

5 Study 2

In this study we wished to explore the behaviour of computer users engaged in a more realistic form of computer-supported collaborative problem-solving. We also wished to explore how gaze was distributed when there was a richer set of task relevant onscreen resources and when the videoconference link was delivered at different quality levels. Study 2 addressed the following questions:

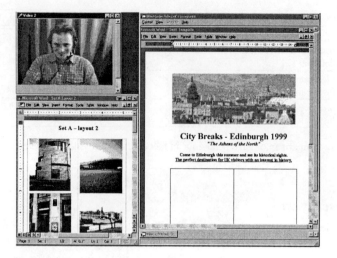

Figure 3: Screen-shot of poster design task.

- Are patterns of onscreen gaze similar for lab-based and realistic collaborative problem-solving?

- As the number of onscreen resources increase does the use of a videoconference link decrease?

- Do users look more at videoconference links delivered at higher levels of quality?

5.1 Methodology

Nineteen volunteers were recruited from students at the University of Glasgow and paid a small fee for participating. They took part in a collaborative design task with a confederate who was unfamiliar with the experimental hypotheses being explored. Their task was to design a tourist poster for the city of Edinburgh. A prize was offered for the best poster. On-screen, participants had a poster shell with blank areas into which they had to place two selected photographs for which they had to type short captions (Figure 3). They had an array of eight on-screen photographs from which to make a selection.

Each participant took part in two versions of the task, once designing a poster for tourists with an interest in history, once for tourists with an interest in the arts. A separate set of photographs was made available for each task. Participants were encouraged to communicate freely with their collaborator and incentives were offered to individual participants to advocate particular options.

The equipment was the same as in Study 1. In Study 2 participants undertook one of their tasks supported by a videoconference link in which the image refreshed, as in Study 1, at over 24 frames a second. In their other task the video image

Video Quality	Video Window	Photo Array	Poster Template
25fps	7.0	32.2	53.2
5fps	8.5	32.2	51.9

Table 3: Participants' gaze by screen location for each frame rate as a % of time spent looking at the screen, over all fixation lengths.

---

refreshed at only 5 frames a second. The order of tasks and quality levels was counterbalanced.

The criteria for retaining or discarding an eye-tracked session were the same as in Study 1. In total, 19 sessions were run with 7 sessions being discarded (36.8%).

5.2 Results

Eye gaze was analysed as in Study 1, with the percentage of subjects' gaze that was directed at either the videoconference window, the window containing the array of photographs and the window containing the poster template. This was calculated for each subject in both frame rate conditions. Table 3 shows the mean percentage of recorded gaze that was directed at each location in each frame rate condition. A small amount of data is lost due to blinks etc. so these figures do not quite total 100%.

Analysis of Variance was performed on the means for each participant. Video quality (25fps & 5fps) and screen location (Video Window, Photo Array & Poster Template) were repeated measures factors. There was no main effect or interactions with video quality ($F < 1$ for all). The main effect of location was significant with each area differing significantly from the others ($p < 0.05$ for all).

In addition to looking at the raw percentage of subjects' gaze directed at the video window, the percentages of gaze that were composed of fixations of different lengths were calculated for each subject to see if the frame rate manipulation affected the lengths of subjects' fixations on the video window. Analysis of these data again showed no significant effects of video quality ($F < 1$).

As well as the percentage of gaze at each location, the total number of glances that subjects made towards the video window in each condition was recorded for each session. Again no significant effects of video quality were found.

5.3 Discussion

From the results we can see that the distribution of gaze is broadly similar to Study 1: onscreen task materials, the map or the poster components, receive the great majority of the participants' visual attention. The richer set of onscreen resources in Study 2, however does seem to impact on the extent to which the participants attended to the video link to their remote collaborator, resulting in even more modest levels of gaze directed to the videoconference window.

There were no observed frame rate effects on participants' gaze behaviour. There were no significant effects of video frame rate on either the total amount of time looked at the video window, the rate at which they looked or in the duration of each glance. Altering the quality of the videoconference link does not seem to affect the frequency with which users will utilise this resource.

6   Conclusion

We feel we have been successful in demonstrating the value of a new form of analysis for exploring computer-supported collaborative working. The methodology is not without its difficulties and we set ourselves particularly difficult challenges by wishing to track computer users for quite lengthy periods of time (up to quarter of an hour in a single trial) while engaged in realistic collaborative tasks. While data loss does occur in quite a substantial proportion of sessions, we nevertheless feel we have demonstrated this is a feasible and valuable additional HCI evaluation technique.

As an illustration of how eye-gaze data can complement other more traditional HCI evaluation techniques we reflected on some of our own recent research. In a previous study we compared the impact on users of multimedia interfaces of different levels of quality of videoconference links, along with a variety of other onscreen resources. We found that markedly different levels of video quality (25 frames per second vs. 5 frames per second) which users could reliably discriminate in isolation, had no significant impacts on their subjective quality ratings in a questionnaire study, (Anderson et al., 2000). The patterns of eye gaze that we have reported in the present studies could explain this surprising finding. The fairly infrequent glances that we record at videoconference windows suggest different quality levels may have little impact on users of such multi-component interfaces.

We also believe these studies have produced some useful scientific insights. We have unambiguous evidence on which components of a multimedia interface are likely to attract most of the users' attention and how visual attention compares in face-to-face and video-mediated interactions. The data from these two studies support the view that, in collaborative problem solving of a variety of kinds, participants make very modest use of video images of their remote collaborator.

There have been very few previous studies of computer users' eye gaze, partly because of the difficulties of conducting such research if eye-tracking technologies are not used. As one part of their investigations of video mediated interactions, Doherty-Sneddon et al. (1997) conducted a small scale analysis of eye-gaze in face-to-face and video mediated interactions. They found rather surprisingly that an apparently high quality video link system, which provided life-size images that allowed users to have direct eye-contact with their remote collaborator, was also found to have unforeseen impacts on communication. Users of this system needed to exchange significantly more talk to complete their task successfully.

One possible explanation of this effect was that, because the novelty of life size images looking the user directly in the eye elicited very substantial amounts of gaze between the interlocutors, this might well have interfered with speech planning. The distracting effect of high levels of interlocutor gaze has been noted in several studies of face-to-face interaction, for example (Beattie, 1981; Ellyson et al., 1981). The smaller more conventional, on-screen video images used in the current studies did not seem to have this distracting effect.

In the present studies, while the visual information relayed via the video conference link was not as rich as that available in face-to-face interaction, it may be adequate for the requirements of interlocutors engaged in collaborative problem solving. Very large differences in quality of computer presented visual information — exceptionally life-like or accompanied by delayed audio signals, can cause impacts on users even in problem-solving collaborations, (Anderson et al., 1997b). The results of the present studies suggest however that desktop on-screen videoconference images, despite their limitations, and over a reasonably wide range of levels of service quality, can offer adequate visual information for the modest demands that collaborative problem solvers require.

The explanation of why these demands are modest can be partly illuminated by some of our earlier research on face-to-face collaborative problem solving. We deduced from very detailed content and gaze analysis of face-to-face interactions, that the main function of instruction givers' gaze in these kinds of problem-solving dialogues, is that of monitoring that a partner appears to understand an instruction and is acting up on it. The video images relayed in the present study may well be adequate for such purposes.

Supporting evidence for this view comes from a separate study we recently conducted with a very similar quality video system, where remote collaborators achieved very good levels of task success with very smooth and efficient dialogues which were comparable with those achieved in face-to-face interactions (Anderson et al., 1999).

There may be other kinds of remote tasks, notably as suggested by early research by Morley & Stephenson (1969), and Short et al. (1976), where a larger social component is involved, which might result in different patterns of eye-gaze. Such tasks might include interviewing, counselling or negotiating, where there could be a requirement for higher levels of visual information about the interlocuter. Investigations of possible task differences in visual attention at the interface are in progress in our eye-tracking lab.

The eye-tracking data have design implications for multimedia service providers. For complex computer-supported collaborative tasks, the onscreen materials that support task completion are by far the most relevant aspects of the interface. As videoconference windows for such tasks seem to be used modestly by users there may be little requirement for delivery at high frame rates.

Acknowledgements

This research was supported by a ROPA award from the UK Economic and Social Research Council (No.R022250151) to AH Anderson and J Mullin.

Matthew Jackson's PhD is supported by UK Engineering and Physical Sciences Research Council award (No.GR/M24462) under the Multimedia Network Applications Programme to A H Anderson and J Mullin.

References

Aaltonen, A., Hyrskykari, A. & Räihä, K.-J. (1998), 101 Spots, or How Do Users Read Menus?, *in* C.-M. Karat, A. Lund, J. Coutaz & J. Karat (eds.), *Proceedings of CHI'98: Human Factors in Computing Systems*, ACM Press, pp.132–9.

Anderson, A. H., Bard, E. G., Sotillo, C., Newlands, A. & Doherty-Sneddon, G. (1997a), "Limited Visual Control of the Intelligibility of Speech in Face-to-face Dialogue", *Perception and Psychophysics* **59**(4), 580–92.

Anderson, A. H., Mullin, J., Katsavras, E., McEwan, R., Grattan, E., Brundell, P. & O'Malley, C. (1999), Multimediating Multiparty Interactions, *in* A. Sasse & C. Johnson (eds.), *Human–Computer Interaction — INTERACT '99: Proceedings of the Seventh IFIP Conference on Human–Computer Interaction*, Vol. 1, IOS Press, pp.313–20.

Anderson, A. H., O'Malley, C., Doherty-Sneddon, G., Langton, S., Newlands, A., Mullin, J., Fleming, A. M. & Van der Velden, J. (1997b), The Impact of VMC on Collaborate Problem-solving, *in* K. Finn, A. Sellen & S. Wilbur (eds.), *Video Mediated Communication*, Lawrence Erlbaum Associates, pp.133–55.

Anderson, A. H., Smallwood, L., MacDonald, R., Mullin, J., Fleming, A. M. & O'Malley, O. (2000), "Video Data and Video Links in Mediated Communication: What Do Users Value", *International Journal of Human–Computer Studies* **52**(1), 165–87.

Argyll, M. (1969), *Social Interaction*, Tavistock Publications.

Beattie, G. (1981), "The Regulation of Speaker Turns in Face-to-face Conversation: Some Implications for Conversation", *Semiotica* **34**(1–2), 55–70.

Benel, D. C. R., Ottens, D. & Horst, R. (1991), Use of an Eye-tracking System in the Usability Laboratory, *in Proceedings of the Human Factors and Ergonomics Society 35th Annual Meeting*, Human Factors and Ergonomics Society, pp.461–5.

Bolt, R. (1981), "Gaze Orchestrated Dynamic Windows", *Computer Graphics* **15**(3), 109–19.

Boyle, E., Anderson, A. H. & Newlands, A. (1994), "The Effects of Eye Contact on Dialogue and Performance in a Cooperative Problem Solving Task", *Language and Speech* **37**(1), 1–20.

Brown, G., Anderson, A. H., Shillcock, R. & Yule, G. (1983), *Teaching Talk: Strategies for Production and Assessment*, Cambridge University Press.

Doherty-Sneddon, G., Anderson, A. H., O'Malley, C., Langton, S., Garrod, S. & Bruce, V. (1997), "Face-to-face Interaction and Video Mediated Communication: A Comparison of Dialogue Structure and Task Performance", *Journal of Experimental Psychology: Applied* **3**(2), 105–25.

Ellis, S., Candrea, R., Misner, J., Craig, S., Lankford, C. & Hutchinson, T. (1998), Windows to the Soul? What Eye Movements Tell Us about Software Usability, *in Proceedings of the Usability Professionals' Association 7th Annual Conference*, Usability Professionals' Association, pp.151–6.

Ellyson, S., Dovidio, J. & Corson, R. (1981), "Visual Differences in Females as a Function of Self-perceived Expertise", *Journal of Non-verbal Behaviour* **5**(3), 164–71.

Gips, J., Oliviera, P. & Tetchi, J. (1995), Direct Control of the Computer through Electrodes Placed Around the Eyes, *in* Y. Anzai, K. Ogawa & H. Mori (eds.), *Proceedings of the 6th International Conference on Human–Computer Interaction (HCI International '95)*, Elsevier Science, pp.630–5.

Goldberg, J. & Schryver, J. (1995), Eye-gaze Determination of User Intention at the Computer Interface, *in* J. Findlay, R. Walker & R. Kentridge (eds.), *Eye Movement Research: Mechanisms, Processes and Applications*, Elsevier Science, pp.491–502.

Jacob, R. J. K. (1991), "The Use of Eye Movements in Human–Computer Interaction Techniques: What You Look At is What You Get", *ACM Transactions on Office Information Systems* **9**(3), 152–69.

Just, M. A. & Carpenter, P. A. (1976), "Eye Fixations and Cognitive Processes", *Cognitive Psychology* **8**(4), 441–80.

Kendon, A. (1967), "Some Functions of Gaze Direction in Social Interaction", *Acta Psychologica* **32**, 1–25.

Morley, I. & Stephenson, G. (1969), "Interpersonal and Interparty Exchange: A Laboratory Simulation of an Industrial Negotiation at Plant Level", *British Journal of Psychology* **60**(4), 543–5.

Rayner, K. (1995), Eye Movements and Cognitive Processes in Reading, Visual Search and Scene Perception, *in* J. Findlay, R. Walker & R. Kentridge (eds.), *Eye Movement Research: Mechanisms, Processes and Applications*, Elsevier Science, pp.3–22.

Schnipke, S. & Todd, M. (2000), Trials and Tribulations of Using an Eye-tracking System, *in* G. Szwillus, T. Turner, M. Atwood, B. Bederson, B. Bomsdorf, E. Churchill, G. Cockton, D. Crow, F. Détienne, D. Gilmore, H.-J. Hofman, C. van der Mast, I. McClelland, D. Murray, P. Palanque, M. A. Sasse, J. Scholtz, A. Sutcliffe & W. Visser (eds.), *Companion Proceedings of CHI2000: Human Factors in Computing Systems (CHI2000 Conference Companion)*, ACM Press, pp.273–4.

Short, J., Williams, E. & Christie, B. (1976), *The Social Psychology of Telecommunications*, John Wiley & Sons.

Sibert, L. & Jakob, R. (2000), Evaluation of Eyegaze Interaction, *in* T. Turner, G. Szwillus, M. Czerwinski & F. Paternò (eds.), *Proceedings of the CHI2000 Conference on Human Factors in Computing Systems*, CHI Letters **2**(1), ACM Press, pp.281–8.

Sibert, L. E. & Jacob, R. J. K. (2000), Evaluation of Eye Gaze Interaction, *in* T. Turner, G. Szwillus, M. Czerwinski & F. Paternò (eds.), *Proceedings of the CHI2000 Conference on Human Factors in Computing Systems*, CHI Letters **2**(1), ACM Press, pp.282–8.

Tannenhaus, M., Spivey-Knowlton, M., Eberhard, K. & Sedivy, J. (1995), "Integration of Visual and Linguistic Information in Spoken Language Comprehension", *Science* **268**, 1632–1634.

Tanriverdi, V. & Jacob, R. (2000), Interacting with Eye Movements in Virtual Environments, *in* T. Turner, G. Szwillus, M. Czerwinski & F. Paternò (eds.), *Proceedings of the CHI2000 Conference on Human Factors in Computing Systems*, CHI Letters **2**(1), ACM Press, pp.265–71.

Traxler, M. & Pickering, M. (1996), "Plausibility and the Processing of Unbounded Dependencies: An eye-Tracking study", *Journal of Memory and Language* **35**(3), 454–75.

Yarbus, A. (1967), Eye Movements during Perception of Complex Objects, *in* L. A. Riggs (ed.), *Eye Movements and Vision*, Plenum Press, pp.171–96.

Zellweger, P., Regli, S., Mackinley, J. & Chang, B. (2000), The Impact of Fluid Documents on Reading and Browsing: An Observational Study, *in* T. Turner, G. Szwillus, M. Czerwinski & F. Paternò (eds.), *Proceedings of the CHI2000 Conference on Human Factors in Computing Systems, CHI Letters* **2**(1), ACM Press, pp.247–55.

Rich Interaction in the Context of Networked Virtual Environments — Experiences Gained from the Multi-player Games Domain

Tony Manninen

Department of Information Processing Science, University of Oulu, PO Box 3000, 90014 Oulun Yliopisto, Finland
Email: *tony.manninen@oulu.fi*

In order to promote richer interaction within Networked Virtual Environment applications, the ambiguous and highly subjective meanings assigned to the word "interaction" require explicit description. The aim of this work is to use ethnographical and constructivist approaches applied to multi-player 3D games domain in order to create a tentative taxonomy and corresponding hierarchical model of interaction in the context of Networked Virtual Environments. The results can be considered as the first step of research towards understanding and innovatively applying the concept of rich interaction. The primary contribution of the models and findings to the people working in areas of human–computer interaction, virtual environments, digital media, and human behaviour is a set of boundaries that direct the discussion and work to the aspects requiring further research.

Keywords: virtual environment, behaviour, action, taxonomy, multi-player games, simulation.

1 Introduction

The aim of this paper is to provide a tentative taxonomy and corresponding hierarchical model of interaction in the context of Networked Virtual Environments (Net-VE). Due to the ambiguous and highly subjective meanings assigned to the word 'interaction', this paper offers one specifically defined scope that will be used as the basis for further research to be conducted in this field. This author believes that the theories and use of virtual environments could be expanded and enhanced if researchers and practitioners were to target their focus towards interactions occurring inside the computerised environments.

According to NRC (1997), the meaning of the word 'interactivity' is not yet fully explored, thus, suggesting the need for further and deeper studies of the multidisciplinary approach. Furthermore, the report states that research should also concentrate on understanding interaction in terms of how it is defined and perceived, what is expected and needed, and what are the analogues, for example, in the theatre, in storytelling, in improvisation, and in the entertainment industry.

The interaction, interactivity, and interactive applications have been widely studied by many disciplines. Still, it would seem that the whole area is not yet covered. Or, if it is covered, it has not been explored in the context of Net-VEs and multi-player games. Researchers representing various disciplines have more often than not worked within their own domains, thus leaving a wide gap between technology and human behaviour. The purpose of this paper is to suggest a new research approach that would contribute in bridging this gap by applying the experience gained from games domain. The emphasis is on combining the expertise and targeting the focus of various areas, such as the entertainment industry, cognitive and behavioural sciences, information processing sciences, and technology.

The **research problem** of this paper is related to the conceptual aspects of interaction. The problem originates from the need to have illustrative models in order to acquire more explicit understanding of the scope. In the search for solution, the main questions to be answered are as follows:

- What is the taxonomy of interaction in the context of Net-VEs (i.e. what components and categories can be explicitly presented) when considering games as a starting point?

- Is it possible to model interaction hierarchically as in robotics and psychology?

The answers to these questions have been searched through conceptual analysis and constructivist approaches. The empirical part of the work consists of ethnographical studies and heuristic evaluations conducted within the area of 3D multi-player games. The work consists of iterative phases of data collection and model construction. The taxonomy has been refined according to the updated information gathered from observations and evaluations.

Although the multi-player games are not an exhaustive area when considering Net-VEs, the games domain provides similar interactions and features that can be found in more 'conservative' virtual environments. The main contribution of this paper is in the positioning and defining of the new research field. It is hoped that this interdisciplinary and inter-cultural approach could be beneficial for other application domains as well.

The remainder of the article consists of seven sections. Section 2 explains the basic features of Net-VEs. Section 3 provides definitions of interaction in the context of this research. Section 4 discusses some of the previous work conducted within the field. Section 5 describes the empirical side of this work by providing the construction and analysis of the interaction taxonomy and hierarchical interaction model. Furthermore, the use of the models in designing and developing a team game is provided. Section 6 raises issues and problems for further research and provides a brief outline of the research to be conducted. Finally, Section 7 presents the findings and results of the paper.

2 Networked Virtual Environments

Net-VEs raise challenging research questions concerning how users interact with objects, applications, and other users. When considering the framework this paper belongs to, it is important to define the concept of Virtual Environments. The majority of the material studied in this work consists of 3D multi-player games, which are one area of Net-VEs. In order to comprehend the main research focus, a general Net-VE description is provided. This definition will also make the conceptual analysis of interaction more focused.

Virtual Environments (VEs) provide another means of simulating real world places and activities. A VE is a computer-generated simulated space with which an individual interacts (Witmer et al., 1996). Further definition and expansion of the term is provided by Singhal & Zyda (1999): Networked Virtual Environment (Net-VE) is a software system in which multiple users interact with each other in real-time, even though those users may be located around the world. These environments aim to provide users with a sense of realism by incorporating realistic-looking 3D graphics and even stereo sound, to create an immersive experience. According to Singhal & Zyda (1999), a Net-VE is distinguished by the following five common features:

1. A shared sense of space (illusion of being located in the same place).

2. A shared sense of presence (avatars of participants).

3. A shared sense of time (real-time interaction possible).

4. A way to communicate (various interaction methods).

5. A way to share (dynamic environment that can be interacted with).

Net-VEs can be considered as applications and extensions of virtual reality technologies. Riva (1999) defines the 'soul' of virtual reality (VR) as a mental experience, which makes the user believe that 'he or she is there', that he or she is present in the virtual world. When interacting with a virtual environment or with other users, the user is no longer a mere observer of that which is happening on the screen. Instead, the user *feels* immersed in that world and can participate in it, in spite of the fact that these worlds are spaces and objects existing only in the memory of the computer and in the user's mind.

VEs may convey information about real world places effectively because they tend to preserve the spatio-temporal aspects and natural modes of interaction characteristic of real world environments. VEs can be used to represent physical spaces which do not exist (e.g. game worlds) or are inaccessible in the real world, or to represent abstract or non-physical concepts (Witmer et al., 1996).

3   Interaction

The importance of understanding the concepts included in interaction encourages researchers to study this field more thoroughly. The research illustrated in this paper starts by describing the concept of interaction in order to lay the basic boundaries for further research. There are several areas of interaction that are not included at this point due to the approach selected. For example, the higher level interaction and group dynamics are not yet fully studied in relation to this work.

3.1   *Definitions*

Interaction techniques are used to map the user input captured by the devices, such as the positions of body parts, voice commands, and hand gestures, into the corresponding control actions and commands. The VE system responds by changing the state of VE, i.e. by modifying the shape, position, colour, and other properties of various entities. Display devices provide sensory feedback to users by stimulating their visual, auditory, and other perceptual systems (Poupyrev & Ichikawa, 1999).

Interaction between a user and the environment, however, involves the use of information that reflects both spatial and temporal changes of the relative environment. It is important that an observer is able to determine where he or she is heading when moving through the world and also to estimate how contact with an object can be made or avoided. Fundamental to most VE settings is the requirement that the users will want to change viewpoint, traverse the three-dimensional structure and position themselves at areas of interest (e.g. action-space in relation to interesting world objects). Where they should stop is dictated by the spatial scale and user intention. The proximity needs to be such that the user can discern relevant visual detail, or activate/manipulate the structure with some input device (Wann & Mon-Williams, 1996).

3.2   *Interaction in the Context of this Research*

The interaction in the context of this research is not directly related to the users ability to make choices when using a computer program. In relation to this, the interface issues, including input/output devices, are not within the main focus area, although their importance and effects cannot be overlooked. Furthermore, as stated by (NRC, 1997), most 'interactive media' is nothing more than multimedia presentations with the ability to click to the next screen of material in order to keep the stream coming. Of course, the definition of interaction differs according to research domain. Behavioural and educational sciences use the word 'interaction' quite differently than it is used in the areas of engineering and information processing sciences.

The definition of interaction in the context of this research can be considered to follow the lines of natural interaction occurring in real life environments. The main focus of this interaction study is **inside** the virtual environment, which means that most of the issues are considered as content matters not necessarily tied to any input/output device or interaction technique. Of course these two worlds of interaction are highly overlapping. Figure 1 illustrates the components of human–computer interaction. The interaction sequence starts, for example, from human action, which is taken by means of input device (such as the mouse in this example). Interaction techniques are used to map the user input from the device to the computer

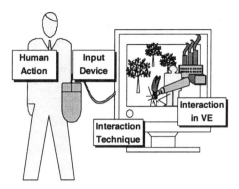

Figure 1: The various components of human–computer interaction.

application. Finally, there is the executed interaction that occurs within the virtual environment. This task can, for example, be acted out by the avatar, or the embodiment, of the user.

3.3   Level of Interactivity

Interactivity is the extent to which the user feels convinced of the mutual effect that he or she and the environment have on one another. Better interactivity produces a more pleasing, better-controlled interaction with the virtual environment. Level of interactivity is a function of the speed of response, the range of possible user interactions and the mapping of controls (Nunamaker, 1997). Rapid response time promotes interactivity by providing immediate feedback to operations performed by the users. Action first-person shooter games like Quake represent the highest level of interactivity attained so far, achieved by pushing I/O devices to their limits in order to provide high speeds of response. The second dimension, or the number of choices that a user can make at any point in time reflects highly on the range of communication technology. Within the application domain of multimedia games, this dimension of interactivity level function is generally dominated by role-playing games and simulators. The third dimension, mapping of controls, is the relationship between the user's physical interactions with the input mechanisms and the changes to the virtual environment. Due to the limitations in user interfaces, this seems to be one of the major problems standing in the way of achieving a high level of interactivity. Fast response action games and simulators are currently operated through the keyboard and mouse, thus requiring complex key mappings in order to provide access to all of the actions. This is still far from the level stressed by Steuer (1992); effective interaction for mapping of controls should be natural and cause predictable outcomes.

With more channels of communicating in current Net-VEs, the ambiguity is reduced by providing more dimensions of elaboration for any message. In recent years, a significant consideration in developing Net-VEs has been to enhance the shared behaviour and interaction within the virtual environment. Even the high-quality environment is still lifeless if it lacks the shared behaviour and interaction among the objects. This means that creating virtual environments that have some realism in them, requires collaborative interaction among humans and machines (Lu et al., 1999). In a way this corresponds, not only to the level, but also to the contextuality of the interaction, cf. (Manninen, 2000a; Manninen, 2000c).

In the context of this work, the term rich interaction could be defined as an interaction set consisting of a large number of individual action and interaction types and possibilities that allows more complex interaction sequences. The complexity refers to the more natural forms of interacting, but due to the limitations in simulations, the virtual counterpart tends to stay far behind from the real-world one.

3.4 *Previous Research*

Human–Computer Interaction (HCI) is the study of how people interact with computers and to what extent computers are or are not developed for successful interaction with human beings. Much of the theoretical framework comes to HCI from cognitive psychology. One relevant theory, when considering interaction issues, is Norman's (1986) theory of action. His theory expresses human task performance from a cognitive engineering perspective — the path from goals to intentions to actions (inputs to the computer), and back to perception and interpretation of the feedback to evaluation of whether the intentions and goals were approached or met.

Much of the earlier research conducted, for example, in the area of computer-supported learning and training, has shown that the interaction and communication occurring in Net-VE has been mainly on a superficial and a relatively modest level. Although the Net-VEs provide tremendous possibilities for time and location independent interaction, they still offer only a very limited set of interactions in terms of actions, reciprocity and social togetherness. The main problem in this area seems to be the gap between cognitive and social psychology and the technical fields (Järvelä, 2000).

The work conducted in Computer Supported Cooperative Work (CSCW) and Management Information Systems (MIS) areas have provided a number of theories and applications that include the aspect of interactivity inside an environment. For example, a group support system (GSS) is a set of techniques, software and technology designed to focus and enhance the communication, deliberations and decision making of groups. Currently, one of the major problems of these systems is the lack of techniques to handle the need for directional changes in the distributed mode. This problem occurs because there are no gestures, no eye-contact, no body language, no pointing, no rolling eyes, and no handshake or pat on the back to signal when to shift gears. These non-verbal cues and other components of body language that encourage engagement in a social interaction situation, such as in a meeting, are absent in existing distributed meeting systems (Nunamaker, 1997).

The research conducted in the field of more technical settings indicates that the possibility to achieve richer interaction is in the foreseeable future. As described by Hagsand (1996), the VEs are able to offer intuitive modes of interaction that are analogous to the ways in which humans communicate with each other or manipulate objects in the real world. VE applications can use 3D spatial properties to represent users and to model interaction, offer direct manipulation interfaces that mimic actions in the real world, and use immersive techniques that give participants the sense of being embedded in the synthetic environments.

Although the possibilities for rich interaction would seem to exist, there still are major drawbacks and limitations in the current applications. One of the problems is that human beings are highly sensitive to seemingly insignificant variations in the facial expressions, gestures, and posture of their conversational partners (Spoelder et al., 1999). This reduces the feeling of presence among the participants and, thus makes the interaction seem unnatural. In order to enhance the sense of presence within Net-VEs, it is important to increase the quality of the physical or social interaction of the participants with each other and with the environment. A virtual environment should give the users a feeling of presence within its environment providing better interaction and intuitive interfaces (Pandzic et al., 1996).

In several games and VR systems, in general, users are able to choose what representation they would like for themselves in the virtual world or, alternatively, to customise a standard avatar so that it suits them. This degree of flexibility widens the scope of control that a user is permitted and encourages a sense of ownership or identification of the avatar. This results in unique avatars becoming associated with the personalities, actions and roles of their controllers (Nunamaker, 1997). One solution to support rich interaction is to provide more detailed and natural-like models and behaviours within the Net-VE. In order to allow users to experiment a higher degree of realism, virtual environments have to go beyond the photo-realism and provide a "physical behaviour-realism" adding kinematic and dynamic behaviour to the primary graphical representations of the avatars (Spoelder et al., 1999).

When considering games and entertainment, for example, Bowman & Hodges (1999) point out that the current applications within entertainment sector do not usually require complex interaction between the user and the system. Although the user may be interacting frequently, the interactions are mostly simple in nature. This may lead to the conclusion, or research hypothesis, that interaction is a major reason for the lack of real-world usage of more complex applications thus suggesting various research topics for the areas such as human–computer interaction and computer-mediated interaction. For example, the enabling nature of rich interaction and the corresponding benefits to the users can be considered as an interesting area of further research.

Interaction has been studied in several fields and under several names. Action, communication, behaviour, manipulation, and simulation can be considered to be closely related to the term interaction as used in the context of this research. The modes and types of interaction have been presented, for example, in the areas of human–computer interaction (Preece et al., 1994), cooperative design processes (Robertson, 1997), affective computing (Picard, 1997), autonomous agents (Maes et al., 1997), virtual environment design (Kaur, 1998) and virtuality (NRC, 1997). Furthermore a hierarchical model of human actions for avatar modelling have been developed by Emering et al. (1998). All these models, although highly beneficial, do not provide adequate details or applicable solutions when considering rich interaction in Net-VEs. The models do provide several guidelines and building blocks that can be used as basis of this work. However, they seem to keep their focus on different issues than it is done, for example, in the area of game design.

In addition to the aforementioned previous research, there are several relevant contributions to the field of interaction in Net-VEs that need to be considered. The work conducted in Benford & Mariani (1993) project describes and analyses the metaphors and requirements of interaction. Gabbard & Hix (1997) describe a very exhaustive taxonomy of usability characteristics in VEs. The taxonomy consists of the complete chain from user to UI to VE and then back to the user. Furthermore, the hierarchical task analysis for collaborative actions in Net-VEs provided by the COVEN project (Tromp, 1998) is an extensive taxonomy of atomic tasks involved in collaboration between multiple users in Net-VE. All of these contributions are partially overlapping with the work described in this paper, although the main focus is somewhat different.

4 Construction and Analysis of the Models

The research material used in the construction of the taxonomy has been collected (video recordings, interviews, walkthroughs, observations, and heuristic evaluations) from a networking game event and from self-arranged gaming sessions. A total of twenty games have been studied and the material has been expanded with heuristic evaluations of a number of Net-VE applications.

The main portion of recorded material was collected during Vectorama 2000 gaming event held in Oulu during June 9–11, 2000. The event was organised by Vector ry, the Network Gaming Association of Finland. The target group for the event was people that were interested in playing multi-player games. The number of participants was over 40 (the average age being around 18). The games played include, for example, the Half-Life multi-player modification called Counter-Strike (CS), thus, corresponding to the fact that CS is one of the most played action games on the Internet at the time. The game is very realistic when compared to the regular Unreal/Quake action games, and players really have to work in teams and think what they are doing to achieve their goals. Counter-Strike can be best described as a "light-weight tactical combat simulation". It modifies the multi-player aspects of Half-Life towards more team-oriented game play. Each team has access to different guns and equipment, as well as different abilities. Game locations have different goals such as: hostage rescue, bomb defusing, terrorist escape, etc. Weapons include the usual assortment of pistols, shotguns, rifles, grenades, etc.

Due to the straight-forward nature of the Counter-Strike, the heuristic evaluation was targeted towards role-playing games and towards games containing aspects of social interaction and constructivism. The research material was selected based on the preliminary survey of multi-player games. The evaluated games were to form as large interaction composition set as possible in this context. The games that have been studied include *action games* (e.g. Action Quake, Counter-Strike, Capture the Flag) and *role-playing games* (e.g. EverQuest, Ultima Online). There are also some material obtained from text-based games and flight simulators.

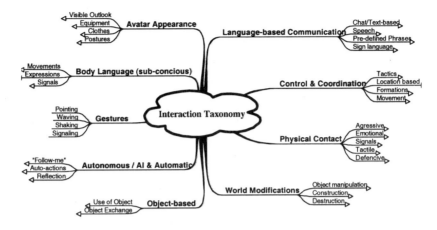

Figure 2: Taxonomy of interaction types.

4.1 Interaction Taxonomy

The following section presents a tentative taxonomy of interaction that has been created based on the data. The main reason for the creation of this interaction classification model is the generally ambiguous understanding of what the concept of interaction exactly includes. This is especially important when considering modern networked multi-user virtual worlds because a major part of the research is tackling the issues of interaction techniques, and thus, are not directly within the same field.

Figure 2 represents a model depicting the first layers of the decomposition that forms the proposed taxonomy. Further decomposition is not presented due to the image size restrictions. The map illustrates the main interaction types that can be found within the current multimedia games. The games domain has been selected as starting point because its limits and numerous applications. The components of this typology have been gathered from gaming session observations, surveys and heuristic evaluations conducted by the research group. The basis for this taxonomy is the categorisation of various interactions in terms of purpose, context, and acting entities (e.g. body parts, fellow team members, etc.). Some of the interactions illustrated by the taxonomy represent the low-level actions that can be considered as signal-type motor skills with relatively simple and straightforward implementations. On the other hand, there are several higher-level interactions that include various degrees of cognitive reasoning and other psychological functions. For example, coordination of a virtual team is a type of interaction that usually requires a higher amount of attributes.

The taxonomy presented here acts as a concrete set of examples and categories of interactions that can be found, not only in games, but also in current Net-VEs. The boundaries of the classes are not necessarily solid, instead there are several occurrences where the overlap is mainly as issue of perspective. The taxonomy resembles an interaction task analysis when considering the actions that occur inside

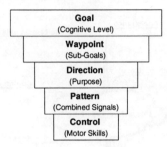

Figure 3: Hierarchical interaction model shown as inverted pyramid.

the virtual environment. This perspective, however, is not always applicable due to the differences in representations of interactions and user tasks — the act of an avatar may not directly correspond to the objectives of the user. The aspects of social theory provide some insight to these relationships between real-world incentives and virtual environment representations. For further discussion about applying social theory to multi-player game research, refer to the previous work conducted by this author (Manninen, 2000b).

The interaction taxonomy can be analysed against the framework proposed by Winograd in (NRC, 1997). Winograd describes three primary modes of interacting with a virtuality that are learned by every normal person in infancy: *manipulation* (perceiving, grasping, modifying, and controlling objects), *locomotion* (observing location and moving from place to place), and *conversation* (using language to communicate with another person in a two-sided discourse). The representatives of these modes can be found from the taxonomy of interaction although there are some contradictions in the classification. Furthermore, the taxonomy presented here describes additional modes of interaction such as non-verbal communication, coordination, appearance, and autonomous actions.

4.2   *Hierarchical Interaction Model*

In order to enhance the dimensionality of the interaction taxonomy, a hierarchical interaction model can be used in parallel with the taxonomy. Figure 3 illustrates the proposed hierarchical interaction model as inverted pyramid structure. The inverted pyramid is used in order to emphasise the number of possible acts, variables, or degrees of freedom in each level. The basis of this model is in human behavioural sciences and there are also elements taken out from emotion management and formulation structures used within the study of affective computing (Picard, 1997). Furthermore, the actions and interactions under discussion in this paper can be considered to be equal to the behaviours as described in related research papers. For example, Maes et al. (1997) provide similar classification of autonomous agent behaviours and motor skills.

The main idea of this structure is to divide and classify the actions included in interaction situations in order to create a hierarchical structure starting from low-level signal-type of actions and going all the way up to the level where the cognitively

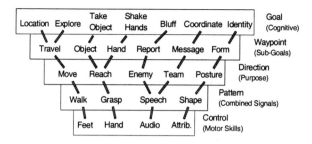

Figure 4: Hierarchical interaction model with some sample interaction chains.

generated goals and objectives define the purpose of the interaction itself. The fields of robotics, artificial intelligence and the game industry have used similar hierarchical structures.

Figure 4 illustrates the proposed hierarchical interaction model with some sample action chains. The lowest level of the model consists of actions that control various parts of the user's motor system (e.g. feet, hand, etc.). The top level includes goal-oriented and usually more generally described interactions which might be compiled from several actions and sub-goals. The number of hierarchical levels is not supposed to be tightly set due to the natural complexity and diversity of interaction types. This complexity can result in chains that can contain only a couple of levels and also chains that can have a number of unique levels or several smaller chains combined together.

The sample interaction chains presented in Figure 4 include the following higher-level interactions or behaviours of the player (from left to right in the figure):

1. Changing of the location within the VE by walking.

2. Exploring the environment by walking.

3. Taking the object by using one hand.

4. Shaking hands with fellow participant (either human player or autonomous agent).

5. Bluffing the opposite team with falsified status reports.

6. Coordinating the team effort through spoken command.

7. Modifying a set of attributes in order to have desired appearance for the avatar.

The lowest level of hierarchy consists of the interactions that are mainly direct manipulations of certain motor systems or attributes of the user's avatar. It should be noted at this point that the model presented here does not include various interaction techniques or human–computer interaction issues. The context of this model is the virtual environment itself with the corresponding entities. The control level can, for example, include the controlling of a character's virtual hand within the

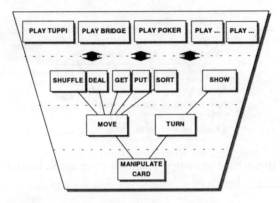

Figure 5: Hierarchical structure of card game interactions.

afforded action space. The pattern level of the model predominantly handles the combinations, or patterns, of various control-level actions. In the hand example, a certain set of hand movements can be recognised as a grasping motion, thus forming a higher level interaction, known as "grasp". The direction level includes the pattern from the previous level but now with a determined overall direction of the interaction. For example, the grasping pattern combined with directional information can create an interaction of reaching out or reaching towards something. The highest levels of the model contain a set of goals that dominate or dictate the interaction in question. For example, the high-level goal of taking an object might include a sub-goal of locating the object to which the reaching interaction can be applied at.

4.3   *Experiments Based on the Models*

The empirical side of this research includes several cases of prototypes that have been designed and constructed based on the aforementioned interaction concepts. One of the cases is part of the University of Oulu coordinated Monica research project and involves the Arctic Bridge (or Tuppi in Finnish), which is a traditional team-based card game which has its origins in northern Finland. The aim of this case was to construct a mobile team game that would not only follow the idea of the original real world version but would also enable location independent gaming using mobile phones. Furthermore, a richer interaction experiment was constructed in the form of 3D representation of the game and corresponding environment.

The hierarchical interaction model is applied in designing a simulated playing card set. The main idea is to start the construction by modelling and programming the lower levels of interactions that are applicable to a deck of cards. The higher levels of interaction are left to the players, thus making it possible to use the same simulator to play almost any card game existing today. This method enables the development of a fully functional card deck with no restrictions to any set of rules. The manipulation of cards follows the lines of natural interactions. Figure 5 illustrates the card game interactions.

5 Further Work

The issues and models represented in this paper should be considered as the starting point for further research. There are many open questions for both researcher and practitioner point of view. This section presents some suggestions and questions that are fruitful ground for research.

One of the main issues is the understanding of interaction in the context of Net-VEs. There is a large amount of work to be conducted in terms of creating and finding new solutions and in terms of closing the gap between technology and humanistic approaches. The detailed questions include team interaction, degrees of freedom, replication of real world interaction, coordination, collaboration and control. These areas can be tackled from different perspectives by using different approaches.

Some practical solutions and problems worth further work include identifiable and customisable avatars (other than VRML-related applications also), AI & agent supported actions and responses in user interface intensive tasks, user profiles as basis of gestures and body language (identification, personalisation), and possibilities for higher level of interactivity.

The refinement of the interaction models will be continued by this author. The problems currently tackled are as follows:

1. Would the support for rich interaction enable more natural ways of interaction?

2. Is the support of lower level interaction a solution that would allow behaviour and cognitive based higher level interactions?

3. Are high-level interactions and communication necessary requirements in achieving adequate training and working in Net-VEs?

6 Conclusions

The research illustrated in this paper starts by describing the concept of interaction in order to lay the basic boundaries for further research. A tentative taxonomy and hierarchical model of interaction in the context of Networked Virtual Environments were created and presented by illustrating some of the drawbacks and difficulties raised in the previous work.

The main purpose of the presented taxonomy is to explicitly illustrate the types and components of the interactions occurring inside Net-VEs. Although some of the components may be trivial or somewhat out of traditional contexts, they provide a set of features that can be considered and evaluated when developing Net-VE applications.

Together with the proposed taxonomy, the hierarchical interaction model provides an explicit two-dimensional perspective to the world of interactions. The application of bottom-up interaction support with a clear understanding of the richer interaction set required can aid in developing more usable and communicative applications.

The second phase of the empirical part of the work provided an example of an experiment in the form of the Mobile Arctic Bridge Case, which provides a brief description of this approach used in designing and developing a team game.

Although successfully applicable, the models were not easily conveyed to the developers. The traditional form of software design seems to be relatively difficult to shake off. Further experiments are required to get full validation of the proposed models.

The results presented in this paper can be considered as a first step of research towards understanding and innovatively applying the concept of interaction in Net-VEs. Although, the usefulness of these models is not yet fully validated, their primary contribution to the field is a set of boundaries that direct the discussion and work to the area requiring further research.

Acknowledgements

This research was conducted with the support of Finnish Academy funded PAULA project, TEKES funded *Monica* project and the Infotech Oulu Virgin Research Group. I would like to thank my supervisor Professor Petri Pulli for his guidance and support during this first phase of research. Furthermore, I am greatly indebted to my research assistants Heikki Korva and Pasi Partanen for their efforts in collecting the research material and in implementing the experiments.

References

Benford, S. & Mariani, J. (1993), Requirements and Metaphors of Interaction, Deliverable 4.1, COMIC Project, Lancaster University.

Bowman, D. A. & Hodges, L. F. (1999), "Formalizing the Design, Evaluation and Application of Interaction Techniques for Immersive Virtual Environments", *Journal of Visual Languages and Computing* **10**(1), 37–53.

Emering, L., Boulic, R. & Thalmann, D. (1998), "Interacting with Virtual Humans through Body Actions", *IEEE Computer Graphics and Applications* **18**(1), 8–11.

Gabbard, J. & Hix, D. (1997), Taxonomy of Usability Characteristics in Virtual Environments, Technical Report 183, Virginia Polytechnic Institute and State University, Virginia, USA. A Report to the Office of Naval Research.

Hagsand, O. (1996), "Interactive Multiuser VEs in the DIVE System", *IEEE Multimedia* **3**(1), 30–9.

Järvelä, S. (2000), "Onko virtuaaliyliopisto todellinen? (Is the Virtual University Real?)", *Kaleva* . 29th April, part 2.

Kaur, K. (1998), Designing Virtual Environments for Usability, PhD thesis, Centre for Human–Computer Interface Design, City University, London.

Lu, T. C., Lin, M. T. & Lee, C. (1999), "Control Mechanism for Large-scale Virtual Environments", *Journal of Visual Languages and Computing* **10**(1), 69–85.

Maes, P., Darrell, T., Blumberg, B. & Pentland, A. (1997), "The ALIVE System: Wireless, Full-body Interaction with Autonomous Agents", *Multimedia Systems* **5**(2), 105–12. Special Issue on Multimedia and Multisensory Virtual Worlds.

Manninen, T. (2000a), Contextual Virtual Reality Prototyping — Cooperative User-centred Design using Distributed Simulations, *in* J. Gulliksen, A. Lantz, L. Oestreicher & K. Severinson Eklundh (eds.), *Proceedings of NordiCHI2000 Conference*, Vol. 2, Swedish Interdisciplinary Interest Group for Human–Computer Interaction, p.2.

Manninen, T. (2000b), Interaction in Networked Virtual Environments as Communicative Action — Social Theory and Multi-player Games, *in Proceedings of Sixth International Workshop on Groupware (CRIWG 2000)*, IEEE Computer Society Press, pp.99–104.

Manninen, T. (2000c), Multimedia Game Engine as Distributed Conceptualisation and Prototyping Tool — Contextual Virtual Prototyping, *in* B. Furht (ed.), *Proceedings of IMSA2000 Conference*, IASTED/ACTA Press, pp.154–7.

Norman, D. A. (1986), Cognitive Engineering, *in* D. A. Norman & S. W. Draper (eds.), *User Centered System Design: New Perspectives on Human–Computer Interaction*, Lawrence Erlbaum Associates, pp.31–62.

NRC (1997), *More Than Screen Deep — Toward Every-citizen Interfaces to the Nation's Information Infrastructure*, National Academic Press. US National Research Council.

Nunamaker, J. F. (1997), "Future Research in Group Support Systems: Needs, Some Questions and Possible Directions", *International Journal of Human–Computer Studies* **47**(3), 357–85.

Pandzic, I. S., Capin, T. K., Magnenat-Thalmann, N. & Thalmann, D. (1996), Motor Functions in the VLNET Body-centered Networked Virtual Environment, *in* M. Göbel, J. David, P. Slavik & J. van Wijk (eds.), *Proceedings of the Eurographics Workshops: Virtual Environments and Scientific Visualization'96*, Springer-Verlag, pp.94–103.

Picard, R. (1997), *Affective Computing*, MIT Press.

Poupyrev, I. & Ichikawa, T. (1999), "Manipulating Objects in Virtual Worlds: Categorization and Empirical Evaluation of Interaction Techniques", *Journal of Visual Languages and Computing* **10**(1), 19–35.

Preece, J., Rogers, Y., Sharp, H., Benyon, D., Holland, S. & Carey, T. (1994), *Human–Computer Interaction*, Addison–Wesley.

Riva, G. (1999), "From Technology to Communication: Psycho-social Issues in Developing Virtual Environments", *Journal of Visual Languages and Computing* **10**(1), 87–97.

Robertson, T. (1997), Cooperative Work and Lived Cognition: A Taxonomy of Embodied Actions, *in* J. Hughes, W. Prinz, T. Rodden & K. Schmidt (eds.), *Proceedings of ECSCW'97, the 5th European Conference on Computer-Supported Cooperative Work*, Kluwer, pp.205–20.

Singhal, S. & Zyda, M. (1999), *Networked Virtual Environments: Design and Implementation*, ACM Press.

Spoelder, H. J. W., Petriu, E. M., Whalen, T., Petriu, D. C. & Cordea, M. (1999), Knowledge-based Animation of Articulated Anthropomorphic Models for Virtual Reality Applications, *in* V. Piuri & M. Savino (eds.), *Proceedings of Instrumentation and Measurement Technology Conference (IMTC'99)*, IEEE Computer Society Press, pp.690–5.

Steuer, J. (1992), "Defining Virtual Reality: Dimensions Determining Telepresence", *Journal of Communication* **42**(2), 73–93.

Tromp, J. (1998), D3.5, Usage Evaluation of the Online Applications — Part B: Collaborative Actions in CVEs, Technical Report AC040-UCL-CS-DS-P-035b.b1, University of Nottingham. ACTS Project AC040 — COVEN (COllaborative Virtual ENvironments).

Wann, J. & Mon-Williams, M. (1996), "What does Virtual Reality NEED?: Human Factors Issues in the Design of Three-dimensional Computer Environments", *International Journal of Human–Computer Studies* **44**(6), 829–47.

Witmer, B. G., Bailey, J. H. & Knerr, B. W. (1996), "Virtual Spaces and Real World Places: Transfer of Route Knowledge", *International Journal of Human–Computer Studies* **45**(4), 413–28.

Using Workflow for Coordination in Groupware Applications

Karim Saïkali & Bertrand David

Laboratoire ICTT, École Centrale de Lyon, 36 avenue Guy de Collongue, BP 163 69131 Ecully Cedex, France
Email: *{Karim.Saikali,Bertrand.David}@ec-lyon.fr*

Workflow is the Information Technology field that is concerned with the management of enterprises' business processes. Unlike groupware, which cover both synchronous and asynchronous aspects of collaborative work, workflow is generally applied to asynchronous cases, and provides functions that are oriented towards coordination and organisation. Groupware is much more oriented towards communication and collaboration support. Because both types of system present complementary features, the tendency is towards the convergence of the two technologies. In particular, there is potential to exploit the coordination functions that workflow systems offer in groupware management. This article proposes a start in this direction.

Keywords: groupware control, workflow, workflow adaptability.

1 Historical Review

The end of the 80's and the beginning of the 90's have witnessed the emergence of the notion of 'work group' and collaborative work in companies. This notion contrasts with the traditional approaches to work organisation and the structuring of enterprises, which consist of compartmentalising the competencies into rather hermetic departments and of achieving work activities in a sequential order. Globally, the origin of collaborative work comes from the observation that introducing various common competencies and knowledge brings improvements to the quality of task performance, and to the speed of task execution. Thus, collaborative work makes it possible to bring together individuals with different skills and specialisations into the same structure that unites its members around the achievement of one common goal. Many management and organising methods concretise this concept, such as, for instance, 'project centric methods' (Zarifian, 1997).

In a complementary way, in parallel to the growth of the notion of group, the importance of enterprise processes has increased. The notion of process takes the individuals, as well as the activities, from the departments and services where they respectively work and are executed, to bring them together into the same structure: the process. This process is associated with a goal that is reached only when all its component activities are executed. Thus, the effective functioning of an enterprise relies on mastering its processes, and consequently methods for optimising and restructuring processes have arisen, such as *Business Process Reengineering* (BPR) or *Continuous Process Improvement* (CPI) (Davenport, 1993, p.11-27).

The increasing need for tools and methodologies to support collaborative work gave birth to a new field of Information Technology: *Computer Supporter Collaborative Work* (CSCW). The French Association for Economical and Technical Cybernetics defines CSCW as:

> "A field that puts together all the techniques and methods that contribute
> to the achievement of an objective that is common to many actors,
> which are separated or reunited in space and time, using any interactive
> computerised device." (AFCET, 1994)

CSCW proposes a set of tools and methods that cover three fundamental aspects:

- Communication: the objective is to enable group members to exchange information and observations, and to converse.

- Cooperation: the objective here is to provide a set of tools allowing the members of a group to work together. This requires a shared workspace, where it is also possible to share the same tools and artefacts (data, files, electronic documents, etc.).

- Coordination: coordination is the key element that manages the interactions between actors and their activities, in order to optimise the course of their cooperation.

In order to support these three aspects, CSCW provides two types of systems: 'groupware' and *Workflow Management Systems* (WMS), which differ in the way they handle the aforementioned aspects.

2 Workflow vs. Groupware

Some specialists, such as Coleman (1997) and Schmidt & Simone (2000), consider that WMS belong to the category of groupware, a name that refers in a generic way to all kinds of software that support collaborative work. For other people, however, these two terms refer to different types of system, although sharing the more global origin of CSCW tools (Joosten & Brinkkemper, 1995; Nurcan, 1996).

Indeed, some differences exist between these two technologies. Thus, in contrast to groupware, which focuses on collaborative work as the main purpose,

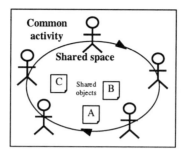

Figure 1: Groupware — Supporting common activity.

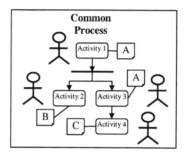

Figure 2: Workflow — Supporting processes.

workflow is oriented towards the management and automation of enterprise processes. This implies a cooperation between many people whose activities must be coordinated, which justifies the inclusion of WMS in the family of cooperative tools.

As shown in Figure 1, groupware requires the presence of tools that allow distant people to interact in a more or less synchronous way, in a common virtual workplace, and to share objects and information in a more or less synchronous way too.

Workflow implies the presence of people interacting in an asynchronous way, in order to achieve a common objective. Synchronisation and coordination in groupware is located at the current activity level, while for workflow it is located at the process level (see Figure 2).

Hence in groupware, the focus is on the group, while in WMS, the focus is on the process. WMS unite the actors and create the group through their coordination capabilities. It is thus the process that defines the group whose members are responsible for executing one or more tasks at a given moment. In contrast, in groupware, it is the group members that define the collaborative activity.

To summarise, the main differences that exist between WMS and groupware are located at four distinct levels:

- At the purpose level: process management and coordination for WMS, vs. group support and sharing for groupware.

- At the interaction granularity level: sharp for groupware, since it is located at activity level, rough for workflow, since it is located at the process level (that is itself composed of activities).

- At the interaction mode level: asynchronous for workflow, synchronous or asynchronous for groupware.

- At the mutual awareness level: although WMS allows the execution of cooperative work, this does not necessarily means that users are aware of each others' activities, in contrast to synchronous groupware — for example, in a cooperative drawing application.

Finally we note that some authors, for example Grudin (1992), classify the two types of systems in the groupware category, but refer to WMS as 'orgwares', to focus on the organisation and coordination dimensions. Other authors also refer to what we call groupware as 'group support systems', to focus on the group support dimension.

3 The Convergence of Workflow and Groupware

In spite of the aspects that make them different, WMS and groupware remain complementary tools. Indeed, apart from sharing the same origin (CSCW) as well as some technical terms (role, actor, activity concepts, etc.) which facilitate communication between specialists of both domains, each type of system proposes functions that could be beneficial to the other.

3.1 Contribution of Groupware to Workflow

One of the problems of WMS comes from their lack of flexibility (Saïkali, 2001; Horn & Jablonski, 1998; Bolcer & Taylor, 1996; Sheth, 1997). This lack of flexibility is due to the fact that many WMS require a strict and detailed modelling of the processes to be managed. Although detailed modelling makes efficient automation and management of the processes possible, it is still quite difficult to take into account process improvements, or to handle unexpected situations. Moreover, it may be necessary to communicate with human actors involved in some kinds of activities, such as decision-making, or to take advice from other people.

We notice in practice that in both cases (exception handling or involvement of many actors in the same activity), it is sometimes necessary to resort to systems that are more flexible than 'traditional' WMS. In the first case, so-called 'ad hoc' WMS are often resorted to. Ad hoc Workflows Management Systems do not base their execution on a precise process model but rely on other concepts like, for instance, the 'folder' metaphor. A virtual folder, in which relevant electronic documents are placed, is passed to each actor, who is thenresponsible for deciding who the next recipient is. Some authors, for example Georgakopoulos et al. (1995), consider that ad hoc workflow is in fact asynchronous groupware.

In the case of an activity that involves many actors, the WMS usually resorts to synchronous groupware, whose functionalities enable more efficient interaction between participants.

Thus for Sheth (1997), WMS should evolve towards what he calls "Work Coordination and Collaboration Systems", that put together the asynchronous dimension of coordination and process management functions of WMS with the synchronous dimension of groupware functions. Mutation or, at least, reflection on a convergence has thus already started.

3.2 Contribution of Workflow to Groupware

On of the most important problems groupware has to face, particularly synchronous groupware, is the control problem (Kanawati, 1997). Tarpin-Bernard (1997) defines seven levels of control in a synchronous groupware application:

- Semantic control: this is related to the management of the relations between the internal data of the functional kernel of the software.

- Interaction control: this is used to manage the effect of users' actions on data.

- Concurrency control: this is aimed towards the coordination of the concurrent users' accesses to shared resources and artefacts.

- Consistency control: this ensures that the last read operation result on a shared object conforms to the last edit operation on this same object.

- Message spreading control: this manages how messages are spread among users in a group.

- Access control over data and transactions: this manages the users' rights and duties according to their role.

- Notification control: this is used to spread notifications about an activity result to users.

Most of these different aspects of control are tightly related, and ensure the coherence of the group's work. To do so, control uses locking mechanisms over shared resources, according to different modes that are described in Kindberg (1996). Control also uses user information and notification mechanisms that allow users to adapt their behaviour, as well as coordination mechanisms to manage actors' activities.

Moreover, as noted by Ferraris & Martel (2000), the way actual groupware allows users to describe their work, setting workgroup rules or organising their activities, is very limited. This very important dimension corresponds to what the authors call 'regulation', which consists of setting rules to coordinate group activities. These rules can be expressed using scenarios describing possible interactions between users who can use them to regulate and coordinate their activities.

From another perspective, existing control and coordination mechanisms only make it possible to manage interactions among small groups of up to a dozen people (Grudin, 1992). Beyond this limit, managing and coordinating exchanges that take place within one activity is very difficult.

Hence, we can see that both coordination and organisation aspects are taken into account in groupware applications, although they do not represent the main focus for such systems. Our idea is thus to take advantage of the intrinsic functions of WMS to satisfy groupware coordination and regulation needs. More precisely, our objective is not to establish a cooperation between two distinct systems but rather to integrate workflow functions (exploiting specialised components) into collaborative applications.

4   Adapting Workflow to Groupware

The scenario and rules mentioned above are not unknown to the workflow field. Indeed, a scenario corresponds to a description of a sequence of steps or milestones, for which the order of execution is either fixed or driven by the occurrence of some events. This definition can be easily applied to the definition of a process model, managed by a workflow system. Without getting into details of existing workflow modelling methods and formalisms, it is worth noting that most of the time, process modelling is done using so-called 'activity-based methods' or 'rule-based methods' (Saïkali, 2001; Eder et al., n.d.; Georgakopoulos et al., 1995).

An activity-based method consists of decomposing a process into activities or sub-processes that are executed on the occurrence of some events. As with rule-based methods, they use ECA (Event Condition Action) rules in order to describe the flow of the process activities. An ECA rule allows the execution of an activity following the occurrence of one or more events, while satisfying a given condition.

To summarise, the proposal to use workflow tools in groupware applications seems coherent since it is possible to establish a connection between the tools and methods that are used on both sides. However, as it is pointed out by Ferraris & Martel (2000), the problem is that in a more or less synchronous common activity, the activity is progressively constructed during the execution of the activity itself. Thus, it is not possible to fix a given scenario or a precise modelling of processes. Consequently, in order to take advantage of workflow properties, it appears to us that two fundamental conditions must be satisfied:

- It is more appropriate to design process models (scenarios) as generic models (patterns) of interaction. These models can later be tailored depending on the users' needs.

- In order to allow the particularisation of patterns or the modification of scenarios during the common activity, it is necessary to have a flexible workflow technology that could allow the creation of adaptable process models. For this purpose, we propose to use the functionalities of a flexible workflow framework that we describe below.

5   FLOW, a Flexible Workflow Framework

The 2FLOW framework Saïkali (2001; Saïkali et al., 1999) has been developed at the ICTT laboratory and is the result of our research in the field of workflow flexibility and adaptability. It has three main purposes:

- To propose mechanisms that allow the setting up of workflow flexibility.

- To provide a set of 'base' adaptable workflow components, allowing non-IT specialists to build functional adaptable workflows by assembling components together.

- In a lesser degree, to provide a methodological framework for designing workflows based on 2FLOW, using specific metamodel and modelling methods.

5.1 Description of the Framework

2FLOW is based on the concept of Object Workflows (Bussler, n.d.), which consists of the integration of object properties into workflow. In other words, the purpose is to provide workflow models of which entities verify the object properties, like inheritance (specialisation) and polymorphism, in order to obtain adaptable models. Thus, the framework proposes a set of components that can be assembled to construct executable workflows. By 'executable workflows', we mean that once the components are put together, no workflow engine is necessary to run the workflow since the components themselves 'are the engine'. Hence in 2FLOW, the responsibility of executing the processes is distributed over the components that build the process. Therefore, the assembly of 2FLOW components defines at the same time the workflow model and the workflow system.

In the following, we briefly describe 2FLOW main components:

- The Process component: this is the basic component of 2FLOW. It is composed of sub-processes and activities.

- The Activity component: this is the representation of an activity that is attributed to a role in a process.

- The Role component: in 2FLOW, we adopt an original approach that conceives an actor's role as an interface (in the object-oriented meaning). Hence, each process activity that is attributed to a role corresponds to one of the role methods. Any actor's class that can take a given role should thus implement the interface methods. This approach is interesting for three main reasons. First, it breaks the dependency between 'what must be done' (the activities) and 'how it is done' (the actor's methods). It is thus possible to replace an actor by another one that takes the same role during the process execution without perturbing its course. A second advantage is that each actor can personalise the way it executes an activity. It is thus possible to have two types of actors, human and automatic ones. Finally, the interface notion ensures that an actor is really capable of taking a certain role since it has to implement its methods.

- The Actor component: this is the computerised equivalent of a real actor. It implements the role methods (although default behaviours are available in the framework).

- The Event component: in 2FLOW, the activity flow is generated by the occurrence of events that are emitted and consumed by activities.

- The Logical Expression component: this makes it possible to allows combine the effects of many events in order to notify one or more activity. Logical expressions are defined using a specific notation that uses classical Boolean operators (OR, AND, XOR).

- The Control Flow Block component (CFB): although the dynamic processes dynamic are event-driven, controlling the execution flow is achieved by specialised components: the CFB. These components exist in three types: sequential CFB, that manage a sequential execution of activities, parallel CFB and loop CFB.

- The Artefact component: this is the computerised equivalent (a 'wrapper') of any object that could be used by the process activities. These components are specialised in other types of components that encapsulate specific behaviours. However, the description of these components is outside the scope of this paper and will not be discussed here.

Notice that models that are built using 2FLOW components can be specialised, at run-time or not, which allows the workflow users to adapt their processes depending on their needs. Moreover, the process components can also be specialised, which makes it possible to sharpen the granularity of adaptation.

5.2   Using the Framework

To use the framework, it is necessary to specialise the components it provides. This specialisation can be done with or without adding new behaviours and/or attributes to the components, or modifying them.

For example, consider a collaborative article-writing process, involving three authors. This process could be composed of three activities: one writing activity that can be executed in parallel and separately by each of the actors; one meeting activity through which the authors agree on miscellaneous aspects of the document; and finally, a submit activity, executed by one of the participants only. It can be looped though the writing activity until the authors reach an agreement during the meeting activity. Figure 3 describes the UML class diagram that corresponds to the writing process.

5.3   Adaptability in 2FLOW

2FLOW adaptability is based on reflexive mechanisms that allow direct manipulation of the component classes. These mechanisms are enabled by a set of tools that we have developed, among which we propose a generic workflow editor with two main functions:

- At build-time, it is used for modelling processes by assembling classes and components of the framework. It also allows reuse and/or specialising of the process components that have already been created by users. The models obtained are used to generate Java classes and files (source and compiled files).

- At run-time, it is possible to modify a process class definition directly, due to its reflexive properties, using the editor services. Any change to a class definition is immediately reflected on the running process instance.

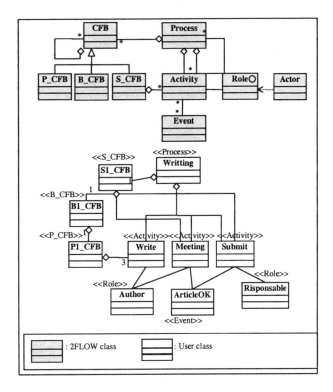

Figure 3: Example of a collaborative process using 2FLOW.

We consider using 2FLOW adaptability mechanisms for the construction of cooperation scenario patterns. Indeed, using the framework will give the ability to instantiate a given pattern into a model that will be specific to a particular collaboration case. Moreover, it will be possible to modify the model obtained according to the construction of the cooperative activity.

5.4 Example of a Cooperation Pattern

In this paragraph, we give a short example of how our framework can be used for the construction of a collaboration pattern. This example is about the management of a dialog among many participants. The dialog can be assimilated to a generic process composed of generic activities that are: 'give hand' (allow a participant to talk or to use a certain tool), 'ask hand', and 'free hand'. However, the execution order of these activities is not known in advance, but the events that initiate them are clearly identified: 'hand released', 'hand requested' and 'hand attributed'. It is also possible to identify two generic roles that can be associated with the activities: 'participant' and 'coordinator'. Notice that an actor can take both roles.

This process can easily be translated into 2FLOW components, as shown in Figure 4.

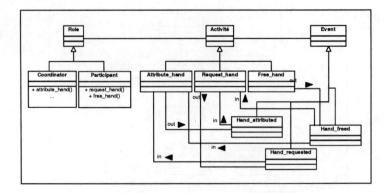

Figure 4: Collaboration pattern — managing a dialog.

2FLOW adaptability mechanisms allow us to instantiate this pattern into different processes that share the same principle of execution. For example, the previous pattern can be specialised into a process for managing shared resources. Moreover, the actor-role-activity approach that we propose makes it possible to involve automatic actors, as well as human actors, in the process. For example, we can consider using a computerised agent in the role of dialog coordinator.

Finally, due to the inherited base behaviours, the pattern and its derived processes are fully functional; they can thus be integrated directly into another application: a collaborative one, for instance.

We are particularly interested in integrating workflow components into other software applications and, more particularly, groupware applications. We develop this aspect in the following paragraph.

6 Integrating 2FLOW in a Multi-agent Architecture: AMF-C Architecture

Most workflow systems are standalone 'heavy' systems that cooperate with other enterprise information systems. One of today's trend is towards the use of lighter workflow applications or workflow engines, which can be integrated into bigger systems for which they can provide coordination and process management functions (zur Muehlen & Allen, 2000).

This new approach is interesting in many cases, particularly when process management and coordination are not the fundamental concerns, but rather the means to reach other objectives. It is, for example, the case for a large number of ERP systems that manage the whole enterprise (SAP, BAAN, etc.) and Product Data Management Systems where it may be possible to manage the engineering data validation processes, etc. So why wouldn't it be the case for synchronous and asynchronous groupware? This is what we propose to do, by integrating 2FLOW in the multi-agent AMF-C architecture.

6.1 AMF-C

Multi-agent systems and architectures are widely used in the field of Man-Machine interfaces and for the development of groupware applications. It is therefore natural to think about using such architectures, especially because they present a major interest by providing 'intelligent' entities, which can be used as run-time environments or as consumers of workflow services and components. Further to this observation, we were interested by the AMF-C architecture (Tarpin-Bernard, 1997; Ouadou, 1994), which was initially developed in our laboratory for the development of Man-Machine interfaces and was later extended to the development of groupware applications.

In the AMF-C architecture, each agent is composed of 'facets', which are components that contain all the data and behaviours that are relevant to a particular functional theme. The number of facets of an AMF-C agent is not limited, and no facet is mandatory. This means that it is possible to have agents with only one specialised facet. Facets support a set of services and communicate with each other through Input/Output ports. Communication between ports is managed by specific facets called 'coordinators' which also manage the allocation of queries that are formulated by a facet, to the services of other facets.

In the case of a collaborative application, agents can be replicated on different parts of the application, and the agent facets can also be distributed over these parts. This is called 'fragmentation'. In both cases, it is necessary to add new facets that act as administrators, which manage the services proposed by the other facets of the agent, as well as version managers for the replicated agent.

Agents are hierarchically organised according to composition rules that express the fact that a parent agent contains a certain number of child agents. Hence, for each application modelled with AMF there is a root agent (generally called 'application'), which is the common ancestor of all the application agents.

6.2 Integration of 2FLOW in AMF-C

Since adding specialised facets to an AMF-C agent is possible, we have proposed introducing a new type of facet, the 'workflow' facet. Depending on the strategy adopted, this facet can play two different roles:

In the first case, it is used as an interface between an agent and a set of underlying 2FLOW components. These components describe one ore more collaboration scenarios between many actors, whose activities will be coordinated by applying the related scenarios. In this case, agents can communicate either directly through their communication facet, or through the workflow facet.

In the second case, we can imagine that the workflow facet enables a specific AMF-C agent to provide a set of coordination services to the other collaborating agents in the application. In this case, this agent plays the role of an administrator. It is in charge of managing the good course of effective interaction between actors. To do so, it uses the services that are implemented in the underlying 2FLOW components.

Whatever strategy is adopted, the integration of 2FLOW and AMF-C relies on the actor-role-activity framework. Each agent (or workflow facet) can be assigned to an actor with a particular role. If an AMF-C agent is associated with each actor of the groupware application, the role corresponds to the one that is taken by the actor in the groupware application, and the associated activities are those that the actor could achieve during the collaboration, via the application tools.

7 Conclusion

This article is based on the idea of a convergence between groupware and workflow. There is indeed a reflection today on what advantages the combined usage of both technologies can bring. In the case of workflow, flexibility seems to be the area where groupware could be used. Conversely, workflow properties could be very beneficial if applied to coordination and regulation in groupware applications. We have shown that these needs exist and that the convergence between the two domains is possible and desirable, partly thanks to a set of concepts already shared by the two technologies. Of course, some adaptation should be made, especially at the workflow level. One solution is to integrate workflow functions into groupware applications, via specific components. We have therefore proposed a preliminary approach, based on the integration of such components in a multi-agent architecture, dedicated to the development of groupware. This approach is an initial attempt at reflection in this field that opens some interesting perspectives, but which still has to be explored further.

References

AFCET (1994), Enquête sur la Pratique de la Collectique (Groupware) en France, Rapport d'Étude, Association Français pour la Cybernétique Economique et Technique.

Bolcer, G. A. & Taylor, R. N. (1996), Endeavors: A Process System Integration Infrastructure, in *Proceedings of International Conference on Software Process (ICSP4)*, IEEE Computer Society Press. Also available at http://www.ics.uci.edu/pub/endeavors/docs/EndeavorsPaper.pdf.

Bussler, C. (n.d.), Towards Workflow Type Inheritance, in *Proceedings of the OOPSLA'98 Workshop on Implementation and Application of Object-oriented Workflow Systems*. http://wwwdb.inf.tu-dresden.de/dokumente/oopsla98-workflow-workshop/buss98a.pdf.

Coleman, D. (1997), *An introduction to Groupware*, Prentice–Hall.

Davenport, T. (1993), *Process Innovation: Reengineering Work through Information Technology*, Havard Business School Press.

Eder, J., Groiss, H. & Liebhart, W. (n.d.), Workflow Management and Databases, in *Proceedings 2éme Forum International d'Informatique Appliquée*. Available via http://www.ifi.uni-klu.ac.at/ISYS/JE/Publications/.

Ferraris, C. & Martel, C. (2000), "Regulation in Groupware: The Example of a Collaborative Drawing Tool for Young Children".

Georgakopoulos, D., Hornick, M. & Sheth, A. (1995), "An Overview of Workflow Management: From Process Modeling to Workflow Automation Infrastructure", *Distributed and Parallel Databases* 3(2), 119–53.

Grudin, J. (1992), "CSCW: History and Focus", *IEEE Computer* **29**(6), 27–35.

Horn, S. & Jablonski, S. (1998), An Approach to Dynamic Instance Adaptation in Workflow Management Application, Paper distributed at the CSCW'98 Workshop on Adaptive Workflow Management, not subsequently published.

Joosten, S. & Brinkkemper, S. (1995), Fundamental Concepts for Workflow Automation in Practice, *in* G. Ariav, C. Beath, J. I. DeGross, R. Hoyer & C. Kemerer (eds.), *Proceedings of the Sixteenth International Conference on Information Systems (ICIS'95)*, Association of Information Systems.

Kanawati, R. (1997), Construction de Collecticiels : Étude d'Architectures Logicielles et de Fonctions de Contrôle, PhD thesis, INPG.

Kindberg, T. (1996), Notes on Concurrency Control in Groupware, Technical Report, Department of Computer Science, Queen Mary and Westfield College.

Nurcan, S. (1996), "Analyse et Conception de Systèmes d'Information Coopératifs", *Techniques et Science Informatiques* **15**(9), 1287–315.

Ouadou, K. (1994), AMF : Un Modèle d'Architecture Multi-agents Multi-facettes, pour Interfaces Hommes–Machines et les Outils Associés, PhD thesis, Ecole Centrale de Lyon.

Saïkali, K. (2001), Le Flexibilité des Workflows par l'Approche Objet, 2FLOW : Un Framework pour Workflows Flexibles, PhD thesis, Ecole Centrale de Lyon.

Saïkali, K., Boutros, N. & David, B. (1999), An Adaptive Workflow Management System for a Semi-automated Disassembly Platform, *in* J. Becker, M. zur Mühlen & M. Rosemann (eds.), *Proceedings of 1999 Workflow Management Conference Workflow-based Applications*, Department of Information Systems, University of Muenster, Germany, pp.54–69. http://www-wi.uni-muenster.de/is/tagung/workflow99/proceedings/WFM99Proceedings.zip.

Schmidt, K. & Simone, C. (2000), Mind the Gap! Towards a Unified View of CSCW, *in* R. Dieng, A. Giboin, L. Karsenty & G. De Michelis (eds.), *Designing Cooperative Systems: The Use of Theories and Models — Proceedings of the 4th International Conference on the Design of Cooperative Systems (COOP2000)*, IOS Press.

Sheth, A. (1997), From Contemporary Workflow Process Automation to Adaptive and Dynamic Work Activity Coordination and Collaboration, Paper distributed at the 8th Workshop on Workflows in Scientific and Engineering Applications.

Tarpin-Bernard, F. (1997), Travail Coopératif Synchrone Assisté par Ordinateur : Approche AMF-C, PhD thesis, Ecole Centrale de Lyon.

Zarifian, P. (1997), L'Émergence de l'Organisation par Processus : À la Recherche d'une Difficile Cohérence, *in Cohérence, Pertinence et Evaluation*, Groupe ECOSIP, pp.65–86.

zur Muehlen, M. & Allen, R. (2000), Workflow Management Coalition Classification: Embedded and Autonomous Workflow Management Systems, White Paper, Workflow Management Coalition.

Mobile Computing

ToyMobile: Image-based Telecommunication and Small Children

Pekka Ketola[†1] & Hannu Korhonen[‡1]

[†] *Nokia Mobile Phones, PO Box 83, 33721 Tampere, Finland*
Email: *{pekka.ketola,hannu.j.korhonen}@nokia.com*

[‡] *Nokia Research Center, PO Box 100, 33721 Tampere, Finland*

Small children are not able to use existing communication devices without errors because they are unable to read and because devices typically require faster input than children are able to provide. If an error-proof communication device is designed for small children, it must contain an extremely simple user interface with visual and auditory input and output. In this study, we identify the interaction capabilities that small children have, show everyday problems that 3 and 5 year old children may have with phone management through simple experiments, and, finally, present a simple prototype, ToyMobile, that is built through cooperative inquiry and design with children.

Keywords: children, design techniques, mobile phone, mobile handset, cooperative design, participatory design, cooperative inquiry, prototyping, ToyMobile.

1 Introduction

Telephones and, especially, mobile handsets are designed for adults. However, some studies show that young children (7–10 years) are already using mobile handsets (Sonera, 1998) and even younger (3–6 years) will have their own mobile handset in the future.

Small children (3–5 years old) are not able to use a standard telephone or a mobile handset without assistance with the functions or without considerable learning time. Still, small children have similar kinds of communication needs as

---

[1] This research was conducted while the authors were students at the University of Tampere.

adults. For example, they often need to contact a parent who is not at home at that moment, or a close relative. Play is also an important element of childhood and this special aspect is not part of current mobile communication devices.

Despite several problems that children face with electronic devices, they are using them amazingly well and independently for some tasks, for example, personal computers for drawing pictures and VCRs for watching their favourite movies.

1.1 Previous Research

The use of mobile handsets by young people and teenagers has been extensively studied in the INSOC (1998) project. The preliminary reports show that the use of mobile handsets is part of everyday activities and that the device is primarily and actively used for maintaining contact with friends. Designing useful and educational devices for children is best performed when children themselves participate in the design process.

Druin (1999) describes the *cooperative inquiry* research approach. This method has been developed to find out and fulfil children's technology needs. She concludes with the notion that this research approach is a thought-provoking experience, and it can lead to exciting results in the development of new technologies and design-centred learning.

Druin et al. (1999) report *applying cooperative* inquiry as design method with children (7–11 years old). The aim of the project was to create storytelling pets with children, for children using low-tech LEGO prototypes. They conclude by stating that this kind of design requires a comfortable environment for common design ground and informal practices in all activities.

Participatory design through games has been used as a design technique for several years. For example, CHI'94 had a tutorial on this method (Muller et al., 1994). This tutorial focused on group design through games.

Cooperative inquiry has been developed on the foundation of Contextual Inquiry (CI). Väänänen-Vainio-Mattila & Ruuska (1998) give an example about applying the CI in the development of mobile communication devices. They conclude with the observation that CI may not be able to cover all aspects of product usage in advance and thus generalisations must be made based on a sample of activities related to the usage of telecommunication services.

The need to involve users in the early phase of design process of technological devices, for example mobile handsets, is described by Väänänen-Vainio-Mattila (2000).

1.2 Approach

In this study we worked both with children and with parents. We conducted a questionnaire-based interview with 7 parents in order to obtain a wider view of small children's abilities and interests with technological devices, and to assess the results obtained from cooperative inquiry. Children were involved through simple phone communication experiments, cooperative inquiry and prototyping. Two children, ages 3 (Heikki) and 5 (Lauri), were observed during a 2 month period at home.

This approach is useful because we receive first-hand knowledge from children about their interest and abilities in using electronic devices in the domestic environment and parents can provide information that the children are not able to tell or express. This approach also helps in evaluating whether the results from a small user group are more generally applicable. The requirement for a comfortable and informal design environment (Druin et al., 1999) is possible through this approach.

Though research exists about cooperative design and technology with children (7–11 years), the active participation of small children (3–5 years) in design and research is not very well covered, especially in the context of telecommunications.

In our research we tried to find out on a limited scale the motoric and cognitive abilities of small children with electronic devices, especially with telephones. With cooperative inquiry and prototyping, our aim was to define an interaction model and set of basic features that small children are able to use and understand in a context of telecommunications. The functionality of the prototype is assessed with a computer simulation that is capable of providing better graphics and audio output.

During the research and design work, we captured both overt and latent user-needs, spontaneous examples of phone usage and problems with phone management. Overt user- needs are those that children directly expressed in different phases of the study. Latent user-needs are those derived from problematic situations and information obtained from parents.

Our findings show that children naturally use basic features of the most common electronic devices and they also have corresponding toys of real devices, which are used in play. Small children use toy mobile handsets or almost any toy as a mobile handset in their play. They also make calls with a real phone but even this simple action often needs adult assistance.

It is possible to build a telecommunication device that small children and analphabetic persons can use without errors in the interaction. The results also show that the basic desired features are very different from an ordinary telephone.

This paper is structured in the following way; Section 2 describes the findings on children's technology use in general. In Section 3 we examine the mobile handset play of the children observed. Section 4 shows the results of the experiments, prototype design and evaluation sessions. In Section 5, we make an analysis of how the results from our research correlate.

1.3   Technology and Small Children

We sent a questionnaire to 7 parents in order to find out what kind of technical abilities their children have and what electronic devices their children use at home. We got answers concerning 11 children (6 girls, 5 boys) from the ages of 3 to 6 years. Most children were either 3 or 5 years old. The families were from different parts of Finland with different backgrounds.

The knowledge of the children is amazing. Usually 3 year old children can not read and the responses indicated the same. Only one child knew some letters and two children knew some numbers. However, 60% of children recognised words. The level of knowledge increases dramatically as the child gets a little older. In our study, all 5 year old children knew letters and recognised written words and one 5 year old child could read. 75% of children knew numbers.

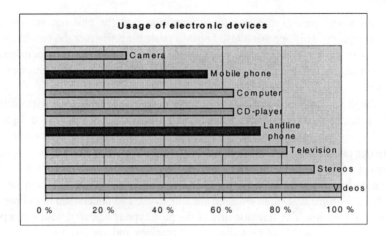

Figure 1: Usage of electronic devices.

The results of the questionnaire showed that children are familiar with the most common devices such as VCRs, stereos and TVs (Figure 1). Land-line phones are used a little bit more than mobile handsets, but this will probably change in the future, because mobile handsets as toys are much more common than land-line phones. In addition to these regular devices, children use computers a great deal. More than 60% of the children have used computers. Usually children like to paint pictures and play simple games with computers. One child even uses a word processing application to write some text or to practice writing. Keyboard, mouse and game controllers are familiar input devices for these children.

Most of the children use basic functions of electronic devices. These functions include turning the device on and off, volume control and playing cassettes. On the other hand, small children do not have any complex needs to use special features of the device. They are happy when they manage to watch their favourite children's programme on TV, a story from videocassette or listen to songs on a tape or CD. These basic functions can be usually carried out with single controls (one button press).

Children use both landline telephones and mobile handsets for telecommunication. Landline telephones are used a little more often than mobile handsets. Parents have the opinion that all the children are able to have a conversation on the phone and parents also think that all the children understand what is happening in the telephone conversation.

Children use the basic features of the landline telephone more often than the same features in mobile handsets. Some children dial numbers or use the quick dial buttons of landline phones by themselves, but only one child dialed numbers using a mobile handset. Our questionnaire did not give any reason for this, but our assumption is that a mobile handset is treated as personal device which is not allowed to be used without permission.

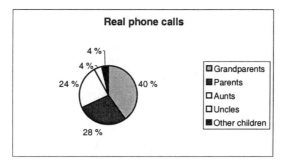

Figure 2: Calls with real phones.

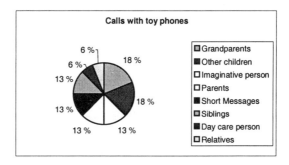

Figure 3: Calls with toy phones.

Small children use phones to call their parents when they are not home and close relatives such as grandparents, aunts and uncles. In a few cases, children call other children in the neighbourhood (Figure 2).

1.4 Communication Is Part of Play

During play, the number of contacts increases significantly. Compared to real use, children use new features of the phones as well. Grandparents and parents still remain important contacts in calls, but also siblings and other children participate these calls (Figure 3).

Phones are part of play and they are used as if they were part of everyday life. When the children play construction workers, police offices and other imaginative characters, the phone is part of that play. During our observations, we received similar findings about the usage of phones. Children make and receive calls and have conversations, but it is also possible that the called party is busy or not reachable. Some children even use text messages (Short Message Service) to send messages during play.

Nowadays mobile handsets are very common toys for children. 73% of the children have a mobile handset as a toy. 45% also have a normal phone and 18%

Figure 4: Toy phones used by the children.

use some other device as a mobile handset. The TV remote control or calculator will work as substitute for a mobile handset for children. Children will use these toys as real ones. They imitate ringing tones of the phones, as if it had real tones and press buttons when dialing. Dialed numbers are sometimes just random numbers, but they can also be real phone numbers. Conversations on the phone are similar to the real ones. They use short replies and other voices, which are typical for phone conversations.

2   Observations

Two Finnish boys, Lauri (5 years) and Heikki (3 years), were observed over a period of two months in order to find out what kind of phone interaction they use in play and who are the people they like to call. Activities related to phone use were recorded.

Both parents have their own mobile handset. There is also one landline phone at the home. Both boys have their own toy mobile handsets (Figure 4) and one real landline phone is available for play.

The parents' daily phone use is based mainly on mobile handsets. Their landline phone use is casual. This tendency was also seen in the children's play. Only one case of landline phone use was recorded during the two months, while there were about 10 observations related to mobile handsets.

Imaginary phone calls that the boys made with toy phones were spontaneous and typically they were made in the middle of another game. A typical phone call is made to or received from a close relative or friend, and it is followed by an explanation of the call to a parent.

Sample calls, Heikki (3 years):

- Real landline phone: "Police! There are burglars here. Come quickly" → "I called the police."

- Toy mobile handset: "Hello, who's there? Bye bye" → "Grandad or somebody called."

Figure 5: Telephone in experiment 1. Quick dial buttons are circled in red.

	Task 1: Dial "I or II"	Task 2: Dial "050002"	Task 3: Dial "0505534783"
Lauri	Ok	Ok	Fail+Ok
Heikki	Ok	Ok with support. Fail (without support)	Fail

Table 1: Results from Experiment 1.

- During car travel, toy mobile handset: "Hi mom. I have something to tell you. I miss you. Bye."

Sample call, Lauri (5 years):

- During a board game, toy mobile handset: "Hi, someone is calling. Uhm. Yep. Bye bye." → "Grandma called and sent her love."

3 Experiments and Prototype

3.1 Experiment 1: Phone Use

An experiment was carried out in order to find out what problems a child faces when using an ordinary telephone (Figure 5). The telephone has a standard telephone user interface and two direct quick dial buttons (I, II). By pressing these buttons, it is possible to establish a phone call without any other key presses. In the test setup, button "I" calls the child's mother and button "II" calls the child's father.

The experiment consisted of three tasks. In each task, the aim was to establish a phone call to the correct number (mobile handset). The task was successfully completed if the correct mobile handset alerted. The interaction consisted of handling the earpiece, dialing and ending the call. The results of the three tasks are summarised in Table 1.

In the first task, Lauri and Heikki were asked to make sequentially 10 calls to their Mother or Father (two mobile handsets) in randomly selected order using quick dial buttons (Figure 5). Both boys could manage the phone calls without errors. The test was repeated 7 days after the first experiment. The result was similar (no errors). However, the order of buttons "I" and "II" was not recalled at first.

The second task was to establish a phone call to a number of six digits (050002). The phone number was on a handwritten paper note. Lauri (5 years) could dial the number independently without errors. Also Heikki (3 years) could dial the number correctly but he needed help from Lauri in identifying the correct number.

In this task we identified two types of problems seen more clearly in the third task. The major problem was that the digits on the note were slightly different to the digits on the phone number pad (for example, $05\,0002$ vs. 050002), especially number 2. The number of zeros was problematic, because in the middle of number input action (primary task) it is difficult for a child to handle the additional cognitive workload that is caused by counting the number of digits ("000") (secondary task).

The third task was similar, except there were more digits in the phone number (10 digits: "0505534783", a typical mobile handset number in Finland). Lauri could dial the numbers correctly, although considerably slower than in the previous task. The first attempt failed because the phone service timed out due to slow input and service information about erroneous phone number was given. Heikki didn't succeed in completing this task. The main problem was that the number was too long to follow, i.e. the mental workload was too high, and numbers were thus pressed in the wrong order. Pressing the same digit too long or twice also produced errors. The identification problem in this task was seen with the number 7 (7 vs. 7).

3.2 Experiment 2: ToyMobile — A Prototype

In the second experiment a phone prototype was built and evaluated with the children. A computer simulation was built and evaluated, too. The prototype building process was based on cooperative inquiry and participatory design.

The design was initiated in a normal play situation when the activity led spontaneously to telephones. Lauri and Heikki were free to propose design and feature ideas. Later they participated in the actual building of the prototype. The prototype was built from cardboard, paper and some other everyday materials. The basic structure was a cardboard box of 10×8×4cm. A picture of the prototype is in Figure 6.

The children set some requirements for the phone: It must contain pictures of people to call and stories. It must fit into a small backpack. "I want to use the phone during a car trip in order to say we are coming. If it is dark outside I want to listen to stories." Lauri also proposed a jigsaw puzzle for the phone but immediately also thought, "we wouldn't be able to use it anyway", and the feature was omitted. Final technical propositions for features that the children made were:

- *Big size* (compared to mobile handsets). Small size was not preferred.

- Big *colour display*.

- *Roller* for up/down scrolling. Lauri invented the idea of roller based on a short experience with the Nokia 7110 (a mobile handset with a roller) a few months earlier.

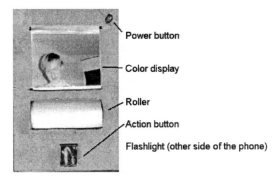

Figure 6: The phone prototype.

Figure 7: A physical piece (long paper slide) of phonebook content in the prototype.

- *Action button* (middle bottom). Originally, separate buttons were designed for phone calls and stories, but finally it was decided to have only one button.

- *Power button* On/Off (upper right corner). However, also the pressing of Action button should also switch the device on.

- *Flashlight* (middle of the reverse).

The two main function of the phone 'ToyMobile' are Phonebook and Stories. Persons in the phonebook are presented as pictures (5 persons) and they are in sequential order 'closest-ones-first' (Figure 7). Set of stories follows the phonebook items separated by a simple start-up screen for stories.

A person from the Phonebook is selected with the roller. The user first scrolls the preferred person from the Phonebook and then presses the action button to establish a call. Pressing the action button again ends the call.

Figure 8: A story picture. Mauri Kunnas' "The Knights of King Arthur". Published with the artist's permission.

A story is a set of pictures (Figure 8) with audio narrative. The user selects a story with roller and presses action button to start a narration. Pressing the action button again ends the narration.

With the rough cardboard prototype, the user actually operates the Phonebook and stories by scrolling the roller and assisting the movement of the paper slide with the other hand. In spite of several interaction problems caused by the cardboard material, both boys used the prototype in daily play and made imaginary phone calls.

A functional computer simulation was made based on the physical prototype. The simulation contained exactly the same content (Phonebook and Stories) and graphical layout as the prototype. It was completed with real audio content for stories.

The simulation was used to assess the usability of the design. Both boys were asked to call close relatives and to listen to stories. No interaction problems related to ToyMobile were seen in these experiments. However, the computer interface (i.e. using the mouse) made the simulation difficult to operate.

3.3   Results from Experiments: Play is Part of Everything

Telephone use is difficult for small children for two reasons. Entering and identifying digits is difficult for people who cannot read (1) and telephone services expect fast-enough input (2). The obvious conclusion of the experiment is that the only reliable method for dialing a phone number requires a single press-to-dial operation (quick dial).

The results of the cooperative inquiry are encouraging. You cannot disagree with the finding that even small children are capable of inventing new interaction methods by combining existing technologies and elements in creative ways. The idea of combining story telling and telephony is a natural reflection of the fact that play is almost always present in a child's life, "play is child's work".

4   Cross Findings in Research

The findings in the parent's interviews, long-term observations with two children and cooperative inquiry in the prototype design correlate at many levels. Parents often mentioned that the use of toy phones is a natural game and this was also seen in our observations.

The findings that real and imaginary phone calls are mostly made to a close relative or friend were also confirmed in the observation. This finding was further verified during the prototype design in the form of preferred Phonebook content.

Stories and fairytales are important for a child's intellectual development. The need to hear and see stories is seen in the high capability rate in using different kind of visual and audio devices (Chart 1). The observers also spontaneously raised this need. Stories were then implemented in ToyMobile.

In information obtained from parents and in dialing experiments we found out that the ability to know and identify characters and numbers was very different between 3 and 5 year old children. This was very clearly seen especially in the number dialing experiment with several digits.

5   Conclusions

Children are not afraid of using electronic devices at home. They use toy telephones and toy mobile telephones spontaneously in games and real technical devices for entertainment and educational purposes.

However, children's needs and cognitive capabilities are often underestimated. In this study we have shown that small children need a simple communication device and the primary task for this kind of appliance is to provide telecommunication with 5–10 close relatives or friends. Almost as important a function, as seen in the use rate of the VCR, is the capability to tell stories and fairytales, which is an essential part of a child's world.

We have also shown with a prototype that it is possible to apply cooperative design method and design a useful mobile communication device that small children can use without errors in communication tasks.

Though the number of parents interviewed (7) and children that participated in the study (2) is low and statistically not significant, it seems that our findings have a highly correlation with the 'real' world and that our results can be applied at a general level.

The prototype designed solves the interaction problems that are met with current telecommunication devices and network features by providing a simple-enough visual interface and function logic that is required by persons who cannot read. Another value of this design is that it downscales the required functionality of current mobile handsets, thus providing easy and cheap implementation. Results obtained by cooperative inquiry with two subjects are generalised and verified with the information that was obtained from a larger parent group.

The limitations of the proposed prototype are related to the configuration of the device. It requires that persons in the phonebook, attached graphics to the phone numbers and stories must be managed via an external device, for example a personal computer.

This design gives an applicable platform to create a reliable and educational mobile telecommunication device for small children.

Further research should verify the usability and usefulness of our approach with a larger user sample, children of different cultural backgrounds and with personal face-to-face parent interviews. For example, there may be major differences in basic telecommunication capabilities of children in different cultures. Also, it should be studied how suitable our design approach is for elderly persons and for persons with disabilities.

Acknowledgements

We thank the children and parents who participated to the surveys and observations. Special thanks to Heikki and Lauri for their enthusiastic participation.

References

Druin, A. (1999), Cooperative Inquiry: Developing New Technologies for Children with Children, *in* M. G. Williams, M. W. Altom, K. Ehrlich & W. Newman (eds.), *Proceedings of the CHI99 Conference on Human Factors in Computing Systems: The CHI is the Limit*, ACM Press, pp.592–9.

Druin, A., Montemayor, J., Hendler, J., McAlister, B., Boltman, A., Fiterman, E., Plaisant, A., Kruskal, A., Olsen, H., Revett, I., Schwenn, T. P., Sumida, L. & Wagner, R. (1999), Designing PETS: A Personal Electronic Teller of Stories, *in* M. G. Williams, M. W. Altom, K. Ehrlich & W. Newman (eds.), *Proceedings of the CHI99 Conference on Human Factors in Computing Systems: The CHI is the Limit*, ACM Press, pp.326–9.

INSOC (1998), Lasten ja nuorten mobiilikulttuuri Suomessa 1998–2000, http://www.info.uta.fi/winsoc/projekti/proj8.htm.

Muller, M. J., Wildman, D. M. & White, E. A. (1994), *Participatory Design Through Games and Other Techniques: CHI 1994 Tutorial Notes*, ACM Press.

Sonera (1998), Matkapuhelimet levinneet Suomessa nuorison keskuuteen kolmena aaltona, Press release http://www.sonera.fi/sijoittajatieto/lehdistotiedotteet/1998/mplevin.html.

Väänänen-Vainio-Mattila, K. (2000), "Ihminen huomioon laitteiden kehityksessä", *Aamulehti* . 10th November.

Väänänen-Vainio-Mattila, K. & Ruuska, S. (1998), User Needs for Mobile Communication Devices: Requirements Gathering and Analysis through Contextual Inquiry, *in* C. Johnson (ed.), *Proceedings of the First Workshop on Human–Computer Interaction with Mobile Devices*, Department of Computing Science, University of Glasgow, pp.113–20. GIST Technical Report G98-1. http://www.dcs.gla.ac.uk/~johnson/mobile.html.

The Reality Gap: Pragmatic Boundaries of Context Awareness

Yun-Maw Cheng & Chris Johnson

Department of Computing Science, University of Glasgow, Glasgow G12 8QQ, UK

Tel: *+44 141 339 8855 ext 0918, +44 141 330 6053*

Fax: *+44 141 330 4913*

Email: *{kevinc,johnson}@dcs.glasgow.ac.uk*

Recent developments in wireless communication and mobile computing have prompted a new vision of the world in which we live. Augmented reality has been proposed as the integration of physical and digital space. This approach is built upon the idea that it is possible to blur the distinctions that currently exist between computers and of artefacts, ranging from household appliances to pieces of furniture. The exchange of digital information both about and between these artefacts creates powerful opportunities for context-aware computing (Ishii & Ullmer, 1997). Inspired by this vision, we decided to engineer a practical and extensible system for augmented reality using 'off the shelf' wireless-enabled computing devices. The first demonstration of this technology was to be the development of electronic notes that could be attached to inanimate objects and read using a PDA. Wireless links were used to trigger the presentation of information when a user approached a 'tagged' object. They were also used to update information on the notes in real-time from any location. Rather than extending this metaphor of augmented reality or proposing further developments to the abstract ideas of context-aware computing, this paper describes the practical challenges of engineering such an interface. The hope is that others might learn from our mistakes.

Keywords: wireless communication, mobile computing, augmented reality.

1 Introduction

Mobile phones and personal digital assistants (PDA) help people to traverse the divide between physical and digital space. These devices enable users to access information from remote servers about the physical location that they are currently in. Such developments form part of a more general trend that is pushing physical and digital environments closer and closer together (Caswell & Debaty, 2000; Oppermann & Specht, 1999). For instance, chat rooms and web-based shopping malls duplicate the physical experience within a digital format. It is a matter of personal experience as to whether these digital developments enhance or parody their physical counterparts. Their success cannot be denied, at least in the short term. Many of these developments have, however, been ad hoc. In consequence, a number of HCI researchers have searched for a more systematic approach to the integration of physical and digital space (Ishii & Ullmer, 1997; Want et al., 1999). This work has developed sophisticated theories and a number of case studies that point to the benefits of tangible bits and augmented reality. A smaller group of studies have pointed to the ethical problems and social exclusion that might result from such development.

Rather than focus on the mass of theoretical and methodological research, this paper examines the engineering challenges that HCI developers must address if they wish to achieve the benefits proposed for augmented reality. Our focus is on systems that will work in an indoor environment. This is appropriate because it is the context in which the greatest benefits have been claimed for augmented reality. It also poses the greatest engineering challenges. Physical barriers prevent GPS, the lingua franca of location detection, from supporting the location detection that is a basic building block for context awareness.

1.1 Previous Work

This section reviews a number of different engineering approaches that have supported the development of augmented reality systems. Brevity prevents a complete overview of the many techniques that have been proposed. We, therefore, focus on the pioneering work of the Active Badge developers. We then go on to consider the Cyberguide approach. It is important to introduce this application because it provided a blueprint for our initial prototypes. However, Cyberguide relies upon specialist hardware. A primary motivation behind this paper is to show how augmented reality systems can be constructed using widely available, off the shelf components. Finally, we describe Hewlett Packard's Cooltown project. This vision of context aware computing is important for the rest of our paper because it forms a contrast with the more prosaic problems that must be addressed before HCI developers can fully achieve the proposed benefits.

The Active Badge system is arguably the first context aware system (Harter & Hopper, 1994). In particular, it provided early demonstrations of 'follow me' and security control applications in the office domain. Using this system, users are required to wear badges. Each badge is able to transmit a periodic infrared signal, which contains a unique code as its identifier. These periodic infrared signals are detected and picked up by networked sensors. Badge sensors are placed at fixed locations around the environment within the host building and are wired into a local area network. The badges' locations can be obtained once the sensors receive the infrared signal. A 'sighting' event is then sent to a server, which hosts the location-dependent information. The server can then provide relevant information to the user based on their current location. Although the Active Badge system can tailor information based on the users' current location, it suffered from a number of problems. Significant installation costs were associated with the sensor network this inevitably involved the use of custom-made hardware. There was also a myriad of social and cultural issues associated with the involuntary disclosure of location information. Users responded by adopting a range of informal protocols to determine when and where a badge would actually be worn.

The Active Badge system exploited sensors that actively detected signals from the users' badges. In contrast, passive location detection relies upon the users' equipment detecting signals that are generated from beacons in their environment. This is an important distinction. These beacons can be low cost signal generators, such as remote control devices, rather than the active sensors of the pioneering systems. For instance, the Indoor Cyberguide system utilised passive infrared sensing technology to demonstrate a context-aware tour guide application (Abowd et al., 1997). It was one of the first attempts to use PDA technology to bridge the divide between physical and digital environments. Unlike the Active Badge system, Cyberguide used infrared transmitters to communicate a unique identifier for each location. It did not use a networked system of base sensors. Each user carries a PDA, which is equipped with an additional specialist infrared sensor using a Motorola 68332 microcontroller. Once the user enters the signal of the infrared transmitter, otherwise known as its cell, the PDA can detect and decode the transmission into a unique identifier. In the original implementation, each PDA cached all of the location dependent information. The infrared location transmission was used to index into this stored data. However, this approach again relied upon a custom infrared unit. This is a significant issue for developers who lack access to specialist hardware or who lack the engineering skills that are necessary to incorporate the signals from these units into existing PDAs. Cyberguide also relied upon cached information. There was no means of dynamically updating information as the user moved around their environment and so the context was essentially frozen once the PDA was disconnected from its network infrastructure.

Hewlett Packard's Cooltown project is based on the idea that every user, every object and every location in physical space will have a web-based representation (Caswell & Debaty, 2000; Hohl et al., 1999; Oppermann & Specht, 1999). For instance, the visitors to Cooltown Museum will be able to access information about the exhibits from their PDA. These devices will automatically download this information from the web using a URL that is associated with an infrared beacon placed close to each exhibit. Visitors implicitly select the web reference by moving within the transmission range of an infrared beacon. This project, therefore, exploits the same passive infrared sensing technology as the Cyberguide system. However, it is augmented with web-enabled devices, such as printers and projectors. Users can exploit their PDAs to print documents by sending their URLs to an appropriate printer.

Similarly, documents might be sent to web-enabled projectors during meetings. This illustrates an important difference between the Cooltown project and the other approaches in this section. It is a pioneering vision rather than an engineering infrastructure. It looks beyond what is currently available to suggest what might be feasible in the short to medium term. There are, however, a number of limitations. For instance, it does not consider the engineering of an appropriate network topology to support the more visionary applications. For instance, what happens when users are out of transmission range? Similarly, although some of the papers assume an infrared architecture, the implementation details are not sufficient for HCI developers to implement a functioning system without recourse to the specialist hardware of previous approaches.

Some of the objections that we have raised will be addressed by technological developments. In particular, Bluetooth devices will enable the transmission and reception of short-range location information without additional hardware. These short-range signals enable users to identify objects that are in their current vicinity, for instance between 2–5 metres away. In contrast, existing commercial radio LANs provide signals that extend from 100–200 meters away. This resolution is not fine enough for most location detection systems. Microsoft is working on triangulation techniques that exploit differing signal strengths from multiple LAN radio beacons to perform fine-grained location detection. Unfortunately, both of these approached face a number of technological challenges. Differential signal detection is subject to distortions from the movement of objects in the environment. The Bluetooth consortium has been working for more than three years and commercial devices are only just beginning to appear on the market. In the meantime, there is a requirement for HCI researchers and developers to have some means of validating the claims for context awareness. Ideally, such a system should be modular, easily extensible and should exploit off the shelf technology.

1.2   The Glasgow Context Server (GCS)

A number of issues exacerbate the development of context aware applications. These can be summarised as follows:

- They have not been integrated with existing mobile computing technology and have relied upon additional hardware.

- The supporting infrastructure has been too costly to deploy and maintain.

- There is no efficient network topology to support disconnected users.

- They have failed to address the social concerns of their users.

The Glasgow Context Server (GCS) system has been developed to address these concerns. GCS uses the existing infrared port on most PDAs. Software has been developed so that the PDA hardware can detect signals from most commercial infrared remote controllers. As a result, it is possible to add a new beacon simply by buying a new remote controller from any one of a number of commercial suppliers at minimal cost. It is possible to cache information on the PDAs, in the manner described for the Cyberguide system. However, the full GCS system

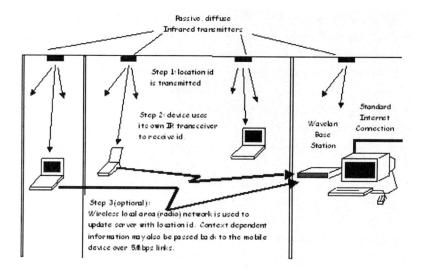

Figure 1: The Glasgow Context Server Architecture.

exploits commercial wireless local area networks. Current implementations use off the shelf systems produced by Apple and Lucent. As a result, PDAs detect their position and the presence of other objects using infrared signals from commercial remote controllers. They can then use the radio network to either communicate their location to a central server or to request information about the objects in their environment. Rather than adopt the active sensing techniques adopted by the Active Badge projects, GCS adopts a passive approach. In other words, GCS will never disclose the users' position unless this is specifically permitted.

2 The Virtual Notelet Case Study

As mentioned, the GCS environment has been developed to enable HCI designers to construct context aware applications using off the shelf technology. In order to demonstrate the application of our techniques, we focussed the initial development work on a proposal made by Baldonado et al. (2000), Pascoe (1997) and others. The idea is to implement a system that enables its users to stick virtual notes to physical objects. These annotations can then be read by holding a PDA close to that object. Alternatively, users might read the virtual notes that others have left for them, for instance on their door, from any location that offered Internet connectivity, following the model proposed by the Cooltown project. Figure 2 illustrates the general architecture for this application.

2.1 Design Overview

The development proceeded by identifying a number of scenarios. We did this by observing how people used these physical notes. An augmented reality system

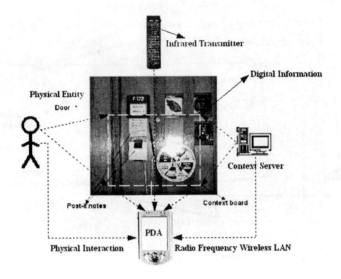

Figure 2: Traditional Notelet (left) and Virtual Notelet (right).

cannot hope to match the flexibility of the physical objects. The ability to hold, fold, interleave and manipulate paper as a physical medium is very difficult to recreate. However, we hoped to offer a range of additional functionality that might blend with, and support, the conventional uses of these physical objects. For instance, we designed a note that users could update with their location as they moved around a building. Another note simply displayed the individuals published diary from a time management system that was already being used within our target organisation. A further template enabled people to link notes to other forms of digital media.

2.2   Pragmatic Concerns and Usability Issues

Many of the concerns that arose in the design of this system had little to do with the underlying communications technology, that is often a focus for work in this area. These concerns had more to do with social and personal issues. For instance, a current problem with existing notes is that they are visible to anyone who might pass a particular door. Users were concerned to associate password protection or other permission mechanisms to the notes that they left. Other concerns related to the longevity of a note. Users wanted to specify when a communication should be removed and so on. More importantly, the initial design activities were dogged by a form of skepticism that is not recognised by many of the more euphoric attitudes expressed by the proponents of augmented reality systems. The earlier proponents of this technology had stressed the benefits of virtual notelets. However, they often failed to recognise the pragmatic barriers. Many people did not posses PDAs. Others forgot to carry them with them or simply did not attempt to access the digital information. Very importantly, an infrared transmitter lacks the affordances provided by a physical note! Many users didn't know that someone had actually left a note for them. Touch sensitive screens in public areas can address some of these problems. However, this again raised security concerns and is far from an ideal solution. An interim conclusion from this work is, therefore, that visionary projects such as CoolTown not only depend on a revolution in the underlying technology. They also require fundamental changes in the way in which people access information as they move around their environment. Our observations revealed a tendency to 'graze' information that was close at hand. Electronic resources, even if they are wireless and Internet enabled, seem to be a last resort for many people.

Many of these insights only emerged as the implementation was developed. This emphasises the key point behind this paper; unless HCI developers have access to off the shelf implementation techniques then systems such as the Virtual Notelet will continue to be proposed with little or no supporting evidence for their usefulness. Section 3, therefore, describes the technical problems that arose during this project.

3 The Technical Challenges for Off the Shelf Systems

This section reviews the technical issues that arose during the development of the GCS and the Virtual Notelet application. Two primary reasons motivate this presentation. The first is that it illustrates the sorts of issues that developers must consider if they want to validate HCI design ideas for context aware computing. The second is that our techniques might act as a blue-print for other HCI developers.

3.1 Infrared

As mentioned, GCS exploits infrared beacons. These are based on domestic remote controls (i.e. TV, CD player remote control). However, there is an important technical obstacle to communication between these infrared devices and mobile devices' existing transceivers. The protocols and standards used by the PDA's built-in IR transceivers are different from the physical and data link layers used by domestic remote controls.

The manufacturer of domestic appliances have exploited three different means of encoding infrared signals in consumer devices. They are pulse coded, space coded, and shift coded (DuBois III, 1991). These coding methods are different from that employed by the infrared transceivers on existing mobile devices. This explains why the Cybergudie system was forced to exploit additional hardware to enable its users to detect infrared signals. The majority of infrared transceivers on mobile devices conform to the Infrared Data Association (IrDA) standard. These standards were developed to support applications whose users needed to frequently transfer significant amounts of data from portable to fixed, portable to portable, and fixed to fixed equipment (i.e. Palm PC to Desktop, Hand-Held PC to Printer, PC to PC) using the serial infrared physical layer specification from IrDA. It utilises a RZI (Return to zero-Inverted) coding scheme (IrDA, 1998). These technical issues might seem to be a very long way from the claimed benefits of context aware computing but they help to illustrate the pressing need for reliable, off the shelf development environments. In passing it is worth noting that we began this project as a study of context awareness and not of infrared transmission standards!

Domestic remote controllers send commands in a low-speed burst for distances of up to 30 feet in one direction (DuBois III, 1991). They use directed IR with Light Emitting Diodes that have a moderate cone angle. In other words, the signal spreads out from the transmitted in a cone shape. This explains why you can change the channel on your television even if the remote control is not directly pointing at the device. In contrast, PDAs rely upon IrDA to transfer point-to-point data. In other words, it is deliberately intended to support line of sight communication. Data transfer is bi-directional. It operates in high-speed bursts over short distances. It uses directed infrared with LEDs having a narrow cone angle (~30 degree cone) (IrDA, 1998). As before, all of these technical considerations might seem to have little to do with mainstream HCI. However, we were again forced to recognise their consequences that they implied for the development of context aware systems. IrDA transmissions require relatively careful aiming; to use this protocol the users of a notelet would have to take careful aim with their device so that it lined up with a transmitter. If any other object comes between the PDA and the transmitter then the signal will fail. These characteristics make it impossible to use IrDA as an architecture for context aware computing, especially given the previous observations about the way in which users require rapid access and low set-up overheads for such information resources.

It is, however, possible to overcome the limitations of the IrDA protocol for our purposes. We have developed software that temporarily disables the protocols for infrared reception through the existing ports on most PDAs. Instead, they are programmed to operate in what is termed 'raw infrared mode'. In raw infrared mode, the infrared port can be accessed as a normal serial port with an infrared transceiver attached. The port is no longer IrDA compliant, however, it is then possible to receive signals directly from a domestic control. This supports the robust transmission of infrared location information and does not force users to carefully position their PDA within the line of sight to an IrDA device.

3.2   Radio frequency Wireless LAN

It should be emphasised that the GCS has a modular design that is consistent with both the Bluetooth standard and with differential radio signal detection. These more elegant approaches can simply be substituted for the infrared beacons that we currently use as a pragmatic alternative.

In the late 1980s, radio frequency based wireless LANs provided a bandwidth of approximately 250kbps. More recent standards support up to 2Mbps (IEEE 802.11). Nowadays, IEEE 802.11b makes a provision of high communication bandwidth up to 11Mbps (Lough et al., 1997). This raises the potential for wireless LANs to replace more traditional alternatives, especially in buildings that are difficult or expensive to rewire such as schools, hospitals, museums and domestic homes. GCS uses a commercial wireless LAN. The wireless LAN adapters that are installed on the users' mobile devices are compatible with most standard platforms. Infrastructure costs depend on the size of the required coverage and the number of users to be served. However, wireless LANs are marketed as a low-cost solution to conventional networks. The user simply inserts a PC card into their mobile device and installs the relevant driver. The system can provide a transparent network connection from then on. This means that users see no difference between wired and wireless based network interaction. In addition, radio frequency base stations can have a range of approximately up to 1500feet depending on the construction of the building.

3.3 Network Topology for Offline Support

The radio frequency local area network (LAN) provides a mobile computing environment for GCS users. However, even with maximal coverage there will be areas in which connection cannot be guaranteed. The physical construction of most buildings creates problems of shielding and interference that cannot easily be resolved. This raises a vast range of usability issues; many of which have not been considered by the more extreme proponents of context aware systems (Ebling & Satyanarayanan, 1998). In particular, it seems unlikely that we will be able to solve the problems associated with partial network coverage for many years to come. This comment applies both to indoor and outdoor systems, to cellular and satellite systems.

The communication technologies in GCS are based on radio frequency and infrared. When the users walk around inside the radio frequency and infrared network coverage, they can access data from the location server without any problem. Unfortunately, however, we initially chose to install our system in what can be described as a 'pathological' environment. We ended up demonstrating the technology in a number of Victorian and Edwardian buildings that contained a large number of computers, monitors, and healthcare equipment. The walls were extremely thick and these were numerous sources of electromagnetic interference. This severely reduced the range of the radio transceivers that formed the backbone of our system. Such factors again might seem to have little relationship to human computer interaction. However, it is precisely these issues that developers must address if they are to realise the more visionary objectives of context aware computing.

Fortunately, a number of features in the architecture of the GCS system enabled us to profit from adversity. The problems of achieving uniform radio coverage forced us to consider the usability issues that arise when people move outside our system. This led to an unsurprising but critically important observation: radio transmitters are expensive but infrared transmitters are cheap. As a result, the GCS system continues to provide context aware services even when users move beyond radio coverage. We can deploy dozens of low cost infrared transmitters that index into pre-cached information on each PDA. The cache is then periodically refreshed when the user moves into radio coverage. Figure 3 shows an example of the distribution of radio transmitters and infrared beacons. It also illustrates how a user can walk from radio coverage in cell 1 through an uncovered area to reach cell 2. On their way, they pass infrared beacons D, B, and A. In order for the user to access information about D, B and A, it must be preloaded before the user leaves cell 1. In other words, GCS must anticipate the users' likely trajectory through the uncovered region. This trajectory is at the heart of the caching mechanisms that support the development of interactive, context aware systems using the GCS.

As mentioned, the users' cache is updated when the system detects a trajectory that will take them beyond radio coverage. This is done by ensuring that infrared

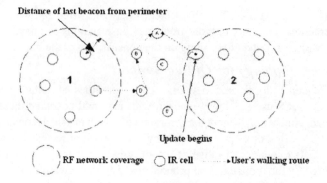

Figure 3: Network topology for offline support.

---

beacons are positioned a short distance inside the perimeter of radio coverage. This distance helps to determine how much time GCS has to finish refreshing the information in the users' cache. It is possible to derive a number of equations that support the installation of the GCS network. It should be noted that the following formulae represent gross simplifications. The time taken to transfer location information from the final beacon and to establish wireless communication is factored into the effective data transfer rate. These equations, however, illustrate important properties of the general architecture:

$$\text{Time required to refresh the cache} = \frac{\text{Quantity of data to be transferred}}{\text{Effective data transfer rate}}$$

Distance of last beacon from perimeter =
Time required to refresh the cache × Users average walking speed

For many applications, this predictive caching relies upon a mixture of task analysis and user modelling. It can also be made more adaptive if the system automatically records information about the user's previous path when they re-enter radio coverage. The practical development of context aware applications, including the Virtual Notelet case study, has also increased our interest in many issues that have not conventionally been part of human computer interaction. For example, we have become acutely interested in the speed at which people walk. As we have seen, this determines how long we have to refresh the cache before a user leaves cellular coverage. We have also become more interested in architectural modelling. It is far easier to cache information if users must follow a single path along a corridor than it is to predict information needs in a less 'confined' architecture.

4 Conclusions

This paper starts from the premise that context awareness offers many potential benefits to future users of interactive systems. It is, however, difficult to validate the many claims that are made about these applications. Very few interface designers possess the necessary resources to build context aware systems and so there is a lack of empirical data or even of direct practical experience with these applications. Previous approaches have relied upon specialist hardware or have involved re-wiring entire buildings. Future technology offers means of avoiding these implementation issues, for instance through the emerging Bluetooth standard or through differential radio signal processing. Unfortunately, technological and commercial difficulties have delayed the delivery óf these potential solutions in a form that can easily be used by HCI developers.

We eventually got tired of waiting for these technologies to mature. This paper, therefore, describes how we set out to engineer an infrastructure for the development of context aware systems. It is worth noting, however, that the GCS has a modular design that is consistent with both the Bluetooth standard and with differential radio signal detection. These more elegant approaches can simply be substituted for the infrared beacons that we currently use as a pragmatic alternative. The design principles behind this architecture were that it should be low cost, should be modular and easily extensible and that, above all, it should exploit 'off the shelf' hardware. The Glasgow Context Server (GCS) satisfies these requirements. However, previous sections have described the many technical difficulties that arose during the implementation of this system. We have also described the implications that these engineering issues have for the development of context aware interactive systems. For example, our use of passive infrared transmitters helps to address some of the security concerns that have been expressed about previous context aware systems.

We have briefly introduced the Virtual Notelet example to illustrate the argument that is presented in this paper. This system is not the central focus for our work. In contrast, the intention has been to demonstrate just how difficult it is to build the context aware applications that many other authors have proposed. These difficulties not only relate to the technical challenges that are addressed by the GCS system. They also relate to the very real human factor issues that are often ignored by the proponents of this technology. In particular, two of these issues stand out. Firstly, users seem reluctant to stand in front of an inanimate object consulting their PDA. There is an inclination to search for immediately accessible information sources, physical notes, notices and other people. The electronic resource is a last resort. Secondly, the use of passive infrared technology does not address all of the security concerns that users have about context aware systems. Tagging inanimate objects with paper notes is a form of social disclosure that is governed by numerous conventions. We have yet to fully understand what those conventions might be like when people from a different organisation or country might read those notes. In closing, it is worth reiterating the key point that such key observations will not emerge from the theoretical analysis of potential technologies. They will, however, become readily apparent if more HCI designers had access to the technological infrastructure that is necessary to support context aware systems.

References

Abowd, G. D., Atkeson, C., Hong, J., Long, S., Kooper, R. & Pinkerton, M. (1997), "Cyberguide: A Mobile Context-aware Tour Guide", *ACM Wireless Networks* **3**(5), 421–33.

Baldonado, M., Cousins, S., Gwizdka, J. & Paepcke, A. (2000), Notable: At the Intersection of Annotations and Handheld Technology, *in* P. Thomas & H. W. Gellersen (eds.), *Proceeding of HUC 2000*, Springer-Verlag, pp.100–13.

Caswell, D. & Debaty, P. (2000), Creating Web Representations for Places, *in* P. Thomas & H. W. Gellersen (eds.), *Proceeding of HUC 2000*, Springer-Verlag, pp.114–26.

DuBois III, J. H. (1991), A Serial-driven Infrared Remote Controller, http://www.armory.com/ spcecdt/remote/Irremote.html.

Ebling, M. R. & Satyanarayanan, M. (1998), The Importance of Translucence in Mobile Computing Systems, *in* C. Johnson (ed.), *Proceedings of the 1st Workshop on Human–Computer Interaction for Mobile Devices*, Department of Computing Science, University of Glasgow, pp.69–72.

Harter, A. & Hopper, A. (1994), "A Distributed Location System for the Active Office", *IEEE Network* **8**(1), 62–70.

Hohl, F., Kubach, U., Leonhardi, A., Rothermel, K. & Schwehm, M. (1999), Next Century Challenges: Nexus — An Open Global Infrastructure for Spatial-aware Applications, *in* T. Imielinksi & H. Korth (eds.), *Proceedings of the Fifth Annual ACM/IEEE International Conference on Mobile Computing and Networking (MobiCom'99)*, ACM Press, pp.249–55.

IrDA (1998), *Serial Infrared Physical Layer Specification v1.3*.

Ishii, H. & Ullmer, B. (1997), Tangible Bits: Towards Seamless Interfaces Between People, Bits and Atoms, *in* S. Pemberton (ed.), *Proceedings of CHI'97: Human Factors in Computing Systems*, ACM Press, pp.234–41.

Lough, D., T. Blankenship, T. K. & Krizman, K. J. (1997), A Short Tutorial on Wireless LANs and IEEE 802.11, Technical Report, The Bradley Department of Electrical and Computer Engineering, Virginia Polytechnic Institute and State University, Blacksburg, Virginia, USA.

Oppermann, R. & Specht, M. (1999), Anomadic Information System for Adaptive Exhibition Guidance, Technical Report, GMD — German National Research Centre for Information Technology Institute for Applied Information Technology.

Pascoe, J. (1997), The Stick-e Note Architecture: Extending the Interface beyond the User, *in* J. Moore, E. Edmonds & A. Puerta (eds.), *Proceedings of the 1997 International Conference on Intelligent User Interfaces*, ACM Press, pp.261–4.

Want, R., Fishkin, K. P., Gujar, A. & Harrison, B. L. (1999), Bridging Physical and Virtual Worlds with Electronic Tags, *in* M. G. Williams, M. W. Altom, K. Ehrlich & W. Newman (eds.), *Proceedings of the CHI99 Conference on Human Factors in Computing Systems: The CHI is the Limit*, ACM Press, pp.370–7.

Data Capture for Clinical Anaesthesia on a Pen-based PDA: Is It a Viable Alternative to Paper?

Martin Gardner, Meurig Sage, Phil Gray & Chris Johnson

Glasgow Interactive Systems Group, Department of Computing Science, University of Glasgow, Glasgow G12 8QQ, UK

Tel: *+44 141 330 4933*

Email: *{martin,meurig,pdg,johnson}@dcs.glasgow.ac.uk*

URL: *http://www.dcs.gla.ac.uk/~{martin,meurig,pdg,johnson}*

Mobile support for medical clinical decision-making and audit faces challenges related to the organisation of information and its presentation. In this paper we describe a document-oriented information design and associated adaptable user interface for pre-and post-operative assessment by anaesthetists. We present the findings of an empirical study comparing the use by real anaesthetists of a prototype of our system with current paper-based techniques for pre-operative data entry tasks.

Keywords: mobile systems, data capture, medical informatics, usability.

1 Introduction

Anaesthetists, like other medical professionals, use computers for many aspects of their work. An anaesthetist can expect to encounter operating theatre management systems that organise operations, automatic anaesthetic operating room systems that capture and record data during anaesthetic delivery and clinical logbooks, based on personal organisers, often used by trainee anaesthetists for audit purposes. Workstations provide access to medical records and, more generally, to online documents and information sources. However, other aspects of an anaesthetist's work, particularly pre- and post-operative assessment of patients and clinical audit, are supported in an ad hoc and sporadic way, if at all. Furthermore, there is little integration of the various existing systems.

Emerging technologies, including palmtop-sized computers, wireless digital communications, location sensors and middleware for nomadic applications, offer opportunities for a new level of support for clinical professions in general and anaesthetists in particular. Success in deploying these technologies will depend, at least in part, on the cost of interaction with these devices and, crucially, the cost-benefit profile of the new technologies compared with existing paper-based methods.

The Paraglide Project is a multidisciplinary project involving anaesthetists, HCI specialists and software engineers, exploring ways of using small mobile context-aware systems to improve pre- and post-operative assessment by clinical anaesthetists. As a first step, we have developed and prototyped an application for capturing pre-operative patient data that integrate existing methods of work with a user interface intended for deployment on a variety of devices with different display capacity.

There are a number of potential benefits of moving anaesthetic assessment data into electronic format and using mobile devices for its entry and access (see Section 2.2). At this stage we do not expect our prototype to match the speed and flexibility of current paper-based practices. However, it is important that the cost of data capture using the hand held computer is not so high, relative to paper, that users would reject computerisation in spite of their awareness of the potential consequent benefits.

In this paper we describe the information and display design for our prototype and present the results of a set of clinically-oriented trials to assess the relative interaction costs of data entry of the prototype compared to conventional paper-based methods. Section 2 introduces the setting in which our investigation is embedded, discussing relevant research that informs and motivates our own work. Section 3 describes the Paraglide system, focusing particularly on the information structures and the user interface design. Section 4 presents a comparative study of data entry with the prototype vs. paper-based methods. Section 5 offers some conclusions.

2 Background

2.1 Clinical Support Systems

Some clinical support systems have improved work efficiency and encouraged evidence-based medical practise (Cutolo et al., 1998). Nevertheless, the history of clinical computer development is littered with examples of systems that have been abandoned after delivery or that have failed live up to expectations (Anderson, 1997; Luff & Heath, 1998). The information structures and interaction techniques associated with current systems can play a part in reducing clinician efficiency, hence reducing the comparative advantage of the computer-based to the paper alternative for information management. For many users, typing is more cognitively demanding than handwriting or dictation, and the use of stylus- small display interaction on palmtops is often even worse. Forms of written expression in patient assessments can be very subtle and complex, typically poorly supported in computer-based medical record interfaces (Heath & Luff, 1996).

Clinical anaesthesia clearly shares many characteristics with other medical professions. However, as will be discussed below, it is important to be aware of the ways in which it differs as well. Professions are in part distinguishable because of the differences in work goals and organisation, interaction with patients and colleagues, document structure and use. There has been some prior work on computerisation of pre-operative assessment (Gibby & Gravenstein, 1998; Essin et al., 1998; Harper et al., 1997). In spite of this, however, pre-operative assessment remains one of the anaesthetic activities least well-served by computerised information systems.

2.2 Clinical Anaesthesia

2.2.1 Context

As is the case for all doctors, anaesthetists have strategic responsibilities for service provision, audit, training, administration and research. For the majority, service provision is their primary role. The services provided by anaesthetists include conducting anaesthetics required in association with certain surgical and medical interventions; obstetric analgesia procedures; acute pain management services; chronic pain management services; emergency resuscitation; and supervision of intensive care units. We are principally interested in the first three of these.

2.2.2 Current Anaesthesia Information Management Systems

Although there are considerable differences between individual hospitals, in the country as a whole, for all types of anaesthesia services, it remains the case that anaesthesia information management is largely reliant on pen and paper, supplemented by unrecorded voice conversations.

There are, however, three types of computerised system available for use in anaesthesia information management:

- theatre management systems — resource scheduling utilities for operating theatre suites; they are used to manage scheduling of cases, rather than handling clinical data;

- logbooks for trainees — used to compile a record of experience for the purpose of accreditation; and

- operating room systems — PC-based systems located on anaesthetic machines inside the operating room, capturing anaesthetic information during operations.

2.2.3 Innovation in Anaesthesia Information Management Systems

Ultimately any innovation in health care can be justified on only three grounds, namely improvements in efficacy, efficiency, and safety. In assessing the potential benefits of innovation in anaesthesia information management systems, it is important to recognise that benefit may accrue not only with respect to the management and outcome of the immediate case, but also with respect to the management and outcome of subsequent cases, either involving the same health care subject, or involving unrelated users, that is, benefit may be ad hoc or post hoc.

Potential ad hoc benefits of improved anaesthesia information management systems include:

- Faster data entry and more accurate data entry.

- Reduced data entry duplication.

- Improved legibility of clinical records.

- Improved distribution of information to collaborators.

- Integrated clinical decision support functionality.

Potential post hoc benefits of improved anaesthesia information management systems include automated support for clinical audit, clinical governance, training and education, resource management, e.g. stock control, knowledge discovery and research. Other than resource management, all of these benefits will be experience directly by the anaesthetists, rather than supplied indirectly to management.

In the work presented here, we have concentrated on the potential benefits of improved data entry and presentation, although we intend to explore other areas of benefit later in our project.

2.2.4   Pre-operative Information Capture

It is evident that many of the above potential benefits are crucially dependent on contemporaneous, near complete, computerised capture and processing of pre-operative assessment information. In crude terms, the pre-operative phase occupies the period between the anaesthetist being notified of a request for service, and the start of the anaesthetic procedure itself. During this phase typically the anaesthetist will make an assessment of the patient's history and clinical state, discuss options with the patient, make a plan, and issue instructions to co-workers.

Although often completed in a short time, pre-operative assessment is in fact a highly skilled task, on which the whole of the subsequent ad hoc management of the case will be predicated. Also post hoc issues such as outcome audit are fundamentally dependent on detailed knowledge of the patient's initial presentation.

The information capture activity is discussed further in Section 4 below.

3   The Paraglide System

3.1   Overview

The goal of Paraglide is to develop a system for the entry, management and communication of pre- and post-operative anaesthetic information. The Paraglide system consists of a network of 'clinical assistants' and a set of remote services allowing electronic access to data from the rest of the hospital. A clinical assistant is an application, intended to be deployed on a small portable computer, holding information about an anaesthetist's current cases requiring assessment. Clinicians use such a clinical assistant to collect additional data, to record their assessments, and to develop plans of drugs and techniques that will be used during the operation.

Clinical assistants communicate, typically using wireless infrastructure[1], with a set of remote services, such as a theatre management system (operating theatre schedules), hospital patient administration system, lab results, staff rotas, in order to

---

[1]We are currently using the SoftWired iBus//MessageServer (http://www.softwired-inc.com) to manage the transfer of data between clinical assistants and remote servers.

collect relevant data related to the anaesthetist's current cases. Clinical assistants can also request information opportunistically from these services, sometimes explicitly and sometimes as the consequence of interaction with the clinical assistant. Further details on the software architecture can be found in (Gray & Sage, 2000).

3.2 Information Design

We have chosen to use an asynchronous 'Document' model in Paraglide in which systems components exchange information by sending and receiving documents (represented in XML) rather than updating a common data structure. This leads to four strategic benefits:

3.2.1 Facilitation of System Evolution

A shared data structure model requires a stable data model capable of representing all the information that any agent may wish to communicate. Effectively it defines the limits of communication at the outset of system development. Relational data models are very difficult to design, especially in domains such as medicine. They are non-intuitive to domain experts, and relatively poor at handling information other than primitive datatypes. If the data structure changes, all potential communicating agents must be updated. In practice, beyond minor additions, any change to the data model is almost impossible.

In contrast, in messaging systems there is no requirement for a shared data model, stable or otherwise, only that each pair of agents in a communication episode can agree on a message format. Internal information representations can be changed at any time without affecting any other agents. Thus evolutionary development of medical information systems is greatly facilitated by 'Document' models.

3.2.2 Opportunistic Communication

British hospitals are highly heterogeneous, in terms of their physical environments; their communication resources; and their work practices. We are concerned with mobile computer devices. It will frequently be that case that mobile applications may have a mutual communication channel (perhaps via a wireless network, or an infrared serial connection), while having no channel to a common data store. In these circumstances the 'Document' model can support opportunistic communications, in contrast to a shared data model.

3.2.3 Clinical User Control of Information Distribution

In a shared data model, access to information is controlled by the data management system. In the 'Document' model, as implemented in Paraglide, the decision to send information to another agent is under direct user control. Thus information distribution is controlled by the clinical generator of that information, not by a remote database programmer.

3.2.4 Parallel Interoperability with Paper-based Environments

Because communication in the 'Document' model is mediated by electronic messages which have paper document analogues in current practice, we have the possibility of parallel interoperability with paper-based working. Depending on circumstances, individual users can choose, on a case-by-case basis, whether to use computer devices or paper records. Indeed, even within a single case, a user

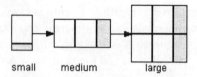

Figure 1: Three display formats.

may choose to communicate part of the case information using a mobile computer device, and part using paper.

3.3 User Interface

We have used a tiled display design basing the unit tile on the minimum height and minimum width of any supported display. Larger displays are handled by combining sets of tiles. Each tile corresponds to a single interactor, where each interactor offers a (possibly editable) view of a component of pre-operative assessment data. The interactors implemented in our prototype have been selected as a result of observational studies and consultation with anaesthetists, in order to support the key features of pre-operative assessment. The interactors correspond to the main sections of current paper-based records. The interactors are:

- Basic patient demographic data.

- Information about the operation.

- Medical history.

- Previous anaesthetic history.

- Physical examination findings.

- Investigation results (e.g. blood tests).

- Pre-anaesthetic instructions.

- Anaesthetic plan.

Our layout approach exploits the fact that current Personal Digital Assistant displays form approximate multiples of one another. Thus, the Vadem Clio and HP Jornada 820 are the same width, but twice the height of the 'clamshell' HP Jornada 620. The clamshell is slightly shorter, but roughly three times the width of the Compaq IPAQ. We also exploit the fact that all tiling designs leave space for a global set of navigation controls.

We first place on the display as many unit tiles as will fit. In the remaining area we place a navigator (mandatory) and a case summary (optional depending on space). Figure 1 illustrates the tiling patterns. Figures 2 & 3 give examples of the smallest and largest display formats.

Figure 2: Smallest display.

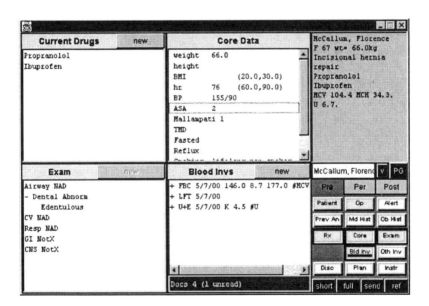

Figure 3: Full-size display.

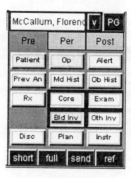

Figure 4: Full-size navigator.

3.4 Navigation

Control of the contents of the display is handled by a navigator component (see Figure 4). In addition to providing control it also supplies a persistent overview of the status and information content of the tile-set. Buttons in the navigator correspond to the potential contents of visible tiles. Pressing a button selects its associated contents for the top left-most tile and fills the remaining tiles with the contents of adjacent buttons.

One desirable feature of the current paper-based anaesthetic record is that all of the pre-anaesthetic assessment notes are continuously in view, on one side of an A4 sheet, so that the user can see immediately which record sections are filled or blank. The importance of this feature became clear as the consequence of early informal user testing. Given that our system is designed to run on large screen and small screen platforms, this feature cannot always be preserved. Therefore we have incorporated dynamic record summary cues into the navigation mechanism. The user always has direct access to a graphic display that indicates for each section of the record one of three states, indicated by colour codes:

- The section has been addressed and contains information (yellow background).

- The section has been addressed and contains an explicit negative (grey background).

- The section has not been addressed (white background).

This scheme has a very simple interpretation, viz. white section surrogates are empty, and still to be addressed, whereas coloured section surrogates have already been addressed. If the colour is grey, the user immediately knows the content of the section (an explicit negative) without having to open the full display of the section.

3.5 Smart Pasting

The interface implements an unusual paradigm for handling document data from external sources. Via visual cues in the interactors and the navigator, it signals the availability of unread information in the form of read-only documents. The user has the option to inspect the data by reading a document (for example, a Full Blood Count report), and may elect to close the document without copying any data into the anaesthetic assessment or 'paste' the information into the assessment with a single button-press. This paradigm is not seen in any other anaesthesia information systems of which we are aware. Although it may appear to place a small but unnecessary burden on the user, the paradigm gives the user control of data entry in a very natural manner, since the task sequence, 'browse documents; select and inspect a document; copy data' mirrors current practice in paper-based working. It also ensures that the user has always inspected and endorsed any information written into the assessment, a desirable situation with respect to clinical records, since the clinical user will have to take full responsibility for the content of the assessment.

4 Evaluation

In current British practice, pre-anaesthetic assessment typically involves:

- Consulting a theatre list.

- Consulting paper case records.

- Talking to the patient.

- Limited examination of the patient.

- Making notes.

An anaesthetist may do 5–15 such assessments per day, taking 2–10mins per assessment.

Paper-based working is flexible, fast, cheap and all too familiar to clinicians. However there is increasing pressure to use clinical information routinely for decision support, audit of techniques, audit of practitioners, education and research. Paper-based working simply cannot adequately support these functions. The acceptability to the user of computer data capture will thus depend on the relation between the additional cost of interacting with computer systems vs. the value of the 'downstream' benefit that would accrue. There are bounds to this equation though. We speculate that if a computerised pre-anaesthetic data capture system added more than approximately 5minutes to the average assessment time using paper, no amount of perceived 'downstream' benefit would justify its introduction.

Thus, in the evaluation of our prototype we are not seeking to show that computerised data capture is faster or cheaper than paper working; rather we wish to estimate the interaction *cost* of data capture in our prototype relative to paper, in terms of time, effort, and the amount of data captured. Most importantly, we are concerned to determine that our approach did not add an unacceptably large cognitive or temporal burden to the data entry process.

4.1   Method

Our evaluation was based on the observation of real users operating with real data in real hospitals[2]. We identified the case notes of seven real patients, such that each patient had undergone an anaesthetic for a common General Surgical procedure approximately 6months before our trial. Relevant information was photocopied and patient identifying data items substituted, to create a set of seven anonymised paper case notes, each consisting of about 3 sides of A4.

We recruited 11 users from 5 different hospitals, all of whom were practising anaesthetists, including 8 Consultants, 1 Staff Grade and 2 Registrars. Six had previous experience of hand held computers (Psion Organiser or Palm Pilot), though only for general applications such as diaries or 'to do' lists.

Each user met one of the researchers for a session of approximately 60mins, which followed the pattern:

- User given a brief introduction to the mobile device used in the trial (a Fujitsu Stylistic, using the larger of the display configurations shown in Figure 3), including its hand writing recognition facilities.

- User undertakes a pre-anaesthetic assessment of Case 0 using the computer, guided by the researcher (this training case data is not used in the analysis below).

- User undertakes 6 further pre-anaesthetic assessments of Cases 1–6, alternating between computer and paper (i.e. 3 on paper, 3 using the computer, in varying order, except for one subject who completed only 2 Paper and 2 Computer assessments). No subject encountered the same case twice. This was important since much of the task involves abstracting information from the case data, rather than explicitly data entry or transcription. Consequently, revisiting the same case would not constitute an equivalent valid comparative task.

- User invited to enter whatever information they felt appropriate for the case in hand, in whatever order they wished. Each assessment was timed, from the presentation of the copied case notes until the subject indicated that they had finished.

- User completes a brief structured assessment form adapted from TLX-style workload ratings (Hart & Wickens, 1990).

- User gives feedback in a semi-structured interview.

This resulted in data on 64 pre-anaesthetic assessments including:

- Timings.

- A detailed transcript of the information entered for each case (either the A4 paper record, or a computer log file in XML of the data entered into the hand held device.

---

[2]Ethical approval was gained from appropriate authorities.

- Ratings comparing use of paper to use of our prototype in terms of six workload-oriented factors.

- The researcher's notes on the users' performance and feedback.

In addition, from the case notes we have the six pre-anaesthetic assessments on paper of the original anaesthetists who actually did the case, though obviously without timings.

4.2 Results

4.2.1 Time

The time taken to complete a pre-anaesthetic assessment is dependent on a number of factors, two of the most important of which are the complexity of the case and the working practice of the individual anaesthetist. For example, a key part of the assessment involves noting details of the patient's regular medications. In many cases, the patient will be found to take no regular medication, but sometimes they might be taking seven or more drugs, all of which must be recorded. The primary reader of a pre-anaesthetic assessment is the anaesthetist who wrote it (typically the day before). Thus it acts as a memory refreshment document. Anaesthetists vary widely in their information recording practices, some being relatively verbose, others relatively terse.

Given that no subject saw the same case twice, we had to accommodate differences in case complexity and in users' working practices in our evaluation. For each of the 32 cases done using Paraglide, we calculated a predicted paper-based assessment time as follows:

$$\text{PPT}(S_x, C_i) = \text{Complexity}(C_i) \times \text{SVF}(S_x)$$

$$\text{Cost}(S_x, C_i) = \text{ParaglideTime}(S_x, C_i) - \text{PPT}(S_x, C_i)$$

where:

- Complexity(C_i) is the average paper-based assessment time for users who did Case i on paper.

- SVF(S_x) is the ratio of the sum of the times S_x took for the 3 cases they did on paper, to the sum of the averages that the other users took for those same cases.

- PPT(S_x, C_i) is the predicted paper-based assessment time for Subject X doing Case I.

Note that no single measured assessment time can contribute to both Complexity(C_i) and SVF(S_x).

So, for example, if S_x did cases 2, 4 and 5 on Paper in a total of 100seconds, and the sum of the averages for all the other users Paper times for cases 2, 4 and 5 is 80seconds, then S_x is generally slower than average by a factor of 1.25. If the average Paper time for Case i is 200seconds, we expect Sx would do it on Paper in $200 \times 1.25 = 250$seconds. Then if S_x takes 300seconds using Paraglide, the

Case 1	286 seconds
Case 2	160 seconds
Case 3	7314 seconds
Case 4	199 seconds
Case 5	215 seconds
Case 6	178 seconds
Mean	225 seconds

Table 1: Mean times for cases done on paper.

Subject A	1.164
Subject B	0.953
Subject C	1.052
Subject D	0.837
Subject E	1.148
Subject F	0.861
Subject G	2.441
Subject H	0.502
Subject I	1.097
Subject J	1.025
Subject K	0.932

Table 2: Subject variability factors.

'time cost' of Paraglide for this assessment is +50seconds. The results are shown in Figures 1 & 2.

The overall mean cost of Paraglide (32 assessments) = 127seconds. Thus on average, using Paraglide for an assessment rather than paper added 127seconds to the estimated time using paper.

After the training case, each subject did three cases using Paraglide (bar one subject who did 2, due to time pressure). In order to investigate the effect of learning from experience, we calculated separate average cost times for three subgroups of the 32 Paraglide assessments, where the assessment was the first, second or third in the sequence of Paraglide assessments done by the subject, shown in Table 3 below.

This demonstrates a strong learning effect — on average a 40% performance improvement resulting from experience of only two previous attempts (after the initial training case). We discuss the potential reasons for this learning effect in Section 4.2.4. There is no speed-up effect within the paper case sequences in this trial, as one would expect, since all of the users have done thousands of assessments using paper.

4.2.2 Data capture

We undertook a detailed assessment of the information items captured in each of the 70assessments (i.e. including the original six paper assessments). In sum the results are as shown in Figure 5.

	Number of Assessments	Overall Mean Cost
1st Paraglide Assessments	11	148
2nd Paraglide Assessments	11	125
3rd Paraglide Assessments	10	106

Table 3: Mean Cost of Using Paraglide by Encounter Order.

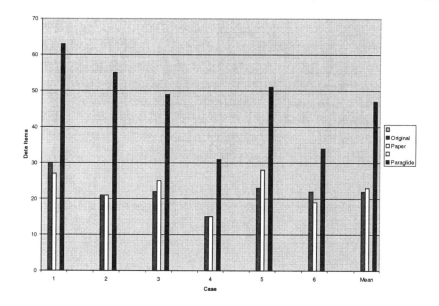

Figure 5: Number of data items entered — paper vs. Paraglide.

On average the computer assessment captures 24 more data items than a paper assessment. However our prototype contains a feature, smart pasting from documents, which biases the data item count in its favour. An example is as follows:

A blood investigation known as a 'Full Blood Count' typically generates 8 numeric measurements, of which 3 are considered particularly important to anaesthetists. If transcribing these results by hand into a paper record, the anaesthetist would rarely enter more than the 3 most relevant. In our prototype, all 8 are entered with a single gesture, thus it might be argued that 5 of these items should not be counted in a comparative analysis of dataentry, as the users would not have bothered to enter them by hand. In order to remove this bias, we compared the number of data items entered excluding any items which could have been transcribed (shown in Figure 6).

This is a surprising result, as we expected the adjusted mean figures for Paper and Paraglide to be similar. In fact we see that even when removing the advantage of one of our prototype's most powerful features, assessments using the prototype still have nearly 50% more data items than assessments recorded on paper.

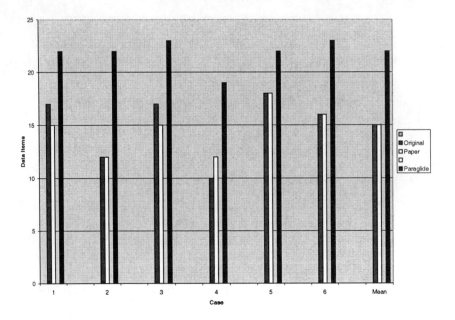

Figure 6: Number of data items entered — paper vs. Paraglide adjusted; note the different scale from Figure 5.

mental demand	Paraglide worse 0.4 (SD=0.43)
physical demand	Paraglide worse 0.3 (SD=0.47)
effort expended	Paraglide worse 1.0 (SD=0.48)
performance achieved	Paraglide **better** 1.0 (SD=0.76)
frustration experienced	Paraglide worse 0.2 (SD=0.38)
annoyance experienced	Paraglide **better** 0.5 (SD=0.46)

Table 4: Workload Ratings.

4.2.3 Workload Ratings

Users compared use of the prototype with use of paper in term of six factors: mental demand, physical demand, effort expended, performance achieved, frustration experienced and annoyance experienced.

For each, they were asked to provide a comparative rating of the prototype against paper on a scale of -5 (prototype worse) to +5. Average results (where 0 indicates no difference between paper and computer) are as shown in Table 4.

These averages must be interpreted cautiously, given that there were a small number of users and there is some variability in their judgements with respect to these scales. See Section 5 below.

4.2.4   Researcher's Observations

It was quite obvious to the researcher present during the trial sessions that the time cost of using Paraglide instead of paper was heavily influenced by two factors:

4.2.5   Handwriting Recognition

Three of the users had prior experience of handwriting recognition (Graffiti on Palm Pilot). None had used the handwriting recognition application on the trial platform (CIC). Two of the users were left-handed.

There was extreme variability in the users' success with character recognition. Some users had to make many attempts to achieve recognition of some characters, notably those with tails, e.g. 'b', 'd', 'g'. Conversely, one subject who had no prior experience of pen input achieved better than 95% character recognition success almost immediately, and could not understand why he was being given even the brief instruction that time afforded. The users with previous experience of Graffiti did not fare especially well. Although they were quick to experiment, they tended to vary the size, shape, speed and pressure of gestures, rather than alter the pattern of the gesture, which would have been more effective.

4.2.6   Synonymy

The prototype contains lists of selectable terms accessible either by browsing or by auto-completion of character input. On a number of occasions users spent considerable time writing in full potentially selectable terms, because of problems with synonymy. For example, dental examination is an important consideration in pre-anaesthetic assessment. Several users wrote the 11-character term 'false teeth', having not found this term in the autocompletion set for dental terms beginning with 'f'. In fact the prototype has a synonym 'edentulous' which could have been entered with one character and one selection gesture.

4.2.7   User Feedback

In general feedback was either positive or strongly positive, although this must be treated with caution due to potential bias given that they knew we were the developers of the Paraglide prototype.

Users identified a number of areas for potential improvement of the prototype, but as expected, most comments concerned handwriting recognition. The navigation mechanism attracted a number of positive comments, focusing especially on the visual cues to overall case context and the simplicity of the interaction. A number of users identified the dynamic case summary as particularly useful feature. Additionally, during the trial, every subject grasped the document pasting paradigm almost immediately, and most users remarked without prompting on the attractiveness of this feature of the system. Manual transcription, particularly of numeric data, is known to be error-prone and any such errors are potentially serious in clinical anaesthesia.

4.3   Discussion

Paraglide is designed for experienced professional practitioners users who are comfortable with the hardware platform, frequent users of handwriting recognition from pen-based input, and very familiar with the functionality of the application and its interface.

Our users are indeed experienced in the domain, but prior to this trial, none had seen a tablet (the type of mobile device used in the trial), none had any experience of the handwriting recognition program used, and none had used mobile computer devices for pre-anaesthetic assessment. Originally we estimated that a user of our system might become 'expert' after approximately 100 cases. Unfortunately, with this user group the time required to complete a training program of this many cases was out of the question.

The average time for completing assessments on paper, and the subject variability in this measure, were as expected on the basis of a prior observational study. The average number of data items entered on paper during the trial is very similar to the average number in the original paper assessments outside the trial. Given that the trial users were novice users with respect to the prototype, the average time cost of using the computer is encouraging. The rapidity of the learning effect we observed is very encouraging, and indicates that our estimate of the experience required to become a fluent user may be too high.

Perhaps the most interesting finding from the trial is that even after removing the effects of facilitated 'pasting' of data items, one of the most powerful and popular features of the prototype, the computer assessments still contained noticeably more data than the paper assessments. (Taken in conjunction with the finding that after experience of two cases done on computer, the time cost had fallen to +50%, this means that at that stage the per-item data entry rate using the computer is equal to that using paper). We speculate that there are two possible explanations for this increased data entry (not mutually exclusive). Firstly, using the computer, important negative findings can be entered very efficiently (for example, the finding 'Normal cardiovascular examination'). On paper, many anaesthetists leave such findings implicit. Secondly, in some screens of the prototype there may be a strong prompting effect. One screen in particular contains 10 entry fields all with fast selection menus. A number of users entered data in most these fields most of the time, whereas there are few paper assessments which give values for more than half of these 10 parameters. Of course, this behaviour may also be explained by simple curiosity. For our users, while paper-based assessment is a daily chore, the computer system is novel and therefore interesting. Perhaps they addressed some data entry fields not because they considered the data item important, but because they were curious as to how the system would behave.

Workload ratings and unstructured feedback were generally very encouraging. Those users responsible for the positive preference for Paraglide on the 'performance achieved' scale were questioned further about this rating. In essence, they interpreted 'performance' in terms of the resulting assessment, rather than in terms of the data entry process, and were clearly aware that they had entered more data in a more structured and accessible manner than would have been the case on paper.

Although handwriting recognition and synonymy caused significant problems for the users, it seems safe to speculate that these are problems which would be cured by experience. Indeed, once users become familiar with the terms in the prototype selection sets, the need for handwriting would be greatly diminished.

In sum, the findings are very encouraging. Although the number of users was small, the cross-over study design and the use of real (anonymised) case data lend weight to our interpretations.

5 Conclusions

The results of our evaluation suggest that the use of a mobile electronic system, such as the Paraglide prototype, featuring a document-based model of information structure and novel interaction techniques, can be a viable alternative to paper for pre-anaesthetic data capture. As anticipated, our initial results reveal that the computer-based system was slower than the more conventional approach. However, more data was entered for each case. It is also important to emphasise that the Paraglide system records the patient data in a consistent, electronic format. This is significant because it more readily supports clinical audit. Additionally, smart pasting proved simple and popular, but users' initial experience of character recognition met with variable success.

There are, however, a range of methodological caveats that affect these conclusions. Firstly, the sample sizes were small. We only examined a relatively small number of anaesthetists interacting with a relatively small number of case notes. This is partly explained by the resource implications involved in gaining the cooperation of nine working anaesthetists and permission to use a sample of data on previous patients. Secondly, the results of the preliminary study indicate that most of the users were still at a relatively low point on the learning curve with the Paraglide system. Data-entry times were still falling in the last of the cases that the anaesthetists entered. Again, this is explained by the difficulty of gaining access to our user sample over a prolonged period of time. For these reasons we view our results as indicative rather than as definitive. We have, therefore, also deliberately refrained from more detailed statistical analysis of our results.

Development of the Paraglide system is continuing, including the addition of further functionality such as post-operative assessment and audit management. A field trial is planned in the near future to examine the use of Paraglide under realistic clinical conditions.

Acknowledgements

This work was funded by EPSRC Grant GR/M53959. We wish to thank the staff who cooperated in our studies (at Glasgow Royal Infirmary, Health Care International, Vale of Leven Hospital, Victoria Infirmary, Western Infirmary). Also, we acknowledge the assistance of Professor Gavin Kenny, our collaborator on the Paraglide project.

References

Anderson, J. (1997), "Clearing the Way for Physicians' Use of Clinical Information Systems", *Communications of the ACM* **40**(8), 83–90.

Cutolo, E. P., Coblio, N. A., McCright, P., McCormick, M. T. & Harris, W. S. (1998), Incremental Improvements in Physician–Computer Interaction in Response to Clinical

Needs and User Feedback, *in* C.-M. Karat, A. Lund, B. Bederson, E. Bergman, M. Beaudouin-Lafon, N. Bevan, D. Boehm-Davis, A. Boltman, G. Cockton, A. Druin, S. Dumais, N. Frischberg, J. Jacko, J. Koenemann, C. Lewis, S. Pemberton, A. Sears, K. T. Simsarian, C. Wolf & J. Ziegler (eds.), *Companion Proceedings of CHI'98: Human Factors in Computing Systems (CHI'98 Conference Companion)*, ACM Press, pp.30 – 31.

Essin, D. J., Dishakjian, R., DeCiutiis, V. L., Essin, C. D. & Steen, S. N. (1998), "Development and Assessment of a Computer-based Preanesthetic Patient Evaluation System for Obstetrical Anesthesia", *Journal of Clinical Monitoring and Computing* **14**(2), 95–100.

Gibby, G. L. & Gravenstein, N. (1998), "Pre-anaesthetic Evaluation", *Baillieres Clinical Anaesthesiology* **12**(3), 503–21.

Gray, P. & Sage, M. (2000), Dynamic Links for Mobile Connected Context-aware Systems, Technical Report TR-2000-73, Computing Science Department, University of Glasgow, UK.

Harper, R., O'Hara, K., Sellen, A. & Duthie, D. (1997), "Toward the Paperless Hospital", *British Journal of Anaesthesia* **78**(6), 762–7.

Hart, S. & Wickens, C. (1990), Workload Assessment and Prediction, *in* H. R. Booher (ed.), *MANPRINT, An Approach to Systems Integration*, Van Nostrand Reinhold, pp.257–296.

Heath, C. & Luff, P. (1996), Documents and Professional Practice: Bad Organisational Reasons for Good Clinical Records, *in* M. S. Ackerman (ed.), *Proceedings of CSCW'96: ACM Conference on Computer Supported Cooperative Work*, ACM Press, pp.354–63.

Luff, P. & Heath, C. (1998), Mobility in Collaboration, *in Proceedings of CSCW'98: ACM Conference on Computer Supported Cooperative Work*, ACM Press, pp.305–14.

Web Design

Interactivity and User Commitment — Relationship Building through Interaction on Websites

Ann Light

School of Cognitive and Computer Science, University of Sussex, Falmer, East Sussex BN1 9QH, UK

Tel: *+44 1273 678 393*

Fax: *+44 1273 673 120*

Email: *annl@cogs.sussex.ac.uk*

Promoting services through networked media requires more than an understanding of commerce. It requires a sense of what user behaviour takes place at the service interface, and how different activities are viewed by potential participants. It also demands knowledge of which of these activities may strengthen users' interest in interacting as the producer wishes. First, a new framework to describe interaction is needed if we are to make connections between activities conducted online. Then, the understanding gained may be used to consider interaction design. A series of studies into the nature of interaction through websites is analysed here to provide modes of description for the particular nature of networked systems. This framework is then used to look at how site activities can be designed to promote participation. It shows that certain design features will promote a more social relationship between producer and user, assisting in the development of trust.

Keywords: interactive mechanisms, ecommerce, relationship-building, websites, design.

1 Introduction

Issues of trust and users' willingness to interact are attracting considerable attention, particularly, now, in the context of online shopping. In fact, many types of website offering services raise similar concerns about use even though their producers have various motivations in offering functionality: to encourage their visitors to vote, build social networks, or test products. Even those hoping to sell services and products accept that shoppers do not spend all their online time buying. As Nielsen says, online shoppers "only buy 5% of the time they visit e-commerce sites" and it is important to facilitate the non-buying tasks that account for 95% of visits to turn people into loyal users (Nielsen, 1999).

The studies described here reveal that a range of website producers have explored interactivity as a way of building user trust and loyalty, but with no certainty about how to do so. Initial hopes that a relationship could be built by encouraging users to respond with discussion and feedback through sites were disappointed. Instead, producers have begun to focus on what makes an effective interface for online services. This paper explores users' behaviour in the context of producers' intentions and discusses the kind of interfaces that optimise producer relations with users. In doing so, it ignores the crucial dimension of providing appropriate domain-specific content and services and concentrates on generic types of interactive behaviour possible through websites and their effect.

1.1 Descriptions of Interactivity

Interactivity is taken here to refer to the quality of systems to respond to a stimulus. The questions asked in this paper introduce a new dimension to these systems, relevant to the world of ecommerce, online democracy and community publishing, by focusing on the opportunity to interact with a remote website producer across a network, or, indeed, with software that might be deemed to be the producer's proxy. In a networked environment, it is time to ask how interaction is promoted, not by the functionality of the machine, but by the relationship between the provider of the system and its user.

Through the last two decades, with the introduction of 'multimedia', or content-based computer systems, there have been two conceptions of the interactions taking place at the computer as a system of:

- the machine and its user; or

- digital material and its interpreter.

For instance, Feldman (1994) uses the term 'interactivity' almost synonymously with non-linearity; defining it as users' potential control of place and pace, saying nothing about users' behaviour. By contrast, Baker-Albaugh (1993) says:

> "Interactivity can be described as the manner in which the learner dialogues with him/herself, with materials, or people during learning's mental activity."

The Internet's rise to prominence and the development of the Web introduced the features of computer-mediated communication to the systems being described and definitions changed a little. Huang & Karmouch (1998) have attempted a new synthesis of the different positions, while introducing the dynamic of interaction *through* the computer. Interactivity, in their work, refers to:

"...the mutual and reciprocal actions and responses between the end-user (especially learners) and the courseware-related entities."

However, the full impact of online exchanges has not yet been felt in an analysis of the interactions between users and computers or in the definitions of behaviour that come out of it. This task is tackled here in the context of the Web, a technology which exploits underlying Internet systems to offer users a chance to participate in remote activities that involve at least the semblance of 'someone at the other end'.

1.2 Community, Loyalty, Trust and Website Interaction

The search for financial success on the Web has prompted many companies to experiment with interactive websites. In 1996, the influential book 'net gain' (Hagel & Armstrong, 1996) was published, reinforcing, if not generating, the belief that the way to exploit the interactivity of the Web commercially was to build communities online and market products to them. At this time, there was a common belief that community building through discussion was the optimum way to establish loyalty among visitors and turn them into purchasers.

As early as a year later, Dyson (1997) was telling publishers:

"A 'community' is about as reliable a business model as a restaurant. ...
We should not talk about online communities, as that is not [visitors']
real interest. Perhaps we should talk about online support, think about
the real people and what online will do for them."

Dyson suggests that individuals' sense of identity with an organisation creates more of a radial model (with the organisation at the centre as recipient of people's interest) than a network, such as underlies the community model.

Since then, promotion of the community–loyalty economic model has given way to pursuit of ecommerce, where services and products are sold through the Web. The Web is being used for relationship marketing, where services are customised on the basis of personal information. This points to a new way of interpreting websites, not only as information repositories, but as the front-end of a service provision network (Wittel et al., 2000).

The area of trust and accountability, especially in privacy matters, has received a growing amount of attention with the rise of ecommerce. Cranor et al. (1999) found that people were comfortable providing information about their preferences on sites, but not personally identifiable information or financial details. Some attention has now been paid to designing sites that promote good relations and overcome people's concerns about trustworthiness. A study by Studio Archetype & Cheskin Research (1999) highlights six aspects which they conclude affect trust, including navigation and customer fulfillment issues. The report stresses that:

"... while trust develops over time, communicating trustworthiness must
occur as soon as interaction with a site begins."

Shneiderman (2000) identifies several ways of increasing trust in site users: disclosing patterns of past performance, providing references from past and current users, getting certification from third parties, and making policies for privacy and security easy to find.

Aaker & Joachimsthaler (2000) develop ideas of relationship building in the context of branding a website with the particular look and feel of the company developing it. websites can motivate customers to get to know the brand and its values, resulting in a deeper relationship:

> "When a brand is conceptually and visually strong and the site is well done, the user should feel that he or she is in the brand's world" (ibid. p.238).

Additionally, there is a considerable literature in the field of social psychology and communication which looks at the nature of relationships between people, for instance Hinde (1979), the development of trust, for instance Goffman (1959; 1969) and its basis in the choice of communication styles (Brown & Yule, 1983).

So the nature of relationship building has been coming under scrutiny from many sides, but there is still little analysis of the range of activities that users can perform on a website and how these activities relate to feelings about the producer 'at the other end'. The next section describes studies carried out so that this analysis might begin.

2   Studies

The work described here is based on two groups of studies of people and websites:

1. The accounts of users – in particular, ones who had been entering text into websites to carry out a range of activities.

2. Studies of producers of large institutional British sites.

The details of these studies are summarised below and given more fully in Light & Rogers (1999), Light (2000; 2001) and Light & Wakeman (2001). All the findings referred to below and used in the discussion are drawn from analysis of these studies.

2.1   Users' Perceptions of Interaction

The user studies upon which this analysis of networked interactions is based were conducted from 1997 to 1999. In a key study, Web users were asked to describe their last experience of entering text into a website, to find out:

- thoughts as they approach and start the task of entering text into websites; and

- how these thoughts compare with thoughts when using other parts of the site.

Accounts were analysed for evidence of apparent changes in perception between descriptions of navigational behaviour, reading information and interaction with forms, fields and comment boxes, where text entry was required.

The interviews followed the 'explicitation post-task interviewing technique' (Vermersch, 1994), which assists participants in recalling the details of their thoughts and behaviour during the performance of a task. Twenty 'experienced' (GVU, 1998)

Web users were interviewed, being asked to describe as fully as possible the last occasion upon which they had entered any text into a website. Participants were picked who used the Web as part of their everyday life, so that unfamiliarity with the medium would not affect the data collected. Participant demographics reflected Web demographics (GVU, 1998), with the exception that all interviewees were European English speakers.

Analysis was concerned with variations within accounts and patterns between accounts. Discourse analysis (Potter & Wetherell, 1987) was used to isolate themes and patterns, with a triangulation of researchers to draw independent conclusions. These concurred.

2.1.1 What Influence Does the Producer Have Upon the User?

In general, the interviews showed that:

- users responded differently at the point where they began to enter text into websites from behaviour with other parts of the site; and

- there were generalisable patterns between accounts about where changes in perception occurred.

Users developed an awareness of the site's producer in responding to requests for text entry. This awareness was not present during navigation, when interface issues were dominant. It was also largely absent when people found information they wanted to read, when their goals were dominant.

The increased awareness of the producer was revealed through a change in people's references to the site as they began entering text, showing a change of perception taking place. There were other changes: at the point when users began the process of deciding what to say in response to search boxes and information requests they became concerned with expression and self-presentation issues, even when they were interacting with software and knew it. Some people visualised 'people at the other end'.

Once obliged to behave in a 'communicative' way by thinking about and entering text, users behaved as if in dialogue with a single human entity, although they could rationalise that the designing of the question fields on pages and the subsequent site information processing were conducted separately, potentially by software.

People considered whether they 'knew' and trusted the producer in a different context before deciding how to view them. Consequently, unfamiliar companies were treated with suspicion and their motives for collecting and giving out data were questioned. If personal data were requested by companies, users became sensitive to the relevance of questions, concerned about further uses of the data, and unsure that the trade-off for what they sought was worth it. For more details of the study, see Light & Wakeman (2001).

In addition to this study, the following findings draw on studies of an online discussion forum (Light & Rogers, 1999) and observations of users examining communication mechanisms on websites (Light, 2001).

2.1.2   *What Influences a Visitor to Use Interactive Mechanisms in a Website?*

Examining the accounts of how users generally approach the interactive elements on websites suggests that the sequence of users' responses can be characterised as:

- Is this for me?

- What do I get?

- Who wants to know about me and why?

This sequence can be used to analyse participants' responses in different contexts.

If we look first at the issue of communicating publicly on a site, we find that different people decided not use the interaction mechanism at different points in this sequence, largely because of uncertainty:

- people without views on the matter under review, or those lacking confidence in expressing them, fall at the first hurdle;

- those who hold confident views but who wonder about the value of the context of display pause next; and

- those who see value or pleasure in contributing, may be deterred by possible negative effects of making personal information publicly available.

The opportunity for public posting was not taken up by most participants in the studies. In fact, taken overall, the activity appears to be unpopular with British Web users for a number of specific reasons, but, overwhelmingly, because there seems nothing to gain by doing so. Most British users, to date, have either been paying for their time online by the minute, or using facilities at work. Both conditions are inhibitory, serving to cut down on activities seen as without specific function or as exploratory. There is limited evidence from the studies that exposure to interaction opportunities might encourage British people to use communication devices, just as seeing others' contributions provides encouragement. Further, analysis of use of a discussion forum found that many people unused to posting first contributed to public debate because they disagreed with a former posting and did not wish to leave it unchallenged (Light & Rogers, 1999).

If we turn now to the effect of being offered the chance to request specific interactive services on site and reapply the same sequence of questions, a change is apparent. The user studies suggest this general model of response:

Q   Is this for me?
A   Yes, if I want the service.
A   No, if I don't want the service. (exit)

Q   What do I get?
A   The service.

Q Who wants to know about me and why?

A If I trust the company from elsewhere, then I'll trust it on the Web.

Likewise, if I've used it before or someone I know has and got good service, then I'll trust it. Otherwise, I may be reluctant to part with financial and personal information as it may be exploited or made public in some way. I may not believe I will get the service promised.

Users are mostly clear about the value of the interaction and their role in the exchange, even if lack of information on most sites muddies their perception of what the producer — or the producer's software proxy — is likely to do.

This can be simply summed up by saying that, as suggested, visitors are only prepared to act on site for what they see as a good reason.

2.2 Producers' Perceptions of Interaction

Users can only interact with what has been provided on a website: producers decide how interactive sites may potentially be. To establish producers' motivations in building relations with users, the producer studies sought to find out:

- how producers employed interaction mechanisms for site visitors to use; and

- their reasons as to why interaction with users might be useful.

Individual website producers from several organisations were studied and compared. Interviews took place over time (1996 to 2000) to see if there was a modification in the function of the sites and the attitudes associated with them. Large British information-producing organisations with websites were chosen as the core sample for interview, to see how they reacted to the interactive challenge of the new medium. Interviewees within these were picked because they had some control of website strategy.

The interviews were semi-structured, in that a specific agenda was set so that similar information could be gathered in each place, but, within this agenda, questioning was flexible to allow interviews to develop (Cordingley, 1989). The interview structure below was followed unless some aspect had been previously covered:

- Who are your target group?

- Are you reaching them?

- How would you describe your relationship with them?

- Do you cultivate it? If so, how?

- What mechanisms do you provide them with for communicating with you?

- Why?

- How effective are they?

- How do you find that the electronic environment differs from other environments?

- What interactivity do you offer?

- What functionality do you offer?

- How is it developed?

For more details of the study's methodology, see Light (2000).

The next section gives details of the relevant findings of the producer studies, relating them to the history of Web development.

2.2.1   What Influences a Producer to Provide Interactive Mechanisms?

Five years ago, many producers were experimenting with new forms of Web interactivity and the new relationships that these might foster. A dominant idea at the time was providing a connection to allow the audience to become more participatory, and this usually involved developing a communication facility, such as a discussion forum, based on the newsgroup model. The problems experienced with this were that:

- to make the discussions work, time and money needed to be invested;

- even successful discussions did not involve many people; and

- there was no apparent financial return in providing forums, despite the prediction of commentators (Section 1.2).

More recently, quite different models of interaction emerged. Corporate goals for Web development, based on the functions and financial needs of the organisation, were drawn up and the new range of functions offered by sites reflect these. It has been recently possible to buy, vote, bet, book, insure or order through sites. The range of services is wide and growing.

While some decisions about how to design sites to support this new functionality were taken through historical happenstance, these arrangements are being reviewed. Instead, a service culture has begun to evolve, which relates individual organisational goals to user needs, and this has started to determine the deployment of interactive mechanisms in site design.

Those producers who wish to provide discursive communication facilities, which are still considered to have a place on some sites, now have greater insight into what can be expected and how to respond. The relative success shown in soliciting contributions by hosts who conspicuously listen and respond demonstrates that acting as an *interested* producer has an effect. But this level of commitment from producers has only been forthcoming where the institution is motivated by core reasons. For instance, producers who are directly accountable to some part of the public for their funding demonstrate a more social basis for interactions with their visitors.

What still eludes producers is a precise understanding of how to achieve their goals in the detail of site design. They do not fully understand how users perceive the different aspects of interaction opportunities. The motivation to involve site visitors in activities online has not yet been interpreted into informed design decisions about what to implement. With the rise of ecommerce, companies have felt this deficiency with a new urgency. However, other professional organisations, with less commercial interests, also hope to benefit from a greater understanding of how design can influence user decisions to interact.

3 Developing a Framework for Exploring Interaction through Websites

It is possible to draw together these two sets of studies and their findings to look further at why and how interaction takes place on websites. We have touched on two kinds of interactions on websites: communication-based exchanges and general purpose service encounters requiring the participation of the user.

User communication with site producers has come in two key forms: private and public (with password-protected communities occupying ground between the two). Discussion forums, hosted by a producer, are an example of the public form and have been used to give opinions, gather information and provide feedback to the producer, while creating content for visitors to the site to read. These functions can be separated, based on whether the user's intended recipient is the producer, or the producer plus the producer's audience, into:

- Private mechanisms, for asking questions of the producer or giving feedback, including complaints and suggestions.

- Public mechanisms, where invited opinions or questions (and their answers) become content, in being selected and displayed for others to read.

The separation of the private and public functions of a forum has clear appeal to producers once the desire to interact becomes more goal-orientated. They can then choose which kind of function, if either, they offer and focus on providing the service effectively in terms of desired outcomes. It also reduces the opportunity for any collective response from visitors attempting publicly to interfere with issues considered to be internal policy, a problem cited by the producers interviewed in the studies.

In addition to communication mechanisms, there are other interactive components on websites that share the feature of requiring text entry by users. These have a different purpose in that they are not offered with the intention of stimulating conversation or feedback or to set up a social relationship, but rather to give the opportunity to perform a function, for instance, to search for information. The interaction may involve software as the other party, rather than a person, and the studies show that users are often aware of this.

The distinction between transactional and phatic communication (Brown & Yule, 1983) is useful here: transactional use is to impart information, whereas phatic uses indicate, for instance, feelings about the recipient of the message, and

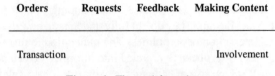

Figure 1: The social continuum.

can be characterised as the social, or bonding, uses of interaction. Communicative acts employ both aspects in some measure, displayed in the choice of expression. The interactions with software described above can be characterised as principally transactional in quality, containing only inadvertent phatic content. By contrast, if people are motivated by a sense of involvement then this can be seen as phatic interaction. They are working *with* the producer to develop a product and an identity linked to the branding of the producer at the same time.

A further complexity is added by the development of services that take place through the site, but not on the site. There is a difference between providing information – even selling it on site – and providing other goods and services that require processing in some kind of back-end activity. In situations where website interactions start a chain of remote activities, the software taking the users' orders might be viewed as the producer's proxy, and further commitment is made by the user and expected from the system dealing with the service. But this interaction is also primarily transactional in its nature, even if there is more clearly a more enduring service relationship developed between customer and provider.

The following subsections explore the relationships developed through these different configurations further.

3.1   A Social Continuum

Types of interaction have to this point been defined as either communicative or not. But there is evidence from the studies that a more subtle interpretation could be employed. We can look at activities on a site in a way that reflects the user's potential for involvement with the producer. Involvement is seen to be a factor in people's self identification with products, by selection and use, such as newspapers or designer-labelled clothing.

With interactive media, it is possible to define involvement in terms of activity and to draw up a list of users' activities positioned on a continuum reflecting the degree to which their motives are social (Figure 1).

Feedback functions occupy a transitional role. Much of the feedback supplied to producers can be regarded as transactional. Increasingly, this is the case as both producers and users develop expectations of professional competency of producers, replacing an earlier view welcoming experiment. In contacting a producer, visitors are often complaining; however, a more 'involved' action might be suggesting an improvement in service. Writing a comment for publication or connecting your site to a portal site — one which links several related sites together — can be seen as a more extreme manifestation of involvement with the site's producer.

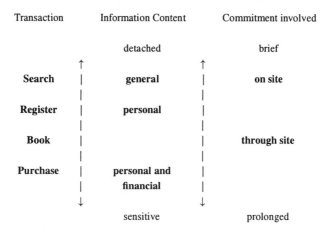

Figure 2: The transactional dimension.

The continuum based on the degree of social motivation is a new way of categorising interactions on websites. It can teach us something about the conditions necessary to encourage participation of different kinds. For instance, it will be evident from looking at it that only activities at the involved end of this spectrum are ever entered into with the intention of being seen publicly. A certain level of identity, or, conversely, fury with the producer and the producer's perceived audience is likely to be involved for people to wish to be seen publicly patronising a producer's site.

Involvement from the target group is, of course, the aim of the subtle marketing strategies that, for instance, Aaker & Joachimsthaler (2000) are discussing: persuading the public to learn more about a brand and using the Web to make that learning experience interactive in the hands-on sense. But these strategies have not been attended to in terms of the different kinds of interactive experience that can be offered on websites or how to persuade visitors to progress on a continuum towards involvement.

3.2 A Transactional Dimension

From the description above, it is also clear there are differences in the kind of transactional interactions that can take place:

- interactions with differing demands in terms of information provision; and

- interactions that begin and end with software on the site and those that involve passing information through the site for action by the producer.

Again continua seem an appropriate way to illustrate the dimensions involved, however, as shown in Figure 2, the transactions do not show users' intentions to commit themselves to some kind of involvement, but rather the engagement with the producer demanded by fulfilling the behaviour in the left hand column.

There are two continua here: one regarding information content that stretches from *detached* to *sensitive* as a way of describing users' feelings about it. Related is the continuum of commitment necessary to see the activity completed: from *brief* to *prolonged*. The most sensitive and prolonged transaction is the one that requires the most trust.

Again, there are transitional states, such as registering, which usually requires some degree of personal information, but which may or may not involve waiting for some response from the producer to allow access to the site or the service requested — such as an email with essential access information. Booking can be seen as transitional too, in that it may or may not require parting with financial details, but it will require the delivery of a service.

These continua also represent a choice of user engagement with the producer. But the activities are all ones which users perform as a by-product of requiring some service and the information handed over and the commitment involved in securing the service are not given with the same social intention that might be apparent in 'involved' activities such as contributing comment. In fact, there may be reluctance on the part of the user to engage in these processes if the information and the commitment required by the producer seem disproportionate to the task involved, or if there is doubt about the integrity of the producer.

By contrast, information giving and commitment behaviours of 'involved' users are not based on a transactional model of give and get, and trust, as such, does not affect users' choice of where to appear on the social continuum, but, rather, whether to engage at all.

The two elements — social and transactional — start to come together in an explicit way (as opposed to being inadvertent features of all communication) when a producer is trusted and becomes a preferred supplier. The producer may begin to take a role in the identity construction of the individual. Then, buying trainers through a site may also be used as an opportunity to be seen to do so, by posting a comment to the site for viewing by other similarly minded shoppers. Can this process be helped on its way?

4 Discussion: Encouraging Users to Interact

From examining the continua above it is possible to see that complex social and practical factors come into play in exploring users' activities with producers on websites and their relation to trust and involvement. The framework can promote the design of sites for user involvement, by making specific the elements of particular kinds of activity that require trust (in terms of the sensitivity of information required and the duration of the relationship) and by offering a view of behaviour as more or less social in intent. This can be interpreted both conceptually in designing the activities offered on site, and in terms of implementing interactive components.

4.1 An 'Inclusive' Design Policy

The text-entering study described above (Section 2.1) showed that users are generally aware of an organisation's goals when visiting its site and cautious if there is no familiar branding. However, the presentation of the site — its approach to visitors and the functionality it offers — will have an impact upon visitors and this experience will serve to build an image for the future. So visitors may be encouraged to become more participative, or become more positively disposed towards site and producer by being offered carefully targetted interaction opportunities.

In interviews with producers (Section 2.2), it became apparent commercial organisations saw little financial motivation for supporting social elements on site. However, the relationship building benefit of supporting user-centred activities need not be restricted to organisations with a public duty. It merely requires the producer to ensure that these functions appear nurtured. And it does not have to involve providing discussion facilities or promoting community.

Some successful tactics have been to:

- display user-generated material as an integral part of the site;

- attempt to link together people with common goals;

- provide material for users to customise and incorporate in their communal activities; and

- conduct consultation exercises on the Web, aimed at groups of users, with a view to developing policy.

Making the website culture collaborative encourages users to identify with, appropriate material from and, occasionally, to contribute material to the site. Producers with this emphasis to their sites have found that some of the feedback they gather is more social than transactional in style. In this respect, they share user features with sites established by community groups and individuals, despite having huge organisations behind them. They will also reap the benefits of bringing in new users through word of mouth.

To solicit content from users, analysis of producers' success shows that the most effective call is for material which is:

- Specific — it has a single function.

- Event-driven — it is topical.

- User-centred — it deals with issues that affect visitors directly.

- Experience-based — it asks for personal accounts.

- Influential — some notice is taken of what transpires, reflected in the body of the site and also elsewhere, if the information provider has other outlets.

This overcomes some of the reservations in contributing that are identified above (Section 3.2), such as indifference to the material or lack of confidence.

An inclusive design policy gives users the opportunity to move further along the social continuum towards involvement, without requiring commitment of other kinds.

4.2   Designing Interaction that Involves

To make specific recommendations in the design of interaction facilities is more complicated because so many other factors intervene that are related to the particular site domain. However, we now can see that interaction opportunities are not necessarily and exclusively presented to be used in the first instance, but also to signal intent. While a primary goal may be selling goods, or encouraging people to vote, secondary goals of encouraging involvement may be promoted with interaction facilities that require less commitment. Of course, this tactic is only effective if the same care is taken in designing all aspects of the site and the associated response procedures.

This approach can be well illustrated with feedback devices. These should be frequent, prominent and labelled as relevant to the material at hand. Their presence is important in showing that the producer wishes to have a relationship with users. If the mechanisms are then also used, this is a stepping stone to further interaction with the client and a build-up of trust, so long as the producer responds effectively. Any offering of feedback by a user, even a complaint, shows the start of 'involved' behaviour.

Providing areas for users to engage interactively with the site by entering information — to customise a service in different ways; to test out aspects of their interest in the site as well as to book or to buy — should also be effective in relationship building, as entering information into a site builds awareness of the producer as an entity (Section 2.1) and makes a good prelude to commitment, especially if the results can be saved.

At the point where user commitment is required, commitments are also needed from the producer along two dimensions to inspire confidence: there must be promises relating to the use of information submitted, and also, if the interaction is to be prolonged (Section 3.2), promises of producer accountability for delivering the service requested. These promises should be accessible at the point where interaction is encouraged, to minimise the fears that undermine trust. Of course, while reassuring on screen, they must be backed by fulfillment if they are to work in the longer term.

5   Conclusion

The analysis of interaction through websites above has shown the complexity of the relationship between behaviour and trust. This analysis has been achieved by examining how producers are hoping to meet their goals with the provision of interaction on websites and by scrutinising users' perceptions of interaction opportunities. The two sets of studies have fed into a new framework for exploring which activities may ultimately strengthen users' interest in interacting as the producer wishes them to in offering services through the Web interface. Throughout, the importance of the social element of the interactions that take place through sites can be seen, with its role in developing trust.

The analytic framework is based on two continua of activities typically offered on websites. The social continuum focuses upon activities as manifestation of users' involvement with the site and its producer. The transactional continua show the kinds of commitment needed from users to take part in site interactions. Between them, they illuminate how relationships underpin activity on site. These insights can be used to explore how the relationship between producers and users of networked media might be changed to promote participation.

Specifically, this framework assists in the design of sites that meet producers' goals to promote services and encourage interactive behaviour in users. It demonstrates that interaction on site is possible without commitment, but that commitment is required from users to engage in much of the activity through sites that producers offer. Two kinds of suggestion are put forward for building involvement without demanding commitment: one regarding how sites communicate their interest in users by adopting an inclusive policy; the other about how interaction opportunities are offered so that they build users' trust in the site and the producer before any trust is asked for.

Unfamiliar site face problems inspiring trust from users. However, implementing interaction design policies which encourage involvement without demanding commitment speed up the positive branding process that builds trust. This can be achieved by designing sites that offer user-centred materials and also by presenting low-commitment interaction opportunities that are seen to value a relationship with users and prepare the way for more committed activities from them.

References

Aaker, D. A. & Joachimsthaler, E. (2000), *Brand Leadership*, Free Press.

Baker-Albaugh, P. R. (1993), "Definitions of Interactive Learning: What We See Is Not What We Get", *Journal of Instruction Delivery Systems* **7**(3), 36–9.

Brown, G. & Yule, G. (1983), *Discourse Analysis*, Cambridge University Press.

Cordingley, E. S. (1989), Knowledge Elicitation Techniques for Knowledge-based Systems, *in* D. Diaper (ed.), *Knowledge Elicitation: Principles, Techniques and Applications*, Ellis Horwood, pp.87–172.

Cranor, L. F., Reagle, J. & Ackerman, M. S. (1999), Beyond Concern: Understanding Net Users' Attitudes About Online Privacy, Research Technical Report, AT&T Labs. available at http://www.research.att.com/library/trs/TRs/99/99.4/99.4/ (as at 2000.05.31) and also at http://www.research.att.com/projects/privacystudy/.

Dyson, E. (1997), Community Building: A Broader Picture, *in Proceedings of the Fourth Interactive Publishing Conference*, Interactive Publishing GmbH/Norbert Specker.

Feldman, T. (1994), *Multimedia*, Blueprint.

Goffman, E. (1959), *The Presentation of Self in Everyday Life*, Doubleday.

Goffman, E. (1969), *The Presentation of Self in Everyday Life*, second edition, Penguin.

GVU (1998), 10th GVU WWW User Survey, http://www.gvu.gatech.edu/gvu/user_surveys/survey-1998-10.

Hagel, J. & Armstrong, A. G. (1996), *Net Gain*, Harvard Business School Press.

Hinde, R. A. (1979), *Towards Understanding Relationships*, Academic Press.

Huang, B. & Karmouch, A. (1998), Enhanced Interactivity in a Multimedia System over Internet, *in Proceedings of the 1998 IEEE Canadian Conference on Electrical and Computer Engineering*, IEEE Computer Society Press.

Light, A. (2000), The Private Life of Websites: British Information Providers on the Web and the Role of their Audience, *in* R. Cheeseman (ed.), *Online Proceedings of the International Symposium on Competencies for New Media*. http://www.cmc.ruc.dk/aktuelt/symp/light-paper.html.

Light, A. (2001), "The Influence of Context on Users' Responses to Websites", *The New Review of Information Behaviour Research* **2**. In press. Paper original presented at the Third International Conference on Information Seeking in Context.

Light, A. & Rogers, Y. (1999), "Conversation as Publishing: the Role of News Forums on the Web", *Journal of Computer-mediated Communication* **4**(4). http://www.ascusc.org/jcmc/vol4/issue4/light.html.

Light, A. & Wakeman, I. (2001), "Beyond the Interface: Users' Perceptions of Interaction and Audience on Websites", *Interacting with Computers* **13**(3), 325–51.

Nielsen, J. (1999), "Why People Shop on the Web", *Alertbox* . http://www.useit.com/alertbox/990207.html.

Potter, J. & Wetherell, M. (1987), *Discourse Analysis and Social Psychology: Beyond Attitudes and Behaviour*, Sage Publications.

Shneiderman, B. (2000), The Future of Web Interfaces, *in* J. Nielsen (ed.), *Ecommerce User Experience Report*, Nielsen Norman Group. Paper presented at the Design for Usability Conference 2000.

Studio Archetype & Cheskin Research (1999), eCommerce Trust Study, http://www.studioarchetype.com/cheskin.

Vermersch, P. (1994), *l'Entretien d'Explicitation*, ESF.

Wittel, A., Lury, C. & Lash, S. (2000), Understanding New Media: from Networks of Virtual Objects to Objects of Virtual Networks, Centre for Cultural Research, Goldsmith's College, University of London, http://www.goldsmiths.ac.uk/cultural-studies/html/under.html.

Evaluating Multi-modal Input Modes in a Wizard-of-Oz Study for the Domain of Web Search

Alexandra Klein, Ingrid Schwank, Michel Généreux & Harald Trost

Austrian Research Institute for Artificial Intelligence, Schottengasse 3, A-1010 Vienna, Austria

Tel: *+43 1 5324621 1*

Fax: *+43 1 5336112 77*

Email: *{alexandra,michel,harald}@ai.univie.ac.at*

URL: *http://ai.univie.ac.at*

Browsing documents in the World Wide Web usually offers little opportunity for real interaction, as user input is often limited to mouse clicks and to filling out forms. By adding language technology, the gap between navigation and interaction can be bridged, which should lead to a more symmetric communicative setting. It means that free typed or spoken utterances can be used as means of access to documents on the Web, in addition to mouse clicks and typed strings as they are used to fill out forms, e.g. in search engines.

A crucial factor in system design is a sound pre-design study, which investigates how users will use typed and spoken queries to complement existing functionality. In this paper, we are going to describe a Wizard-of-Oz (WoZ) study which has shown that users tend to prefer multi-modal input over traditional input modes in search tasks concerning German newspaper texts, and that they were generally faster in completing the tasks whenever they were allowed to use free typed and spoken input. Additionally, users were grouped according to previous experience with search engines and the Internet. It can be shown that non-expert users expressed a stronger preference for multi-modal interaction than expert users and that, with multi-modal interaction, task completion times were reduced more significantly among non-experts than among experts users.

Generally, we interpret these effects as an indication that multi-modal access to the Web may result in higher usability, especially for non-expert users.

Keywords: natural language processing, multi-modality, usability, Wizard-of-Oz experiments.

1 Introduction

While developers of Web pages may use any combination of text, audio, pictures and video in their presentations in order to address the user effectively — thus fully exploiting the multimedia possibilities of the Web — the users' reactions are much more limited in being restricted mainly to point-and-click operations. It is to be expected that users can overcome this communicative asymmetry better if they are offered a greater variety of input modes, namely multi-modal interaction including free typed and spoken utterances. In the project which is described in this paper, we concentrate on the role of multi-modal queries posed to a search engine from the point of view of usability and its implications for the system architecture and the interface.

Recently, first steps have been taken by augmenting the Web by search engines which accept words or even phrases entered by the user and which are then matched with the stored information. We argue that these input options are still far too formal and too different from natural conversations to achieve high user acceptance once more and more interaction is carried out on the Web.

There are also structural arguments for using free spoken or written language. Complex types of action cannot be handled by mouse clicking and typing simple phrases, as these two types of input usually only refer to visible entities. Therefore, it is not possible to express e.g. indirect relations occurring throughout natural speech. furthermore, simple reference modes like single-word search or point-and-click are often particularly inadequate as a lot of information on the Web is textual which suggests also textual access. By using the latter, the gap between navigation and interaction in a communicative setting can be bridged. Textual queries also provide the advantage of reaching through the hypertext structure directly to the required (textual) information. This frees the user from a dependence on the document structure offered by the content provider, which is advantageous because often, users' and content providers' intentions may differ. At the same time, the user is not restricted to any predefined wording of the query.

2 Multi-modal access to texts on the Web

In order for the user action to be interpreted correctly, the constraints, which are imposed by the communicative setting, need to be recognised and represented. This suggests an action-centred model which treats user action, be it by spoken or written input or by point-and-click operations, as instances of information requests in the specific communicative context. This way, the expressive power of user requests is acknowledged by not restricting the user like in command-and-control systems.

At the same time, regarding user action in its situational contexts helps reduce the ambiguities and errors which are introduced by the results of speech recognition (Oviatt, 2000b).

Research and development in speech recognition has recognised the advantages and challenges of multi-modal interaction. System design has mostly focused on integrating various input modes, paying special attention to speech as the most relevant one. In these systems, browsing functionality can be accessed by appropriate speech commands. This approach is sensible, e.g. for offering additional browsing functionality over the telephone and for providing a restricted speech recognition vocabulary, resulting in better system performance. Yet these systems are still far from a real integration of reference to form, content and structure, as it is natural for any interaction in the context of hypertext documents. Therefore, it is the aim of the described project to point out new ways of integrating speech and language with classical access methods, and to investigate the respective shortcomings and advantages of different combinations of input modes. In contrast to commercial systems, not a broad solution will be reached. Rather, a situation with complex interaction is created and analysed in terms of usability, while the domain is limited in this research scenario.

In order to gain insight into the possibilities of speech access to the Web, from a practical point of view, the project is concerned with building the prototype of an interactive system for Web browsing and search, which integrates the processing of spoken and typed queries with the usual point-and-click commands of a GUI.

While the functionality of the GUI part will be standard, natural language queries can concern any combination of the following:

- what some particular piece of information refers to (i.e. content);

- how this information is presented (i.e. structure); and

- how this information is connected (i.e. document hierarchy).

Accordingly, we expect the system to handle (the German equivalents of) spoken browser commands, e.g. *back*, as well as content queries, e.g. *more about soccer*, and combinations of the two, e.g. *back to the page about the soccer game*. Natural language queries are to be interpreted in the appropriate contexts as they can be derived from the current communicative setting. The language processing module distinguishes queries referring to content, structure or document hierarchy and determines the new appropriate system states, e.g. by displaying text segments.

In the system architecture, on the other hand, the functionality of the GUI is enhanced and complemented by the possibility to use language commands. It seems plausible to stipulate that adding spoken and typed natural utterances to the input media of a Web browser will generally lead to a higher usability. This hypothesis was supported by the Wizard-of-Oz experiments which were carried out in the pre-design study. Therefore, it is very important to integrate the three input modes speech, text and point-and-click operations in a way that is perceived as natural by the user, in order to achieve high usability. Thus, the contrastive functionality (Oviatt & Olsen, 1994) of the input modes concerning interaction with the system is considered.

3   The Wizard-of-Oz Study

3.1   *Aims*

In the context of the project, the pre-design study aims at three main goals:

- research on the role of speech input in a multi-modal system;

- the adaptation to user needs; and

- the creation of a corpus.

A prominent aim in usability testing is the investigation of mode preference and coordination. Generally, researchers agree that a contrastive functionality of several input modes including speech guarantees highest performance as well as user acceptance (Oviatt & Olsen, 1994). The experiments are designed to investigate how system functionality is addressed by the input mode and which function is fulfilled by speech with respect to the other variants.

The investigation parallels research on speech input as opposed to other input modes in the domain of map tasks (Cohen et al., 1994), dialogue agents (Litman, 1998) and multi-modal access to timetable information (Quarfordt, 1998).

Experience with multi-modal interfaces integrating speech has generally shown that only a cyclic development process results in a usable system, cf. (Mariani, 1997). At several stages of the development process, user responses have to be considered and evaluated.

Furthermore, it is another important aim of usability testing in the proposed project to collect a corpus for user interaction in the specific domain of German search requests for news texts on the Web.

It was decided to use Wizard-of-Oz experiments (Fraser & Gilbert, 1991) in the pre-design study. Wizard-of-Oz experiments imply that the test persons are given tasks for interaction with a system, but they are not aware of the fact that the system is at least partly simulated by human(s), the *wizard(s)*. Wizard-of-Oz experiments are often used in the development of Natural Language Processing systems because with them, it is possible to test functionality, user behaviour and interfaces for systems which have not yet been fully implemented. The results of the Wizard-of-Oz tests can then be incorporated into the design of the actual systems.

We are well aware of the problems associated with WoZ experiments in a speech environment, particularly the simulation of speech recognition errors (Aust et al., 1994;   Oerder & Aust, 1994) and possibly the lack of relation to real-world tasks. Yet, testing the usability of the interface and obtaining a corpus is an important impulse for the development of the system. For the experiments, we decided to simulate almost perfect speech understanding. Naturally, errors in speech understanding and recognition are an important aspect in user interaction with the system (and in usability). Yet, it is very difficult to adequately simulate speech understanding errors, particularly speech recognition errors, and consequently, we decided not to model this part of system behaviour.

3.2 The Setup of the experiments

The four performance dimensions in the evaluation are task completion (determined in retrospect), task completion speed (which will be measured), complexity of interaction (derived from logging the interaction) and the user response to the system (evaluated by means of questionnaire-based satisfaction ratings (Litman, 1998)).

The subject's utterances were recorded, and typed input and mouse clicks were logged in order to assess task complexity. These sources can be synchronised via time stamps. Variance among the performance dimensions is evaluated according to standard methods of empirical evaluation (Preece et al., 1994).

The interface was built using Netscape Navigator 4.73 as a browser. The interface consists of two frames. One frame was simply used for displaying the resulting pages as provided by the more important control frame. To avoid the activation of links in the display frame by the user, the control frame had to intercept all sorts of unwanted events that could accidentally be triggered by the user. This was achieved by the use of an *applet*, a Java program associated with the page. Because the applet had to cope with all sorts of events which are usually handled naturally by the browser, and also because we wanted to limit user interference, the editor was made very simple. The applet was also responsible for triggering a commercial speech synthesis tool. It uses the Java Speech Application Programmer Interface, which allows for smooth interaction with commercial speech products. The applet was also responsible for producing a log file containing the user's and wizards' keyboard actions (the wizard's actions were limited to displaying Web pages and error messages, both triggered by key combinations).

The Wizard-of-Oz effect was produced by another computer connected to the same network as the computer used by the test person. A freely available program called PC Remote allowed the wizard to view and control the user's interface via a set of keys. The test persons' spoken utterances were recorded using a free software called STX, from the Austrian Academy of Sciences.

3.3 Test persons

43 test persons participated in the experiments. Before the start of the tests, they filled out a questionnaire asking for information on previous experience with search engines and the Web in general. According to the degree of familiarity with search engines and the Web, users were grouped as *experts* and *non-experts*. Familiarity was measured with the help of questions concerning expertise with traditional search engines, mainly concerning knowledge and use of logical operators. As is has been postulated that especially non-expert users benefit from multi-modal interaction (Oviatt, 2000a), for a Wizard-of-Oz study in our context, these two users groups were evaluated comparatively in addition to the comprehensive evaluation of all users. Overall, experts as well as non-experts had various professional backgrounds and belonged to all age groups between 18 and 62.

3.4 Tasks

Each test person was assigned 12 tasks. In each task, one newspaper text had to be searched in a large databases of German newspaper texts. The documents looked like texts on the Web but were stored locally on our server and where not changed

	general reaction	dialogue	interface	overall
non-experts	1.6	1.8	1.9	1.8
experts	2.1	2.3	2.4	2.3
average	1.9	2.1	2.1	2.0

Table 1: User ratings concerning general topics.

	System 1 spoken + mouse	System 2 spoken + written + mouse	System 3 written + mouse
non-experts	1.77	1.90	1.93
experts	2.00	2.13	2.34
average	1.88	2.01	2.10

Table 2: User ratings concerning systems.

during the course of the experiments. In the specification of the tasks, each text was summarised in two sentences, and the test persons had to formulate adequate queries based on these summarisations.

The twelve tasks were grouped according to combinations of input modes, during the course of the experiments, all tasks appeared with all input modes. We called the three different combinations 'systems'. One system accepted only spoken input and mouse clicks, one system accepted only typed input and mouse clicks, and one system accepted spoken and typed input as well as mouse clicks.

Each test person was given an instruction sheet, but was advised to use free spoken and typed input. The interface was explained, but no demonstrations were given. Assistance was available on demand, but only help concerning the interface or formal issues was given. Error messages were displayed whenever test persons mixed up the systems or formulated requests completely irrelevant to the tasks. This way, test persons were discouraged to explore the limits of the 'system' as this would have led to problems for the evaluation.

After completion of all tasks, the test persons filled out another questionnaire. This questionnaire focused on usability of the system as a whole as well as the different combinations of input modalities. This way, it is possible to compare users' preferences with task completion times under different constraints for the input modalities.

3.5 Results

Overall, the test persons stated that they consider the system usable (cf. Table 1). On a scale between 1 (highest grade) and 5 (lowest grade), the mean grade is 2.049. Generally, non-experts liked the system more than experts. This supports the hypothesis that the combination of traditional input modes with free typed and spoken input is appealing particularly to non-expert users, as it is a more natural way of interaction (cf. Table 2).

	System 1 spoken + mouse	System 2 spoken + written + mouse	System 3 written + mouse
non-experts			
average number of interactions	24	22	22
average time in seconds	553	514	1000
experts			
average number of interactions	26	25	26
average time in seconds	593	427	758

Table 3: Number of interactions and time used.

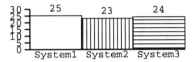

Figure 1: Number of interactions (mean).

Regarding specific aspects of usability of the system, the results can be compared to the overall grades given to the system. Efficiency received the grade 2.05 in overall average.

Furthermore, it can be said that on average, test persons needed less time for the completion of the task if they were allowed to use spoken or spoken and written language. Generally, task completion times were longer if the test persons only used written input (cf. Table 3). Expert users improved less by the use of spoken language than non-experts users did. For System 1 (spoken input and mouse clicks), there is no significant difference between non-expert and expert users. For System 2 (spoken and written input as well as mouse clicks), there is a significant difference. The same can be said for System 3. Generally, expert and non-expert users were faster using all three input modes (cf. Table 1 and Table 2).

So far, results indicate that multi-modal interaction can provide a usable and efficient access to documents on the Web, especially for non-experts. Further analysis of the experiments will focus more on the role of free spoken and written input. It has to be determined which functions these input modes tend to fulfill: whether they are fall-back modes, a general alternative or means of getting a shortcut to the requested information. In our tests, only a fraction of users replaced mouse clicks with spoken commands. Some extremely unexperienced users, however, relied solely on spoken commands and chose not to use mouse clicks. Search commands were usually spoken rather than typed. There was a significant growth in competence for the users during the tests. Again, these results show that using multi-modal interaction is an efficient means of accessing the Web, particularly for non-expert users.

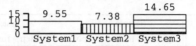

Figure 2: Number of minutes (median).

---

4   Conclusion

The Wizard-of-Oz study has shown that users, particularly non-expert users, prefer multi-modal interaction over traditional written input modes and point-and-click operations as they are used in Graphical User Interfaces, at least in the domain of searching newspaper texts and under idealised speech recognition conditions. Furthermore, it can be shown that users tend to perform faster if they are able to use spoken-language queries, and also then, non-expert users had a greater gain in task completion times. This is crucial as documents in the Internet have become an important source of information in both professional and private contexts, and access should be as efficient, open and natural as possible, not only from a technical but also from a communicative point of view.

The results from the Wizard-of-Oz experiments are considered in the design of the system, and users' comments will influence a new version of the interface. While there are results of Wizard-of-Oz experiments e.g. for multi-modal access to timetables (Quarfordt, 1998), there is no sound empirical foundation for usable interaction schemes accessing pages in the Web.   Empirical evidence from this domain will contribute to research on multi-modal interfaces and speech understanding for different applications. From the point of view of natural language processing, the obtained empirical data has two interesting dimensions. On the one hand, the corpus will provide important insights into the structure of communication, in this case the interaction with the Web as a multi-modal environment, and how it is mirrored in user action (speech, typing, point and click). On the other hand, from a more application-oriented point of view, empirical results can provide a valuable link between natural language understanding components and objectives of software usability.

Acknowledgements

The Austrian Research Institute for Artificial Intelligence is supported by the Austrian Federal Ministry of Education, Science and Culture; the project is supported by the Austrian Science Fund (P13704-INF). The authors would like to thank the users who participated in the study as well as the anonymous reviewers for their comments.

References

Aust, H., Oerder, M., Seide, F. & Steinbiss, V. (1994), Experience with the Philips Automatic Train Timetable Information System, *in Proceedings IVTTA'94 the 2nd IEEE Workshop on Interactive Voice Technology For Telecommunications Applications*, IEEECSP, pp.67–72.

Cohen, P., Johnston, M., McGee, D., Oviatt, S., Clow, J. & Smith, I. (1994), The Efficiency of Multimodal Interaction: A Case Study, *in Proceedings the International Conference on Spoken Language Processing (ICSLP'94)*, Acoustics Society of Japan, pp.249–52.

Fraser, N. M. & Gilbert, G. N. (1991), "Simulating Speech Systems", *Computer Speech and Language* **5**(1), 81–99.

Litman, D. L. (1998), Evaluating Response Strategies in a Web-based Spoken Dialogue Agent, *in 36th Annual Meeting of the Association for Computational Linguistics and 17th International Conference on Computational Linguistics*, Vol. II, Université de Montreal, Morgan-Kaufmann, Montreal, Quebec, Canada, pp.780–6.

Mariani, J. J. (1997), "Spoken Language Processing and Multimodal Communication: A View from Europe", Plenary Talk, NSF Workshop on Human-centered Systems: Information, Interactivity, and Intelligence (HCS), Arlington, VA, USA.

Oerder, M. & Aust, H. (1994), A Real-time Prototype of an Automatic Inquiry System, *in Proceedings the International Conference on Spoken Language Processing (ICSLP'94)*, Vol. 2, Acoustics Society of Japan, pp.703–6.

Oviatt, S. L. (2000a), Multimodal Interface Research: A Science without Borders, *in* B. Z. Yuan, T. Y. Huang & X. F. Tang (eds.), *Proceedings of the 6th International Conference of Spoken Language Processing (ICSLP2000/Interspeech 2000)*, China Military Friendship Publishers.

Oviatt, S. L. (2000b), "Taming Recognition Errors with a Multimodal Interface", *Communications of the ACM* **43**(9). Special Issue on Spoken Language Interfaces.

Oviatt, S. L. & Olsen, E. (1994), Integration Themes in Multimodal Human-Computer Interaction, *in Proceedings the International Conference on Spoken Language Processing (ICSLP'94)*, Vol. 2, Acoustics Society of Japan, pp.551–4.

Preece, J., Rogers, Y., Sharpe, H., Benyon, D., Holland, S. & Carey, T. (1994), *Human–Computer Interaction*, Addison–Wesley.

Quarfordt, P. (1998), Usability of Multimodal Timetables: Effect of Different Levels of Domain Knowledge on Usability, Master's thesis, Linköpings Universitet, Sweden.

Dynamic Information Presentation through Web-based Personalisation and Adaptation — An Initial Review

Diana Bental, Lachlan MacKinnon, Howard Williams, David Marwick, Daniel Pacey, Euan Dempster & Alison Cawsey

Department of Computing and Electrical Engineering, Heriot-Watt University, Riccarton, Edinburgh EH14 4AS, UK

Tel: *+44 131 451 3410*

Fax: *+44 131 451 3431*

Email: *lachlan@cee.hw.ac.uk*

URL: *http://www.cee.hw.ac.uk/~jdp/dip/index.htm*

Personalisation and adaptation of information and information presentation to reflect user needs and interests is an area in which there is considerable interest. DIP, Dynamic Information Presentation, is a research project that focuses on problems in this area. As part of this research a review has been conducted of existing Web-based information applications from a variety of domains that use such techniques, and a set of dimensions proposed as a basis for analysing and comparing them. The applications fall naturally into three categories. The results provide a useful step towards a general framework for classifying these approaches.

Keywords: personalisation, adaptation, dynamic information presentation, transformation framework.

1 Introduction

There has been considerable research in recent years on the retrieval of information from distributed heterogeneous databases, specifically focused on overcoming the problems of heterogeneity in data model, data representation, database structure and varied technologies (Sheth & Larson, 1990; Williams & Hu, 1992,

MacKinnon et al., 1998). This research has led naturally to work on providing more comprehensive and coherent responses to user requests for information on almost any topic. However, the nature of the data stored in databases and users requirements for the representation of that data have changed significantly. The prevalence of multimedia and hypermedia presentations, typified by the exponential growth of the World Wide Web, indicates a requirement by users for more flexible and dynamic presentation models than those provided by conventional database approaches. This requirement demands that information be transformed and presented appropriately according to the users preferences, the volume of data retrieved, the nature of both the data and the original request, and potentially any further requirements imposed by the information provider or the application itself (Cawsey, 1992; Bental et al., 1999; McNee et al., 1995; MacKinnon & Wilson, 1996; Rock et al., 1999). A number of applications have been developed to address these issues, with advanced search engines focusing primarily on user preferences and data volumes, while e-Commerce applications operate according to information provider requirements.

In both of the cases described information may be tailored along several dimensions:

- Content may be selected and filtered.

- Content may be differently structured and organised.

- Different presentation styles or modes can be adopted.

Each of these types of tailoring may be influenced by properties of the data, and by user preferences and selection. While there has been significant research effort on specific parts of this problem, e.g. selection of style of graphical presentation depending on properties of information (Bordegoni et al., 1997; Wilson & Marwick, 1997); combining information from heterogeneous sources (MacKinnon et al., 1998), there is no existing work that provides a coherent model for combining and integrating these different types of personalisation. DIP, Dynamic Information Presentation, is a research project that aims to address this problem and to develop a general solution for it.

One particular problem we will address lies in the interaction or interference that can arise between the different types of selection and personalisation. One simple example of this occurs in the use of search engines. These may lead the user to the middle of what is a coherent presentation, targeted at a particular audience, with resultant loss of context and coherence — and potentially serious consequences. This problem will be exacerbated by improved dynamic presentation techniques in which information is re-ordered and restructured for presentation. It will be further compounded if some form of intelligent filtering is applied by the user's system to the results returned. In this case there are potentially three different processes attempting to transform the information in different ways. This underlines the need for a general solution to the problem.

DIP will help to provide a better understanding of the techniques for dynamic presentation of information, and of how to deal with interference/cooperation between the processes manipulating such information to achieve a balance between their different attempts to transform the presentation. From a better understanding of these processes and how they can interact a more general approach to dynamic information presentation can be developed that will benefit both heterogeneous database/general search presentations as well as personalised presentations. This could lead to the development of more powerful intelligent display tools in the future. Within the DIP framework the design of usable systems will be enhanced by clarifying which personalisation transformations are being made, where they are made and who controls them.

2   Proposed Dimensions

In a simple model of information flow over the Web, information is passed directly from a server to the user's browser. Increasingly information may be processed through a sequence of different intermediaries, each of which will perform different operations on the information. Search engines are an example of one such intermediary; they collect information from many sources and serve it in response to the user's query. (A general architecture for intermediaries is proposed by Maglio & Barrett (2000) and Maglio & Farrell (2000)). Each intermediary may have a different model of the user's information needs and preferences. Even in the simplest case of a single server and browser, the user's preferences (as expressed in their browser settings) may make nonsense of the layout determined by the server. Where information has passed through a sequence of different intermediaries, we need some way to ensure that the models of the user that are held by each intermediary, and the operations performed as a result of these models, do not conflict and do not result in an incoherent display to the user. In order to derive a framework which could support coherence, we need to describe the models that are used for personalisation and the ways in which they affect the data passing through them. We have so far identified the following dimensions: the application area; the factors that are **input** to the model (such as the user's information needs, preferences, or behaviour; this may extend to knowledge about other similar users for collaborative models); the **source** of the model (e.g. from preferences directly expressed by the user, or from observation of the user's behaviour); whether the stored information is used directly, or whether inferences are made about the user; the output transformations that are applied as a result of the model (such as filtering or sorting the information). Other factors include the **control** and openness of the model (can the user see the model's settings, or change them); the system technology (a WAP interface does not support the setting of many explicit preferences); and finally, timing (a model may be intended for use just once, or may build up a picture of the user over time). This list is provisional, but we expect that it will lead to a better understanding of how user models compare, of the ways in which they may be applied, and of the ways in which different models may interact with each other.

2.1   Application Area (Area)

This paper concentrates on Web-based applications but related technologies such as email filters are also relevant. These applications include: daily news services; digital TV schedules; personalised Web search engines; shopping services; recommender systems; medical information extraction.

2.2 Input Factors

Input factors include:

- Personal state, history and preferences. These are factors about the user's preferences, knowledge and behaviour which are being observed or otherwise recorded.

- Collaborative models/factors. Collaborative models gather and analyse information about other users' behaviour and preferences in order to compare them with the current user and make inferences about the current user.

- External or environmental factors. These factors are not directly part of the user model, but are relevant to specific users. For example, GUIDE (Cheverst et al., 2000) adapts according to whether visitor attractions are open at the current time.

- System state. Some systems assume only a single user interface (e.g. a PC and browser), whereas others are adapted to run on a variety of hardware and software systems. Features may include fixed static features, such as the type of interface being used, the browser, the line speed; and dynamic features such as system loading or whether the connection is active or not at any particular time (e.g. the GUIDE system).

In the intelligent agents world (e.g. intelligent agents to assist with IR on the Web) a distinction is made between content-based and collaborative or social learning approaches (Mladenic, 1999). In a content-based approach, the system searches for items which are similar to the ones that the user has already liked. Some criteria are needed for similarity — similarity of texts or keywords in texts, say. Using keywords in this way can lead to confusion due to synonyms (different words, same meaning) and polysemy (same word, multiple meanings). In order to allow the system to learn which pages (and features) the user wants, the user may be required to rate explicitly the quality of the information returned, or alternatively the user may give some explicit criteria. In a collaborative or social learning approach, the system uses information about other users and their choices. Rather than looking for similar documents, the system looks for other users with similar interests and then for the documents that they have chosen or rated highly. Collaborative approaches can avoid the problems of polysemy and synonyms, on the assumption that similar user groups will use similar terminology and therefore rate similar search results as relevant. They can also be used for resources which do not contain text (e.g. videos, audio). Collaborative approaches require access to models of many individual users, so we record whether a collaborative approach is being used.

2.3 Model Source

We can distinguish four main sources of information, which may be combined:

- The user, in order to obtain a set of explicit preferences, e.g. GUIDE (Cheverst et al., 2000).

- Giving the users specific tasks to fulfil in order to infer their knowledge or preferences. For instance, asking people who want to search a document database to rate a set of sample pages from the database in order to infer their interests (Balabanovic & Shoham, 1997; Benaki et al., 1997), or giving students exercises to infer how well they have understood the material (Boticario et al., 2000).

- Directly observing the user's behaviour and using some learning mechanism to infer preferences or predict future behaviour. Observation-based models may be built from the user's interactions with the system or with other online systems, or even by reacting to other physical behaviour or state (e.g. the users' physical location in GUIDE).

- External information sources, such as a patient's medical record, e.g. the TIGGER (Bental et al., 2000) system.

2.4   Model Content, Structure and Inferences (Model Content)

Some models simply record information about the user, such as explicitly stated preferences. Others use the recorded information to make other inferences about the user which are then used to transform the output. These models may base their inference on fixed stereotypes of different users' behaviour, or they may use learning algorithms to adapt constantly to the users' preferences and behaviour.

2.5   Transformations (Transforms)

There are a number of ways in which the model can affect the output. These include:

- Selection — select different content for inclusion; include or reject items in a list, links, sections of text, images etc.

- Compression — include a link rather than the text or image; summarise information in briefer text; use a thumbnail image for a graphic or a screen shot from a video.

- Reordering — e.g. place the most relevant items where they are most quickly accessed.

- Alternatives — use different wordings or pictures to convey similar information; convey different information in different situations.

- Layout — elements may be presented differently on the screen.

Most of these transformations can affect both the content of the information presented and also its surface appearance, although layout and reordering are surface transformations.

2.6   Model Control and Openness (Openness)

As described above, a user model may be built explicitly by the user, or implicitly by the system. Related to this is the question of where the model is held, who controls the model and who can see its workings. Models may be maintained on the server or the client. The user may be able to see the model, or the model may be completely invisible to the user who is only able to observe its effects. The user may or may not be able to override the settings provided by the model.

2.7   System Technology (Technology)

The technology being used affects the kind of personalisation that is feasible and necessary. A PC and browser can easily be used to set up an explicit profile, whereas the limited display and key set of a WAP phone makes it more difficult for the user. Conversely, the small screen and difficult navigation of a WAP phone makes personalisation essential if we are to make the most relevant information accessible to the user. There are also other technologies such as specialised kiosks (which may have touch screens), PDAs and portable PCs.

2.8   Timing

Some systems are intended for single or occasional use (e.g. tourist information), while others are expected to be used daily or more frequently (daily news service, stock updates). Repeated uses may occur over a few days or else over weeks or months (e.g. TIGGER).

3   Application Review

3.1   Personalised Web Browsing and Recommender Systems

There are a large number of adaptive tools designed to assist with web browsing. In general, these offer lists of links to potentially relevant pages. These systems may be content based, typically with an explicit model of the user's information needs (such as a list of keywords obtained from the user) which are sought among the documents. Alternatively they may be collaborative, in which case the user's profile is matched with the profile of other users doing similar searches. Table 1 describes five of these systems in terms of our dimensions, and Table 2 briefly describes several other Web recommender systems.

3.2   Personalised and Adaptive Systems

We describe various other personalised and adaptive web applications in terms of our dimensions.

Table 3 describes:

- An online tourist guide (GUIDE) and a job search tool (CASPER).

- Two medical information systems for patients (TIGGER and DynaCat).

- Three Web shopping assistants (SETA, TELLIM and Web Assistant).

- Two educational systems (STIA and Hyperflex).

- Three listings and news services (PTV for TV listings, ANATAGONOMY for news, My Yahoo! information service).

Table 4 briefly describes applications from various application domains — calendar management, electronic news filters, expert identification, question answering.

Application	Area	Input Factors	Model Source	Model Content	Transforms	Openness	Technology	Timing
Personal Web-watcher (Mladenic, 1999)	Assists web browsing. Highlights useful links from current page.	Personal history (contents of pages visited).	Observation (of pages visited by the user).	Machine learning. Content of web pages is analysed and user profile maintained.	Anticipatory feedback — adds icons to links on web pages, to reflect user interest.	Intermediary. Autonomous agent, cannot be inspected or changed by user.	Web browser, proxy server.	Intended for multiple uses by a single user.
FAB (Balabanovic & Shoham, 1997)	Assists web search. Personalises the results of a query.	Personal history and preferences. Collaborative (contents & ratings of pages visited).	Observation (of pages visited by the user). Rating task (users rate titles returned).	Machine learning. Combines content-based and collaborative models.	Presents list of recommended URLs, derived from topic list by user interest.	Intermediary. Model controlled by web agent, adaptive for multiple users	Web browser.	
HUMOS/WIFS (Ambrosini et al., 1997)	Assists web search. Personalises the results of a query — front end to AltaVista.	Personal history and preferences. Collaborative (contents & ratings of pages visited).	Observation (of pages visited by the user). Rating task (users rate titles returned).	Case-based stereotypes, learning mechanism.	Ordering of results returned by AltaVista	Intermediary. Model controlled by web agent, adaptive for multiple users	Web browser.	Single, occasional or frequent use. Relies multi-users making similar queries
Letizia (Lieberman, 1997)	Assists web search. Offers personalised list of URLs close to page being read.	Personal state, history and preferences of current page and pages visited)	Observation (of pages visited by the user, and linked pages)	Inference of user interest, query or page analysis on keyword basis.	Selection. Offers user list of recommended titles in own browser window.	Autonomous agent, controlled by web agent. User control on number of titles.	Web browser.	Single, occasional or frequent use.
ECRAN/UMIE (Benaki et al., 1997)	Information extraction from company news and information.	Personal preferences (interest in a topic).	Rating tasks (users rate set of topics and titles returned) User can request topic.	Stereotypes.	Information extracted from documents placed in alternative templates.	User ratings override stereotype information.	Web browser.	

Table 1: Web browsing and recommendation applications.

Application	Description
Musag (Mladenic, 1999)	Application: Document search User model source: Content based Musag takes keywords from the user and searches for documents relevant to those keywords.
ApWeb (Bollen, 2000)	Application: Document search in an electronic journal library User model source: Collaborative ApWeb creates a group user model using spreading activation. Identifies documents that other users doing similar searches have downloaded.
Syskill & Webert (Mladenic, 1999)	Application: Document search User model source: Content based Asks the user to rate pages that it returns in order to learn a user profile. It autogenerates improved queries to a search engine.
Internet Fish (Mladenic, 1999)	Application: Document search User model source: Content based Proposal for web browsing using the user's own ratings.
Siteseer (Rucker & Polanco, 1997)	Application: Document search User model source: Collaborative Siteseer uses the user's bookmark file and other people's bookmark files to give priority to URLs that appear in 'similar' bookmark files.
Lifestyle Finder (Mladenic, 1999)	Application: Document search User model source: Content based and Collaborative User profiles are generated from (demographic) questionnaires. These profiles are used to identify similar users and recommend 15 Web pages that those users have rated highly.
PWW (Kushmerick et al., 2000)	Application: Document search User model source: Browsing history Uses a representation of the user's browsing context (i.e. either the previous URL itself or else the previous Web page) to infer the user's interests and retrieve relevant pages.

Table 2: Other Web document recommender applications.

3.3   Web Intermediaries

Web intermediaries are tools which operate on and possibly change the data flowing between the server and browser. An example of a general architecture for intermediaries is WBI (Maglio & Barrett, 2000),(Maglio & Farrell, 2000). WBI operates as a proxy server with plugins. Two of the transformations which it supports are:

- Customisation using information about the user for tailoring.

- Annotation using information about the outside world for tailoring (e.g. to highlight popular links, or to indicate how long a link will take to download).

For instance, LiveInfo is a plugin which changes text on the screen to a link to a window which contains more information about the text, and can be customised insofar as the user may choose different ways to break up the text for annotation. The Traffic Lights plugin adds green, yellow or red images next to a hyperlink to indicate

Application	Area	Input Factors	Model Source	Model Control	Transforms	Openness	Technology	Timing
GUIDE (Cheverst et al., 2000)	Tourist information, a mobile guided tour.	Personal preferences, state and history (places already visited) External and System information also.	Profile supplied by tourist. Cell-based wireless communication.	Direct from profiles and inputs.	Selection from nearby attractions list, and alternatives.	Tourist creates profile, may change itinerary.	Portable PC, specialised browser, local cells.	Single use, may be extended to occasional use.
CASPER (Bradley et al., 2000)	Identify suitable jobs from a database for applicants	Personal state & preferences. Collaborative.	Observation of applicants.	Machine learning.	Selection, from personalised list provided from server.	Model is maintained by the information provider.		Multiple uses over weeks.
TIGGER (Bental et al., 2000)	Information for cancer patients.	Personal state.	External electronic source (online medical record).	Interests inferred from medical records.	Selection (of texts). Re-ordering (of topics and texts).	Medical record viewable by patient, who cannot alter it or change options.	PC & Web browser.	Occasional use over months.
DynaCat (Pratt et al., 1999)	Front end to medical bibliographic database, supports information search.	Personal interests.	Explicit. Patient supplies query, terminology model and FAQ list.	Patient's query is interpreted in terms of the FAQ list.	Selection & Classification (of documents). Patients see list.	Model is held by provider, does not reflect individual user.	PC front end to MEDLINE.	Single or occasional use.

Table 3: Various personalised and adaptive applications.

Application	Area	Input Factors	Model Source	Model Control	Transforms	Openness	Technology	Timing
SETA (Ardissono & Goy, 1999)	Electronic shopping assistant	Personal preferences and history (general needs, domain expertise, lifestyle).	Explicit questions to user. Observation of user behaviour.	Stereotypes, with separate models for user and user buying others.	Customisation of presentation. Selection from recommended list.	Multi-agent architecture, all agents controlled by information provider.	PC type Web browser.	Occasional or frequent use.
TELLIM (Joerding, 1999)	Electronic shopping.	Personal preferences for products and presentation. System — plug-ins.	Observation of browsing behaviour.	Machine learning, inference from rules about behaviour.	Alternative presentation methods. Selection of items.	Interactions registered on client side, history list kept on server.	Web browser, Java.	Single use, no longer term modelling.
Web Assistant (Aberg & Shahmehri, 1999)	Human assistant for electronic shopping.	Personal state, tastes and preferences.	Explicit questionnaire. Conversation with the Web Assistant.	Web Assistant is a human being.	Selection of items to offer/recommend.	Web Assistant acts for the vendor.	Email plus human advisor.	Single use, multiple planned.
STIA (Mladenic, 1999)	Education — adaptive guidance for tutoring chess.	Students personal state and history.	Student tasks (multiple choice & problem solving). Observation.	Overlay model, infers which pages student can access.	Tutor may grant or deny access or recommend pages.	Provider controls model. Student navigates alone or with advice, see aspects of model.	Web browser.	Multiple uses by a single user.

Application	Area	Input Factors	Model Source	Model Control	Transforms	Openness	Technology	Timing
WebDL (Boticario et al., 2000)	Education — Web-based adaptive model for distance learning.			Agent architecture. Modelling agent infers accessible pages.	Link annotation. Selection of tasks in different windows and presentation styles.	Provider controls model. Students can annotate pages, but system controls visibility.	Web browser with multiple windows.	
PTV (Smyth & Cotter, 2000)	Personalised TV listings service.	Viewer's personal preferences. Collaborative.	Explicit identification by user. Users rate programmes for interest. Observation planned.	User profile compared to program profile by conversion to feature schema	Selection/ ordering of programmes. Compression for WAP.	User can inspect and change their preferences.	WAP phone or PC browser.	Frequent use.
ANATAGONOMY (Kamba et al., 1997)	Personalised online newspaper.	Personal reading history and topic preferences.	Explicit selection of layout. Users rate articles for interest. User observation.	Single user, content based. System rates user interests, by browsing behaviour and preferences.	Selection and presentation of articles.	Provider controls content model User can choose layout.		Occasional or daily use.
My Yahoo (Manber et al., 2000)	Online news, TV guide, local information, etc.	Personal preferences and history.	Explicit customisation by user selection. Reuse of information from user queries.	Direct.	Topic and content selection. Layout.	Explicit customisation of model by user. Layout can follow user to different machines.	PC browser.	Occasional or frequent use.

Application	Description
Calendar Apprentice (Mladenic, 1999)	Application: Automated Calendar User model source: Content based Learns by observing user's electronic diary/calendar and helps user to schedule new meetings. Integrates information about schedules of other meeting attendees.
Newsweeder (Mladenic, 1999)	Application: Electronic news filter User model source: Content based Filters electronic news based on user's rating of articles. Offers feedback on each article. Using predefined ratings can return 'top fifty' list.
GroupLens (Konstan et al., 1997)	Application: Electronic news filter User model source: Collaborative (no knowledge of content)
ContactFinder (Mladenic, 1999)	Application: Identify expertise User model source: Content based Categorises messages and extracts topic areas to identify experts in particular areas. Analyses user queries to match them to suitable topic experts.
Referralweb (Kautz et al., 1997)	Application: Identify expertise User model source: Collaborative Incrementally constructs map of relationships between individuals
FAQFinder (Mladenic, 1999)	Application: Answer questions on the Web User model source: Content based Matches user questions to FAQ questions and returns the 'top five'.

Table 4: Various other recommender applications.

how quickly the server can respond to that link. Table 5 describes WBI in terms of our dimensions. The WBI architecture and related research in web intermediaries may inform solutions for DIP.

4 Conclusions and Future Work

This paper has described a review of existing Web-based information applications, from a variety of domains, that provide personalisation and adaptation of information and presentation. In order to conduct the review we have proposed a set of dimensions that have provided a useful model by which an analysis and comparison of these applications has been supported. From the details set out in the tables in the preceding sections it is clear that the dimensions we have selected provide good evidence of the potential for interchange of information and interoperability between applications, while also highlighting the significant level of heterogeneity to be overcome to achieve this. This review has been an extremely useful starting exercise for the DIP project, identifying the range and diversity of applications in this area, and confirming a research agenda based on our existing experience in heterogeneity, interoperability and information personalisation.

However, as indicated earlier, this set of dimensions is an initial list and, although it has proved both useful and sufficient for this review, it is not exhaustive

Factor	WBI/LiveInfo
Area	Development kit for Web intermediaries
Input Factors	Supports personal, external system. Traffic lights plugin adds coloured images to hyperlink to indicate download time. LiveInfo plugin converts words to dictionary definition hyperlinks.
Model Source	Observation or explicit. Personal or external.
Transforms	Modifies page markup. Transforms existing text to links. Adds annotations.
Openness	Model controlled by intermediary, but possible to build plugins which are user controlled or customisable.
Technology	Proxy server with plugins.
Timing	Variable.

Table 5: WBI Web Intermediary Development Kit.

enough to support a general framework for the classification of approaches to the generation of such applications. We aim to provide a coherent framework to integrate the different aspects of personalisation that we have identified. We are currently working on a more detailed framework which defines a set of functions to describe personalisation of Web information. These functions will be used to describe existing personalised Web sites and to specify and develop a demonstrator Web site for personalised health information.

The taxonomy presented here supports the development of the general classification framework, which will in turn support the collaboration and interoperation of adaptive and personalised information applications.

Acknowledgements

This work has been funded by the Engineering and Physical Science Research Council, grant reference GR/N22229/01 Dynamic Information Presentation, and we gratefully acknowledge their support.

References

Aberg, J. & Shahmehri, N. (1999), Web Assistants: Towards an Intelligent and Personal Web Shop, Proceedings of the Second Workshop on Adaptive Systems and User Modelling on the World Wide Web, http://www.contrib.andrew.cmu.edu/~plb/wwwum99_workshop/aberg/aberg.html.

Ambrosini, L., Cirillo, V. & Micarelli, A. (1997), A Hybrid Architecture for User-adapted Information Filtering on the World Wide Web, *in* A. Jameson, C. Paris & C. Tasso (eds.), *Proceedings of the Sixth International Conference on User Modelling, UM'97*, Springer-Verlag, pp.59–61.

Ardissono, L. & Goy, A. (1999), Tailoring the Interaction with Users in Electronic Shops, *in* J. Kay (ed.), *Proceedings of the Seventh International Conference on User Modelling, UM'99*, Springer-Verlag, pp.35–44.

Balabanovic, M. & Shoham, Y. (1997), "Content-based Collaborative Recommendation", *Communications of the ACM* **40**(3), 66–72.

Benaki, E., Karkaletsis, V. & Spyrolopoulos, C. (1997), Integrating User Modelling into Information Extraction: The UMIE Prototype, *in* A. Jameson, C. Paris & C. Tasso (eds.), *Proceedings of the Sixth International Conference on User Modelling, UM'97*, Springer-Verlag, pp.55–7.

Bental, D., Cawsey, A. & Jones, R. (1999), "Patient Information Systems that Tailor to the Individual", *Patient Education and Counselling* **36**(2), 171–80.

Bental, D., Cawsey, A., Pearson, J. & Jones, R. (2000), Adapting Web-based Information to the Needs of Patients with Cancer, *in* P. Brusilovsky, O. Stock & C. Strapparava (eds.), *Adaptive Hypermedia and Adaptive Web-based Systems*, Springer-Verlag, pp.27–37.

Bollen, J. (2000), Group User Models for Adaptive Hyperlink Recommendation, *in* P. Brusilovsky, O. Stock & C. Strapparava (eds.), *Adaptive Hypermedia and Adaptive Web-based Systems*, Springer-Verlag, pp.38–50.

Bordegoni, M., Faconti, G., Feiner, S., Maybury, M., Rist, T., Ruggieri, S., Trahanias, P. & Wilson, M. (1997), "A Standard Reference Model for Intelligent Multimedia Presentation Systems", *Computing Standards and Interfaces* **18**(6-7), 477–96.

Boticario, J., Gaudioso, E. & Hernandez, F. (2000), Adaptive Navigation Support and Adaptive Collaboration Support, *in* P. Brusilovsky, O. Stock & C. Strapparava (eds.), *Adaptive Hypermedia and Adaptive Web-based Systems*, Springer-Verlag, pp.51–61.

Bradley, K., Rafter, R. & Smyth, B. (2000), Case-based User Profiling for Content Personalisation, *in* P. Brusilovsky, O. Stock & C. Strapparava (eds.), *Adaptive Hypermedia and Adaptive Web-based Systems*, Springer-Verlag, pp.62–72.

Cawsey, A. (1992), *Explanation and Interaction: The Computer Generation of Explanatory Dialogues*, MIT Press.

Cheverst, K., Davies, N., Mitchell, K. & Smith, P. (2000), Providing Tailored (Context-aware) Information to City Visitors, *in* P. Brusilovsky, O. Stock & C. Strapparava (eds.), *Adaptive Hypermedia and Adaptive Web-based Systems*, Springer-Verlag, pp.73–85.

Joerding, T. (1999), A Temporary User Modelling Approach for Adaptive Shopping on the Web, Proceedings of the Second Workshop on Adaptive Systems and User Modelling on the World Wide Web, http://www.contrib.andrew.cmu.edu/~plb/wwwum99_workshop/joerding/joerding.html.

Kamba, T., Sakagami, H. & Koseki, Y. (1997), "Anatagonomy: A Personalized Newspaper on the World Wide Web", *International Journal of Human–Computer Interaction* **46**(6), 789–803.

Kautz, H., Selman, B. & Shah, M. (1997), "Referralweb: Combining Social Networks and Collaborative Filtering", *Communications of the ACM* **40**(3), 63–4.

Konstan, J., Miller, B., Maltz, D., Herlocker, J., Gordon, L. & Riedl, J. (1997), "Grouplens: Applying Collaborative Filtering to Usenet News", *Communications of the ACM* **40**(3), 77–87.

Kushmerick, N., McKee, J. & Toolan, F. (2000), Towards Zero-input Personalization: Referrer-based Page Prediction, *in* P. Brusilovsky, O. Stock & C. Strapparava (eds.), *Adaptive Hypermedia and Adaptive Web-based Systems*, Springer-Verlag, pp.133–43.

Lieberman, H. (1997), Autonomous Interface Agents, *in* S. Pemberton (ed.), *Proceedings of CHI'97: Human Factors in Computing Systems*, ACM Press, pp.67–74.

MacKinnon, L. & Wilson, M. (1996), User Modelling for Information Retrieval from Multidatabases, *in* C. Stephanidis (ed.), *Proceedings of the 2nd ERCIM Workshop on User Interfaces for All*, ERCIM.

MacKinnon, L., Marwick, D. & Williams, M. (1998), "A Model for Query Decomposition and Answer Construction in Heterogeneous Distributed Database Systems", *Journal of Intelligent Information Systems* **11**(1), 69–87.

Maglio, P. & Barrett, R. (2000), "Intermediaries Personalize Information Streams", *Communications of the ACM* **43**(8), 96–101.

Maglio, P. & Farrell, S. (2000), Liveinfo: Adapting Web Experience by Customization and Annotation, *in* P. Brusilovsky, O. Stock & C. Strapparava (eds.), *Adaptive Hypermedia and Adaptive Web-based Systems*, Springer-Verlag, pp.144–54.

Manber, U., Patel, A. & Robison, J. (2000), "Experience of Personalisation on Yahoo!", *Communications of the ACM* **43**(8), 35–9.

McNee, C., Behrendt, W., Wilson, M., Jeffrey, K. & Hutchison, E. (1995), "Presenting Dynamically Expandable Hypermedia", *Information and Software Technology* **37**(7), 339–50.

Mladenic, D. (1999), "Text Learning and Related Intelligent Agents", *IEEE Intelligent Systems and their Applications* **14**(4), 44–54.

Pratt, W., Hearst, M. & Fagan, L. (1999), A Knowledge-based Approach to Organising Retrieved Documents, *in* J. Hendler & D. Subramanian (eds.), *The Proceedings of the 16th National Conference on Artificial Intelligence*, MIT Press, pp.80–5.

Rock, S., Cawsey, A., McAndrew, P. & Bental, D. (1999), The MIRADOR Project: Metadata Improved Relevance Assessment through Descriptions of Online Resources, Notes from the Workshop on Virtual Documents, Hypertext Functionality and the Web held at the 8th International World Wide Web Conference.

Rucker, J. & Polanco, M. (1997), "Siteseer: Personalised Navigation for the Web", *Communications of the ACM* **40**(3), 73–6.

Sheth, A. & Larson, J. (1990), "Federated Database Systems for Managing Distributed, Heterogeneous and Autonomous Databases", *ACM Computing Surveys* **22**(3), 183–232.

Smyth, B. & Cotter, P. (2000), "A Personalized Television Listings Service", *Communications of the ACM* **43**(8), 107–11.

Williams, M. & Hu, J. (1992), "Communication between Heterogeneous Medical Databases", *Journal of Information Science and Technology* **2**, 12–30.

Wilson, M. & Marwick, D. (1997), "Describing the MIPS Multimedia Presentation System with the IMMPS Reference Model", *Computing Standards and Interfaces* **18**(6-7), 623–30.

Speech and Audio

Speech Output for Older Visually Impaired Adults

M Zajicek & W Morrissey

School of Computing and Mathematical Sciences, Oxford Brookes University, Headington Campus, Oxford OX3 OBP, UK

Tel: *+44 1865 483683*

Fax: *+44 1865 483666*

Email: *mzajicek@brookes.ac.uk*

URL: *http://www.brookes.ac.uk/speech*

The ageing process affects an individual's ability to use the standard Graphical User Interface (GUI). In fact the facilities, which are required for successful use of a GUI, are the very ones that deteriorate most markedly with age. Visual impairment, together with memory loss in particular, reduce the user's ability to build conceptual models of the working of the interface. The ability to navigate successfully and build strategies also deteriorates with age, an aspect which is especially important when moving from page to page on the World Wide Web. Interface design for older adults should acknowledge these factors. This paper reports the results of experiments, which show that there is a significant difference in spoken information retention between older and younger adults and that older visually impaired users retain more information from shorter messages in a speech output Web browser with voice help. The paper also discusses optimum levels of functionality for older adults, an important consideration when designing interfaces for Web access for this user group.

Keywords: interface design, older adults, memory loss, visual impairment, functionality, Web.

1 Introduction

Older adults find computers difficult to use (Zajicek & Hall, 2000). The ageing process affects an individual's ability to function successfully with the standard graphical user interface. In fact the facilities, which are required for this kind of interaction, are the very ones that deteriorate most markedly with age.

Deteriorating visual acuity makes the interface difficult or impossible to see. Memory impairment reduces the ability to build conceptual models of the working of the interface since this activity relies on remembering sequences of actions and reasoning about them. In addition the ability to navigate successfully and build strategies, deteriorates with age (Wilkniss et al., 1997) an aspect which is especially important when moving from page to page in the World Wide Web environment. Manual dexterity is also affected (Walker et al., 1996) making mouse use difficult and user's confidence in tackling new situations diminishes with age (Zajicek & Arnold, 1999) promoting a reluctance to tackle new and demanding tasks.

It is generally agreed that older people are still able to learn but knowledge of the effects of age associated memory impairment indicates the need for a different type of interaction, which uses aspects of cognition that are less likely to be impaired.

This paper describes interface design approaches which support those with visual impairment and memory loss and reports experiments carried out to determine optimum amounts of information that can be absorbed from voice help designed to support older adults at the interface. A control experiment was performed to determine whether these considerations are also relevant to younger adults. The paper also discusses levels of functionality, and the concept of increasing functionality in particular, for older adults.

2   The Experimental Interface

The aim of this work is to enable older adults who have not used computers before to be included in Information Technology and get up and running on the World Wide Web. These users will become increasingly marginalised as more information such as bus timetables and doctors surgery hours is placed on the Web for general consumption.

The platform application used to evaluate interface design approaches which improve usability for older adults was a Web browser developed at Oxford Brookes University for blind and visually impaired users, called BrookesTalk.

3   Supporting Visual Impairment

BrookesTalk is a stand-alone Web browser for visually impaired people. It can be used in speech output only mode or with a large text window, which displays the words as they are spoken. The size of text can be adjusted to suit the user. BrookesTalk also incorporates a standard visual browser so that visually impaired people can work with sighted colleagues. Consequently a range of visual impairment can be accommodated.

The innovative feature of BrookesTalk is the way it enables partially sighted users to move quickly around the Web searching for information in the same way as sighted users. BrookesTalk gives information on the page from different view points, headings, links, keywords and provides an abstract (Zajicek et al., 1998) so that blind and visually impaired users do not have to listen to the whole page in order to decide whether it is useful to them. The design was informed by experiments with sighted users, which showed that in assessing the usefulness of a page they looked first at images then links and then heading, before reading the text.

Abstracting of the Web page is designed to imitate the visual scanning of pages that sighted users do. BrookesTalk also has a special search facility, which when a search has been submitted, retains the real search results in a separate menu so that they can be distinguished from other information on the search results page.

These facilities are designed to compensate for the lack of visual clues and the requirement of using synthetic speech as output, which is slow and often tedious to listen to.

Keys used in BrookesTalk are:

F1:	load a URL
F2:	perform a search
F3:	hear the headings in the current page
F4:	Hear the links in the current page
F5:	hear the jumps in the current page
F7:	change browser settings
F8:	hear more details about the options available
F9:	hear the keywords in the current page
F11:	hear summary of the current page
F12:	hear abstract of the current page
Shift F:	select from results of the last search
Shift F4:	select a link from the current page
Shift F2:	select search results from the last search
Right arrow:	read out the page in the mode selected
Back arrow:	go back in the page in the mode selected
Up and down arrow:	cycle through word mode, sentence mode, document mode
B:	move backwards through pages
F:	move forwards through pages

4   The Voice Help Interface

Many factors affect the take up of the Internet by elderly visually impaired users (Zajicek & Hall, 2000). However memory loss and visual impairment are the two factors addressed in the enhanced BrookesTalk system described below, both of which reduce the user's ability to benefit from visual clues and contexts. To accommodate memory loss and visual impairment, a voice help facility was built onto BrookesTalk. The idea is to support the user in their construction of conceptual models by 'talking' them through their interaction.

For each possible state of BrookesTalk an optional spoken output is provided. The user is informed as to where they are in the interaction and which actions are possible at this point. Optional further details are also available to describe the consequences of each action. After listening to the message the user chooses an option, presses the appropriate function key and then receives another message describing the new state of the system.

For example the spoken output for those who have just started up BrookesTalk would be:

> 'Welcome to BrookesTalk your speaking web browser.   There is currently no page loaded. Would you like to:
>
> Enter the URL of a page, press F1
> Start an Internet search, press F2
> Change the settings of the browser, press F7
> Hear more details about options available to you, press F3
> Repeat the options, press return'

Under the 'Hear more details …' it is possible for the user to access further expanded details which describe the options in more detail and in language further removed from computer terms. An example is given below.

> 'You have just started the browser and have no page loaded. You might want to first change the setting for the browser such as the speed of the voice, the size of the text and other things which affect how the browser works, or you might want to load a page.
>
> Which of the three would you like to do: ……'

These messages reinforced the users' knowledge of the state of the system and explained what they can do next. It was hoped that the development of conceptual models would be supported through repetition and that the user would no longer need to rely on short term memory. The user can function initially with virtually no conceptual models, by using the system like a telephone answering system by simply answering questions. The aim of the speaking front end was to familiarise the user with the steps needed to achieve Web interaction goals so that eventually the spoken instructions would be superfluous and the user would 'know' which function key to press for the required result.

The system described above was used in a pilot study of eight users who had previously been unable to get up and running on their own with the non-enhanced version of BrookesTalk. The aim was to determine the effects of personal support in developing confidence and whether people who could use BrookesTalk with voice help could move on to standard BrookesTalk.

The results of the study are published in detail elsewhere (Zajicek & Hall, 2000). They showed that personal support is very important for elderly visual impaired users using a computer application for the first time. They also indicate voice help has a part to play where memory impairment precludes the building of strategies and experimental learning at the interface. 63% of subject users were able to improve their performance using voice help.

5   Reducing Memory Overload

It was clear from observation of users struggling to recall the long synthetic speech messages in enhanced BrookesTalk, that for these people, messages should be simpler and shorter since they cannot absorb or remember large amounts of spoken information. Therefore, despite the proven benefits users gained from voice help it was felt that the length of spoken output message had to be reduced.

5.1 Conceptual Grouping and Functionality

BrookesTalk is operated using twelve function keys, which means that voice help describes twelve different actions using speech output. The reader can imagine the amount of time and synthetic speech involved. In order to reduce the time taken to output instructions voice help described function keys in two conceptual groups. The first group contained functions that were involved with page retrieval i.e. F1 'Enter a URL' and F2 'perform a search'. The second group contained functions that were concerned with different views of the page once it was loaded, i.e. F3 'hear the headings in the current page', F4 'hear the links in the current page', F5 'hear the jumps in the current page', F11 'hear summary of the current page', F12 'hear abstract of the current page'. F7 change settings was made available at logon only.

Grouping functions provides for a smaller set of function keys to select between at any one time and therefore shorter messages and less to remember. However conceptual groupings rely on the user understanding the concepts behind the groupings in order to know where the functions may be found. This knowledge cannot be assumed with first time Internet users and is not required of sighted users making selections on a graphical user interface as they can see the selection and refer back to it at any time.

It was observed that a smaller number of selections in any one message makes operation easier. However a smaller numbers of selections means a larger number of groupings with attendant grouping conceptualisation problems. It was seen that the ideal choice is a selection between two functions with the most commonly required option appearing last.

5.2 Reducing Functionality

It was decided that as reduction in selection is paramount to reduce the message length, the functionality of the system must also be reduced. The advantage gained by presenting several different views of the page is lost when the user cannot even load a page. There is little gain in providing a wide range of views of the Web page to elderly users if they cannot visualise the advantage or build strategies to use the different views.

6 Experiments with Different Message Lengths

The observations above indicate that dialogues, for older adults, should be designed with the messages of the shortest possible length, which also allow enough functionality for successful interaction. It is important that those designing interfaces for this user group are aware of how much advantage is gained by shortening messages whether contained in speech or visual output. The authors performed the experiment described below with lengths of speech message, to determine if older subjects will remember more when presented with shorter messages for communicating information.

To reduce the number of variables in the experiment pre-recorded speech messages were used rather than the synthetic speech output used by BrookesTalk. Previous work had shown that synthetic speech requires more cognitive processing for some older adults and could influence levels of understanding (Zajicek, 2000).

6.1   Subject Users

The subjects used for the experiment were older adults all aged over seventy years who attend day centres run by 'Age Concern' in Oxfordshire. They were not ill and showed normal age related sensory impairment. None of them had used a computer before and they had rather sketchy ideas of what the World Wide Web might be about.

Thirty subjects were randomly allocated to two groups. Group 1 whose average age was 81.74 years, were given shorter messages to listen to and Group 2 with average age 80.74 years, were given longer messages.

6.2   Pre-test Procedure

A pre-test exercise was carried out to allow subjects to practice so that they knew what to expect in the real experiment. It also acted as a control test to ensure that there was no significant difference in memory impairment between the two groups.

Each subject performed a pre-experimental test to set volume levels for output. They all then listened to the introductory message:

> 'Welcome to BrookesExplained. Please listen carefully to the following instructions. It will make using the Internet easy. Don't worry about making mistakes or pressing the wrong key — you cannot damage the computer. To pause, to give you time to collect your thoughts, press the space-bar on the keyboard. The space-bar is the long horizontal bar below the lettered keys. Press the space-bar again to continue listening.
>
> To repeat the instructions press the letter R.
> To cancel the instruction, press the ESCape key'

For this experiment extra information about the location of space bar and not being able to break the computer was included as previous work (Zajicek, 2000) had shown that users were confused about key presses. It had also been found that those with no previous experience of computers borrowed conceptual models from the interfaces of electrical goods such as video recorder to help them in their interaction. And of course some of these mechanical goods can break with wrong use.

In this pre-test users were then asked the following questions orally:

- Can you cause any harm to the computer?

- Which key do you press to stop the voice help?

- Which key do you press to start again?

- What letter do you press to repeat the instructions?

- What key do you press to cancel an instruction?

A one-tailed t-test showed that the mean scores for Group 1 and Group 2 were not significantly different $p = 0.34$ at 5% level of significance.

6.3 Sample Messages

When it had been shown that the two groups had comparable memory levels, the subject users were given messages to listen to as follows:

Group 1 were given the two short messages below which represented output for BrookesTalk with reduced functionality. Here users are no longer able to change settings or hear headings, summary or abstract:

> *Message 1A*
> This is the main menu.
> There is currently no page loaded:
> To enter an Internet address, press F1.
> To perform an Internet search, Press F2.
> To repeat these instructions press R.

> *Message 1B*
> You have a page loaded:
> To read the current page, press the right arrow key.
> To follow the links on this page, press F4.
> Go back to the main menu, press M.
> To repeat these instructions, press R.

Group 2 were given the longer messages in the original enhanced BrookesTalk system as follows:

> *Message 2A*
> There is currently no page loaded:
> To enter the URL of a page, press F1.
> To perform an Internet search, Press F2.
> To change the settings of the browser, press F7.
> To hear more details about options available to you, Press F8.
> To repeat these instructions press R.

> *Message 2B*
> You have a page loaded:
> To read the current page, press the right arrow key.
> To hear the headings on this page, press F3.
> To follow the links on this page, press F4.
> To hear the page summary, press F11.
> To hear the page abstract, press F12.
> To repeat these instructions, press R.

6.4   Testing for Information Retention

After listening to each message the subject was asked a set of questions orally.

Group 1, those who listened to shorter messages, were asked the following:

For Message 1A
Is there a page loaded?
Which key do you press to enter an Internet address?
Which key do you press to perform an Internet search?
What letter do you press to repeat the instructions?

For Message 1B
Is there a page loaded?
How do you read the current page?
Which key do you press to follow a link?
Which key do you press to go to the main menu?
What letter do you press to repeat the instructions?

Group 2, those who listened to longer messages, were asked the following:

For Message 2A
Which key do you press to enter the URL of a page?
Which key do you press to perform an Internet search?
Which key do you press to change the settings?
Which key do you press to hear more options?
What letter do you press to repeat the instructions?

For Message 2B
Is there a page loaded?
How do you read the current page?
Which key do you press to hear the headings?
Which key do you press to hear a list of links?
Which key do you press to hear a page summary?
Which key do you press to hear an abstract?
Which key do you press to hear more options?
What letter do you press to repeat the instructions?

7   Results of Experimentation

The percentage of correct responses for each subject were computed. In the case of Group 2 two percentages were worked out. The percentage of all correct responses and the percentage correct responses of only those questions, which were also asked of Group 1. Ranked percentages are shown in Table 1.

Percentages were tested for normality and a one-tailed t-test carried out on the means to see whether they were significantly different, with 0.95 confidence.

	Group 1 Short message	Group 2 Long message All	Group 2 Long message Same as Group 1
	11	0	0
	22	7	11
	33	7	11
	33	7	11
	33	14	22
	56	14	22
	56	14	22
	56	14	22
	56	21	33
	67	21	33
	78	50	44
	78	50	44
	78	50	56
	78	64	89
	89	64	100
Mean	54.81	26.87	34.8
St. Dev.	23.56	22.34	28.4

Table 1: Percentage of correct responses.

A one-tailed t-test showed that the average of percentage correct responses for Group 1 questions (54.81) and all Group 2 questions (26.67) were significantly different, $p = 0.001$ at 5% level of significance.

A second one-tailed t-test showed that the average of percentage correct responses for Group 1 questions (54.81) and those Group 2 questions which were the same as Group 1's questions (31.1) were also significantly different, $p = 0.003$ at 5% level of significance.

8 Analysis of Results

Users are able to answer significantly more questions correctly when messages are shorter in both cases, where more questions are asked of those with longer messages and when both sets of messages are the same. This means that more information is being retained from shorter messages.

We also see that the average of percentage correct responses in column 3 Table 1 (34.8) is significantly higher than that of column 2 in Table 1 (26.67). This means that the questions based on the shorter Messages 1A and 1B were easier to answer than the extra questions based on Messages 2A and 2B.

This concurs with our observation of users where they found difficulty relating to function keys and finding them on the keyboard. They appear to be happier with letter keys for commands.

Main points are:

- Shorter messages are more easy to remember

- Unfamiliar instructions involving function keys are more difficult to remember

- Instructions involving letter key presses rather than function keys were more easy to remember

9   Are Shorter Messages Better for All Users?

To determine whether the issue of message length and information retention is particular to older visually impaired users, rather than all users, the experiments described above were performed with a control group of young adults.

A total of 30 young adults were divided into two groups Group 1 for shorter messages and Group 2 for longer messages. They were given the preliminary test to ensure that they had similar memory levels. A one-tailed t-test showed that there was no significant difference in the means of their percentage correct responses, $p = 0.29$ at 5% level of significance.

The two groups were then tested on the shorter and longer messages respectively. Those listening to shorter messages scored an average correct response of 91.98% and those listening to longer messages scored 90.13%. A one-tailed t-test showed that there was no significant difference between the percentage correct responses, $p = 0.3$ at 5% level of significance.

Therefore shorter messages are not significantly helpful for younger users. If we also factor in the reduced functionality required for shorter they are even less useful.

10   Conclusion and Discussion

We have shown that memory retention at the interface works differently for older and younger adult users. While younger adults are able to accommodate differences of length of output message, older adults are not. This indicates that there are important factors playing their part in interface design for older adults with visual impairment which make the difference between a usable and unusable interface. We have identified at this point message length and level of functionality. There may be other equally important factors at work.

A new version of BrookesTalk is currently under construction in which the functionality is dictated by the shorter Messages 1A and 1B. When these users have become familiar with this low functionality system, our work indicates (Zajicek & Hall, 2000) that they should be able to progress to standard BrookesTalk.

Other research into interfaces for older adults points to the need for low functionality systems, with the possibility of adding in extra facilities when a few simple ones are mastered. For example Czaja et al. (1990) found that older adults were happy to add extra facilities once they had mastered a reduced functionality email system.

An investigation is also under way into the most appropriate key presses for BrookesTalk commands. The mnemonic value of letters compared with function keys, appears to be significant with older adults.

References

Czaja, S., Clark, C., Weber, R. & Nachbar, D. (1990), Computer Communication Among Older Adults, *in Proceedings of the Human Factors and Ergonomics Society 34th Annual Meeting*, Human Factors and Ergonomics Society, pp.146–8.

Walker, N., Millians, J. & Worden, A. (1996), Mouse Accelerations and Performance of Older Computer Users, *in Proceedings of the Human Factors and Ergonomics Society 40th Annual Meeting*, Human Factors and Ergonomics Society, pp.151–4.

Wilkniss, S. M., Jones, M. G., Korol, D. L., Gold, P. E. & Manning, C. A. (1997), "Age-related Differences in an Ecologically Based Study of Route Learning", *Psychology and Ageing* **12**(2), 372–5.

Zajicek, M. (2000), The Construction of Speech Output to Support Elderly Visually Impaired Users Starting to Use the Internet, *in* B. Z. Yuan, T. Y. Huang & X. F. Tang (eds.), *Proceedings of the 6th International Conference of Spoken Language Processing (ICSLP2000/Interspeech 2000)*, Vol. 1, China Military Friendship Publishers, pp.150–3.

Zajicek, M. & Arnold, A. (1999), The 'Technology Push' and The User Tailored Information Environment, *in* A. Kobsa & C. Stephanidis (eds.), *Proceedings of the 5th European Research Consortium for Informatics and Mathematics Workshop on 'User Interfaces for All'*, GMD Forschungszentrum Informationstechnik GmbH, pp.5–11.

Zajicek, M. & Hall, S. (2000), Solutions for Elderly Visually Impaired People Using the Internet, *in* S. McDonald, Y. Waern & G. Cockton (eds.), *People and Computers XIV (Proceedings of HCI'2000)*, Springer-Verlag, pp.299–307.

Zajicek, M., Powell, C. & Reeves, C. (1998), A Web Navigation Tool for the Blind, *in* A. Karshmer & M. Blatner (eds.), *Proceedings of the 3rd ACM/SIGRAPH on Assistive Technologies*, ACM Press, pp.204–6.

Using Non-speech Sounds to Improve Access to 2D Tabular Numerical Information for Visually Impaired Users

Rameshsharma Ramloll, Stephen Brewster, Wai Yu & Beate Riedel

Glasgow Interactive Systems Group, Department of Computing Science, University of Glasgow, Glasgow G12 8QQ, UK

Tel: *+44 141 330 4256*

Fax: *+44 141 330 4913*

Email: *{ramesh,stephen,rayu}@dcs.glasgow.ac.uk, beate@psy.glasgow.ac.uk*

URL: *http://www.dcs.glasgow.ac.uk/~stephen*

We investigated two solutions for numerical (2D) tabular data discovery and overview for visually impaired and blind users. One involved accessing information in tables (26 rows x 10 columns containing integers between and including 0 and 100) by this target user group using both speech and non-speech sounds. The other involved accessing similar information in tables of the same size through speech only by the same user group. We found that opportunities to access data through non-speech sounds result in a highly significant decrease in the overall subjective workload, more specifically in the mental, temporal, performance and frustration workload categories. This subjective workload assessment was supported by our quantitative results which showed a highly significant decrease in the average time taken to complete a given data comprehension task and a significant increase in the number of successfully completed tasks.

Keywords: data visualisation, sound graphs, subjective workload assessment, non-speech sounds, 2D tables, speech output.

1 Introduction

This paper describes the design and evaluation of a tool for improving access to numerical information in 2D tables by visually impaired and blind people. Our early experimentation with homegrown prototypes for accessing data in tables suggests that tabular data discovery and overview rapidly becomes overwhelming especially for large tables when access occurs solely through the speech medium. We propose that that this is because it takes an impractically long time to listen to the whole data set in speech and secondly, it is hard to construct meaningful meta-information, e.g. trend information, about the data presented in this manner because of the limitations of human working memory (Gomez et al., 1994). In this paper, we report the results of our evaluation carried out to verify formally these insights.

1.1 Issues Relevant to Cell-by-cell Access in Speech

The present de-facto standard for accessing numbers in 2D tables is through synthetic speech. Many blind and partially sighted people use screen reader applications to listen to the contents of a table on a cell-by-cell basis. The speech synthesiser reads out the cell, selected through cursor key presses. Discussions with visually impaired users accessing tables using this approach reveal three central issues:

Awareness of their current position within the table: Users   get   quickly discouraged when they are lost. The 'Where am I?' information has to be made readily available to avoid any unsettling uncertainties about their current location in the table.

Overloaded speech feedback resulting from their navigational moves: The common approach of associating every cursor key press with speech feedback describing the current row index, column index of a cell followed by its contents, may be inappropriate. All this information is not needed all the time and loads unnecessarily the short-term memory of users.

Lack of overall picture of the data structure containing information of interest: Users need to be aware of the overall size of the table and need to have some idea of peripheral cell contents in addition to that of the currently selected one. This concern about the importance of the context of a local piece of information on its role in the overall data representation is in general relevant to most representation media (Kurze, 1998; Alty & Rigas, 1998).

The three issues just mentioned reflect clearly the users' need to remember more than what is immediately accessible at any point in time. According to Ben Shneiderman's (1994) mantra of "overview first and filter to reveal detail", data browsing scenarios typically involve shifts between data overviews and data inspections. Unfortunately, producing data overviews in the auditory medium is currently not as clear as it is in the visual medium. A number of designers have tackled this problem through the use of non-speech sounds but not specifically for 2D tables containing numbers (Gardner et al., 1998). While the core of our approach is not radically different, right from the beginning, we aim at evaluating our application at the level of the real world tasks they are designed for rather than at the level of narrowly defined ones more suitable for psycho-acoustic experiment designs.

1.2   Motivation for Using Non-speech Sounds

There have been a number of earlier attempts at providing users with access to trend information about a sequence of numbers (Mansur, 1975). A common approach is to represent a given number using the pitch of non-speech sounds. The use of pitch to represent data was shown by Pollack & Ficks (1954) to have a lower error rate in comparison to other auditory dimensions such as sound duration, repetition rate, or loudness. A central aspect of our approach is the assumption that if overview information becomes important at some point during a data comprehension task, then opportunities should be provided to allow numerical values to be accessed in pitch. When a numerical sequence is accessed as a series of pitches, the resulting 'signature tune' can presumably inform the listener about its contents quicker than if its contents were to be read out one at a time in speech. An early investigation showed that there is a natural tendency to perceive a pitch that is higher in frequency to be coming from a source that is vertically higher in space when compared to some lower tone (Roffler & Butler, 1968). This result encourages us to map low numerical values to low pitches and to increase the latter as the numerical values increase perhaps to maintain some congruity with the visual graphical representations we are accustomed to.

This approach is not without problems. While the human ear is very good at detecting small differences of pitch at a high temporal resolution, the ability to make absolute judgment is a very rare skill (1% of the population have perfect pitch) (Moore, 1982). Fortunately, we are not interested in replacing the representation of numerical values with pitch. We do not expect users to make correct numerical value estimations based on pitch perceptions. In addition, experiments have shown that there is no linear relationship between pitch perception and the frequency of the auditory signal (Stevens et al., 1937). Indeed, any relationship that exists is user specific. This non-linear relationship between the number and mapped pitch makes accurate meaningful comparisons between pitches hard. To clarify this issue further with an example, it is quite difficult to listen to two pitches, perceive the first to be twice higher than the second and deduce that the value associated with the first one is 2 times higher than that associated with the second one.

In our design we do not make use of pure sine waves to generate the tones. Instead we use sounds produced by a MIDI synthesiser. The main advantage of this approach is that the tones produced have intrinsically a more complex spectrum and therefore are more easily distinguishable. In addition, Brewster et al. (1993) found they are more pleasant and this is known to have important implications for long-term use. It is interesting to note that we are using the familiar technique used by Mansur to map line graphs to sound graphs to represent numerical values in tables. Thus, traditional boundaries between data representations in the visual medium (e.g. graphs and tables are commonly accepted to be in different data visualisation categories) are not maintained in the auditory medium.

1.3   Our Evaluation Strategy

We are interested in finding out whether there is any value in exploiting the fairly widespread ability to perceive pitch differences for improving the accessibility of tables containing numerical information to the visually impaired people. So far, there is little evidence showing convincingly whether this strategy can work for realistic data comprehension tasks tackled by visually impaired or blind users on their own. In order for our evaluation to produce useful results we adopted the following policies:

- The participants of our experiments have to be representative of our target users. In that respect, we contacted institutions (Royal National Institute for the Blind in Peterborough and Royal Blind School in Hereford) engaged in the education of the visually impaired students to draw our pool of participants.

- Our design has to be tested under realistic data comprehension task conditions. In principle, the investigation cannot focus on only one intermediate step in the data comprehension process that we assume to be most relevant.

Our main reason for adopting the second policy is that narrowly focused evaluations often examine isolated aspects of an application. For example, one could devise experiments where participants are made to listen to a sequence of tones and asked to draw a sound graph. From a human computer interface evaluation perspective, the success of such an exercise does not necessarily extrapolate to a successful technique for tackling data comprehension in the auditory medium. For example, while providing users with the ability to browse data mapped to non-speech sounds, the interface of the application has to be made more complex in order to accommodate the facilities that enables the user to choose the browsing mode, e.g. speech or non-speech, she wants to be in. A more complex interface inevitably makes its learning curve steeper. In addition, the user will require more careful planning before accessing information because she now has to decide the relevant mode she wants to be in prior to the data access. Before the experiments, we had no idea how these various factors would play out and we did not have enough evidence to make assumptions about the impact of these unavoidable modal shifts on the usability of our application.

2 Apparatus and Stimuli

The Microsoft SAPI4.0 (Speech Application Program Interface) was used to implement the speech functionalities of the application. The application sends MIDI messages to a synthesiser to generate non-speech sounds. Participants have access to the auditory messages through headphones and navigate the table through key presses of a numeric keypad. Table 1 illustrates the typical table that is accessible in the auditory medium using our application. In this paper, we use the following conventions to simplify our descriptive and explanatory stories. $X_1 \ldots X_C \ldots X_M$ are the labels of the columns, X_1 is the first column, X_C refers to the current column and X_M refers to the last. $Y_1 \ldots Y_C \ldots Y_N$ are the labels of the rows, Y_1 is the first row, Y_C refers to the current row and Y_N refers to the last. The pair (X_C, Y_C) refers to the current cell of interest i.e. the cell in focus.

2.1 Sound Mapping Strategy

The mapping of numbers to musical note in the version of the application used in our experiments is straightforward. Every number (integer between and including 0 and 100) in a cell of a table is used as a MIDI pitch parameter. A more general

	Column referents					
	X_1	X_2	...	X_C	...	X_M
Y_1						
Y_2						
...						
Y_C				X_C, Y_C		
...						
Y_N						

(Row referents, left side)

Table 1: A Typical 2-dimensional table that can be accessed using our application.

Note	A	A#	B	C	C#	...	F	F#	G
MIDI pitch	0	1	2	3	4	...	125	126	127

Table 2: MIDI pitch parameter to musical note mapping.

mapping from integers to musical notes implemented in the latest version of our application is given by the following function:

$$y = \left(\frac{x - S_{min}}{S_{max} - S_{min}} \right) \times 127$$

where y is rounded to the nearest integer and is the value of the MIDI pitch parameter representing an integer x in an arbitrary set of integers ranging from S_{min} to S_{max}. We select the MIDI piano instrument for rendering the notes mainly because of its wide range of audible notes in our MIDI synthesizer.

The mapping also involves panning of the representative non-speech sound sources. The latter are localised along a line joining the left and right ears and positioned according to the position of their relevant cell in its row or column. When moving down a column, the first value is associated with a pitch heard in the left ear, the subsequent values are associated with pitches localised on a line between the left and right ear, and finally, the last value of the column is perceived in the right ear. The same effect is obtained while navigating across a row. The first value is heard to the left, the last value is heard to the right and the intermediate values are heard in between the left and right ears.

We use the coarse panning instructions to place the sound sources in the appropriate locations. Coarse panning in MIDI ranges from 0 to 127, with 0 representing left and 127 right. The following simple function is used to set the location of the sound sources; $P = \left(\frac{R}{N} \right) \times 127$ rounded to the nearest integer, where P is the panning number, R the rank (starting with 0) of the cell in the current column or row and N is the number of cells in the current column or row. Thus every cell is associated with two panning numbers, one based on the row and the other on the column on which the cell is found. During navigation along a row, row panning numbers are triggered and during navigation along a column, column panning numbers are triggered.

2.2   Interface (Re)Design Based on Output from Initial Pilot Studies

Before carrying out our experiment, 16 sighted pilot participants tried accessing the tabular information through the auditory medium alone in order to identify early on any obvious problems with the application and with the data comprehension tasks. Our choice of a 2×2 factorial experiment design meant that 4 treatment groups were required. Since we planned to allocate 4 subjects to each group, we therefore needed 16 participants in all. The pilot study was the dress rehearsal for the real experiment to be carried out with the visually impaired and blind users.

2.2.1   To Cross or Not To Cross Table Boundaries

Participants were initially allowed to cross table boundaries and move out of them. Once this happened the application triggered speech messages to navigate them back into the table. This strategy was intended to inform users of the limits of every row and column. Once participants were out of a table, pressing a key to reveal their current location caused the 'not in table' message to be read out. When users wandered away from the contents of the table, clicking on an arrow keys produced messages such as 'move left', 'move right', 'move up' and 'move down' which was intended to guide them back into the table. Trials showed that this strategy was confusing to the users. Thus, instead of allowing the user to venture out of a table, we restricted any navigation outside the table boundaries. In the version used for our experiments with the visually impaired, whenever users attempted to cross a table boundary an appropriate non-speech message was generated to highlight the fact that a boundary has been reached. Any further key presses for navigation in the inappropriate direction repeated the boundary sound without any change in their current position.

2.2.2   Optimising Speech Feedback

Most users found speech information that they really can do without annoying. Our initial design was judged to be over verbose because the application read out the name of the current row and column before presenting its contents in speech whenever a cell was brought into focus. Unnecessary information was distracting and overloaded unnecessarily the short-term memory of users. Our application therefore makes use of two different speech modes to optimise the speech output. In the 'labels' mode, whenever a cell of the table is brought into focus, its column name and row name (the cell referents) are read out only when the key 5 is pressed, the column name is only read out with vertical (Up and Down) cursor key presses and row name with horizontal (Left and Right) cursor key presses. In the 'value' mode, only the content of the cell in focus is read out. In the current design, the user does not need to wait for an auditory speech message to complete before initiating a key press. Ongoing auditory messages are simply flushed once a key press is detected. These simple strategies prove to be effective in providing the user with better control on the amount of speech feedback.

We also provide users with redundant information about the mode they are currently in by making voice characteristics (e.g. pitch and speed) mode specific. For

Key	Function	Output	Cell information revealed by key press
/	Enter labels mode	Speech	Either row, column or both read out
*	Enter value mode	Speech	Cell content read out in speech
-	Enter pitch mode	Pitch	Cell content mapped to pitch

Table 3: Modal keys to select 'value', 'pitch' or 'labels' mode.

example, in a given mode, the speech feedback sounds feminine; while in another, the feedback sounds masculine.

During our pilot studies, we found that the spatial cues we provided using the MIDI coarse panning parameter helped users identify approximately their current position in the current row or column. Pilot users also did not report any confusion with the mapping and thus cleared some concerns that the spatial encoding might not be readily understood during a task.

2.2.3 Key Descriptors in Speech to Facilitate the Learning of the Interface

In order to facilitate the learning of the interface, and the recall of the functionality of input keys in various modes, we develop a key descriptor facility. Our application includes a help mode triggered by holding down the Insert key. This mode allows users to press any key of interest and to be informed of the key functionality in speech. These messages also change to match the relevant mode in which the user is currently in as the functionality of the keys is mode dependent. This facility has proved to be very useful to participants during the training phase of the experiment.

3 Functionality of Numeric Pad Keys

Pressing the Delete key produces a high level description of the data, e.g. "table contains information about number of reported cases in London, columns represent type of crime and rows represent years". The keypad keys have been grouped into groups: modal keys (Table 3), navigation keys (Table 4), shortcut keys (Table 5) and overview keys (Table 6). Note that (X, Y) indicates that the contents of the cell in column X and row Y read out in speech, $[X, Y]$ indicates that the contents of the same cell is represented as a non-speech sound. The Key-functionality map we present here is not the first one we have come up with. The inclusion of three navigation modes in our design namely, labels, value and pitch is the result of a number of refinements to provide users with better control on the auditory output.

It is worth mentioning here that in any of the modes keeping the keys pressed (with the exception of key 5) will cause the cell in focus to change repeatedly. Thus in the pitch mode, keeping the cursor keys pressed will generate an overview similar to that obtained when the overview keys are pressed. The main difference is that when cursor keys are used to generate overviews, the user can control the direction and span of the overview. When the overview key is used the current position of the user is not changed in table so that the user can fall back to where he was before the onset of the overview.

Key	Function	Labels	Value	Pitch
↑	Move to cell above	Y_{C-1}	(X_C, Y_{C-1})	$[X_C, Y_{C-1}]$
←	Move to left cell	X_{C-1}	(X_{C-1}, Y_C)	$[X_{C-1}, Y_C]$
→	Move to right cell	X_{C+1}	(X_{C+1}, Y_C)	$[X_{C+1}, Y_C]$
↓	Move to cell below	Y_{C+1}	(X_C, Y_{C+1})	$[X_C, Y_{C+1}]$
5	Reveal info about current cell without moving elsewhere	X_C, Y_C	(X_C, Y_C)	$[X_C, Y_C]$

Table 4: Navigation keys allowing user to move from cell to cell.

Key	Function	Labels	Value	Pitch
Home	Jump to top left corner of table	X_1, Y_1	(X_1, Y_1)	$[X_1, Y_1]$
PgUp	Jump to beginning of current column	X_C, Y_1	(X_C, Y_1)	$[X_C, Y_1]$
End	Jump to beginning of current row	X_1, Y_C	(X_1, Y_C)	$[X_1, Y_C]$
PgDn	Jump to bottom right corner of table	X_M, Y_N	(X_M, Y_N)	$[X_M, Y_N]$

Table 5: Shortcut keys for moving quickly to strategic positions in table.

4 Comparing the Effect of Non-speech Sounds on the Accessibility of 2D Tabular Numeric Information

The purpose of this experiment was to evaluate how successfully visually impaired and blind participants tackled data comprehension tasks under two auditory conditions namely:

1. speech only referred in this paper as (Speech); and

2. speech and pitch referred to as (Pitch).

In the speech only condition, the 'Enter pitch mode' key was disabled. Thus, users had access to the contents of the table only in speech, i.e. they could navigate the table in the 'value' or 'labels' modes only. In the Pitch condition, the user was able to navigate the table in all three modes, namely the 'labels' mode, the 'value' mode and the 'pitch' mode.

4.1 Hypotheses

Access to numerical information in tables is improved when opportunities to access numerical information both in speech and pitch are provided:

H.1. The overall subjective workload is reduced under the pitch condition.

H.2. There is a decrease in the time participants take to tackle set data comprehension tasks.

H.3. There is a decrease in the number of errors under the pitch condition.

Key	Function	Labels	Value	Pitch
+	Overview of current column without moving elsewhere	$Y_1 \ldots Y_N$	$(X_C, Y_1) \ldots$ (X_C, Y_N)	$[X_C, Y_1] \ldots$ $[X_C, Y_N]$
Enter	Overview of current row without moving elsewhere	$X_1 \ldots X_M$	$(X_1, Y_C) \ldots$ (X_M, Y_C)	$[X_1, Y_C] \ldots$ $[X_M, Y_C]$

Table 6: Overview keys allowing user to trigger an overview output with a single key press.

	Demonstration and Training	Session I	Session II	NASA TLX Explanation	NASA TLX Administration	Debriefing
A.1		(Speech) Crime Statistics	(Pitch) Students Statistics			
A.2		(Speech) Student Statistics	(Pitch) Crime Statistics			
B.1		(Pitch) Crime Statistics	(Speech) Students Statistics			
B.2		(Pitch) Student Statistics	(Speech) Crime Statistics			

← . . . . 1 hour 30 . . . . →

Table 7: Experiment schedule.

4.2 Experimental Design

16 participants were subjected to the speech and pitch conditions as described in Table 7. The order in which the tasks and auditory conditions were presented to the participants ensured that any effects due to inherent task difficulty levels and practice (i.e. increase in task tackling efficiency due to increase in familiarity) were minimised.

4.3 Experimental Procedure

The data analysis and inspection tasks that participants had to tackle were designed according to a number of requirements. Firstly, the data analysis should not be so complicated that the focus of the task was on the interpretation of the question rather than on how the tabular data is perceptualised or accessed. Secondly, the questions should not favour a single class of data comprehension task e.g. overview tasks over data discovery tasks.

The two sets of questions that participants face in this experiment relate to Crime and Student statistics. During the training phase, participants had our non-speech mapping strategy explained to them. Through examples, we made sure they had a reasonable understanding of what we meant by pitch, *this concept cannot be assumed to be known by participants*, how the values were mapped to pitch and the spatialisation of the non-speech sounds to give them a cue about their current position in the current row or column. Participants were then allowed to experiment with a data set different from those used in the experiment. This provided them with the opportunity to familiarise themselves with the interface and to ask the experimenter for any clarifications they needed. Also any major hearing impairment would have become apparent during this exercise.

During the next two sessions, participants were administered the relevant tasks in the required order. The time taken for tackling each question was noted. They were free to ask clarifications about questions they felt were not clear. They were encouraged to make a best guess of the solution whenever they felt any question was too hard to tackle. Participants were free to leave during the experiments whenever they wanted.

In the next stage, the experimenter explained the various factors contributing to the workload variable in the NASA task load index (Hart & Wickens, 1990). After the meanings of the various variables were clarified, the pair wise comparison step of the NASA TLX was performed to determine the weight of each contributing factor for each participant. This step allowed us to compare workload values obtained with this experiment to other values obtained form other independent experiments (e.g. a similar experiment but administered to sighted users). The participants were then asked to rate each factor for every task under the relevant condition.

4.4   Construction of Queries

The data comprehension tasks constituted of queries constructed in the same spirit as exercises used to test the basic graph or table analytic skills of late primary or early secondary school students in the UK. We adopted this approach firstly because we wanted to avoid tasks, which were so difficult to understand that participants would find it hard to construct a meaningful goal before interacting with the application, and secondly to increase the size of our pool of participants who had a wide variety of education backgrounds. Our aim was not to make an exhaustive evaluation of data comprehension tasks. They were used mainly for motivating meaningful interactions with our application. We reproduce here the two sets of questions in our experiments regarding two tables of 260 cells containing fictitious numerical data.

4.4.1   Student Statistics: Student Performance Analysis

This dataset is about the performance of a number of students in various subjects. Answer the following questions based on the information available in the table.

- Name the student or students scoring the highest marks for Biology?

- The list of student is presented in ascending order of marks for a given subject. Name the subject?

- Name the subject most likely to have the highest number of passes, note that the pass mark is greater than 40?

- Name the student or students scoring the lowest marks for the Assembly course?

- In which course is performance particularly poor, that is, most marks are less than 40?

- Name the student most likely to have the highest total marks?

4.4.2 Crime Statistics: London Crime Statistics

This table is about the type of crime and the number of cases reported in London from 1974 to 2000. Answer the following questions based on the information available in the table.

- State the year or years in which the highest number of murder cases was or were reported?

- State the year or years in which the highest number of robbery cases was or were reported?

- Which type or types of crime had a consistently high number, consider this number to be greater than 50, of cases reported?

- Which type or types of crime shows or show a consistent increasing trend?

- State the year or years in which the numbers of hate crime cases was or were lowest.

- Which type or types of crime shows or show a consistent decreasing trend?

5   Results

We now compare the various scores obtained for the individual workload categories as defined by the NASA Task Load Index.

5.1   Participants

The age of the participants ranged from 23 to 57. There were 7 women and 9 men in the experiment. The subjects had diverse visual impairment conditions (e.g. aniridia, optic atrophy, congenital rubella, colaboma etc. ...) but none used any residual vision for tasks relevant to our experiment. Most participants were comfortable with the notion of tables and what they are used for. The majority did not have special musical skills with the exception of three subjects who were musicians (one claimed to have perfect pitch). The notion of pitch however was new for some subjects and had to be explained during the training session with examples. The majority of our subjects were familiar with screen reader applications; some also had access to Braille displays. Few were expert users spreadsheet applications and some 'played around' with spreadsheet without really using them. Two of the participants were programmers and appeared to be very comfortable with the numeric keypad.

5.2   Comparing Workload Categories

Figure 1 illustrates the average values for the various workload categories for the NASA TLX for visually impaired users. For completion, we have also included the results obtained for an earlier similar experiment with sight users who could access information in the tables only in the auditory medium.

Table 8 shows the results of a t-test (paired two sample for means) on the workload categories. Our results show a highly significant decrease in the mental ($T_{15} = 4.46$, $p < 0.01$), temporal ($T_{15} = 4.00$, $p < 0.01$), performance ($T_{15} = 3.70$,

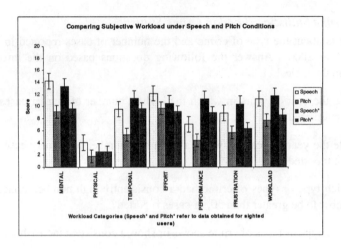

Figure 1: Results showing the impact of pitch on workload categories (standard error bars are shown).

	Mental	Physical	Temporal	Effort	Perform--ance	Frustr--ation	Workload
p	0.0002	0.0237	0.0006	0.0238	0.0011	0.0087	0.0003
T_{15}	4.4636	2.1594	4.0026	2.1568	3.6958	2.6709	4.2836
(Sighted) p	0.0044	0.5000	0.0725	0.0574	0.0939	0.0032	0.0082
(Sighted) T_{14}	3.0389	0.0000	1.5432	1.6813	1.3844	3.1916	3.5475

Table 8: Summary of t-test results (the cells containing $p < 0.01$ are highlighted.

$p < 0.01$), frustration ($T_{15} = 2.67$, $p < 0.01$), and overall subjective workload ($T_{15} = 4.28$, $p < 0.01$) in the pitch condition. Hypothesis H.1 is thus confirmed.

The reader should note that the conditions for these two groups of participants were not identical. In the experiment with sighted users, data was obtained from only 15 participants. Also, an earlier version of the application was used: there was no key descriptor facility and participants had access only to one speech and one pitch mode. While direct comparisons cannot strictly be made, the results does provide us insights about how visually impaired users compare to their sighted counterparts and also perhaps about the effect the interface design has on the workload experienced by users. For example, the bar chart shows that sighted users experienced more temporal and frustration workload as compared to their visually impaired counterparts. This may be due to the fact the version of the application the sighted participants used had only one speech mode which made it over verbose. This might have slowed down their interaction.

5.3 Analysis of the Average Time Taken per Question

Visually impaired users on the average took 133 seconds to tackle a question in speech (standard deviation = 55.033) and on the average took only 44 seconds to tackle a question in pitch (standard deviation = 14), this difference was statistically significant ($T_{15} = 6.2$, $p < 0.01$). In the case of the experiment with sighted users, no temporal information was captured. On the average participants got 4.6 correct in the speech condition and got 5.3 in the pitch. This difference was statistically significant ($T_{15} = 2.2$, $p = 0.0219 < 0.05$). Our quantitative evaluation strongly supports hypotheses H.2 and H.3.

5.4 Participant Feedback and General Discussions

The majority of participants found that commands and modes of interaction were easy to understand and remember. The ability to learn the interface quickly and get on with the task was a definite plus.

We have collected here the most positive and the most negative of user's comments.

Positive comments:

'thought it was another gimmick, once I started using it to tackle tasks, it is quite useful . . . '
'the pitch facility is absolutely fantastic . . . '
'. . . pitch was easier on the memory . . . '
'was not convinced with the idea but it works . . . '
'it is so clear it is easier in pitch'
'in pitch, I see a picture . . . '

Negative comments:

'not really useful for low values . . . '
'difficult to distinguish between low notes'
'. . . pitch makes it slightly easier? can't say . . . '

Our quantitative results reveal that when low values were involved in a data comprehension task, the benefits of the pitch mode decreased. This observation ties well with the feedback we got from some participants who stated that low pitches were difficult to distinguish. In our data comprehension tasks, the lowest frequency presented to participants by our application was 8.18Hz (Midi pitch parameter 0). Earlier guidelines for the design of earcons suggest that the pitch used should be no lower than 125–150Hz (the octave of C4) so that the sounds are not easily masked and are within the hearing range of most listeners (Brewster et al., 1995). Our results confirm that pitch discriminations at lower frequencies is problematic and we plan to use an improved number to pitch mapping in forth coming experiments to tackle this issue.

The majority of participants were pleased with the panning effects of the pitches during table navigation and none found the mapping confusing. One participant was oblivious to the panning effects and failed to detect spatialisation; we did not test spatial hearing ability during this experiment. However, she was still able to complete the data comprehension tasks using pitch information alone. In our opinion, this mapping is an effective way of introducing spatial cues in the representation without having recourse to expensive sound rendering hardware to produce realistic out of the head spatialisations.

Our data reveals that, in rare cases, there is little difference on average between the time taken to tackle a question under the speech condition and the pitch condition. This may be due to the fact that introducing a number of modes in for browsing the table may impose extra strategy building load on participants attempting a data comprehension task. Most participants found choosing the right mode at the right time during the task solving process straightforward. The evidence is that there were a very small number of participants who found meaningful mode transitions difficult and were often engaged in inefficient transitions.

6 Conclusions

In summary, we investigated whether there are grounds to introduce pitch to make the experience of data browsing more effective. Arguably, the obvious way to represent a table in sound is to use speech feedback to inform the user where she is in the table and what is available there. We have demonstrated through rigorous evaluation of our application that non-speech sounds if introduced with care in a data visualisation application can have a significant impact on making it accessible to the visually impaired user. Many participants were eager to find our approach integrated in commercial products, more so, because it is simple and should not be difficult to implement in spreadsheet or screen reader applications. We hope that our work will provide some useful pointers to commercial software developers engaged in making data visualisations accessible to the visually impaired.

7 Acknowledgements

We wish to thank the funding bodies of the MultiVis project namely EPSRC, ONCE (Spain) and Virtual Presence. This work would not have been possible without the collaboration of the enthusiastic staff and students from Royal National Institute for the Blind (Peterborough) and the Royal Blind School (Hereford).

References

Alty, J. & Rigas, D. (1998), Communicating Graphical Information to Blind Users Using Music: The Role of Context, *in* C.-M. Karat, A. Lund, J. Coutaz & J. Karat (eds.), *Proceedings of CHI'98: Human Factors in Computing Systems*, ACM Press, pp.574–81.

Brewster, S. A., Wright, P. C. & Edwards, A. D. N. (1993), An Evaluation of Earcons for Use in Auditory Human–Computer Interfaces, *in* S. Ashlund, K. Mullet, A. Henderson, E. Hollnagel & T. White (eds.), *Proceedings of INTERCHI'93*, ACM Press/IOS Press, pp.222–7.

Brewster, S. A., Wright, P. C. & Edwards, A. D. N. (1995), Experimentally Derived Guidelines for the Creation of Earcons, *in* G. Allen, J. Wilkinson & P. Wright (eds.), *Adjunct Proceedings of HCI'95*, BCS, pp.155–9.

Gardner, J. A., Lundquist, R. & Sahyun, S. (1998), TRIANGLE: A Tri-modal Access Program for Reading, Writing and Doing Math, *in Proceedings of CSUN International Conference on Technology and Persons with Disabilities*, Center on Disabilities, California State University, Northridge, California, USA. http://www.dinf.org/csun_98/csun98_104.htm.

Gomez, C., Shebilske, W. & Regian, J. (1994), The Effects of Training on Cognitive Capacity Demands for Synthetic Speech, *in Proceedings of the Human Factors and Ergonomics Society 38th Annual Meeting*, Human Factors and Ergonomics Society, pp.1229–39.

Hart, S. & Wickens, C. (1990), Workload Assessment and Prediction, *in* H. R. Booher (ed.), *MANPRINT, An Approach to Systems Integration*, Van Nostrand Reinhold, pp.257–296.

Kurze, M. (1998), TGuide: A Guidance System for Tactile Image Exploration, *in Third Annual ACM Conference on Assistive Technologies*, ACM Press, pp.85–91.

Mansur, D. (1975), Graphs in Sound: A Numerical Data Analysis Method for the Blind, Master's thesis, University of California.

Moore, B. (1982), *An Introduction to the Psychology of Hearing*, Academic Press.

Pollack, I. & Ficks, L. (1954), "Information of Elementary Multi-dimensional Auditory Displays", *Journal of the Acoustical Society of America* **26**, 155–8.

Roffler, S. & Butler, R. (1968), "Localisation of Tonal Stimuli in the Vertical Plane", *Journal of the Acoustical Society of America* **43**, 1260–6.

Shneiderman, B. (ed.) (1994), *Sparks of Innovation in Human–Computer Interaction*, Ablex.

Stevens, S., Volkmann, J. & Newman, E. (1937), "A Scale for the Measurement of the Psychological Magnitude of Pitch", *Journal of the Acoustical Society of America* **8**, 185–90.

Diary in the Sky: A Spatial Audio Display for a Mobile Calendar

Ashley Walker, Stephen Brewster, David McGookin & Adrian Ng

Glasgow Interactive Systems Group, Department of Computing Science, University of Glasgow, Glasgow G12 8QQ, UK

Tel: *+44 141 330 4966*

Email: *stephen@dcs.glasgow.ac.uk*

URL: *http://www.dcs.glasgow.ac.uk/~stephen*

We present a spatial audio display technique that overcomes the presentation rate bottleneck of traditional monaural audio displays. Our compact speech display works by encoding message semantics into the acoustic spatialisation. In user testing, this display facilitated better recall of events than a conventional small screen visual display. Moreover, results showed that this mapping aided in the recall of the absolute position of events — as opposed to merely their relative orders — in a temporally ordered data set.

Keywords: planar 3D audio, non-speech sounds, mobile devices, PDAs spatial mapping, earcons, sound, interface sonification.

1 Introduction

We live in a visual culture. The great worth of pictorial representations are reaffirmed over and over in the achievements of the 20th century — on billboards and the big screen, by graphic artists mousing over digital canvases, and school children clicking at multimedia PCs. As technology evolves in the 21st century, however, we may begin to see things differently. At least, we are likely to see things through a smaller display. As the mobile and miniature devices of the new millennium replace older forms of communication and computation, the fabric of our visual culture must stretch to accommodate other display and interaction techniques.

Concerns about the limits of the visual display are not new. We have known for decades that visual representations of information, including graphics and written text, can be hard to read — causing 'eye-strain' and visual overload. This is particularly true in multi-tasking computer interfaces involving many windows of information. Moreover, people who interact with information 'on the go' — via the small screen of a personal digital assistant (PDA) or mobile phone — have further reduced visual (and attentional) resources. Mobile phone displays, in particular, have a small fraction of the pixel display space of desktop monitors and they are employed in use-contexts that are themselves visually intensive. One place in which we can seek display alternatives — alternatives not wed to the diminishing resource of screen space — is in the audio domain.

Sonic displays have been developed in a number of special purpose application areas (Gaver, 1989; Schmandt & Mullins, 1995; Kobayashi & Schmandt, 1997; Crease & Brewster, 1998; Mynatt et al., 1998; Sawhney & Schmandt, 1999; Walker & Brewster, 2000). Where these have succeeded, they have been based upon a firm understanding of hearing. Where audio displays have failed, they have naively attempted to translate a (visual) stream of information into an audio one — ignoring important differences between how the eye and ear process information.

The ear differs from the eye in that it is omni-directional — a true three-dimensional (3D) display space that does not suffer from occlusion. Its fabric is course grained — with angular resolutions approximately 10 times more coarse than the eye across the sensorially richest regions (Howard & Templeton, 1966). However, what the ear lacks in spatially sensitivity, it more than makes up for in temporal sensitivity (try watching an action movie with the sound turned off: the eye rarely perceives a punch land, but the ear satisfies your need to know that justice has been served).

The ear analyses information temporally; and this is both its strength and weakness. Audio displays involving speech are often dismissed as too slow because of the supposed delay involved with rending a stream of text (or, worse, a description of a graphic). A simple translation of information into a single audio stream, however, fails to exploit the third important strength of the ear: its ability to simultaneously monitor more than one stream of information (Cherry, 1953; Arons, 1992). Compare the layers of audio in a movie soundtrack — including music, dialogue, ambient sounds, auditory feedback from footsteps, dripping faucets, gun-shots, etc.— with the single layer of visual information on the screen (Chion, 1990).

Here we present a novel audio display technique that overcomes the presentation rate bottleneck of traditional monaural audio displays by spatialising audio streams. Moreover, we encode message semantics into the spatialisation to further increase presentation rate. This display technique is general and may be used in a variety of application interfaces. To test the utility, however, we built a prototype that encompassed the same functionality as a popular mobile device application: the *DateBook*, or calendar. This paper covers design and implementation (Section 2) of that prototype, as well as user-testing (Section 3 and 4). In Section 5 and 6, we draw together insights.

2   Materials

Here we describe an experiment to investigate the usability of an auditory interface to a DateBook application. We chose to work with the DateBook Application in

Figure 1: Palm DateBook visual display.

particular because the inherent temporal separation of the data (i.e. DateBook events) is naturally amenable to the mappings described below. We chose to compare our audio DateBook interface with a model of the visual DateBook interface that runs on Palm, Inc. PDAs because of the wide user-base of the latter (Palm, Inc.) — at the present time these are the most popular PDAs on the market.

The Palm is a small and light PDA with a 6cm×6cm rectangular screen (see Figure 1). Most applications — including the DateBook — present their data vertically in scrollable lists. In the case of the DateBook, events are typically displayed in 1 hourly denominations in a long vertical list. Due to the screen size limitations, approximately half a day's worth of events is typically visible at one time. Scrolling between events, however, requires some visual attention, due to the problem of mating the tip of a stylus with the small scroll bar area.

These limitations are inherent in a small screen device and can only be overcome via alternative display techniques. Figure 2 shows a mapping of DateBook events onto an alternative audio display space. In this space, an imaginary clock-face is projected onto a slice of the auditory sphere surrounding a user's head — with 9am/pm as the extreme left, 12am/pm as the direct front, 3am/pm as the extreme right and 6am/pm as the direct back. The mapping is displayed within the horizontal plane containing a listener's ears because this is the most sensorally rich listening region (Begault, 1994).

We hypothesised that this horizontal ('clock-face') display orientation was more natural — exploiting existing knowledge of time-space mappings — than a vertical list of time-ordered data or a stream of non-spatialised audio items. Given the limitations of current spatialisation technology it is much harder to make a solution for the general population that works well in azimuth (due to pinnae differences between listeners); the transverse plane is much easier to work with for a general solution. In particular, we hypothesised that such a clock-face display would facilitate better recall of events and incur lower workloads. A description of hypothesis testing is given in the next section.

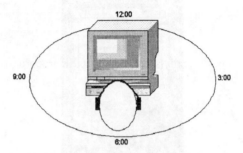

Figure 2: Time-space mapping of the auditory DateBook display.

3   Methods

3.1   Experimental Design

Sixteen students from University of Glasgow served as participants. This group comprised six women and ten men between the ages of 18 and 24. Participants were paid. The experiment was a counter-balanced within-groups design with modality of cue as the single independent variable. Each of the participants performed the task described below using a visual display and the spatial audio display. Dependent variables included recall performance (of four diary items) and several subjective workload measures. Participants also gave informal feedback following the experiment.

3.2   Experimental Scenario

Users were presented with DateBook contents and told that they would be asked to perform a series of recall questions about the day's events. Events consisted of simple keyword phrases of 4 words or less, preceded by a verbal or written time stamp. Care was taken to ensure that the semantics did not overlap with those in a participant's real-life by telling participants that they were seeing/hearing the diaries of a variety of professionals (e.g. Surgeon, Reporter, Circus Clown, etc.). After being exposed to each condition as described below, the display was hidden/muted and the participant was asked four recall questions — one per calendar item. The responses were verbally cued and tested relative recall of item order ("Did A occur before or after B?") as well as absolute recall of the temporal ordering of items ("What time did X occur?" or "What occurred at Y time?"). The questions were equated in that they sampled the entire temporal window in an effort to control for memory order effects that could favour recall of primacy/recency items over items from the middle of the list. Following this recall test, workload ratings were collected. Each participant performed the experiment three times and the order of presentation of each modality was varied.

In the visual condition users were presented with the interface to the standard Palm DateBook. As the Palm is the biggest selling PDA its diary application is one of the most commonly used. Diary applications on many other PDAs follow a very similar list-based design so we took this as the control condition. Participants were allowed to scroll between events over a period of 8 seconds (this period was chosen to correspond with the two seconds per event playback scheme used in the audio condition). Events were vertically separated by space proportional to their temporal separations. Users had to scroll between events, as they did not all fit on one screen. Because the Palm device does not yet support audio of the type required by this study, the experiment ran in a 6×6cm rectangular window on the screen of a desktop computer. Participants scrolled between events using a standard desktop mouse. To make the audio and visual conditions consistent both used this desktop simulation.

In the audio condition events were speech synthesised sequentially using Lucent's Text-to-Speech technology (Lucent Technologies, 1999) in intervals of two seconds (none of the audio cues lasted more than 1.5seconds). In this condition events were spatialised via convolution with head-related transfer functions (HRTFs) included with Microsoft's Direct X multimedia API and a Creative Labs SoundBlaster Live! Platinum soundcard. Events were not preceded by a verbal time stamp, as that information was available in the semantics of the spatial audio mapping. The sounds were presented through a pair of Sennheiser HD25 headphones. There was no visual display in this condition.

3.3 Measures

Recall performance was calculated using the percentage correct in each condition, as well as an intra-condition performance comparison of absolute vs. relative event knowledge. Subjective workload assessments — on a modified set of NASA TLX scales (Hart & Staveland, 1988) — were collected after each condition. The workload ratings included mental and physical demand, time pressure, effort expended, frustration and performance. We added a seventh factor: Annoyance. This is one of the main concerns that users of auditory interfaces have with the use of sound. In the experiment described here annoyance due to auditory feedback was measured to find out if it was indeed a problem. We also asked our participants to indicate overall preference, i.e. which of the two interfaces they felt made the task easiest. Participants had to fill in workload charts after both conditions of the experiment.

4 Results

4.1 Recall

Recall rates were significantly affected by modality, with users performing better in the audio than the visual condition ($T_{15} = 4.49$, $p = 0.0002$). The mean percentage of correct recalls was 88.3% and 70.2% in the audio and visual conditions respectively.

Analysis of a subset of the data showed that, in both conditions, recall of the absolute time of an event was worse than recall of an event's order relative to other events. However, in the case of absolute event time recall, the mean percentage of correct recalls dropped more markedly in the visual than the audio conditions (84.4% and 64.6% in the audio and visual conditions, respectively).

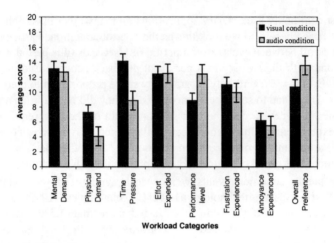

Figure 3: Average workload scores including annoyance and overall preference. Standard error bars are shown.

4.2 Subject Workload Ratings

The audio condition resulted in significantly lower subjective workload ratings in three of the six workload categories measured. Participants reported that the audio condition caused significantly less physical demand ($T_{15} = 2.31$, $p = 0.018$) and time pressure ($T_{15} = 3.97$, $p = 0.0006$). This ultimately resulted in a significantly higher sense of performance in the audio condition ($T_{15} = 2.98$; $p = 0.005$). As shown in Figure 3, the other workload ratings are fairly equal across the conditions. The audio condition was not rated as more annoying than the visual.

5 Discussion

5.1 Spatial Axes

Many participants said that the audio condition required less 'interpretation'. Some participants explained that event time came 'for free', thereby reducing the task to memorising a keyword associated with an easily recalled spatial landmark. By contrast, the visual condition required the memorisation of 'two things': time and event. This insight could be valuable in visual layout design as well. Although one could argue that a list of items is spatially extended, the vertical extendedness of such a space does not inherently encode the relevant semantics of this task as effectively as a horizontal, clock-face space.

5.2 Audio

On top of advantages associated with an audio DateBook display, a number of participants also said that audio, *per se*, registered more automatically ("like someone telling you what to do"). Many participants admitted to feeling surprised that an apparently visual task could be performed without much effort using the auditory cues.

Although most participants found that heard (as opposed to read) events were easier to memorise/recall in a verbally cued recall test, it is not necessarily the case that a well-designed written recall test would elicit the same response.

5.3 Serial vs. Parallel Presentation

The audio and visual conditions differed in the presentation bandwidth. In the visual condition, users could see several events at once; while, in the audio, events were presented serially. We expected that this would frustrate audio users, but only a minority complained that the audio was presented too fast or that they only had 'one chance' to memorise the audio events.

In pilot studies, we broadcast spatial audio events in parallel and tracked users' head movements — adjusting the volume (audibility) of each event depending upon listening behaviour. However, this volume control mechanisms appeared to be too crude and listeners felt overloaded. Certainly more training in this technique — or more sophisticated volume control (Schmandt & Mullins, 1995) — could yield better results.

5.4 Active and Passive Displays

The audio and visual conditions differed in the degree of interactivity. While we expected users to prefer some control over the display, a few complained about losing time scrolling through the visual list. Recall that users experienced significantly greater time pressure and physical demand in the visual condition. Moreover, one participant highlighted a potential difficulty: although the event list was sorted according to time of occurrence, the order of events appeared reversed when he scrolled back up through it. Again, this may be more a reflection of the difficulty of scrolling as opposed to a commentary on control in general. Good audio interaction techniques — i.e. input devices symmetrical to the 3D display space — are certainly worth pursuing in future work.

5.5 Laboratory vs. Mobile Interface Testing

Applications with great potential to enhance mobile device interfaces should be tested on those devices to confirm that they work as well in the field as they do in the lab. We regret that we did not have the technology to conduct a field study in this case. From other fieldwork on mobile audio, e.g. Brewster (2001), we expect that the following factors would bear on the same study conducted there.

First, it is well established that device interface tasks with a high visual load and manual input requirement are difficult to perform when walking or driving. In this regard, we expect results of a field study to further accentuate the suitability of audio (indeed, such a belief motivated this study). Brewster (2001) showed that a real sonically-enhanced Palm PDA significantly improved usability and mobility in a real mobile situation. It is not possible to do more sophisticated audio interfaces on the Palm platform as it has only basic audio capabilities. The next stage of our work in this area is to use a wearable PC with soundcard that will allow us to run the type of experiment discussed here on a real mobile device in a real mobile situation.

Nevertheless, there remains an open question as to how the introduction of additional audio stimuli, on top of environmental sounds, will impact on the perception of those sounds and vice versa. We performed the present study in a laboratory where there was no environmental sound targeted at the participant. The number and content of environmental plus artificial/display streams competing for a user's attention appears, to us, to be a more relevant issue than 'lab' vs. 'field' noise. This issue certainly requires more sophisticated and systematic study than any field test report available in the literature.

5.6   Conclusions

We consume audio and visual information in different ways, and different techniques are required for displaying to the ear and eye. GUI design, in collaboration with visual display hardware, has evolved to exploit the narrow-field, high resolution, space-scanning proclivity of the eye. Here we presented a simple and effective audio display device that exploits the ear's omni-directionality, its sensitivity to coarse-scale spatialisation, and its temporal sensitivity. In doing so, we constructed a display that overcomes some of the bandwidth limitations of traditional (monaural) speech displays and provided a more effective interface to an existing PDA application.

Acknowledgements

This work was funded by EPSRC GR/L79212 and a New Discoveries grant from Microsoft Corporation.

References

Arons, B. (1992), "A Review of the Cocktail Party Effect", *Journal of the American Voice I/O Society* **12**(7), 35–50.

Begault, D. (1994), *3-D Sound for Virtual Reality and Multimedia*, Academic Press.

Brewster, S. A. (2001), Overcoming the Lack of Screen Space on Mobile Computers, Technical Report TR-2001-87, Department of Computer Science, Glasgow University, Glasgow, UK.

Cherry, E. C. (1953), "Some Experiments on the Recognition of Speech", *Journal of the Acoustical Society of America* **25**, 975–9.

Chion, M. (1990), *Audio-Vision: Sound on Screen*, Columbia University Press.

Crease, M. & Brewster, S. (1998), Making Progress With Sounds — The Design And Evaluation Of An Audio Progress Bar, *in* A. Edwards & S. Brewster (eds.), *Proceedings of the International Conference on Auditory Display (ICAD'98)*, BCS. http://www.ewic.org.uk/.

Gaver, W. W. (1989), "The SonicFinder: An Interface that Uses Auditory Icon", *Human–Computer Interaction* **4**(1), 67–94.

Hart, S. & Staveland, L. (1988), Development of NASA-TLX (Task Load Index): Results of Empirical and Theoretical Research, *in* P. Hancock & N. Meshkati (eds.), *Human Mental Workload*, North-Holland, pp.139–83.

Howard, I. P. & Templeton, W. B. (1966), *Human Spatial Orientation*, John Wiley & Sons.

Kobayashi, M. & Schmandt, C. (1997), Dynamic Soundscape: Mapping Time to Space for Audio Browsing, *in* S. Pemberton (ed.), *Proceedings of CHI'97: Human Factors in Computing Systems*, ACM Press, pp.194–201.

Lucent Technologies (1999), Lucent Speech Solutions, http:// www.lucent.com/speech.

Mynatt, E. D., Back, M., Want, R., Baer, M. & Ellis, J. (1998), Designing Audio Aura, *in* C.-M. Karat, A. Lund, J. Coutaz & J. Karat (eds.), *Proceedings of CHI'98: Human Factors in Computing Systems*, ACM Press, pp.566–73.

Sawhney, N. & Schmandt, C. (1999), Nomadic Radio: Scalable and Contextual Notification for Wearable Messaging, *in* M. G. Williams, M. W. Altom, K. Ehrlich & W. Newman (eds.), *Proceedings of the CHI99 Conference on Human Factors in Computing Systems: The CHI is the Limit*, ACM Press, pp.96–103.

Schmandt, C. & Mullins, A. (1995), AudioStreamer: Exploiting Simultaneity for Listening, *in* I. Katz, R. Mack & L. Marks (eds.), *Companion Proceedings of CHI'95: Human Factors in Computing Systems (CHI'95 Conference Companion)*, ACM Press, pp.218–9.

Walker, V. A. & Brewster, S. (2000), "Spatial Audio in Small Screen Device Displays,", *Personal Technologies* 4(2), 144–54.

Novel Input Devices

Input Device Selection and Interaction Configuration with ICON

Pierre Dragicevic & Jean-Daniel Fekete

*École des Mines de Nantes 4, rue Alfred Kastler, La Chantrerie,
44307 Nantes Cedex 3, France*

Tel: *+33 2 51 85 82 08*

Email: *{dragice,fekete}@emn.fr*

This paper describes ICON, a novel editor designed to configure a set of input devices and connect them to actions into a graphical interactive application. ICON allows 'power users' to customise the way an application manages its input to suit their needs. New configurations can be designed to help physically challenged users to use alternative input methods, or skilled users — graphic designers or musicians for example — to use their favourite input devices and interaction techniques (bimanual, voice enabled, etc.).

ICON works with Java Swing and requires applications to describe their input needs in terms of ICON modules. By using systems like ICON, users can adapt more deeply than before their applications and programmers can easily provide extensibility to their applications.

Keywords: multiple inputs, input devices, interaction techniques, toolkits, assistive technologies.

1 Introduction

Today, interactive desktop applications manage a very limited set of input devices, typically one mouse and one keyboard. However, the population of users requiring or simply possessing alternative input devices is growing, as well as the number of new devices available.

Given the proliferation of input devices and the importance of tasks performed by users on a computer, being able to adapt an existing application to one or several input devices is an important issue for physically challenged users, musicians, video game players, graphic artists etc. These users find their environment more usable or simply improved when they use their favourite input devices with existing applications.

However, the complexity of supporting alternative input devices is currently very high: each application has to explicitly implement some code to manage each device and all the desired interaction techniques using these devices. At best, specialised applications support a limited set of devices suited to their task. Some systems provide extensibility through plug-in mechanisms, but writing plug-ins require expert programming skills.

On the user side, most applications provide simple but limited input configurability, usually through control panels. *Power users*, i.e. users willing to invest their time to customise and improve computer tools, are a growing category of users due to the widespread use of computers, but which still has little recognition from software vendors.

In this paper, we describe ICON (Input Configurator), a system for selecting alternative input devices and configuring their interaction techniques interactively. Using ICON, power users can connect additional input devices — such as tablets, voice recognition software, assistive devices or electronic musical instruments — to an ICON aware application and/or assign specific interactive behaviour to connected devices. Figure 1 shows a typical configuration.

ICON is implemented using Java Swing and requires applications to externalise their interaction tools to be effective. The effort required to do so is very modest compared to the benefits. Typical ICON users need not be computer scientists; a good understanding of computer systems is sufficient. Users with disabilities or special requirements may need the help of such power users to configure their application.

This paper first describes a typical scenario a user would follow to edit the input configuration of a simple application. After comparing ICON to related work, we describe the ICON editor in details; we give then more implementation details and discuss practical issues for the use of ICON in applications.

2 Scenario

In this section, we show how John, a typical ICON power user, may adapt a sample application called 'ICONDraw' that can draw lines, rectangles and freehand curves. By invoking the 'configure' menu of ICONDraw, John starts ICON that displays the current configuration as in Figure 1. This dataflow diagram shows several connected blocks called modules. Each module has input or output slots where links can be connected. Only connected slots are displayed in the figures. The two input devices of the default configuration — the mouse and the keyboard — are on the left, connected to some processing modules and finally to ICONDraw's interaction tools appearing as output modules.

In ICONDraw's standard configuration, the mouse is connected to a cursor module, which displays feedback and is used as a virtual device. The right mouse button is used to cycle through the drawing tools. Keyboard keys are used to change the colour and size of the lines. John can then change the configuration, save it to a file or load it from the configuration files available for ICONDraw.

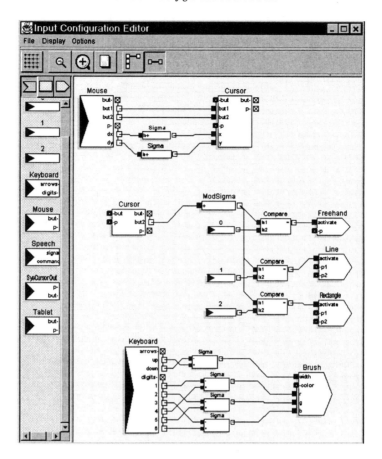

Figure 1: Screenshot of ICON showing part of the configuration of a drawing editor. The right mouse button changes the selected tool and keypad keys change the colour an line width attributes. Mouse relative positions are added and sent to a 'cursor' model that abstracts a 2D locator device.

2.1 Stabilising the Mouse Position

John remembers his friend Jane wants a drawing program but couldn't use a regular one because she suffers from Parkinson's disease that provokes uncontrollable hand shaking. With ICON, he can stabilise the pointer position by inserting a low-pass filter — averaging pointer positions to remove quick moves — between the mouse device and the cursor as shown in Figure 2.

To insert a LowPass module, John drags it from the left pane — where all existing modules are shown — and drops it in the editor pane. Clicking on one slot and dragging into another creates a connection. The configuration is effective immediately in ICONDraw. When finished, John saves the configuration and sends it by email to Jane.

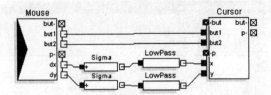

Figure 2: Low-pass filters are inserted between the mouse an the cursor to stabilise the position.

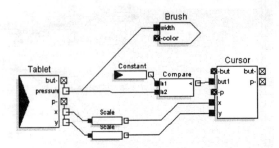

Figure 3: Adding a pressure sensitive stylus to ICONDraw where the pressure changes the line width of the drawing.

John is a graphic designer and has a tablet with a pressure sensitive stylus. To use it inside ICONDraw, he needs to disconnect the mouse, drag the tablet module in the ICON pane and connect it to the cursor through scale modules.

To further use the pressure for changing the line width when drawing, he needs to connect the pressure slot of the stylus to the size slot of the brush used by the drawing tools, as shown in Figure 3. Brushes abstract graphic attributes just like cursors abstract positional devices. John can now draw with the stylus and have varying width strokes when using the freehand drawing tool.

2.2 Configuring for Bimanual Interaction

Figure 4 shows part of the configuration controlling ICONDraw's interaction tools (Figure 1 only represents the tool selection part). John now wants to use both his mouse and the stylus. A bimanual configuration requires a second pointer that can be dropped from the left pane into the ICON pane. Figure 5 shows the configuration required to create a line using bimanual interaction: one should be connected to the 'p1' slot and the second to the 'p2' slot. A combination of Boolean modules determines when the creation mode is triggered and when it is finished.

2.3 Other Configurations

Current input modules also include voice and gesture recognition. John could use it to control the selected tool or to change the colour if he wishes, effectively adapting

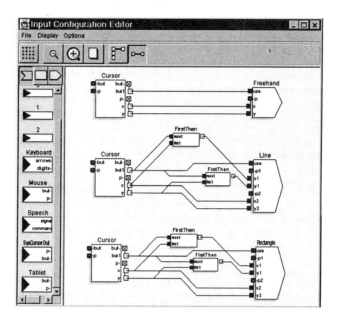

Figure 4: Creation tools of ICONDraw represented as output modules.

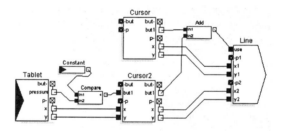

Figure 5: Configuration for creating a line with bi-manual interaction.

the program to his skills and environmental particularities such as limited desk space or noisy environment.

3   Related Work

There have been several attempts at simplifying the connection of alternative input devices or specifying the configuration of interactive applications.

3.1   *Assistive Technologies*

Assistive technologies include hardware devices and software adapters. They are designed to allow disabled users to work on a desktop computer. Software adapters can be external applications that take their input from various special hardware devices and translate them as if they were actions on the mouse and keyboard. NeatTool (Carbone et al., 2000) is such a system and configurations are designed using a rich graphical dataflow system. However, systems like NeatTool are limited to using existing interaction techniques of an application. More generally, external software adapters have problems when they need to maintain the internal states of an application like the current selected drawing tool.

In contrast, internal software adapters are becoming more common. Microsoft Active Accessibility (Microsoft Corporation, 1999) and Java Swing (Andrews, 1999) have provisions for accessibility and programmers can modify existing applications to adapt them to various input and output configurations. However, accessibility functions are not well designed for continuous interaction such as drag and drop or line drawing, and no graphical configuration tools exist yet, requiring a programmer's skill and sometimes source access to use them.

3.2   Games

Most current games offer some configuration options and all 3D video games offer a large choice of supported input devices. However, most of the games have a set of standard configurations and adapt alternative devices by compatibility. A regular action game will provide one configuration using the keyboard and another using positional devices (mouse, joystick or any compatible device). Sometimes, very specific devices are also managed like a force feedback joystick for flight simulators or a driving wheel for car racing. However, no general mechanism could allow a pianist to use a midi keyboard on a car-racing program for example. The configuration is usually done through a simple form-based interface or a simple script-like language which only allows direct bindings of device channels (Honeywell, 1999).

Furthermore, alternative input devices can only be used to play the game but other controls such as menus or dialogs can only be controlled by the regular mouse and keyboard.

3.3   3D Toolkits

3D toolkits and animation environments are usually aware of alternative input devices. The AVID/SoftImage system implements a 'channel' library to connect any valuator device as a set of channels cc. These channels can in turn be connected to internal values inside 3D models or trigger the internal constraint solver to perform sophisticated direct animations. However, channels are limited to these direct animations and cannot be used to enhance the interaction of the 3D-modelling tool itself for instance. The World toolkit (Sense8 Corp., 1999) can use any kind of device if it is described as an array of relative positional values. Again, this view of input device is meant for animation or direct control in VR environments but not for the interactive creation of objects or control of menus. Furthermore, the configuration of these input devices has to be programmed.

Recently, Jacob proposed a new architectural model to manage the interaction (Jacob et al., 1999) using VRED, a dataflow system similar to ICON. Due to its complexity, VRED is meant to be used by expert programmers since it interacts deeply with the internals of animation programs.

3.4 2D Toolkits

There has been some attempts at simplifying the integration of alternative input devices in applications, such as the X Input Extension (Ferguson, 1992). However, very few 2D programs use it and, when they do, their level of configuration is very limited. The X Toolkit (Nye & O'Reilly, 1992) specifies a textual format to configure application bindings but its syntax is complex and requires the application to be restarted when it changes.

Myers (1990; 1991) described an interactive system for visual programming of interactions using interactors in the Garnet environment. Garnet is still oriented towards programmers and interaction techniques cannot be changed dynamically during the execution of an application. Furthermore, Garnet only manages one mouse and one keyboard.

Other systems for managing multiple devices exist such as MMM, Chatty's two-handed aware toolkit and Hourcade's MID library (Hourcade & Bederson, 1999; Bier & Freeman, 1991; Chatty, 1994) but they all offer tools to programmers instead of users.

3.5 Classification

Table 1 summarises this section, classifying existing systems in term of support for configurability and multiple input devices (MID). Configurability is classified in 6 categories: (1) none, (2) direct binding from device and events to program actions (i.e. without higher level control such as conditional binding), (3) environments configurable by users, (4) environments configurable by a programmer using a specialised language, (5) environments requiring a regular programming language for configuration, and (6) for completeness, adaptive environments that could automatically adapt interaction techniques and input devices to user's needs. No existing systems belong to this category yet. MID are classified in 4 categories: aware of only a fixed set of devices, aware of accessibility services and aware of many (a fixed set of classes) or any alternative devices.

4 The ICON System

The ICON Editor allows users to view and edit the mappings between all the available input devices and an application. It is based on a dataflow model, with the underlying semantics of reactive synchronous languages such as Esterel (Berry & Cosserat, 1984) or Lustre (Halbwachs et al., 1991). In this dataflow model, modules are input devices, processing devices, and application objects. Links are connections between input and output slots of the modules. A configuration is built by dragging modules into the ICON workspace and connecting them to perform high level actions, expressed as output modules. This section first describes how to use ICON, then how to design an ICON Aware application.

4.1 Using ICON

Modules that can be used to build an input configuration are available in three repositories: an input module repository, a processing module repository and an output module repository (see Figure 1). Each type of module has its own graphical representation. New compound modules can also be created at will.

Configure	MID			
	Fixed set	Accessibility	Many	Any
None	Most applications			
Direct binding	Video games		Midi configuration	
User oriented	Hardware accessibility NeatTool	Software accessibility	Softimage Channels	ICON
Limited programmer oriented	Garnet interactors			VRED
Programming	Most toolkits	Java Swing MFC	World Tk	MMM Chatty MID
Adaptive				

Table 1: Classification of current systems in term of support for configuration and multiple input devices.

Input module repository: When the editor is launched, it asks the input APIs — WinTab (LCS/Telegraphics, 1999) for the tablets, JavaSpeech (Sun Microsystems Inc., 1998) for the voice recognition engine, Direct Input (Kovach, 2000) and USB (Axelson, 1999) for yet other devices — for the set of connected input devices, and their capabilities. Device's capabilities are interpreted as a set of typed channels. For each detected device, a module is created and filled with output slots (corresponding to the device's channels), and is added to the input module repository. Timer modules also belong to this repository. With timer modules, users can detect timeouts, idle cursors, perform auto-repeat or other time-oriented constructs.

Processing module repository: The editor contains a set of processing modules loaded from a library. A processing module has both input and output slots. There are currently three categories of processing modules: control modules, primitive modules and utilities. Control modules are useful to implement tests and control switches. Primitive modules include arithmetic, Boolean operations, comparisons and memorisation of previous values. Utilities include debug modules, feedback modules, and modules that could be built by composing primitives but are faster and smaller as primitives themselves.

Output module repository: This repository contains application-specific modules that are loaded when the user chooses an application to edit. These output modules show what the application needs in terms of input. It also contains global output devices such as the standard text output, the system cursor, or a Text-To-Speech engine.

Applications choose the level of granularity and how they describe their interactions in term of output modules. For example, all the atomic commands usually attached to menu items or buttons can be exposed as single output modules or can be grouped and exposed as one larger module. Exposing control objects as output modules is supported at the toolkit level. For application specific interactions, programmers have to provide suitable output modules according to the level of configurability they want to provide. More details are given in the next section.

Compound modules: Part of an input configuration can be used to create a user-defined module, by simply selecting a group of modules and issuing the 'create compound' command. Selected modules and all the connections between them are moved into a new compound module. External connections are also preserved: slots are automatically created on the compound device to enable external connections to internal modules.

Module properties: In addition to slots, some modules have properties that can be edited in a separate window. All modules have the *name*, *help*, and *enabled* properties. Other properties are mostly numerical parameters in mathematical processors.

Properties can also exist in input modules depending on the input API. As an example, recogniser devices issued from the JavaSpeech API have an array of string describing their vocabulary (empty by default). The properties describing the way an input module interprets user's actions to generate data is sometimes called the device context. Several instances of the same input module can live separately, each having its own *device context*.

Module cloning and shortcuts: Modules and groups of modules can be cloned in the workspace by dragging them while holding the control key. During this operation, all property values are copied. For example, cloning a processing module is useful when we have to perform the same operations elsewhere in the configuration. But an input module such as a mouse has a unique data source, and its clone will produce exactly the same data. However, cloning an input module can be useful to describe different device contexts (e.g. different working vocabularies for the same speech recogniser). The semantics of cloning an output module depends on how the application manages several instances of this module.

Another useful feature is module shortcuts. They allow the user to display the same device in different places of the workspace, so that an input configuration looks much clearer (Figures 1–5 use shortcuts). A shortcut is made by dragging a device while holding both the shift and control keys.

Connections: Connections are created by dragging from one slot to another. Inconsistent connections — i.e. connections between input or output slots, type-incompatible slots, or connections that generate a cycle — are forbidden. Only authorised slots are highlighted during the dragging operation. ICON provides facilities for modifying connections, such as group deleting or fast reconnecting (changing one side of an existing connection).

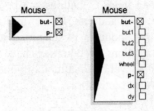

Figure 6: Hierarchical slots of the mouse device.

Hierarchical slots: The configuration editor has a hierarchical representation of slots (Figure 6), which facilitates browsing of numerous slots. This also allows the structure of input devices to be preserved. Furthermore, hierarchical slots can be used to manipulate complex types.

Extended/Minimal Display: There are two display modes for modules. Extended mode shows all slots. Minimal mode shows only used slots, which reduces the visual complexity of a configuration. Entering a module with mouse cursor automatically displays it in extended mode.

Panning/Zooming: The user can pan and zoom on the workspace, and easily work on large configurations. It is also possible to enlarge and shrink individual modules.

4.2 Designing ICON-*Aware Applications*

ICON changes the programming paradigm used by interactive systems. Current systems rely on an event-based model, an event dispatching strategy and a state management programmed in a general-purpose language such as Java or C. ICON uses another paradigm where values are propagated through a network of operations directly into actions. This paradigm is used extensively and successfully in automatic control systems, a domain we consider close to input configuration management.

Configurations in ICON are very similar to controllers in the traditional Smalltalk Model View Controller (MVC) triplet (Krasner & Pope, 1988). Externalising the controller requires externalising a protocol to communicate between a Model and a View. This protocol is modelled as input and output modules.

Concretely, new modules have to be programmed in three circumstances: for a new application that needs to export some new Views and Models, when an unimplemented input device is available and when a new processing is required such as a gesture classifier. The next paragraph shows the code for implementing an output module displaying the currently selected tool in ICONDraw:

```
public class ToolModule extends Module {
    // INPUT SLOTS
    protected final IntSlot tool = new IntSlot("tool");
```

```
protected ToolBox toolbox;

public ToolModule(String name) {
  super(name);
  addInSlot(tool);
  toolbox = (Toolbox) getComponentNamed("ToolBox");
}

public void changed(Change change) {
  if (change. hasChanged(tool)) {
  toolbox. setTool(tool. getIntValue());
  }
}
}
```

Programming a new module involves modest efforts. Existing modules have an average size of 50 lines, the largest being the speech recognition module, 512 lines long.

5 Implementation Issues

ICON is currently implemented in Java 1.2 and relies on Java Swing (Geary, 1999) with some specific extensions. Connections to the low level input APIs are usually implemented in C++ using the Java Native Interface (Liang, 1999). The implementation is divided in three parts: the reactive language interpreter, the native modules API and the graphical editor ICON.

5.1 *The Reactive Language Interpreter*

The language underlying the execution of ICON is derived from Lustre and Esterel (Halbwachs et al., 1991; Berry & Cosserat, 1984). Instead of defining a new semantics, we have relied on the well-established synchronous reactive language semantics for the propagation of values and the flow control. Modules are like digital circuits and connections are like wires. Values are propagated during a clock tick that occurs at regular intervals or when a device requests it and at least one value has changed in the network. We have adapted and improved the value model of these languages by introducing hierarchical compound slots. A slot can either be of atomic type like integer or string, or by a collection of named slots. These compound or hierarchical slots simplify greatly the readability and construction of configurations. The interpreter is 4000 lines of source code long.

5.2 *The Module API*

A module is implemented as a Java object with a list of input and output slots:

```
class Module {
  attribute String name;
  attribute boolean enabled;
  void addInSlot(InSlot s);
  void removeInSlot(InSlot s);
  InSlot[] getInSlots();
  void addOutSlot(OutSlot v);
  void removeOutSlot(OutSlot v);
  OutSlot[] getOutSlots();
  boolean open(Frame f);
  protected boolean doOpen(Frame f);
  void close();
  protected void doClose();
  abstract void changed(Change c);
}
```

The interpreter calls the 'changed' method of the object at each internal clock tick when at least one of its input slots has received a new value. The method can then compute new values for its output slots and the signal propagates through connections. New modules are simple to implement with this interface.

5.3   The Configuration Editor

The configuration editor modifies the reactive network interactively and relies on the reflection mechanisms of Java to expose module internals to the users. It represents about 4000 lines of source code.

6   Discussion

The use of ICON on real programs raises several important issues that we discuss here. Among them, one can wonder about the practicality of the approach from the programmer point of view, the expressive power of configurations edited with ICON, and the kind of users who will use ICON.

6.1   Practicality

From an application programmer's point of view, interaction tools can be exposed with any level of granularity and abstraction, providing a smooth transition path from no ICON support at all to full ICON support and extensibility. For example, the programmer can partially connect an existing word processor to ICON by exposing global actions such as performing some menu commands, scrolling the active document, or changing current font size. This only requires writing output modules which call methods of an external API every time their input values change. This basic ICON support is sufficient to allow alternative input techniques such as cut-and-paste with additional mouse buttons or voice commands, changing font size with mouse wheel, or scrolling through the document with head tilt using a 6-DOF tracker. For some applications like action games, full ICON support is easy to provide, since all actions are non-contextual.

ICON is currently in early stages: most of the specification of the interaction of interactive graphical applications can be configured outside the application but we haven't modified all the Swing components yet to be ICON-aware. Instead, we have modified the Java Swing architecture to suit our needs and these modifications are quite small and not intrusive. We believe modern toolkits could benefit from this externalisation of the interaction in terms of modularity and extensibility. For example, the support of text input methods is currently implemented at a very low level in Java Swing and requires a complicated internal mechanism that could be more simply described using ICON. The same is true for some aspects of accessibility.

6.2   Expressive Power

ICON is a full language, although it doesn't allow run-time created modules or recursion. Considering the experience in the field of reactive synchronous languages, we have chosen to stay away from these run-time modifications. We also believe this is not a serious issue because users are not expected to build large dynamic configurations. As for the readability of dataflow systems, we haven't conducted

Task	Skills involved	Targeted users
1. Selecting among different available configurations.	None.	Any user.
2. Customising a module by changing its parameters.	Locating the right module in the configuration.	Power users.
3. Shifting compatible modules or slots.	Basic understanding of slots (device channels).	Power users.
4. Inserting additional processing modules.	Basic understanding of dataflow paradigm, data types and available processing modules.	Power users.
5. Using an extended input device to control compatible parameters.	Basic understanding of input and application modules.	Power users.
6. Using any input device to control any application tool.	Good knowledge of control and processing modules, and dataflow paradigm.	Scientific users and programmers.
7. Building or adapting a full input configuration.	Full knowledge of ICON system.	Scientific users and programmers.
8. Writing an input or a processing module.	Knowledge of the Java language and the Module interface.	Programmers.

Table 2: Tasks that can be performed while customising an input interaction using ICON, ranging from easy to difficult.

---

experiments but they seem quite readable for the configurations we experienced. For larger configurations, the textual form of the ICON language could be better for some users, although compound modules, hierarchical slots and online help enhance the readability by hiding details.

6.3 ICON *Users*

Table 2 gives a list of different tasks that can be performed by the user to customise input interaction with ICON, in increasing order of difficulty. Each task has prerequisites: performing a task requires the specified skill, plus all previously listed skills. We also give an idea of the kind of users we think will be able to perform each task.

The most basic task (Task 1) is choosing among different existing configurations, for example replacing a standard configuration by a configuration designed for disabled users. This task can be performed by any user, provided that available configurations are properly listed and explained.

The second task (Task 2) is customising a module by changing its parameters. One example is changing the language or the vocabulary of a speech recognition module. This supposes that the user is able to find where the speech recognition module resides in the input configuration. This is currently done by looking at module labels. We plan to make this task easier by adding module ToolTips, and online configuration help from the configuration designer. The next task (Task 3) consists in interchanging compatible input modules or slots. For example, replacing a mouse by a trackball for controlling the cursor, replacing an input method by another one, or customising key shortcuts. This task is currently quite straightforward using slot reconnections, though we could make it easier by adding support for full device reconnection. We are also investigating more interesting substitutions using device emulation modules: for example replacing the mouse by the keyboard for pointer control, or replacing the keyboard by a positional device using an 'on-screen keyboard' module (as on stylus-based computers). The next task (Task 4) involves the addition of a new device to the configuration, but is not much more technical. One example is given in Section 2.1. This task currently requires slot reconnection, but again, it can be made quite straightforward by adding support for automatic drag and drop module insertion. The next task (Task 5) is using an extended input device by connecting its channels to compatible parameters or actions of the application. For example, issuing special commands with mouse buttons, or controlling the zoom factor of a drawing application with the mouse wheel. Another example is using the stylus pressure to control the brush size, as shown in Section 2.1. The main difficulty here comes from domain incompatibilities, but we are investigating the use of automatic scaling modules which should help a lot.

Compared to previous tasks, Task 6 is much more technical: incompatible types and higher level control adds complexity. For example, connecting the stylus pressure to mouse click requires additional processing devices, compared to X/Y connection (see Figure 3). Furthermore, performing high-level control to trigger contextual actions can be quite difficult for those who never worked on dataflow systems (see the tool selection example on Figure 1). Although providing specialised control modules and converters may help, we don't expect all users to perform tasks like designing new interaction techniques (see bimanual example in Section 2.2, Figure 5). Those tasks can range from tricky to very difficult for the non-specialist, especially if he has to redesign a large part of the configuration (Task 7). Input configuration design is more a job for computer scientists. Programmers may also find useful to design their own modules in Java (Task 8). As shown before, designing a processing module involves modest efforts. However, writing an input module to interface an exotic input device can be more technical, especially if it implies the use of the Java Native Interface (JNI).

In short, we think that the Tasks 1–5 can be performed on small portions of configuration by power users who understand the basic principles of ICON. We also think that this remains true for large configurations since compound modules allow those configurations to be structured and complex parts to be hidden. Typically, a configuration will provide virtual devices to allow independent device-side configuration (see the use of pointer abstraction in the examples of Section 2.1 and 2.2). However, this still has to be validated on real applications.

We don't expect all users to design large specific configurations of their applications with ICON. Instead, applications should come with a set of sensible configurations and users should usually modify small portions to suit their needs. However, with the possibility of sharing configurations with other users, we expect configurations to improve incrementally.

Some users may need special configurations, either because they have disabilities or because they have particular skills with some set of devices. These users will need the help of expert ICON users or programmers but still, they could adapt the programs to their abilities.

7 Conclusion and Future Directions

We have shown how ICON enables power users to adapt applications to available devices as well as to their skills. Those adaptations previously required access to the source code of the application and were impossible to improve incrementally.

Such a system not only opens applications to the use of alternative, better suited devices but also tremendously simplifies the integration of new interaction techniques published each year on conferences like CHI (Hinckley & Sinclair, 1999; Frohlich & Plate, 2000;   Myers et al., 2000) but very seldom implemented on commercial products.

Furthermore, new devices or interaction modes can be tested and adapted to existing programs. This is even more important for combined devices and their interaction techniques. When a voice recognition software is used in conjunction with a pressure and tilt-sensitive stylus, a large number of attributes are produced continuously and the best way to use them together has to be tested by trials and errors. Currently, this kind of testing can only be done by the application's programmers. ICON transfers this effort to any power user who is motivated.

For future directions, we are currently enhancing ICON's editor to improve scalability and transparency of the interface, and are planning to validate its usability on different kinds of users. We are also enriching our collection of supported input device managers to play with more exotic devices, including force feedback.

References

Andrews, M. (1999), Accessibility and the Swing Set, Sun Microsystems Inc, http://java.sun.com.

Axelson, J. (1999), *USB Complete : Everything You Need to Develop Custom USB Peripherals*, Lakeview Research.

Berry, G. & Cosserat, L. (1984), The Synchronous Programming Languages Esterel and its Mathematical Semantics, *in* S. Brookes & G. Winskel (eds.), *Seminar on Concurrency*, Springer-Verlag, pp.389–448.

Bier, E. A. & Freeman, S. (1991), MMM: A User Interface Architecture for Shared Editors on a Single Screen, *in* J. MacKinlay (ed.), *Proceedings of the ACM Symposium on User Interface Software and Technology, UIST'91*, ACM Press, pp.79–86.

Carbone, M., Ensminger, P., Hawkins, T., Leadbeater, S., Lipson, E., O'Donnell, M. & Rajunas, J. (2000), NeatTool Tutorial, Pulsar Project, http://www.pulsar.org/neattools.

Chatty, S. (1994), Extending a Graphical Toolkit for Two-handed Interaction, *in* S. Feiner (ed.), *Proceedings of the ACM Symposium on User Interface Software and Technology, UIST'94*, ACM Press, pp.195–204.

Ferguson, P. (1992), "The X11 Input Extension: Reference Pages", *The X Resource* **4**(1), 195–270.

Frohlich, B. & Plate, J. (2000), The Cubic Mouse: A New Device for Three-dimensional Input, *in* T. Turner, G. Szwillus, M. Czerwinski & F. Paternò (eds.), *Proceedings of the CHI2000 Conference on Human Factors in Computing Systems*, *CHI Letters* **2**(1), ACM Press, pp.526–31.

Geary, D. M. (1999), *Graphic Java 2: Mastering the JFC – Volume 2, Swing Components*, The Sun Microsystems Press Java Series,, third edition, Prentice–Hall.

Halbwachs, N., Caspi, P., Raymond, P. & Pilaud, D. (1991), "The Synchronous Dataflow Programming Language Lustre", *Proceedings of the IEEE* **79**(9), 1305–20.

Hinckley, K. & Sinclair, M. (1999), Touch-sensing Input Devices, *in* M. G. Williams, M. W. Altom, K. Ehrlich & W. Newman (eds.), *Proceedings of the CHI99 Conference on Human Factors in Computing Systems: The CHI is the Limit*, ACM Press, pp.223–30.

Honeywell, S. (1999), *Quake III Arena: Prima's Official Strategy Guide*, Prima Publishing.

Hourcade, J. P. & Bederson, B. B. (1999), *Architecture and Implementation of a Java Package for Multiple Input Devices (MID)*, University of Maryland.

Jacob, R. J. K., Deligiannidis, L. & Morrison, S. (1999), "A Software Model and Specification Language for Non-WIMP User Interfaces", *ACM Transactions on Computer–Human Interaction* **6**(1), 1–46.

Kovach, P. J. (2000), *Inside Direct3D*, Microsoft Press.

Krasner, G. E. & Pope, S. T. (1988), "A Cookbook for Using the Model-View-Controller User Interface Paradigm in Smalltalk-80", *Journal of Object Oriented Programming* **1**(3), 26–49.

LCS/Telegraphics (1999), The Wintab Developers' Kit, http://www.pointing.com/WINTAB.HTM.

Liang, S. (1999), *The Java Native Interface : Programmer's Guide and Specification*, Addison–Wesley.

Microsoft Corporation (1999), "Active Accessibility SDK 1.2".

Myers, B. A. (1990), "A New Model for Handling Input", *ACM Transactions on Office Information Systems* **8**(3), 289–320.

Myers, B. A. (1991), The Garnet User Interface Development Environment, *in* S. P. Robertson, G. M. Olson & J. S. Olson (eds.), *Proceedings of CHI'91: Human Factors in Computing Systems (Reaching through Technology)*, ACM Press, p.486.

Myers, B. A., Lie, K. P. & Yang, B.-C. (2000), Two-handed Input Using a PDA and a Mouse, *in* T. Turner, G. Szwillus, M. Czerwinski & F. Paternò (eds.), *Proceedings of the CHI2000 Conference on Human Factors in Computing Systems*, *CHI Letters* **2**(1), ACM Press, pp.41–8.

Nye, A. & O'Reilly, T. (1992), *Volume 4M: X Toolkit Intrinsics Programming Manual*, second edition, O'Reilly.

Sense8 Corp. (1999), *The World Toolkit Manual*.

Sun Microsystems Inc. (1998), Java Speech API Programmer's Guide, http://java.sun.com/.

Measuring the Usability of Text Input Methods for Children

Janet Read, Stuart MacFarlane & Chris Casey

Department of Computing, University of Central Lancashire, Preston PR1 2HE, UK

Tel: *+44 1772 893 276*

Fax: *+44 1772 892 913*

Email: *{jcread,sjmacfarlane,ccasey}@uclan.ac.uk*

This paper describes an experiment in which children aged between 6 and 10 entered text into a word processor using four different input methods, mouse, keyboard, speech recognition, and handwriting recognition. Several different measures of usability were made in an attempt to assess the suitability of the input methods in this situation. The paper describes and discusses the measures and their use with very young children.

Measures of effectiveness were affected by a number of different types of error that occurred during text input. Following an analysis of these errors, six types of error were identified. This analysis should help in the construction of more discriminating measures. Efficiency measures were sometimes affected by the distracting effect of novel input methods. Satisfaction measures were particularly problematic; several methods were used, with the repertory grid technique appearing the most promising.

Keywords: evaluation, children, text, speech, handwriting.

1 Introduction

This work is part of a wider project looking at alternative text input methods. Young children have relatively advanced verbal language skills yet they find spelling difficult and have difficulties constructing good written language.

Several studies have shown that the use of a word processor can assist in developing written language skills (Sturm, 1988; Newell et al., 1992). A study by

Kurth (1987) suggested that although the use of a computer did not always improve the literal quality of children's writing, the high visibility of text on the screen fostered more conversation about the writing, and the spelling was improved. In his book 'Mindstorms', Papert (1980) suggests that a computer with word processing software affords the child the luxury of being able to revise and rework their ideas, and therefore becomes a powerful intellectual product.

2   Input Methods

Children in school are encouraged to use word processors to produce electronic text where possible. However, access to the software is traditionally via a QWERTY keyboard which novices find difficult to master. Herrmann (1987) suggested that handling the keyboard interferes with the writing process, and if this is the case, then the use of more natural interfaces, such as speech and handwriting recognition may be desirable. There is also a case to consider whether or not children prefer to use a pointing device for text entry, this could be a touch screen or a mouse. Special keyboards are used in a few primary schools, however they have many of the same features as QWERTY keyboards and as they are not in widespread use and are considerably more expensive than the natural language interfaces they are not considered in this study. For similar reasons, touch screens are not included.

Children are able to speak fluently at an early age, and they are taught handwriting as part of the early curriculum. This suggests that the natural language technologies of speech and handwriting recognition may suit young users. Snape et al. (1997) use the term 'disobedient interface' to describe this sort of technology where a correct action by the user can result in an incorrect outcome by the software.

Studies of speech recognition have reported levels of recognition as high as 95%, but these have not been with children. O'Hare & McTear (1999) used speech recognition with secondary school age children with accuracy rates of 82%. They also reported much faster input with rates of 50wpm, compared with 10wpm at the keyboard.

Handwriting recognition is a newer technology; in order to participate, the user needs a 'pen' and a graphics tablet. An earlier experiment by the present authors (Read et al., 2000) gave an encouraging picture in relation to handwritten input with young children. In this study, children's handwriting was traced onto the machine by an adult and a Character Recognition Rate recorded. The average recognition rates exceeded 80%.

3   Design of the Experiment

The experiment was designed to compare four input methods; QWERTY keyboard, mouse clicking using an on screen alphabetic keyboard, speech input and handwritten input. These four methods were seen to be affordable to implement in a classroom and sufficiently easy to master by children of the target ages. Of interest was the comparative strengths and weaknesses of the methods, and particularly issues raised from measuring usability with children.

The experiment was carried out in a small primary school over a two-week period. Children aged between 6 and 10 were arranged in age order and systematic sampling was used to select twelve children covering all ages and abilities. Each child in the experiment did a task using each of the four input methods, but the order in which the methods were presented varied across the sample. Children did only one task a day, and at least two days separated each task. There were three parts to each task; initial orientation and/or training; copying text which was put in front of the children, and adding their own text to a story which had been introduced to them.

The text which was to be copied was constructed using words from the Key Stage 1 reading list (DfEE, n.d.) (a list of words with which children aged between 6 and 8 are expected to be familiar), and was similar in structure to text which the children would have met in their school's reading scheme. Each task had its own story and this was used by all the children. The Microsoft Word grammar checking tool, was used to ensure that readability and word length were consistent across all the stories. The words used in each task were very similar. After copying each story, the children were asked to write about what happened next.

During the tasks, recordings of the children were made using a video camera.

3.1 Training

Each task required different training. The training needs had been established by discussing the interfaces with four children prior to the experiment and determining what was required. The intention was to ensure that the child was comfortable with the hardware and the software interface. A training activity was defined for each input method, and children stopped doing this activity when it was seen that they were sufficiently competent. The keyboard was familiar to all the children, so they simply typed their name and then continued with the task. The mouse interface had an alphabetic keyboard and a text display box. It did not have the extra symbols and functions which are a feature of the QWERTY keyboard as it was only being used for simple text entry. Children were shown how to select characters and were then asked to input their name. This highlighted those who were unsure about the manoeuvrability of the mouse, and they were then shown how to proceed.

The speech recognition software used was IBM ViaVoice Millennium version 7, which had been previously trained with a young female with a local accent. The children used a headset microphone. The children tried out the software by reading some text, and were told to enunciate in a clear way, pronouncing the beginnings and endings of words clearly (Caulton, 2000). Handwriting was done using a Wacom tablet and pen, and with Paragraph Pen Office software. The software was set up for online recognition. Initially the children were encouraged to use the pen to trace over letters which were on the screen, and then they wrote a few words. They were given advice relating to the size and orientation of their script (Read et al., 2000).

3.2 Problems with the Experiment

Following the selection process, one child was identified by the class teacher as having special educational needs and it was thought that she would be unable to manage the tasks set. A second child became ill after having completed just one task; both of these children were replaced with the adjacent child from the age ordered list.

4   What was Measured?

The measurements of the usability of the four methods were based on the standards suggested in Part11 of ISO 9241 (ISO, 2000).

Usability objectives include suitability for the task, learnability, error handling, and appropriateness (Dix et al., 1998). Some of these were inappropriate in relation to the input methods used and the user group. Learnability and appropriateness were difficult to assess given the brevity and simplicity of the tasks which were carried out. Measuring error handling would have muddled the input methods, as an attempt to correct errors created by the speech recogniser would have been difficult without using the keyboard; similarly correcting at the keyboard may have involved the mouse. The suitability of the method for the task was evaluated using Effectiveness, Efficiency and Satisfaction measures.

4.1   *Effectiveness Measures*

The mouse, keyboard and handwriting interfaces were all character based. The discrete characters were entered, selected, or recognised. To measure the effectiveness of these methods a Character Error Rate (CER) metric was used:

$$CER = \frac{s+d+i}{n} \times 100$$

where s = number of substitutions, d = number of deletions, i = number of insertions and n = number of characters. (A substitution counted as one error, not as a deletion plus an insertion.)

In the character systems, a decision had to be made regarding spaces. Firstly, it was noted that younger children were unlikely to put spaces in copied or composed text when using the keyboard and the mouse. Secondly, it was observed that when children put spaces in, they were as likely to put three spaces as one. Thirdly, the handwriting recogniser inserted its own single space when the pen was lifted from the tablet for a certain duration. This happened frequently with younger children, particularly when they copied text. For these reasons spaces were disregarded in the effectiveness measures.

The speech recognition was measured using 'word error rate' (WER):

$$WER = \frac{s+d+i}{n} \times 100$$

where s = number of substitutions, d = number of deletions, i = number of insertions and n = number of words. (A substitution counted as one error, not as a deletion plus an insertion.)

The CER and WER measures give a rating for the failings of the system. As effectiveness is a positive concept, a new metric, 'percentage correctness measure' (PCM) was defined:

$$PCM = 100 - (\text{either } CER \text{ or } WER)$$

4.2 Efficiency Measures

There are two measures of efficiency; these are 'characters per second' (CPS) and 'words per second' (WPS):

$$CPS = \frac{Characters\ input}{Time\ taken}$$

$$WPS = \frac{Words\ input}{Time\ taken}$$

The WPS was multiplied by the average characters per word (3.33 in this instance) to give an approximate CPS for the speech recognition.

The time taken was recorded from the start of the activity to the close. Two separate times were recorded, one for the copying exercise and one for the composing exercise. During the copying, children were generally on task for the whole time, but on four occasions, hardware and software problems caused an interruption, and this time was deducted.

During composing, children were inclined to 'pause for thought' or ask for spellings; this time was included. The rationale for this is discussed in Section 6.2.

4.3 Satisfaction

The user satisfaction was expected to be problematic with regard to the ages of the children. Satisfaction is an adult concept that correlates with a feeling that something is good enough. It is typically measured by observations and questionnaires. For adults 'Very satisfied' is used on Likert scales to refer to the best that one can get.

Watching children it soon becomes evident that 'satisfaction' is not an appropriate word for what they may be experiencing, they appear to have wider extremes of feelings than adults. Children have a different perception of the world, their cognition is less well developed which makes it difficult for them to articulate likes and dislikes (Druin et al., 1999). Evaluation techniques that work for adults may work badly or may be wholly inappropriate for children of this age.

The work of Beyer & Holtzblatt (1998) suggests that children need to have satisfaction measured in their own environment and so a suite of specially designed satisfaction metrics was developed (Read & MacFarlane, 2000).

To measure expectations, a discrete scale using a series of 'smiley' faces (Figure 1) was used (Read & MacFarlane, 2000). This was repeated after the task in order to measure the effect the activity had on the child's prior and subsequent perception of it. Selections on this scale were scored from 1 (Awful) to 5 (Brilliant).

During the task, observations of facial expressions, utterances and body language were used to establish a measure for engagement. Positive and negative signs were counted, and the balance of positive vs. negative instances was recorded (Read & MacFarlane, 2000).

When all four tasks had been completed, the children were presented with a repertory grid test (Fransella & Bannister, 1977) that had been developed with the four children who had piloted the experiment. This was used to provide comparative scores. The children were given icons representing the four methods and were asked to place them in order from best to worst in respect of the four constructs on the grid

| Awful | Not very good | Good | Really good | Brilliant |

Figure 1: The 'smiley' faces representing the Likert scale.

Name of child............................. Age........... Sex...........

	Best			Worst
Worked the best				
Liked the most				
Most fun				
Easiest to do				

Figure 2: The repertory grid.

(Figure 2). The method was given a score by summing the positions from 4 (best) to 1 (worst) for each attribute.

Following the repertory grid evaluation, children were asked to asked to rate each input method using a vertical 'funometer' (Figure 3) similar to the one developed by Risden et al. (1997). Each column on the grid measured 10cm, so a score out of ten was obtained for each method.

5   Results of the Experiments

Results for the four different text input methods are given in the tables below. The figures for Effectiveness and the first three satisfaction metrics are given as a percentage of the optimum score. The observations are absolute figures, and the Efficiency measures are in Characters per Second.

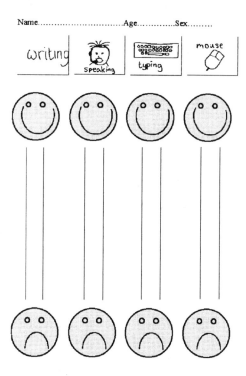

Figure 3: A prepared funometer.

	Effectiveness	Efficiency	Satisfaction			
	PCM	CPS	Rep Grid	Expec- tations	Fun- ometer	Obser- vations
Copying	90%	0.25	57%	82%	84%	20
Composing	97%	0.26				

Table 1: Keyboard input.

	Effectiveness	Efficiency	Satisfaction			
	PCM	CPS	Rep Grid	Expec- tations	Fun- ometer	Obser- vations
Copying	99%	0.14	61%	78%	77%	8
Composing	99%	0.15				

Table 2: Mouse input.

	Effectiveness	Efficiency	Satisfaction			
	PCM	0.33 × WPS	Rep Grid	Expec-tations	Fun-ometer	Obser-vations
Copying	36%	5.74	67%	82%	85%	11
Composing	44%	6.26				

Table 3: Speech input.

	Effectiveness	Efficiency	Satisfaction			
	PCM	CPS	Rep Grid	Expec-tations	Fun-ometer	Obser-vations
Copying	73%	0.24	64%	88%	77%	20
Composing	86%	0.34				

Table 4: Handwriting input.

6 Observations on the Results

From this pilot study it appears that handwriting recognition closely matches keyboard entry in terms of efficiency and effectiveness. There may be considerable potential in handwriting as a text input method for young children.

It appears that the mouse is not sufficiently different from the keyboard to make it worthwhile pursuing as an alternative text input device, although there may be special cases where it is a desirable alternative.

The repertory grid and the observations both suggest that children enjoyed the handwriting and speech more than the other methods. Further work is required to establish the reasons for this.

7 Discussion of the Measures used in the Experiment

7.1 Effectiveness

Both the CER and WER are measures of errors found in the finished text. To evaluate the efficacy of these measures it is necessary to examine how each character or word is transformed into its on-screen representation. This transformation is made up of a sequence of processes which are different for 'obedient interfaces' and 'disobedient interfaces'. Additionally, copying text and composing text have unique processes which contribute to the transformation.

Each process within these transformations has a capacity for error. In the table below, six different types of error are identified.

The individual processes and the errors associated with them can be seen in Figures 4 & 5. Figure 4 illustrates the errors that can occur when using an obedient interface, while Figure 5 shows the slightly different possibilities for error when using a disobedient interface.

The standard PCM measure tells us very little about which type of error has occurred. In addition, there are errors that are averted at the last minute, which

	Example	Observations
Error 1 **Cognition error**	Child misreads a word or cannot distinguish letters.	This only happened when copying.
Error 2 **Spelling error**	Child misspells words or mispronounces a word that they know.	Rarely occurred in speech, as the children only spoke words they knew. More likely to occur in character based entry where children were unable to spell words that they wanted to use. This only happened when composing.
Error 3 **Selection error**	Child picks 'l' for 'i'.	This happened, as did 'o' for '0'. Only relevant for obedient interfaces.
Error 4 **Construction error**	Child cannot form the letter or word correctly. In handwriting, 'a' may look like 'd'. In speech, 'dragon' becomes 'dwagon'.	Only relevant with disobedient interfaces.
Error 5 **Execution error**	The child presses for too long, fails to click, or hits the adjacent character. The microphone or pen may be out of range.	This could happen with all the methods, but was less likely to occur in speech and handwriting.
Error 6 **Software induced error**	The software misrecognises the word or character.	Only a problem with disobedient interfaces.

Table 5: Classification of errors.

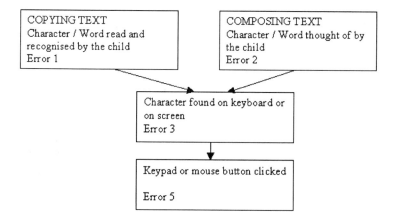

Figure 4: Processes and potential errors with obedient interfaces.

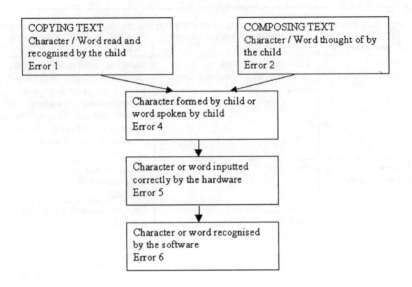

Figure 5: Processes and potential errors with disobedient interfaces.

could give us information about usability. It was observed during this experiment that children sometimes intended writing something, and then changed their minds. This could be attributed to the child realising that the word they had intended was too difficult to spell, and so a substitute word was used, which masked a potential spelling error (Error 2). This didn't happen with the speech recognition software as the child was thinking and composing using words that he or she could speak (but not necessarily spell).

The speech and handwriting recognition processes are based on subcomponents of characters and words, namely strokes and phonemes. The combination of strokes or phonemes enables the recogniser to 'predict' the letter or word intended. If an error is caused by the recogniser (Error 6), then the traditional CER and WER measures will take no account of how 'close' recogniser was. The error that the speech recogniser makes in turning 'playing' into 'played in' is as bad as the one which makes 'the dragon' into 'murder again' (both are examples from this experiment). For a user, these errors are very similar, as they both require similar correction. For a researcher, trying to measure the success of an input method, the WER and CER measures cause a lot of information to be lost.

In speech recognition there have been some attempts made to address the failings of WER. A method known as phonological scoring as developed by Fisher et al. (1995) would go some way to measuring the 'closeness' of the recogniser. With this scoring method, 'playing' to 'played in' would be credited with having recognised 'play' and 'in' correctly.

Cox et al. (1998) proposed a interesting measurement based on human performance, where the question 'How much better is it than me?' would be asked, instead of 'How accurate is it?' The underlying issue is to see how much better or worse the recogniser is at recognising words than a human would be. This measure was originally designed for speech recognition, but may also be useful when evaluating handwriting recognisers, as a human reader may interpret characters written by a child incorrectly, especially if they are viewed out of context.

7.2 Efficiency

The efficiency measure used was to do with time taken to input. On four occasions there were problems with the hardware or software, and in these instances, the time taken to repair the problem was subtracted from the overall time on task measurement.

Sovik & Flem (1999) describe how writing has three aspects, the motor skill, the cognitive-linguistic (thinking) process and the linguistic-semantic (spelling and grammar) process. When the child was copying text, the time taken was a measure of the motor activity associated with the task. During composition, the other aspects extended the duration of the activity. Children sometimes 'paused for thought' and it was noted that when children used the character based devices, they sometimes asked for spellings, or waited while they found a way of writing what they wanted to say using words which they were able to spell. This linguistic-semantic pausing was not evident during the speech input task. Cognitive-linguistic processing occurred during all the composition activities but generally it was more prolonged with the character devices. These times were included in the efficiency measures as they were seen to be part of the task of composition (Andreissen, 1993).

The children were sometimes distracted by the interface when it behaved differently than they had expected. This was particularly true of the handwriting tablet, when letters were misrecognised, the child often stopped and remarked on what had happened. It was less of a problem with the speech recogniser, partly because the children realised quite quickly that it was not showing the words they were saying, and partly because the words displayed were often incomprehensible to the children.

The distracting effect of the handwriting recogniser could possibly be masked by using 'Lazy recognition' wherein the text is recognised online, but is displayed after the writer has finished (Nakagawa et al., 1993). This is an interesting idea, but it would significantly change the interface, removing the potential for interactive corrections and immediate feedback.

7.3 Satisfaction

The satisfaction measures could be divided into three types; child created, child created but controlled, and observation.

There were considerable problems with some of the child created satisfaction measures. When children were presented with a Likert scale, they were generally 'very kind' to the activity, in that they typically thought things were going to be brilliant! The average score on the funometer was 81%. They appeared to lack the adult tendency to avoid picking the extreme values in a Likert scale. This was also the case with the discrete expectations scale, with the average being 82%.

It is likely that these measures were in part influenced by the combined effects of several factors including the desire of the child to please, the child's perception of computers, the perceived novelty of the activity and the excitement or irritation at being taken from a class activity to take part in this experiment.

Some of these factors were ameliorated in the repertory grid scoring. However, the younger children had a limited understanding of the differences between constructs like 'Worked the best' and 'Liked the most' and so some of the ratings were likely to be unreliable. One child admitted to wanting to be fair, when it appeared that the mouse was getting a poor score!

The observations were based on negative and positive actions, these were largely beyond the child's control; and the children did not know in advance what was being observed. Assumptions had to be made about the origin of facial expressions and positive instantiations, and some children were more expressive than others.

8   Conclusions

The early intention of this study was to evaluate the usability of the four input methods. Given the small size of the user sample, it is not easy to make general statements about usability, but the results do highlight a number of areas for further study. One area is the optimisation of the recognition technologies for young children.

The inherent differences between obedient and disobedient interfaces seem to make comparisons between them difficult. There is clearly a trade off between efficiency and effectiveness. However, for children, tolerance of errors may be higher than for adults, and it may be that children prefer to use interfaces which are 'easier' and need correcting, than 'harder' interfaces which are generally more reliable.

The measures of satisfaction that were used with the children were experimental, and it seems that together the metrics can give a fairly consistent picture. It may have been illuminating to include a question / answer sheet at the end of each activity. The repertory grid test would have been improved by allowing the child to look at only one row at a time, this would have helped the child focus on one construct at a time.

Many of the considerations of error handling, efficiency and effectiveness can be applied to applications where adults rather than children are the users. Often children demonstrate exaggerated versions of adult mistakes, and they may help us to model adult behaviour.

References

Andreissen, J. E. B. (1993), Episodic Representations in Writing and Reading, *in* G. Eigler & T. Jechle (eds.), *Writing: Current Trends in European Research*, Hochschulverlag, pp.71–83. Revised versions of papers presented at the Third meeting of the European Writing SIG.

Beyer, H. & Holtzblatt, K. (1998), *Contextual Design: Defining Customer-centered Systems*, Morgan-Kaufmann.

Caulton, D. (2000), Can Voice Recognition Work for Computer Users? The Effects of Training and Voice Commands, *in* S. Turner & P. Turner (eds.), *Proceedings of HCI'2000: Volume 2*, BCS, pp.77–81.

Cox, S., Linford, P., Hill, W. & Johnston, R. (1998), "Towards Speech Recognizer Assessment Using a Human Reference Standard", *Computer Speech and Language* 12(4), 375–91.

DfEE (n.d.), The National Literacy Strategy — Framework for Teaching Yr to Y6, Department for Education and Employment, http://www.standards.dfee.gov.uk/literacy (Accessed 7th November 2000).

Dix, A., Finlay, J., Abowd, G. & Beale, R. (1998), *Human–Computer Interaction*, second edition, Prentice–Hall Europe.

Druin, A., Bederson, B., Boltman, A., Miura, A., Knotts-Callaghan, D. & Platt, M. (1999), Children as Our Technology Design Partners, *in* A. Druin (ed.), *The Design of Children's Technology*, Morgan-Kaufmann, pp.51–72.

Fisher, W. M., Fiscus, J. G. & Martin, A. (1995), Further Studies in Phonological Scoring, *in Proceedings of the ARPA Spoken Language Workshop*, Morgan-Kaufmann, pp.181–6.

Fransella, F. & Bannister, D. (1977), *A Manual for Repertory Grid Technique*, Academic Press.

Herrmann, A. (1987), Research into Writing and Computers: Viewing the Gestalt, Presentation at the Annual Meeting of the Modern Language Association of America.

ISO (2000), "ISO 9241 International Standard. Ergonomic Requirements for Office Work with Visual Display Terminals (VDTs). Part 11: Guidance for Specifying and Measuring Usability". International Organization for Standardization, Genève, Switzerland. http://www.iso.ch (Accessed 6th November 2000).

Kurth, R. (1987), "Using Word Processing to Enhance Revision Strategies During Student Writing Activities", *Educational Technology* 27(1), 13–9.

Nakagawa, M., Machii, K.and Kato, N. & Souya, T. (1993), Lazy Recognition as a Principle of Pen Interfaces, *in* S. Ashlund, K. Mullet, A. Henderson, E. Hollnagel & T. White (eds.), *Proceedings of INTERCHI'93*, ACM Press/IOS Press, pp.89–90.

Newell, A. F., Boothe, L., Arnott, J. & Beattie, W. (1992), "Increasing Literacy Levels by the Use of Linguistic Prediction", *Child Language Teaching and Therapy* 8(2), 138–87.

O'Hare, E. A. & McTear, M. F. (1999), "Speech Technology in the Secondary School Classroom, an Exploratory Study", *Computer and Education* 33(1), 27–45.

Papert, S. (1980), *Mindstorms. Children, Computers, and Powerful Ideas*, Basic Books.

Read, J. C. & MacFarlane, S. J. (2000), "Measuring Fun", *Interfaces* 46, 6–7. Paper presented at the "Computers and Fun 3" Workshop.

Read, J. C., MacFarlane, S. J. & Casey, C. (2000), Postcards to Grandad — A Study of Handwriting Recognition with Young Children, *in* S. Turner & P. Turner (eds.), *Proceedings of HCI'2000: Volume 2*, BCS, pp.51–2.

Risden, K., Hanna, E. & Kanerva, A. (1997), "Dimensions of Intrinsic Motivation in Children's Favorite Computer Activities", Poster session at the meeting of the Society for Research in Child Development, Washington, DC, USA.

Snape, L., Casey, C., MacFarlane, S. & Robertson, I. (1997), Using Speech in Multimedia Applications', *in Proceedings of TCD Conference on Multimedia*, Vol. 7(7) of *Teaching Company Directorate Seminar Proceedings*, TCD, pp.50–60. ISBN 1 901255 08 5.

Sovik, N. & Flem, A. (1999), "The Effects of Different Tasks on Children's Process and Product Variables in Writing", *Learning and Instruction* 9(2), 167–88.

Sturm, J. (1988), "Using Computer Software Tools to Facilitate Narrative Skills", *The Clinical Connection* 11, 6–9.

Beyond the 10-bit Barrier: Fitts' Law in Multi-Scale Electronic Worlds

Yves Guiard*, Frédéric Bourgeois*, Denis Mottet† & Michel Beaudouin-Lafon‡

* Mouvement et Perception, CNRS & Université de la Méditerranée, 163 avenue de Luminy, CP 910, 13288 Marseille Cedex 09, France

Tel: *+33 491 172 257*

Fax: *+33 491 172 252*

Email: *{guiard,bourgeois}@laps.univ-mrs.fr*

† Faculté des Sciences du Sport, Université de Montpellier, 700 avenue du Pic Saint Loup, 34090 Montpellier, France

Tel: *+33 467 415 703*

Fax: *+33 467 415 708*

Email: *dmottet@sc.univ-montp1.fr*

‡ Laboratoire de Recherche en Informatique, Université de Paris Sud, Bât 490, 91405 Orsay Cedex, France

Tel: *+33 169 156 910*

Fax: *+33 169 156 586*

Email: *mbl@lri.fr*

Multi-scale interfaces make it possible to investigate Fitts' law beyond 10 bits, so far an inviolable barrier of difficulty. We had computer users, equipped with a zoom, point at visual targets whose index of difficulty (*ID*) varied between 3 and 30 bits. The zoom was ignored for easy targets and began to be used at *ID* = 8bits, with zooming amplitude then increasing linearly with the *ID*. A linear, zero-intercept Fitts' law equation was

found to accurately model target acquisition time throughout our extended spectrum of *ID*s. Some implications of these findings for human–computer interaction and basic research are discussed.

Keywords: input, Fitts' law, pointing, multi-scale pointing, navigation in electronic worlds, zooming interfaces, two-handed input.

1 Introduction

Fitts' law (Fitts, 1954; Fitts & Peterson, 1964) is the well known empirical relationship that links target acquisition time (or movement time, *MT*) to the ratio of target distance (*D*) and width (*W*). The most widely accepted definition of the law is:

$$MT = k_1 + k_2 \log_2(D/W + 1) \tag{1}$$

with k_1 and k_2 standing for adjustable constants (MacKenzie, 1992) and the term $\log_2(D/W + 1)$ representing the index of difficulty (*ID*), measured in bits of information (Fitts, 1954). Since Card et al.'s (1978) first application of Fitts' law to human–computer interaction (HCI), the law has abundantly served to quantify and predict users' performance. Fitts' law has proved particularly useful to evaluate the ever increasing variety of analogue input devices like mice, tablets, joysticks, trackballs, or trackpads (Accot & Zhai, 1999; Kabbash et al., 1993; Zhai et al., 1999) and to optimise the layout of characters in soft keyboards (MacKenzie & Zhang, 1999; Zhai et al., 2000). Recently, ISO standards for the objective evaluation of computer input devices were defined on the basis of Fitts' law (Douglas et al., 1999).

It is not fortuitous that these two decades of Fitts' law research in HCI have coincided with the advent and the development of graphical user interfaces. The reason why hand pointing has become relevant to HCI is because these interfaces have allowed users to interact with electronically generated objects very much as they do with real objects. The so-called WIMP interfaces (Windows, Icons, Menus, and Pointers) reproduce the laws that govern the interactions of humans with their natural environment, making the behaviour of virtual objects on a screen closely resemble that of real objects on a flat horizontal surface. So HCI researchers have approached Fitts' law in much the same way as psychologists of basic-research laboratories, e.g. Guiard (1997), Meyer et al. (1990), Schmidt et al. (1979), Welford (1968). After all, for the student of Fitts' law, no matter whether the task is to reach and select a menu item or an icon on a virtual desktop, using some remote-controlled cursor, or to tap on some mark on a tabletop with the tip of a hand-held stylus as in Fitts' original experiments, as the problem, conceptually, is essentially the same: from the moment *D* and *W* can be experimentally manipulated and *MT* is measured, Fitts' law should, and does, hold. Not only is it essentially the same problem that HCI and classic experimental psychology have been studying, but up until the recent past the two fields have been in similar positions to progress in the understanding of Fitts' law.

However, dramatic changes have occurred recently in HCI that are liable to renew the theme of target-directed movement. With the advent, during the nineties, of multi-scale or zooming interfaces (Furnas & Bederson, 1995), interface designers have been able to give birth to *multi-scale* navigation. With a zooming interface, not only can users move a cursor (an analogue to hand motion in the real world), not only can they move their view in the electronic world (an analogue to locomotion in the real world), but now they are allowed to freely adjust the scale at which they wish to interact with the electronic world at hand. It must be emphasised that this is an entirely novel category of user action, one that has no counterpart in the real world

Suppose you are exploring the zoomable maps of an electronic world atlas. The screen is showing you, for example, a city map of Wellington, New Zealand, but you decide to look for another, remotely located place, say, the Jardin du Luxembourg in Paris — at a distance of over 19,000km. You will first zoom out to see a large-scale view of the Earth, then perform a rapid pan across the continents and the seas to position your view over Europe, and finally plummet down to France and then Paris by performing intricate zooms in and pans. When, in the end, you are facing a detailed map of Paris, you will be able to click on the Jardin du Luxembourg, perhaps to request some information about this public garden. The whole sequence, down to the final click, will have lasted just a few seconds.

The above example is perfectly well defined in terms of Fitts' aimed movement paradigm, with D = 19,000km, W = 0.4km, and hence ID = 15.5bits. It must be realised that while handling this high a level of ID for target selection is commonplace for users of multi-scale electronic worlds[1], it is just an impossible task in the real world.[2] A recent survey of the literature has shown that Fitts' law experiments so far have used ranges of ID that never extend beyond 10bits, corresponding to a D/W ratio of about 1,000 (Guiard et al., 1999). The explanation is straightforward. So long as an aimed movement is confined in a single level of scale (the fate of real-world movements), it is constrained by the tight functional limitations of the human perceptual-motor system (Guiard et al., 1999). In a tapping task (Fitts, 1954; Fitts & Peterson, 1964), for example, humans cannot cover a D larger than about one meter with the hand, for simple anatomical reasons[3], and on the other hand they are unable to cope with a W smaller than about one millimeter. So the D/W ratio, owing to both the upper limit of its numerator and the lower limit of its denominator, cannot exceed 1,000 — hence the 10-bit barrier of the ID.

In contrast, as one explores a multi-scale electronic world, one can deal with however large values of D and however small values of W one likes, thanks to the zoom. Indeed, there are ultimate limits to the D/W ratio — those imposed by the amount of information stored and the technology — but these limits are quite remote in comparison with those of real-world pointing.

---

[1] An analogous example is navigation among the 5,000,000 pages made accessible by the Web site of the Library of Congress (Shneiderman, 1997).

[2] Obviously, we do cover this sort of distances in the real world, but this requires concatenating a series of transportation acts (e.g. a walk + a taxi ride + a walk + a flight, etc.), none of which, it must be realised, obeys Fitts' law.

[3] Of course, a human can run to reach with the hand a target placed, say, at a D of 100m. In such a case, however, Fitts' law will no longer hold because MT will be mainly a function of D, not D/W.

It is a new and important fact for Fitts' law research that in target acquisition tasks humans are actually able to deal smoothly with *ID*s far higher than 10bits provided the world they interact with is zoomable — see (Guiard et al., 1999) for a recent demonstration that, with just two levels of scale, humans can already handle an *ID* of over 12bits. Let us examine more closely the case of pointing in an electronic atlas. The user's action has three degrees of freedom (DOF): two for panning, that is, moving the latitude and longitude of one's view (controlled, e.g. by mouse translations), and a third one for zooming (controlled, e.g. by mouse-wheel rotations).

Zooming electronic maps in and out feels like changing one's altitude, hence the temptation to use flight metaphors like plummeting to describe zooming. However, this third DOF of the user's action is scale, and it must not be confused with a spatial dimension (Furnas & Bederson, 1995). In the real world, changing one's altitude does entail a re-scaling for vision, but this is *not* the case for action. The farther from a surface, the larger and less detailed one's view of this surface, but one's ability to *move* oneself remains constant. Therefore, the more distant objects in the real world, the more time consuming one's motion relative to them.

In sharp contrast, it is the hallmark of multi-scale electronic worlds that they keep the speed of one's displacements (i.e. those of the view) proportional to viewing distance, so that the rate of optical flows generated on the screen by the user's action remains essentially constant across magnification changes. In a zooming interface, movement capabilities, at all levels of zoom, remain always scaled to the perceived objects — if the map you are watching shows you hundreds of meters, your panning speed will be on the order of several hundreds of meters per second; but if it extends over thousands of kilometers, then you will just as easily move at a speed of several thousands of kilometers per second. This desirable property is absent in real-world movement constrained by the limits of energetic resources.

If humans actually can, in multi-scale electronic worlds, successfully carry out target acquisition tasks with *D/W* ratios far higher than 1,000 and hence *ID*s far higher than 10bits, an important question arises: does Fitts' law, admittedly one of the most general and robust empirical relationships in the whole field of experimental psychology, hold *in general*, that is, beyond the so far inviolable 10-bit barrier? This is the question we addressed in the present exploratory study.

2 The Experiment

Our goal was to investigate Fitts' law with a selection of *ID*s that extended far beyond the traditional 1–10bit range. To this end, we used a highly simplified experimental paradigm, à la Fitts, except that our participants were provided with a powerful zooming facility. Thanks to the zoom, we were able to expose our participants to a selection of *ID*s ranging from 3.2bits ($D/W = 8$) up to 30bits ($D/W = 10^9$).

2.1 Multi-Scale Pointing as Tree Traversal

One difficulty typical of zooming interfaces which we had to circumvent for this experiment is that known as the *desert fog* problem: one gets lost if one zooms in an empty region of an electronic world (Jul & Furnas, 1998). To simplify our pointing

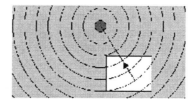

Figure 1: A schematic illustration of the array of concentric circles surrounding the target, shown located out of sight. The view (unfilled rectangle) is shown intercepting a number of arcs that specify target direction and distance (the radius and the arrow are shown only for the sake of the explanation).

paradigm as much as possible, our first intention was to display just the targets in an otherwise completely empty environment, and so the desert fog problem was likely to jeopardise task performance.

In fact, the present study was concerned with the basic sensory-motor processes involved in target reaching rather than the higher cognitive processes of orientation — i.e. tree traversal rather than navigation, to use the terminology of Furnas & Bederson (1995). Therefore, we set out to preclude disorientation altogether. This was achieved by using a background of equidistant concentric circles centred around the target (see Figure 1). Zooming in caused a radial expansion of this pattern with fewer and fewer circles remaining on the screen — note, however, that depending on mouse position, the focus of this radial expansion (i.e. the target) was not necessarily visible in the view. Zooming out caused a radial contraction of the pattern, with more arcs popping in from the periphery of the view. By a mechanism similar to that known to guide as simple organisms as bacteria in a gradient of chemical concentration (Benhamou & Bovet, 1992), such a pattern provided our participants with permanent knowledge of target direction and distance, regardless of view position and zoom level. They always knew the direction to take because target azimuth was specified by the perpendiculars to all the tangents to all the arcs intercepted by the view. They always knew target distance because the current value of D, a radius of the concentric array, equalled the inverse of arc curvature.

2.2 Methods

2.2.1 Apparatus and Parameter Setting

The program, written in DirectX 7, was run on a Windows98 operated Dell Inspiron 5000 laptop computer with a 15-inch screen set at 1024×768 pixels. The display was in full-screen mode, over a black background. A Microsoft IntelliMouse, whose gain was set to four times its default value, and a Saitek Cyborg 3D USB joystick game controller were connected to the computer. The throttle of the game controller, which discriminates 65,536 positions over a course of about $110°$, was used to control the zoom (each throttle position corresponding to a certain level of zoom). The screen magnification M of the document (i.e. of both target distance D and target size W) was computed as $M(Z) = (1 + \varepsilon)^Z$ with ε representing a fixed magnification increment and Z standing for the zoom level controlled by the throttle. However, to avoid the desert fog problem at high magnification levels, the distance between two adjacent arcs of the concentric background was made to depend linearly on Z.

2.2.2   Task and DOF Assignment

We adapted Fitts' (1954) classic reciprocal tapping task for the purpose of this study. Participants had to record as many hits as possible for a variable, pre-determined period of time (henceforth called a trial) by clicking alternatively on two differently coloured discs, one blue and the other green. Between-target distance varied from trial to trial, but the movement always had to proceed through the document in a 45° direction, heading alternatively to the North East (to reach the green target) and the south West (to reach the blue target). This movement, unlikely to involve the shoulder joint, was particularly easy to perform with a right-hand held mouse. The current target was a coloured disk surrounded by the pattern of concentric circles drawn in the same colour.

In fact, the targets proper were not visible at low levels of magnification. Instead, small square marks whose size remained constant across zoom variations indicated their approximate locations — just like dots show the location of cities on a large-scale continental map. A zoom-in threshold had to be passed through to see the real target — a characteristic reminiscent of semantic zooming (Furnas & Bederson, 1995; Perlin & Fox, 1993). When this occurred, the small square turned into a disc, which, unlike the square, was zoomable as well as responsive to clicks.

No cursor was displayed on the screen. Rather, a stationary cross hair permanently apparent at the centre of the screen served for aiming, like in shooting games. Moving the mouse resulted in the screen image moving in the opposite direction, and so subjectively it felt like the cross hair (i.e. the view) was actually moving across a stationary world. Once the cross hair was judged to be on the target, validation had to be performed by pressing the left button of the mouse. A hit caused the current array of concentric circles to be replaced at once by the alternate array centred on the other target (located a long way away, out of the view, for difficult trials) and shown in the same colour as the new target (see Figure 1). A miss was ineffective, and so an error always had to be corrected before the next movement could start.

Participants were asked to control panning with the mouse assigned to their right, preferred hand and zooming with the throttle assigned to their left, non preferred hand (see Figure 2). Three-DOF tasks like that of the present experiment can be carried out with a single hand, using a wheel mouse. For the present experiment, however, we resorted to two-handed input because we had found in pilot testing that panning and zooming could proceed more smoothly, in a partly parallel fashion. We assigned the zooming component of the task to the left hand and the panning component to the right hand, rather than vice versa, in keeping with the principles of Guiard's (1987) kinematic chain model — see also Guiard & Ferrand (1996). Since setting the interaction scale determines the context for the immediately subsequent panning act, the latter task component is dependent on the former — an argument for assigning the panning component to the participants' right, preferred hand.

Figure 2: The experimental setup.

2.2.3 Independent Variables

Beside practice, the experiment involved a single independent variable, manipulated in a within-participant design: *task difficulty*, quantified by the *ID* (MacKenzie, 1992). Seven levels were chosen on this variable: 3.2, 5.1, 8, 12, 17, 23 and 30 bits (for a *W* of 1pixel, these *ID*s corresponded to distances of 8.5, 32.5, 257, 4,097, 31,073, 8,388,608 and 1,073,741,825 pixels, respectively)[4]. It should be realised that pointing with an *ID* of 30bits is equivalent to reaching and selecting a 1-inch target at a distance of over 12,500miles — half the circumference of our planet. At the first two levels of *ID* (3.2 and 5.1 bits), zooming was not necessary because at the outset of a trial the zoom could be preset so as to show both targets with a size compatible with acquisition. For *ID* = 8bits, the zoom began to be very useful, and beyond it became indispensable.

2.2.4 Procedure, Design, and Task Instructions

Seven healthy right-handed adults, five male and two female, with a mean age of 26.0 years (*SD* = 1.15 years), volunteered for the experiment. Each participant received seven trials for each level of the *ID*, yielding a total of 49 trials per participant in a single session. Practice was balanced using a 7×7 Latin square, whose lines where permuted from one participant to the next. Trial duration was varied according to the *ID*, so as to obtain an approximately equal number of movements in all *ID* conditions (by offering more time for trials with longer *MT*s). From the lowest to the highest *ID*, trial duration was 7.5s, 12.2s, 19.2s, 28.6s, 40.4s and 70.8s.

The participants were tested individually. They began the session with several familiarisation trials at various levels of difficulty. They were carefully shown how to use the zoom command, but they were left free to use it or not during experimental trials. Upon completion of each trial, the program displayed the shortest as well as the mean value of *MT* to encourage the participants to improve their speed.

---

[4]Note that no absolute measurement of variables *D* and *W* can be made in a multi-scale interface, these quantities being zoom dependent. The variable that can be quantified is the critical, zoom-independent ratio D/W, the determiner of the *ID*.

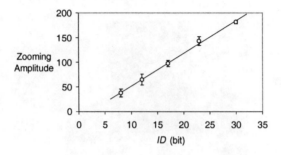

Figure 3: Mean zooming amplitude as a function of task difficulty for $ID \geq 8$bits. Error bars represent 95% confidence intervals based on between-participant standard deviations.

2.3 Results

2.3.1 Sample Size

Similar movement-sample sizes were obtained at the seven levels of task difficulty. With all 49 trials included, data points for our overall estimate of Fitts' law were each based on 300 to 450 individual measurements of *MT* — 215 to 320 measurements with the first two trials discarded as warm up (see below).

2.3.2 Utilisation of the Zoom

For the first two levels of difficulty (ID = 3.2 and 5.1 bits), the zoom facility was systematically ignored by the participants, who were content to carry out the task with just the mouse[5]. For higher levels of the *ID*, all the movements of all the participants involved the zoom.

Using as our metric the output value of the zoom command (Z, which was made to vary between -150 and $+50$), we defined zooming amplitude (A_Z) as the difference between the zoom level reached at hit time and the subsequent peak of zoom out (Z_{min}). As shown in Figure 3, the relation between zooming amplitude and task difficulty was rigorously linear ($A_Z = 6.6\ ID - 14.8$, $r^2 = 0.997$). The more difficult the task, the larger the zooming amplitude.

2.3.3 Movement Time

We defined *MT* as the amount of time elapsed between two consecutive hits. Computed over all trials and all participants, the *MT* vs. *ID* curve was almost perfectly modelled by Equation 1. A linear regression yielded $MT = 0.33\ ID + 0.004$ ($r^2 = 0.995$), with each of the seven participants exhibiting a very good fit ($0.984 < r^2 < 0.997$). Notice also the virtually zero (4ms) intercept. Keeping in mind that we used seven data points over a very wide-ranging selection of *ID*s, such a fit is remarkable.

However, a 7×7 repeated-measures analysis of variance performed on mean *MT* with the *ID* (3.2, 5.1, 8, 12, 17, 23 and 30 bits) and practice (Trials 1–7)

---

[5]The only exception was one participant occasionally trying to zoom for a few movements at ID = 5.1bits, during his second and third trials.

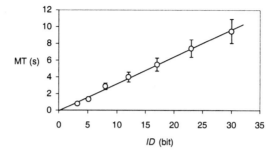

Figure 4: Fitts' law assessed over a selection of *ID*s ranging far beyond 10bits, thanks to the zoom facility.

Participant	r^2	Slope (s/bit)	Intercept (s)
1	0.999	0.30	−0.08
2	0.992	0.24	0.08
3	0.993	0.41	−0.27
4	0.995	0.40	−0.04
5	0.997	0.34	−0.15
6	0.981	0.32	0.15
7	0.988	0.25	0.02
all	0.995	0.32	−0.04

Table 1: Goodness of fit and linear regression coefficients of Fitts' law for each individual participant.

treated as within-participant factors revealed a considerable *ID*×practice interaction ($F(36,216) = 2.88$, $p = 0.000001$). This interaction reflected a consistent reduction, as participants familiarised themselves with the task, of the slope of Fitts' law, which declined on average from 0.38s/bit on Trial 1 to 0.33s/bit on Trial 3, where it stabilised. In view of this pattern of results, we resolved to treat the first two trials as warm-up. So below we will be considering exclusively the data from Trials 3–7, assuming these trials offer a relatively steady-state picture of performance after a moderate amount of practice.

Figure 4 shows the curve linking *MT* to the *ID*, computed over all participants. The figure shows that *MT*, estimated thanks to the zooming facility over a wide-ranging selection of task difficulties, still varies as predicted by Equation 1 ($MT = 0.32\ ID - 0.04$, $r^2 = 0.995$), that is, as a logarithmic function of the ratio D/W. The fit was excellent not only for the mean curve shown in Figure 4, but also for each of the seven participants, with $0.981 < r^2 < 0.999$ (see Table 1).

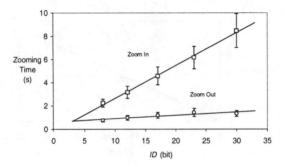

Figure 5: Mean zooming-out and zooming-in time as functions of task difficulty.

Interestingly, the five data points corresponding to difficult, multi-scale pointing (8- to 30-bit range) were found to be approximately aligned with the two data points corresponding to easy pointing without the zoom. There was, in particular, no evidence of a difference in the slope of Fitts' law (0.30 and 0.29s/bit for multi-scale and single-scale pointing, respectively).

Finally, Figure 4 shows that Fitts' law intercept (-0.04s for the overall data of Figure 4) was close to zero, consistent with the simplest possible version of the law, of the form $MT = k \times ID$.

2.3.4   Zooming-Out and Zooming-In Time

We parsed MT into *zooming-out time* (Z_oT), the time separating a successful click from the subsequent peak of zoom out (Z_{min}), and zooming-in time (Z_iT), the time separating a peak of zoom out from the subsequent hit. It should be remarked that while Z_oT corresponded to a virtually pure zooming time (with little or no panning), Z_iT represented the duration of a composite process made up of a series of intricately alternating pans and zooms, which started invariably with a large-scale pan.

As shown in Figure 5, most of the time elapsed between two consecutive hits consisted of Z_iT, with the initial zoom-out phase accounting for a smaller and smaller proportion of MT as task difficulty increased. The two components of MT were linearly dependent on the ID, with markedly different slopes ($Z_iT = 0.28\ ID - 0.16$, $r^2 = 0.997$, and $Z_oT = 0.03\ ID + 0.63$, $r^2 = 0.809$).

2.3.5   Index of Performance

Fitts (1954) proposed to use the ratio ID/MT, referred to as the index of performance (IP) — 'throughput' in the terminology of MacKenzie (1992) — to evaluate the rate of information transmission in the spirit of Shannon's communication theory. Fitts' initial hypothesis was that the IP (dimensionally, in bit/s) should be invariant along the continuum of task difficulty, but his own data (Fitts, 1954; Fitts & Peterson, 1964) showed the IP to decrease monotonically with task difficulty, as has been repeatedly found in Fitts' law research ever since — e.g. Gan & Hoffmann (1988), Guiard (1997; 2001).

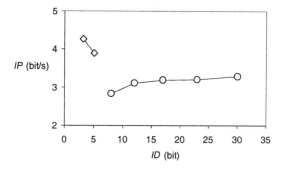

Figure 6: Index of performance as a function of task difficulty.

Consistent with previous observations, the *IP* declined from the first to the second level of difficulty, where the zoom was useless (see Figure 6). This effect, evident in all participants, was highly significant. For the higher five levels of difficulty, which required zooming, no more decrease in the *IP* was obtained. On the contrary, we observed a slight but significant improvement of the *IP* as pointing became more difficult ($F(4,24) = 10.38$, $p = 0.00005$). However, Newman-Keuls post-hoc tests revealed that this effect was essentially due to the *IP* value at 8bits being located lower than the other four — an effect that presumably reflects the sub-optimal size of the screen we used. So, focusing on the 12- to 30-bit range — a respectably large range, after all — it seems fair to conclude that in this experiment the processing rate for multi-scale pointing was essentially *insensitive* to task difficulty, in keeping with Fitts' (1954) initial expectation.

3   Overview of the Results

To sum up, the present exploratory study shows that Fitts' law can be investigated, within zooming interfaces, far beyond the classic 10-bit barrier, without altering the essence of Fitts' aimed-movement paradigm. Our data show that while the zoom resource started to be useful at 8bits, zooming amplitude was linearly dependent on task difficulty. Perhaps the most dramatic outcome of the experiment was the finding that all our *MT* measures, over an unusually large selection of *ID*s ranging from 3 to 30 bits, could be accurately modelled with a single Fitts' law equation (Equation 1), with no evidence of any discontinuity with regard to the coefficients of the equation. That is, the same equation turned out to account for both extremely difficult pointing aided by a powerful zoom and very easy, single-scale pointing. Moreover, the data were consistent with the simplest possible version of Fitts' law, of the form $MT = k \times ID$. In difficult, zoom-aided conditions, the participants spent most of their time zooming-in. The relative contribution of $Z_i T$ to *MT* strongly increased with the *ID*, and $Z_i T$ (along with $Z_o T$, but to a lesser extent) increased linearly with the *ID*. A final result was that for difficult, multi-scale pointing, processing rate, quantified by Fitts' *IP*, appeared constant across variations of the *ID*.

4   Basic Research Perspectives

Perhaps the main potential interest of the present exploratory work, from a basic-research viewpoint, lies in its suggesting new avenues for theorising and experimenting on human aimed movement. The designers of multi-scale interfaces have begun to create, for the performance of goal-directed movements, radically novel environments and conceived interaction principles that are without precedents in the real world. In the near future, such changes are likely to elicit substantial conceptual revisions in human movement science.

The present study was exploratory, and more work is needed to test the robustness of our findings (especially that of a zero intercept in the generalised version of Fitts' law). What seems already reasonably clear is that for modelling Fitts' law in general (i.e. with multi-scale pointing included) a power relationship (Meyer et al., 1990) will not do[6]. Second, kinematic — more accurately, space-scale-time — analyses of the actual movements of users are needed, in the spirit of Furnas & Bederson (1995), to fully understand the coordination of panning and zooming. Recently, we have started to tackle this problem experimentally (Bourgeois et al., 2001) in relation with the issue of two-handed input (Guiard, 1987).

5   Some Implications for HCI Design

Since Card et al. (1978), recourse to Fitts' law for modelling target-selection performance in graphic user interfaces has become a norm in HCI. It is noteworthy, however, that over the past few years evaluation studies concerned with multi-scale interfaces in HCI have squarely abandoned Fitts' law, as though inapplicable or irrelevant, and retreated to raw measurements of task completion times — e.g. compare Zhai & Selker (1997) vs. Accot & Zhai (1999). In fact, the present work suggests that Fitts' paradigm, as an evaluation tool, has not said its last word in the face of multi-scale electronic worlds.

2D interfaces enriched with a third dimension of scale have proliferated during the nineties. Currently, most major commercial applications like word processors, spreadsheets, and photograph processors offer zoomable displays. Such a success reflects the remarkable ease with which users integrate the dimension of scale with two dimensions of space, as well as the possibility of efficiently navigating a theoretically unlimited information space, enhanced by semantic zooming and filtering (Bederson & Hollan, 1994; Furnas & Bederson, 1995; Perlin & Fox, 1993). In view of these advantages, which may be contrasted with the difficulty of controlling, with inherently 2D tools like screens and mice, the third spatial dimension in 3D interfaces, e.g. Robertson et al. (2000), 2D zooming interfaces do seem to have a future.

---

[6]Meyer et al. (1990) model $MT = k_1 + k_2 \times (D/W)^{1/n}$, in which n stands for the number of sub-movements involved, approaches a logarithmic function as parameter n grows larger than 1. However, the relation approaches $MT =$ a constant when n becomes very large, and so this model seems unsuitable to accommodate difficult multi-scale pointing.

Acknowledgments

We gratefully acknowledge the generous financial support of the French Ministry of Defense (DGA Grant #96.34.058.00.470.75.65 to the first author) and of the Programme Cognitique of the French Ministry of National Education and Research (Grant #ACI-COG101 to the first author). We thank Reinoud Bootsma and Andy Slifkin for helpful discussions, and Christophe Prudhomme for programming the experiment.

References

Accot, J. & Zhai, S. (1999), Performance Evaluation of Input Devices in Trajectory-based Tasks: An Application of Steering Law, *in* M. G. Williams, M. W. Altom, K. Ehrlich & W. Newman (eds.), *Proceedings of the CHI99 Conference on Human Factors in Computing Systems: The CHI is the Limit*, ACM Press, pp.466–472.

Bederson, B. B. & Hollan, J. D. (1994), Pad++: A Zooming Graphical Interface for Exploring Alternate Interface Physics, *in* S. Feiner (ed.), *Proceedings of the ACM Symposium on User Interface Software and Technology, UIST'94*, ACM Press, pp.17–26.

Benhamou, S. & Bovet, P. (1992), "Distinguishing between Elementary Orientation Mechanisms by Means of Path Analysis", *Animal Behavior* **43**, 371–7.

Bourgeois, F., Guiard, Y. & Beaudouin-Lafon, M. (2001), Pan-zoom Coordination in Multi-scale Pointing, *in* J. A. Jacko & A. Sears (eds.), *Companion Proceedings of CHI2001: Human Factors in Computing Systems (CHI2001 Conference Companion)*, ACM Press, pp.157–8.

Card, S., English, W. & Burr, B. (1978), "Evaluation of Mouse, Rate-controlled Isometric Joystick, Step-keys and Text Keys for Text Selection on a CRT", *Ergonomics* **21**, 601–13.

Douglas, S., Kirkpatrick, A. & MacKenzie, I. (1999), Testing Pointing Device Performance and User Assessment with the ISO 9241, Part 9 Standard, *in* M. G. Williams, M. W. Altom, K. Ehrlich & W. Newman (eds.), *Proceedings of the CHI99 Conference on Human Factors in Computing Systems: The CHI is the Limit*, ACM Press, pp.215–22.

Fitts, P. M. (1954), "The Information Capacity of the Human Motor System in Controlling Amplitude of Movement", *British Journal of Educational Psychology* **47**(6), 381–91.

Fitts, P. M. & Peterson, J. R. (1964), "Information Capacity of Discrete Motor Responses", *Journal of Experimental Psychology: General* **67**(2), 103–12.

Furnas, G. W. & Bederson, B. B. (1995), Space-scale Diagrams Understanding Multiscale Diagrams, *in* I. Katz, R. Mack, L. Marks, M. B. Rosson & J. Nielsen (eds.), *Proceedings of CHI'95: Human Factors in Computing Systems*, ACM Press, pp.234–41.

Gan, K. C. & Hoffmann, E. R. (1988), "Geometrical Conditions for Ballistic and Visually Controlled Movements", *Ergonomics* **31**(5), 829–39.

Guiard, Y. (1987), "Asymmetric Division of Labor in Human Skilled Bimanual Action: The Kinematic Chain as a Model", *Journal of Motor Behaviour* **19**(4), 486–517.

Guiard, Y. (1997), "Fitts' Law in the Discrete vs. Continuous Paradigm", *Human Movement Science* **16**, 97–131.

Guiard, Y. (2001), Disentangling Realtive From Absolute Amplitute in Fitt's Law Experiments, *in* J. A. Jacko & A. Sears (eds.), *Companion Proceedings of CHI2001: Human Factors in Computing Systems (CHI2001 Conference Companion)*, ACM Press, pp.315–8.

Guiard, Y. & Ferrand, T. (1996), Asymmetry in Bimanual Skills, *in* D. Elliott & E. Roy (eds.), *Manual Asymmetries in Motor Performance*, CRC Press, pp.175–95.

Guiard, Y., Beaudouin-Lafon, M. & Mottet, D. (1999), Navigation as Multiscale Pointing: Extending Fitts' Model to Very High Precision Tasks, *in* M. G. Williams, M. W. Altom, K. Ehrlich & W. Newman (eds.), *Proceedings of the CHI99 Conference on Human Factors in Computing Systems: The CHI is the Limit*, ACM Press, pp.450–7.

Jul, S. & Furnas, G. W. (1998), Critical Zones in Desert Fog: Aids to Multiscale Navigation, *in* B. Schilit (ed.), *Proceedings of the ACM Symposium on User Interface Software and Technology, UIST'98*, ACM Press, pp.97–106.

Kabbash, P., MacKenzie, I. & Buxton, W. (1993), Human Performance Using Computer Input Devices in the Preferred and Non-preferred Hands, *in* S. Ashlund, K. Mullet, A. Henderson, E. Hollnagel & T. White (eds.), *Proceedings of INTERCHI'93*, ACM Press/IOS Press, pp.474–81.

MacKenzie, I. (1992), "Fitts' Law as a Research and Design Tool in Human–Computer Interaction", *Human–Computer Interaction* **7**, 91–139.

MacKenzie, I. & Zhang, S. (1999), The Design and Evaluation of a High-performance Soft Keyboard, *in* M. G. Williams, M. W. Altom, K. Ehrlich & W. Newman (eds.), *Proceedings of the CHI99 Conference on Human Factors in Computing Systems: The CHI is the Limit*, ACM Press, pp.25–31.

Meyer, D., Smith, J., Kornblum, S., Abrams, R. & Wright, C. (1990), Speed-accuracy tradeoffs in aimed movements: Toward a theory of rapid voluntary action, *in* M. Jeannerod (ed.), *Attention and Performance XIII*, Lawrence Erlbaum Associates, pp.173–226.

Perlin, K. & Fox, D. (1993), Pad: An Alternative Approach to the Computer Interface, *in* *Proceedings of SIGGRAPH'93 20th Annual Conference on Computer Graphics and Interactive Techniques, Computer Graphics (Annual Conference Series)* **27**, ACM Press, pp.57–64.

Robertson, G., van Dantzich, M., Robbins, D., Czerwinski, M., Hinckley, K., Risden, K., Thiel, D. & Gorokhovsky, V. (2000), The Task Gallery: A 3D Window Manager, *in* T. Turner, G. Szwillus, M. Czerwinski & F. Paternò (eds.), *Proceedings of the CHI2000 Conference on Human Factors in Computing Systems, CHI Letters* **2**(1), ACM Press, pp.494–501.

Schmidt, R., Zelaznik, H., Hawkins, B., Frank, J. & Quinn Jr., J. (1979), "Motor Output Variability: A Theory for the Accuracy of Rapid Motor Acts", *Psychological Review* **86**, 415–51.

Shneiderman, B. (1997), Designing Information Abundant Websites: Issues and Recommendations, http://www.cs.umd.edu/hcil/members/bshneiderman/ijhcs/ijhcs.html.

Welford, A. (1968), *Fundamentals of Skill*, Methuen.

Zhai, S., Hunter, M. & Smith, B. (2000), The Metropolis Keyboard: An Exploration of Quantitative Techniques for Virtual Keyboard Design, *in Proceedings of the 13th Annual ACM Symposium on User Interface Software and Technology, UIST2000, CHI Letters* 2(2), ACM Press, pp.119–28.

Zhai, S., Morimoto, C. & Ihde, S. (1999), Manual and Gaze Input Cascaded (MAGIC) Pointing, *in* M. G. Williams, M. W. Altom, K. Ehrlich & W. Newman (eds.), *Proceedings of the CHI99 Conference on Human Factors in Computing Systems: The CHI is the Limit*, ACM Press, pp.246–53.

Zhai, S. Smith, B. A. & Selker, T. (1997), Improving Browsing Performances: A Study of Four Input Devices for Scrolling and Pointing Tasks, *in* S. Howard, J. Hammond & G. K. Lindgaard (eds.), *Human–Computer Interaction — INTERACT '97: Proceedings of the Sixth IFIP Conference on Human–Computer Interaction*, Chapman & Hall, pp.286–93.

Author Index

Abed, Mourad, 331
Adams, Anne, 49
Al-Qaimari, Ghassan, 153
Anderson, A H, 367
Antunes, H, 139

Barbosa, Simone D J, 279
Beaudouin-Lafon, Michel, 247, 573
Beaudoux, Olivier, 247
Bental, Diana, 485
Bourgeois, Frédéric, 573
Bourguin, Grégory, 297
Brewster, Stephen, 515, 531

Calvary, Gaëlle, 349
Casey, Chris, 559
Cawsey, Alison, 485
Chaillou, Christophe, 83
Cheng, Yun-Maw, 427
Cockton, Gilbert, 171
Cordier, Frédéric, 31
Coutaz, Joëlle, 349

David, Bertrand, 399
de Souza, Clarisse Sieckenius, 279
Dearden, Andrew, 213
Degrande, Samuel, 83
Dempster, Euan, 485
Denley, Ian, 125
Derycke, Alain, 297
Dragicevic, Pierre, 543
Dubois, Emmanuel, 65
Dye, Ken, 3

Fekete, Jean-Daniel, 543

Gardner, Martin, 439
Gray, Phil, 439
Guiard, Yves, 573

Généreux, Michel, 475

Hailing, Mario, 107
Hourizi, Rachid, 229

Iivari, Netta, 193

Jackson, M, 367
Johnson, Chris, 427, 439
Johnson, Peter, 229
Jokela, Timo, 193

Kaindl, Hermann, 107
Katsavras, E, 367
Ketola, Pekka, 415
Klein, Alexandra, 475
Korhonen, Hannu, 415
Kramer, Stefan, 107

Le Mer, Pascal, 83
Lee, WonSook, 31
Light, Ann, 459
Long, John, 125

MacFarlane, Stuart, 559
MacKinnon, Lachlan, 485
Magnenat-Thalmann, Nadia, 31
Mahfoudhi, Adel, 331
Manninen, Tony, 383
Marwick, David, 485
McCall, Rod, 267
McGookin, David, 531
McRostie, Darren, 153
Morrissey, W, 503
Mottet, Denis, 573
Mullin, J, 367

Nevakivi, Katriina, 193
Ng, Adrian, 531

Nieminen, Marko, 193

Pacey, Daniel, 485
Paris, Cécile, 313
Perron, Laurence, 83
Pestina, S, 139

Rabardel, Pierre, 17
Radhakrishnan, T, 139
Rajanen, Mikko, 193
Ramloll, Rameshsharma, 515
Read, Janet, 559
Riedel, Beate, 515

Sage, Meurig, 439
Sasse, Martina Angela, 49
Saugis, Grégory, 83
Saïkali, Karim, 399
Schwank, Ingrid, 475
Seffah, A, 139
Seo, HyeWon, 31

Silveira, Milene Selbach, 279
Smallwood, L, 367

Tabary, Dimitri, 331
Tarby, Jean-Claude, 297, 313
Thevenin, David, 349
Trost, Harald, 475
Turner, Phil, 267
Turner, Susan, 267

Vander Linden, Keith, 313

Walker, Ashley, 531
Watts, Leon, 65
Williams, Howard, 485
Woolrych, Alan, 171

Yu, Wai, 515

Zajicek, M, 503

Keyword Index

2D tables, 515
3D clothing, 31

action, 247, 383
activity theory, 297
adaptation, 349, 485
affordance, 17
artefact, 17
assistive technologies, 543
augmented reality, 427
automation surprise, 229
aviation, 229

behaviour, 383
body cloning, 31

CASE tools, 107
CAUsE tools, 153
children, 415, 559
co-evolution, 297
cognitive walkthrough, 153
collaborative virtual environments, 83, 267
communicability utterances, 279
complexity evaluation, 331
compound document, 247
conceptual model, 247
context of use, 349
cooperative design, 415
cooperative inquiry, 415
CSCW, 367

data capture, 439
data visualisation, 515
design, 459
design method, 297
design models, 213
design space analysis, 213

design techniques, 415
desktop environment, 247
development tools, 107
document-centred interaction, 247
DR-AR model, 171
dynamic information presentation, 485

earcons, 531
ecommerce, 459
environment, 349
evaluation, 153, 171, 367, 559
evolving system, 297
exception, 297
eye-tracking, 367

Fitts' law, 573
foeld research, 3
formal method, 331
formative model, 17
function allocation, 213
functionality, 503

generic database, 31
generic garment, 31
gesture, 83
GOMS, 153
grounded theory, 49
groupware control, 399

handwriting, 559
HCI specification, 331
help systems design, 279
help systems model and architecture, 279
heuristic evaluation, 171
human-centred design, 17
human-to-human communication, 139
human/avatars/human interaction, 83

IDA-S, 213

input, 573
input devices, 543
instrument, 17
instrumental interaction, 247
interaction techniques, 543
interactive mechanisms, 459
interactive work-space, 247
interface design, 503
interface sonification, 531
Internet, 31

knowledge structures, 229

made to measure, 31
media space, 65
mediation, 17
medical informatics, 439
memory loss, 503
metaphor, 247
mobile computing, 427
mobile devices, 531
mobile handset, 415
mobile phone, 415
mobile systems, 439
mode error, 229
multi-modality, 475
multi-player games, 383
multi-scale pointing, 573
multidisciplinary practice, 125
multimedia, 367
multimedia communication environments,
     65
multimedia communications, 49
multiple inputs, 543

narrative, 267
natural language processing, 475
navigation in electronic worlds, 573
non-speech sounds, 515, 531
non-verbal communication, 83

object approach, 331
older adults, 503

paradigms, 125
partial automation, 213
participatory design, 415
PDAs spatial mapping, 531
perception, 247
personal view, 17

personalisation, 485
Petri nets, 331
place, 65
planar 3D audio, 531
plasticity, 349
platform, 349
pointing, 573
privacy, 49, 65
process guide, 107
product design, 3
prototyping, 415

reflective system, 297
relationship-building, 459
requirements, 267
requirements analysis, 313
requirements engineering, 125

safety, 229
scenarios, 3, 107
semiotic engineering, 279
simulation, 383
social identity theory, 65
software design, 3
software development lifecycle, 139
sound, 531
sound graphs, 515
speech, 559
speech output, 515
subjective workload assessment, 515
system design, 313
systems engineering, 213

tailoring activities, 17
task, 297
task analysis, 331
task and strategy, 229
task modelling, 313
taxonomy, 383
text, 559
toolkits, 543
ToyMobile, 415
transformation framework, 485
trust, 49
two-handed input, 573

ubiquitous computing, 65
UCD, 193
usability, 3, 439, 475
usability capability, 193

usability capability assessment, 193
usability engineering, 139, 171
usability inspection methods, 171
usability maturity models, 193
use cases user-centred design, 139
user interface redesign, 229
user-centred design, 49, 267
utilisation scheme, 17

videoconferencing, 367
virtual environment, 383

virtual try-on, 31
visual impairment, 503

Web, 31, 503
websites, 459
wireless communication, 427
Wizard-of-Oz experiments, 475
workflow, 399
workflow adaptability, 399

zooming interfaces, 573